Soviet Economic Structure and Performance

FOURTH EDITION

Paul R. Gregory
University of Houston

Robert C. Stuart
Rutgers University

1817

HARPER & ROW, PUBLISHERS, New York
Grand Rapids, Philadelphia, St. Louis, San Francisco,
London, Singapore, Sydney, Tokyo

For Annemarie, Andrei, and Mischa;
Beverly, Andrea, and Craig

Sponsoring Editor: John Greenman
Cover Design: Heather A. Ziegler

Soviet Economic Structure and Performance, Fourth Edition

Library of Congress Cataloging-in-Publication Data

Gregory, Paul R.
 Soviet economic structure and performance / Paul R. Gregory,
Robert C. Stuart.   —4th ed.
  p.   cm.
 Includes bibliographical references.
 ISBN 0-06-042506-7
 1. Soviet Union—Economic conditions—1918– 2. Soviet Union—
Economic policy—1917– I. Stuart, Robert C., 1938– .
II. Title.
 HC335.G723   1990
 330.947´054—dc20   89-38408
90 91 92 93 9 8 7 6 5 4 3 2 1   CIP

Contents

Preface

The first, second, and third editions of this book described and evaluated the Soviet economy. Their primary focus was on Soviet organizational arrangements for allocating scarce resources and on how well such arrangements have worked over the years. We found, as have most writers on the Soviet economy, that Soviet organizational arrangements have been remarkably resilient to significant change. The founders of the Soviet planning system in the late 1920s and early 1930s would feel quite at home with the contemporary Soviet economic system.

The growth rate of Soviet GNP and productivity, which has not been healthy since the 1960s, continues its long-term downward trend, while the capitalist economies (after ironing out the effects of the business cycle) have experienced rather stable long-term growth. The American economy is approaching the 1990s with an ongoing business expansion that has lasted over seven years. The Soviet satellites in Eastern Europe, with few exceptions, have shared in declining Soviet economic fortunes. The majority of the Eastern European countries have experienced episodes of negative growth in the late 1970s and 1980s. The Reagan years saw a marked buildup in real U.S. defense spending, which placed added strain on the already burdened Soviet economy. There are few signs that the Soviet Union is overcoming its technological backwardness vis-à-vis the Western world; the Soviet Union remains dependent on the capitalist West for innovations and new technology. Soviet agriculture continues to suffer from weather and organizational problems, and Soviet dependence on massive grain purchases in the world market is now taken for granted. Moreover, the Soviets' military and ideological rivals to the east, the Chinese, have experienced rapid economic growth since their own liberalizing reforms of the post-Mao era. Growing Chinese economic power is not a welcome sign to Soviet leaders trying to deal with their own lagging economy. Falling relative oil prices and gold prices in international markets have taken away the significant windfalls that boosted Soviet economic performance in the 1970s.

Since the death of Brezhnev, Soviet leadership has changed hands three times. The Andropov and Chernenko interregnums were years of marking time and waiting for sickly, incapacitated leaders to pass from the scene. The appointment of a young and vigorous leader, Mikhail Gorbachev, in 1985 presented the Soviet Union with an opportunity to address its long-term problems. The problems are apparent; the solutions are obscure. On the one hand, the Soviets have the liberalizing example of the Hungarians, who have been trying for over 20 years to combine their market and their plan without sacrificing party control. On the other hand, the Soviets have the example of the Chinese, who have reintroduced private ownership into agriculture. Neither reform charts the waters for the Soviet leadership. The Hungarian experiment is troubled by inflation, consumer resistance, and balance-of-payments difficulties. The Chinese have had difficulty in extending their reform beyond agriculture.

Gorbachev's vaunted perestroika (restructuring) and glasnost (openness) programs have justifiably captured the world's imagination. They represent what may be the most significant social experiment of the second half of the twentieth century. If perestroika and glasnost do indeed result in significant changes in the Soviet economic and political system, the course of the twenty-first century will be altered. The Soviet Union could indeed become a part of the world economic system. The political and economic realignment of Eastern Europe could take place. In general, the world might become a better and safer place in which to live.

Observers of the Soviet economy have learned to approach the subject of Soviet reform with caution and skepticism. It is far too early to decide the success or failure of Gorbachev's "radical" reform program. There is little questioning of the seriousness of intent. What is questioned is whether the Soviets can "pull it off." Can Gorbachev devise a new economic system that reintroduces incentives, allows local decision making in a rational context, and promotes technological progress while it retains the fundamental elements of the Soviet economic system that the Communist Party leadership finds essential?

There is agreement among Soviet specialists that the glasnost experiment has proceeded more rapidly than the perestroika experiment. The gains in freedom of expression that have occurred during the first four years of the Gorbachev regime have been truly remarkable, judged by historical standards. Yet Soviet specialists agree that economic restructuring has lagged behind glasnost. The economic reforms remain to be implemented, and they face substantial opposition in the form of an entrenched bureaucracy.

The main focus of this fourth edition is, inevitably, perestroika. Why is a serious restructuring of the Soviet economic system taking place at this time? What parts of the Soviet economic system does perestroika aim to change? What parts of the Soviet economic system are immutable? The most significant questions this edition addresses are these: What are the chances for a successful reform of the Soviet economic system? Will the Soviet economic system of the early twenty-first century be markedly different from the system devised by Stalin in the late 1920s, which has been so resistant to change over the years? Will the Soviet leadership abandon this reform as they have previous reforms and be forced to settle for the familiar "muddling through" approach of the past? Can the Soviet leadership afford to fail in this restructuring experiment?

ORGANIZATION OF THE TEXT

The present work on Soviet planned socialism is designed to serve as a basis for introductory courses in Soviet economics, comparative economic systems, and the economics of socialism. In the latter two courses, it would be combined with readings on other models of socialism.

We assume a level of sophistication generally acquired in a one-year introductory economics course. We emphasize the broad issues in the operation of the Soviet planned economy: In what manner and how effectively are resources allocated by the Soviet command economy?

The book consists of four parts. Part One, titled "Origins of the Soviet Economy," focuses on the economic history of the Soviet Union from the tsarist period to the mid-1980s. Chapter 2 recounts the nature and extent of Russian economic development prior to the revolution of 1917. The objectives of this chapter are to determine the nature of the economic base inherited from the tsars, to facilitate an evaluation of the achievements of the Soviet period, and to allow comparisons with the developing countries.

Chapter 3 deals with the period from 1918 to 1928, that is, War Communism and the New Economic Policy. This chapter examines the two Soviet economic organizations of this period and their roles in the evolution of the Soviet planned economy.

Chapter 4 describes the Soviet Industrialization Debate that preceded the adoption of the first Five Year Plan in 1928. The outcome of the debate is evinced by a discussion of the vast institutional and structural changes that occurred during the 1930s once the all-out industrialization decision had been made.

Chapter 5 deals with the foundations of the Soviet planned economy by considering the evolution of central planning in the Soviet Union during the late 1920s and early 1930s and the introduction of collective agriculture into the Soviet countryside. It recounts the formation of the ministerial system and the role of *Gosplan* in economic planning. The most important topic of this chapter is the Soviet development model, the most conspicuous feature of which was the forced collectivization of agriculture. The effects of collectivization on short-run and long-run economic performance are considered. Chapter 5 ends with a discussion of the Soviet economy during World War II.

Chapter 6 highlights the major events of the postwar era from the end of World War II to the late 1980s. It begins with the transition to a peacetime economy—an event accompanied by the change from the Stalin dictatorship to the Khruschev years. Economic performance during the Khruschev years is discussed along with the organizational changes and experiments in both agriculture and industry initiated by Khruschev. Soviet economic performance in the Brezhnev and Gorbachev years is the focus of the remainder of the chapter.

Part Two, "How the Soviet Economy Operates," focuses on the process of resource allocation in the Soviet command economy. Chapter 7 deals with the functioning of the Soviet economy in terms of the planning structure, industrial planning, and price setting. The informal "second economy" is also discussed. Chapter 8 continues this topic in a discussion of decision making by the Soviet manager, of labor allocation, and of the investment decision.

Chapter 10 discusses resource allocation in Soviet agriculture. The characteristics of Soviet collectivized agriculture are considered. The Soviet search for long-run solutions to agricultural problems is the main focus of this chapter.

Chapter 11 is about Soviet foreign trade. The institutional planning and operation of foreign trade is first considered both in terms of the Soviet foreign trade monopoly and of the Council for Mutual Economic Assistance (COME-CON) organization. The results of the Soviet foreign trade sector are then examined, especially as they bear on the role of foreign trade in the course of Soviet industrialization and its impact on economic integration within the Soviet bloc.

Part Three deals with Soviet economic performance. Chapter 12 considers Soviet economic performance in terms of a series of performance indicators: economic growth, dynamic efficiency, static efficiency, income distribution, consumer welfare, and economic stability. Chapter 13 continues the evaluation of Soviet performance by considering further indicators: military power, technological performance, and environmental quality.

Part Four analyzes Soviet economic reform and future prospects. Past attempts at economic reform are considered in Chapter 14, and in Chapter 15 Gorbachev's restructuring program is evaluated and its chances of success are discussed. Chapter 16, the final chapter, examines the Soviet economy and its prospects for the future.

ACKNOWLEDGMENTS

The authors would like to thank a large number of scholars for their direct and indirect participation in this project. In the latter category, Abram Bergson and David Granick must be singled out for their guidance during our years of graduate study, and the Harvard University Russian Research Center must be noted as having provided the intellectual stimulation that played an important role in the project's original conception in 1970. In the direct participation category, thanks are due to Carl McMillan, Franklyn D. Holzman, Holland Hunter, Keith Bush, and H. Peter Gray, all of whom kindly commented on some aspect of the first edition of this study. Valuable suggestions for revision of the first edition were supplied by James Millar, Thomas Wolf, Edward Hewett, Earl Brubaker, Vladimir Treml, Gertrude Schroeder Greenslade, Frank Durgin, Anna Kuniansky, and Susan Linz. A number of scholars provided valuable suggestions that improved the third edition. We would like to acknowledge the assistance of Judith Thornton, Gertrude Schroeder Greenslade, Holland Hunter, Susan Linz, Hugh Neary, Ken Gray, Morris Bornstein, Marvin Jackson, and Fyodor Kushnirsky. Valuable suggestions for the fourth edition were made by Yasuhiko Yoshida, John P. Farrell, and Morris Bornstein. For the conception, development, and presentation of this work, the authors bear sole responsibility.

PAUL R. GREGORY
ROBERT C. STUART

Origins of the Soviet Economy

Chapter 1

The Setting of the Soviet Economic System

*I*n the late 1980s, two new terms entered our vocabulary—perestroika and glasnost. Both are Russian. The first is translated as "restructuring"; the second as "openness." Restructuring and openness signify the policies initiated by General Secretary Mikhail Gorbachev in the late 1980s to alter radically the way the Soviet system works.

PERESTROIKA

Perestroika refers to the restructuring of the Soviet economy to make it more efficient, and glasnost refers to the opening up of Soviet society to new ideas and new freedoms of expression. This book is largely about perestroika. To understand why the Soviet leadership has chosen to embark upon a course of radical reform, one must understand Soviet economic history, the tenacious resource allocation arrangements put in place in the 1930s, and Soviet economic performance. Moreover, one must understand earlier reform efforts designed to correct—through less radical means—the same problems that contemporary perestroika addresses.

Russia became a socialist nation (the USSR, or Union of Soviet Socialist Republics) in 1917, after the Bolshevik revolution led by Vladimir Ilich Lenin. However, the Soviet economic system as we know it today dates from the years 1928–1929, when Joseph Stalin moved forcefully to abolish market allocation and introduce command planning to coordinate economic activity. Stalin also vigorously pursued collectivization of agriculture, a traumatic transformation of the countryside in which private agriculture was replaced by the collective and state farm systems. By the mid-1930s, the "second Soviet revolution" was essentially complete.[1]

Following the Bolshevik revolution of 1917 and prior to the dramatic changes introduced in 1928, the Soviet Union operated under two very different economic regimes. Between 1917 and 1921, the system of War Communism included nationalization of the means of production; a lessening of monetary incentives as a means to motivate workers; and, possibly most important, forced requisitioning of grain from the peasants. This was a period of civil war and sharp retrogression in both industry and agriculture. Nevertheless, the civil war was won by the Red Army organized by Leon Trotsky, and the power of the new regime was consolidated.

The period of War Communism came to an end with the introduction of the New Economic Policy (NEP), in 1921. Although the so-called commanding heights (major sectors) of industry, transportation, and banking remained nationalized, the market was reintroduced, money incentives returned, and a more or less orderly tax system and state purchases replaced the forced requisitioning of agricultural products. The 1920s were a period of economic relaxation and modernization, and by 1928 the economy had basically recovered from the losses of earlier years.

The NEP period was one of significant economic progress under a system more or less coordinated by the market mechanism. In light of the consolidation of political power and rapid economic recovery, why did Stalin decide to disrupt the status quo in the late 1920s? The 1920s were a battleground of conflicting ideologies and development strategies advanced by different factions within the Communist Party. It was also a period of relatively open discussion and debate. Despite the fact that the basic development alternatives were all discussed in a lively debate, the participants did not foresee the draconian alternative that would be chosen by Stalin.

The introduction of a socialist planned economy in the late 1920s was the Soviet leadership's response to the perceived need for rapid industrialization. In addition to the creation of state and collective farms to guide economic activity in rural areas, the economic system put in place by Stalin was characterized by public ownership of the means of production and the allocation of resources by means of a national economic plan, not the market. Both of these features became hallmarks of the Soviet (and later other) socialist economic systems.

Transformations of the 1930s were of major proportions. The consumer-oriented economy of the 1920s was transformed into a heavy-industry-oriented economy. Moreover, Stalin clearly viewed the peasants, through their production of grain, as holding the key to future Soviet industrialization. However history may judge this choice, the Soviet leadership clearly envisioned the new arrangements in agriculture as providing the means to harness grain production to the needs of rapid industrialization.

To understand the Soviet economic system, it is necessary to look both backward and forward. The Soviet Union was, at the time of the Bolshevik revolution in 1917, a relatively primitive country by the standards of Western Europe and the United States. However, the years following the Emancipation Act of 1861, and especially after the 1880s, witnessed significant economic growth of both industry and agriculture. The Russian economy was already moving in the typical directions associated with the early stages of economic development. An important, albeit relatively small, industrial base had already been put in place by the outbreak of World War I, not to mention a rail system that compared favorably with those of its more advanced neighbors. Prior to the Bolshevik revolution Russia was the major European exporter of grain. It is important that we understand these early developments if we are to assess the base upon which later socialist policies would build.

In historical perspective, Stalin is remembered for more than the dramatic events of the late 1920s and early 1930s. In particular, he is remembered for the draconian measures used to achieve a decade of exceedingly rapid economic growth and structural change in the Soviet Union. These transformations were interrupted by the incredible Soviet human and economic losses of World War II. However, the recovery of the late 1940s restored the economy to prewar levels without the introduction of major new initiatives. Stalin died in 1953. The Stalin years represent an exceedingly difficult period in Soviet history. They saw massive loss of human life through collectivization, repression, and political terror. On a more ordinary level, economic sacrifices were required to finance the rapid transformation of the economy. Earlier soviet accounts of the Stalin years have admitted the harshness of this period but have argued that the sacrifices of that time made life better for future generations. The questioning of this interpretation in writings of the late 1980s must be traumatic to the older generation; they suggest that their immense sacrifices were in vain.

The death of Stalin ushered in a new era. While the political and economic system in place since the late 1920s remained intact, Stalin's immediate successor, Nikita Khrushchev, presided over a period of relative relaxation and reform. The sacrifices demanded of the Soviet people became less severe. The restraints on agriculture were somewhat relaxed without returning to private ownership. The output of consumer goods increased. If anything, the 1950s and early 1960s were the golden age of Soviet economic performance, with a confident Khrushchev declaring that the Soviet Union would overtake the United States before the last decade of the twentieth century. Khrushchev also embarked on a series of organizational and structural economic reforms, which proved of little consequence in the long run but at least opened the door to reform discussion. As Khrushchev's reform schemes became more erratic and as Soviet economic performance slipped, Khrushchev was deposed in a party coup. Khrushchev's bloodless overthrow provided forceful evidence of the turn away from Stalin terror as Khrushchev and his allies were put out to a pasture of complete obscurity.

The Brezhnev era began on a promising note. With economic matters under the supervision of an experienced technocrat, Alexei Kosygin, a modest state-sponsored reform was begun in the mid-1960s. The reform, which was supposed to elevate Soviet economic performance after a transition period, failed to do so, and it was abandoned for all practical purposes by the start of the 1970s. The long Brezhnev era (from 1964 to his death in 1982) is characterized as an era of intensifying stagnation. With no bold reform initiatives, the rigid party and state bureaucracy continued to direct economic activity through traditional planning practices. Growth and productivity declined steadily; corruption was rampant, and Soviet consumers and producers increasingly turned to the underground economy.

In March 1985, the relatively young and vigorous Mikhail Gorbachev ascended to power following the deaths of two aged and incapacitated general secretaries, Yuri Andropov and Konstantin Chernenko. Deriding the two decades of economic stagnation under Brezhnev, Gorbachev began building the political power base for a radical restructuring of the Soviet system. Gorbachev moved to discredit the Brezhnev regime and had succeeded in removing most of the old guard from leadership positions by 1988. Gorbachev rehabilitated a number of figures from the past (including Khrushchev and the old Bolshevik theorist Nikolai Bukharin) whose reform ideas have provided justification for Gorbachev's own reform thinking.

Gorbachev differentiated between moderate reform (such as the partial reforms and experiments tried by his predecessors) and the "radical" reform course upon which he was embarking. Although many of Gorbachev's reform ideas can be traced to earlier reform experiments, his restructuring program appears to be different both in terms of seriousness of intent and in its scope.[2]

Of course, the main questions this or any book on the contemporary Soviet economy must ask are, will Gorbachev's reform create a new and more efficient Soviet economic system? Can perestroika reverse the long-term decline of Soviet economic performance? We cannot go directly to our answers to these questions. Considerable groundwork is required. We must first study Soviet economic history and the resource allocation problems that perestroika seeks to correct.

THE SOVIET NATURAL SETTING

The Soviet economic system organizes the economic activity of a very large, resource-rich, and diverse nation.[3] Analysis and assessment of the economic system cannot be readily isolated from its setting, influenced by national, human, political, ideological, cultural, and historical factors.

In terms of land area, the Soviet Union is almost three times the size of the United States (excluding Alaska and Hawaii', with a land area of approximately 8.6 million square miles. The Soviet Union has a population of over 270 million, 65 percent of whom live in urban areas. This compares to a United States population of over 245 million, 78 percent of whom live in urban areas.

The Soviet Union is a northerly country, with significant regional variations in resources, climate, topography, and population settlement. In the most general terms, the Soviet Union can be divided into three major regions. The bulk of the Soviet population and economic activity (see Figure 1.1) is located in the first major region—the plains of the West and European Russia. This is the most densely populated region of the USSR. As one moves east, the Ural mountains, a major source of mineral wealth and hence economic activity, form a major barrier to the vast and sometimes inhospitable expanses of Siberia. Siberia is itself a vast region with substantial natural resources, in effect, the frontier area of Soviet economic development. The area east of the Urals is the most sparsely populated major region of the USSR.

As one moves south, a third major region, Central Asia, is a warm but mostly dry region. This part of the Soviet Union is less developed from an economic standpoint, and it is predominantly Moslem. It has the most rapidly growing population of the USSR owing to its relatively high birthrates.

In terms of natural resources, the Soviet Union is a very wealthy nation. Although natural conditions (inadequate warmth, inappropriate moisture, permanently frozen subsoil) constrain Soviet agriculture, the country nevertheless has a substantial endowment of good agricultural land. Possibly the best known agricultural land is the black earth zone in West Central Russia. Although agricultural activity is spread over many areas of the Soviet Union, many parts of the country, while able to grow crops and raise animals, must nevertheless overcome natural disadvantages, thus making agricultural activity in those areas expensive. Whether it is irrigation in the south or drainage in the north, these natural limits are important in assessing Soviet agricultural performance.

Soviet timber reserves are vast, among the best in the world. It is difficult to name a mineral or fuel that the Soviet Union does not have in significant amounts, whether it be coal, iron ore, natural gas, or oil. This extensive natural resource base means that, in practice, the Soviet Union can be (and has been) largely self-sufficient in raw materials. However, this is only part of the story. Whether judged in terms of domestic needs or in terms of participation in markets, the exploitation of Soviet natural resources present a major challenge. First, most of the natural wealth is located in areas of inhospitable natural conditions. The bulk of new raw material is in Siberia, with inherent climate and

Figure 1.1. Administrative divisions of the Soviet Union.

transportation problems. The regional distribution of natural resources plays a major role. Soviet oil from Siberia costs much more than that delivered from the traditional but waning fields of the Caspian Sea. Second, as the Soviet Union increases its participation in international markets, its exports are dominated by raw materials, a pattern more typical of less-developed nations and carrying the risks inherent in volatile world raw material markets. Undoubtedly, the Soviet Union would like to modernize its export sector to reduce its reliance on raw material exports.

Natural wealth is an obvious plus for the Soviet Union, and the management of this wealth under socialist planning is a distinct, important, and interesting issue. Has the Soviet planned economy exploited effectively the natural resource wealth of the Soviet Union?

SOVIET REGIONAL DIVERSITY

Soviet regional diversity can be characterized in differing ways.[4] Indeed, we have already simplified our overall picture of the Soviet Union by looking at a tripartite regional classification. Another mode of classification is the administrative/political subdivision of the Soviet Union.

The Soviet Union is divided into 15 union republics. Below the level of these republics, the administrative/political units are called provinces (the *oblast'*), and finally, at the lowest level, the districts (*raion*) and/or city (*gorod*). In fact, the Soviet political/administrative apparatus is more complex than this simple description suggests. Table 1.1 shows key demographic and economic characteristics of the 15 union republics.

Soviet republics vary significantly in many dimensions. They differ greatly in size. The Russian Republic (formally the RSFSR, or Russian Soviet Federated Socialist Republic) is by far the largest, representing just over 52 percent of the total Soviet population according to the 1979 census. The next largest republic by this measure is the Ukraine, representing just over 14 percent of the Soviet population. The remaining republics account for 34 percent of the USSR population and are substantially smaller.

Soviet regional diversity is also reflected in the ethnic composition of the population. While the Russian population accounts for slightly over half of the Soviet population, its share is declining. According to the 1959 Soviet census, the Russian population represented 55 percent of the aggregate Soviet population. This number had declined to 52 percent in the most recent (1979) census. Moreover, the Russian population is unevenly distributed throughout the country, ranging from over 82 percent of the population in the Russian Republic to a very small 2 percent in Armenia. Although issues relating to the ethnic composition of the Soviet population would take us beyond the central issues of this book, they are nevertheless important to an understanding of the Soviet people as both producers and consumers. The fastest-growing republics are the largely Moslem republics of Central Asia, most of which have relatively small

Table 1.1 THE SOVIET UNION: SELECTED REGIONAL INDICATORS

	Population			Per Capita nominal income (1978: USSR = 100)	Per Capita fixed capital (1975: USSR = 100)
	In millions (1980)	Percent urban	Percent Russian		
USSR	264.5	63	52.3	100.0	100
RSFSR	138.4	70	82.5	110.9	115
Ukraine	49.9	62	21.0	95.9	90
Belorussia	9.6	56	11.9	97.9	80
Moldavia	3.9	40	12.8	89.9	69
Kazakhstan	14.8	54	40.8	88.4	102
Transcaucasia					
Georgia	5.0	52	7.4	93.6	75
Azerbaidzhan	6.1	53	7.8	63.6	64
Armenia	3.0	66	2.3	86.7	73
Central Asia					
Uzbekistan	15.7	41	10.8	71.6	54
Kirgizstan	3.5	39	25.8	69.7	60
Tadzhikistan	3.9	35	10.3	59.9	51
Turkmenistan	2.8	48	12.6	75.1	73
Baltic					
Estonia	1.4	70	27.9	126.9	137
Latvia	2.5	69	32.8	113.7	117
Lithuania	3.4	62	8.9	115.1	101

Sources: Population data are from *Narodnoe Khoziaaistvo SSR v 1979 g.* [The national economy of the USSR in 1979] (Moscow: Statistika, 1980), p. 10; *Chislennost' i sostav naseliniia SSSR* [The number and composition of the population of the USSR] (Moscow: Finansy i statistika, 1984), Tables 13-35; per capita income data from G. E. Schroeder, "Regional Living Standards," in I. S. Koropeckyi and G. E. Schroeder, eds., *Economics of Soviet Regions* (New York: Praeger, 1981), p. 120; capital stock data from J. W. Gillula, "The Growth and Structure of Fixed Capital," in I. S. Koropeckyi and G. E. Schroeder, eds., *Economics of Soviet Regions*, p. 160.

nonnative populations. Moreover, ethnic differences, such as between the Armenians and Moslems or between the Balts and Russians, have led to well-publicized friction and strife in the 1980s.

The USSR achieved this regional diversity in two historical steps. The expansionary policies of successive tsarist regimes pushed out the frontiers of the Russian Empire into Central Asia with the support of garrisons operated by the Russian military. Territory was added to the USSR as a consequence of the annexation of the Baltic republics during the Second World War and the acquisition of former German and Polish territories at the end of the war. Events of the late 1980s have brought into the open the regional and ethnic divisions of the Soviet Union that could hamper the implementation of economic reform in the late 1980s and early 1990s.

The USSR is characterized by strong regional differences in per capita income (Table 1.1). The relatively rich Soviet republics are located in the RSFSR, the Ukraine, and the Baltic republics. The poorest republics are in Central Asia.

Although it has long been Soviet policy to decrease regional differentials in the level of living , Table 1.1 suggests that substantial differentials remain. In the late 1970s, per capita nominal income varied from a high of 126.9 in Estonia (USSR average = 100) to a low of 59.9 in Tadzhikistan. Data for the two most populous republics show the RSFSR per capita income is 11 percent above the USSR average and that the Ukraine per capita income is 4 percent below the USSR average. The RSFSR is more abundantly endowed with fixed capital than the Ukraine. The republic richest in fixed capital per person is Estonia, and the poorest republic is Tadzhikistan in Central Asia. The distribution of fixed capital reflects roughly the distribution of economic activity in the USSR.

Urbanization is another important aspect of Soviet regional development.[5] To appreciate the magnitude of the Soviet urban transformation, it is important for the reader to know that in 1926, just before the beginning of the Stalinist industrialization drive, just 18 percent of the Soviet population was classified as urban. By 1979, in the most recent census, 65 percent of the population was classified as urban. Through both natural urban growth and migration from rural to urban areas, Soviet urban growth has been rapid over the past half-century. Although the share of population remaining in the countryside remains high for a country that has attained significant economic development, we must treat contemporary Soviet society as an urban-based society, understanding both the problems and the prospects that this raises for the planned socialist economic system.

SOVIET ECONOMIC ACHIEVEMENTS AND FAILURES

Russia became a socialist economy with the October Revolution of 1917 and instituted central planning in 1928 under the first Five Year Plan. We have a long time period for viewing the Soviet system in perspective. Yet unbiased evaluation of Soviet economic performance is difficult, since many in the West are unsympathetic to the Soviet political system. Nevertheless, there is substantial agreement concerning the following achievements of the first 70 years of Soviet power.

Possibly the most notable achievement from the Soviet viewpoint is a political one—the expansion of communism. The magnitude of this achievement becomes evident when one compares the tenuous control exercised by the Bolshevik regime over the former Russian Empire in 1918—encircled by unfriendly capitalist countries and plagued by civil war, foreign intervention, and a shaky economy—with the current situation in which roughly one-third of the world's population lives under some form of communism. The Soviet Union is no longer encircled by unfriendly capitalist countries; rather, it has fashioned a bloc of (sometimes reluctant) socialist allies in Eastern Europe to act as buffers between itself and the capitalist world. Ironically, a major political threat to the Soviet Union—the People's Republic of China—comes from within the socialist world.

Second, the speed with which the Soviet Union transformed itself from relative economic backwardness into industrial and military strength must be listed as a major achievement. Russia in 1917 was predominantly agricultural, with high mortality rates, especially among infants. Nearly 60 percent of the population was illiterate. The industrial sector's shares of output and labor force were quite small, and the domestic machinery sector was poorly developed, requiring heavy dependence upon the capitalist world for capital equipment. By 1937, most of the indicators had been reversed; the USSR had been transformed into an industrial economy without reliance on foreign aid or extensive imports from the West (with the exception of industrial technology). Both during and after the period of rapid industrialization, Soviet GNP grew at high rates by international standards, albeit declining in recent years. Commenting on the speed of Soviet industrialization in the 1930s, Simon Kuznets, a Noble laureate scholar of modern economic growth, writes:

> As in all countries, economic growth in the USSR meant a decline in the shares of national product originating in, and labor force attached to, the A [agriculture] sector. But the rapidity of this shift was far greater in the USSR than in the other developed countries ... the shift of labor force out of agriculture of the magnitude that occurred in the USSR in the 12 years from 1928 to 1940 took from 30 to 50 years in other countries ... and the same was true of the decline in the share of the A sector in national product. A comparable shift took from 50 to 60 years in most other countries.[6]

Third, by devoting a larger share of resources to defense than do the United States and Western Europe, the Soviets have produced a defense capability equivalent or superior to that of the United States. Over the past decade, the Soviet Union has outspent the United States by substantial amounts both in the aggregate and in the important areas of strategic and general-purpose forces. Thus, the Soviets have been able to achieve military parity vis-à-vis the United States and Western Europe, utilizing an economic base 55 percent that of the United States and 33 percent that of the North Atlantic Treaty Organization (NATO) countries combined.[7]

The weaknesses of the Soviet economic system are not seriously contested: the Soviet economy's inability to provide consistent increases in living standards, especially during the initial Five Year Plan periods, and its inability to produce an assortment of consumer items corresponding to the demands of the population for quantity and quality are serious problems. Second, in terms of absolute economic efficiency, the Soviets have tended to generate less output per unit of input, by their own admission, than the American and most Western European economies. This relative economic inefficiency has become more bothersome with the slackening pace of population and labor force growth, rising defense spending, and the growing reluctance of Soviet consumers to accept low-quality merchandise. Various attempts to solve the problems of consumers supply and industrial inefficiency through experiments and reform have not proved successful. Third, Soviet economic successes have often been achieved at the cost of human life, political freedom, and material deprivation, making an overall evaluation of the system extremely difficult. The most immediate cost of rapid industrialization was the establishment of dictatorial control over the population in order to implement the extreme austerity of the first Five Year Plan.

Also, the agricultural sector has thus far failed to be an adequate and reliable supplier of meat and vegetable products. In addition, the output of the major grain corps is still subject to large annual fluctuations, and the regime has been forced to negotiate long-term agreements to import substantial amounts of grain from the West. While these imports do not necessarily prove the failure of Soviet agriculture (most industrialized countries import food products), they are nevertheless a disappointment to a Soviet leadership that has devoted considerable resources to improve agricultural performance. The increased reliance on the West for basic food supplies and the periodic shortages of food staples in a large country with a high concentration of employment in agriculture point dramatically to the Soviet Union's unresolved agricultural problem.

The Soviet economy has not succumbed to the internal contradictions that the early critics of planned socialism predicted would cause the Soviet planned economy to fail. The experience of more than 60 years of planned socialism in the USSR has shown that this type of economic system can survive. What is increasingly in doubt is whether such an economic system—in its original form—can provide an economic performance that is sufficiently good to warrant the continuation of the economic system in the face of available alternatives. The deterioration of Soviet growth and productivity performance that has continued throughout the 1970s and 1980s, the inability of the system to satisfy its consumers despite a rich raw material base, and the persistent failures of agriculture have caused the new Soviet leadership to search for viable alternatives. Table 1.2 provides comparisons to show the economic position of the Soviet Union relative to the United States.

This book will demonstrate that this search for alternatives is a more difficult process than is widely recognized. The present system of planned socialism does not work well, but there are no safe blueprints explaining how to move to an alternate economic system that is acceptable to the Communist leadership and reverses the economic fortunes of the Soviet Union.

THE SOVIET POLITICAL SYSTEM[8]

In the Soviet Union, the crucial economic decisions—the allocation of output among consumption, investment, and defense, and the rates of expansion of different sectors—are made administratively, not by the market. Whereas in the United States about one-quarter of the GNP is allocated by administrative decisions through the public sector, in the Soviet Union most output is allocated administratively. There are exceptions, such as underground economic activity, private-plot agricultural production, and nonplanned activities of some state enterprises, but by and large, planners decide how resources are to be allocated.

Table 1.2 ECONOMIC INDICATORS—USSR AND USA COMPARISONS, 1987

	USSR	USA
GNP (billion 1987 U.S. $)	2,375	4,436
Population, midyear (million persons)	284	244
Per capita GNP (1987 U.S. $)	8,363	18,180
Grains (million metric tons)	211	281
Milk (million metric tons)	103	65
Potatoes	76	16
Meat (million metric tons)	19	27
Crude oil (million barrels per day)	11.9	8.3
Natural gas (trillion cubic feet)	25.7	17.1
Electric power (billion kilowatt-hours)	1,665	2,747
Coal (million metric tons)	517	760
Crude steel (million metric tons)	162	81
Cement (million metric tons)	128	63.9
Aluminum (million metric tons)	3.0	3.3
Refined copper (million metric tons)	1.0	1.6
Iron ore (million metric tons)	114	44
Plastics (million metric tons)	6	19
Bauxite (million metric tons)	7.7	0.5
Tractors (thousands)	569	38
Automobiles (million units)	1.3	7.1
Trucks, including buses (million units)	0.9	3.8
Housing (million sq. m)	129	224
Rubber tires (million)	68	204
Gold production (million troy ounces)	10.6	5.0

Source: National Foreign Assessment Center, *Handbook of Economic Statistics*, 1988, U.S. Government Printing Office, September, 1988.

Planners' preferences supplant *consumer sovereignty* by taking resource allocation out of the hands of the market and placing it under the control of an administrative apparatus. By *planners' preferences*, we mean a mechanism for guiding the economic system so that the decisions as to what to produce, how to produce, and who gets the output are made by planners rather than by the dollar (and political) votes of consumers in the marketplace. Although perestroika proposes to move more resource allocation decisions to local levels, the Soviet system as of the late 1980s remained a system of planners' preferences.

Nominally, the Soviet Union is governed by an elected government that is subject to the Soviet constitution. The highest organ of the state is the *Supreme Soviet*, which is comprised of directly elected deputies. Because the Supreme Soviet meets infrequently (and then only to ratify automatically decisions of the party), the *presidium* appointed by the Supreme Soviet carries on the work of the Supreme Soviet between sessions. The *Council of Ministers* is the government bureaucracy of the USSR and is elected by the Supreme Soviet. Each of the 15 union republics of the Soviet Union has a state apparatus that parallels the national apparatus. Beneath the union, republican governments are the provincial (*oblast'*) governments, the local (*raion*) governments, and the city (*gorod*) governments.

Parallel to the state apparatus is the Communist Party of the Soviet Union (CPSU).[9] The supreme authority over the party organization is exercised nominally by the Party Congress, made up of delegates from all levels of the party hierarchy. Party congresses are held only at infrequent intervals, and they serve to elect (often perfunctorily) the *Central Committee* of the CPSU, which in turn appoints the *Politburo*—the most important policy-setting body in the Soviet Union. The general secretary of the CPSU (currently Mikhail Gorbachev) is the most powerful political figure in the Soviet Union.

At the republican, regional, and local levels, departments of the CPSU duplicate the various state agencies; thus, for each state agency there is a parallel party branch. The CPSU has committees at the province, or *oblast'* level (*obkom*), the regional, or *raion*, level (*raikom*), and the city level (*gorkom*). The first secretary of each of these party committees exercises considerable control in that area. At the enterprise level, a party cell supervises enterprise operations. In large enterprises, the head of the party cell tends to be a full-time party employee. In small enterprises, the job tends to be a part-time activity. Unlike the state apparatus, where lines of authority generally run from the local to the provincial to the republican to the national level, all lines in the party apparatus run directly to Moscow, suggesting a significant centralization of power.

One of the principal functions of all branches of the CPSU is the control and supervision of the economy. This control is exercised in several ways. Many branches of government report directly to the party. The State Planning Committee, for example, reports directly to the Politburo of the CPSU. At lower levels, building projects are first submitted to the party (to the *obkom* or *gorkom*, for example) before being submitted to the appropriate government office. Typically, a party committee will sign off completed construction projects. At the enterprise level, the party organization serves two functions—one, to mobilize the workers to fulfill the plan (often through the enterprise trade union that the party dominates), and the other, to check on the enterprise manager. These are just isolated examples of party supervision.

A potent tool used by the CPSU to influence the economy is the *nomenklatura* system. The *nomenklatura* is a comprehensive list of appointments that are controlled by the party. It is the party that nominates individuals for all important posts in the CPSU, state, industry, and army. At the national level, the Central Committee Cadres Department exercises this function. Party control over *nomenklatura* is crucial insofar as it is party nominees who run for elective office and become enterprise directors and farm managers. It is not surprising to find that while roughly 10 percent of the Soviet population belongs to the CPSU, very few agricultural or industrial managers are not members of the party.

The dominant role of the Communist Party in the Soviet Union is envisioned in Article 6 of the Soviet Constitution:

The leading and guiding force of Soviet society and the nucleus of its political system, of all state organizations, is the Communist Party of the Soviet Union.[10]

The military also carries out control activities over economic units. In enterprises that produce for the military, an autonomous military representative (the *Voenpred*) is responsible for signing off on military goods. Large enterprises may have a permanent military representative assigned to them. Smaller enterprises are supervised by a military representative responsible for several factories. Enterprises that produce both civilian and military production have their production broken down into a "first department" (*pervy otdel*) and civilian production. The planning and supply of the first department tends to be handled directly by the Ministry of Defense, while the civilian department is handled by the planning apparatus described below. The Military-Industrial Commission (VPK) reports directly to the Politburo.

THE ECONOMIC BUREAUCRACY

We turn now from party and military control to the state apparatus to consider the planning and organization of the economy. Throughout most of the plan period (1928 to present), the Soviet economy has operated under a ministerial system in which individual enterprises belonging to a particular branch of the economy (aviation, chemicals, metallurgy, etc.) are subordinated to a single ministry. There are three types of ministries: The *all-union ministry* runs the enterprises under its control directly from Moscow, and its enterprises are not answerable to regional authorities. The *union-republican ministry* has offices both in Moscow and in the various republics, and the enterprises under its control are subject to the dual authority of Moscow and the republican Councils of Ministers. The *republican ministry* directs enterprises within the republic and has no direct superior in Moscow. In recent years, republican ministries have been limited primarily to directing enterprises that produce for the local economy. The heads of these ministries are members of the Council of Ministries of the USSR and of the republican Councils of Ministers, respectively.

The ministerial system was introduced in 1932. Initially, three ministries were created—for the heavy, light, and timber industries. Since then, the number has fluctuated from a high of 32 in the late Stalin years, to 11 immediately after Stalin's death, to around 40 in the late 1960s. In 1987, there were 61 ministries, not counting other agencies with ministerial status. The ministries possess considerable power: they control a network of productive enterprises and have tended to develop their own supply and disposal agencies.[11]

An organization chart of the Soviet economic-administrative structure is provided in Figures 1.2 and 1.3 to illustrate the organization of the Soviet economy according to its ministerial system. The ministries are comprised of summary departments (such as finance and pricing departments) and of chief administrations (*glavks*). The chief administrations are responsible for enterprises producing specific product lines. For example, one chief administration in the construction materials ministry is in charge of metal pipes; another is in charge of cements; and so on. The functional departments implement general plans (such as the ministry's profit and cost plan or the balance plan for the distribution of equipment) that transcend the boundaries of the functional chief administrations. From the perspective of the enterprise, day-to-day control is carried out by the responsible chief administration.

There are a number of functional state committees and other agencies whose job it is to coordinate activities among ministries on an economywide basis. As of 1987, there were 38 state committees. The most important state committee is the State Planning Commission, or *Gosplan*. Established in 1921, *Gosplan* is responsible for drawing up national economic plans. *Gosplan* has a close association with the Politburo of the CPSU and is seen as representing the interests of the CPSU in its dealing with other organizations in the Soviet economy. *Gosplan* is charged with setting output targets for the various ministries and for working out materials and financial balances at the economywide level. In its planning activities, *Gosplan* works together with the ministries. *Gosplan* hands down the aggregate targets and approves resource "limits" for the ministries. The ministries work out the finer details of the plan and allocate tasks among enterprises.

There are other state committees that deal with economywide issues. The State Bank (*Gosbank*) monitors enterprise bank accounts and provides working capital credits. The Central Statistical Administration collects economic statistics and monitors plan fulfillment. The State Committee for Material and Technical Supply (*Gossnab*) works out the detailed material supply plans and allocations based on the more general supply and delivery plans of *Gosplan*. The State Committee for Construction Affairs (*Gosstroi*) coordinates construction activity for the entire economy. Although the task of coordinating the national economy is shared by a number of state committees and other agencies, it is clear that *Gosplan* is the dominant planning organ in the Soviet economy. Our later discussion of Soviet economic planning focuses primarily upon the planning activities of *Gosplan*.

The productive enterprises (*predpriiatie*) occupy the lowest level in the planning hierarchy. They are distinct economic entities operating under an independent accounting system (called *khozrashchet*). Soviet enterprises are supposed to cover their costs from their sales revenue and to earn a planned profit, a portion of which is turned over to the state in the form of a profit tax.

Since 1973, intermediate bodies, called industrial associations (or *obedineniia*), occupy an intermediate managerial position between the enterprises and the ministry. The industrial associations were created through the horizontal or vertical merger of enterprises working in related activities. The notion behind the formation of industrial associations was to improve the economic coordination of the economy by having the ministries and *Gosplan* work more with the management of industrial associations than with the individual enterprises. Routine operations were to be dealt with by the management of the industrial associations, freeing higher bodies to handle more aggregate planning tasks.

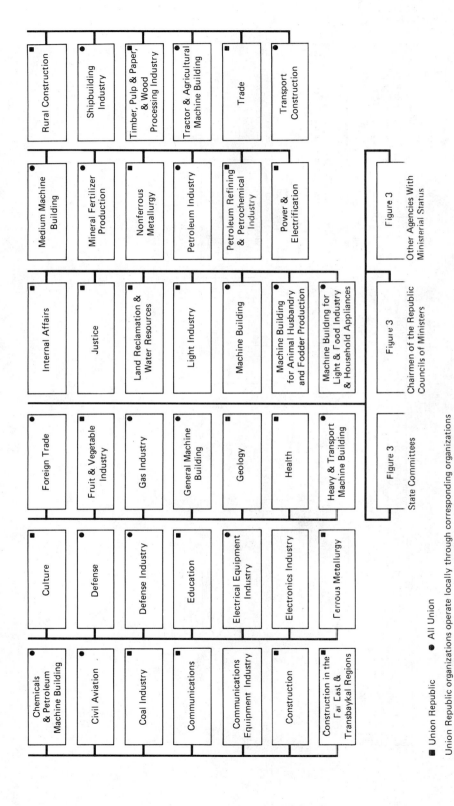

■ Union Republic   ● All Union

Union Republic organizations operate locally through corresponding organizations on the republic level. All union organizations have no such regional counterparts.

Figure 1.2. The USSR Council of Ministers: ministries. *Source:* Paul K. Cook, "The Political Setting," in U.S. Congress Joint Economic Committee, *The Soviet Economy in the 1980s: Problems and Prospects* (Washington, D.C.: U.S. Government Printing Office, 1982), pp. 19–20.

19

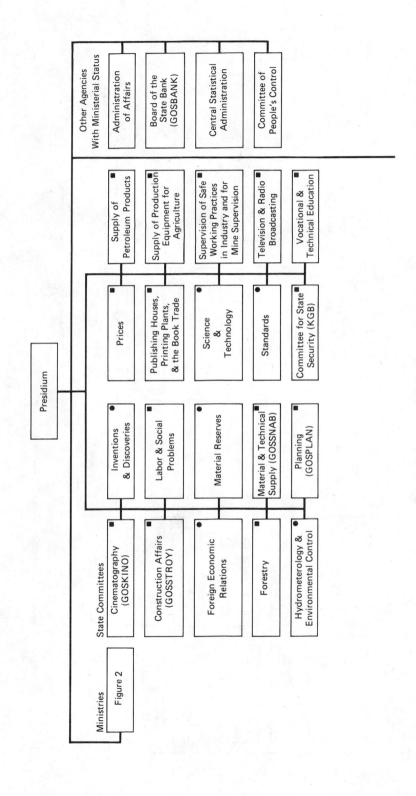

Figure 2

Ministries

State Committees

Other Agencies With Ministerial Status

Presidium

Cinematography (GOSKINO)

Construction Affairs (GOSSTROY)

Foreign Economic Relations

Forestry

Hydrometerology & Environmental Control

Inventions & Discoveries

Labor & Social Problems

Material Reserves

Material & Technical Supply (GOSSNAB)

Planning (GOSPLAN)

Prices

Publishing Houses, Printing Plants, & the Book Trade

Science & Technology

Standards

Committee for State Security (KGB)

Supply of Petroleum Products

Supply of Production Equipment for Agriculture

Supervision of Safe Working Practices in Industry and for Mine Supervision

Television & Radio Broadcasting

Vocational & Technical Education

Administration of Affairs

Board of the State Bank (GOSBANK)

Central Statistical Administration

Committee of People's Control

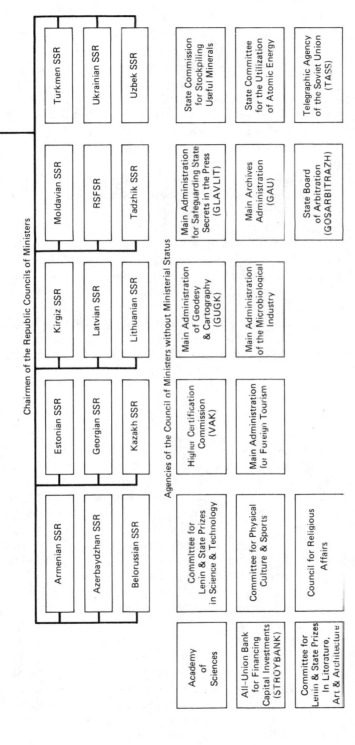

Figure 1.3. The USSR Council of Ministers: state committees and other agencies. *Source:* Paul K. Cook, "The Political Setting," in U.S. Congress Joint Economic Committee, *The Soviet Economy in the 1980s: Problems and Prospects* (Washington, D.C.: U.S. Government Printing Office, 1982), p. 21.

■ Union Republic   ● All Union

Union Republic organizations operate locally through corresponding organizations on the republic level. All union organizations have no such regional counterparts.

Soviet economic bureaucrats work in a hierarchy, ranging from the top elite to those who occupy responsible professional (but not managerial) positions within the bureaucracy.[12] The political or executive elite is comprised of members of the political elite (from the Central Committee down to first secretaries of provinces, regions, and cities) and the executive elite (from members of the Supreme Soviet and Council of Ministers, to minister presidents of the republics, chairmen of regional and city executive committees, down to the directors of the hundred or so largest enterprises). Less than 1000 individuals belong to this top elite.

Below the top elite is the middle elite. According to Soviet statistics, more than 10 million persons work in the sphere of administration (*upravlenie*) of the economy, which amounts to 14 percent of employment. This 10 million figure includes the numerically insignificant top elite, the middle elite, and the millions of clerks, statisticians, economists, and accountants working in nonleadership positions in the economic bureaucracy. Soviet statistics place 2.2 million persons as members of higher organs of state administration.

As these figures show, millions of persons are involved in the administrative allocation of resources in the Soviet Union. Gorbachev has been critical not only of the size of this bureaucracy but also of its tendency to dictate to lower units when such dictation is not necessary. Finding the appropriate bureaucratic structure is one of the prime tasks of the restructuring effort.

VALUE JUDGMENTS

Discussions about the Soviet economy inevitably turn to value considerations: Is a predominately private-enterprise economy, such as we have in the United States and much of Western Europe, superior to the Soviet economy? Although the question is legitimate, the answer must ultimately reflect subjective individual biases (personal value judgments) and cannot rest on objective grounds. The question of the ends or goals of a society serves as an illustration. It is generally assumed that a private-enterprise society satisfies consumer wants concerning the production and distribution of goods and services. In other words, consumer satisfaction is the end of such an economy, and consumer sovereignty is said to prevail. If the demand for a particular product increases, more of that commodity will be produced, probably at a slightly higher price. Consumers (assuming a given set of supply relationships) determine the output mix of the economy by exerting effective demand in the marketplace.

The ends of society in a centrally planned socialist economy are pictured quite differently. The goal of such a society is said to be the satisfaction of planners' preferences. A central plan, which administratively determines the current output mix and then distributes it between current consumption and investment, substitutes planners' preferences for consumers' preferences. This does not necessarily mean that consumer desires will be wholly neglected. In fact, it is theoretically possible for the planning agency to plan output to fit consumers' preferences by employing a complex market research network. In practice, however, there generally has been a dichotomy between consumers' and planners' preferences. In fact, a basic rationale for the planners' preferences system is that it enables the planners to do as they, not the consumers, see fit.

Can we judge the superiority of one economic system over the other on the basis of the goals of the two societies? The answer, we think, is no—for to do so would require a weighting system that could gauge the relative importance of the goals of each so that the aggregate achievement of one society could be compared with that of the other society. Pure objectivity in either direction is impossible, because the weighting itself implies an existing preference for one set of goals over the other. Insofar as value judgments differ among individuals, there is no scientific or objective basis for such a conclusion.

Using strictly economic criteria, the superiority of one economic system over another can only be demonstrated when one or more individuals feel themselves better off and no one feels worse off under the one system relative to their perceptions of their own welfare under the other system. But such cases are not likely to be found in the real world.[13] One might argue that the Soviet system involves a reduction in current welfare since Soviet planners have generally opted for high investment and low consumption ratios; therefore, the private-enterprise system provides higher levels of welfare and is thus superior. The Soviets could reply to this contention that the welfare of future generations has been enhanced as a result of their investment policy and that their system is superior. The whole argument would then hinge on whose welfare should be valued more highly—the welfare of the present generation or of future generations—which again would involve a value judgment.

An alternative approach would be to evaluate economies according to whether they derive maximum output from their limited resources. To do so would be to judge an economic system solely on the basis of its *technical efficiency* with the goals of the society accepted as givens.

The matter of technical efficiency can be illustrated using the familiar Production Possibilities Schedule (PPS) in Figure 1.4. The graph pictures a hypothetical economy that produces two types of goods: (1) producer and defense goods, and (2) consumer goods. This economy is endowed with a fixed stock of land, labor, and capital, which producers employing the available technology convert into output. Insofar as total resources are limited, the economy cannot produce unlimited quantities of output; instead, it must choose among a large number of maximum combinations of goods that the economy can produce. A technically efficient economy, which generates a maximum amount of output from its stock of inputs, is said to be operating on its Production Possibility Schedule. Let us say that a consumer-oriented economy would choose point *A* and a planned socialist economy would choose point *B* on the PPS. One cannot say that *A* is superior to *B* or that *B* is superior to *A* because both statements would be personal value judgments, which vary according to individual preferences and prejudices.

Figure 1.4 Economic priorities and the production possibilities frontier.

The criterion of technical efficiency can be objected to on the grounds that a technically efficient economy producing that mix of output designated by either planners or consumers can have an extremely "poor" distribution of income among the members of society and is therefore "inferior" to a less efficient economy having a "better" distribution of income. This, of course, brings us back to close the circle—"better" or "inferior" distributions of income can only be determined by specific value judgements.

We are not suggesting that value judgments should not be made in comparing economic systems; rather, we are pointing out that such judgments must be made with the explicit understanding that they *are* value judgments. For example, the substitution of planners' for consumers' preferences in the USSR was accomplished by imposing a dictatorship that subjected the Soviet population to considerable suffering and discomfort during the 1930s. Moreover, democratic political principles, defined in the Western sense of the word, remain foreign to the modern Soviet system even in the late 1980s. Any reader might find these facts personally objectionable. Nevertheless, such an objection rests upon personal value judgments, and it should be recognized that others (Soviet planners, for example) may subjectively argue that dictatorship (the "dictatorship of the proletariat") and deprivation were the necessary price of building a socialist society. It is difficult to prove one viewpoint right or wrong on purely objective grounds. Some might find this proposition difficult to accept in view of what they consider to be obvious deficiencies of the Soviet economic and political system.

REFERENCES

1. For historical overviews, see A. Nove, *An Economic History of the USSR* (New York: Penguin, 1969); and Roger Munting, *The Economic Development of the USSR* (London: Croom Helm, 1982).
2. Timothy J. Colton, "Approaches to the Politics of Systemic Economic Reform in the Soviet Union," *Soviet Economy*, vol. 3, no. 2 (April–June 1987), 145–170.

3. R. G. Jensen, T. Shabad, and A. W. Wright, eds., *Soviet Natural Resources in the World Economy* (Chicago: University of Chicago Press, 1983).

4. For literature devoted to regional aspects of the Soviet economy, see V. N. Bandera and Z. L. Melnyk, eds., *The Soviet Economy in Regional Perspective* (New York: Praeger, 1973); I. S. Koropeckyj and G. E. Schroeder, eds., *Economics of Soviet Regions* (New York: Praeger, 1981); and NATO, *Regional Development in the USSR: Trends and Prospects* (Newtonville, Mass.: Oriental Research Partners, 1977).

5. For a survey of urban issues, see H. W. Morton and R. C. Stuart, eds., *The Contemporary Soviet City* (Armonk, N.Y.: M. E. Sharpe, 1984).

6. S. Kuznets, "A Comparative Appraisal," in A. Bergson and S. Kuznets, eds., *Economic Trends in the Soviet Union* (Cambridge, Mass.: Harvard University Press, 1963), pp. 345, 347.

7. *Soviet Defense Trends*, a staff study prepared for the use of the Subcommittee on International Trade, Finance, and Security Economics of the Joint Economic Committee of Congress, Washington, D.C., U.S. Government Printing Office, September 1983.

8. This discussion is based on J. F. Hough and M. Fainsod, *How the Soviet Union Is Governed* (Cambridge, Mass.: Harvard University Press, 1979); A. Bergson, *The Economics of Soviet Planning* (New Haven, Conn.: Yale University Press, 1964), chap. 3; A. Nove, *The Soviet Economic System* (London: Allen & Unwin, 1977); F. Kushnirsky, *Soviet Economic Planning, 1965–1980* (Boulder, Colo.: Westview Press, 1982); W. J. Conyngham, *The Modernization of Soviet Industrial Management* (New York: Cambridge University Press, 1982); and P. R. Gregory, *The Soviet Economic Bureaucracy* (New York: Cambridge University Press, Forthcoming).

9. For treatments of party structure and functions, see L. Shapiro, *The Communist Party of the Soviet Union* (New York: Random House, 1971); and T. H. Rigby, *Communist Party Membership in the U.S.S.R., 1917–1967* (Princeton, N.J.: Princeton University Press, 1968). For the official Soviet view (subject to change in different editions), see *History of the Communist Party of the Soviet Union* (Moscow: Foreign Languages Publishing House, 1960). For more evidence, see T. H. Rigby, "Soviet Communist Party Membership Under Brezhnev," *Soviet Studies*, vol. 28, no. 3 (July 1976), 317–337; T. H. Rigby, "Addendum to Dr. Rigby's Article on CPSU Membership," *Soviet Studies*, vol. 28, no. 4 (October 1976), 613; and A. L. Unger, "Soviet Communist Party Membership Under Brezhnev: A Comment," *Soviet Studies*, vol. 29, no. 2 (April 1977), 306–316. For a discussion of the more general question of political participation, see J. F. Hough, "Political Participation in the Soviet Union," *Soviet Studies*, vol. 28, no. 1 (January 1976), 3–20. For a general discussion of the role of the party in the economy, see P. Rutland, *The Communist Party and Economic Management in the USSR*, typescript, 1988.

10. *Constitution (Fundamental Law) of the Union of Soviet Socialist Republics* (Moscow: Novosti Press Agency Publishing House, 1978), p. 21.

11. "Ubytochnye, no svoi [unprofitable but our own]," *Trud*, June 2, 1987.

12. Figures on the size of the Soviet bureaucracy are from G. Meyer, *Buerokratischer Sozialismus: Eine Analyse des sowjetischen Herrschaftssystem* (Stuttgart-Bad Cannstatt: Friederich Frommann Verlag, 1977), pp. 143–149; D. M. Gvishiani, "Problemy upravleniia sotsialisticheskoi promyshlennosti," [Problems of management of socialist industry] *Voprosy filosofii*, no. 11 (1956), 7; and D. B. Averianov, *Funktsii i organizatsionnaia struktura organov gosudarstvennogo upravleniia*

[Function and organizational structure of organs of state administration] (Kiev: Akademiia Nauk, 1979), pp. 132–133.

13. For a discussion of welfare criteria and their applicability to comparing economic systems, see, for example, A. Bergson, "Market Socialism Revisited," *Journal of Political Economy,* vol. 75, no. 5 (October 1967), 655–672; and M. Dobb, *Welfare Economics and the Economics of Socialism* (Cambridge: Cambridge University Press, 1969). For a discussion of criteria for comparing economic systems, see B. A. Belassa, "Success Criteria for Economic Systems," in M. Bornstein, ed., *Comparative Economic Systems, Models and Cases,* rev. ed. (Homewood, Ill.: Irwin, 1969), pp. 2–18; for more detailed treatments, see A. Eckstein, ed., *Comparison of Economic Systems* (Berkeley: University of California Press, 1971), pp. 25–240; M. Bornstein, "Comparing of Economic Systems," in M. Bornstein, ed., *Comparative of Economic Systems, Models and Cases,* 4th ed. (Homewood, Ill.: Irwin, 1979), pp. 3–18; and J. M. Montias, *The Structure of Economic Systems* (New Haven and London: Yale University Press, 1976), chap. 4.

Chapter 2

Economic History of Russia to 1917

*T*he economic record of the Soviet period cannot be evaluated in proper perspective without knowing the economic base the Bolsheviks inherited from the tsars. If economic development during the tsarist period had been extensive, then the rapid industrialization of the 1930s would be merely a continuation of past development. If, on the other hand, the Bolsheviks inherited a backward and stagnant economy, then their achievements must be gauged differently.

Both the rate and the level of Russian economic development prior to 1917 are matters of some controversy. Lenin proclaimed the backward tsarist economy, with its isolated pockets of modernity, as the "weakest link" in the capitalist chain; official Soviet ideology argues that the economic backwardness inherited from the tsarist period made the sacrifices of the 1930s necessary. Were it not for the dramatic restructuring of the economic system in the 1930s, today's Soviet economy would not be as far advanced as it is. Western economic historians (such as Alexander Gerschenkron and W. W. Rostow) have tended to focus on the rapid industrial growth achieved after 1880 while emphasizing the feudal problems of Russian agriculture.[1] Other Western economic historians have tended to view tsarist agriculture in a more favorable light.

Our approach to the question of Russian economic development is to first consider the development of industry and agriculture during the last half-century of tsarist rule, and then turn to other factors, such as growth of per capita GNP, changes of industrial structure, and demographic characteristics, suggested by Simon Kuznets as being indicators of "modern economic growth."[2]

INDUSTRIAL GROWTH UNDER THE TSARS

Although it is usually difficult to trace the development of the industrial sector in a country as ancient as Russia, the reign of Peter the Great (1698–1725), an important turning point in Russian economic history, provides us with a convenient place to begin.

Peter the Great, impressed by the technology and industrial expertise he observed during his extensive early travels in Western Europe, determined to industrialize Russia by importing Western technology and technicians en masse. Military considerations played an important role in this decision. Peter the Great provided the initial impetus to move the backward Russian economy toward the development of an increasingly modern industrial sector, by eighteenth-century standards. As a result, eighteenth-century Russia acquired a nascent industrial capacity that, when combined with its vast natural and manpower resources, enabled it to compete militarily with the West for nearly two centuries despite a succession of less vigorous Russian tsars. After Peter the Great, however, a gap began to widen between the Russian economy and its industrializing Western European competitors, especially during the nineteenth century.[3] In fact, during this two-century period, industrialization came to be regarded in Russia as a threat to the autocracy. Tsarist authorities feared that railroads would spread egalitarianism and that the growth of factory towns would spawn a rebellious proletariat.[4] One of history's great ironies was the firm entrenchment during the reign of Peter the Great of feudalism, a retrogressive social institution that later was to become a great obstacle to long-term economic development. Serfdom was used by Peter the Great to finance his military ventures; and, indeed, he staffed his new factories, mines, and postal system with serf labor to implement his progressive industrial policies.

The Crimean War (1854–1856) forced Russian leaders to realize the relative industrial backwardness of Russia vis-à-vis the industrializing Western powers. The potential dangers of this gap were painfully obvious, especially to an empire-conscious country accustomed to respect as a formidable military power. As a result, the Russian government began to promote industrialization in a reversal of its earlier anti-industrialization stance, especially under the forceful leadership of Count Sergei Witte, the minister of finance from 1892 to 1903. Industrial development was fostered by the government in a variety of ways. The state sponsored massive railroad construction, spurred by the obvious military importance of railway transport in a land as massive as the Russian Empire. In 1860, the Russian rail network consisted of 1,600 kilometers of track. By 1917, 81,000 kilometers had been built.[5] This new transportation network opened up the iron and coal resources of the Ukraine, which soon overtook the Ural region as the metallurgical center of the Russian Empire. In addition, it opened up world markets for Russian wheat. Russian exports of wheat products increased five times between the 1860s and 1900, competing with North American wheat, which had also been made available to the world market by the railroads.[6] The state acted as guarantor of bonds, thereby promoting the widespread participation of foreign capital in industrial development. A succession of finance ministers pursued a conservative monetary policy, which stabilized the ruble exchange rate and allowed Russia to join the international gold standard in 1897. Domestic heavy industry was promoted by a series of measures such as high protective tariffs, profit guarantees, tax reductions and exemptions, police help in labor disputes, and government orders at high prices to ensure adequate demand for domestic production. In addition, the state actively recruited foreign entrepreneurs for Russian industry. The military objectives of the state are seen in the ministry of finance's promotion of heavy industry over the small-scale light industry during this period.[7]

A modern entrepreneurial class began to form in nineteenth-century Russia. Russian entrepreneurs were drawn from the civil service and nobility as well as the ranks of Jewish merchants and Old Believer sects.[8] Russian entrepreneurs, like the Western entrepreneurs working in Russia, operated in a legal setting that was ambivalent toward private enterprise. The tsar's signature was required on the charter of every joint-stock company, placing the tsarist bureaucracy in a position to determine who would be allowed to form limited liability corporations. Russian industrialists often got their start in business through state subsidies, tariffs, or preferential state orders. Corrupt practices were common, with industrialists purchasing state favors with bribes. Bribery appeared to be one of the ordinary costs of conducting business in bureaucratic Russia. For its part, the Russian economic bureaucracy, under the leadership of the finance ministry, was ambivalent in its attitude toward modern capitalist institutions. On the one hand, the succession of able finance ministers understood the importance of promoting private initiative and attempted by and large to recruit entrepreneurs on the basis of talent rather than family connections. On the other hand, the Russian state feared the consequences of unbridled capitalism. Russian industrialists, who banded into lobbying organizations such as the Association of Industry and Trade, shared this ambivalence. They argued for fewer restrictions on their activities while at the same time continuing to rely on state protection, subsidies, and state credits.

The Russian legal and state system at the turn of the twentieth century was not unusual for a relatively backward country with great economic potential and a firmly entrenched state bureaucracy. The economic potential was sufficiently great to bring in foreign capital from abroad, attracted primarily by the higher rates of return in Russia. The profit potential was sufficiently great to cause the emergence of a class of home-grown entrepreneurs, while at the same time promoting bureaucratic corruption that added to the business costs of Russian industrialists. The entrenched Russian bureaucracy, unlike the less well-entrenched British bureaucracy, found it difficult to sit on the sidelines. As a result, there was more active bureaucratic meddling in economic affairs.

In the 1880s, an acceleration in the rate of growth of industrial output took place. There has been considerable debate about the causes of this acceleration. Some economic historians, such as Arcadius Kahan, have argued that the upturn in industrial growth was a consequence of natural market forces, spurred by the enormous profit potential of the resource-rich Russian empire.[9] Kahan and others maintain that state activities either hampered (or did not contribute to in a significant way) industrial growth, and they cite the fact that state subsidies to industry were actually quite modest during this period. Others have argued that the acceleration (or "spurt") in industrial growth was the direct result of state intervention.

A prominent scholar of Russian economic history, Alexander Gerschenkron, has proposed the relative backwardness hypothesis to explain this spurt.[10] He suggests that whenever the gap between economic potential and economic actuality of a nation becomes too great, that is, whenever a nation with great economic promise as measured by its total resource endowment becomes backward relative to other countries (as Russia was around 1860), tension is created, new institutions are substituted for missing preconditions, and a spurt of industrial growth occurs. In the case of Russia, the tension was great, the resulting industrial spurt was significant, and the Russian state, which acted as a substitute for missing entrepreneurial resources and deficient demand, was the instigator of industrialization.

Between 1880 and 1900, industrial production more than tripled, accelerating again between 1906 and 1914 after the depression at the turn of the century and the political instability of the 1905 revolution.[11] The extent of Russian industrial progress between 1861 and 1913 is shown in Table 2.1, which indicates that by 1913, Russia had risen to become the world's fifth largest industrial power, behind the United States, England, Germany, and France, and had succeeded in narrowing the gap between itself and the leading producers of key industrial products.

These aggregate figures mask the low per capita output of Russian industry, which can be inferred from the population and output figures in Table 2.1. Despite the considerable growth of industrial output, Russia on the eve of World War I belonged to the group of poor Western European countries (Spain, Italy, and Austria-Hungary) in terms of industrial output per capita.

Russian industrial growth between 1880 and 1913 was rapid, and the industrial gap between Russia and the more advanced industrialized countries, although it remained significant, was narrowed. For this reason, economic historians who have concentrated on Russian industrial development prior to 1917 have traditionally taken a fairly sanguine view of Russian economic development during the last three decades of tsarist rule.

Is this conclusion justified? While significant industrial development is a necessary condition, it is not sufficient in itself to produce overall economic development. Insofar as the growth of GNP (industry, agriculture, services) and per capita GNP—not industrial growth alone—are the most generally accepted indicators of the rate of economic development, we must focus upon the performance of the second major sector, agriculture, during this period of rapid industrialization before a balanced picture of Russian economic development can be obtained.

RUSSIAN AGRICULTURE UNDER THE TSARS

The agricultural revolutions that accompanied the industrialization of Western Europe and England were generally preceded by the breakdown of feudalism, which prepared the way for a modern agriculture unfettered by traditional cultivation methods and restrictions. Feudalism developed rather late in Russia, at a time when this institution was declining or extinct in the more advanced Western nations. Perhaps as a result of its late emergence, feudalism in Russia embodied particularly odious forms of servitude in which serfs were bound to the soil, could be deported to Siberia, were conscripted virtually for life into the army, and were sold on the open market by their masters. Depending on the region of the country, Russian serfs were either required to provide labor services on the landlord's land (*barshchina*) or to make payments in kind from their crops (later money) for the use of their allotted land (*obrok*). In addition, peasant land was held communally and was periodically redistributed by the village elders, who constituted a form of village self-government.

Russian feudal agriculture provided little incentive for the individual peasant. Serf labor was so inefficient that it became customary to call *barshchina* "all that is done slowly, incorrectly, and without incentive."[12] Mobility from the countryside to the town was limited. A peasant working in the town not only had to pay a large portion of his earnings to his master but also had to return to his village if so ordered, unlike the earlier Western European practice whereby serfs could gain their freedom by living in the town.

The Emancipation Act of 1861, which freed the serfs and divided the land holdings of the landed aristocracy (the gentry) between the peasant and the gentry, was a significant watershed, for it provided a unique opportunity to establish the foundations for a modern Russian agriculture. However, the primary objective of the Russian emancipation, initiated by the tsar himself, was not to promote economic development but to prevent further peasant revolts and preserve the autocracy while retaining a form of agriculture that could still be controlled. The vested land interests were favored. While the peasants received their juridical freedom, they were allotted plots of gentry land to be "redeemed"

Table 2.1   SELECTED ECONOMIC AND SOCIAL INDICATORS, RUSSIA AND OTHER COUNTRIES, 1861 AND 1913

	Population (millions)	National Income, 1913 rubles (million)	Per capita national Income	Grain output (100 metric tons)	Coal output (million metric tons)
1861					
Russia	74	5.269	71	41,500	0.38
United Kingdom	20	6.469	323	n.a.	85.0
France	37	5,554	150	26,220	9.4
Germany	36	6,313	175	28,706	18.7
United States	32	14,405	450	39,318	13.3
Netherlands	3	n.a.	n.a.	292	n.a.
Norway	2	331	166	802	n.a.
Sweden	4	449	112	1,265	0.03
Italy	25	4,570	183	6,455	0.03
Spain	16	n.a.	n.a.	n.a.	0.35
Austria-Hungary	35	n.a.	n.a.	20,745	2.5
1913					
Russia	171	20,266	119	123,000	36.1
United Kingdom	36	20,869	580	8,948	292.0
France	39	11,816	303	30,870	40.8
Germany	65	24,280	374	85,445	277.3
United States	93	96,030	1,033	146,100	517.0
Netherlands	6	2,195	366	3,686	1.9
Norway	2	918	659	1,076	n.a.
Sweden	6	2,040	340	4,979	0.36
Italy	35	9,140	261	13,128	0.7
Spain	20	3,975	199	9,025	3.9
Austria-Hungary	50	9,500	190	38,953	54.2

[a]1871.

[b]Average 1867–1869.

Source: P. R. Gregory, *Russian National Income, 1885–1913* (Cambridge: Cambridge University Press), pp. 155–156; n.a. denotes figure not available.

by the holder. The remaining gentry land (well over 50 percent) was retained by its original owners. The peasants were generally dissatisfied with the size of their plots; many were too small to provide earnings for the redemption payments due to the state (which had purchased the land from the gentry).

Some peasants accepted "beggar's allotments"—small plots of land free from all obligations—and became small freeholders. The state peasants received land as well, under more generous terms; but as late as 1877, the crown and the state treasury still owned almost 50 percent of the land in European Russia.

Let us now consider the principal features of the Emancipation Act of 1861 from the viewpoint of economic efficiency.[13] While the reform did contain positive elements—an increase in the large estates that created export surpluses, the introduction of a money economy into the countryside via redemption pay-

Pig iron (1000 metric tons)	Crude steel (1000 metric tons)	Raw cotton (1000 meters)	Rail network (1000 km)	Infant mortality (per 1000)
320	7	43.0	2.2	239[b]
3,772	334	456.0	14.6	148
967	84	110.0	9.6	190
592	143	74.0	11.5	260
830	12	213.0	50.3	n.a.
n.a.	n.a.	3.6	0.34	196
0	n.a.	n.a.	0.07	113
170	0	7.7	0.57	124
27	0	12.0	2.8	232
67	n.a.	27.0	2.9	174
315	22	44.0	3.2	264
4,641	4,918	424	70.2	237
10,425	7,787	988	32.6	108
5,207	4,687	271	40.7	112
16,761	17,609	478	63.4	151
34,700	31,800	1,458	400.0	115
n.a.	n.a.	36	3.2	91
n.a.	0	n.a.	3.1	64
730	591	22	14.3	70
427	934	202	18.3	138
425	242	88	15.1	155
2,381	2,611	210	23.0	190

ments, and the psychological impact of emancipation—it placed serious constraints on agricultural development. Communal agriculture was retained, as a means of control over the rural population, in the institution of the *mir* or *obshchina* (the village communal organizations). The agricultural communes were held responsible for the debts of their individual members; therefore, the more prosperous commune members were liable for the defaults of the poorer. With this feature, there was reduced incentive to accumulate wealth within the commune.[14] The peasant family could not officially withdraw its land from the commune until all debts on the land were met and then only with a two-thirds vote of the membership. Nor could the peasant leave agriculture permanently for the city until his land was free of obligations—the rigid internal passport system was supposed to ensure peasant compliance. In addition, the land was to be redistributed periodically within the commune, thereby reducing incentives to improve a particular plot. In short, the Emancipation Act made it difficult for the peasant to develop both a sense of private property and an interest in long-term productivity improvements, factors that had proved crucial in the agricultural revolutions of other countries.

According to Gerschenkron, the guiding principles of the Russian agrarian program between 1861 and 1906 were:

> To preserve the *obshchina* until the liquidation of the redemption debt, to prolong the amortization of that debt so as to protect the *obshchina*, and at the same time to continue to hold the peasantry in the vise of ruinous aggregate taxation.[15]

Gerschenkron has argued (along with Lenin and Soviet scholars) that massive peasant dissatisfaction with the Emancipation Act was a significant cause of the Revolution of 1905. Peasant unrest during this period bordered on spontaneous armed rebellion in the countryside, which prompted the state to enact measures to improve the lot of the peasant: joint responsibility was abolished in 1903, and 50 percent of peasant indebtedness was forgiven in 1906 and finally canceled fully in 1907. From the point of view of long-run economic development, the Stolypin Reforms of 1906 and 1910 were significant government measures because they sought to weaken communal agriculture and to create a class of small peasant proprietors. Their principal provision made it easier for individual peasants to withdraw from the commune, which—combined with the reduced indebtedness of the peasantry—opened the way for private agriculture in Russia. Heads of households could demand their portion of commune land and withdraw from the commune. They could further demand consolidation of their land into a single area.

It is difficult to predict what impact the Stolypin Reforms would have had on the Russian economy had they been given sufficient time to take effect. Most authorities agree that they would have strengthened Russian agriculture. Western authorities (Gerschenkron, Lazar Volin, Jerome Blum, and G. T. Robinson) have joined tsarist and Soviet scholars in emphasizing the poor performance of Russian agriculture after 1861. These authorities point to a possible decline in per capita grain availability between 1870 and the 1890s, accounts of appalling poverty in the Russian village,[16] rising peasant tax arrears, and the increasing number of mortgaged estates as evidence of an "agrarian crisis." Moreover, the existence of an agrarian crisis provides a convenient explanation for the Revolution of 1905 and support for the Gerschenkron proposition that the burden of industrialization was borne by the Russian peasant.

This entirely pessimistic picture of Russian agriculture has been questioned by a number of scholars. Internal passport data have been analyzed to demonstrate that the Russian peasant was relatively free to go to the city or to outlying provinces, despite official restrictions on such movements. Analyses of peasant taxes reveal that the growing arrears may not be indicative of the exhaustion of the taxpaying capacity of the Russian village. In fact, Russian peasants may have adjusted their tax payments automatically according to their sense of social justice.[17] Most importantly, recent studies demonstrate that the output and marketing performance of Russian agriculture was much better than the earlier literature had suggested.

Basically, the more recent studies of Russian agricultural output and peasant living standards find that, on average, Russian peasants were experiencing rising living standards (alongside urban workers) during the period of rapid industrialization. Over the 1885–1913 period, there does not appear to have been a noticeable shift in the distribution of consumption expenditures between the city and countryside. The growth rates of agricultural output and of output per capita were quite respectable by Western European standards, lagging only slightly behind the growth rate of total output. There was positive growth of agricultural labor productivity, at perhaps two-thirds the rate in industry.[18] The aggregate figures point to rising peasant living standards, rising agricultural productivity and rising per capita agricultural output. Agricultural progress was, however, quite uneven. The Russian grain market was not integrated (there was substantial regional variation in agricultural prices); the regional distribution of transportation services was uneven; and significant resources continued to be devoted to agriculture in grain deficit regions ill-suited by climate and soil conditions to agriculture pursuits.[19] A generally rising trend in agriculture is quite consistent with the accounts of regional and individual poverty that abound in the Russian and Soviet literatures (see reference 16, for example).

The conclusion that Russian agriculture performed reasonably well despite the strictures placed upon it by the 1861 emancipation is not surprising. In a country as vast as Russia, it would have been difficult for the bureaucracy to restrain peasant mobility (as the passport data demonstrate). An artificial separation of the economy into a prosperous and growing industrial sector and a backward and stagnant agricultural sector would be an unexpected economic result. Unless the agrarian population could be rendered immobile, the natural tendency would be for labor to seek out its highest return, and this tendency would lead to a rough equalization of real wages between the city and countryside in the long run. It would also be difficult to keep Russian agriculture, with its close ties to world markets, isolated from the agricultural revolutions of Western Europe, North America, and Australia. It should also be remembered that Russian agriculture was expanding extensively during the late nineteenth century into new areas not subject to the restrictions of the peasant emancipation.

ECONOMIC GROWTH UNDER THE TSARS

Russian industrial growth was more rapid than that of its European neighbors after 1880. Russian agricultural performance, according to recent evidence, was better during the industrialization era than had been thought by earlier historians. To provide some perspective on the issue of modern economic growth in Russia, an assessment of Russian economic performance relative to that of the industrialized countries is required. In such an assessment, the position of the Russian Empire at the beginning of the "modern era" (1861) and on the eve of World War I must be established, and the Russian record of economic growth and structural change must be considered.

Data on population, national income, and various output series have been assembled (see Table 2.1) for Russia and other countries for the years 1861 and 1913. These figures allow one to draw a general picture of the Russian economy at the end of the tsarist era and to trace its progress from the emancipation to the eve of World War I.

On the eve of the war, Russia was one of the world's major economic powers, but the dichotomy between the country's aggregate economic power, as dictated by the magnitude of the Russian Empire, and its relative poverty on a per capita basis is striking. Russia began its modern era with a population twice as large as its next most populous neighbor (France) and ended the era three times as large as its largest European neighbor (Germany). This increase indicates the more rapid growth of population in Russia than in Europe. Russian population growth was much like that in the European offshoots, Australia and North America, with a crucial difference. Russia's rapid population growth was due entirely to high rates of natural increase, while immigration played an important role in North America and Australia.

With such a large population, exceptionally low per capita output levels would be required to prevent Russia from being one of the world's major economic powers. This point is confirmed by the national income rankings. By 1913, Russia's national output was above France's, equal to England's, 80 percent that of Germany, and twice that of Austria-Hungary. In relative terms, the only decline between 1861 and 1913 was vis-à-vis the United States, a country that experienced a rapid growth of population and national output during this period.

Russia's economic power was concentrated in agriculture. In 1861, Russia produced more grain than any other country and was surpassed only by the United States in 1913. On a per capita basis, however, Russia ranked well behind the more advanced grain-producing countries, such as the United States and Germany, but was roughly on a par with countries such as France and Austria-Hungary. Russia's position as a major industrial power was less well established. In 1861, Russia was a minor producer of major industrial commodities (coal, iron, and steel) and had only a rudimentary transportation system, despite its vast territory. By 1913, Russia's relative position had improved somewhat, especially relative to France and Austria-Hungary, but Russia still lagged seriously behind the major industrial powers. It was only in textiles that Russia occupied a position roughly equivalent to that of Germany, the continent's largest industrial producer.

The relative backwardness of the Russian economy is masked by aggregate figures but is evident from per capita comparisons. Russia began its modern era with a per capita income one-half France's and Germany's, one-fifth England's, and 15 percent that of the United States. By 1913, Russia's relative position had declined, due primarily to rapid population growth and slow output growth until the 1880s. Russia's 1913 per capita income was less than 40 percent that of France and 33 percent that of Germany, still one-fifth England's, and one-tenth that of the United States. On a per capita income basis, 1913 Russia was a poor European country, ranking well below Spain, Italy, and Austria-Hungary.

Russia's most important relative achievement was the development of a rail network that was Europe's largest by 1913 and was comparable on a per capita basis to countries like Italy and Austria-Hungary. The one social indicator in Table 2.1, infant mortality, shows that the advances in public health experienced in other countries were not shared by the masses in the Russian village. Russia entered its modern era in 1861 with a rate of infant mortality not much different from that of Western Europe. Yet 50 years later, infant mortality was virtually unchanged in Russia, while in other countries it had declined significantly.

Growth of Per Capita NNP

A distinctive feature of modern economic growth is accelerated and sustained growth of per capita output. This rapid growth contrasts with the secular stagnation of the premodern period. Annual rates of growth of Russian net national product (NNP), population, and per capita NNP are given in Table 2.2. These figures suffer from several weaknesses, yet they should be accurate within a reasonable margin of error.

The growth of Russian NNP was relatively slow from the emancipation to the early 1880s, but this was prior to the establishment of a modern transportation system. Between 1861 and 1883, the growth rate of per capita income was negligible, and labor productivity apparently failed to increase. However, in assessing tsarist economic growth, one should focus on the "industrialization era" from the mid-1880s and compare Russian growth performance with that of the industrialized countries.

During Russia's industrialization era, the growth of Russian national income was above average when compared to other countries during the same period. The Russian growth rate of 3.3 percent per annum was equaled or surpassed by only four countries and exceeded the growth rate of the two other "follower" countries, Italy and Japan.[20] Russian growth was similar to that of

Table 2.2   PATTERNS OF RUSSIAN GROWTH (Percent per Annum)

	NNP	Population	Per capita NNP	Labor force	NNP per worker (1–4)
1861–1863 to 1881–1883	1.8	1.1	0.7	1.9	0.1
1883–1887 to 1909–1913	3.3	1.6	1.7	1.7	1.6

Sources: The 1861–1883 figures are for the 50 European provinces and are from P. R. Gregory, "Economic Growth and Structural Change in Tsarist Russia: A Case of Modern Economic Growth?' *Soviet Studies,* vol. 23, no. 1 (January 1972), 422. The 1883–1913 figures are for the Russian Empire and are from P. R. Gregory, "Economic Growth and Structural Change in Tsarist Russia and the Soviet Union: A Long-Term Comparison," in S. Rosefielde, ed., *Economic Welfare and the Economics of Soviet Socialism* (Cambridge: Cambridge University Press, 1981).

the European offshoots in North America and Australia, which also experienced rapid population growth.

On a per capita and per worker basis, Russian output growth was average relative to the industrialized countries. Thus, Russia's above-average output growth was largely the consequence of relatively rapid population and labor force growth. Russian economic growth was, therefore, of a largely "extensive" character, that is, was caused principally by the growth of inputs rather than the growth of output per unit of input. The less reliable evidence on tsarist capital stock suggests that roughly two-thirds of Russian output growth was accounted for by the growth of conventional labor and capital inputs.[21] Again, the Russian experience is similar to that of the European offshoots, which also grew "extensively" during this period.

The conclusion follows from this evidence that after 1885, the Russian Empire grew at total, per capita, and per worker rates that were at least average relative to those of the industrialized countries. Although Russian growth over the entire 1861 to 1913 period was indeed relatively slow,[22] this was due to the slow growth until the 1880s. During the industrialization era, Russian growth appears to have taken on the classical features of modern economic growth.

Structural Change

Another means of establishing whether Russia was indeed undergoing the initial stages of modern economic growth after the mid-1880s is to compare Russian structural change with that of the industrialized countries during the early phases of modern economic growth. In Table 2.3, shifts in the structure of Russian national income both by producing sector and by final use are shown. These shifts reveal the expected modern economic growth pattern of structural change—rising shares of industry, falling shares of agriculture, rising shares of net investment, and falling shares of personal consumption.

One way to assess these changes is to compare them with the structural shifts experienced by the industrialized countries during their first 30 years of modern economic growth. Utilizing data from Kuznets,[23] one finds that the amount of structural change experienced in Russia during its industrialization era was about average (or perhaps slightly below average) for a country undergoing the initial stages of modern economic growth. Thus, the evidence on structural change supports the proposition that Russia was in the process of embarking upon a path of modern economic growth during its industrialization era.

Investment in Human Capital

Between the emancipation and the 1880s, labor productivity failed to increase; thereafter, it grew at an average rate relative to that of the industrialized countries. One possible explanation for the initiation of productivity growth is the increased public and private investment in human capital after 1880. There is little firm evidence on literacy rates prior to 1897, but data on the literacy rates

Table 2.3 RUSSIAN ECONOMIC STRUCTURE DURING THE INDUSTRIALIZATION ERA

	Shares in national product by producing sector (percentages)		
	Agriculture	Industry, construction, transportation, and communication	Trade and services
1883–1887	57.5	23.5	19.0
1909–1913	51.0	32.0	17.0

	Shares in national product by final use (percentages)			
	Personal consumption	Government	Net domestic investment	Net foreign investment
1885–1889	83.5	8.1	8.1	0.3
1909–1913	79.6	9.7	12.1	−1.5

Source: P. R. Gregory, "Economic Growth and Structural Change in Tsarist Russia and the Soviet Union: A Long-Term Comparison," in S. Rosefielde, ed., *Economic Welfare and the Economics of Soviet Socialism* (Cambridge: Cambridge University Press, 1981).

of military recruits and in St. Petersburg and Moscow show that the increase in literacy was barely perceptible prior to the early 1880s.[24] From the mid-1880s on, however, the growth of literacy rates accelerated. Between 1884 and 1904, the literacy rates of military recruits more than doubled, from 26 percent to 56 percent. For the country as a whole, the 1897 illiteracy rate was 72 percent (see Table 2.4), with urban literacy almost three times rural literacy. Between 1897 and 1913, further progress was made in providing education to the population, and a rough estimate places Russian illiteracy in 1913 at 60 percent of the over-10-year-old population. For comparison, we note that U.S. illiteracy in 1900 was only 11 percent of the over-10 population.

The low literacy rates of the Russian population prior to the revolution is a fairly convincing indicator of the social backwardness of the economy. The limited pool of educated workers constrained overall industrialization and may have forced Russian industry to adopt capital-intensive production techniques

Table 2.4 ILLITERACY RATES: RUSSIA IN 1897 AND 1913—UNITED STATES IN 1900
Percent of Total Population over 10 Years of Age

		Urban	Rural	Total
Russia	1897	55[a]	83[a]	72
	1913	—	—	60
United States	1900	—	—	11

[a] Percent of entire population.

Source: A. G. Rashin, *Formirovanie rabochego klassa v Rossii* [The formation of the working class in Russia] (Moscow: 1958), pp. 579–581.

to utilize more efficiently the limited supply of skilled industrial laborers (some of whom were imported from abroad).[25] The extremely low rural literacy rates show that while the pool of rural labor was substantial, it was not perhaps suited for employment under modern factory conditions.

Although the *level* of human capital remained low, Russian human capital was indeed growing at a relatively rapid rate. Arcadius Kahan has emphasized the rising investment in primary education, the 2560 percent increase in the number of elementary schools, and the 3.5-fold increase in primary school enrollment between 1890 and 1914.[26] In fact, Kahan argues that the growth of human capital was more important than that of physical capital to Russia's growth during this period.

Demographic Patterns

Modern economic growth has characteristic demographic patterns as well. As Kuznets[27] notes, the dominant trend in birthrates is downward throughout the modern period, although changes in premodern institutional practices may create initial increases in birthrates. The death rate declines rapidly during modern economic growth, being the principal factor behind the acceleration of population growth. The most conspicuous benefactors of the declining death rate are the younger age groups, owing to increased control over infant mortality. Comparing premodern and modern rates, Kuznets notes that premodern birthrates varied substantially among countries, ranging from highs of 55 per 1000 to lows of 31 per 1000. The average premodern death rate was around 30 per 1000 in Western Europe and somewhat lower in the areas of European settlement in North America and Australia. From these initial levels, birth and death rates declined, the death rate approaching a lower limit of around 10 per 1000 in recent times.

Russia began the postemancipation development in 1861 with a demographic base like that of Western Europe and North America some 75 to 100 years earlier (see Table 2.5). The Russian birthrates of the early 1860s were exceeded only by the U.S. rates of the 1790–1800 period. The Russian 1861 death rate was well above the eighteenth-century Western Europe average of approximately 30 per 1000. The Russian death rate began to decline steadily during the late 1890s but remained high relative to Western European standards. The 1913 Russian death rate of 27 per 1000 was still more than double the Western European average of 13 per 1000 for that same year.

The high Russian death rate can be explained by the high rate of infant mortality—27 deaths per 100 during the 1867–1871 period and 24 deaths per 100 in 1911. This limited decline over a 40-year period indicates the meager success that tsarist Russia had in reducing infant mortality.[28]

The Russian birthrate hovered around 50 per 1000 from 1860 to 1900, after which it declined steadily; but in 1913, it was still twice the Western European average of the same year. Thus, although Russian birth and death rates began to conform to modern economic growth patterns around the turn of the century,

Table 2.5   BIRTHRATES, DEATH RATES, AND RATES OF NATURAL
INCREASE: 50 EUROPEAN RUSSIAN PROVINCES, 1861–1913
Per 1000

	Birthrate	Death rate	Rate of natural increase
1861–1865	51	37	14
1866–1870	50	37	12
1871–1875	51	37	14
1876–1880	50	36	14
1881–1885	51	36	14
1886–1890	50	35	16
1891–1895	49	36	13
1896–1900	50	32	17
1901–1905	48	31	17
1906–1910	46	30	16
1910–1913	44	27	17

Source: A. G. Rashin, *Naselenie Rossii za 100 let* [The population of Russia for 100 years] (Moscow: Sotzekizdat, 1956), p. 155.

they still roughly corresponded to premodern levels at the time of the Revolution.

RUSSIA'S DEPENDENCE ON THE WEST

Tsarist Russia's economic dependence on the West was a topic of considerable importance during the Soviet industrialization debates of the 1920s (Chapter 3). Russia's dependence on foreign capital goods bears on our discussion of Russia's economic development because heavy dependence is accepted as an indicator of underdevelopment.[29] As an economy develops, it becomes able to produce domestically the capital equipment that it had been required to import earlier (import substitution) and thus to reduce its dependence on foreign capital.

To determine Russia's dependence on foreign technology, one must first consider its domestic production of capital equipment. A possible rough indicator of Russia's domestic machinery-producing capacity was the relative importance of metal products (engineering) in the tsarist Russian economy. In 1913, metal products accounted for 10 and 12 percent of manufacturing net output and labor force, respectively. During that same period, the average manufacturing product share of engineering in England, the United States, and Germany was 21 percent.[30] Russia in 1913 devoted less than half as much of its manufacturing resources to machinery as did the major industrial powers of the West. Inasmuch as Russia in 1913 devoted a much smaller proportion of total resources to manufacturing than the three major industrial powers, the share of total resources devoted to the production of capital equipment was even smaller.

The relatively small portion of resources devoted to capital goods is perhaps surprising in view of the apparent zeal with which the Russian state one-sidedly promoted the investment goods industries at the expense of consumer goods industries during the 1890s, which, according to Gerschenkron, resulted "in the relative top-heaviness of the Russian industrial structure as well as its relative concentration upon producer goods."[31]

It is clear that the development of the tsarist economy was dependent on the transfer of foreign technology and equipment. The data also show that Russian development was aided by the receipt of savings from abroad to finance domestic capital formation. Russia was, in fact, a large debtor country during the 1880–1913 period, receiving significant capital inflows from France, England, and Belgium. Foreign capital probably accounted for 40 percent of industrial investment, 15 to 20 percent of total investment, and about 2 percent of NNP at the end of the tsarist era.[32]

As a frame of reference, one might compare the Russian foreign debt experience with that of two other large countries, the United States and Japan, both of which were debtor countries at early stages of their economic development. Foreign capital accounted for about 1 percent of U.S. GNP and 10 percent of investment during the mid-1880s, when U.S. dependence on foreign capital was at its peak. It accounted for 0.2 percent of Japanese GNP between 1887 and 1896, rising briefly to a high of 4 percent between 1897 and 1906, after which Japan became a capital exporter.[33] This comparison suggests that tsarist Russia was more dependent on foreign capital in both magnitude and duration than were either the United States or Japan during their dependence periods. The inability of the domestic economy to meet the needs of industrialization and the resulting extensive dependence on foreign capital left a deep impression on the Bolshevik leaders and played an important role in Stalin's industrialization and collectivization decisions of 1928 and 1929 (Chapter 4).

WAS RUSSIA UNDERDEVELOPED IN 1914?

Imperial Russia began the initial phases of modern economic growth during the industrialization era after the early 1880s. Prior to 1880, the rate of growth of national output was quite slow in aggregate and per capita terms, and labor productivity was not increasing. During the industrialization era, the growth of national output was rapid relative to the industrialized countries, while per capita and per worker growth rates were average vis-à-vis the industrialized countries. Suggested causes of the improvement in Russian growth performance are the creation of a modern transportation network and the growing investment in human capital. In addition to the acceleration in growth rates and efficiency characteristic of modern economic growth, Russia experienced between the 1880s and 1913 the structural shifts typical of modern economic growth. The Russian economy was well integrated into the world economy by the 1880s. Russia and the United States were the major suppliers in world wheat markets, a relatively modern rail and shipping network linked Russia with world markets, and the Russian economy participated in the booms and busts of the European business cycle.

Despite this sustained progress over a 30-year period, the tsarist economy was still relatively backward on the eve of World War I. Russia's per capita income ranking placed it among the poorest countries of Europe. The sheer size of the Russian Empire and the magnitude of Russian agricultural output masked the per capita weakness of industrial outputs. The peasant, not the industrial worker, was still the dominant figure in the Russian economy. A minority of the population—and therefore the labor force—was literate, indicating poorly developed human capital; illiteracy was nearly complete among the vast, underemployed peasant population. Russia's demographic pattern was still roughly comparable to that of the developed countries during their premodern periods. Birthrates, death rates, and especially, rates of infant mortality remained stubbornly high. Industrialization remained dependent on foreign capital. It is not clear whether the most highly organized institution, the tsarist bureaucracy, was a help or hindrance to economic development.

The formidable task of creating a modern industrialized economy still lay ahead when the Bolsheviks came to power in 1917. The Soviets directed themselves to their task in 1928, after recovery from the ravages of World War I and the civil war (1917 to 1920), and came to grips with the universal economic and political problems of economic development that the developed countries had faced before them. The Soviet response to this task was distinctive in that the Soviets chose to combine nonmarket forces with political dictatorship to generate rapid development, whereas other countries chose to rely primarily upon market forces and some form of political representation.

The assessment of economic performance during the late tsarist era is important for two reasons. The first is that it permits us to evaluate economic performance during the Soviet era. Without knowing the economic base and the growth tradition inherited by the Soviet leadership, one cannot judge properly the achievements of the Soviet period. For this reason, we shall return to the tsarist period base in our assessment of Soviet economic performance. The second reason is that one cannot judge the relevance of the Soviet development model for use by contemporary less-developed countries (LDCs) without knowing the starting point of the Soviet experiment. Did the Soviet leadership launch its industrialization drive in 1928 from an economic base superior to that of today's LDCs?

In many respects, the similarities between the Russian economy in 1914 and the contemporary LDCs are striking: the low literacy rates, the high rates of birth and infant mortality, the concentration of the labor force in agriculture, and the dependence on foreign capital. Yet despite these features of relative backwardness, the evidence suggests that the Russian economy did have a substantial head start when compared to that of today's LDCs.

First, Russia in 1914 was a much richer country on a per capita income basis than most LDCs today. In 1914, Russian per capita income was some 33 to 40 percent that of its richest European neighbors, whereas per capita incomes in contemporary LDCs are only a small fraction of those in industrialized countries. Although one cannot compare income levels of countries 65 years apart, it is nevertheless informative to note that 1913 Russian per capita income in 1988 U.S. dollars was in the range of $750 to $1334,[34] figures that would place it in the middle range of contemporary LDCs. Moreover, 1913 Russian per capita income was not notoriously high or low compared with the modern economic growth starting points in Europe and North America.[35]

A second advantage vis-à-vis the contemporary LDCs relates to agricultural marketings. During the industrialization era, Russian agriculture tended to market a fairly substantial portion of its output outside of villages. For grain, the marketed portion averaged a fairly steady 25 percent from the 1880s to 1913.[36] Thus, Russian agriculture was able to produce a marketed surplus available for export and industrial raw materials, and was able to feed the urban population—a crucial requirement for successful economic development. In the poorer LDCs, agriculture tends to operate closer to peasant subsistence levels and is unable to provide the margin so crucial to industrial development.

A third advantage inherited by the Soviet regime was the Russian experience with rapid industrial growth and infrastructure investment, especially after 1880. In fact, we have argued that the beginnings of modern economic growth can be discerned during this period. This industrialization provided the nucleus of a factory labor force and management personnel, and the rail network served as a valuable asset for an industrializing country. Few LDCs can launch industrialization from such a favorable base.[37]

Russia's comparatively favorable starting point relative to the LDCs should not obscure the basic point of its relative poverty to the industrialized countries of Europe and North America in 1914. Life expectancy in Russia was still below what it had been in colonial America 150 years earlier. Russia was still subject to plagues and famine, while the industrialized countries had developed a strong degree of immunity. Russia had still to create a rule of law conducive to contract enforcement. There is not doubt that the Bolshevik leadership inherited one of the most backward economies of Europe despite the impressive progress after 1880.[38]

REFERENCES

1. A. Gerschenkron, *Economic Backwardness in Historical Perspective* (Cambridge, Mass.: Harvard University Press, 1962), chap. 1; W. W. Rostow, *The Stages of Economic Growth* (Cambridge: Cambridge University Press, 1965), p. 67; W. W. Rostow, *The World Economy: History and Prospect* (Austin and London: University of Texas Press, 1978), pp. 426–429; M. E. Falkus, *The Industrialization of Russia, 1700–1914* (London and Basingstoke: MacMillan, 1972), pp. 1–25; and V. I. Lenin, *The Development of Capitalism in Russia* (Moscow: Progress Publishers, 1977).

2. S. Kuznets, *Modern Economic Growth* (New Haven, Conn.: Yale University Press, 1966), chap. 1.

3. A. Kahan, "Continuity in Economic Activity and Policy During the Post-Petrine Period in Russia," in W. L. Blackwell, ed., *Russian Economic Development from Peter the Great to Stalin* (New York: New Viewpoints, 1974), pp. 51–70.

4. A. Gerschenkron, "Russian Agrarian Policies and Industrialization, 1861–1917," in *Continuity in History and Other Essays* (Cambridge, Mass.: Harvard University Press, 1968), pp. 144–147.

5. P. A. Khromov, *Ekonomicheskoe razvitie Rossii* [The economic development of Russia] (Moscow: 1967), p. 280.

6. Ibid., pp. 361–362; M. E. Falkus, "Russia and the International Wheat Trade, 1861–1914," *Economica*, vol. 33, no. 132 (November 1966), 416–429; and J. Metzer, "Railroad Development and Market Integration: The Case of Tsarist Russia," *Journal of Economic History*, vol. 34, no. 3 (September 1974), pp. 529–550.

7. A. Gerschenkron, "The Early Phases of Industrialization in Russia: Afterthoughts and Counterthoughts," in W. W. Rostow, ed., *The Economics of Takeoff into Sustained Growth* (New York: St. Martin's Press, 1963), pp. 152–154; and J. P. McKay, *Pioneers for Profit: Foreign Entrepreneurship and Russian Industrialization, 1885–1913* (Chicago: University of Chicago Press, 1970).

8. For a collection of authoritative studies of Russian entrepreneurship, see G. Guroff and F. V. Carstensen, eds., *Entrepreneurship in Imperial Russia and the Soviet Union* (Princeton, N.J.: Princeton University Press, 1983). In particular, see the studies by Thomas Owen, Arcadius Kahan, Boris Anan'ich, Fred Carstensen, and Ruth Amende Roosa.

9. Arcadius Kahan has examined the pattern of state expenditures during the period of rapid industrialization and found that only a very small portion of the imperial budget was devoted to promoting industrialization. It is primarily for this reason that Kahan has disputed the fact that the Russian state played a crucial role in promoting Russian industrialization. For further information, see A. Kahan, "Government Policies and the Industrialization of Russia," *Journal of Economic History*, vol. 27, no. 4 (December 1967).

10. Gerschenkron, *Economic Backwardness*, chap. 1.

11. R. Goldsmith, "The Economic Growth in Tsarist Russia, 1860–1913," *Economic Development and Cultural Change*, vol. 9, no. 3 (April 1961), pp. 462–463; and A. Gerschenkron, "The Rate of Growth in Russia Since 1885," *Journal of Economic History* (supplement), vol. 7 (1947), pp. 144–174.

12. M. V. Dovnar-Zapol'skii, *Na zare krestianskoi svobody* [At the daybreak of peasant emancipation] (Kiev: 1911), p. 179.

13. The following discussion is based primarily upon Gerschenkron, "Russian Agrarian Policies," pp. 140–256; and Lazar Volin, *A Century of Russian Agriculture from Alexander II to Khrushchev* (Cambridge, Mass.: Harvard University Press, 1970), part I.

14. Olga Crisp argues that this provision served to introduce a form of income tax, graduated according to ability to pay within the commune: O. Crisp, *Studies in the Russian Economy Before 1914* (London and Basingstoke: Macmillan, 1976), essay 3.

15. Gerschenkron, "Russian Agrarian Policies."

16. We relate a couple of examples of rural poverty in Russia during the 1870s and 1880s. In the Kazan province, it was estimated that the yield per *desiatin*, on fertile land was about 1.9 rubles. Obligations (taxes, redemption payments, etc.) per *desi-*

atin, however, were 2.8 rubles, which means that the peasant had to make up the difference by gainful employment either in industry or as a hired hand: Yu. Yanson, *Opyt statisticheskogo isledovaniia o krestianskikh nadelakh i platezhakh* [Experience of statistical investigations of peasant plots and payments] (St. Petersburg: 1877), pp. 75–85. A study of the Novgorod province revealed that total peasant income was 8.8 million rubles, of which 70 percent was earned outside agriculture. Bread purchases, taxes, and other obligations came to 6.3 million rubles, leaving a remainder of 2.6 million rubles, or 12 rubles per household for other consumption items: A. A. Kornilov, *Krestianskaia reforma* [The peasant reform] (St. Petersburg: 1905), pp. 194–195.

17. Crisp, *Studies in the Russian Economy*, essays 1 and 3; and J. Simms, "The Crisis in Russian Agriculture at the End of the 19th Century," *Slavic Review*, vol. 36, no. 3 (September 1977), pp. 377–398. For more on this point, see the discussion between J. Sanders and J. Simms in "Once More into the Breach, Dear Friends: A Closer Look at Indirect Tax Receipts and the Condition of the Russian Peasantry, 1881–1899," *Slavic Review*, vol. 43, no. 4 (Winter 1984), pp. 657–671.

18. The available studies of Russian national income point to agricultural output rising more rapidly than the rural population. Studies of Russian capital stock find that agricultural capital stock (livestock, structures, and equipment) was rising on a per capita basis. Available statistics also point to agricultural exports rising more rapidly than agricultural output. A study of Russian peasant living standards points to rising per capita consumption of the Russian agrarian population. On these points, see A. Kahan, "Capital Formation During the Period of Early Industrialization in Russia 1890–1913," *Cambridge Economic History of Europe*, vol. VII, part II (Cambridge: Cambridge University Press, 1982), appendices 8 and 9; Goldsmith, "Economic Growth in Tsarist Russia"; P. Gregory, "Grain Marketings and Peasant Consumption, Russia, 1885–1913," *Explorations in Economic History*, vol. 17, no. 2 (April 1980) pp. 135–164; and Gregory, *Russian National Income* (Cambridge: Cambridge University Press, 1982), chap. 6. Curiously, statistical studies conducted by Russian economists in the early twentieth century generally find rising per capita output in agriculture. For the most authoritative sources, see P. I. Liaschenko, *Ocherki agrarnoi evoliutsii Rossii* [Studies of the agrarian evolution in Russia] (Petersburg: no publisher given, 1908); and S. N. Prokopovich, *Opyt ischisleniia narodnogo dokhoda 50 gubernii Evropeiskoi Rossii v. 1900–1913 gg.* [An attempt to estimate the national income of the 50 European Russian provinces in the years 1900 and 1913] (Moscow: Soviet Vserossiiskikh Kooperativnykh Siezdov, 1918).

19. For authoritative studies of regional aspects of Russian agricultural production, see A. I. Chuprov and A. S. Posnikov, eds., *Vliianie orozhaev i khlebnykh tsen na nekotoryie storony russkago narodnogo khoziastva* [Influence of harvests and grain prices on several aspects of the Russian national economy] (Petersburg: Kirshbaum, 1897); and I. D. Koval'chenko and L. V. Milov, *Vserossiisky agrarny rynok XVIII–nachalo XX veka* [The all-Russian agrarian market from the eighteenth to the beginning of the twentieth century] (Moscow: Nauka, 1974).

20. P. R. Gregory, "Economic Growth and Structural Change in Tsarist Russia and the Soviet Union: A Long-Term Comparison," in S. Rosefielde, ed., *Economic Welfare and the Economics of Soviet Socialism* (Cambridge: Cambridge University Press, 1981).

21. Ibid.

22. Goldsmith, "The Rate of Growth in Tsarist Russia," pp. 441–443.

23. These results are reported in Gregory, "Economic Growth and Structural Change in Tsarist Russia and the Soviet Union."

24. Data on investment in schooling in Russia are summarized in O. Crisp, "Labor and Industrialization in Russia," *Cambridge Economic History of Europe* (Cambridge: Cambridge University Press, 1978), vol. 7, part 2, pp. 387–399; and in A. Kahan, "Capital Formation During the Period of Early Industrialization in Russia," in the same volume, pp. 293–295.

25. Gerschenkron writes, "[the] labor supply to Russian industry was inadequate in quantity and inferior in quality. . . . Therein lies the explanation for the paradoxical situation that a country, so poor in capital and holding much of its accumulated wealth in hands that would not make it available for industrial venture, contrived to build up . . . a modern industrial structure . . . [which] compared favorably with those of economically advanced countries." In Gerschenkron, "Russian Agrarian Policies," pp. 210–211. For a contrary interpretation, see P. Gregory, "Some Empirical Comments on the Theory of Relative Backwardness: The Russian Case," *Economic Development and Cultural Change*, vol. 22, no. 4 (July 1974), pp. 654–665.

26. Kahan, "Capital Formation During the Period of Early Industrialization in Russia," p. 307.

27. Kuznets, *Modern Economic Growth*, pp. 40–51.

28. In 1886, the average life span was 29 years for males and 32 for females, which shows the marked effect of the high rate of infant mortality on age structure. See A. G. Rashin, *Naselenie Rossii za 100 let* [The population of Russia for 100 years] (Moscow: Gostatizdat, 1956), p. 205.

29. See in particular H. Chenery, "Patterns of Industrial Growth," *American Economic Review*, vol. 50, no. 4 (September 1960), pp. 624–653.

30. P. Gregory, *Socialist and Nonsocialist Industrialization Patterns* (New York: Praeger, 1970), pp. 28–29, 34, 171–174.

31. Gerschenkron, "The Early Phases of Industrialization in Russia," pp. 152–154. For a study that seeks to demonstrate that Russian industry was not top-heavy in heavy industry, see Gregory, "Some Empirical Comments."

32. These figures are from B. Bonwetsch, "Das ausländische Kapital in Russland" [Foreign capital in Russia], *Jahrbücher für die Geschichte Osteuropas* [Yearbooks for the History of Eastern Europe], Band 22, Heft 3, 1974, pp. 416–418; and P. Gregory, "The Russian Balance of Payments, the Gold Standard, and Monetary Policy," *Journal of Economic History*, vol. 39, no. 2 (June 1979), pp. 379–399.

33. Kuznets, *Modern Economic Growth*, pp. 332–334.

34. S. Cohn, *Economic Development in the Soviet Union* (Lexington, Mass.: Heath, 1970), p. 111.

35. S. Kuznets, *Economic Growth of Nations* (Cambridge, Mass.: Harvard University Press, 1971), p. 24.

36. S. G. Wheatcroft, "The Reliability of Russian Prewar Grain Output Statistics," *Soviet Studies*, vol. 26, no. 2 (April 1974), pp. 157, 180; Gregory, "Grain Marketings and Peasant Consumption."

37. C. Wilber, *The Soviet Model and the Underdeveloped Countries* (Chapel Hill: University of North Carolina Press, 1969), disagrees with this assessment. He argues that the combined populations of LDCs with economic bases at least equal to the Soviet Union's 1928 base number more than 900 million. This conclusion is based upon physical indicators—literacy, wheat yields, energy consumption, and so on.

38. For a comparison of the economic development of Russia and America from the seventeenth to nineteenth centuries, see Colin White, *Russia and America: The Roots of Economic Divergence* (Beckenham, Kent: Croom Helm, 1987).

SELECTED BIBLIOGRAPHY

Non-Soviet Sources

A. N. Antsiferov, *Russian Agriculture During the War* (New York: Greenwood Press, 1930).

W. Blackwell, ed., *Russian Economic Development from Peter the Great to Stalin* (New York: New Viewpoints, 1974).

J. Blum, *Lord and Peasant in Russia* (New York: Atheneum, 1965).

O. Crisp, *Studies in the Russian Economy Before 1914* (London and Basingstoke: Macmillan, 1976).

M. E. Falkus, *The Industrialization of Russia, 1700–1914* (London and Basingstoke: Macmillan, 1972).

P. Gatrell, *The Tsarist Economy, 1850–1917* (New York: St. Martin's Press, 1986).

A. Gerschenkron, "Russian Agrarian Policies and Industrialization, 1861–1917," *The Cambridge Economic History of Europe,* vol. 6 (Cambridge: Cambridge University Press, 1965), pp. 706–800.

———, "The Early Phases of Industrialization in Russia: Afterthoughts and Counterthoughts," in W. W. Rostow, ed., *The Economics of Takeoff into Sustained Growth* (New York: St. Martin's Press, 1963).

———, "The Rate of Growth in Russia Since 1885," *Journal of Economic History* (supplement), vol. 7 (1947), pp. 144–174.

D. Geyer, ed., *Wirtschaft und Gesellschaft in vorrevolutionären Russland* [Economy and society in prerevolutionary Russia] (Cologne: Kiepenheuer & Witsch, 1975).

R. Goldsmith, "The Economic Growth of Tsarist Russia, 1860–1913," *Economic Development and Cultural Change,* vol. 9, no. 3 (April 1961), pp. 441–476.

P. R. Gregory, *Russian National Income, 1885–1913* (Cambridge: Cambridge University Press, 1982).

G. Guroff and F. V. Carstensen, *Entrepreneurship in Imperial Russia and the Soviet Union* (Princeton, N.J.: Princeton University Press, 1983).

W. Kirchner, *Die Deutsche Industrie und die Industrialisierung Russlands 1815–1914* (St. Katharinen: Scripta Mercaturae Verlag, 1986).

J. P. McKay, *Pioneers for Profit: Foreign Entrepreneurship and Russian Industrialization, 1885–1913* (Chicago: University of Chicago Press, 1970).

R. Munting, *The Economic Development of the USSR* (London: Croom Helm, 1982), chap. 1.

J. Nötzold, *Wirtschaftspolitische Alternativen der Entwicklung in der Ära Witte und Stolypin* [Economic political alternatives in the era of Witte and Stolypin] (Berlin: Duncker & Humblot, 1966).

T. C. Owen, *Capitalism and Politics in Russia: A Social History of the Moscow Merchants* (Cambridge: Cambridge University Press, 1981).

R. Portal, "The Industrialization of Russia," *The Cambridge Economic History of Europe,* vol. 6 (Cambridge: Cambridge University Press, 1965), pp. 801–872.

M. M. Postan and Peter Mathias, eds., *The Cambridge Economic History of Europe,* vol. 7, part 2 (Cambridge: Cambridge University Press, 1978), section on Russia.

G. T. Robinson, *Russia Under the Old Regime* (New York: Macmillan, 1949).

M. I. Tugan-Baranovsky, *The Russian Factory in the 19th Century,* translated by A. and C. Levin (Homewood, Ill.: Irwin, 1970).

L. Volin, *A Century of Russian Agriculture* (Cambridge, Mass.: Harvard University Press, 1970).

T. von Laue, *Sergei Witte and the Industrialization of Russia* (New York: Columbia University Press, 1963).

C. White, *Russia and America: The Roots of Economic Divergence* (Beckenham, Kent: Croom Helm, 1987).

Soviet Sources

V. I. Bovykin, *Formirovanie finansogo Kapitala v Rossii* [Formation of financial capital in Russia] (Moscow: Nauka, 1984).

P. A. Khromov, *Ekonomicheskoe razvitie Rossii* [The economic development of Russia] (Moscow: 1967).

———, *Ekonomicheskoe razvitie Rossii v 19. i 20. vekakh* [The economic development of Russia in the 19th and 20th centuries] (Moscow: Gospolitizdat, 1950).

V. I. Lenin, *Development of Capitalism in Russia* (Moscow: Progress, 1977).

P. I. Lyaschenko, *History of the National Economy of Russia to the 1917 Revolution* (New York: Macmillan, 1949).

B. N. Mironov, *Khlebnye tseny v Rossii za dva stoletiia* [Grain prices in Russia for two centuries] (Leningrad: Nauka, 1985).

A. G. Rashin, *Formirovanie rabochego klassa v Rossii* [The formation of the working class in Russia] (Moscow: Sosteklitizdat 1958).

———, *Naselenie Rossii za 100 let* [The population of Russia for 100 years] (Moscow: Gostatizdat, 1956).

Chapter 3

War Communism and the New Economic Policy (1918–1928)

*T*his chapter considers the events of the period 1918–1928 and their impact on later Soviet economic policies. During this period, the economy operated under two quite different administrative regimes—War Communism and the New Economic Policy (NEP)—which provided experience to assist in making the final choice of comprehensive central planning (1928) and collectivization of agriculture (1929).

The lessons of War Communism and the New Economic Policy provide insights into the evolution of the Soviet economic system. The Soviet planning system did not appear from a vacuum; rather, it emerged as a response to the practical economic problems of earlier periods. The impact of the early Five Year Plan period (the 1930s) and World War II upon the evolution of the current system are discussed in Chapter 5.

WAR COMMUNISM (1918–1921)[1]

War Communism was an abortive attempt by the inexperienced Bolshevik leadership to attain full communism without going through any preparatory intermediate stages: money was virtually eliminated, private trade was abolished, workers were militarized and paid virtually equal wages in kind, and farm output was requisitioned. Were these war measures the product of the ideological intent of the Bolshevik leadership to establish full communism directly, or were they forced responses to the civil war? The most generally accepted view, as postulated by the well-known British authorities on War Communism, Maurice Dobb and E. H. Carr, is that War Communism was forced upon the Bolshevik leadership by the Russian civil war and that the various theoretical arguments posited by the Bolshevik leadership in support of War Communism were "no more than flights of leftist fancy." In fact, Lenin—and Leon Trotsky—often referred to War Communism as the measures of a "besieged fortress." Other scholars argue that Lenin originally conceived War Communism, with its elimination of market institutions and its introduction of administrative controls, as a necessary step in the socialist revolution.[2] War Communism was adopted for ideological reasons as a product of Marxian ideas (as interpreted by Lenin), not as a forced response to the wartime emergency. In fact, the Bolshevik regime sought to strengthen the War Communism system at the end of the Civil War, only to be forced to abandon it by growing civil unrest.

The roots of War Communism can be traced to the October Revolution. One of the first actions of the fledgling Bolshevik regime was to nationalize the remaining large estates (the Land Decree of November 8, 1917) and to sanction the distribution of this land among the peasants. This action legalized in part the spontaneous appropriation of land by the peasantry, a process that had already taken place to a large degree. Irrespective of its causes, this change in land tenure was to have a far-reaching impact upon economic policy throughout the 1920s. In their enhanced capacity as full proprietors, the peasants were no longer obligated to deliver a prescribed portion of their output either to the landlord (as a rental payment) or to the state (as a tax or principal payment). Now they, not the state or landlord, made the basic decisions about how much to produce and what portion of this output would be sold. Thus, the total agricultural output and the *marketed portion* thereof became dependent for the first time upon the Russian peasant. Moreover, the 1917 revolution essentially did away with large farm production units. Before the revolution, 4 percent of the farm households farmed more than 13 *desiatins* of land and another 13 percent were landless. By 1922, virtually no farm families had land holdings of more than 13 *desiatins*, and only 5 percent were without land.[3]

There was a revival of the *mir* during and after the Revolution. The *mir* was the institution that had confiscated and redistributed the land of the gentry, and it remained the principal voice of legal and administrative authority within the village during the early years of Soviet rule.[4] The village assembly settled most of the questions of interest to the peasants and was able to steer a course independent of the *selsovet*, the local administrative arm of the Bolshevik government. However, as M. Lewin writes, one should not overemphasize the socialist instincts of the peasants.[5] The peasants remained attached to their village communities, and in their eyes, the purpose of the revolution was to give them their own farms. That the land was nationalized and belonged to the *mir* did not detract from the peasants' conviction that the land was theirs to farm and manage as they saw fit.

The initial Bolshevik attitude toward private industry was cautious and restrained, since an uneasy truce between Bolshevik and capitalist was required to prevent a drop in industrial output. Trade unions were formed after the October Revolution, 2000 in the first two months. Workers' Committees in privately owned enterprises were given the right to supervise management, but at the same time, the proprietor received the executive right to give orders that could not be countermanded by the Workers' Committees. Also, the Workers' Committees were denied the right to take over enterprises without the permission of higher authorities. Only enterprises of key importance—such as banking, grain purchasing and storage, transportation, oil, and war industries—were nationalized, establishing a form of state capitalism based on state control of key positions in the economy, mixed management of enterprises, and private ownership of agriculture, retail trade, and small-scale industry.

The uneasy truce between the Bolsheviks and the capitalists and the peasants did not last long. By 1918, the Bolsheviks were locked in a struggle for survival with the White Russian forces supported in part by foreign powers. The Germans were in possession of the Ukraine, while the White Russian armies occupied the Urals, Siberia, North Caucasus, and other economically important regions. Poland invaded in May 1920. At one time, the Bolsheviks retained only 10 percent of the coal supplies, 25 percent of the iron foundries, less than 50 percent of the grain area, and less than 10 percent of the sugar beet sources of the former Russian Empire.[6] At one point, three-quarters of USSR territory was occupied by opponents of Soviet authority.

To divert industrial and agricultural resources from private into military uses, the Bolsheviks, lacking a domestic tax base and access to foreign aid, resorted to printing money. This expansion of the money supply combined with shrinking supplies of consumer goods created hyperinflation. On November 1, 1917, the amount of money in circulation was 20 billion rubles. The rate of monetary emission accelerated thereafter, and by July 1, 1921, 2.5 trillion rubles were in circulation. In the spring of 1919, printing presses could no longer print money at a fast enough pace. Supplies of consumer goods offered for sale dwindled as materials were diverted to military uses, and prices rose more rapidly than the rate of growth of the money supply. Between 1917 and 1921, prices increased 8000-fold.[7]

The hyperinflation resulted in the near destruction of the market exchange economy. Peasants were reluctant to exchange their products for depreciating money, as were manufacturers and artisans. The economy increasingly employed barter to effect transactions, and this led to what the Soviets call the "naturalization" (demonetization) of the economy. This naturalization process was welcomed by the left wing of the Bolshevik party, which termed the government printing press "that machine gun which attacked the bourgeois regime in its rear, namely, through its monetary system."[8] The naturalization of the economy created, however, an immediate crisis for the Soviet leadership. The central government found itself powerless to obtain through the market those goods, food supplies in particular, that it needed to fight the war.

War Communism Policies

The Bolshevik leadership under Lenin responded by introducing War Communism, a system by which the leaders attempted to substitute administrative for market allocation to marshal resources for the war. The crux of War Communism was its policy of forcibly requisitioning agricultural surpluses. Police (the *Cheka*) and party activists were sent into the countryside to collect the "surpluses" of the rich and middle peasantry—a policy that severed the existing market link between industry and agriculture. In theory at least, the link was to be maintained by state allocation of manufactured products to the peasants and barter transactions for the remaining agricultural output. In fact, the peasants received only from 12 to 15 percent of prewar supplies of manufactured goods. Initially, the regime had hoped to preserve the market link with agriculture by setting aside manufactured commodities to promote exchange with the countryside, but the peasants failed to respond. On May 9, 1918, the system of requisitioning (called the *prodrazverstka*) was initiated, and the commissar for food was invested with extraordinary powers to confiscate food products from the farm population. Thus, a "food dictatorship" was established, and the Bolshevik government took over the task of collecting and distributing agricultural products. The distribution of manufactured goods to rural areas was based on the food requisitioned from the community, not on that delivered by individual production units. This system broke the link between agricultural deliveries and rewards for those deliveries.[9]

Nationalization of the economy was the second major policy of War Communism. The sugar industry was the first to be nationalized in the spring of 1918, and by the autumn of 1920, a total of 37,000 enterprises had been nationalized, of which roughly half were small-scale businesses that did not use mechanical power. This pervasive nationalization of industry may be regarded in part as a crisis response, for a large number of former industrial proprietors had gone over to the White Russian side, and there was widespread fear of German takeovers of German-owned enterprises. Also, "punitive" nationalization from below by workers had been proceeding at a rapid pace despite government attempts to control unauthorized worker takeovers. On the other hand, the excessive nationalization from above down to enterprises employing only one worker may perhaps be regarded as an ideological response not to be justified by the crisis situation. Nominally, the nationalized enterprises were subject to central direction by the state budget and national industrial boards.

In actual practice, centralized coordination was generally lacking.

The abolition of private trade was the third cornerstone of War Communism policy. Private trade was regarded as incompatible with the War Communism system of centralized requisitioning and allocation. Government trade monopolies and monopsonies (mainly the Commissariat of Supply and the Comissariat of Agriculture) were set up to replace private organizations and concentrate commodity distribution in the hands of the state. In November 1918, all private internal trade was abolished, and the state ostensibly became the sole supplier of consumer goods to the population. In fact, the black market continued to supply a significant portion of total consumption goods and was unofficially tolerated by the authorities, especially up to 1920.[10] In the most critical moments of 1918, the Soviet government made it legal for workers to purchase up to 20 kilograms of grain directly from peasants, but this provision was quickly rescinded when it threatened to disrupt government requisitioning.[11]

Semimilitary controls over industrial workers became a major means of labor allocation. The movement of industrial workers was restricted, and they could be mobilized for special work. In some cases, army personnel were used for special projects. Labor deserters received severe penalties according to a decree of November 28, 1919, which placed the employees of state enterprises under military discipline.

The mobilization of labor was managed in large part by Leon Trotsky, the organizer of the Red Army. Trotsky's intention was to create a system of universal labor mobilization, and by the end of 1918, his mobilization plans were being put into effect. Labor was decreed to be compulsory for all able-bodied persons, compulsory labor service was declared for the peasantry, labor armies (one under the leadership of Stalin in the Ukraine) were created by delaying demobilization, and the Commission for Universal Labor Service was created with Trotsky at its head.[12] In 1920, railway workers, firemen, miners, construction workers, metal workers, and shipbuilders were mobilized. The Siberian labor army was engaged in coal mining, forestry, and rail construction; and the Caucasian labor army was charged with rail construction and crude oil extraction.[13]

The War Communism system of distribution attempted to apply class and social principles to distribution. Under the "class ration," introduced in 1918, wages were to be based on the type of work being done. Since money wages had lost most of their meaning as a consequence of hyperinflation, the highest ration (wage) would go to workers performing heavy work under dangerous conditions; the lowest, to the free professions and the unemployed. The highest category was to receive a ration four times that of the lowest category. The wartime chaos of the period made it difficult for the state to adhere to these class ration principles because in most regions state supply agencies were doing well to keep the population above subsistence. Special rations were used, however, to supply the workers of priority industries, and in 1919, 30 categories of workers were placed on preferential rations.[14]

The final feature of War Communism was the naturalization of economic life. The procurement of agricultural products through requisitioning and confiscation replaced the market link between the city and countryside. Every citizen had to be registered with a state or cooperative shop to obtain legal rations. Settlements among state enterprises were made via bookkeeping transactions that had little real meaning. In 1920, postal services, housing, gas, electricity, and public transportation were made available free of charge, and it was decided that foodstuffs supplied through the Food Commissariat should also be free of charge.[15]

An Evaluation of War Communism

Any evaluation of War Communism must emphasize a frequently neglected point made by the Soviet literature: War Communism did enable the Bolsheviks to muster sufficient resources to win the civil war. In this sense, War Communism may be viewed as an important political and military success. It is easy to overlook this basic point and to concentrate instead on the system's many weaknesses. We seek rather to evaluate War Communism in terms of the question, Was War Communism a viable economic system for coping with the long-term problems of economic growth and development facing the Soviet regime during the 1920s?[16]

As one might expect, War Communism's replacement of market exchange by administrative resource allocation created several serious problems. First, there was a sharp decline in both agricultural output and marketings to the state during the 1918—1921 period, even after adjustment for war devastation. Peasants were holding back grain in storage, were planting less, and were selling to private traders. The area of Siberia sown in wheat was halved and in the Volga and Caucasus regions was reduced to as little as one-quarter of previous levels. Actual sowing concealed from authorities was reported to be as high as 20 percent of sown area in some regions.[17] Since agricultural surpluses in excess of family subsistence were requisitioned, there was no incentive to produce a surplus. Instead, the peasants, if they could not conceal their surplus from the authorities, restricted output to the subsistence needs of their family. Thus, War Communism's agrarian policy estranged Russian peasants from the Bolshevik regime and encouraged them to engage in dysfunctional behavior, such as restricting output and hoarding or concealing surpluses during a period of agricultural shortages.

Soviet industry was also faced with serious problems. Almost all enterprises, with the exception of certain small-scale handicraft shops, had been nationalized without first establishing a suitable administrative structure to coordinate their activities. The industrial census of 1920 showed over 5000 nationalized enterprises employing only one worker.[18] The abolition of private trade, which was to be superseded by state rationing, removed the existing market link between consumer and producer. Producers, except those selling to the black market, therefore, were no longer directed by the market in their production decisions.

Ostensibly, large-scale industry was to be coordinated by the Supreme Council of the National Economy (VSNKh), which was broken up into departments (*Glavki*), each of which was to direct a particular industry. The *Glavki* were usually grouped into trusts. For example, the mining trust contained six *Glavki*. By 1920, there were over 50 *Glavki* charged with controlling production and distribution.[19] In addition, the provincial economic councils (*Gubsovnarkhozy*) were the local organs of VSNKh. This arrangement bordered on chaos. In 1920, there were over 37,000 nationalized enterprises. The *Glavki* possessed insufficient information about local enterprises to direct them effectively—to such a degree that an investigative committee of 1920 found that many *Glavki* not only "do not know what goods and in what amounts are kept in warehouses under their control, but are actually ignorant even of the numbers of such warehouses."[20] As a result, the directives that the *Glavki* issued to the local authorities rarely corresponded to local capacities and requirements, causing a prolonged struggle between central and local administrations. Often, local authorities merely gave formal compliance to directives from above and then countermanded them, knowing they could do so with impunity.

VSNKh was the principal champion of centralized control during War Communism, and under its influential chairman, Aleksei Rykov, it fought against the "Left Communist" contingent, which favored workers' control of factories. Rykov also attacked the concept of trade union control of enterprises, citing Lenin's opposition to workers' control and Lenin's support of rational one-man management. Nevertheless, VSNKh's success in establishing centralized control was modest. Individual industries were being run independently by the *Glavki* and local authorities with virtually no centralized coordination. Various national and local organizations had overlapping and conflicting responsibilities concerning the distribution of consumer and producer goods. Primitive plans were drawn up for particular industries, but these plans were not presented in the form of a national plan to be approved by government. The first effort at national economic planning was the general electrification plan (GOELRO), completed in December 1920.

In sum, War Communism industry operated essentially without direction, either from the market or from planners. Bottlenecks were eliminated by employing "shock" (*udarny*) methods, which meant that whenever congestion in a particular sector became alarming, it would receive top priority in the form of adequate supplies of fuels, materials, and rations. The shock system provided a means of establishing priorities and was beneficial in this sense. However, while the concentration of resources in the shock industries allowed them to surge ahead and overcome the original bottleneck, the nonshock industries had in the process fallen behind and had created new bottlenecks, which would then be attacked by additional shock methods. In this manner, some weak sense of general direction was supplied to the economy to replace total chaos. The shock system was somewhat effective as long as it remained undiluted, which meant that the number of shock industries at one time had to be limited. As time went by, the agitation for widening the shock categories became so intense that eventually even the manufacture of pens and pencils was included, thus destroying the whole purpose of the shock method—to set up a system of priorities.

Finally, the lack of an adequate system of incentive wages led to industrial labor supply problems. The government controlled the legal distribution of consumer commodities among members of the industrial labor force, thereby controlling a significant portion of real industrial wages. The Bolshevik party never officially subscribed to a utopian view of income distribution according to need; instead, it was realized that wage differentials were important in attracting labor in skilled and/or arduous jobs. For example, the Ninth Congress of the Communist Party in 1920 resolved that the food supply system should give preference to the industrious worker, and the Third Trade Union Conference of the same year proposed incentive premiums in kind to be paid to diligent workers.

The result, however, contradicted the intention and was one reason Trotsky referred to War Communism wage policy as the measure of a "besieged fortress." In fact, wages were rationed out to industrial workers on a fairly equal basis because, first, shortages were so severe that local supply authorities were content to keep the working force at subsistence, and second, it proved too complex to devise a system of incentive wages to be paid in kind.

The result of this egalitarianism was an insufficient pool of qualified labor in industry. Instead of being drawn into factories, labor was flowing out of them during War Communism. The number of townspeople declined from 2.6 million in 1917 to 1.2 million in 1920.[21] Morale was poor, worker sabotage was rampant, absenteeism was high, and the tenuous loyalty of specialists was slipping. These developments were especially ominous in view of the dearth of skilled industrial laborers during this early period. Strikes became quite common during the latter part of 1920.

The Soviet regime had succeeded in solidifying its position by the end of 1920. A peace treaty had been signed with Poland, and the White Russian army had been driven out of the crucial industrial and agricultural regions that it had occupied earlier. The crisis under which War Communism had come into existence had been overcome, and the dangers of continuing that economic policy were growing more apparent. The still powerful trade unions were revolting against the crippling centralization of industry and the conscription of labor. The alienated peasant population called for abolition of the state grain monopoly. Industrial workers were restive, the military was in a rebellious mood, and the Soviet regime was in danger of falling victim to internal discontent. Factory output had fallen to less than 15 percent of its prewar level.[22] Table 3.1 shows the extent of the drops in industrial and agricultural output, the decline in transportation services, and the USSR's virtual withdrawal from export and import markets. At the end of 1920 and the beginning of 1921, there were peasant uprisings in the countryside against the continuation of requisitioning after the end of hostilities. Supplies to Moscow and Petrograd collapsed. The final blow was the Kronstadt Uprising of March 1921, when the sailors of the Kronstadt naval base revolted in support of the Petrograd workers. The Soviet

Table 3.1   PRODUCTION AND TRADE INDEXES, USSR: 1913 AND 1920
1913 = 100

	Industry	Agri-culture	Trans-portation	Exports	Imports
1913[a]	100	100	100	100.0	100.0
1920	20	64	22	0.1	2.1

Sources: G. W. Nutter, "The Soviet Economy: Retrospect and Prospect," in D. Abshire and R. V. Allen, eds., *National Security: Political, Military, and Economic Strategies in the Decade Ahead* (New York: Praeger, 1963), p. 165; M. Kaser, "A Volume Index of Soviet Foreign Trade," *Soviet Studies,* vol. 20, no. 4 (April 1969), 523–526.

[a]The 1913 figures refer to interwar territory of the USSR.

leadership moved quickly to dispel this discontent by replacing War Communism with the New Economic Policy (NEP) in March 1921.

THE NEW ECONOMIC POLICY (1921–1928)

Just as War Communism may have been thrust upon the Soviet regime by the civil war in 1918, the New Economic Policy was forced upon the Soviet leadership by the excesses of War Communism. For whatever its reasons, the Soviet leadership at the time took pains to stress the temporary nature of both periods. Lenin declared that "War Communism was thrust upon us by war and ruin. It was not, nor could it be, a policy that corresponded to the economic tasks of the proletariat. It was a temporary measure."[23] In the same vein, Lenin described NEP as a temporary step backward (away from socialism) in order later to take two steps forward. From the viewpoint of the Bolshevik leadership, NEP was a transitional step backward because of the important roles that "antisocialist" institutions, such as private ownership, private initiative, and capitalist markets, were allowed to play during this period.

The most striking feature of NEP was its attempt to combine market and socialism: agriculture remained in the hands of the peasant, and the management of industry (with the exception of the "commanding heights") was decentralized. Market links between industry and agriculture and between industry and consumer replaced state control of production and distribution. Most industrial enterprises were denationalized. But many of the largest enterprises—the so-called commanding heights—remained nationalized and encompassed about three-quarters of industrial output. In this manner, it was thought that the state could provide general guidance by retaining direct control of the commanding heights of the economy—heavy industry, transportation, banking, and foreign trade—while allowing the remainder of the economy to make its own decisions.

The political basis of NEP was the *Smychka,* or alliance, between the Soviet regime (supposedly representing the urban proletariat) and the peasant.

An important political objective of NEP was to regain the political and economic support of the peasant. Thus, the War Communism policy of requisitioning agricultural surpluses had to be abandoned, for the peasants would never ally themselves with a regime that confiscated their surpluses. Market agriculture had to be reestablished in its place, freeing the peasant both to sell surpluses freely and to buy industrial products freely.

The *Smychka* strategy represented a significant concession from the Bolshevik leaders, whose freedom of action was accordingly severely restricted because they were limited to policies that would not alienate the peasant. This at times placed them in the tenuous position of having to choose between the support of the peasantry and the attainment of basic party objectives. However, there was even a more fundamental contradiction. The reestablishment of market agriculture would serve to create a commercially minded peasantry and an environment that would reward success and penalize failure. The very success of NEP would require increasing economic differentiation among the agricultural population and the emergence of a class of relatively prosperous peasants, who would produce the critical market surpluses. Marx had condemned the wealthy and middle peasant as adamant opponents of socialism, but NEP would serve to promote this class. Thus, the ideological concession underlying NEP was apparently very great.[24]

NEP Policies

The cornerstone of NEP was the proportional agricultural tax (the *prodnalog*) introduced in March 1921 to replace the War Communism system of requisitions. First paid in kind, and by 1924 in money, it was a single tax, based upon a *fixed proportion* of each peasant's *net produce*. The state now took a fixed proportion of production, and the peasant again had an incentive to aim for as large a surplus as possible. The *prodnalog* was differentiated according to income level (as dictated by the size of the landholding and farm animals) and by family size. In 1923, for example, the *pradnalog* varied from 5 percent (landholdings less than one-quarter hectare) to 17 percent (more than three hectares) of annual income. Throughout the NEP period, the burden of the *prodnalog* was shifted increasingly to the middle and upper peasants, and it accounted for some one-quarter of state revenues during NEP. According to studies conducted in the mid-1920s, this percentage was below 10 percent. More recent studies by Western historians find that the tax burden during NEP was about the same as in 1913 when all forms are considered.[25]

The agriculture tax was the first step in reestablishing a market economy; it, in turn, necessitated further measures. Unless the peasants could dispose profitably of their after-tax surplus, they would have little incentive to produce above subsistence. Therefore, the state granted the peasants commercial autonomy to sell their output to the buyer of their choice, be it the state, a cooperative, or a private dealer. This measure required the legalization of private trade, which was again permitted to compete with state and cooperative trade organizations. Now the peasants could market their after-tax surplus at terms dictated by market forces, not by a state monopoly. The resurgence of private trade provided a further incentive for peasants to market their surplus, for they no longer faced a state supply monopoly, rationing out industrial products to them. Finally, peasants were allowed to lease land and hire farm laborers, both of which had been forbidden under War Communism.

Within one year, private activity dominated Soviet retail trade and restored the market link between consumer and producer. By the end of 1922, nine-tenths of all retail trading outlets were private, and they handled about three-quarters of the value of all retail trade turnover, with state and cooperative outlets handling the balance.[26] The private trader, or *Nepman*, was less strongly entrenched in wholesale trade, which remained dominated by state and cooperative organizations.

NEP also brought about significant changes in Soviet industry. The majority of industrial enterprises were permitted to make their own contracts for the purchase of raw materials and supplies and for the sale of their output; during War Communism, the state had performed these functions. Small enterprises employing 20 persons or less were denationalized, and a small number of them were returned to their former owners. Others were leased to new entrepreneurs, thereby re-creating a class of small-scale capitalists. The Bolsheviks even granted a limited number of foreign concessions. (The lessee typically signed a contract of six years' duration obligating the enterprise to sell a prescribed portion of its output to the state.) Denationalization was limited to small-scale enterprises, and the overwhelming portion of industrial production during NEP was turned out by nationalized enterprises. The industrial census of 1923 showed that private enterprises accounted for only 12.5 percent of total employment in "census" establishments.[27] In addition, only 2 percent of the output of large-scale industry was produced by the private sector in 1924–1925.[28]

While much of large-scale industry remained nationalized, decision making throughout industry was decentralized to a great extent. Nationalized enterprises were divided into two categories: the commanding heights of the economy—fuel, metallurgy, war industries, transportation, banking, and foreign trade—were not separated from the state budget and remained dependent on centralized allocations of state supplies. The remaining nationalized enterprises were granted substantial financial and commercial autonomy from the state budget. The latter enterprises were instructed to operate commercially, that is, to maximize profits and sell to the highest bidder, be it state or private trade. Most important, they were not obligated to deliver output according to production quotas to the state, as under War Communism.

The nationalized enterprises of this second category were allowed to federate into trusts, which soon became the dominant form of industrial organization during NEP. By 1923, the 478 chartered trusts accounted for 75 percent of all workers employed in nationalized industry.[29] These trusts were given the legal authority to enter into independent contracts. They were to be supervised loosely either by VSNKh or by the *Sovnarkhozy* (the regional economic councils), but their commercial independence was protected in that the state was not allowed to acquire the property or products of a trust except by contractual agreement. The most powerful trusts remained under the direct administration of VSNKh. About 25 percent of industrial production (mainly light industry) remained under Sovnarkhoz supervision. In light industry the trusts were largely independent of state control other than the usual forms of fiscal and monetary intervention. In some key sectors of heavy industry, VSNKh exercised much stricter controls over trusts in the form of specific production and delivery targets. The profits of trusts were subject to property and income taxation in the same manner as private enterprises. The monopoly State Bank controlled trust commercial credit. Although the commanding-heights enterprises remained within the state budget, they also were instructed to operate as profitably as possible to eliminate reliance on subsidies. Emphasis on capitalist-type cost accounting was the order of the day.

NEP was not a command economy. Planning authorities generally provided trusts with "control figures," which were to be used as forecasts and guides for investment decisions. Mandatory output plans were drawn up only in the case of a few key sectors in heavy industry. The limited physical planning and distribution was carried out through the Committee of State Orders (representing the commissariats), which placed orders through VSNKh, which in turn negotiated the orders with the producer trusts. During the major part of NEP, the most important force of economic control and regulation was the People's Commissariat of Finance (*Narkomfin*), which exerted its influence through the budget and credit system (the so-called dictatorship of finance). Planning during the NEP period was carried out by a variety of organizations—VSNKh, the State Planning Committee (*Gosplan*, established in 1921), the commissariats, and local authorities. Until the late 1920s, planners limited themselves primarily to forecasting trends as dictated by market conditions. Also, there was a notable lack of coordination among the various planning agencies until *Gosplan* established itself as the dominant coordinating planning body after 1927.[30]

One basic notion of a way to guide the economy during NEP was to amalgamate producing enterprises in order to simplify control and coordination. An important phenomenon was the amalgamation of trusts into syndicates, initially to coordinate industry sales. In addition to easing the planning burden, trusts and syndicates were favored by the Soviet leadership's ideological preference for large-scale industry.[31] By the late NEP period, the syndicates came to dominate the sales of state industry, accounting for 82 percent of state industry sales in 1927–1928 and for all sales of ferrous metal.[32] The trusts and syndicates acquired considerable commercial autonomy. Syndicates were allowed to enter directly into foreign trade agreements (without permission of the state foreign trade monopoly) and had the right to receive credit from credit institutions in the Soviet Union and in some instances from foreign banks. The growing autonomy of trusts and syndicates had its disadvantages for the Soviet leadership, particularly when the trusts attempted to charge monopoly prices for their products, as we shall discuss below.

Use of money had been virtually eliminated during War Communism as a result of hyperinflation and had been replaced by a system of barter and physical allocation. Such a system, however, would have been too clumsy for the new market system of NEP. To avoid this obstacle, the Soviets reintroduced the use of money with the reopening of the State Bank in 1921 for the expressed purpose of aiding the development of the economy. Both public and private enterprises were encouraged to deposit their savings in the State Bank; limitations on private bank deposits were removed, and safeguards were established to protect such deposits from state confiscation. A new stabilized currency, the *chervonets*, was issued by the State Bank in 1921, a balanced budget was achieved in 1923–1924, a surplus in 1924–1925, and the old depreciated paper ruble was withdrawn from circulation in the currency reform of May 1924. Thereby a relatively stable Soviet currency was created, which for a time was even quoted on international exchanges. Money transactions between state enterprises replaced earlier barter transactions.

NEP also witnessed an attempt to reestablish relatively normal trading relations with the outside world.[33] A state monopoly over foreign trade had been established shortly after the Bolshevik takeover, and foreign trade virtually disappeared during the civil war. During NEP, the Soviet leadership was reluctant to become dependent on capitalist markets, which they believed would suffer from increasingly severe crises. Rather, the NEP strategy of trade was enunciated in Lenin's dictum of "learning from the enemy as quickly as possible." Thus, the trading monopoly aimed at the importation of capitalist technology (and foreign experts) and of equipment that could not be produced at home. With this strategy in mind, foreign concessions were granted and credits from the capitalist world were sought. It was thought that in their scramble for Russian markets, the capitalist countries would mute their political hostility to the Soviet regime, which had repudiated tsarist Russia's foreign debt.

The volume of foreign trade grew rapidly during NEP, from 8 percent of the prewar level in 1921 to 44 percent in 1928.[34] Yet unlike the production figures, which showed a recovery to prewar levels, the volume of foreign trade throughout NEP remained well below half that of the prewar level. Credits from the capitalist nations were not forthcoming, and foreign policy failures made them even less likely. The concessions program never got off the ground; at the end of NEP, there were only 59 foreign concessions, accounting for less than one percent of the output of state industry.

The Economic Recovery of NEP

Just as War Communism provided the means for waging the civil war, NEP provided the means for recovery from the war, and in this sense, it was an important strategic success for the Soviet leadership. The economic recovery during the NEP was impressive (see Table 3.2.).

In 1920, production statistics (Table 3.1) indicated the low level of economic activity that existed at the end of War Communism. Industrial produc-

Table 3.2   SELECTED INDICATORS OF SOVIET OUTPUT LEVELS IN 1928
            RELATIVE TO 1913
            1913 = 100

National income		Selected physical production series	
1913 prices	117	Grain production	87
1926/27 prices	119	Pig iron	79
		Steel	102
		Coal	122
Industrial production		Cotton cloth	104
1913 prices	129	Freight turnover	104
1926/27 prices	143–139	Electric power	203
		Foreign trade	
Agricultural production		Exports	38
1926/27 prices	111	Imports	49

Sources: A. I. Vainshtein, *Narodny dokhod Rossii i SSSR* [National Income of Russia and the USSR] (Moscow: Nauka 1969), p. 102; Gosplan SSSR, *Kontrol'nye tsifry narodnogo khoziaistva SSSR na 1928/29 g.* (Moscow: Izdatel'stvo Planovoe Khoziaistvo, 1929), p. 68; R. W. Davies, "Soviet Industrial Production, 1928–1937: The Rival Estimates," *Centre for Russian and East European Studies Discussion papers,* no. 18 (University of Birmingham, 1978), p. 63; S. G. Wheatcroft, "Grain Production Statistics in the USSR in the 1920s and 1930s," *Centre for Russian and East European Studies Discussion Papers,* no. 13 (University of Birmingham, 1977), p. 23; Wheatcroft, "Soviet Agricultural Production, 1913–1940" (mimeographed, 1979); A. Bergson, *The Real National Income of Soviet Russia Since 1928* (Cambridge: Harvard University Press, 1961), p. 7; M. Kaser, "A Volume Index of Soviet Foreign Trade," *Soviet Studies,* vol. 20, no. 4 (April 1969), 523–526.

tion and transportation were both only one-fifth of the prewar level. The shortage of fuel threatened to paralyze industry and transportation, and industry was living on dwindling reserves of pig iron. The food shortage led to the exhaustion and demoralization of the labor force. Agricultural production was 64 percent of the prewar level. Foreign trade had virtually disappeared.

In 1928, on the eve of the first Five Year Plan and at the end of NEP, the official statistics provide a striking contrast: both industry and agriculture had surpassed their prewar levels. Foreign trade remained well below prewar levels but had recovered substantially from the negligible War Communism volumes.

More recent calculations suggest that official Soviet figures may have overstated the extent of recovery during NEP and that Soviet national income in 1928 was still below 1913 levels. Surprisingly, this position appears to be supported by A. L. Vainshtein, the noted Soviet authority on Soviet national income.[35] Subsequent research may be able to determine more precisely the extent of the economic recovery during the NEP period. The recovery from the economic devastation shown by the figures for 1920 was impressive irrespective of which set of statistics one chooses to use. Although the NEP recovery was impressive, particularly as judged by official statistics, one should note that high rates of growth during recovery periods are to be expected once a suitable economic environment is established. NEP policies provided this suitable framework for recovery.

The End of NEP

According to Soviet statistics, the highest level of NEP is usually dated to 1926, when prewar production levels were generally surpassed. The absolute growth of the nonagricultural private sector stopped in 1926.[36] At that time, all seemed to be going well; yet two years later, NEP was abandoned in favor of the radically different system of state central planning, collectivization of agriculture, and nationalization of industry and trade. This radical turn of events seems puzzling in view of the impressive NEP successes. Why was NEP abandoned? Several considerations stimulated the decision.

First, a large number of party members viewed NEP as a temporary and unwelcome compromise with class enemies. Now that the state was stronger, they argued, the offensive against class enemies could be resumed.[37] Second, the Soviet authorities feared that economic policy might become dominated by the growing numbers of prosperous peasants and *Nepmen*. Increasingly, policies were being dictated to suit the needs of the peasants, not the objectives of the state. A prime example of this was the "Scissors Crisis" of 1923, which forced the Soviet regime into the paradoxical stance of favoring private agriculture over socialist industry. The Scissors Crisis merits a slight digression at this point.

According to Soviet figures, the total marketed surplus of agriculture in 1923 was 60 percent of the prewar level, with grain marketings falling even below this figure. On the other hand, industrial production was only 35 percent of the prewar level.[38] The more rapid recovery of agriculture placed upward pressure on industrial prices relative to agricultural prices. The different sectorial recovery rates were not the sole determinants of relative price movements. A portion of the already limited output of industry was being withheld from the market by the industrial trust and syndicates, who were using their monopoly power to restrict trust sales to raise prices. The net result was an even more rapid rise of industrial prices relative to agricultural prices. The relative price movements between early 1922 and late 1923 (Figure 3.1) take on the shape of an open pair of scissors, hence the term *Scissors Crisis*.

The Soviet authorities viewed the opening price scissors with alarm, for they expected the peasants to react by refusing to market their surpluses as their terms of trade with the city fell. Moreover, Soviet authorities were very sensitive to signs of peasant unrest. In 1924, there were a number of disturbing developments. In August, there was an uprising of Georgian peasants. There was also a ground swell to form a peasant association that would represent peasant interests against the party, and in the elections to the Soviets in the fall of 1924, the peasant turnout was under 30 percent (despite party efforts to have mass peasant participation).[39] During the prewar period, Russian peasants marketed (outside of the village) on the average 30 percent of their output. In early 1923, before the price scissors had opened sharply, they marketed about 25 percent, and Soviet authorities feared a further drop. It is uncertain what did happen to peasant marketings as the scissors opened, since statistics for this early period are difficult to find. A student of the scissors crisis, James Millar, sug-

Figure 3.1 The Scissors Crisis. *Source:* A. L. Vainshtein, *Tseny i tsenoobrazovanie v SSSR v vosstanovitel, 'ny period* [Prices and price formation in the USSR in the transition period] (Moscow: Nauka, 1972), pp. 158–167.

gests that the Bolsheviks mistakenly *expected* peasant marketings to decline as agricultural prices fell in relative terms.[40] In fact, Millar argues, the peasants had traditionally responded to a decline in the terms of trade with the city by selling more to the city in order to maintain their standard of living. The Millar argument is supported by evidence showing that prewar grain marketings were not significantly affected by the terms of trade.[41] Grain marketing statistics for the Ukraine do, however, suggest a reduction in peasant marketings between 1923 and 1925, but such evidence is quite fragmentary,[42] and it is difficult to determine whether Millar's or the Soviets' perception of peasant behavior is correct.

Rightly or wrongly, the Soviet government viewed this development as a threat to the NEP recovery, for the industrial worker had to be fed and light industry required agricultural raw materials. The regime's reaction to a similar problem in 1918 had been to requisition agricultural surpluses, which resulted in a costly reduction of agricultural output; a return to requisitioning would jeopardize the progress made by NEP between 1920 and 1923. Further, influential party officials, particularly Nikolai Bukharin, feared (probably irrationally) an insufficient aggregate demand if the Scissors Crisis continued: if the peasants refused to market their output, peasant demand for industrial commodities would shrink, thereby causing an eventual glut of industrial commodities, which would also threaten the industrial recovery.

In essence, the Scissors Crisis forced the Soviet leadership to choose between two alternatives: to abandon NEP and return to requisitioning, or to retain NEP and to favor agriculture over industry to preserve the tenuous peace with the peasantry.

A third source of dissatisfaction with NEP was the conviction at that time that economic recovery had reached its limits and that further advances could be achieved only by expanding the capacity of the economy, that is, by accumulating capital. NEP statistics revealed that much capacity had been lost as a result of World War I and the civil war: the capital stock of heavy industry as of 1924 was estimated to be 23 percent below its 1917 peak, and this capital equipment was on the whole old and outmoded. In 1924, the output of steel, a principal component of investment equipment, was 23 percent of 1913 output. Thus, industrial capacity had been lost between 1917 and 1924 and little had been done to replace it, although the building of socialism in the Soviet Union and expansion of military capacity were priority objectives of the Soviet state. After eight years of Soviet rule, investment and military commodities accounted for the same proportion of industrial output as they had prior to the revolution. For example, 28 percent of manufacturing net output was devoted to heavy industry in 1912, and this share had only risen to 29 percent by 1926.[43] To a regime already committed to the ideological primacy of large-scale heavy industry, this was an unacceptable outcome.

In spite of their dissatisfaction with the course of industrial development during the 1920s, the Soviet leaders viewed their hands as tied as long as NEP was retained. They feared that a drive to increase industrial capacity—that is, to increase the share of heavy industry—would reduce the availability, and consequently raise the prices, of manufactured goods in the short run and would further turn the terms of trade against agriculture, thus creating an additional agricultural supply crisis that would impede industrialization.

Moreover, the NEP period demonstrated to the Soviet leadership its inability to make policy in a market environment. First, the Soviet authorities failed to understand normal speculative behavior in a world of fluctuating prices. Particularly in agriculture, products will be withheld from the market when producers believe that prices are temporarily low. Thus, when Soviet pricing authorities would set low agricultural prices, grain producers would withhold their products from the market in expectation that the lower prices would not hold. It was primarily the more affluent agricultural producers who could afford to withhold grain from the market (to wait for better prices); therefore, most speculative grain stockpiling would naturally be done by the upper peasants. Second, Soviet authorities failed to appreciate fully the general inflationary pressures of the mid-1920s. Between 1924 and 1927, the money supply rose by 2,665 percent, which meant that there were strong inflationary pressures both in industry and agriculture. Many of the Soviet pricing policies (both in agriculture and in industry) were simply undertaken to hold down the rate of inflation. However, economic history tells us that, whenever price controls are introduced in tandem with excessive monetary growth, economic distortions of all sorts are bound to emerge. Third, Soviet authorities failed to understand common notions of opportunity costs. There were several instances in the mid-1920s when the state prices for grains were set below the opportunity costs of producing the grains. It is not unexpected that peasants would reduce their production and marketings of grains with prices below opportunity cost. Fourth, Soviet authorities appeared to be much more interested in grain collected by the state than in the total amount of grain offered to the market. Soviet authorities throughout the 1920s were much more interested in how much grain they were able to obtain from the peasants than in total grain marketings (both to the state and to the population).[44]

The handling of the Scissors Crisis described above is a classic case of these points. Although the scissors probably would have closed by themselves when (and if) the peasants reduced their marketings, the Soviet government intervened directly to improve the peasants' terms of trade. First, maximum selling prices were set for industrial products and price cuts for selected products were ordered. Second, imports of cheaper industrial commodities were allowed to enter the country. Third, the State Bank restricted the credit of the industrial trusts to force them to unload excess stocks. VSNKh even began to use quasi-antitrust measures against the syndicates, and some were abolished.[45] The substantial closing of the scissors (Figure 3.1) by mid-1925 indicates the apparent success of these measures.

However, the setting of maximum industrial selling prices in a period of rising wage and price inflation had an important side effect: an excess demand for industrial products was soon created, which could not be eliminated through price increases, as ceilings had been set. Despite this excess demand and its resulting shortages, no formal rationing system was in effect, which meant that lucrative profits could be made by the *Nepmen* by selling at prices in excess of ceiling prices. This general shortage of industrial commodities has been called the "goods famine," and the peasants, because of their isolation from the market, were hit especially hard.[46] Despite the efforts of the People's Commissariat for Trade to sell in the village at the established ceiling prices, the peasants had to buy primarily from the *Nepman*, who sold at much higher prices. Thus the peasants, despite the nominal closing of the scissors, still lacked incentive to market their surplus. In fact, there is some evidence to suggest that grain marketings were falling as the scissors were closing.[47] The *net* marketings of grain in 1926–1927 were between 50 and 57 percent of prewar levels, although grain output was close to the prewar level.[48]

The state's pricing policy had another serious side effect that eventually destroyed the market orientation of NEP. Initially, two sets of industrial and agricultural prices coexisted side by side: the higher prices of the *Nepmen*, who sold to a great extent in the villages, and the official state ceiling price. In 1927, prices in private stores were 30 percent higher than in state stores. By the end of 1928, they were 63 percent above official state prices.[49] The *Nepman* soon came to be regarded as a black marketeer and an enemy of the state. Beginning in late 1923, policies were adopted to systematically drive out the *Nepman* and widen the state's control over trade. This objective was pursued through the control of industrial raw materials and goods produced by state industry, surcharges on the rail transport of private goods, and taxes on profits of *Nepmen*. In 1926, it became a crime punishable by imprisonment and confiscation of property to make "evil intentioned" increases in prices through speculation. Finally, in 1930, private trade was declared a crime of speculation.

Similar phenomena can be noted in agriculture. After 1926–1927, the state lowered grain procurement prices (which eventually caused peasants to divert production to higher-priced crops and livestock), and a larger gap between state procurement prices and private purchase prices developed. Statistical studies undertaken during this period show that state procurement prices for the four major grains were below production costs in 1926 and 1927. Due to the higher production costs of small and middle peasants, the losses on sales to the state were highest for small and middle peasants.[50] The peasants responded by refusing to market their grain to state procurement agencies, creating the "grain procurement crisis" discussed in Chapter 5. Again, the private purchaser was systematically forced out of the agricultural market by the state. This trend culminated in 1929, when compulsory delivery quotas replaced the agricultural market system.

Such actions effectively signaled the end of NEP, for the market on which NEP primarily depended was no longer functioning. Prices were set by the state, acting through the *Glavki*, trusts and syndicates, and they no longer reflected supply and demand. The economy was without direction from either market or plan—a situation that was not to be tolerated long.

The high unemployment rate of the mid- and late 1920s was yet another reason for official dissatisfaction with NEP. Rising unemployment was supposed to be a problem that troubled only capitalist societies; yet rural underemployment was estimated to be between 8 and 9 million, and there were well over a million unemployed in the cities.[51] The existence of such high unemployment was not only ideologically embarrassing to the Soviet leadership, but the social unrest it engendered represented a real political threat to the regime.

A final source of dissatifaction with NEP relates to national security problems. The fear of imperialist conspiracies, England's breaking off of diplomatic relations in 1927, and concern over Japanese activities in the Far East prompted the Soviet leaders to realize that rapid industrialization would be required to meet the security needs of the Soviet Union and that NEP was not well suited to generate such rapid industrialization. The Soviet leadership in 1927 expected a war with the capitalist West, and panic purchases by the population worsened the supply situation.[52]

THE PRECEDENTS OF THE 1920s

During the 1920s, the economic problem of resource allocation was dealt with by using two radically different economic systems. The first—War Communism—relied heavily upon command elements, whereas the second —NEP—attempted to combine market and command methods. The experiences of this early period tended to establish precedents that had a visible and lasting impact upon the eventual organizational structure of the Soviet planned economy. These precedents are introduced at this point as recurring themes throughout the ensuing chapters.

First, we emphasize the Soviet experiences with central planning during the 1920s. War Communism indicated that the market cannot be eliminated by fiat, for unless an enforceable plan is introduced in its place, the economy will be without direction other than that provided by the "sleepless, leather-jacketed commissars working around the clock in vain effort to replace the market."[53] To use Trotsky's apt description: "Each factory resembled a telephone whose wires had been cut."[54] The "paper" planning of War Communism was shown to be virtually no plan at all, and unless planners have detailed and coordinate information from the enterprise level and up and the political and economic muscle to ensure compliance, planning will be ineffective. To quote one expert on War Communism: "War Communism cannot be considered a centrally planned economy in any meaningful sense."[55] A further precedent in the area of planning was the importance of shock tactics in a world of deficient information and imperfect control. Thus, the concentration of resources on priority projects to eliminate bottlenecks was seen as a way to guide the planned economy in accordance with politically determined priorities. It was also noted that the success of shock tactics depended on their limited application. This precedent can be seen in the "storming" tactics and the practice of singling out a few key branches for preferential treatment that persist until today. The 1920s also introduced the issue of central versus regional direction, which was to become a recurring theme throughout later periods. The friction between central and regional planning authorities (the *Glavki*, the *Sovnarkhozy*, and local authorities) throughout the 1920s revealed an imperfect harmony of national and regional interests that persists to the present. Thus, the vacillation between ministerial an regional planning, a particularly important issue during the Khrushchev years, had its roots in the 1920s. The NEP period also witnessed the growing reliance on amalgamations of state enterprises into trusts and syndicates. These amalgamations, forerunners of the modern Soviet industrial associations, were a link between the central administrators and the producing enterprises and thus eased the burden on the administrators.

Second, the Soviet leadership's experiences with peasant agriculture during the 1920s also set important precedents. It was widely feared that peasant agriculture could be a thorn in the side of rapid industrialization, for the success of industrialization was seen as being dependent on peasant marketing to the state. It was thought that attempts by the state to extract surpluses from the peasantry without offering economic incentives in return would be met by reductions in agricultural output and/or marketings. The Soviet leaders' apprehension was the impetus for the introduction of force into the countryside with the collectivization of agriculture in 1929 and provides an explanation for the continuing reluctance of the leadership to reinstate individual peasant farming (other than the small household plot), despite the often disappointing performance of collective agriculture.

The third important precedent of this early period was the development of an ingrained mistrust of the market that persists to the present. Most of the experiences with the market during the late NEP period were negative. The predominant trusts used their monopoly power to restrict output and withhold stocks. The *Nepmen* sold at high market prices despite the efforts of state pricing authorities to set limits on industrial prices. The peasants withheld their output whenever they deemed market incentives insufficient. For these and other reasons, the market was virtually abolished after 1929, with only such minor exceptions as the collective farm market, the "second economy," and, in part, the labor market. It is in this context that one can better understand the Soviet leadership's inbred opposition to fluctuating prices, output and input decisions based on profit maximization, and other market phenomena that still persists. Yet both War Communism and NEP convinced the Soviet leadership of the inevitability of an uneasy truce between the market and the central authorities. Throughout the transition period, the bulk of consumer goods continued to be supplied by private markets, even during periods when market transactions of this type were proscribed. During War Communism, the Soviet state continued to print money, whose use was proscribed in legal transactions, knowing full well that it was destined for illegal private markets. During NEP, the *Nepmen* were tolerated because the state knew that it would be unable to supply populations living in remote areas.

A fourth precedent, which can be related directly to the experiences of War Communism labor policies, was the evident necessity of freedom to choose occupations. If workers are to be productive, they must be allowed to choose their occupation on the basis of economic incentives. The militarization of labor attempted under War Communism proved to be an ineffective tool for allocating labor. Not only must wages be differentiated, but the resultant money income must have meaning in terms of real purchasing power; that is, a consumer goods market must exist. The labor experiences of War Communism set an important precedent in favor of free occupational choice—a precedent followed in subsequent periods except when temporarily abandoned during the late 1930s and 1940s in response to the tremendous turnover of the inexperienced factory labor force and wartime emergency.

A final precedent was the need to establish state control over the trade unions and other worker groups. During both War Communism and NEP, powerful forces within the party favored worker or trade union control over enterprises and trade union protection of worker interests. Opponents of these positions argued for the "statization" of the trade unions, for example, that the trade union should be the representative of state interest and that there should be "one-man management" in the enterprise. By the end of NEP, the statization of the trade unions was virtually complete and the doctrine of one-man management was firmly entrenched. The reasons for party distrust of independent trade unions and worker councils are clear. Immediately after the revolution, the central authorities had been unable to restrain wildcat nationalizations and worker takeovers. Moreover, in the absence of a coordinated central planning system, worker-dominated enterprises were operated in the interest of local workers, not in the interest of the party.

The year 1928 found the Soviet Union on the eve of the Five Year Plan period, about to embark on an ambitious program of forced industrialization. It was during this period that the Soviet command system evolved in large part into its present form. The period that we have just discussed, from the revolution to the first Five Year Plan, is important because of its impact on this command system. One might in fact argue that War Communism and NEP represented a practical learning experience for the Soviet leadership. Chapter 4 describes another (more theoretical) learning experience that also had a significant impact on the evolution of the Soviet command system: the Soviet Industrialization Debate.

NEP AND PERESTROIKA

Gorbachev's perestroika program has caused the Soviet leadership to reevaluate NEP's attempt to combine market and plan. The increased freedom of expression of the 1980s has allowed Soviet scholars to question seriously whether NEP could have served as an alternative to the forced collectivization ordered by Stalin in 1929. Official Soviet writings on NEP represent a calculated attack on the remnants of Stalinism, but they also appear to be a sincere effort to learn more about combining market and plan in a setting of predominantly public ownership.

Official Soviet writings on this subject conclude that NEP was an unsuccessful attempt to find the optimal proportion between private initiative based on market relations and administrative allocation[56] The use of market relations and private initiative in light industry and handicraft is viewed as a positive feature of NEP. The use of administrative-command allocation in light industry, services, and handicraft is viewed as inappropriate. The failure to find an appropriate formula for motivating the state-directed sector is criticized. Soviet writers see in NEP a basic contradiction that caused it to carry the seeds of its own destruction. Basically, the failure to find ways to channel initiative and risk in the state sector resulted in an expansion of the administrative-command system of resource allocation far beyond its necessary bounds.

On the matter of private ownership in agriculture, official Soviet writings maintain that private peasant agriculture was not a viable long-run alternative but that Stalin's use of force to collectivize was premature. With private ownership, market allocation in agriculture would have created a series of grain collection crises that could have been handled only by inflationary monetary expansion. The appropriate course of action, in the absence of crises, would have been to cultivate the natural cooperative tendencies of peasants as reflected in the continued strength of the village commune. By encouraging what Lenin called "civilized cooperatives" based on state ownership of land and high degrees of cooperation, Soviet agriculture would have evolved into sufficiently large-scale production units. Stalin's decision to collectivize was premature because it preceded the development of necessary cooperative tendencies.[57]

Although some Soviet writers see NEP as an appropriate model for current Soviet economic reform, official Soviet writers have remained cautious and are willing to accept only selected parts of the NEP program. Private ownership of agricultural land has been ruled out; cooperative tendencies are to be encouraged based on state ownership of capital; and more market allocation is to be used in place of the discredited administrative-command system. Most of all, appropriate incentive mechanisms are to be found to guide the activities of state enterprises.

REFERENCES

1. The discussions of War Communism and NEP are largely based on the following sources: A. Nove, *An Economic History of the USSR* (London: Penguin, 1969), chaps. 3 and 4; E. Zaleski, *Planning for Economic Growth in the Soviet Union, 1918–1932* (Chapel Hill: University of North Carolina Press, 1971), chap 2; M. Dobb, *Soviet Economic Development Since 1917*, 5th ed. (London: Routledge & Kegan Paul, 1960), chaps. 4–9; E. H. Carr and R. W. Davies, *Foundations of a Planned Economy, 1926–1929*, vol. 1, part 2 (London: Macmillan, 1969), chaps. 33–35. M. Lewin, *Russian Peasants and Soviet Power* (London: Allen & Unwin, 1968), chaps. 1–15; Y. Avdakov and V. Borodin, *USSR State Industry During the Transition Period* (Moscow: Progress Publishers, 1977); L. Szamuely, *First Models of the Socialist Economic Systems* (Budapest: Akademiai Kiado, 1974); V. A. Vinogradov et al., eds., *Istoriia sotsialisticheskoi ekonomiki SSSR* [History of the socialist economy of the USSR] (Moscow: Nauka, 1976), vols. 1 and 2; V. P. Diachenko, *Istoriia finansov SSSR* [History of USSR finance] (Moscow: Nauka, 1978), chaps. 2–4; and S. Merl, *Der Agrarmarkt und die Neue Ökonomische Politik* [The agrarian market and the new economic policy] (Munich: Oldenbourg Verlag, 1981).
2. The position that Lenin adopted War Communism for ideological reasons is supported by the Hungarian authority Szamuely, *First Models of the Socialist Economic Systems*, pp. 7–62. This interpretation is bitterly opposed by Soviet ideology. For a typical attack on "bourgeois falsifications," see Vinogradov et al., *Istoriia sotsialisticheskoi ekonomiki SSSR*, vol. 1, pp. 251–252. Also see the discussions in Silvana Malle, *The Economic Orgaization of War Communism 1918–1921* (Cambridge: Cambridge University Press, 1985), chap. 1.
3. Merl, *Der Agrarmarkt*, p. 411.
4. See V. P. Danilov, *Rural Russia Under the New Regime* (translated and introduced by Orlando Figes) (Bloomington: Indiana University Press, 1988), chap. 7.
5. Lewin, *Russian Peasants and Soviet Power*, pp. 26–28.
6. Dobb, *Soviet Economic Development*, p. 98; Vinogradov et al., *Istoriia sotsialisticheskoi ekonomiki SSSR*, vol. 1, p. 236.
7. Szamuely, *First Models of the Socialist Economic Systems*, p. 21; Diachenko, *Istoriia finansov SSSR*, pp. 54–55.
8. A statement of E. Preobrazhenzy quoted in Zaleski, *Planning for Economic Growth*, p. 20. See Malle, *The Economic Organization of War Communism*, p. 174, for further discussion of hyperinflation as a means of destroying a money exchange system.
9. Danilov, *Rural Russia Under the New Regime*, chap. 7.
10. Nove, *An Economic History of the USSR*, p. 62. Estimates of the period suggest that in the large towns only 31 percent of all food came through official channels (1919). Szamuely, *First Models of the Socialist Economic Systems*. p. 18, supplies

similar estimates showing that most consumption requirements were satisfied in the free (black) market.

11. Vinogradov et al., *Istoriia sotsialisticheskoi ekonomiki SSSR*, vol. I, p. 374.

12. R. Day, *Leon Trotsky and the Politics of Economic Isolation* (Cambridge: At the University Press, 1973), chap. 2.

13. Szamuely, *First Models of the Socialist Economic Systems*, pp. 12–14.

14. Ibid., pp. 14–17.

15. Ibid., pp. 17–18.

16. Soviet doctrine depicts War Communism as a genial tactical victory by Lenin to win the civil war, while conceding that the USSR was not yet prepared for the elimination of capitalist vestiges. On this, see Vinogradov et al., *Istoriia sotsialisticheskoi ekonomiki SSSR*, vol. I, pp. 244–246.

17. Dobb, *Soviet Economic Development*, p. 117.

18. Nove, *An Economic History of the USSR*, p. 70.

19. For accounts of the organization of the War Communism economy, see Zaleski, *Planning for Economic Growth*, pp. 27–29; S. Oppenheim, "The Supreme Economic Council, 1917–21," *Soviet Studies*, vol. 2, no. 1 (July 1973), 3–27; and Malle, *The Economic Organization of War Communism*, chaps. 5–6.

20. Dobb, *Soviet Economic Development*, p. 112.

21. Nove, *An Economic History of the USSR*, pp. 66–67.

22. Ibid., p. 94.

23. Quoted in Dobb, *Soviet Economic Development*, p. 130. According to P. C. Roberts, *Alienation and the Soviet Economy* (Albuquerque: University of New Mexico Press, 1971), pp. 36–41, this quote is not reflective of Lenin's true position during War Communism. Instead, Lenin tended to view War Communism as a basically correct movement in the direction of revolutionary socialism, which he was forced to back away from by the strikes and civil unrest of 1920. Roberts points out the pains taken by Lenin during this period to justify the abandonment of War Communism on ideological grounds, which would have been unnecessary if War Communism had simply been a temporary wartime measure.

24. A quote from Stalin on this point (from the late 1920s, after he adopted his antipeasant stance): "What is meant by not hindering *kulak* farming? [The term *kulak* refers to the prosperous peasant.] It means setting the *kulak* free. And what is meant by setting the *kulak* free? It means giving him power." I. V. Stalin, *Sochinenia* [Collected works] (Moscow: 1946–1951), vol. XI, p. 275. Quoted in A. Erlich, *The Soviet Industrialization Debate, 1924–1928* (Cambridge, Mass.: Harvard University Press, 1960), pp. 172–173.

25. Vinogradov et al., *Istoriia sotsialisticheskoi ekonomiki SSSR*, vol. 2, pp. 37–38; and S. Merl, *Der Agrarmarkt und die Neue Ökonomische Politik* (Munich: Oldenbourg Verlag, 1981), pp. 305–308.

26. Dobb, *Soviet Economic Development*, p. 143; and Merl, *Der Agrarmarkt*, p. 56.

27. Dobb, *Soviet Economic Development*, p. 142. Census establishments were those employing 16 or more persons along with mechanical power or 30 or more without it. G. W. Nutter, *The Growth of Industrial Production in the Soviet Union* (Princeton, N.J.: Princeton University Press, 1962), pp. 187–188.

28. Nove, *An Economic History of the USSR*, p. 104.

29. Dobb, *Soviet Economic Development*, p. 135. Also see W. Conyngham, *Industrial Management in the Soviet Union* (Stanford: Hoover Institution Press, 1973), pp. 17–24.

30. Carr and Davies, *Foundations of a Planned Economy*, pp. 787–836.

31. Avdakov and Borodin, *USSR State Industry*, chaps. 3 and 4.

32. Ibid., p. 339.

33. For discussions of NEP trade policy, see M. R. Dohan, *Soviet Foreign Trade in the NEP Economy and Soviet Industrialization Strategy*, unpublished doctoral dissertation, Massachusetts Institute of Technology, 1969; L. M. Herman, "The Promise of Economic Self-Sufficiency Under Soviet Socialism," in M. Bornstein and D. Fusfeld, *The Soviet Economy: A Book of Readings*, 3rd ed. (Homewood, Ill.: Irwin, 1970), pp. 260–290; and W. Beitel and J. Nötzold, *Deutsch-Sowjetische Wirtschaftsbeziehungen in der Zeit der Weimarer Republik* [German-Soviet economic relations in the time of the Weimar Republic] (Ebenhausen: Stiftung Wissenschaft und Politik, 1977).

34. M. Kaser, "A Volume Index of Soviet Foreign Trade," *Soviet Studies*, vol. 20, no. 4 (April 1969), 523–526.

35. See M. E. Falkus, "Russia's National Income, 1913: A Revaluation," *Economica*, vol. 35, no. 137 (February 1968), 61. This position is also supported in P. R. Gregory, *Russian National Income, 1885–1913* (Cambridge: Cambridge University Press, 1982), chap. 5. For Vainshtein's position, see A. L. Vainshtein, *Narodny dokhod Rossii i SSSR* [National income of Russia and the USSR] (Moscow: Nauka, 1969), p. 106.

36. Nove, *An Economic History of the USSR*, p. 137.

37. Ibid., p. 138.

38. Cited in Dobb, *Soviet Economic Development*, pp. 161–162.

39. Merl, *Der Agrarmarkt*, pp. 40–43.

40. J. R. Millar, "A Reformulation of A. V. Chayanov's Theory of Peasant Economy," *Economic Development and Cultural change*, vol. 18, no. 2 (January 1970), 225–227.

41. P. R. Gregory, "Grain Marketings and Peasant Consumption, Russia, 1885–1913," *Explorations n Economic History*, vol. 17, no. 2 (April 1980), 135–164.

42. J. F. Karcz, "Thoughts on the grain Problem," *Soviet Studies*, vol. 18, no. 4 (April 1967), 407. Unfortunately, the one effort to test Russian peasant behavior in response to changing relative prices using modern econometrics failed to yield decisive answers. On this, see R. M. Harrison," Soviet Peasants and Soviet Price Policy in the 1920s," *CREES Discussion Papers*, SIPS, no. 10 University of Birmingham, 1977.

43. Erlich, *The Soviet Industrialization Debate*, pp. 105–106; P. R. Gregory, *Socialist and Nonsocialist Industrialization Patterns* (New York: Praeger, 1970), p. 28.

44. For an account of the thinking of Soviet authorities on these points see Merl, *Der Agrarmarkt*, pp. 50–140. The monetary growth figures cited above are from *Statisticheski spravochnik SSR za 28 1928* [The USSR Statistical Handbook 1928] (Moscow: Ts.S. Ul, 1929), p. 600.

45. Avdakow and Borodin, *USSR State Industry*, pp 196–198.

46. Karcz, "Thoughts on the Grain Problem," p. 419.

47. The marketed share of grain for the Ukraine between 1923 and 1926 was: 1923–1924, 26%; 1924–1925, 15%; 1925–1926, 21%.

48. R. W. Davies, "A Note on Grain Statistics," *Soviet Studies*, vol. 21, no. 3 (January 1970), 328. The controversy over grain marketings during the late 1920s will be discussed in Chapter 4.

49. *Statisticheski spravochnik SSR za 1928* [The USSR Statistical handbook 1928] (Moscow; Ts.S.U, 1929), p. 727.

50. These studies are cited by Merl, *Der Agrarmarkt*, p. 104.

51. L. M. Danilov and I. I Matrozova, "Trudovye resursy i ikh ispol'zovanie" [Labor resources and their utilization], in A. P. Volkova et al., eds , *Trud i zarabotnaia plata v SSSR* [Labor and wages in the USSR] (Moscow: Nauka, 1968), pp. 245–248.

52. M. Reiman, *Die Geburt des Stalinismus* [The birth of Stalinism] (Frankfurt/Main:EVA, 1979), chap. 2.

53. Nove, *An Economic History of the USSR*, p. 74.

54. Quoted in Szamuely, *First Models of the Socialist Economic Systems*, p. 97.

55. Malle, *The Economic Organization of War Communism*, p. 318.

56. Official statements on the NEP economy are published in G. L. Smirnov, ed., "Vremiia trudnykh voprosov, Istoriia 20-30-x godov i sovremennaia obshchestvennaia mysl" [Time of difficult questions, history of the 20s and 30s in contemporary social thought] *Pravda*, September 30, 1988; October 3, 1988.

57. It is understandable that Soviet authorities have encouraged the publication of V. P. Danilov's classic studies of Russian agriculture during the NEP period. Danilov emphasizes the natural cooperative tendencies of the NEP peasant and objects to the premature forced collectivization move. See V. P. Danilov, *Rural Russia Under the New Regime*.

SELECTED BIBLIOGRAPHY

Non-Soviet Sources

W. Betel and J. Nötzold, *Deutsch-Sowjetische Wirtschaftsbeziehungen in der Zeit der Weimarer Republik* [German-Soviet Economic Relations in the Time of the Weimar Republic] (Ebenhausen: Stiftung Wissenschaft und Politik, 1977).

E. H. Carr and R. W. Davies, *Foundations of a Planned Economy, 1926–1929*, vol. 1, parts 1, 2 (London: Macmillan, 1969).

R. W. Davies, "Soviet Industrial Production, 1928–1937: The Rival Estimates," *CREES Discussion Papers, SIPS*, no. 18, University of Birmingham, 1978.

R. Day, *Leon Trotsky and the Politics of Economic Isolation* (Cambridge: Cambridge University Press, 1973).

M. Dobb, *Soviet Economic Development Since 1917*, 5th ed. (London: Routledge & Kegan Paul, 1960), chaps. 4–9.

A. Erlich, *The Soviet Industrialization Debate, 1924–1928* (Cambridge, Mass.: Harvard University Press, 1969).

M. Harrison, "Why Was NEP Abandoned?" in R. Stuart, ed., *The Soviet Rural Economy* (Totowa, N.J.: Rowman & Allanheld, 1984), pp. 63–78.

M. Lewin, *Russian Peasants and Soviet Power* (London: Allen & Unwin, 1968).

S. Malle, *The Economic Organization of War Communism 1918–1921* (Cambridge: Cambridge University Press, 1985).

S. Merl, *Der Agrarmarkt und die neue Ökonomische Politik* [The Agrariam Market and the New Economic Policy] (Munich: Oldenbourg Verlag, 1981).

A. Nove, *An Economic History of the USSR* (London: Penguin, 1969), chaps. 3–6.

S. Oppenheim, "The Supreme Economic Council, 1917–21," *Soviet Studies*, vol. 25, no. 1 (July 1973), 3–27.

M. Reiman, *Die Geburt des Stalinismus* [The birth of Stalinism] (Frankfurt/Main: EVA, 1979).

M. Reiman, *Lenin, Stalin, Gorbachev: Kontinuität und Brüche in der sowjetischen Geschichte* (Hamburg: Junius Verlag, 1987).

P. C. Roberts, *Alienation and the Soviet Economy* (Albuquerque: University of New Mexico Press, 1971).

L. Szamuely, *First Models of the Socialist Economic Systems* (Budapest: Akademiai Kiado, 1974).

S. G. Wheatcroft, "A Reevaluation of Soviet Agricultural Production in the 1920s and 1930s," in Robert Stuart, ed., *The Soviet Rural Economy* (Totowa, N.J.: Rowman Allanheld, 1984), pp. 32–62.

S. G. Wheatcroft and R. W. Davies, eds., *Materials for a Balance of the National Economy, 1928–1930* (New York: Cambridge University Press, 1985).

E. Zaleski, *Planning for Economic growth in the Soviet Union, 1918–1932* (Chapel Hill: University of North Carolina Press, 1971), chaps. 1 and 2.

Soviet Sources

Y. Avdakov and V. Borodin, *USSR State Industry During the Transition Period* (Moscow: Progress Publishers, 1977).

V. P. Danilov, *Rural Russia Under the New Regime,* translated and introduced by Orlando Figes (Bloomington: Indiana University Press, 1988).

V. P. Diachenko, *Istoriia finansov SSSR* [History of USSR finance] (Moscow: Nauka, 1978).

E. G. Gimpel'son, *Veliki Oktiabr i stanovlenie sovetskoi sistemy upravleniia narodnym khoziastvom* [The great October and the creation of the Soviet system of regulation of the national economy] (Moscow: Nauka, 1977).

S. G. Strumilin, *Na planovom fronte* [On the planning front] (Moscow: Nauka, 1963).

A. L. Vainshtein, *Narodny dokhod Rossii i SSSR* [National income of Russia and the USSR] (Moscow: Nauka, 1969).

V. A. Vinogradov et al., eds., *Isotoriia sotsialisticheskoi ekonomiki SSSR* [History of the socialist economy of the USSR], vols. 1–3 (Moscow: Nauka, 1976).

Chapter 4

The Soviet Industrialization Debate (1924–1928)

*A*n extraordinary debate on how to initiate economic development took place in the Soviet Union between 1924 and 1928[1] that anticipated Western discussion on the same topic by some 25 years. Its participants ranged from leading party theoreticians to nonparty economists, and its audience included almost everyone of political and intellectual importance in the Soviet Union. The most remarkable feature of this debate was that it raised a multitude of questions concerning development strategy—issues of balanced growth versus unbalanced growth, agricultural savings, the proper scope of planning, taxation, and inflation to promote development—that are still widely debated among Western students of economic development. The debate focused on the alternative development strategies open to the Soviet economy in the late 1920s. An important point is that Stalin, who actually made the eventual choices of central planning and collectivization in 1928 and 1929, respectively, was an observer of and a participant in this debate.

In this chapter, we consider the major issues of the Soviet Industrialization Debate, without undue emphasis on details and biographical information. The Marxist-Leninist legacy provides the ideological foundation of the debate and is discussed first. We limited ourselves to the views of spokesmen for three important factions: Lev Shanin and N. I. Bukharin representing different views within the right wing of the Bolshevik party, and E. A. Preobrazhensky, the economic spokesman of the left wing of the party. We omit mention of significant contributors such as Bazarov, Rykov, Groman, Sokolnikov, and many others, not because they are unimportant but because of space limitations and because the three views presented cover a broad spectrum of the debate, subsuming many of the ideas of other participants.

THE SETTING OF THE SOVIET INDUSTRIALIZATION DEBATE

The rate of economic recovery of NEP probably reached its peak in 1926, but the industrial capacity lost during World War I had not been replaced by the limited industrial investment during NEP. Therefore, industrial capacity during the late 1920s was probably below prewar levels. The investment rate in 1928 was likely near that of 1913. Depending on the prices used, 1928 investment proportions were either slightly above or slightly below those of 1913.[2] The economic instability of the 1920s—the Scissors Crisis and the goods famine, the desire for rapid industrialization, and concern with defense—pointed to the need for massive capital accumulation in industry.[3] Yet could this capital accumulation occur without ruinous inflation? This was the inflationary imbalance dilemma that initially sparked the Soviet Industrialization Debate.

The rapid NEP recovery had brought the economy to its capacity limits. With the loss of industrial capital stock and the limited net investment of the 1920s, the fact that industrial output had regained prewar levels indicates that industrial capacity was probably already being overtaxed by the recovery of the mid-1920s. If, in this situation, an investment drive was undertaken to raise industrial capacity, additional income would be created through the multiplier, thereby generating severe inflationary pressures. This was the Soviet inflationary imbalance in a nutshell: industrial investment was required to raise industrial capacity, yet the capacity-creating effect of investment would be felt only after a period of time. The income-generating effect of investment, however, would be felt almost immediately, thus creating an inflationary problem.

If this inflation were to occur, the peasant would again be alienated by the increasing prices of manufactured goods, which would rise rapidly as capacity was diverted to producing investment goods. The terms of trade would again move against agriculture and another Scissors Crisis would ensue. It was felt that an industrialization drive would redistribute wealth away from the peasant (through declining terms of trade) and that such a redistribution could have disastrous effects on political stability and grain marketings. The *Smychka* basis of NEP would be jeopardized, and some alternative system would have to be substituted to feed the industrial workers.

The second alternative, a slow rate of capital accumulation, would avoid excessive inflation and preserve the alliance with the peasant On the other hand, the basic problem—the low capacity of the economy—would not be addressed. The economy would remain on the brink of inflation without achieving long-run objectives. This inflationary imbalance dilemma was the spark that ignited the Soviet Industrialization Debate in 1924. The scope of the debate then broadened to include far-reaching discussions of long-run development alternatives.

The political background of the debate should be outlined as well.[4] After Lenin's death in January 1924, the leadership of the Communist Party was split by a bitter factional debate. The "united opposition" of the left, led by Leon Trotsky, Grigory Zinoviev, and Lev Kamenev, opposed the NEP concessions to the peasant and to private trade and was a persistent critic of the foreign policies of the party leadership. The left opposition advocated "superindustrialization" and harsh discriminatory measures against the more prosperous peasants and resisted the notion of "building socialism in one country." The party leadership consisted of a coalition between the Bolshevik "moderates"—Nikolai Bukharin, the editor of *Pravda*, who was a recognized Marxist theoretician and a popular revolutionary figure; Mikhail Tomsky, the trade union leader; and Aleksei Rykov, the head of the government bureaucracy—and Joseph Stalin, the general secretary of the Communist Party. This ruling coalition favored the continuation of NEP, the avoidance of a superindustrialization drive, the preservation of the *Smychka*, and efforts toward rapprochement with the capitalist world.

The leadership coalition had a vested interest in the success of the NEP experiment and the policy of rapprochement with the West. The latter policy was important because through it they hoped to attract foreign credits to bolster the NEP recovery. Serious setbacks occurred on both fronts in 1927: voluntary grain marketings fell well below government targets, and the government suffered serious foreign policy setbacks—the British broke off diplomatic relations, there were troubles in Poland, and Chiang Kai-shek turned on the Chinese Communists. The Soviet Union was gripped by a war scare, and it was felt that a major war with the capitalist West was imminent. Sensing a weakening in the political base of the ruling coalition, Trotsky and the left opposition chose to challenge the leadership, a challenge that was successfully repulsed and resulted in the expulsion of Trotsky from the party in December 1927.

This recitation of the political setting of the mid-1920s is relevant to a discussion of the Industrialization Debate because it shows that the debated issues were the very ones that divided the leadership of the Communist Party. The debate was much more than an abstract theoretical discussion concerning development alternatives. Rather, it was a debate that dealt with the most pressing political issues of the day.

THE MARXIST-LENINIST LEGACY

The participants in the Soviet Industrialization Debate addressed themselves to the proper way to industrialize the Soviet economy. The debate centered largely on sectorial growth strategies, that is, on whether industry (the "state sector") or agriculture (the "private sector") should be favored or whether sectorial growth should be balanced.* This same question has been widely discussed by Western economists in the postwar period and has been called the "balanced versus unbalanced growth controversy."

The Soviet Industrialization Debate of the mid-1920s drew upon the theoretical legacies of Marx and Lenin. All participants in the debate had as their goal the "building of socialism," all agreed the state (society) should own the means of production at least in industry, and all used appropriate quotations from Marx and Lenin to support their programs.

Marx

The Marxist legacy consists of Marx's (and Friedrich Engel's) limited instructions concerning the shape of the future socialist society and of Marx's model of expanded reproduction, a model that states the conditions for a growing economy.[5] Marx's expanded-reproduction scheme is of direct relevance to the Industrialization Debate, for it provided a conceptual model for determining sectoral priorities. A further Marxist legacy that was to achieve considerable prominence in the debate was Marx's notion of primitive capitalist accumulation, the process by which capital initially came to be controlled by the capitalist class. The primitive capitalist accumulation notion was important to the debate insofar as Soviet socialist thinkers sought after socialist parallels to primitive capitalist accumulation.

Marx's instructions concerning the shape of future socialist societies are quite brief because he believed that the details of the future communist society were unforeseeable. According to the Marxian dialectic, societies must inevitably evolve into higher-order economic systems. Feudalism must inevitably replace slavery, capitalism must inevitably replace feudalism, and socialism must inevitably replace capitalism, for each system possesses internal contradictions that eventually explode into qualitative changes, that is, the rapid transition from one economic system to the other. The basic contradiction of capitalism, the class struggle between the worker and the capitalist, would

---

*The discussion of sectorial priorities can be cast in terms of either industry and agriculture or the state sector and the private sector. During the debate, industry (in particular, heavy industry) was owned primarily by the state and agriculture had private owners. It may be more accurate to picture the debate over priorities as a battle between the state-owned and the private sectors. On this, see Millar, "A Note on Primitive Accumulation," pp. 387–392.

inevitably lead to the violent overthrow of capitalism and the establishment of a socialist society. The first phase of the new socialist society would consist of a transition period that would vary from society to society depending upon the legacy of the proceeding stage of capitalism. Only when communism, the final stage of social evolution, had been reached would differences among societies be eliminated. Marx had remarkably little to say about the critical period of transition from capitalism to communism.

Marx believed that the socialist revolution would occur in the advanced capitalist countries, in societies that had already developed a powerful productive apparatus. The new socialist government could, therefore, take charge of this productive apparatus and free it from the wastes of capitalist crises and costly imperialist competition. Thus, the period of transition to communism, the stage of abundance where members of society can be rewarded according to wants and needs, would not be too long in duration. In the meantime, the transition period would be characterized by the distribution of goods to individuals according to their contribution to the productive process. Those who contribute more in terms of labor services should receive more back from society. Workers would receive vouchers from society indicating the amount of work they had performed. The workers would then be entitled to withdraw from society's production a value of goods (after deductions for investment, depreciation, etc.) equivalent to their contribution to society's output. The distribution of income would, therefore, remain unequal during the transition period, a defect inevitable during the first phase of communist society, but this system is fair in that it involves an exchange of equivalent values (labor for labor).

Marx felt that planning would play a key role during the transition period. He emphasized the chaos of the market and the fact that market allocation creates economic crises. Planning would allow a socialist society to avoid the disproportions that plagued capitalist societies. Socialist societies would have greater foresight, and he advocated central control over resource allocation in his famous critique of the Gotha Program.[6]

During the transition period, the objective of socialist planners should be to accelerate the rate of economic growth and thus shorten the waiting time for the abundant communist society. In his model of expanded reproduction, Marx described the necessary relationship among economic sectors required to bring about economic growth. It might be noted that these are physical relationships, independent of the society's economic system; therefore, they would hold in socialist as well as capitalist societies. The condition for economic growth (expanded reproduction) can be illustrated by beginning with a stationary economy that is not growing (simple reproduction).[7]

Marx divided the economy into two broad sectors: Sector I, in which the means of production are produced, and Sector II, in which consumer goods are produced. For our purposes, we equate Sector I with heavy industry and Sector II with agriculture and light industry. Using Marx's labor theory of value, which states that the value of output will equal the value of direct and indirect labor inputs plus surplus value (profits), we can write the value of each sector's output as

$$V_1 = c_1 + v_1 + s_1$$

$$V_2 = c_2 + v_2 + s_2$$

(4.1)

where   V = value of sector output
c = fixed capital costs and depreciation
v = variable costs, primarily labor costs
s = surplus value (or profits) of each sector

The subscripts 1 and 2 refer to Sector I and Sector II, respectively.

In a stationary economy, the output of Sector I (investment goods) equals the depreciation requirements of Sectors I and II, or

$$V_1 = c_1 + c_2$$

(4.2)

and this is Marx's condition of simple reproduction. On the other hand, the economy will grow if the net capital stock of the economy expands, and this occurs when the output of Sector I exceeds the depreciation expenses of I and II or

$$V_1 > c_1 + c_2$$

(4.3)

This is Marx's condition of expanded reproduction.

For the economy to be in equilibrium (an equilibrium of supply and demand for the output of Sector I), capital accumulation (saving) equal to $V_1 - c_1 - c_2$ must take place. Marx assumed that, in capitalist societies, workers (the recipients of v) would be at subsistence and would thus not be a source of capital accumulation. The capitalists, the recipients of surplus value s, would, therefore, be the source of capital accumulation. Marx did not expand upon the sources of capital accumulation during the transition period, a topic of heated controversy during the Industrialization Debate, but he did describe the process of capital accumulation during the early phases of capitalism, called *primitive capitalist accumulation*.[8]

In the Marxian schema, the notion of primitive capitalist accumulation is used to explain how capital came to be controlled by a capitalist class in the first place. Marx rejected the argument that capitalists acquired capital through their own (or their ancestors') abstinence from consumption. Instead, he argued that this process occurred primarily through expropriation of the property of the weak (the serfs, the urban workers, etc.) by the strong (the state, the church, robber barons, the merchants). In this manner, the poorer segments of society were divorced from the means of production and were forced to offer their labor to the capitalist class.

What directions could the new Soviet leadership draw from the Marxist legacy in preparing their blueprints from the new socialist society? The first directive is that during the period of transition to communism, distribution should be according to one's contribution to production. The second is that some form of planning should replace the anarchy of capitalist markets. The third instruction follows from Marx's model of expanded reproduction, namely, that growth can be accelerated by giving priority to the investment goods sector over the consumer goods sector. One may care to read a final directive into Marx concerning the initial stages of capital accumulation in a new socialist state. Insofar as capitalists initially gained control of capital by expropriation (primitive capitalist accumulation), the socialist state may adopt the same method to expropriate capital from the remaining capitalists (primitive socialist accumulation).

Lenin

In his theoretical writings, Lenin had to reconcile the socialist revolution in Russia with Marx's clear prediction that it would occur in the advanced capitalist countries. Lenin's explanation represents a basic revision of Marxism in that he argued that the socialist revolution would occur, for a variety of reasons, in the "weakest link" in the capitalist chain and that Russia was that weakest link.[9] Russia's economic backwardness presented further theoretical problems for Lenin, for Marx felt that the task of making the transition from capitalism to communism would be eased by the inheritance of an advanced industrialized economy. This was not the case of Russia in 1917.

Lenin argued that the backward nature of the Russian economy required a transition period between capitalism and socialism, which he called state capitalism.[10] In Lenin's view, a strong Soviet state would be required to capture the commanding heights of the economy. By having the state nationalize and control banking, transportation, utilities, and heavy industry, the Soviet state would be in a position to exercise control over the nonstate sector (light industry and agriculture), which would remain temporarily in private hands. With this strategy, the Soviet government would obtain the many benefits capitalism had to offer (the services of specialists, foreign concessions, private trade) while exercising overall control over economic affairs. Lenin, in justifying why the socialist revolution would start in Russia, put a great deal of effort into demonstrating the advanced nature of Russia's commanding-heights industries. Lenin pointed to the high concentration ratios of Russia's heavy industries and emphasized the role of foreign capital in promoting this concentration. In Russia, the Bolshevik state inherited pockets of advanced capitalism when they took over the country. These pockets of advanced capitalism, which would spawn the revolutionary proletariat, would provide the heavy-industry base for building socialism. The enormous productive potential of capitalism, admired by Marx, would thus be put to the benefit of the working classes. In advocating state capitalism, Lenin was opposed by Nikolai Bukharin, who argued that the state should be "smashed," for Bukharin feared that a strong state might lead to the restoration of capitalism.

Although the state would control the commanding heights, light manufacturing and handicraft could remain (at least temporarily) in private hands. In agriculture, farming could remain in the hands of private peasants. Over time, however, peasants would recognize the advantages of large-scale mechanized farming, and they would voluntarily join large collective farms.

The failure of the Russian socialist revolution to spark the world revolution predicted by Marx presented Lenin with further doctrinal difficulties.[11] Was it possible to "build socialism in one country" (in relatively backward Russia), or would socialism in Russia have to wait on a successful socialist revolution in the advanced capitalist countries? This was a doctrinal issue that split the Bolshevik leadership. On the one side, Leon Trotsky argued for a "permanent revolution," maintaining that Russia could not hope to build socialism successfully without the assistance of more advanced socialist nations. Nikolai Bukharin (and later Stalin) opposed Trotsky by arguing that the Soviet Union's resource base and potential economic power were sufficiently strong to build socialism in Russia, isolated from the outside capitalist world. Lenin failed to make a definitive statement in this controversy, although he appeared to believe that the success of the Soviet experiment would eventually depend on the spread of the revolution to the advanced nations. He did, however, argue that "breathing spells" would be required to allow consolidation of revolutionary gains before the permanent revolution could continue. Thus, contrary to Trotsky, Lenin did not believe that the world socialist revolution would be a continuous process.

Defining Lenin's legacy to the participants in the Industrialization Debate is difficult because Lenin, as a practical politician, was forced to justify Marxist theory to a wide range of conflicting policies. In the early months after the revolution, Lenin laid out his blueprints for the fledgling Soviet regime (the "April theses"), in which the basic features of state capitalism were outlined. Shortly thereafter, he was obliged to justify War Communism and then, three years later, to explain the advent of NEP.

The Soviet Industrialization Debate began in earnest shortly after the death of Lenin. To a great extent, the debate was about the type of economic system—NEP or a War Communism-like system—that would be best suited to building socialism. When NEP was abandoned in 1928, the outcome of the debate was clear.

PREOBRAZHENSKY—UNBALANCED GROWTH OF INDUSTRY

E. A. Preobrazhensky, the vocal spokesman of the left wing of the Bolshevik party, took up where Marxian expanded reproduction left off and argued that a discontinuous spurt in the output of investment goods was required to attain rapid industrialization.[12] Preobrazhensky envisioned two possible courses of action at the end of the 1920s: the Soviet economy could either continue to stagnate or even retrogress to lower levels of capacity, or a "big push" to expand capacity could be undertaken. In taking this latter step, which he supported, halfway measures would not be advisable, for a spurt below the crucial minimum effort of investment would be self-defeating.

Preobrazhensky based this conclusion on several factors. He thought that the inflationary imbalance had two causes: the low capacity of the industrial sector, and a loss of saving ability—the latter being a consequence of institutional change in agriculture. Before the revolution, the peasants had been forced to "save" in real terms a substantial portion of their output, which was delivered either to the state or to the landlord. This forced saving limited their capacity to purchase industrial products. The revolution, however, established them as free proprietors. Rent payments were eliminated and agriculture taxes (in 1924–1925) were less than one-third of prewar obligations.[13] The peasants became accustomed to receiving industrial commodities in return for the sale of their agricultural surplus. According to Preobrazhensky, this caused a "drastic disturbance of the equilibrium between the effective demand of the village and the marketable output of the town."[14] The effective demand of the peasant had increased substantially without a substantial increase in industrial capacity, creating an inflationary gap.

Preobrazhensky suggested that net investment in industry must be raised significantly to close the gap between effective demand and capacity and that the inflationary effects of this action must be neutralized by altering the structure of demand significantly away from consumption and toward saving. Once the new industrial capacity has been created, private consumption could again be free to approach its previous position.

As far as the sectoral allocation of this net investment was concerned, Preobrazhensky argued for unbalanced growth to favor industry in general and heavy industry in particular on the grounds that the short-run benefits of investment in agriculture and light industry would be well outweighed by the long-run benefits of investment in capacity-expanding heavy industry. Thus, he emphasized that investment goods and consumer goods industries must be arranged in "marching combat order," in keeping with the Marxian theory of economic dynamics.*

---

*This conclusion follows the Fel'dman growth model of 1928. Employing Marx's division into an investment goods section (Department A) and a consumption goods sector (Department B), G. A. Fel'dman developed a mathematical model for the USSR State Planning Commission that made a stronger case for unbalanced growth in favor of Department A than the original Marxian model of expanded reproduction outlined above. Fel'dman made several implicit and explicit assumptions in deriving his model: (1) that the state had the power to control the division of total investment between Department A and Department B; (2) that once investment had been made in one sector, this capital could not be shifted later for use in the other sector; (3) that the economy was closed to trade with the outside world; (4) (implicitly) that the state rather than individuals controlled aggregate

In arguing in favor of a big push, Preobrazhensky stressed that moderate increases in the capacity of the capital goods sector would be self-defeating: the technological gap between the USSR and the advanced capitalist powers had become so wide that it was now impossible to adopt advanced technology gradually. Second, he echoed a view widely held at the time that the replacement requirements of the Soviet economy had become so immense that a significant increase in investment was required just to keep industrial capacity from falling.

According to Preobrazhensky, foreign trade could, to some extent, substitute for domestic capital production by importing foreign capital. However, the Soviets' capacity to import was limited by the lack of foreign credits (which would probably not be offered by capitalist foes) and by the small size of the exportable agricultural surplus. A foreign trade monopoly would be essential to ensure that machinery and not luxuries would be imported. In any case, considering the massive capital requirements of the Soviet economy in the 1920s,

---

consumption and saving (given a particular aggregate investment goal, the state could make saving equal that amount); and (5) that capital was the sole limiting factor of production and that labor was overabundant.

Given these assumptions, Fel'dman concluded that the rate of growth of GNP in the long run depends on the proportion of output of the investment goods sector that is back into that sector. If a substantial portion of the Department A output goes into the consumer goods sector, then the rate of growth of total output will be small. The long-term rate of growth of consumption also depends on reinvestment in the investment goods sector. A high reinvestment ratio will yield high rates of growth of consumption in the long run, whereas a low reinvestment ratio will yield a relatively high short-term rate and a relatively low long-term rate of growth of consumption. That is, current consumption must be sacrificed in order to obtain a maximum rate of growth of both output and consumption in the long run. In sum, Fel'dman's model concludes that the bulk of investment must flow into the capital goods sector at the expense of consumer goods sectors if the growth rate of consumption and GNP is to be maximized in the long run. The partial derivation of the Fel'dman model is given below:

$$I_t^1 = \alpha I_t$$

$$I_t - I_{t-1} = \frac{\alpha I_{t-1}}{V_1}$$

$$I_t = \left(1 + \frac{\alpha}{V_1}\right) I_{t-1}$$

$$= I_o \left(1 + \frac{\alpha}{V_1}\right)^{t-1}$$

$$C_t - C_{t-1} = \frac{(1 - \alpha) I_{t-1}}{V_2}$$

Preobrazhensky felt that the foreign sector could only play a limited role in the Soviet capacity buildup.[*]

The long-run payoff of Preobrazhensky's policy of one-sided reinvestment in the capital goods sector would be an enhanced capacity to produce manufactured consumer goods and industrial farm machinery. Yet he recognized that it would take years for this to happen:

> ...a discontinuous reconstruction of fixed capital involves a shift of so much means of production toward the production of means of production, which will yield output only after a few years, that thereby the increase of the consumption funds of the society will be stopped.[15]

To dampen the interim inflationary pressures, Preobrazhensky proposed the system of primitive socialist accumulation, which was to replace the market so as to force the economy to save more for capital investment than it would have had the market prevailed. Instead of the market, state trade monopolies would set prices. By purchasing at low delivery prices and then selling at higher retail prices, the state would be able to generate a form of profit or forced saving that would reduce inflationary pressures. Preobrazhensky further suggested that during the period of primitive socialist accumulation, the main burden of industrialization should be placed on the peasantry in the form of low state pur-

$$C_t - C_{t-1} = \frac{I_1(1-\alpha)\left[1+(\alpha/V_1)\right]^{t-2}}{V_2}$$

where
I = total investment
I^1 = investment allocated to A
C = total consumption
a = portion of I allocated to A
V_1 = capital coefficient of A
V_2 = capital coefficient of B
t = time subscript

See E. Domar, "A Soviet Model of Growth," *Essay in the Theory of Economic Growth* (New York: Oxford University Press, 1957), pp. 223–261.

[*]Apparently, Preobrazhensky's view of the role of foreign trade did not coincide with the views of the political leader of the left wing, Trotsky. Trotsky's belief in the inability of the Soviet Union to build socialism on its own forced him to argue that the USSR remain integrated in the world economy. He felt that economic and political events would be dictated by events in the outside world and that Russia's economic weakness could be ameliorated by exchange with the more advanced world, especially when capitalist crises forced the advanced capitalist countries to compete for the Russian market. For these reasons, Trotsky attacked the trade policies of the ruling coalition as being too autarkic. Preobrazhensky may have agreed with Trotsky on these points, but he felt that a major capitalist crisis was imminent and would destroy the Soviet industrialization drive if the USSR were integrated into the world economy. For discussions of Trotsky's views on economic integration, see Day, *Leon Trotsky and the Politics of Economic Isolation,* part 2; and Nove, "A Note on Trotsky," pp. 582–584.

chase prices and high manufactured consumer goods prices, thereby extracting forced saving through a reduced peasant living standard.

In addition to his ideological preference for state industry, Preobrazhensky chose to burden the peasants because of the high potential of their saving capacity as exhibited prior to the revolution and because of peasant agriculture's ability to be independent of industry. The overall purpose of primitive socialist accumulation was to let the state, not private individuals, decide how much would be saved. In doing so, the state would try to equate real saving (composed of both voluntary and involuntary savings) with the output of the capital goods sector (real investment).

Preobrazhensky's notion of primitive socialist accumulation contained ideological as well as economic motives. On the ideological front, the battle would be waged between the state sector (nationalized heavy industry) and the private sector (agriculture and handicraft manufacturing), and Preobrazhensky believed that the state must ensure the victory of the socialist sector. Primitive socialist accumulation would transfer resources out of the private sector (primarily agriculture) and into the state sector by imposing "nonequivalent exchanges" between the city and countryside. The exchange of industrial and agricultural commodities would be nonequivalent because of the state's manipulation of agricultural prices. Once the state had eliminated the private sector as a viable threat, the socialized sector would become the source of capital accumulation.[16]

Preobrazhensky clearly recognized the dangers of primitive socialist accumulation. Given the large volume of savings that had to be extracted from agriculture, extremely low agricultural purchase prices would have to be set. The peasant would again be faced with deteriorating terms of trade and would withdraw from the market, alienated from the Soviet regime. In Bukharin's words, primitive socialist accumulation would "kill the goose [agriculture] that laid the golden eggs." This was the weakest point of his program and proved the focus for strong attacks by his opponents. How was the industrialization drive to be sustained if agricultural supplies were not available? The platform of the left wing did call for increased emphasis on collective and state farming, but the development of socialized agriculture would be a slow evolutionary process.[17]

SHANIN—UNBALANCED GROWTH OF AGRICULTURE

Lev Shanin, a representative of the extreme right wing of the Bolshevik party, favored a program of unbalanced growth of agriculture within an essentially free market environment. The inflationary imbalance of the mid-1920s also provided the point of departure for Shanin. In view of this imbalance, Shanin thought that the Soviet economy should adopt a short-term horizon in planning policy. If massive investments were made in heavy industry with its long gestation periods, demand-creating income would be released without a parallel increase in capacity except in the long run, and by that time it would be too late. Shanin emphasized the income-generating side of capital investment, whereas

Preobrazhensky emphasized its capacity-creating aspect.

The difficult transition from NEP recovery to new construction capacity could be smoothed, according to Shanin, by adopting an agriculture-first policy. There were several reasons for this conclusion.

First, Shanin argued that the short-term increment in real output to be derived from an additional ruble of investment (the marginal output-capital ratio) in agriculture far exceeded that of industry, especially in view of agriculture's surplus population and low capital intensity.[18]

Second, Shanin believed that there was a higher propensity to save in agriculture than in industry. According to this assumption, aggregate saving (a crucial factor in an inflation-prone economy) would be enhanced by a redistribution of money income in favor of agriculture.[19] Using these two assumptions, Shanin derived his agriculture-first policy.

Shanin presented his arguments by contrasting two alternative investment programs: one channeling investment into industry, the other channeling investment into agriculture. Investment of a given amount in agriculture would generate a relatively large increase in capacity because of agriculture's low marginal capital-output ratio. In addition, the increased investment in agriculture would increase agricultural incomes, and because of the high marginal propensity to save in agriculture, this increase in income would create a relatively large amount of incremental saving and inflationary pressures would be reduced. On the other hand, an equivalent amount of investment in industry would not only generate a smaller increase in capacity but would also fail to create as large an increase in saving because of the industrial worker's high marginal propensity to consume. In this matter, Shanin's invest-in-agriculture policies would allow the economy to expand through additional investment and without inflation.

According to Shanin, two benefits would be derived from investment in agriculture. First, the capacity of the economy would be increased by a larger amount and in a shorter period of time, thereby ameliorating the short-term inflationary imbalance. Second, the creation of additional income in agriculture would generate a larger amount of incremental saving that could be used to finance additional investment without inflation.

Finally, Shanin emphasized the benefits to be gained from foreign trade. By trading according to its comparative advantage in agriculture, the Soviet Union could exchange agricultural products for industrial capital equipment, thereby building up the capital stock of industry while avoiding the inflation that would have occurred had the investment initially been in industry.[20]

Shanin envisioned that his policies would have to be carried out within an essentially free market environment to ensure the support of the peasantry and thereby the efficient utilization of investment in agriculture. He was sufficiently realistic to see that his proposals would have to be altered in the case of an imminent military threat, which would require the short-run enhancement of industrial capacity irrespective of the economic consequences. He also saw that certain industrial investments, such as in transportation, would be required to carry out his agricultural programs.[21] Therefore, industrial investment could not be neglected entirely. Another circumstance mitigating against the full-scale adoption of his agriculture-first program would be the exhaustion of foreign markets for Soviet agricultural products. Nevertheless, he minimized the importance of these exceptions and did not allow them to materially alter his main conclusions.

In the long run, after the initial inflationary imbalance had been eliminated, Shanin proposed a shift in emphasis toward industry, a shift toward reinvesting in capital goods which could be now accomplished free of inflationary pressures. At this time, the building of socialism could begin in earnest, unhindered by short-term inflationary problems.

BUKHARIN—BALANCED GROWTH

Nikolai Bukharin was the official spokesman of the right wing of the Bolshevik party. A close associate of Lenin and possessing credentials as a leading Marxist theoretician, Bukharin remained a potent individual force in Soviet politics until the Stalin purges of the 1930s.[22] Prior to NEP, Bukharin's ideas were closely attuned to those of the left wing of the party, and he even co-authored a standard textbook on communism with Preobrazhensky. But NEP brought about a significant change in Bukharin's thinking. Throughout the NEP period, he remained an influential supporter of the NEP economic system and acted as its advocate in the face of attacks from the left wing.

Whereas Preobrazhensky felt that the victory of socialist ownership over private property had to be engineered by the state through unequal exchanges between the city and countryside, Bukharin felt that this outcome would be ensured by the natural superiority of socialist ownership.[23] The proletariat was in a position to exercise political control over the country and would thus be able to contain the antisocialist tendencies of the peasant, but market relations between the city and countryside would ensure that harmony between the peasant and the industrial worker (the *Smychka*) would be maintained. Any effort to introduce nonequivalent exchanges would destroy the foundation of economic development.

Unlike the left wing, Bukharin and his followers felt that socialized industry did not require discriminatory government action to assert its superiority. Rather, state industry would naturally grow more rapidly than the rest of the economy, and its share would inevitably increase. In this manner, the superiority of socialist ownership would be demonstrated to those outside the state sector, and they would gradually be attracted to join the state sector voluntarily. The peasants would increasingly join consumer and producer cooperatives, and the state would encourage agricultural cooperation through favorable credit terms granted by the State Bank. Eventually, the peasants would join collective farms voluntarily. This action, however, would have to be noncoercive, for it would be counterproductive to impose collectivization on the peasantry before the peasants themselves were convinced of the superiority of the socialist form.

So much for the political side of the Bukharin program. On strictly economic grounds, he argued in favor of the balanced growth of industry and agriculture, granting that socialized industry would grow more rapidly than the economy as a whole. According to Bukharin, any investment policy that one-sidedly favors agriculture over industry or vice versa, or one branch of industry over another, will fail because of the interdependence of economic sectors.[24] First, industry cannot function successfully without agricultural supplies: the productivity of the industrial worker depends on the availability of marketed agricultural foodstuffs. Further, industrial capacity will be reduced greatly if agricultural raw materials are not available for sale. Industry requires sophisticated capital equipment, which it initially cannot produce domestically and which cannot be purchased abroad if agricultural surpluses are not exported to finance such imports. Agricultural producers, on the other hand, depend on industry for hand tools, agricultural machinery, and manufactured consumer goods. If these goods are not forthcoming, the peasants will retaliate by not supplying agricultural products for industry.

Bukharin recognized the need for capital accumulation but argued that it should be kept within manageable proportions. The overextension of one sector or subsector of the economy at the expense of other sectors would create critical bottlenecks—steel shortages, deficits of vital agricultural raw materials, insufficient foreign exchange earnings—that would inevitably retard overall economic development. According to Bukharin, any formula calling for maximum investment in heavy industry without a corresponding expansion of light industry would not only aggravate the goods famine, owing to the channeling of investment resources into time-consuming capital goods industries, but would also threaten to undermine the NEP recovery.

Because he emphasized economic interrelationships, Bukharin's program called for the gradual expansion of all sectors simultaneously. The critical link between agriculture and industry would be maintained by creating a favorable atmosphere for peasant agriculture. Instead of setting low agricultural delivery prices and high industrial prices, the state should do the opposite: first, to provide an incentive for the peasant to produce and market a larger output, and second, to pressure state enterprises to lower costs. It would not be necessary to force saving from agriculture as Preobrazhensky proposed; instead, only a stable economic environment free of the uncertainties of War Communism and NEP would be needed. In such a situation, the peasants would return to their traditional frugality, creating the savings to finance further expansion of capacity. Bukharin's advice to the peasant was to "get rich," a slogan from which Stalin carefully disassociated himself.[25]

To resolve the incongruence between limited industrial capacity and his call for moderate capital investment to be spread evenly among economic sectors, Bukharin proposed a series of measures to economize and utilize the available capital more fully. Small-scale manufacturing and handicrafts were to undergo a technological "rationalization" and be transformed into supposedly more efficient producers' cooperatives. Large-scale investment projects were to be made more efficient by better planning and more efficient construction work. Maximum attention was to be accorded to the speedy completion of investment projects. The available capital equipment was to be used more exhaustively by employing multiple shifts. Attention was to be given to appropriate factor proportions; that is, capital was not to be invested in areas where labor could do the job as efficiently. The state pricing policy should stimulate cost economies and more efficient use of available resources by eliminating monopoly profits.[26] Nevertheless, Bukharin was forced to admit that balanced growth meant steady but slow progress toward socialism. His own expression was "progress at a snail's pace," a phrase that was used against him in his struggles against the left wing and then later with Stalin.[27]

Although Trostsky had criticized the foreign trade strategy of the right wing as too autarkic, the trade policies advocated by Bukharin and his associates recognized the Soviet Union's initial dependence on the advanced capitalist power.[28] Bukharin argued that during the early stages of industrialization, the USSR must import large quantities of industrial equipment from abroad and pay for those commodities with agricultural exports. Yet the long-term goal must be independence from the capitalist world and the "building of socialism in one country." Thus, the Soviet Union's dependence on foreign imports should be of limited duration, lasting only until domestic industry would be capable of producing the necessary capital equipment at home.

In sum, Bukharin favored the balanced expansion of both industry and agriculture under a general policy of moderate capital accumulation financed by the voluntary saving of the peasantry. This balanced growth was to be fostered by an environment that would encourage the peasantry to produce and sell their surplus to the city. State pricing policy would be used to gain the favor of the peasants by setting low industrial and high agricultural prices. By fostering methods to increase the efficiency of capital utilization, a return to the goods famine of the 1920s could be avoided without resorting to the massive industrialization drive favored by the superindustrialists of the left wing. The foreign sector would play an important role in that it would provide the foreign machinery to sustain the growing capacity of industry.

STALIN'S CONSOLIDATION OF POWER

In a series of adroit political maneuvers, Stalin consolidated his power within four years after Lenin's death in 1924. First, he allied himself with the right wing of the party (Bukharin, Rykov, and Tomsky) to purge the leftist opposition led by Trotsky from positions of power—a phase completed in late 1927. Then, Stalin turned his attention to the "right deviationist" Bukharinites, who were denounced by the Central Committee of the Communist Party in November of 1928. This occurred just one month after Stalin's adoption of the more ambitious alternative draft of the first Five Year Plan, which supported the original left-wing industrialization program.[29]

The variant of the first Five Year Plan adopted in 1928 and formally approved in April 1929 staggered the imagination of even the superindustrialists. The low capacity of the Soviet industrial sector was to be subjected to an all-out attack: the Soviet fixed capital stock was to double within five years to provide the industrial base for building socialism. The first Five Year Plan also called for a 70 percent expansion of light industry, which was quite unrealistic in view of the limited industrial capacity in 1928.[30]

Stalin's changeover from his alliance with the Bukharinites and their pro-NEP policies to an acceptance of the program of the already purged left wing should be described.[31] During the Industrialization Debate, Stalin was clearly aligned with the Bukharin position. Stalin emphasized the achievements of NEP and ridiculed the left's superindustrialization proposals and demand that "tribute" (primitive socialist accumulation) be paid by the peasants. Although Stalin underscored the advantage of large-scale farming, he made it clear that any movement in the direction of collective farming would be gradual and voluntary. Throughout the Industrialization Debate, Stalin refrained from making independent contributions that could later be attributed to him alone, and even the doctrine that socialism could be built in one country that is generally credited to Stalin was in reality Bukharin's contribution.

The foreign policy setbacks and the grain collection problem of 1927 emboldened Trotsky and the left opposition to challenge the ruling coalition. Stalin, allied with the moderates, was able to repulse the attack, but he came to believe that the left had correctly foreseen the crises encountered in 1927, in particular the problem of state grain collections from a reluctant peasantry. To increase grain collections, Stalin came to rely more and more on coercion and emergency measures, personally directing state grain collections in Siberia. The coalition with Bukharin was kept intact by carefully timed concessions to the right wing concerning the lifting of force in the countryside. Stalin came away from his experiences in 1927 with the conviction that force was the answer to the agrarian problem, for primitive socialist accumulation without the power to force peasant deliveries would not work. From this point on, Stalin ceased to serve as defender of the NEP system and began instead to criticize lagging NEP performance and to call for a superindustrialization drive. Moreover, he began to reiterate Trotsky's call for tribute from the peasants and to warn of *kulak* sabotage of grain collections. Encouraged by Stalin's move to the left, former Trotskyites such as Preobrazhensky returned to the party fold, only to perish later in the purges.

The first Five Year Plan was adopted in October 1928, amidst a new grain collection crisis that was to have a crucial impact on subsequent events. According to Stalin, the success of the industrialization program was clearly jeopardized, for it was dependent on an increasing supply of food products and agricultural raw materials from the countryside. As long as the peasants refused to turn over such deliveries to the city, they held the power to halt the entire industrialization program.[32] The peasants' reluctance to sell their output to the state was understandable in light of the low purchase prices paid by the state and the increasing use of coercion to collect grain.

Stalin's answer to the crisis he perceived was to mount a counteroffensive designed to break once and for all the peasants' hold over the pace of industrialization. In the autumn of 1929, he ordered the wholesale collectivization of agriculture. Peasant landholdings and livestock were forcibly amalgamated into collective farms, which were obligated to deliver to the state planned quotas of farm products at terms dictated by the state.

The ensuing turmoil was great not only in the countryside, which burst into open rebellion, but also in Soviet cities, which received a vast influx of workers from the countryside and saw a significant redistribution of labor among industrial branches as enterprises attempted to fulfill their taut production targets.

THE OUTCOME OF THE SOVIET INDUSTRIALIZATION DEBATE

The actual Soviet industrialization pattern that emerged after 1928 (A, B, and C, Table 4.1) bears a close resemblance to Preobrazhensky's industrialization program: Soviet economic growth between 1928 and 1940 was heavily biased in favor of industry in general and of heavy industry in particular. Industrial production grew at an annual rate of 11 percent, whereas agricultural production grew at an annual rate of only one percent between 1928 and 1937 (C 3 and 4). The negative rate of growth of livestock graphically indicates the impact of collectivization upon agricultural performance. The same trends are apparent in the differential rates of growth of the agricultural and nonagricultural labor forces between 1928 and 1937 (C 2): the former declined, while the latter expanded rapidly at an annual rate of almost 9 percent.

The structural transformations resulting from these differential sector growth rates are impressive (B). Agriculture's shares of net national product and labor force declined from 49 percent and 71 percent, respectively, in 1928 to 29 and 51 percent, respectively, in 1940, whereas the increase in industry's product and labor force shares was from 28 and 18 percent, respectively, to 45 and 29 percent, respectively, during the same period.

The most remarkable feature of the 1930s was the extent to which the pro-heavy-industry bias asserted itself (as Preobrazhensky said it should). Between 1928 and 1937, heavy manufacturing's net product share of total manufacturing more than doubled, from 31 percent to 63 percent, whereas light manufacturing's product share fell from 68 percent to 36 percent.

The impact of this production program on real consumption levels in the absence of significant foreign trade (the ratio of imports plus exports to GNP sank to one percent by 1937, E) had already been foreseen by Preobrazhensky. Between 1928 and 1937, household consumption scarcely grew (at an annual rate of 0.8 percent), and the share of consumption in GNP (in 1937 prices) declined markedly, from 80 percent to 53 percent. During the same period, gross

Table 4.1 OUTCOME OF THE SOVIET INDUSTRIALIZATION DEBATE
The Industrialization Drive of 1928–1940

	1928	1933	1937	1940
A. Changes in manufacturing				
1. Heavy manufacturing ÷ overall manufacturing				
Net product share (1928 prices)	31	51	63	—
Labor force share	28	43	—	—
2. Light manufacturing ÷ overall manufacturing				
Net product share (1928 prices)	68	47	36	—
Labor force share	71	56	—	—
B. Changes in major economic sectors, structure of output				
1. Share in net national product (1937 prices)				
Agriculture	49	—	31	29
Industry	28	—	45	45
Services	23	—	24	26
2. Share in labor force				
Agriculture	71	—	—	51
Industry	18	—	—	29
Services	12	—		20
C. Rates of growth (1928–1937)				
1. GNP (1937 prices) (%)			4.8	
2. Labor force				
Nonagriculture (%)			8.7	
Agricultural (%)			−2.5	
3. Industrial production (1937 prices) (%)			11.3	
4. Agricultural production (1958 prices) (%)			1.1	
Livestock (%)			1.2	
5. Gross Industrial capital stock (1937 prices)				
(billion rubles)	34.8	75.7	119	170
D. Changes in the structure of GNP by end use (1937 prices)				
1. Household consumption ÷ GNP	80	—	53	49
Annual growth rate (1928–1937) (%)			0.8	
2. Communal services ÷ GNP	5	—	11	10
Annual growth rate (1928–1937) (%)			15.7	
3. Government administration and defense ÷ GNP	3	—	26	21
Annual growth rate (1928–1937) (%)			15.6	
4. Gross capital investment ÷ GNP	13	—	26	19
Annual growth rate (1928–1937) (%)			14.4	
E. Foreign trade proportions				
1. Export + imports ÷ GNP (%)	6[a]	4	1	—
F. Shares of the socialist sector in				
1. Capital stock (%)	65.7	—	99.6	—
2. Gross production of industry (%)	82.4	—	99.8	—
3. Gross production of agriculture (%)	3.3	—	98.5	—
4. Value of trade turnover (%)	76.4	—	100.0	—
G. Prices				
1. Consumer goods prices				
(state and cooperative stores, 1928 = 100)	100	400	700	1000
2. Average realized prices of farm products (1928 = 100)	100	—	539	—

Sources: A: P. R. Gregory, *Socialist and Nonsocialist Industrialization Patterns* (New York: Praeger, 1970), pp. 28–29, 36. Heavy manufacturing is defined according to the International System of Industrial Classification as ISIC 30–38. Light manufacturing is defined as ISIC 20–29. B: S. Kuznets, "A Comparative appraisal," in A. Bergson and S. Kuznets, eds., *Economic Trends in the Soviet Union* (Cambridge, Mass.: Harvard University Press, 1963), pp. 342–360. C. Bergson and Kuznets, *Economic Trends*, pp. 36, 77, 187, 190, 209. D: A. Bergson, *Real Soviet National Income and Product Since 1928* (Cambridge, Mass.: Harvard University Press, 1961), pp. 217, 237. E: Bergson and Kuznets, *Economic Trends*, pp. 288–290. F: *Narodnoe khoziaistvo SSSR v 1958 g.* [The national economy of the USSR in 1958], p. 57. G: F. D. Holzman, Inflationary Pressures, 1928–1957: Causes and Cures," *Quarterly Journal of Economics*, vol. 74, no. 2 (May 1960), 168–169.

[a]1929.

capital investment grew at an annual rate of 14 percent, and the ratio of gross investment to GNP doubled, from 13 percent to 26 percent. If we define total consumption expenditures to include both private consumption and communal services, and nonconsumption expenditures to include investment, government administration, and defense, then total consumption fell between 1928 and 1937 from 85 percent of GNP to 64 percent of GNP (D).

The changing institutional setting within which these transformations were occurring should also be noted (Table 4.1, F): between 1928 and 1937, the socialist sector share of total capital stock, industry, agriculture, and trade expanded sharply, so that by 1937 the socialist sector totally dominated all economic activity.

Part G in Table 4.1 has special relevance to the outcome of the industrialization debate. Consumer prices rose by 700 percent between 1928 and 1937 and probably would have risen even faster without the extensive rationing of the period. Average realized prices of farm products, which are weighted averages of the extremely low state procurement prices, the above-quota state delivery prices, and collective farm market prices, on the other hand, rose by 539 percent, which indicates a reopening of the price scissors against agriculture between 1928 and 1937. An examination of some partial data (Figure 4.1) suggests that, in fact, the scissors did reopen and were not closed again until the mid-1950s, with a resultant squeeze on the agricultural sector in terms of low procurement prices.

In sum, the left opposition program was the model for the Soviet industrialization drive. The pro-industry and pro-heavy-industry bias of the first two Five Year Plans is clearly shown in Table 4.1 and was implemented at the expense of the agricultural sector and the consumer. The expected deterioration in the agricultural terms of trade occurred, but it did not halt the industrialization drive, possibly owing to the forced collectivization of agriculture.

THE INDUSTRIALIZATION DEBATE AND CURRENT SOVIET IDEOLOGY

The Soviet industrialization debate was really about two interrelated issues: sectorial priorities, and the economic system. The party's right wing offered one view of the future; the left wing offered an alternate view. Stalin followed the program of the left wing—only in a form more extreme than that envisioned by its designers—and instituted the Stalinist economic model, now called the administrative-command system by the new Soviet leadership. The sacrifices that the Stalinist model extracted from the Soviet population were immense. In strictly technical economic terms, living standards stagnated at a time when real economic growth was rapid. Although both industrial workers and peasants shared in the burden, it is probably true that peasants suffered disproportionately through the system of unequal exchange. Although there have been endless debates over magnitude, the loss of life associated with the catastrophes of Stalinism—forced collectivization, famine, purges—was in the millions.

The official rehabilitations of some of the major figures in the industrialization debate, such as Bukharin, Tomsky, and Rykov, have refocused attention on the alternatives put forward by the losing side. This attention has forced the Soviet leadership to deal with the thorny question of whether Stalin was really necessary. Would the right-wing program of balanced growth, continuation of NEP, and a more gradual transformation of property relations have resulted in a more prosperous and stable Soviet Union in the late 1980s?

The new Soviet leadership is apparently not willing to dismiss the accomplishments of the Stalinist model out of hand. They note the incredibly rapid

Figure 4.1 State wholesale prices for objects of mass consumption and purchase price of wheat (USSR 1929 = 100). (These figures are not directly comparable to those in Figure 3.1, which relate an index of agricultural prices to an index of all prices, because of the vast change in agricultural prices after 1929, when procurement prices began to diverge significantly from the retail prices of agricultural commodities, and because this figure refers only to wheat prices, not to a more general farm price index.) *Source:* A. N. Malafeev, *Istoriia tsenoobrazovaniia v SSSR* [The history of price formation in the USSR] (Moscow: 1964), p. 286.

transformation of the Soviet industrial structure and of property relations. They also speak more openly about the immense costs of Stalinism and strictly differentiate Stalinism from socialism.[33]

The official Soviet reevaluation of the industrialization debate appears to credit Bukharin with a better sense of the appropriate pace of the transformation of the Soviet system. There appears to be support for Bukharin's argument for a balance between state-planned heavy industry and light industry and agriculture directed by market forces. Bukharin's apparent emphasis on allowing the natural cooperative tendencies of the peasantry to develop without being forced by "extraordinary measures" has also found a sympathetic response among the contemporary Soviet leadership, as has Bukharin's point that resource allocation cannot be permanently based on commands, administrative interference, and extraordinary measures.

On the other hand, current Soviet ideology is not prepared to say that collectivization was a mistake. It is prepared to admit that collectivization was carried out prematurely and that Stalin's extraordinary measures were costly, extreme, and antidemocratic. Current Soviet ideology holds to the belief that private peasant agriculture was incompatible in the long run with rapid industrialization and that the emergencies perceived by Stalin and his associates were real, not imagined. In this sense, Bukharin's faith in peasant agriculture is viewed as misguided, even though Bukharin's long-run solution called for socialization of property rights in agriculture.

REFERENCES

1. Our discussion of the Soviet Industrialization Debate is drawn primarily from the following sources: A. Erlich, *The Soviet Industrialization Debate, 1924–1928* (Cambridge, Mass.: Harvard University Press, 1960); N. Spulber, *Soviet Strategy for Economic Growth* (Bloomington: Indiana University Press, 1964); N. Spulber, ed., *Foundations of Soviet Strategy for Economic Growth* (Bloomington: Indiana University Press, 1964); A. Erlich, "Stalin's Views on Economic Development" in E. Simmons, ed., *Continuity and Change in Russian and Soviet Thought* (Cambridge, Mass.: Harvard University Press, 1955), pp. 81–99; M. Lewin, *Russian Peasants and Soviet Power* (London: Allen & Unwin, 1968), chaps. 6–9; S. F. Cohen, *Bukharin and the Bolshevik Revolution* (New York: Knopf, 1973); M. Reiman, *Die Geburt des Stalinismus* [The birth of Stalinism] (Frankfurt/Main: EVA, 1979); A. Nove, "A Note on Trotsky and the 'Left Opposition,' 1929–31," *Soviet Studies*, vol. 29, no. 4 (October 1977), 576–589; J. R. Millar, "A Note on Primitive Accumulation in Marx and Preobrazhensky," *Soviet Studies*, vol. 30, no. 3 (July 1978), 384–393; and R. Day, "Preobrazhensky and the Theory of the Transition Period," *Soviet Studies*, vol. 27, no. 2 (April 1975), 196–219.

2. P. Gregory, *Russian National Income, 1885–1913* (Cambridge: Cambridge University Press, 1982), pp. 185–186.

3. The growth models developed during this period by V. A. Bazarov and V. G. Groman predicted a declining growth rate as the Soviet economy approached its prewar equilibrium. For a discussion of these models, see L. Smolinski, "The

Origins of Soviet Mathematical Economics," in H. Raupach et al., eds., *Yearbook of East-European Economics*, Band 2 (Munich: Gunter Olzog Verlag, 1971), p. 144.

4. For discussions of the political setting, see Cohen, *Bukharin and the Bolshevik Revolution*, chaps. 7–9; Reiman, *Die Geburt des Stalinismus*, chaps. 1–6; and Lewin, *Russian Peasants and Soviet Power*, chaps. 6–12.

5. This discussion is based on P. M. Sweezy, *The Theory of Capitalist Development* (New York: Modern Reader Paperbacks, 1968), chaps. 5 and 10; Day, "Preobrazhensky and the Theory of the Transition Period," pp. 196–199; and F. Engels, *Anti-Dühring* (Moscow: Progress Publishers, 1975).

6. S. Malle, *The Economic Organization of War Communism 1918–1921* (Cambridge: Cambridge University Press, 1985), chap. 6; and K. Marx, *Critique of the Gotha Program* (Moscow: Progress Publishers, 1971), pp. 9–21.

7. Sweezy, *The Theory of Capitalist Development*, pp. 75–95, 162–169.

8. This discussion of primitive capitalist accumulation is based primarily upon Millar, "A Note on Primitive Accumulation," pp. 384–392.

9. For a discussion of Lenin's revision of Marx in light of the Russian experience, see P. R. Gregory and R. C. Stuart, *Comparative Economic Systems*, 3rd ed. (Boston: Houghton Mifflin, 1989), chap. 4.

10. In addition to the references already cited in this chapter, see H. Ray Buchanan, "Lenin and Bukharin on the Transition from Capitalism of Socialism: The Meshchersky Controversy, 1918," *Soviet Studies*, vol. 28, no. 1 (January 1976), 66–82. For a Soviet author's modern study of industrial concentration in Russia prior to the revolution, see V. I. Bovykin, *Formirovanie finansovo kapitala v Rossii* [Formation of financial capital in Russia] (Moscow: Nauka, 1984).

11. For a detailed discussion of this controversy, see R. Day, *Leon Trotsky and the Politics of Economic Isolation* (Cambridge: Cambridge University Press, 1973).

12. Preobrazhensky's views are outlined in his famous work, *Novaia ekonomika* [The new economics], which is available in English translation. See E. A. Preobrazhensky, *The New Economics*, translated by B. Pierce, (Oxford: Oxford University Press, 1964).

13. Erlich, *The Soviet Industrialization Debate*, p. 35.

14. Ibid., p. 35.

15. Quoted in Erlich, *The Soviet Industrialization Debate*, pp. 56–57.

16. Lewin, *Russian Peasants and Soviet Power*, pp. 146–152; and Millar, "A Note on Primitive Accumulation," pp. 387–393.

17. Stalin's solution to this dilemma—collectivization of the peasantry, which eliminated the peasant's freedom to dispose of surpluses—did not occur to Preobrazhensky. Several years after the collectivization decision, Preobrazhensky declared in a speech: "Collectivization—this is the crux of the matter! Did I have this prognosis of the collectivization? I did not." Quoted in Erlich, *The Soviet Industrialization Debate*, p. 177. Erlich adds to this: "He [Preobrazhensky] was careful not to add that neither did Stalin at the time when the industrialization debate was in full swing. And he was wise not to point out that the decision to collectivize hinged not on superior intellectual perspicacity but on the incomparably higher degree of resolve to crush the opponent..."

18. L. Shanin, "Questions of the Economic Course," in N. Spulber, ed., *Foundations of Soviet Strategy for Economic Growth* (Bloomington: Indiana University Press, 1964), p. 219.

19. Ibid.
20. Erlich, *The Soviet Industrialization Debate,* pp. 140–141.
21. Ibid., p. 132.
22. Cohen, *Bukharin and the Bolshevik Revolution.*
23. Lewin, *Russian Peasants and Soviet Power,* pp. 132–142.
24. Erlich, *The Soviet Industrialization Debate,* pp. 82–83.
25. Ibid., pp. 86–87.
26. Ibid., pp. 84–86.
27. Lewin, *Russian Peasants and Soviet Power,* p. 139.
28. Day, *Leon Trotsky and the Politics of Economic Isolation,* chap. 7.
29. Ibid., chap. 9. It was not until the Stalin purges in the late 1930s that this political process was complete. Preobrazhensky, Shanin, and Bukharin all lost their lives in the purges.
30. Ibid., p. 166.
31. Accounts of Stalin's move to the left are found in Erlich, "Stalin's Views on Economic Development," pp. 81–99; Reiman, *Die Geburt des Stalinismus,* chaps. 5–8; and Lewin, *Russian Peasants and Soviet Power,* chaps. 9–17.
32. According to Jerzy Karcz, there was no real agricultural crisis during this period. The grain collection "crisis" was precipitated by the lowering of state grain procurement prices in 1926–1927, while procurement prices for animal products were raised. Peasants shifted their attention to animal products, fed grain to livestock, and held grain in stock, waiting for grain prices to be increased. Total agricultural sales did not fall during this period. Thus the "crisis" was caused not by the weakness of peasant agriculture but by the ineptitude of state pricing policy. In addition, Karcz raises the question of deliberate falsification of grain statistics by Stalin to gain support for collectivization. J. F. Karcz, "Thoughts on the Grain Problem," *Soviet Studies,* vol. 18, no. 4 (April 1967), 399–434. For a different view, see R. W. Davies, "A Note on Grain Statistics," *Soviet Studies,* vol. 21, no. 3 (January 1970), 314–329. This controversy will be discussed in detail in Chapter 5.
33. G. L. Smirnov, ed., "Vremiia trudnykh voprosov, Istoriia 20–30–x godovi sovremennaia obshchestvennaia mysl" *Pravda,* [Time of difficult question, history of the 20s and 30s and contemporary social thought], September 30, 1988; October 3, 1988.

SELECTED BIBLIOGRAPHY

N. Bukharin, *The Politics and Economics of the Transition Period,* Kenneth Tarbuck, ed., (London: Routledge & Kegan Paul, 1979).

S. F. Cohen, *Bukharin and the Bolshevik Revolution* (New York: Knopf, 1973).

R. Day, *Leon Trotsky and the Politics of Economic Isolation* (Cambridge: Cambridge University Press, 1973).

M. Dobb, *Soviet Economic Development Since 1917,* 5th ed. (London: Routledge & Kegan Paul, 1960), chap. 8.

F. Engels, *Anti -Dühring* (Moscow: Progress Publishers, 1975).

A. Erlich, "Stalin's Views on Soviet Economic Development," in Ernest Simmons, ed., *Continuity and Change in Russian and Soviet Thought* (Cambridge, Mass.: Harvard University Press, 1955), pp. 81–99.

————, *The Soviet Industrialization Debate, 1924–1928* (Cambridge, Mass.: Harvard University Press, 1960).

N. Jasny, *Soviet Economists of the Twenties: Names to Be Remembered* (Cambridge: Cambridge University Press, 1972).

V. I. Lenin, *Imperialism, the Highest Stage of Capitalism* (Moscow: Progress Publishers, 1970).

M. Lewin, *Russian Peasants and Soviet Power* (London: Allen & Unwin, 1968), chaps. 6–9.

K. Marx, *Critique of the Gotha Program* (Moscow: Progress Publishers, 1971).

J. R. Millar, "A Note on Primitive Accumulation in Marx and Preobrazhensky," *Soviet Studies*, vol. 30, no. 3 (July 1978), 384–393.

A. Nove, "A Note on Trotsky and the 'Left Opposition,' 1929–31," *Soviet Studies*, vol. 29, no. 4 (October 1977), 576–589.

————, *An Economic History of the USSR* (London: Penguin, 1969), chap. 5.

M. Reiman, *Die Geburt des Stalinismus* [The birth of Stalinism] (Frankfurt/Main: EVA, 1979), chaps. 3–9.

N. Spulber, ed., *Foundations of Soviet Strategy for Economic Growth* (Bloomington: Indiana University Press, 1964).

————, *Soviet Strategy for Economic Growth* (Bloomington: Indiana University Press, 1964), chaps. 1–4.

P. M. Sweezy, *The Theory of Capitalist Development* (New York: Modern Reader Paperbacks, 1968).

R. C. Tucker, ed., *The Lenin Anthology* (New York: Norton, 1975).

Chapter 5

The Foundation of Planning, Collectivization, and War (1928–1945)

*W*e have already described the precedents of the 1920s and the impact of the Soviet Industrialization Debate on the course of Soviet industrialization during the 1930s. Our attention now turns to the creation of the Soviet command economic system during the early plan era, specifically to the development of a coordinated central planning apparatus and to the introduction of forced collectivization into the countryside. World War II provided a stern test of the command economy put in place in the 1930s. The war imposed enormous costs on the Soviet Union and also caused some changes in the resource allocation system.

The 1920s witnessed two significant struggles over the nature of economic planning in the Soviet Union. The first was the debate over the theory of planning in a socialist economy—the debate between the so-called *genetic* and *teleological* schools of planning. The second was the struggle among the various planning bodies in existence during the 1920s for ascendancy in the planning hierarchy—a battle eventually won by *Gosplan* (the State Planning Committee). Let us first turn to the planning debate.

THE PLANNING DEBATE: THE GENETICISTS VERSUS THE TELEOLOGISTS[1]

During NEP, an important controversy arose concerning the conception of economic planning in the Soviet Union. The debate focused on the issue of whether planning was to be directed (and limited) by market forces or molded by the will of planners, unconstrained by market forces and limited only by the physical constraints of the economy. The first approach was advocated by the *geneticists*, the most notable being N. D. Kondratiev (the prominent Russian authority on business cycles), V. A. Bazarov, and V. G. Groman, the latter two being *Gosplan* economists. The geneticists argued that economic planning should be directed by consumer demand, which would dictate to planners the needed direction of the economy.

The principal function of the planner would be to forecast and project market trends to aid central and local administrators in their decision making; the geneticists envisioned a form of *indicative* planning, as it is called today. In drawing up such plans, authorities should always make sure of their internal consistency, for the geneticists viewed the economy as a vast complex of interrelated sectors (a general equilibrium system), the balance of which would be disturbed if planners neglected sectorial interrelationships. For example, to expand the heavy-industry sector without concern for the resulting impact on the equilibrium of other interrelated sectors would create disproportions that would impede overall development. Thus, the geneticists advocated a form of planning that was largely consistent with the precepts of NEP, in view of the dominant role that market forces would be allowed to play in the planning process. The advocates of genetic planning, therefore, were supportive of NEP and were associated with the party's right wing.

The *teleological* approach to planning, as advocated by S. Strumilin, G. L. Pyatakov, V. V. Kuibyshev, and P. A. Fel'dman, stated that the economic plan should be consciously formulated by social engineers and shaped by national goals established by the state. Such planning should seek to *overcome* market forces rather than be directed by them as the geneticists argued. The market and finance, according to the teleologists, should *follow* the plan rather than dictate the plan. Planning should begin only after national economic goals have been set by the political authorities. Then, the planners should form economic strategy, largely in terms of binding targets for basic industries, limited only by the availability of investment, and such investment should be allocated to meet the needs of industry independently of market forces.

In drawing up output and investment plans, the teleologists argued that planners need not be constrained by the need to preserve the general equilibrium of the economy, for to do so would be to subject the growth of the economy to the spontaneous forces of the market. Instead, the concept of equilibrium should be denounced as an unnecessarily severe constraint on the flexibility of planners. As stated by one teleologist, to accept the direction of the market meant acceptance of the "genetic inheritance" of 300 years of tsarism.[2]

According to the teleologists, the actual process of plan construction should proceed according to a system of "successive approximations." First, plans for the leading branches (namely, heavy industry) were to be drawn up; then, the plans for other sectors (light industry, agriculture, trade, etc.) would be molded into the framework of the first set of plans. In this manner, the plans of lower priority sectors would be predetermined by the plan for heavy industry, not by the market.

The late 1920s witnessed the conclusive victory of the teleological viewpoint. As the NEP system was gradually abandoned, the advocates of the genetic approach, tied as it was to a market-directed system of planning, saw their support within the party deteriorate. From the summer of 1927, actual planning paid little attention to market equilibrium and financial stability as advocated by the geneticists. Instead, attention turned to physical planning involving a "ferocious straining of effort," the outcome of which would be "decided by struggle."[3] The teleological approach to planning is obviously consistent with the superindustrialization notions of the left adopted by Stalin in 1928. Eventually, the geneticists came to be accused of counterrevolution and rightwing Menshevism. The advocates of the teleological approach, namely, Strumilin, Krzhizhanovsky, and others, remained prominent in the *Gosplan* apparatus during the 1930s and played a guiding role in the planning for rapid industrialization.

THE EVOLUTION OF THE PLANNING STRUCTURE[4]

A variety of agencies dealt with planning problems throughout the 1920s—VSNKh (the Supreme Council of the National Economy), the People's Commissariat of Finance, the People's Commissariat of Transportation, *Gosplan* USSR (State Planning Committee of the USSR), the regional *Gosplans*, the *Sovnarkhozy*, local authorities, and many others. However, of these agencies, only *Gosplan* was explicitly and exclusively concerned with economic planning. *Gosplan's* duties (according to a 1922 decree) were "the preparation not only of a long-range plan but also of an operational plan for the current year."[5]

From modest beginnings in February 1921 (in 1925, *Gosplan* employed only around 50 economists and statisticians[6]), *Gosplan* gradually came to be accepted by the late 1920s as the planning agency in charge of coordinating economic planning for the entire economy. Much of this recognition emerged as a consequence of *Gosplan's* work on the annual *control figures,* or tentative output targets, for the various branches of the economy. The first control figures were prepared covering the year 1925–1926, and while they did not initially prove important in directing economic activity, the figures were used to establish the principle that economic policy should be guided on an annual basis by control figures prepared by *Gosplan.* In this manner, *Gosplan* came to play a supervisory role in the preparation of plans by other administrative bodies. The early control figures had a definite geneticist flavor, as they were designed to forecast rather than manipulate. The growing importance of *Gosplan's* control figures is clear: by 1926, the control figures were the first order of business of the Central Committee meeting of the party. In 1927, the party gave full compulsory status to the 1927–1928 control figures, which had taken on a strong teleological character.

While *Gosplan's* role as the coordinator of all planning was developing, it had little to do with the actual operational planning of the economy, especially at the enterprise and trust levels. Such work was primarily performed by the central planning staff of VSNKh and by the *Glavki* planning offices of VSNKh. In this manner, annual plans, including production and financial targets known as *promfinplans,* were drawn up. The major problem with the *promfinplans* was that they tended to be compiled on a sector-by-sector basis, with little attention given to the overall result when these plans were combined. *Gosplan,* which was charged with overall planning, complained that it received the *promfinplans* too late to coordinate them with the overall control figures. All *Gosplan* could do was to accept the *promfinplans* as an accomplished fact. Gradually, the *promfinplans* drawn up by VSNKh were merged into the control figures compiled by *Gosplan.* Beginning in 1925, VSNKh was instructed to prepare its *promfinplans* on the basis of *Gosplan's* 1925–1926 control figures. By 1926–1927, VSNKh was in the habit of compiling a comprehensive *promfinplan* for all industry, to be scrutinized by *Gosplan* and the People's Commissarist of Finance, and it was established that the *promfinplan* was clearly dependent on the control figures.

During this period, the machinery for physical planning—the system of *material balances*—was also being developed. As certain basic industrial commodities came to be in short supply and the administrative allocation of commodities increased, planning bodies began compiling balances for critical industrial materials. In 1925, a balance for iron and steel was compiled; and in 1927, an energy balance of fuel and power consumption was drawn up. The balance system was extended to building materials in 1928.[7] In charge of coordinating these balances through the *promfinplan* and control figure system were VSNKh and *Gosplan,* but initially this coordination proved too complex in the absence of detailed statistical information, and most of these early material balances were poorly prepared.

The plan period began with the adoption of the first Five Year Plan in 1928, with the following planning principles established: First, *Gosplan* was to be the central coordinating planning body to which all other planning bodies were to submit their proposals. Second, the annual control figures prepared by *Gosplan* were to provide the general direction for the economy on an annual basis. Third, the actual detailed operational plans for industries and for enterprises (the *promfinplans*) were to conform to the control figures prepared by *Gosplan*. Fourth, materials were to be allocated through a system of balances, compiled from the control figures and *promfinplans*, which would elaborate the supplies and uses of basic industrial materials.

Gosplan's elevation to full planning authority came in 1932 with the development of the ministerial system. Between 1928 and 1932, the functions of VSNKh had grown increasingly complex and confused; and in 1932, VSNKh was, in effect, dissolved as a central coordinating agency for industry. Its chief departments, the *Glavki*, which later became ministries, were allowed to take direct power over planning and administering their enterprises. Earlier, VSNKh had served to coordinate the activities of the industrial departments—a role that *Gosplan* now inherited. VSNKh itself became three separate ministries (Commissariats): heavy industry, light industry, and wood-working.

The ministries became the operational links between *Gosplan* and the actual production units. The ministries became co-planners with *Gosplan*, and the operational plans drawn up by *Gosplan* were in fact ministry plans. Input plans were also compiled on a ministerial basis with general allotments of materials apportioned to the ministries. The ministries then made the actual distributions of industrial materials to the enterprises they directed.

During the late 1920s and early 1930s, party control over economic affairs was solidified. Major economic powers resided in the Politburo under Stalin. Direct central committee control was applied to major construction and industrial projects. Stalin immersed himself in overseeing even minor economic details. The party cadres department handled the task of providing nominations for important positions in the economy. The party served, at all levels, as a general troubleshooter to deal with bottlenecks. Local party officials were charged with mobilizing the masses to plan fulfillment.

Soviet authorities recognized the need for long-range planning to serve as a guide for annual plans.[8] After some experimentation with long-range sectorial plans (for metals, industrial branches, transportation, and agriculture), *Gosplan* assumed responsibility in 1925 for drawing up Five Year Plans for the national economy. The five-year period was chosen because major construction projects in industry, transportation, and construction were felt to have a five-year gestation period and because annual fluctuations in agriculture could be smoothed out over this time interval. After some experimental efforts at five-year planning, *Gosplan* initiated the practice of developing the long-range plan in two variants: a minimum variant based on cautious assumptions, and a bold maximum variant.

The maximal variant of the plan for 1928–1933 (the first Five Year Plan) was formally adopted by the party in April 1929 and reflected the teleological thinking of Stalin. It was a 2000-page document, authored by the leading proponents of the teleological approach, G. M. Krzhizhanovsky and S. Strumlin, and it called for the industrialization of the country at a maximum pace, as was discussed in Chapter 4.

The breaking down of Five Year Plans into annual operational segments and the enforcement of economic plans were resolved during the early Five Year Plan era. One lesson learned early was that Five Year Plans cannot be written in stone, for circumstances change over a five-year period. Five Year plans were never neatly divided into five annual plans. Instead, the Five Year Plan had to be constantly revised, so that the end result often bore little resemblance to the original targets. As Eugene Zaleski describes it, the Five Year Plan represented "a vision of growth, itself at the service of development strategy."[9] As the objectives of the long-range and annual plans were not necessarily compatible, it was decided that the state agencies controlling material supplies and credits were the ones to determine what parts of the "vision" were to be realized. For example, the first Five Year Plan (maximum variant) called for a quadrupling of investment in state industry, an 85 percent increase in consumption expenditures, a 70 percent increase in real wages, and a 30 percent increase in peasant incomes. These targets represented the planners' vision, but it was the responsibility of the economic administrators in charge of material allocations to ensure that priority targets (industrial investment) were fulfilled.

This period also witnessed the evolution of a centralized administration for the setting of prices. Extensive centralized price setting and regulation , introduced during the early plan era, proved to be a complex task involving issues well beyond the setting of prices per se and requiring the expansion of administrative arrangements.[10] Although the setting of prices was largely decentralized during the NEP period (typically reflecting cost-price relationships of the pre-Soviet period), the Commission for Internal Trade and VSNKh gained increasing authority toward the end of NEP. This tendency toward the centralization of price formation and related functions was greatly enhanced after the introduction of comprehensive central planning in 1928. Not only were internal prices subsequently shielded from world prices through the creation of a state monopoly in foreign trade, but also a series of decrees in the late 1920s and early 1930s harnessed the price system toward the achievement of state goals. Price discrimination in state purchases (buying the same product at different prices—determined by factory costs of production—and then selling at one set price) was introduced, as were multiple pricing (charging different retail prices for the same product), profit margin controls, and differentiated sales taxes (the so-called turnover tax), the last serving as a primary mechanism for generating state revenues.

The early 1930s witnessed the significant expansion of the number of administrative organs concerned directly or indirectly with price formation, although during the 1930s there was a measure of consolidation with VSNKh and later with the ministries that became the main price-setting bodies.[11] This period also witnessed the tightening of financial controls over enterprises. Commercial credits between enterprises were forbidden, and *Gosbank* (the State Bank) and various specialized banks controlled all credit operations.

Moreover, direct grants from the state budget became a major source of investment finance.

CENTRALIZED MANAGEMENT

We have described the creation of the Soviet planning apparatus in the late 1920s and early 1930s. From this discussion, one might view the Soviet economy as being thoroughly under the control of the planning mechanism. In fact, this was not the case. It would soon become evident that the Soviet economy was more of a managed than a planned economy.[12] Let us review the evidence.

There were three major Five Year Plans between 1928 and 1942, the first for 1928 through 1933, the second for 1934 through 1937, and the third for 1938 through 1942. Although the implementation of planning in this period necessarily captures much of our attention, in fact, the planning system was rather less than a full-blown administrative and managerial system. Indeed, the plan periods themselves were less than firm; the first Five Year Plan ended early largely due to pressure for overfulfillment. The second plan was late being developed, as pressure mounted for ever-increasing levels of achievement. The third plan was disrupted by military preparations and, ultimately, the beginning of World War II.

During this period, economic policy for the development of the Soviet economy was part of the Five Year Plans. However, as Eugene Zaleski has emphasized, resources were extremely limited.[13] Planning in the 1930s reflected political and ideological aspects of change. Plans were used to motivate the population.

Cast in this perspective, the performance of the Soviet economy in the 1930s cannot be assessed simply by looking at plan targets and plan results. Multiple plan variants were prepared, and frequent changes were made as fulfillment difficulties were encountered. Plan fulfillment during the first two Five Year Plans is shown in Table 5.1. The first Five Year Plan (1928–1932) was quite ambitious. Western estimates of plan fulfillment show that the economy came closer to meeting its industrial production and producer goods targets (60–72 percent fulfillment) than its labor productivity (36–42 percent fulfillment), agricultural production (50–52 percent fulfillment), or retail trade targets (39 percent fulfillment).

The fulfillment of the second Five Year Plan was better than the first, although there were still substantial deviations between targets and fulfillment. Industrial production and producer goods targets were basically met; there was a smaller (14 percent) shortfall in labor productivity targets. Although agricultural production and retail trade targets came closer to fulfillment, shortfalls remained substantial.

The first Five Year Plan was clearly beyond the capacity of the Soviet economy. It was an unrealistic plan, but the achievements of the economy during this period were substantial. The second Five Year Plan was also ambitious, but it proved to be more realistic.

Table 5.1   SOVIET PLAN FULFILLMENT IN THE 1930s
Percent Fulfillment

Objective	First Five Year Plan (1928–1932)	Second Five Year Plan (1933–1937)
National income		
Official estimate	92	96
Western estimate	70	67
Industrial output		
Official estimate	101	103
Western estimate	60–70	76–93
Producer goods		
Official estimate	128	121
Western estimate	72	97
Consumer goods		
Official estimate	81	85
Western estimate	46	68
Agricultural production		
Official estimate	58	63–77
Western estimate	50–52	66–78
Labor productivity		
Official estimate	65	
Western estimate	36–42	86
Retail trade		
Western estimates	39	54

Sources: N. Jasny, *Essays on The Soviet Economy* (New York: Praeger, 1962), p. 266; E. Zaleski, *Stalinist Planning for Economic Growth: 1933–1952* (Chapel Hill: University of North Carolina Press, 1980), p. 503; A. Nove, *An Economic History of the USSR* (London: Penguin, 1969), p. 353.

THE DECISION TO COLLECTIVIZE

Developments in the agricultural sector during the late 1920s were as significant in the evolution of the Soviet planned economy as was the formation of the centralized planning structure. War Communism and NEP pointed to the crucial nature of the relationship between the peasant and the state. This relationship, the subject of continuing discussion in the 1920s, was abruptly formalized by the Communist Party under Stalin's leadership when the historic collectivization movement (the forcing of the collective farm, the *kolkhoz*, on the countryside) was begun in 1929.

Underpinnings of the Collectivization Decision

The focus of the Soviet Industrialization Debate of the 1920s was the strategy of industrialization; the desire to industrialize was not a matter of contention among the participants. From this discussion and the fact that the Soviet Union was in the 1920s primarily an agricultural economy, it is not surprising that alternative roles for the agricultural sector in the development process would be a point of focus for the participants.[15]

Preobrazhensky had argued that the rate of saving had to be increased as industrial investment rose. The peasant, according to Preobrazhensky, should bear the burden of this increase in the savings rate through the system of primitive socialist accumulation, whereby savings would be extracted from the countryside by setting low agricultural prices. How to ensure the critically needed peasant marketings under such a system was a question that Preobrazhensky was unable to answer. Bukharin, on the other hand, argued that any system designed to extract involuntary savings from the peasants would destroy any positive relationship between peasant and state and lead to active peasant resistance in the form of reduced peasant marketings. Instead, Bukharin argued, it would be better to adopt a slower rate of economic growth and set prices to favor the peasant. The perceived behavior of the peasants during the Scissors Crisis was thought to underscore this view, that is, the falling trend in peasant marketings as relative agricultural prices dropped.

Against this background, it should be pointed out that Lenin had long stressed the need to take advantage of economies of scale in agricultural production. Although there was experimentation with various forms of agricultural collectives in the 1920s, these were largely unsuccessful.[16] It was evident that the peasants would not join collective farms voluntarily in the short run. Although both wings to the party favored the growth of agricultural collectives, leading party officials realized that voluntary collectivization would be at best a slow and evolutionary process. The right wing of the party was not distressed by the fact that the regime would have to rely on peasant farming in the near term, for it was felt that a workable alliance (*Smychka*) with the peasant could be maintained. The left wing, on the contrary, was alarmed by the growing reliance on peasant farming, especially on the prosperous *kulak*, who was regarded as a dangerous counterrevolutionary threat.[17] Thus, in 1928, collectivization was regarded by the different party factions as a desirable long-term solution to the agrarian problem, but few could have foreseen (or would have supported) the forced collectivization drive that was to follow shortly.

Stalin used as a major justification for instigating collectivization the *grain procurement crisis* of 1928.[18] According to the best evidence available (see Table 5.2), the output of key agricultural products, for example, grain, was significantly below the 1913 levels in the early 1920s.[19] However, the indices of both gross agricultural production and livestock production were higher (though not by much) in 1928 than in 1913.

Stalin, in a now famous presentation made in May 1928, put forward data to suggest that 1926–1927 *grain* output (considered a critical indicator by the Soviet leadership) was slightly below 1913 but that the *marketed share* of grain had declined substantially.[20] According to Stalin's data, between 1913 and 1926–1927, gross output of grain declined slightly, but the marketed share declined by roughly 50 percent. In addition, while grain production and marketings by the *kulaks* fell sharply (both had declined to less than one-third of pre-

Table 5.2   SOVIET AGRICULTURAL PRODUCTION
1913–1938[a]

Year	(1) Gross agricultural production (1928 = 100)	Grain variants[b] High	Low	Cotton	Sugar beets	Potatoes	Meat	Milk	Eggs	(2) Livestock production (1928 = 100)
1913	96	92.7	79	0.5	10.8	29.9	4.0	25.1	10.2	87
1924	—	51.4	44	n.a.	3.5	35.3	3.3	26.3	n.a.	—
1925	—	72.5	62	0.6	9.1	38.4	3.7	28.2	9.6	—
1926	—	76.6	66	0.6	6.4	42.8	4.1	30.5	10.5	—
1927	—	71.7	62	0.7	10.4	42.5	4.3	30.6	10.5	—
1928	100	73.3	63	0.8	10.1	45.2	4.9	31.0	10.8	100
1929	93	71.7	62	0.9	6.3	45.1	5.8	29.8	10.1	87
1930	88	78.0	67	1.1	14.0	44.6	4.3	27.0	8.0	65
1931	84	68.0	62	1.3	12.1	40.6	3.9	23.4	6.7	57
1932	76	68.0	62	1.3	6.6	37.2	2.8	20.6	4.4	48
1933	82	74.0	68	1.3	9.0	44.0	2.3	19.2	3.5	51
1934	86	75.0	68	1.2	11.4	44.2	2.0	20.8	4.2	52
1935	99	80.0	75	1.7	16.2	53.8	2.3	21.4	5.8	74
1936	93	66.0	60	2.4	16.8	44.7	3.7	23.5	7.4	76
1937	116	100.0	95	2.6	21.9	58.8	3.0	26.1	8.2	83
1938	107	76.0	70	2.6	16.7	37.5	4.5	29.0	10.5	100

[a] All data are million tons, except eggs, which are billions, and agricultural production and livestock production, which are constant price indexes.

[b] The grain variants are based on differing views in the comparability of pre- and post collectivization series. The high variant has been adjusted, the low variant has not been adjusted.

Source: From S. G. Wheatcroft, "A Reevaluation of Soviet Agricultural Production in the 1920s and 1930s," in R. C. Stuart, ed., *The Soviet Rural Economy* (Totowa, N.J.: Rowman & Allenheld, 1984), 11. 42–3, 49. n.a. = not available.

war levels), output and marketings of the middle and poor peasants had expanded. For Stalin, this was evidence of the need to move against the *kulaks*. The talk of moving against the *kulaks* made for good window dressing, but Stalin was well aware that the bulk of grain supplies was in the hands of the middle peasants. In the turmoil that followed, it was, therefore, necessary to blur the distinction between the *kulak* and the middle peasant (the *seredniak*). In fact, in the heat of the collectivization campaign, a *kulak* became any peasant who resisted collectivization.

There are, however, two important reservations to Stalin's data. First, as Jerzy Karcz has pointed out, Stalin's grain information was ". . . completely misleading and presents an exceedingly distorted picture of the relation between 1913 and 1926–1927 grain marketings."[21] According to Karcz, these data, when appropriately reconstructed as grain balances for these years, show that, in fact, gross grain output had, by 1928, all but recovered to prewar levels and that the problem was the definition of marketings. Thus, in Stalin's data, *gross market-*

ings for 1913 were compared with *net marketings* for 1926–1927.[22] Stalin's case for collectivization as the answer to the marketing problem was based on incomparable data.

A second and related factor, according to Karcz, was the role of government policy in bringing about the grain procurement "crisis." In years immediately preceding collectivization, net grain marketings did decline precisely because the state lowered grain procurement prices in 1926–1927, naturally encouraging peasants to market their grain through other than state channels—that is, where prices were more attractive—and to hold back their grain in anticipation of higher prices. Chapter 4 noted that state grain procurement prices were below the production costs of small and middle peasants. At the same time, peasant taxes were lowered, as were the prices of manufactured goods, thus stimulating peasant demand. The lower state grain procurement prices encouraged peasants to shift into the production of meat and related products, the prices of which were generally rising. Although peasant marketings of grain were falling, the output and marketings of *other* farm products were rising in response to more favorable prices and were offsetting the declining grain marketings.

The immediate justification for collectivization may, therefore, have been based on inadequate statistical information and Stalin's will to impose adverse state policy on the peasants, in addition to ideological underpinnings and the drive for large-scale production units.[23] As S. G. Wheatcroft has shown, comparisons of output and marketings of the twenties with prewar figures are subject to wide margins of error; so the controversy over Stalin's statistics will probably never be resolved. However, from the vantage point of the state, the grain crisis was real. State grain collections from the peasants (*zagotovki*) were alarmingly low (the peasants were selling on the private market), and the government had to undergo the humiliating experience of importing grain.[24] Even Bukharin became convinced that harsher methods were necessary. At this time, Stalin unleashed an emergency campaign to increase state grain collections, dispatching trusted party officials to supervise the campaign. Grain supplies were confiscated, roadblocks were set up, and peasants holding grain were charged as speculators. Stalin suspended these emergency measures in 1928 to quiet down the alarmed Bukharinites, but he came away from the experience convinced that force and coercion could be applied successfully in the countryside once the Bukharinites were destroyed.

The Collectivization Process

While the discussion of collectivization and Stalin's arguments on its behalf were well under way in 1928, it was not until mid-1929 that central control over existing cooperatives was substantially strengthened and the system of grain procurements changed—in short, the beginning of the process of mass collectivization.[25] By the latter part of 1929, an all-out drive for collectivization had been initiated by the Communist Party, becoming in large measure an organized movement against the *kulaks* and the middle peasants. Lacking strength in the countryside (less than one percent of the farm population belonged to the party or *komsomol*), the party sent 25,000 representatives, drawn largely from the ranks of industrial workers, to oversee collectivization. The most burning issue, once the all-out collectivization decision has been made, was whether or not to admit *kulaks* to the collectives. In a speech before the November party plenum, Stalin spoke for the first time of eliminating the *kulak*.

There were significant regional differences in the speed of collectivization and also a continuing debate over the precise organizational form to be utilized. Table 5.3 shows the speed of collectivization. Between July 1, 1929, and March 1, 1930, the proportion of peasant households in collective farms increased from 4 percent to 56 percent.[26] In effect, the collective farm had supplanted the centuries-old *mir* form of village government within a year's time.

Although the fiction was maintained that collectivization was a spontaneous action on the part of the peasantry, resisted only by the "*kulak* saboteurs," there can be little doubt that collectivization was imposed on an unwilling peasantry by brutal force. Vague definitions of what constituted a *kulak* household were employed to justify the arrest and deportation of peasants resisting collectivization. Militia and the secret police (then called the GPU) were sent into the countryside to force peasants into collectives along with thousands of armed party faithful from the city. The "dekulakization" drive resulted in the flight, execution, deportation, and resettlement of millions of peasants and provided the initial manpower for a vast army of penal labor. According to one estimate, 3.5 million peasants became a part of the *gulag* penal labor force, 3.5 million were resettled, and another 3.5 million died during forced collectivization.[27] There is considerable controversy over the number of victims of collectivization, but there is little doubt that it was in the millions.

Table 5.3   EXPANSION OF THE COLLECTIVE FARM SECTOR, 1918–1938
Selected Years

Year	Collective farms (in thousands)	Households in collectives (in thousands)	Peasant households collectivized (percentage)
1918	1.6	16.4	0.1
1928	33.3	416.7	1.7
1929	57.0	1,007.7	3.9
1930	85.9	5,998.1	23.6
1931	211.1	13,033.2	52.7
1932	211.1	14,918.7	61.5
1935	245.4	17,334.9	83.2
1938	242.4	18,847.6	93.5

Source: L. Volin, *A Century of Russian Agriculture* (Cambridge, Mass.: Harvard University Press, 1970), p. 211.

Although Stalin, in a famous speech in March 1930, warned against proceeding too rapidly and blamed local party leaders for the excesses that had occurred, in fact, the pace of collectivization remained rapid, and by the mid-1930s the process was basically completed.[28] The role of the Communist Party in the countryside was formally strengthened when in 1933 political departments (*Politotdely*) were established in the machine tractor stations (MTS). The MTS had themselves been established in 1930; and, in addition to supplying machinery and equipment to the collective farms (for which payment in kind would be made to the state), they were to play a significant role in the management of collective farms.[29] Informal party control in the countryside had also been strengthened considerably by collectivization, through the party's placing of "reliable" people in the posts of collective farm chairmen.

THE IMMEDIATE IMPACT OF COLLECTIVIZATION

The most immediate result of collectivization was a decline in agricultural output. Although there were year-to-year fluctuations, the general decline is unmistakable (see Table 5.2). The index of gross agricultural production (1928 = 100) declined from a precollectivization high in 1928 to an immediate postcollectivization low of 76 in 1932.[30] In large part this can be accounted for by a sharp decline in gross production of livestock products to 48 in 1933.[31] In general, the decline in meat, dairy, and egg production was more severe than the decline in cultivated crops. Although grain output declined in the initial years of collectivization (1928 through 1932, with the exception of 1930), both gross and net marketings of grain increased between 1928–1929 and 1931–1932, due to some extent to a sharp decline in the number of cattle for which grains for fodder were now not necessary.[32] The worsening of agricultural performance during the first Five Year Plan (1928–1932) plus the losses from state reserves were major factors contributing to the famine that reached a peak in 1932–1933.

The loss of lives (especially severe in grain-producing regions) from both the collectivization process *per se* and the famine thereafter (the famine being the major factor) has been the subject of considerable discussion, but very little hard data are available by which to assess its severity. The most frequently quoted estimate of lives lost is five million, although the estimates vary from one to ten million.[33]

In addition to the loss of life and the decline in agricultural production, there was a sharp decline in agricultural capital stock, most notably caused by the mass destruction of animal herds as the peasants vented their hostility toward the collectivization process by slaughtering their livestock rather than bringing them into the collective farms. The impact of this development can be observed in Table 5.4. In addition, Naum Jasny, one of the research pioneers in

Table 5.4   NUMBERS OF LIVESTOCK IN THE SOVIET UNION, 1928–1935
In Millions of Head

Year	Cattle (total)	Cows	Pigs	Sheep	Goats	Horses
1928[a]	60.1	29.3	22.0	97.3	9.7	32.1
1929	58.2	29.2	19.4	97.4	9.7	32.6
1930	50.6	28.5	14.2	85.5	7.8	31.0
1931	42.5	24.5	11.7	62.5	5.6	27.0
1932	38.3	22.3	10.9	43.8	3.8	21.7
1933	33.5	19.4	9.9	34.0	3.3	17.3
1934	33.5	19.0	11.5	32.9	3.6	15.4
1935	38.9	19.0	17.1	36.4	4.4	14.9

[a]Borders of the Soviet Union as of 1939.

Source: E. Strauss, *Soviet Agriculture in Perspective* (London: Allen & Unwin, 1969), p. 307.

this area, has indicated that other forms of capital stock, notably buildings and machinery, simply disappeared during the turmoil of collectivization. The impact of collectivization upon per capita incomes of the farm population was predictable: they fell sharply to perhaps one-half the 1928 level.[34]

COLLECTIVIZATION AND ECONOMIC DEVELOPMENT

Official Soviet ideology admits that collectivization had substantial immediate costs. Livestock herds were decimated, there was armed resistance, output declined, and lives were lost. Collectivization, however, created an appropriate set of property relations within agriculture (it solved the problem of private peasant holdings), and it contributed to industrial transformation of the Soviet Union. The need for collective or state ownership has not been questioned; what has been questioned in recent years is whether collectivization was prematurely carried out and whether Stalin acted more for political motives than for the needs of economic development.[35]

In the course of economic development, agriculture contributes to the development process by supplying labor and capital resources to the rest of the economy. Agriculture performs four supportive functions:[36]

1. Provision of manpower for industry.
2. Expansion of output and marketings to supply foodstuffs for the expanding nonagricultural sector and raw materials for industry.
3. Provision of agricultural products for export to earn foreign exchange to pay for importation of machinery and equipment.
4. Assistance to capital accumulation in the industrial sector by the transfer of savings from the rural to the industrial sector.

As far as the first supportive role is concerned, Soviet agriculture did without a doubt provide a vast amount of manpower to industry within a relatively brief amount of time. Between 1926 and 1939 alone, the urban population increased from 26.3 million to 56.1 million—a net gain of some 30 million—and by 1959, this figure had increased to 100 million—a net overall increase of over 73 million, of which 43.4 million (well over one-half) can be accounted for by migration from rural to urban areas.[37] This internal migration, along with the increasing participation rates of the urban population, sustained an average annual rate of growth of the nonagricultural labor force of 8.7 percent between 1928 and 1937, while the agricultural labor force declined at an annual rate of 2.5 percent during the same period. This vast transformation was effected by both market and nonmarket forces: First, a substantial gap between urban and rural incomes was created, thereby promoting movement out of agriculture. Second, massive recruitment campaigns were carried on in the countryside to facilitate the transfer.

Most experts would agree that collectivization was at least in part responsible for the flow of labor from rural areas to industry in the 1930s. In effect, collectivization "pushed" labor out of agriculture, rather than the more common case of industrial prosperity "pulling" labor from the countryside. The contemporary debate over the merits of Soviet collectivization focuses on whether collectivization was necessary to promote this outflow or, if not necessary, whether it was the most efficient mechanism to facilitate the labor outflow from the rural areas.

In this debate, Michael Ellman has argued that collectivization was necessary to generate sufficient supplies of urban (industrial) labor. Given the vast manpower needs of Soviet industry, sufficient labor would not have been available without collectivization. James Millar, on the other hand, maintains that in this respect collectivization was both unnecessary and undesirable. Millar maintains that flows of labor from rural to urban areas have always been adequate (in fact, frequently more than adequate) in countries experiencing development. Moreover, the urban unemployed or underemployed could have been mobilized to meet additional industrial manpower needs if the influx from agriculture had not been sufficient.[38]

In sum, while collectivization, combined with a fair measure of state control, led to an outflow of labor from rural areas in the 1930s, the necessity and effectiveness of the use of forced collectivization for this purpose is still under debate. Although labor flows voluntarily into industry during economic development, the Soviet process is distinguished by the great speed of this flow.

How well Soviet agriculture performed the second supportive function during the crucial early years of industrialization is also the subject of controversy. The figures on grain marketings (Table 5.5) provide valuable insights.

The evidence presented in Table 5.5 supports the view that from the late 1920s through the late 1930s, grain procurements generally increased more rapidly than grain production. Grain procurements increased from a low of roughly 16 percent in 1929 to a high of roughly 43 percent in 1938.

Table 5.5   SOVIET GRAIN PRODUCTION AND PROCUREMENT, 1929–1938a

Year	Grain[b] production (million metric tons)	Grain procurement[c] (million metric tons)	Procurement production
1929	66.8	10.8	16.2
1930	71.0	16.0	22.5
1931	65.0	22.1	34.0
1932	65.0	23.7	36.5
1933	71.0	23.3	32.8
1934	71.5	26.0	36.4
1935	77.5	28.4	36.6
1936	63.0	25.7	40.8
1937	97.5	31.8	32.6
1938	73.0	31.5	43.1

[a]These data should be interpreted with caution as representing general trends. There are important and controversial issues of definition and measurement.

[b]Simple average of the high and low variants from Table 5.2.

[c]Procurements (actually grain collections) 1929–1931 are for the agricultural year (i.e., 1929 = 1928–1929), while procurements for 1932–1938 are for plan (calendar) years.

Sources: Grain production data from S. G. Wheatcroft, "A Reevaluation of Soviet Agricultural Production in the 1920s and 1930s," in R. C. Stuart. ed., *The Soviet Rural Economy* (Totowa, N.J.: Rowman and Allanheld, 1984), pp. 42–43; procurement data 1929–1932 from R. W. Davies, *The Industrialization of Soviet Russia* (Cambridge, Mass.: Harvard University Press, 1980), vol. 1, Table 8; procurement data for 1932 from J. F. Karcz, "Khrushchev's Agricultural Policies," in M. Bornstein and D. F. Fusfeld, eds., *The Soviet Economy: A Book of Readings*, 3rd ed. (Homewood, Ill. Irwin, 1970), p. 44; procurement data 1933–1938 from E. Zaleski, *Stalinist Planning for Economic Growth,1932–1952* (Chapel Hill: University of North Carolina Press, 1980), Statistical Appendix.

Jerzy Karcz has attempted to show that the entire increase in gross grain marketings between 1928 and 1933 can be accounted for not by the ability of the state to gather additional grain *per se* from *kolkhozy*, but by the reduction in animal herds, which would otherwise consume grains, that took place during collectivization.[39] However, one may question this conclusion in the light of the large state exactions during poor harvest years that exacerbated the famine of 1932–1934. Also, the drastic decline in peasant living standards during the 1930s might be cited as counterevidence to Karcz's conclusions.

As far as the third function is concerned, Soviet agriculture did earn crucial foreign exchange to pay for machinery imports during the first Five Year Plan. Between 1929 and 1931, Soviet imports increased by over 60 percent in volume despite the worsening terms of trade resulting from the collapse of agricultural prices in the world market. In fact, Soviet imports were severely limited by balance-of-payments constraints given the Western countries' unwillingness to grant long-term credits to the fledgling Communist regime. The Soviet government's sole recourse, therefore, was to continue to market abroad the traditional Soviet export commodities—grain and wheat, timber, and petroleum. Between 1929 and 1931, Soviet exports expanded about 50 percent, and this expansion was spearheaded by an increase in the proportion of the total domestic output of agricultural products exported. In 1928, for example, less than one percent of the domestic output of grain, wheat, and corn was exported; yet by 1931, 14 percent of the output of grain, 18 percent of wheat, and 2 percent of corn was exported. Thus, agricultural exports were used to finance machinery and ferrous metals imports, which rose from one-third of total Soviet imports in 1928 to almost three-quarters by the end of the first Five Year Plan.[40] The costs of maintaining agricultural exports were considerable, for they worsened the famine of 1932–1934. As one student of this famine writes:

> The immediate cause was not poor harvests but the requisitioning of grain from moderate harvests in such quantities that not enough was left for the peasants themselves. The main reasons for this drastic policy appear to have been, first the attempt to maintain exports of agricultural produce and hence imports of machinery. . .[41]

The most controversial role of Soviet agriculture in economic development relates to the fourth function, namely, the transfer of savings from the countryside to the city. On the surface, it would appear that the Preobrazhensky model of primitive socialist accumulation was indeed used successfully in forcing savings from the rural population during the early years of industrialization. While estimates of the extent of decline must be quite crude, Naum Jasny has estimated that per capita income of the farm population had fallen to 53 percent of the 1928 level by 1932–1933, which perhaps is not too unrealistic in view of the fact that the peasants' standard of living during the best prewar year for the Russian peasantry (1937) was still only 81 percent that of 1928.[42] Although it would appear from such figures that Soviet agrarian policies succeeded in marshaling forced savings from the rural sector, such a judgement may be premature for reasons discussed below. In any case, the burden of industrialization was also borne by the urban sector. Mindful of the significant decline in urban living standards during the 1930s, Abram Bergson notes the following:

> Contrary to a common supposition, the industrial worker fared no better than the peasants under Stalin's five year plans. Indeed, he seemingly fared worse, although I believe he was able to maintain in some degree the margin he enjoyed initially in respect to consumption per capita.[43]

It may be as well that the decline in both urban and rural standards during the first Five Year Plan has been underestimated, so that the savings "forced" from the Soviet population were indeed quite significant.[44]

However, the fundamental issue here is the role of collectivization in the extraction of a surplus from the countryside to form the basis of the industrial expansion of the Soviet economy in the 1930s and thereafter. That savings were forced via reductions in living standards is not at issue, for investment rates (saving rates) did explode during the early 1930s as a consequence of transferring income from individuals to the state. The issue instead is, Was the collective farm responsible? Although the Western assessment of collectivization has generally been negative, especially in a long-run perspective, the *kolkhoz* has been credited by some as being the mechanism that served to extract a surplus from the countryside and hence played a crucial role in the accumulation process.[45]

Although it has proved difficult to achieve precision in defining and measuring an agricultural surplus, evidence provided by the Soviet economist A. A. Barsov and by James Millar appears to demonstrate that during the crucial period of the first Five Year Plan, Soviet agriculture was a net *recipient* of resources.[46] For surpluses to be transferred from agriculture to industry, the flow of deliveries from agriculture to industry must exceed the flow of deliveries from industry to agriculture (grain for tractors, if you will). As these are flows of physical commodities, the outcome will depend on the prices applied. Millar uses the prices of 1928 (which place a low relative valuation on agriculture) and finds an inflow to agriculture on a net basis. Michael Ellman uses modified 1913 prices (which place a higher relative valuation on agriculture prices) and obtains a net outflow. But the crucial point is that both Millar and Ellman find that the advent of collectivization failed to alter the magnitude of the surplus, however it is measured. Thus, one cannot argue that collectivization was responsible for any significant change in the surplus. Millar summarizes his view as follows:

> Ultimately, therefore, although the state did succeed in raising real resources from the peasantry for investment purposes, the destruction occasioned by resistance to collectivization obliged it to turn around and use those resources for replacement investment in agriculture. This inflow, together with the net inflow to the private sector that was financed by the favorable change in the terms of trade with the nonrural population, caused the agricultural sector taken as a whole to become a net recipient of resources during the first Five Year Plan Whatever its merits may have been on other grounds, mass collectivization of Soviet agriculture must be reckoned as an unmitigated economic policy disaster.[47]

COLLECTIVIZATION: AN ASSESSMENT

Collectivization ranks among the most controversial events in contemporary history. From an economic viewpoint, the usual Western literature on collectivization focuses on two major themes. First, collectivization is viewed as a major disaster, inflicting major costs, both short-term and long-term, on the Soviet peasant population and the economy as a whole.

Second, collectivization is viewed as introducing a unique if brutal mechanism for harnessing the agricultural surplus (and the rural population) to the service of the industrial sector. Doubt has been cast upon collectivization's contribution to industrial capital formation in the form of the Millar-Barsov hypothesis, which claims that agriculture at best provided a very small net positive flow, one that changed little if at all during the collectivization drive. If we accept this proposition, it must change the traditional view of collectivization, specifically the view of agriculture as a contributor of a large net surplus to the industrialization drive. There is little dispute that collectivization lowered Soviet agricultural productivity in both the short and long run. Moreover, if sufficient labor would have migrated voluntarily to the cities anyway, collectivization would not have been necessary to meet the manpower needs of industry. The major lasting benefit the Soviet regime obtained from collectivization would have been the imposition of political control over the countryside and the changes in property relations. The political benefits to a Stalin of bringing a potentially unruly and unfriendly segment of the population under control were considerable.

Prior to the Barsov-Millar hypothesis, it was felt that, because a surplus was extracted from agriculture, it was the agricultural sector that bore a major burden of the industrialization drive. The peasants gave up the grain they would have eaten and/or converted into consumer goods. The revisionist view of the surplus does not really alter the question of burden to any appreciable degree. To the extent that offsetting flows from nonagriculture to agriculture were agricultural inputs, they would do little for the immediate peasant standard of living, particularly given state exactions at low prices. In this sense, the peasants must have borne a burden even thought the newly supplied inputs to agriculture may have improved the long-term prospects for improved agricultural production.

The Soviet investment rate doubled between 1928 and 1937 (Table 4.1). The industrial capital stock almost quadrupled over the same period. The investment rate in 1913 was likely not much below that of 1928.[48] Thus, it is clear that massive capital accumulation, concentrated primarily in industry, took place in the 1930s. The agricultural surplus controversy does not dispute this basic point. At issue rather is whether the agricultural population bore a disproportionate share of this accumulation burden. The evidence presented in Table 4.1 suggests that,despite rapid economic growth, both urban and rural living standards stagnated, the agricultural more than the urban. The burden was heavy, and both urban and rural workers shared the forced savings that made this rapid capital accumulation possible.

THE STALINIST DEVELOPMENT MODEL

By the late 1930s, the Stalinist model was firmly entrenched. An administrative-command system had replaced market resource allocation; private ownership of the means of production had virtually disappeared; the private peasant had been forced into collective farms. The economic system installed by Stalin for allocating resources has been resistant to significant change, as subsequent chapters will show.

The glasnost and perestroika programs of the late 1980s have prompted Soviet ideologists to ask, What elements of the Soviet economic system are "Stalinist," and what elements are inherent to socialism? By asking this question, Soviet reformers are placed in a position to change the "Stalinist" elements of the system and to retain those elements that are inherent to socialism.

It is worthwhile at this point to describe in a more complete way the features of the Stalinist model of economic development at the end of the 1930s. Most of these elements have already been described—the ministerial planning system, collectivization, structural shifts of resources. We delineate seven basic features of the Stalinist development model:[49]

1. Planners' preferences , dictated by the Communist Party through the planning hierarchy, replaced consumer preferences. This changeover was made possible by the establishment of a political dictatorship that placed the means of production in the hands of the state. As a response to the imposition of planners' preferences, the structure of demand was changed dramatically within a brief period of time in favor of selected (priority) heavy-industry branches, in particular, metallurgy, machine building, and electricity. The allocation of resources to light industry and agriculture was severely restricted. These two trends were reflected in prominent structural shifts: the aggregate investment rate rose markedly and rapidly, while the share of GNP devoted to personal consumption fell. The share of communal consumption (public health, education, etc.) rose at the expense of private consumption. The rise in public consumption, however, was not sufficient to counter the relative decline in total consumption (as a percentage of GNP) (Table 5.6).

The growth of the service sector was retarded despite the rise in health and education services, thereby limiting the flow of resources into "nonproductive" sectors. Development of commerce was especially restricted because the limitations placed on consumer goods retarded the growth of retail trade; the absence of property ownership limited the need of banking, legal, and other com-

Table 5.6   STRUCTURAL CHANGE OF SOVIET ECONOMY IN THE 1930s

	1928	1937
Sector shares of NNP (%)		
Agriculture	49	31
Industry	28	45
Services	23	24
End use shares of NNP (%)		
Consumption	82	55
Government	8	22
Net domestic investment	10	23
Foreign trade		
Exports + imports/NNP	6.2	1
Economic growth (average annual %)		
Total product: 1928–1940	5.1	
Per capita product: 1928–1940	3.9	

Source: P. R. Gregory, "Economic Growth and Structural Change in Czarist Russia and the Soviet Union: A Long-Term Comparison" in S. Rosefielde, ed., *Economic Welfare and the Economics of Soviet Socialism* (New York: Cambridge University Press, 1981), p 39.

mercial services; and the material balance system in large measure replaced the wholesale trade network.

2. Sectorial relationships changed. Agriculture was collectivized and private trade was virtually eliminated. In this way, the state could ensure deliveries of agricultural products to the cities by making the deliveries mandatory. The prices at which farms had to sell produce to the state were set at low levels for two purposes. The first was to force a transfer of savings from the countryside to industry to finance the industrial investment (via the turnover tax on food products). The second purpose was to reduce rural real incomes to facilitate the transfer of labor out of agriculture into higher-priority industrial occupations offering relatively higher real wages. The depression of rural living standards encouraged the more productive age groups to leave the collective farms for the city, and organized state recruitment campaigns in the countryside were used to promote this movement.

3. In industry, especially in high-priority branches, highly capital-intensive factor proportions were adopted. In this manner, the movement of population from the rural to urban areas, though quite rapid, was held down. The result was a below-average ratio of urbanization, relative to the level of development, which enabled planners to restrict the flow of resources into nonproductive municipal services. Urbanization was also held down by encouraging high labor participation rates among the existing urban population, especially women. The low absolute real income levels and (in later years) laws against parasitism and absenteeism were used to encourage such high labor participation rates.

The rapid expansion of priority industrial branches was made possible by generous allocations of scarce capital by planning authorities. In addition, in the priority areas, relatively high wages were set to attract skilled industrial workers. On the other hand, the most neglected light industrial sectors were those with high capital-output ratios, notably printing, paper, and food products.

Not having developed sophisticated planning techniques, the Soviets used "campaigns" to eliminate bottlenecks that arose as a result of taut planning. In addition, industrial planning was simplified by limiting product differentiation. This product strategy was expected to encourage standardization, limit the spare parts problem, and facilitate maintenance and repair. Scarce industrial capital was stretched by multiple shift arrangements (often three per day) and by utilizing capital until it was totally worn out. Further capital-saving techniques involved the combining of advanced capital-intensive Western technology in primary processes with old-fashioned labor-intensive methods in auxiliary processes and the limiting of social overhead investment in transportation, roads, apartment buildings, schools, and hospitals. Instead, social overhead capital carried over from earlier periods was simply utilized more intensively.

Large scale integrated plants were chosen. This gigantomania was sanctioned for reasons of international prestige (having the world's largest dam, for example) and because it was hoped that unit costs would eventually be lower owing to economies of scale.[50] Furthermore, a long planning time horizon was adopted and interest rate calculations were not used, both of which condoned the long gestation periods involved in such projects. Highly integrated plants were chosen because of the primitive state of the material supply system, a factor that made less integrated plants vulnerable to supply interruptions. Machinery plants, for example, produced their own steel and shipped their finished products.[51] The integrated nature of industrial plants enabled planners to limit the size of wholesale trade.

4. Inflation, monetary controls, and the "money illusion" played important roles. The shift of resources away from consumer goods meant that the growth of real income would be held below the overall growth rate or, in its extreme manifestation, would even decline. However, it was necessary to preserve worker incentives. Wages were allowed to rise out of pace with consumer goods, thereby creating inflation. Prices of consumer goods were raised at a more rapid rate than wages, on the grounds that workers would be more concerned with what was happening to their *money* wages than to their *real* wages. To preserve equity during this period of rapid inflation, some rationing of necessities was implemented. Sales at above-rationing prices were permitted—in fact, a complex multiple price system was used—to preserve the incentive effect of differential wages.

Personal income taxes were not used as a major source of state revenue because it was assumed that indirect taxes better preserve worker incentives. The form of indirect taxation adopted, the turnover tax, was a hidden tax, and consumers were unaware of the extent to which they were bearing the burden of industrialization.[52] In addition, the multiple price system was a rich source of tax revenue.

Tax revenues gathered in this fashion were then used to finance investment, the funds for which were allocated by an investment plan. Very little, if any, investment was determined at the plant level. The State Bank monitored the cash in the hands of the public through its control of enterprise cash accounts and —via its control over credit and transactions—monitored plan fulfillment, thus providing a secondary source of information on enterprise operations for the planning apparatus.

5. A significant portion of government expenditure was used to finance industrial investment. The remainder served to finance defense, administration, and public consumption expenditures. Considerable public resources were channeled into public health and education, on the grounds that a healthy and well-trained labor force was required to man the economy. The focus of education was on technical specialization. The state embarked on a mass campaign of vocational education that took place to a great extent on the job. In this manner, the state saved scarce capital by not having to build additional schools, universities, and technical institutes. A further device to stretch educational resources was the emphasis on night school training, correspondence courses, and self-instruction. Throughout, the worker was encouraged to acquire additional training by highly differentiated wages that favored the skilled worker.

6. The expansion of transport capacity was limited to restrict investment in social overhead capital. Planners counted on substantial improvements in lev-

els of *utilization*, coupled with a pattern of industrialization designed to minimize the need for transport services. To achieve this latter objective, strong emphasis was placed on locating industrial establishments at the site of raw materials.[53] A further aspect was the emphasis on railways as opposed to other forms
of surface transportation, thereby enabling authorities to avoid highway
construction.

7. The economy's relationships with the outside world changed as well.
The state established a foreign trade monopoly to ensure that dealings with the
outside world were in accordance with the needs of industrialization. Initially,
agricultural products were exchanged for the machinery—in particular, machine tools that could be used to make other machinery—vital to the early
stages of industrialization, and heavy reliance was placed on imports of foreign
technology. However, the long-term emphasis was placed upon lessening dependence on the rest of the world, for such reliance was viewed as incompatible
with the planned nature of the economy. This autarky approach dictated that a
complete range of industrial and agricultural products should be produced domestically. Domestic production was, therefore, substituted for imports, and
specialization according to comparative advantage was neglected.

Some features of the Stalinist development model are not new. Others,
such as material balance planning, the substitution of planners' preferences, the
collective farm, and the deemphasis of services, are new features. One important fact, however, should not be neglected: the Stalinist model involved considerable differences in magnitude and timing in the implementation of these
common elements. The following differences in magnitude should be noted.

1. The relative increase in heavy industry that generally occurs during development was greater in both *magnitude* and *speed* in the Soviet Union. The
increase in the combined metallurgy and engineering product share of manufacturing in the USSR of 26 percentage points (from 19 percent to 45 percent) between 1928 and 1937 required from 50 to 75 years in other countries, and many
industrialized Western countries have yet to attain a heavy-industry share as
large as the USSR's in 1937.[55]

2. The rapidity of the increase in the investment rate in the Soviet Union is
another distinctive feature. In 1928, gross investment as a percent of GNP
(measured in 1937 factor costs) was 12.5 percent; by 1937, this figure was 25.9
percent, after peaking at 32 percent in 1935.[56] Such high investment rates have
been matched and even surpassed by several Western countries. However, in
Western countries, the rise in the investment rate was gradual and began several decades after industrialization was under way, not during its initial stages.

3. Extremely rapid shifts of resources out of agriculture into industry were
also characteristic of the Stalinist model. In the course of Western development, the labor force and product shares of agriculture generally declined, but
the decline in the Soviet Union between 1928 and 1940 (Table 4.1) required
from 30 to 50 years in other countries.

4. As far as sectorial productivity relationships are concerned, the Soviet experience was distinctive for the relatively low output per worker in agriculture
compared to industry. In fact, ratios of sectorial product per worker were quite

similar to the LDCs, where traditional and backward agricultural sectors prevail. There is evidence that labor productivity (in full-time equivalents) in Soviet agriculture actually declined between 1928 and 1940, quite in contrast to the industrialization experiences of other countries, where agricultural labor productivity generally kept pace with the overall productivity growth of the economy.

5. The Stalinist model also differed from the Western experience with respect to private consumption. In the West, the GNP share of private consumption normally declined. The distinctive feature of the trend in private consumption in the Soviet Union was the magnitude and rapidity of its relative decline, not to mention the *absolute* decline. In 1928, private consumption accounted for 80 percent of Soviet GNP. By 1940, this figure had dropped to 50 percent (Table 4.1). In other countries, the drop was from 80 percent to between 60 and 70 percent, a decline that required from 30 to 80 years to be completed versus 12 years in the Soviet case.

6. A further distinctive feature was the rapid rise in the labor participation rate. Between 1928 and 1940, the Soviet population grew at 1.2 percent annually, while the labor force grew at 3.7 percent. Thus, there was a 2.5 percent annual rate of growth of the labor participation rate. As Simon Kuznets notes: "No such accelerated use of labor relative to population appears to have occurred in other countries."[57]

7. The relatively low Soviet foreign trade proportions during industrialization were also a distinctive feature. Commonly, a country's dependence on foreign trade is gradually reduced in the course of development. In the Soviet case, the ratio of exports to national income dropped dramatically, from 3.5 percent in 1930 to 0.5 percent in 1937. Part of this drop can be explained by the collapse of world prices of primary products during the world depression, but Soviet trade ratios to and after the depression remained quite low by international standards. As Kuznets notes: "[The low Soviet foreign trade proportions] reflect a forced isolation of a large population from contact with the rest of the world, not paralleled in any non-Communist country within modern times."[58]

8. A final distinctive feature of the Stalinist model was the extent to which the service sector, especially commercial services such as trade, banking, and insurance, was depressed below "normal" levels in the Soviet Union. When compared with the development experience of Western countries, a Soviet service gap is evident in the sense that the labor force share of services was much below that expected of a market economy at a similar level of development. Thus, the Soviet economy developed without devoting as much resources to services as have "normally" been required in the West.

The Soviet leadership of the early 1990s must decide what features of the Stalinist model to keep and which to discard. As the preceding list shows, some of the features of the Stalinist model are institutional, for example, the type of resource allocation system. Others, such as the choice of sectorial priorities or plant sizes, are strategic. Others relate to the fundamental character of the economic system, for example, choice of property relations in agriculture. We shall return to these issues when we discuss economic reform in Chapter 14.

THE SOVIET ECONOMY DURING WORLD WAR II

The impact of World War II on the Soviet Union in general and the Soviet economy in particular[59] is a subject that has been receiving increasing attention from both Soviet and Western scholars. The subject is of immense contemporary interest in the Soviet Union, where the war achievements are viewed as demonstrating the viability of the Soviet social and economic system even under the most extreme conditions.

Our interest in World War II centers not only on the costs of the war to the Soviet system, but also on the short- and long-term adjustments that resulted and the resiliency of the planned socialist economy under new and very different conditions from those prevailing earlier.

The impact of World War II on the Soviet economy was immense. For example, in terms of loss of life, Soviet authors frequently cite a figure of 20 million, or approximately 10 percent of the 1940 Soviet population, of which roughly one-half was from military action. However, if one were to count indirect losses, for example, early deaths from war-related injuries, prisoners of war who chose not to be repatriated, and those entering the *gulag* camps, the figure for loss of life would undoubtedly be much higher. In a recent survey of the impact of World War II on the Soviet economy, James Millar has suggested a figure of 30 million, or approximately 15 percent of the Soviet population as of 1940.[60] As we shall see shortly, much more than loss of life was involved.

In addition to population loss of the sort noted above, the war losses imposed major and long-standing demographic changes on the Soviet population. Specifically, war losses resulted in a substantial male deficit (much greater than would be anticipated under more normal conditions), leading to other important changes, for example, in marriage rates and birthrates and hence population growth. Moreover, as Barbara Anderson and Brian Silver note, the war-related male deficit resulted in a substantial increase in russification through intermarriage.[61] These and related demographic trends would persist long after the end of the war.

Germany invaded the Soviet Union in June 1941. Soviet territorial losses resulting from this invasion were sudden and large. In a recent study of the economic impact of World War II on the Soviet economy, Susan Linz indicates that between July and November 1981, 1523 major industrial enterprises were moved eastward along with 6 million people. While this eastward movement facilitated later production, it resulted in immediate disruption. The Soviet economy, after the German invasion, did not recover production levels of 1940 until 1942; by the end of the war, output levels were 20 percent below those of the prewar period, not to mention an estimated 30 percent destruction of the Soviet capital stock.[62]

The aggregate cost of the war to the Soviet economy has been estimated in a number of different ways. The official Soviet claim is that the war cost the USSR "two Five Year Plans," not including the loss of life noted above. Recent

Western estimates confirm this sort of magnitude. Linz and Millar find that losses range from four to ten years of effort by the labor force available in 1940 or 1945. Summarizing the issue of war losses, Millar notes: "Put differently, the economic cost of the war was equal to, and possibly even greater than, the total wealth created during the industrialization drive of the 1930s."[63]

How was this war effort financed by the Soviet Union? Again, Millar notes that "...the population as a whole increased its work effort and reduced its claim on current output during the war years."[64] Specifically, a number of important changes were made. First, resource allocation priorities were obviously changed. The share of national income devoted to the war effort increased sharply, from about 10 percent in 1940 to slightly under 50 percent by 1943.[65] This change was in part facilitated by the nature of the Soviet economic system and the extraordinary mechanisms (about which more later) put in place during the war years. In general, there was a major shift of resources away from traditional uses (especially consumption and investment) toward war uses.

Second, consumer demand was effectively constrained in a number of ways, although not all efforts in this area worked smoothly and effectively. Rationing of consumer goods was introduced in July 1941 in successive stages. In addition, the distribution of key consumer goods was centralized. However, Soviet efforts to control wages were not always effective. This fact, in combination with the existence of various retail markets under differing degrees of control, meant that, in fact, multiple prices existed for the same goods. For example, the prices in collective farm markets in 1943 were higher than state ration prices by a factor of 14.[66]

Third, labor allocation procedures were changed. While we shall leave the general issue of labor allocation for a subsequent chapter, suffice it to say here that the importance of administrative controls in the labor allocation process increased significantly. Direct mobilization of labor was introduced in December 1941, with strong disciplinary measures enforced. These measures were in large part a response to severe labor shortages imposed by the war effort. For example, the magnitude of the Soviet civilian labor force decreased from 31 million in 1941 to 18 million in 1942.[67] This labor shortage had serious repercussions on the economy, not the least important of which was a tendency for wage inflation, which necessitated offsetting tax increases.

How was the Soviet economy administered during the war? Western observers have noted that, while there were important wartime changes in the administrative structure of the Soviet economy, these changes were for the most part superimposed on top of existing arrangements and were derived from previous experience, for example, the civil war period.[68] A series of new agencies was created, effectively centralizing power and facilitating rapid shifts of resources. For example, the overall war effort was directed by the State Committee for Defense headed by Stalin. Regional shifts were directed by the Evacuation Committee. Moreover, while the planning and materials allocation system put together in the 1930s remained intact, Zaleski has pointed out that, in fact, much less attention was paid to national plans, and much more attention was paid to specific plans for war-related activities. The more limited number of specific, defense-related plans allowed the planners to control defense production more closely. The remainder of the economy was guided not only by general plans but was also regulated by the state budget and the use of newly imposed rationing powers.

Gosplan and the war-related ministries and commissions gained power through the increased importance of the material balances. Thus, at the height of the war effort, central plans were being drawn up for 30,000 materials and supplies to be allocated to 120 large users.

The administrative response to the war was quick and effective, using previously demonstrated strengths (for example, the priority principle) to shift resources into the war effort.

Thus far, we have focused on the costs of the war and the manners in which the economic system was altered to handle the war effort. But how were these costs borne by the Soviet people? In contrast to market economies where the concern focuses on market methods to maintain labor discipline in the face of limited growth of rewards, Soviet leaders resorted to strict administrative methods to enforce labor discipline.[69] At the same time, taxes were increased as a means of restricting consumer demand and financing the war effort. Both direct and indirect taxes were increased. In addition to the increase in the rates for existing taxes, new taxes (notably the war tax) were introduced along with other exactions through bond purchases, multiple levels of distribution in retail trade, and the like. Deficit financing was used, as the government printed money to pay for the war effort. In a sense, Soviet financing of the war effort was based on the use of familiar tools, though possibly with greater emphasis on direct taxation than that generally found in market systems.

In sum, World War II imposed a tremendous burden on the Soviet Union. The economic system was effectively transposed to handle that burden by shifting resources into the successful war effort. All sectors of Soviet society, whether the ministries, the Communist Party, or transportation, were geared to the war effort. While we will pursue postwar economic development in Chapter 6, it is useful to note here that the Soviet postwar transition to a peacetime economy was not easy, nor was it the same as transitions in other war-ravaged economies.

While controls were relaxed, other controls were implemented, and the Stalinist mode of operation would remain in effect until the Khrushchev era of the 1950s. The problem of pent-up demand, which stimulated the postwar growth of consumption (and hence consumer goods production) in market systems, was effectively curtailed in the Soviet Union. While rationing and other such direct controls were relaxed and removed, the currency reform of 1947 proved to be a more direct means to extract currency from the population.[70] Thus, one new ruble was given for each old ruble in a generally complicated currency reform. In addition, the prewar priorities were generally reasserted, such that the Soviet consumer would have to wait for the anticipated postwar relaxation.

THE SOVIET ECONOMY THROUGH WORLD WAR II:
A SUMMARY

The contemporary Soviet economy as we presently know it dates from the very end of the 1920s. In this period, as the NEP system came to an abrupt end, Stalin, firmly in command, introduced two major changes into the Soviet economy: national economic planning and collectivization. Both would be cornerstones of an economic system vastly different from that prevailing earlier, a system that, with changes over the years, exists to the present day.

In this chapter, we have examined the underpinnings of both the planning decision and the collectivization decision. We have emphasized that planning was introduced as a means to control both the pace and the directions of economic development. At the same time, collectivization was introduced as a means to harness the peasants, indeed the rural sector, to the industrialization drive, although, as we have seen, collectivization and its use as a mechanism to finance the development process have been called into question in recent years.

In addition to our examination of these two major decisions, we have examined the Soviet economic system in its formative years, the 1930s and thereafter in the tumultuous years of World War II. By most standards, the 1930s well earned their reputation as a period of unprecedented economic growth and structural change in the Soviet Union—forced-draft industrialization, to be sure.

The costs were high, yet the achievements were, by most standards, great. Indeed, a severe test of these achievements came when the Germans invaded the Soviet Union in 1941. This event, which would foreshadow a conflict of immense proportions, placed a large burden on the Soviet Union and the Soviet economic system; and yet, as we have seen, the system proved capable of meeting the challenge. Although the losses were great and the postwar conversion slow, nevertheless, the 1950s ushered in a new era, particularly after the death of Joseph Stalin in 1953. We now turn our attention to the development of the Soviet economy in the postwar era.

REFERENCES

1. Our discussion of the planning debate of the 1920s is based on the following sources: E. H. Carr and R. W. Davies, *Foundations of a Planned Economy, 1926–1929*, vol. 1, part 2 (London: Macmillan, 1969), pp 787–801; and N. Spulber, *Soviet Strategy for Economic Growth* (Bloomington: Indiana University Press, 1964), pp. 101–111.

2. Statement of P. Vaisburg in *Planovoe khoziastvo* [The planned economy], no. 4 (1928), 167. Quoted in Carr and Davies, *Foundations of a Planned Economy*, p. 793.

3. *Pravda*, September 14, 1927. Quoted in Carr and Davies, *Foundations of a Planned Economy*, p. 818.

4. Our discussion is based on the following sources: Carr and Davies, *Foundations of a Planned Economy*, chaps. 33–35; A. Nove, *An Economic History of the USSR* (London: Penguin, 1969), pp. 212–215, 263–267; M. Dobb, *Soviet Economic Development Since 1917*, 5th ed. (London: Routledge & Kegan Paul, 1960), chap. 13; E. Zaleski, *Planning for Economic Growth in the Soviet Union, 1918–1932* (Chapel Hill: University of North Carolina Press, 1971), pp. 40–73; Y. Avdakov and V. Borodin, *USSR State Industry During the Transition Period* (Moscow: Progress Publishers, 1977); and W. Conyngham, *Industrial Management in the Soviet Union* (Stanford, Calif.: Hoover Institution Press, 1973), pp. 34–42.

5. Zaleski, *Planning for Economic Growth*, p. 41.

6. Carr and Davies, *Foundations of a Planned Economy*, p. 802.

7. Ibid., pp. 830–831. Also see Z. K. Zvezdin, *Ot Goelro k planu pervoi piatiletki* [From Goelro the first Five Year Plan] (Moscow: Nauka, 1979).

8. Zaleski, *Planning for Economic Growth*, pp. 29–73.

9. E. Zaleski, *Stalinist Planning for Economic Growth, 1933–1952* (Chapel Hill: University of North Carolina Press, 1980), p. 483.

10. The discussion here is based on R. Hutchings, "The Origin of the Soviet Industrial Price System," *Soviet Studies*, vol. 13, no. 1 (July 1961), 1–22.

11. For details of the organizational arrangements, see Hutchings, "The Origin of the Soviet Industrial Price System," pp. 13–14.

12. In this section, we rely on Zaleski, *Planning for Economic Growth*; and Nove, *An Economic History of the USSR*.

13. Zaleski, *Planning for Economic Growth*, chap. 19.

14. For details of plan fulfillment in the 1930s, see Zaleski, *Planning for Economic Growth*, Statistical Appendices.

15. In this section, we rely heavily on the following sources: J. F. Karcz, "From Stalin to Brezhnev: Soviet Agricultural Policy in Historical Perspective," in J. R. Millar, ed., *The Soviet Rural Community* (Urbana: University of Illinois Press, 1971), pp. 36–70; J. F. Karcz, "Thoughts on the Grain Problem," *Soviet Studies*, vol. 18, no. 4 (April 1967), 399–434; M. Lewin, *Russian Peasants and Soviet Power* (London: Allen & Unwin, 1968); J. R. Millar and C. A. Guntzel, "The Economics and Politics of Mass Collectivization Reconsidered: A Review Article," *Explorations in Economic History*, vol. 8, no. 1 (Fall 1970), 103–116; A. Nove, "The Decision to Collective," in W. A. D. Jackson, ed., *Agrarian Policies and Problems in Communist and Non-Communist Countries* (Seattle: University of Washington Press, 1971), pp. 69–97; E. Strauss, *Soviet Agriculture in Perspective* (London: Allen & Unwin, 1969), chaps. 5–6; L. Volin, *A Century of Russian Agriculture* (Cambridge, Mass.: Harvard University Press, 1970), chaps. 10–11; R. W. Davies, "A Note on Grain Statistics," *Soviet Studies*, vol. 21, no. 3 (January 1970), 314–329; S. G. Wheatcroft, "The Reliability of Russian Prewar Grain Output Statistics," *Soviet Studies*, vol. 26, no. 2 (April 1974), 157–180; A. Vyas, "Primary Accumulation in the USSR Revisited," *Cambridge Journal of Economics*, vol. 3 (1979), 119–130; and R. W. Davies, *The Industrialization of Soviet Russia*, vols. 1 and 2 (Cambridge, Mass.: Harvard University Press, 1980).

16. The reader interested in the agricultural collectives of the 1920s should consult D. J. Male, *Russian Peasant Organization Before Collectivization* (Cambridge: Cambridge University Press, 1971); R. F. Miller, "Soviet Agricultural Policy in The Twenties: The Failure of Cooperation," *Soviet Studies*, vol. 27, no. 2 (April 1975), 220–244; S. Merl, *Der Agrarmarkt und die Neue Ökonomische Politik* (Munich:

Oldenbourg Verlag, 1981), chap. 5; and R. G. Wesson, *Soviet Communes* (New Brunswick, N.J.: Rutgers University Press, 1963).

17. Class stratification played an important role in the thinking about collectivization and its actual implementation. Although census data from the 1920s suggest that the wealthy peasants (*kulaks*) were a very small proportion of the total peasant population, they were nevertheless seen as politically unreliable at best and enemies of the Soviet industrialization program at worst. For a detailed discussion of the problems of class stratification in this case, see Lewin, *Russian Peasants and Soviet Power*, chaps. 2 and 3.

18. Millar and Guntzel, "Economics and Politics of Mass Collectivization," 112.

19. For a discussion of various output series, see S. G. Wheatcroft, "A Reevaluation of Soviet Agricultural Production in the 1920s and 1930s," in R. C. Stuart, ed., *The Soviet Rural Economy* (Totowa, N.J.: Rowman Allanheld, 1984), pp. 32–62.

20. For details of Stalin's argument and related data, see Karcz, "Thoughts on the Grain Problem," pp. 399–402.

21. Karcz, "Thoughts on the Grain Problem," p. 403.

22. *Ibid.*, pp. 403–409. Gross marketings include sales to other peasants within the village. Net marketings include only sales outside of agriculture.

23. Karcz's analysis of grain marketings and agricultural performance during the late 1920s has been disputed by R. W. Davies. Thus, we cannot know for sure whether Stalin's analysis of the agricultural "crisis" was erroneous. For example, Davies estimates that the 1926–1927 net grain marketings were slightly more than half of prewar marketings—a figure close to Stalin's. See Davies, "A Note on Grain Statistics," p. 328; also S. G. Wheatcroft, "A Reevaluation of Soviet Agricultural Production in the 1920s and 1930s."

24. Lewin, *Russian Peasants and Soviet Power*, pp. 214–244.

25. Ibid., p. 409.

26. Volin, *A Century of Russian Agriculture*, p. 222.

27. S. Swianiewicz, *Forced Labor and Economic Development* (London: Oxford University Press), p. 123.

28. Volin, *A Century of Russian Agriculture*, pp. 228–229.

29. For a detailed account of the history and functions of the MTS, see R. F. Miller, *One Hundred Thousand Tractors* (Cambridge, Mass.: Harvard University Press, 1970), especially chap. 2.

30. Wheatcroft gives a high and low variant calculation. The difference between the two is minimal. Wheatcroft, "A Reevaluation of Soviet Agricultural Production in the 1920s and 1930s."

31. For an alternate livestock index, see Strauss, *Soviet Agriculture*, p. 303.

32. Karcz, "From Stalin to Brezhnev," p. 42.

33. For detailed discussion of various estimates, see D. G. Dalrymple, "The Soviet Famine of 1932–1934," *Soviet Studies*, vol. 15, no. 3 (January 1964), 250–284.

34. N. Jasny, *The Socialized Agriculture of the USSR* (Stanford, Calif.: Food Research Institute, 1949), p. 323; Jasny, *Essays on the Soviet Economy* (New York: Praeger, 1962), p. 107. Jasny's figures on per capita income of the Soviet farm population in constant prices reveal the following picture: 1928, 100; 1932–1933, 53; 1936, 60; 1937, 81; 1938, 63.

35. G. L. Smirnov, ed., "Vremiia trudnykh voprosov, Istoriia 20-30-x godov i sovremennaia obshchestvennaia mysl" [Times of difficult questions, history of the 20s and 30s in contemporary social thought], *Pravda*, September 30, 1988; October 3, 1988.

36. For a detailed discussion of the role of agriculture in economic development, the reader is referred to J. W. Mellor, *The Economics of Agricultural Production* (Ithaca, N.Y.: Cornell University Press, 1966).

37. W. Eason, "Labor Force," in A. Bergson and S. Kuznets, eds., *Economic Trends in the Soviet Union* (Cambridge, Mass.: Harvard University Press, 1963), pp. 72–73.

38. See J. R. Millar, "Views on the Economics of Soviet Collectivization: The State of the Revisionist Debate," in R. C. Stuart, ed., *The Soviet Rural Economy*, pp. 109–117.

39. J. F. Karcz, "From Stalin to Brezhnev: Soviet Agricultural Policy in Historical Perspective," in J. R. Millar, ed., *The Soviet Rural Community* (Urbana: University of Illinois Press, 1971), p. 42.

40. F. D. Holzman, "Foreign Trade," in A. Bergson and S. Kuznets, eds., *Economic Trends in the Soviet Union* (Cambridge, Mass.: Harvard University Press, 1963), pp. 294–295.

41. P. Hanson, *The Consumer Sector in the Soviet Economy* (Evanston, Ill.: Northwestern University Press, 1968), p. 36.

42. N. Jasny, *The Soviet Economy During the Plan Era* (Stanford, Calif.: Food Research Institute, 1951), p. 107.

43. A. Bergson, *The Real National Income of Soviet Russia Since 1928* (Cambridge, Mass.: Harvard University Press, 1961), p. 257.

44. S. Rosefielde, "The First Great Leap Forward Reconsidered: The Lessons of Solzhenitsyn's Gulag Archipelago," *Slavic Review*, vol. 39, no. 4 (December 1980), 559–587. See also comments by H. Hunter, R. W. Davies, and S. Wheatcroft, Igor Birman, and P. Gregory on this subject in the same issue.

45. In addition to earlier writings by Maurice Dobb, another exposition of this viewpoint is: M. Ellman, "Did the Agricultural Surplus Provide the Resources for the Increase in Investment in the USSR During the First Five year Plan?" *Economic Journal*, vol. 85, no. 4 (December 1975).

46. For a summary of the evidence and appropriate references, see J. R. Millar, "Mass Collectivization and the Contribution of Soviet Agriculture to the First Five Year Plan: A Review Article," *Slavic Review*, vol. 33, no. 4 (December 1974), 750–766; J. R. Millar, "Soviet Rapid Development and the Agricultural Surplus Hypothesis," *Soviet Studies*, vol. 22, no. 1 (July 1970). For the original data and discussion, see A. A. Barsov, *Balans stoimostnykh obmenov mezhdu gorodom i derevnei* [Balance of the value of the exchange between the city and the country] (Moscow: Nauka, 1969); A. Vyas, "Primary Accumulation in the USSR Revisited," *Cambridge Journal of Economics*, vol. 3, no. 3 (1979), 119–130; and J. Millar, "Views on the Economics of Soviet Collectivization of Agriculture: The State of the Revisionist Debate," in R. C. Stuart, ed., *The Soviet Rural Economy*, pp. 109–117.

47. Millar, "Mass Collectivization," p. 764. For a contrary view, see David Morrison, "A Critical Examination of A. A. Barsov's Empirical Work on the Balance of Value Exchanges Between the Town and the Country," *Soviet Studies*, vol. 34, no. 4 (October, 1982), pp. 570–584.

48. P. Gregory, *Russian National Income 1885–1913* (Cambridge: Cambridge University Press, 1982), pp. 185–186.

49. Our elaboration of the components of the SDM is drawn from the following studies: Wilber, *The Soviet Model and Underdeveloped Countries* (Chapel Hill: University of North Carolina Press, 1969), part I; G. Ofer, *The Service Sector in Soviet Economic Growth* (Cambridge, Mass.: Harvard University Press, 1973); G.

Ofer, "Economizing on Urbanization in Socialist Countries," in A. A. Brown and E. Neuberger, eds., *Internal Migration: A Comparative Perspective* (New York: Academic Press, 1977), pp. 277–304; G. Ofer. "Industrial Structure, Urbanization, and the Growth Strategy of Social Countries," *Quarterly Journal of Economics*, vol. 90, no. 2 (May 1976), 219–243; P. R. Gregory, *Socialist and Nonsocialist Industrialization Patterns* (New York: Praeger, 1970); F. L. Pryor, *Public Expenditures in Communist and Capitalist Nations* (Homewood, Ill.: Irwin, 1968); F. D. Holzman, "Foreign Trade," in A. Bergson and S. Kuznets, eds., *Economic Trends in the Soviet Union* (Cambridge, Mass.: Harvard University Press, 1963); pp. 283–332; H. Hunter, *Soviet Transportation Policy* (Cambridge, Mass.: Harvard University Press, 1957); E. W. Williams, Jr. *Freight Transportation in the Soviet Union* (Princeton, N.J.: Princeton University Press 1962); S. Kuznets, "A Comparative Appraisal," in A. Bergson and S. Kuznets eds., *Economic Trends in the Soviet Union* (Cambridge, Mass.: Harvard University Press, 1963); and C. K. Wilber, *The Soviet Model*. Other authors making significant contribution are O. Hoeffding, "State Planning and Forced Industrialization," *Problems of Communism*, vol. 8, no. 6 (November–December 1959); N. Spulber, *Soviet Strategy for Economic Growth* (Bloomington: Indiana University Press, 1964); A. Nove, "The Soviet Model and Underdeveloped Countries," *International Affairs*, vol. 36, no. 1 (January 1961); and N. Dodge and C. K. Wilber, "The Relevance of Soviet Industrial Experience for Less Developed Economies," *Soviet Studies*, vol. 21, no. 3 (January 1970), 330–349.

50. An empirical study of the costs of gigantism is provided by B. Katz, "'Gigantism' as an Unbalanced Growth Strategy: An Econometric Investigation of the Soviet Experience, 1928–1940," *Soviet Union*, vol. 4, part 2 (1977), 205–222. For a statistical comparison of the scale of Soviet industrial establishments with American establishments, see A. Woroniak, "Industrial Concentration in Eastern Europe: The Search for Optimum Size and Efficiency," *Notrwendigkeit und Gefahr der Wirtschaftlichen Konzentration* (Basel: Kyklos Verlag), pp. 265–284.

51. D. Granick, *Soviet Metal Fabricating and Economic Development* (Madison: University of Wisconsin Press, 1967).

52. F. D. Holzman, "Financing Soviet Development," in M. Abramovitz, ed., *Capital Formation and Economic Growth* (Princeton, N.J.: Princeton University Press, 1955), pp. 229–287.

53. Soviet planners have long stressed the need for economic development in all regions of the country. The Ural-Kuznetsk Combine was designed to tap the mineral resources of the Ural mountains and the coal resources of the Kuznetsk area and to be appropriately combined to form a large industrial center. For a detailed discussion of the program, see, for example, F. D. Holzman, "The Soviet Ural-Kuznetsk Combine: A Study of Investment Criteria and Industrialization Policies," *Quarterly Journal of Economics*, vol. 71, no. 3 (August 1957), 367–405.

54. S. Kuznets, *Modern Economic Growth* (New Haven, Conn.: Yale University Press, 1967), pp. 300–303.

55. Gregory, *Socialist and Nonsocialist Industrialization Patterns*, pp. 28–29, appendix B.

56. R. Moorsteen and R. Powell, *The Soviet Capital Stock, 1928–1962* (Homewood, Ill.: Irwin, 1966), pp. 358, 361. The 1935 figure is estimated by applying the Moorsteen and Powell investment rate index to the Bergson 1937 figure.

57. Kuznets, "A Comparative Appraisal," p. 341.

58. Ibid., p. 367.
59. This discussion of World War II is based largely on the following sources: Nove, *An Economic History of the USSR*, chap. 10; Zaleski, *Stalinist Planning for Economic Growth*, chaps. 14 and 15; J. R. Millar, "Financing the Soviet Effort in World War II," *Soviet Studies*, vol. 32, no. 1 (January 1980); J. R. Millar and S. J. Linz, "The Cost of World War II to the Soviet People," *Journal of Economic History*, vol. 38, no. 4 (December 1978), 959–962; N. A. Voznesensky, *Soviet Economy During the Second World War* (New York: International Publishers, 1949), translated from the Russian; S. J. Linz, ed., *The Impact of World War II on the Soviet Union* (Totowa, N.J.: Rowman & Allanheld, 1985); and T. Dunmore, *The Stalinist Command Economy* (New York: St. Martin's Press, 1980).
60. J. R. Millar, "Conclusion: Impact and Aftermath of World War II," in S. J. Linz, ed., *The Impact of World War II on the Soviet Union*, p. 292.
61. B. A. Anderson and B. D. Silver, "Demographic Consequences of World War II on the Non-Russian Nationalities of the USSR," in S. J. Linz, ed., *The Impact of World War II*, pp. 211–249.
62. S. J. Linz, "World War II and Soviet Economic Growth, 1940–1953" in S. J. Linz, ed., *The Impact of World War II*, pp. 11–34.
63. Millar, "Conclusion: Impact and Aftermath of World War II," p. 291.
64. Ibid., p. 292.
65. Millar, "Financing the Soviet Effort."
66. Zaleski, *Stalinist Planning for Economic Growth*, p. 326.
67. Ibid., p. 311.
68. Ibid., chap. 14; Millar, "Conclusion: Impact and Aftermath of World War II," pp. 292 ff.; S. R. Lieberman, "Crisis Management in the USSR: The Wartime System of Administration and Control," in S. J. Linz, ed., *The Impact of World War II*, pp. 61–78.
69. Zaleski, *Stalinist Planning for Economic Growth*, p. 287.
70. For a discussion of the relaxation of controls and the currency reform in particular, see Zaleski, *Stalinist Planing for Economic Growth*, chap. 18; also S. Fitzpatrick, "Postwar Soviet Society: The 'Return to Normalcy'" in S. J. Linz, ed., *The Impact of World War II*, pp. 131–158.

SELECTED BIBLIOGRAPHY

Y. Avdakov and V. Borodin, *USSR State Industry During the Transition Period* (Moscow: Progress Publishers, 1977).

E. H. Carr and R. W. Davies, *Foundation of a Planned Economy, 1926–1929* vol. 1, parts 1 and 2. (London: Macmillan, 1969).

R. W. Davies, *The Industrialization of Soviet Russia*, vols. 1 and 2 (Cambridge, Mass.: Harvard University Press, 1980).

M. Dobb, *Soviet Economic Development Since 1917*, 5th ed. (London: Routledge & Kegan Paul, 1960).

T. Dunmore, *The Stalinist Command Economy* (New York: St. Martin's Press, 1980).

A. Erlich, *The Soviet Industrialization Debate, 1924–1928* (Cambridge, Mass.: Harvard University Press, 1960).

M. Harrison, *Soviet Planning in Peace and War: 1938–1945* (Cambridge: Cambridge University Press, 1985).

N. Jasny, *Soviet Industrialization 1928–1952* (Chicago: University of Chicago Press, 1961).

———, *The Socialized Agriculture of the USSR* (Stanford, Calif.: Food Research Institute, 1949).

J. F. Karcz, "From Stalin to Brezhnev: Soviet Agricultural Policy in Historical Perspective," in J. R. Millar, ed., *The Soviet Rural Community* (Urbana: University of Illinois Press, 1971), pp. 36–70.

———, "Thoughts on the Grain Problem," *Soviet Studies*, vol. 18, no. 4 (April 1967), 399–434.

M. Lewin, *Russian Peasants and Soviet Power* (London: Allen & Unwin, 1968).

———, "The Immediate Background of Soviet Collectivization," *Soviet Studies*, vol. 17, no. 2 (October 1965), 162–197.

S. J. Linz, ed., *The Impact of World War II on the Soviet Union* (Totowa, N.J.: Rowman & Allanheld, 1985).

J. R. Millar, "Financing the Soviet Effort in World War II," *Soviet Studies*, vol. 32, no. 1 (January 1980).

A. Nove, *An Economic History of the USSR* (London: Penguin, 1969), chaps. 7–10.

———, *Economic Rationality and Soviet Politics* (New York: Praeger, 1964), pp. 17–40.

L. Smolinski, "Planning Without Theory, 1917–1967," *Survey*, no. 64 (July 1968), 108–128.

———, "Soviet Planning: How It Really Began," *Survey*, no. 64 (April 1968), 100–115.

N. Spulber, ed., *Foundations of Soviet Strategy for Economic Growth* (Bloomington: Indiana University Press, 1964).

———, *Soviet Strategy for Economic Growth* (Bloomington: Indiana University Press, 1964).

V. A. Vinogradov et al., eds, *Isotoriia sotsialisticheskoi ekonomiki SSSR* [History of the socialist economy of the USSR], vols. 1–5 (Moscow: Nauka, 1976).

L. Volin, *A Century of Russian Agriculture* (Cambridge, Mass.: Harvard University Press, 1970), chaps. 9 and 10.

N. A. Voznesensky, *Soviet Economy During the Second World War*, translated from the Russian edition (New York: International Publishers, 1949).

E. Zaleski, *Planning for Economic Growth in the Soviet Union, 1918–1932* (Chapel Hill: University of North Carolina Press, 1971).

———, *Stalinist Planning for Economic Growth, 1933–1952* (Chapel Hill: University of North Carolina Press, 1980).

Chapter
6

The Soviet Economy in the Postwar Era: The Road to Perestroika

*T*hus far, we have examined the historical underpinnings of the Soviet economic system. This story has been developed through the momentous organizational changes of the 1930s and the crushing impact of World War II. Before we turn to an in-depth analysis of how the Soviet economy works, it is appropriate that we bring the story of Soviet economic development up to date.

The period between the 1950s and the end of the 1980s is obviously of importance to the assessment of the Soviet economy. This is, after all, the era in which the Soviet Union came to enjoy world status as a superpower. Moreover, it is as close as we can come to a period of "normal" operation for the Soviet system, a period in which we can begin to isolate and identify the forces contributing to the Soviet economic performance.

Possibly most important, this period represents a gradual end to the forced-draft industrialization of the 1930s and an attempt to achieve maturity. Both in terms of our understanding of the planned socialist system and in terms of projections of Soviet economic prospects, it is imperative that we understand the Soviet economy in its contemporary setting, in its drive for maturity through efficiency.

The Soviet Union entered the postwar era with its command planning system in place. Prior to Stalin's death, it was not possible to criticize the economic system. Failures were attributed to human error or even human malice; the economic system itself was sound. Yet from its very inception, the inherent weaknesses of the command system were apparent. As these weaknesses resulted in performance downturns, the Soviet leadership began to permit and even encourage consideration of how the command system might be changed. The perestroika program of the late 1980s is the latest of a series of reform efforts and experiments that have been attempted over the years. In its search for maturity, the Soviet Union has allowed tinkering with the Stalinist economic system. This tinkering, or reform process, must be understood in its entirety. It must be tied to postwar economic performance and to the sequence of events leading up to Gorbachev's *perestroika*.

It has been customary to periodize economic history, that is, to identify policies and performance with prevailing political leaders. This approach may be somewhat artificial, since, in fact, there is a good deal of continuity of basic economic policies from one Soviet leader to the next. However, to simplify our presentation in this chapter, we will follow this practice, beginning with the post-Stalin transition (Malenkov and Khrushchev), the long tenure of Brezhnev, the short tenures of Andropov and Chernenko, and finally the present era of Gorbachev in the late 1980s.

THE EARLY YEARS—POSTWAR TRANSITION

After the end of world War II, a transition period saw much of the war-related administrative structure dismantled. The State Committee of Defense was abolished in late 1945. The fourth Five Year Plan for the period 1946–1950 was a plan of reconstruction. The postwar recovery was rapid. As Table 6.1 suggests, by 1950, most prewar indices had been exceeded, in some cases by substantial amounts. There were two major exceptions to this record of rapid postwar recovery. Grain production in 1950 was well below the level of production achieved in 1940. In part, this resulted from the depressed conditions in rural areas and possibly from the low priority accorded to agriculture during the war years.[1] It is worth noting that the share of total investment devoted to agriculture declined steadily from 15.5 percent during the first Five Year Plan (1928–1932) to 9.3 percent during the war years.[2] While this trend would be reversed after the war, it would take time to rebuild the agricultural capital stock. According to the official Soviet capital stock series, the share of agricultural

Table 6.1   THE SOVIET ECONOMY: SELECTED INDICATORS, 1940–1950

	1940	1945	1946	1950
National income (1940 = 100)	100	83	—	161
Industrial production	100	91	76	172
Heavy industry (Group A)	100	112	82	204
Light industry (Group B)	100	59	67	122
Gross agricultural product	100	60	—	99
Steel (million tons)	18,317	12,252	13,346	27,329
Oil (million tons)	31,121	19,436	21,746	37,878
Electricity (million kWh)	48,562	43,257	48,571	91,226
Transport (billion tons km)	494.4	374.8	395.5	713.3
Fertilizer (standard units)	3,290	1,121	1,711	5,497
Grain (million tons)	95.6	47.3	39.6	81.2
Meat (tons slaughter wt.)	4,695	2,559	—	4,867
Money wage (avg. monthly)	33.1	—	48.1	64.2

Source: Official Soviet series from *Narodone khoziaistvo SSSR za 60 let* [The national economy of the USSR over 60 years] (Moscow: Statistika, 1977). Data on meat production from *Sel'skoe khoziaistvo SSSR* [Agriculture of the USSR] (Moscow: Statistika, 1971).

capital stock declined from roughly 31 percent in 1929 to 16 percent of the total in 1941 and remained at 14 percent throughout the 1950s.[3] In any event, agricultural production in general and grain production in particular would become the subjects of major concern in the 1950s and thereafter.

The early postwar years saw a continuation of the priorities established in the 1930s. The difference in performance between heavy industry and light industry was striking. For industrial output in the aggregate, the fourth Five Year Plan (1946–1950) was fulfilled by 117 percent. However, heavy industry (Group A) was fulfilled by 128 percent, while light industry (Group B) was fulfilled by 95 percent.[4] On the surface, this evidence seems to confirm the widely held view that in the immediate postwar years, the primacy of heavy industry so firmly established in the 1930s was not challenged. However, the issue of sectorial priorities was complex, involving such issues as a weakening of Stalin's personal authority, changing distribution of power among Soviet administrative agencies, and economic problems such as materials allocation.[5] Moreover, the issue of industrial priorities did not disappear with Stalin's death. Prior to Nikita Khrushchev's final ascendancy to power in the mid-1950s, he would vie for power with Georgi Malenkov, a major issue being the appropriate roles for the light and heavy industrial sectors in the Soviet economy.

The postwar transition of the Soviet economy was, in a number of respects, different from that experienced in other countries. The impact of shortages of labor, destruction of capital, and the general disruption of economic activity continued to be felt long after the cessation of hostilities. The wartime economic system that had been successful in winning the war was gradually dismantled. The Communist Party was once again established as an overseer of economic activity, budget allocations on both the income and expenditure side changed, and the labor force was gradually shifted back to civilian employment.

The transition was not easy, nor did it take place in an unchanged economy. It was a time of rising consumer expectations, a sense of uncertainty as to whether Stalin would return to the policies of the 1930s. Joseph Stalin, who would be discredited for his draconian measures of the 1930s, died in March 1953. His last major program was the 1948 Stalin program for the transformation of nature. These programs reflected the Stalinist thinking of the 1930s; they were grandiose projects calling for major alterations to the Soviet countryside in the form of irrigation projects, shelter belts, and the like. While they were criticized in the subsequent Khrushchev era, substantial portions of these programs were, nevertheless, carried out in a less grandiose framework. For example, the expansion of irrigated farmlands remains as an important ingredient of Soviet agricultural policy to the present day. Moreover, the major expansion of sown area, ultimately to come to an end in the 1960s would nevertheless be a key part of the Khrushchev program.

THE KHRUSHCHEV YEARS

Nikita Khrushchev rose to power in the early and mid-1950s and was ousted in October 1964, being labeled a "hare-brained schemer" in an era of "subjectivism." However history may judge the Khrushchev years, many features make it distinctive.

From the standpoint of economic performance, the 1950s were years of rapid growth, judged by international standards. In fact, Soviet rates of economic growth would never be as good again. The 1950s were a "golden era" for Soviet economic performance. However, a close look at the record (see Table 6.2) indicates that the early years were very good years, the latter years markedly less so. Many have argued, that Khrushchev's downfall in 1964 was at least in part based on declining economic growth.

At the peak of Soviet economic performance (the late 1950s), a confident

Table 6.2   AGGREGATE ECONOMIC PERFORMANCE: THE KHRUSHCHEV YEARS

	Average annual growth		
	1951–1955	1956–1960	1961–1965
Gross national product	5.5	5.9	5.0
Industry	10.2	8.3	6.6
Agriculture	3.5	4.2	2.8
Services	1.9	3.5	4.4
Consumption	4.9	5.7	3.7
Investment	12.4	10.5	7.6

Source: U.S. Congress, Joint Economic Committee, *USSR: Measures of Economic Growth and Development, 1950–80* (Washington, D.C.: U.S. Government Printing Office, 1982).

Khrushchev boasted that the Soviet Union would overtake the United States well before the turn of the century. The 1950s were definitely a heady period for the Soviet Union.[6]

Khrushchev left his mark on the Soviet Union in several ways. First, he began the de-Stalinization process. Khrushchev denounced Stalin's "personality cult" in a secret speech to the twentieth party congress in 1956. Although complete de-Stalinization has yet to be achieved, Khrushchev initiated the first step of this process. Second, Khrushchev began the reform process. He allowed open discussion of the defects of the Soviet economic system, and he permitted a limited amount of tinkering with the Soviet economic system. It was Khrushchev's penchant for reform and experimentation that contributed to his downfall. Many of his reform ideas were ill prepared and ill conceived. Alarmed party colleagues worried that eventually his hare-brained schemes would lead to economic disaster. Third, the Khrushchev years saw a rise in Soviet living standards and real wages after two decades of stagnation or decline.

In the agricultural sphere, Khrushchev rose to power as an outspoken critic of Soviet agricultural performance at the Twentieth Congress of the Communist Party in 1953.[7] As a self-proclaimed agricultural specialist, Khrushchev would stake his career, in part, on his ability to solve the Soviet Union's agricultural problems. Khrushchev's agricultural policies can be marked as campaigns, organizational changes, and economic adjustments.

Agricultural Campaigns

Khrushchev's most famous agricultural campaign was the virgin lands campaign.[8] Begun in 1954, the goal was initially quite modest, namely, to reclaim 13 million hectares (1 hectare is 2.47 acres) of land by 1955 in Siberia and Kazakhstan, using state farms as the mode of organization. As we shall see later, state farms are those farms owned and operated directly by the state, using state employees paid a guaranteed wage. However, by 1960, 42 million hectares, representing some 20 percent of all sown area in that year, had been seeded.[9] The vision was grandiose, but the results were less so. Although these new lands received substantial capital investment, the marginal soil and the variable climate resulted in modest yields and a fluctuating (and gradually declining) output. However, the program did contribute roughly 25 million tons of grain annually between 1958 and 1963, though performance in the early years of the program was generally better than in the later years.[10] It is interesting to note that this program, generally attributed to Khrushchev, was in fact, an acceleration of a long-term trend. In part, it continued the eastward shift of agricultural activity begun much earlier and, in addition, replacement of sown area lost during the war years.[11] It was also representative of the extensive strategy of agricultural development that would persist through the 1950s into the 1960s.

A second major program initiated by Khrushchev was the corn program. Begun in 1955, it was intended to imitate practice in the United States, where corn has been a major source of animal fodder. This program also expanded rapidly. In 1954, 4.3 million hectares were sown to corn, while corn sowings would reach 37 million hectares by 1962.[12] As a portion of total sown area, the importance of corn increased from just under 10 percent in 1955 to over 17 percent in 1962. Corn has become an important element in Soviet fodder supplies, although Khrushchev's initial vision was overly grandiose and, moreover, neglected important differences between the U.S. and the Soviet cases, namely, U.S. development of hybrids and the fact that climatic conditions in the USSR were ill suited to the production of corn.

Finally, Khrushchev's "plow up" campaign, begun in 1961, was designed to eliminate or sharply reduce the grassland system of crop rotation by drastically cutting the land area devoted to fallow. Undoubtedly, such a policy would have had beneficial short-run effects on production but with serious long-term consequences as soil nutrients were gradually used without adequate replacement.

These programs did alter the nature of Soviet agriculture and became the focus of controversy. Undoubtedly, they were overly grandiose in conception and, in some cases, lacked a sound scientific basis, not to mention readily available complementary inputs. On the other hand, they did represent a strategy of long-term standing, namely, an extensive strategy of development or the expansion of output by the expansion of inputs, a reasonable approach given the prevailing Soviet stage of economic development. If intensification would come later, these programs did, in a sense, help to buy time until agricultural modernization could become a major focus of Soviet policy in the 1960s and thereafter.

Organizational Changes in Agriculture

While the flamboyance of the campaigns caught the spotlight, Khrushchev's far-reaching organizational changes were no less important.[13] One change that would continue (though at a much reduced pace) in the post-Khrushchev era was the amalgamation of collective farms and the conversion of a number of collective farms to state farms. For example, between 1940 and 1969, the number of collective farms declined from 236,900 to 34,700, while the sown area per farm increased from approximately 500 hectares to 2,800 hectares.[14] The pace of amalgamation varied, as did the regional impact. Nevertheless, the pattern was similar: several collectives would be combined to form a new larger collective farm, with the original collective farms becoming brigades in the new larger units. The pursuit of scale economies was a major force motivating these amalgamations.

In addition to the changing organizational structure of the typical *kolkhoz*, also other important changes were introduced. Khrushchev placed great emphasis on improvement of the quality of farm management personnel. Along with this emphasis on greater quality was a tendency to enhance the decision-making power within the farm, especially at the brigade level, and to use new tools, especially accounting. The brigade grew in size over these years. Moreover, the abolition of the machine tractor stations in 1958 and the placement of agricultural specialists directly on the farms improved the technical input available to collective farms to some degree.[15] Although it is difficult to characterize the extent to which these changes actually decentralized decision making, they must have moved in this general direction. An effort was made to begin targeting output (letting local managers decide details) rather than have central planners involved in every detail of land use, sowing, harvesting, and the like. There was also an effort to pay more attention to serious long-term planning—all themes that would surface again in the post-Khrushchev years.

Economic Adjustments in Agriculture

Khrushchev undertook major economic adjustments within Soviet agriculture. Improved collective farm management became a major focus. For example, cost-accounting methods were introduced on a major scale in an effort to improve farm decision making. The discovery that, in many cases, procurement prices did not cover production costs led to substantial increases in farm prices. At the same time, peasant rewards were changed. Historically, rewards to collective farmers had generally been paid in kind and on a very uncertain schedule. Increasingly, these rewards came to be paid at least partially in money form and on a more regular and frequent basis. During the decade after 1953, peasant incomes increased significantly. Although industrial incomes were also increasing, they rose at a much slower pace, which substantially reduced the rural/urban difference.[16] This policy with regard to incomes was part of a more general strategy of making rural life more attractive and to stem the rapid flow of the labor force (especially the young labor force) out of rural areas and strengthen rural production incentives.

Khrushchev also acted to increase agricultural inputs, such as chemical fertilizers. The chemical industry received major attention. Prior to the 1950s, the Soviet chemical industry was neglected, especially its ability to bring much-needed chemical fertilizers to agriculture. The growth of output of chemicals and petrochemicals increased from an average annual rate of 9.8 percent in 1951 to a high of 14.9 percent in 1955.[17] Investment in chemicals and petrochemicals increased at an average annual rate of 18.3 percent between 1951 and 1960, compared to an overall annual average investment increase of 11.7 percent for the same period.[18] This priority would be relaxed in the 1960s.

The output of mineral fertilizers increased from 5.5 million tons in 1950 to 13.8 million tons in 1960 and 31 million tons in 1965.

Khrushchev's agricultural policies represented a clear reversal of the Stalinist policy of "uneven exchange" between the countryside and the city. During the 1930s, agriculture was viewed as a source of resources to be extracted and transferred into industry. Agricultural living standards, accordingly, were allowed to decline relative to those of the city population. Khrushchev's farm policies recognized that the deprivation of farmers via low state procurement prices depressed output and marketings. Khrushchev reinjected economic incentives into agriculture—a policy that was continued by his successors.

Organizational Change: The Sovnarkhoz Reform

Although Khrushchev became closely associated with reform of agriculture, he experimented with organizational change of the planning system. Much of this change was motivated by a desire to improve the planning of Soviet industry. The first major planning reform was Khrushchev's Sovnarkhoz Reform of 1957. The Sovnarkhoz Reform, subsequently abolished by Brezhnev in 1965, was an attempt to change Soviet planning from a ministerial to a regional basis.[19] Khrushchev argued that the industrial ministries had created planning problems: empire building within ministries, lack of attention to regional coordination, and bureaucratic delays, especially in the material technical supply system. Khrushchev sought to correct these deficiencies by revamping the planning system along regional lines. Accordingly, in 1957, the ministries were abolished (except the ministries supervising the nuclear sector and electricity) and a system of 105 *sovnarkhozy* (regional economic councils) was introduced. Enterprises were subordinated to a regional council rather than a ministry.

After Khrushchev's ouster, the *Sovnarkhozy* were replaced by the former ministries. While the ministries had been blamed for empire building and bureaucratic inefficiencies, the regional economic councils, *Sovnarkhozy*, were criticized for favoring regional interests, for "localism." Khrushchev's *Sovnarkhozy* experiment and its abandonment by his successors reflected a long-standing conflict in the Soviet system of planning. With a ministerial system, economic activities that transcended ministry boundaries proved difficult to coordinate. Ministries preferred to look after the affairs of enterprises falling within the ministry boundary; "foreign" enterprises outside the ministry tended to be ignored. The parochial tendencies of ministries caused Khrushchev to experiment with territorial planning organizations—the *Sovnarkhozy*. Yet parochial tendencies plagued regional planning organizations, which tended to give the interests of the territory top priority. Obtaining supplies from enterprises in other regions had proved just as difficult as obtaining supplies from enterprises of another ministry.

Economic Reform Under Khrushchev

The Stalinist system of planning and resource allocation, put in place in the 1930s, had weaknesses that were apparent by the early 1930s. The highly centralized system required that higher bodies exercise "petty tutelage" (*opeka*) over productive enterprises. This petty tutelage (exercised primarily by the ministries) was reflected in a series of centralized targets that the enterprises were expected to fulfill. Faced with a large number of targets sent down by authorities who did not know the local circumstances of the enterprise, enterprise managers found that they could satisfy their superiors by engaging in actions that were actually contrary to their superiors' interest (and contrary to the interests of society). Managers found it in their interest to produce low-quality goods, to shun innovation, and to combine resources in an inefficient manner. Moreover, the Stalinist system judged enterprises primarily in terms of quantity targets (such as tons of steel produced), not in terms of efficiency of resource use or profitability.

Chapters 7 and 8 discuss how resources are allocated in the Soviet Union; they demonstrate why Soviet enterprises have been encouraged by the system to engage in dysfunctional behavior. For now, it is sufficient to note that Khrushchev was the first Soviet leader to allow open discussion of the deficiencies of the Stalinist system of resource allocation. In 1962, a paper by the then-obscure Kharkov economist, Evsei Liberman, entitled "The Plan, Profits, and Bonuses," was published in *Pravda*. Its publication signaled an official sanctioning of reform discussion by Khrushchev and the party leadership.[20]

Although a lively discussion of reform alternatives ensued between 1962 and Khrushchev's ouster in 1964, very little in the way of real reform occurred during Khrushchev's tenure in office. The official government reform, the response to the reform discussion initiated under Khrushchev, was announced in September 1965, about one year after Khrushchev's fall from power. The 1962–1964 reform discussion, however, set the agenda for reform discussion in the Soviet Union and established its basic outlines. It was established that economic reform should take place within a planned-economy system. The reform should reduce the amount of petty tutelage from above and should allow more local decision making. The individual actors in the economy should respond to economic incentives, such as profits and bonuses.

Living Standards

Georgi Malenkov, Khrushchev's rival for power after Stalin's death, had, in the earlier 1950s, emphasized the need to expand consumer goods production, a move generally seen as an attempt to enhance his political fortunes. In spite of Khrushchev's reassertion of the primacy of heavy industry, he nevertheless did take steps to improve the position of the consumer in Soviet society. In addition to reducing compulsory bond purchases and lowering some consumer goods prices, he increased the production of consumer durables and introduced limited credit provisions to make these products more readily available. To the extent that these moves represented a concession to the consumer, they were generally thought to have arisen out of a debate about consumer goods in the early 1950s.

In the period between 1951 and 1955, per capita consumption grew at an average annual rate of 4.5 percent, while for the period 1956–1960, it grew at 4.0 percent. For these same periods, consumer durable output grew at rates of 17.7 and 10.4 percent, respectively.[21] These were exceptionally rapid rates, especially after the deprivation of the 1930s and 1940s.

Khrushchev emphasized the expansion of services, for example, educational facilities and medical services, though not without controversy. For example, in an attempt to emphasize technical education, compulsory schooling was reduced from ten years to eight years, a move that would later be reversed.[22]

Khrushchev devoted considerable attention to housing, a much neglected sector of the Soviet economy. The average annual growth rate of housing increase steadily from a low of 2.6 percent in 1951 to a high of 5.9 percent in 1959.[23] Indeed, in retrospect, the 1950s would turn out to be a golden age for housing construction, the only period in the entire postwar era in which the growth of housing construction in Soviet urban areas would exceed the growth of urban population demanding this housing. For the period 1951–1960, there was an average annual increase of fixed investment in the construction materials sector of the Soviet economy of 22.8 percent. The comparable figure for the period 1961–1965 was –2.8 percent.

Foreign Trade

Soviet foreign trade reemerged in the 1950s.[24] Foreign trade will be discussed in depth in Chapter 10. After the formation of the Council for Mutual Economic Assistance (CMEA, or COMECON) in 1949, the Soviet Union promoted increasing integration with Eastern Europe and increasing participation in world markets in the 1950s. Although such efforts were limited in these years, the expansion of Soviet foreign trade and the various problems that this effort would encounter were important issues throughout the postwar period.[25]

The volume of Soviet foreign trade (imports plus exports) increased significantly during the Khrushchev years. Although the bulk of Soviet foreign trade during these years was with other socialist countries, the growth of Soviet trade with capitalist countries was more rapid than that with socialist countries. Thus, Soviet trade with capitalist countries accounted for a growing portion of total Soviet trade. Moreover, a basic pattern persisted: soviet exports of raw materials in return for imports of machinery and equipment. Although the events of the early 1960s (the U-2 incident and the Cuban missile crisis) chilled trade relations between the Soviet Union and the United States, the Soviet need for grain would soon be a new factor in expanding East-West trade.

THE KHRUSHCHEV YEARS: AN ASSESSMENT

Considering the changes outlined above, how might we assess the Khrushchev years? The Khrushchev record had two rather distinct phases.[26] In the first phase, from the mid- through the late 1950s, Khrushchev could ride a crest of generally expanding economic performance. However, in the second phase, the late 1950s and early 1960s, there was a slackening of economic growth.

The aggregate evidence presented in Table 6.2 support the conclusion of slackening performance in the later years. To what extent these reverses were associated specifically with policies implemented by Khrushchev or with other influences outside his immediate control (for example, climatic reverses affecting agriculture) is difficult to say. Whatever the case, Khrushchev would bear the burden of failure.

For example, the newly cultivated virgin lands came to be a major contributor to Soviet total grain output, but with sharp year-to-year fluctuations. In 1956, for example, fully 68 percent of state grain purchases would come from these lands, while by 1963 this figure would drop to 36.4 percent.[27] While the contribution of this program of new cultivation continued to expand, yields and output were variable, and a good year in 1964 was too late to save Khrushchev.

Khrushchev's reorganization of industry was the subject of attention and controversy. The problems of the newly created *Sovnarkhozy* were in large part similar to those of the ministries they had replaced. Rather than pursue fundamental changes suggested in 1962 by Evsei Liberman, Khrushchev pursued further organizational changes.[28] In 1961, some *Sovnarkhozy* were combined with coordination councils being set up to administer the economy in 17 large economic regions.[29] This was yet another attempt to discover the optimum set of organizational arrangements. In addition, Khrushchev split the Communist Party into an agricultural and an industrial branch and in 1963 established yet another superagency for economic coordination, the Supreme Council of the National Economy. Khrushchev continued to voice criticism of arrangements in agriculture and arrangements in industry. Doubtlessly, he would have continued to shuffle the arrangements had he not been removed in 1964. Whether Khrushchev would have gone beyond organizational shuffling to meaningful reform will never be known.

THE BREZHNEV YEARS

Leonid Brezhnev came to power after Khrushchev's ouster in October 1964. He remained as general secretary of the Communist Party until his death in November 1982. Brezhnev was succeeded by the ailing Yuri Andropov, the former head of the KGB, who died in February 1984. Konstantin Chernenko succeeded Andropov, only to die in March 1985 after only 13 months in office. The 54-year-old Mikhail Gorbachev was chosen to replace Chernenko in March 1985. Although Brezhnev died in 1982, it is appropriate to call the entire period from 1964 to 1985 the Brezhnev era. By the time of Brezhnev's death, the Soviet Union had established a form of collective leadership, which became increasingly evident as the Communist Party continued to conduct its business despite the obvious incapacitation of three general secretaries. The Andropov and Chernenko years were far too short to alter the basic policies and strategies put in place during Brezhnev's 18-year tenure.

Declining Economic Performance

The most important feature of the Brezhnev era was the declining economic performance of the Soviet Union. Table 6.3 compares economic growth during the Khrushchev years (1955–1965) with those of the Brezhnev era and early Gorbachev years (1966–1987). The pattern of decline is obvious. From and an-

Table 6.3   AGGREGATE ECONOMIC PERFORMANCE: 1955–1965 versus 1966–1987

	Average annual growth					
	1955–1965	1966–1970	1970–1975	1976–1980	1981–1983	1984–1987
Gross national product	5.4	5.2	3.7	2.7	2.3	1.6
Industry	7.5	6.3	5.9	3.4	1.5	2.1
Agriculture	3.5	3.5	–2.3	0.3	4.2	0.8
Services	4.0	4.2	3.4	2.8	2.1	
Consumption	4.7	5.3	3.6	2.6	1.7	2.4
Investment	9.1	6.0	5.4	4.3	4.2	3.0

Source: U.S. Congress, Joint Economic Committee, *USSR: Measures of Economic Growth and Development, 1950–80* (Washington D.C.: U.S. Government Printing Office, 1982); *Handbook of Economic Statistics* (Washington, D.C.: Directorate of Intelligence, 1983 and 1988 editions).

nual GNP growth rate of over 5 percent, GNP growth dropped close to 2 percent during the 1980s. Industrial growth declined from near 8 percent in the 1950s to mid-1960s to around 2 percent in the 1980s. The agricultural growth rate showed extreme volatility, even declining at over 2 percent per year from the beginning to the middle of the 1970s. Both investment and consumption growth rates faltered, with investment falling from 9 percent annual growth to 3–4 percent in the 1980s.

The decline in growth rates was due to deteriorating productivity growth after 1970. From 1970 to 1987, productivity growth was actually negative in most years. Output per unit of labor and capital input was actually declining; for the period 1970–1987 as a whole, output per unit of input declined at a rate of more than one percent per year.

Economic Reform During the Brezhnev Years

Khrushchev initiated the reform discussion by encouraging open discussion of change in the Soviet economic system between 1962 and his ouster in 1964. It was the task of the Brezhnev team to decide the issue of economic reform. In September 1965, the Soviet leadership announced the official government reform, often called the Kosygin Reform after Alexei Kosygin, Brezhnev's chief economic official.[30]

Kosygin announced a general reform to be gradually implemented over the next five years. In light of the high expectations for significant change raised by the debates of the preceding years, the official response must have been disappointing to the proponents of significant reform. However, the conservatism and caution of the party leadership should have been anticipated, given the power of the forces in support of the status quo.

The basic thrust of the 1965 reform was a reduction in the number of enterprise targets to be set from above and, most important, replacement of gross output by "realized output" (sales) as the primary indicator of success for an enterprise. In addition, the number of indicators for labor planning—previously four—was to be reduced to a single indicator: the magnitude of the wage fund. An enterprise manager was now to face the eight targets established within the central plan, compared to the earlier system of 20 to 30 targets. Enterprises were to be allowed to keep more of their profits to be used for incentive payments and to finance investment. One-fifth of investment was to be determined by the enterprises themselves.

The 1965 reform recentralized the Soviet economic bureaucracy. Power was returned to the ministries, and the regional economic councils (the *Sovnarkhozy*) created by Khrushchev in 1957 were abolished. Decision-making authority shifted from regional authorities to national authorities. The 1965 reforms called for a variety of organizational changes in the economic management and planning system. Key functions were centralized in three powerful new state committees: the State Committee for Material-Technical Supply (*Gossnab*), the State Committee for Prices (*Gostsen*), and the State Committee for Science and Technology (*Gostekhnika*). Industrial enterprises were to be combined into large associations, called "production associations," and research enterprises and institutes were to be grouped into "science-production associations." The rationale given for these associations was that they would yield economies of scale, reduce the bureaucracy, and assist in the planning process. *Gossnab* was given the primary responsibility for allocating producer goods, and the ministerial supply organizations that had dominated the rationing of funded goods were largely to disappear. *Gossnab* was to apply itself to the creation of a wholesale trade system based on direct contracting arrangements among suppliers and buyers.

Movement Away from Reform

The 1965 reform is a valuable case study of the barriers that stand in the way of Soviet economic reform. It reveals those areas of the Soviet economic system most resistant to change. Initially, two phases of implementation of the reform were anticipated. The first, or "extensive," phase was to be the phased conversion of nonagricultural enterprises to the new system. The second, or "intensive," phase, scheduled to begin in 1970, would be the one in which the true potential of the reform would be realized. In terms of the original format, all industrial enterprises were to be converted to the new system by the end of 1968 and the remainder of the economy by the end of 1970. The basic thrust of the 1965 reform program was a reduction in the tutelage of the enterprise manager by higher planning organs. The idea was to create a system whereby managers would be encouraged to respond spontaneously to various economic "levers"—profits, bonuses, increased authority over investment, and so on—so as to make the Soviet enterprise more efficient and release "hidden reserves." The number of plan targets was to be reduced, reliance was to be placed on better success indicators such as sales and profitability, and managers and workers were to become materially interested in the outcome of enterprise performance by the tying of bonus funds to enterprise activity.

Between 1965 and 1971, there was evidence of greater managerial spontaneity in response to economic levers. As managers began to exercise their new-found authority, planners and bureaucrats began to react against "undesirable" spontaneous enterprise actions and to press for amendments to the 1965 rules. During the very period when the reform was scheduled to move into its "intensive" phase, amendments and modifications were introduced that significantly altered the original reform. The particular shortcomings these amendments sought to correct were the unduly large shares of new bonus funds received by managerial personnel, the lack of attention to labor productivity and quality improvement, the unwillingness of managers to request difficult production targets or to economize costs—many of the very shortcomings that the 1965 reform had sought to correct.

Between June 1971 and January 1978, changes were introduced that significantly modified the spirit of the reform. First, rigid regulations governing the size of enterprise incentive funds replaced the original, more flexible system. The ministry was to determine the size of enterprise incentive funds by fixing planned incentive fund targets. Incentive funds were also to depend on three additional targets: the plan for key products in physical units, the plan for consumer goods, and the plans for changes in product quality and new products. Furthermore, the size of the incentive fund was tied to the difficulty of the enterprise plan. These restrictions restored most authority to the ministries. The ministry again had the authority to determine the conditions under which incentive funds would be accumulated and disbursed. Enterprises could be punished by fund reductions for failing to meet specific targets set by the ministries.

The number of enterprise targets was expanded. New targets were reinstated after 1970: labor productivity, gross output, consumer goods assignments in heavy industry, quality targets, material and fuel economy targets, delivery obligations, new products, and the size of basic incentive funds.

Many of the administrative changes proposed by the 1965 reform were thwarted. During the early years of the reform, enterprises did not amalgamate into productive associations; but after a party-government decree in April 1973, the formation of production associations proceeded at a rapid pace. In the early 1980s, production associations accounted for some three-quarters of industrial output. The purposes of the production association were to gain the advantages of economies of scale in management through the amalgamation of firms involved in similar lines of business and to economize on administrative personnel. In practice, the formation of industrial associations meant little more than "changing the names on doors" in Moscow; supervisory power continued to remain in the hands of the chief administrations of the ministries, and there was a 60 percent expansion in the bureaucracy between 1966 and 1977. The ministries continued to be the centers of economic power, allocating materials and equipment, dictating the incentive systems of enterprises and industrial associations, and controlling investment.

Strengthening Central Planning

By the early 1970s, there was little doubt that the main features of the 1965 reform had been abandoned or never implemented. It had not succeeded in reducing the amount of tutelage from above, and the decision-making freedom of enterprise managers had not increased. With the reform abandoned and economic growth continuing to decline (see Table 6.3), the Brezhnev team sought to improve economic performance through other means. From the mid-1970s to Brezhnev's death in 1982, scarcely a year would pass without the announcement of some "reform" or "experiment" that would solve the nation's economic problems.

It is not worthwhile to review all these reforms or experiments. Some will be mentioned in Chapters 7 and 8. Their common ground appears to have been the desire to make centralized planning work better. Rather than seeking to reduce the role of planning from above, the efforts of the last decade of the Brezhnev era were directed toward improving Soviet planning. Considerable emphasis was placed on devising "scientific" input norms, computerized planning systems, and qualitative indicators. The culmination of this effort was the July 1979 decree, clumsily entitled "On Improving Planning and Strengthening the Economic Mechanism's Influence on Raising the Effectiveness of Production and the Quality of Work."[31] The July 1979 program specified a number of ways to make the planning system more effective: systems for gathering better information on enterprise capacity were to be created; scientific norms were to replace directive indicators; enterprises were to be encouraged to take on more difficult "counterplans"; greater emphasis was to be placed on long-term plans; and the material supply system was to be improved through the greater use of contracting between enterprises. New plan indicators of enterprise success were to be based more on net outputs than on gross outputs, and greater emphasis was to be placed on the quality of outputs.

The reforms and experiments of the late Brezhnev years did not change the Soviet resource allocation system in any material way. One observer assessed the net impact of the 1979 decree as follows: "Planning is more centralized, rigid, and detailed than ever; the scope for initiative of the producing units is more circumscribed; producer goods are more tightly rationed."[32]

Although the Brezhnev team sought to improve the Soviet planning system, the evidence points more toward declining performance of the planning system. Table 6.3 shows that growth rates continued to decline throughout the long Brezhnev tenure in office. The ambitiousness of Soviet economic plans also declined throughout this period. Table 6.4 shows that Soviet planners aimed for higher growth rates in the late 1960s and early 1970s than in the late 1970s and mid-1980s. However, as growth targets became less ambitious, plan fulfillment performance deteriorated. Whereas actual growth was three-quarters of planned growth in the second half of the 1960s, it fell to less than 50 percent of planned growth in the mid-1970s and early 1980s.

Table 6.4   PLAN FULFILLMENT: PLANNED VERSUS ACTUAL GROWTH

	Average annual growth			
	1966–1970	1971–1975	1976–1980	1981–1985
Gross national product				
Plan	6.5–7.0	5.8	5.0	4.0
Actual	5.0	3.1	2.2	1.8
Industry				
Plan	8.2	8.0	6.5	4.9
Actual	6.3	5.4	2.6	1.8
Agriculture				
Plan	5.5	3.7	5.0	5.0
Actual	3.7	–.6	0.8	2.1

Source: *Handbook of Economic Statistics 1988,* CPAS 88-10001 (September 1988), 62.

THE BREZHNEV YEARS: AN ASSESSMENT

General Secretary Gorbachev inherited a difficult legacy from his predecessors. Growth of output and productivity were declining in a monotonic fashion, yet there was no serious effort being undertaken to reverse this alarming trend. The one serious reform effort had been abandoned, and a series of innocuous partial reforms and experiments were being offered as palliatives.

Why did the Brezhnev team not mount a serious reform program in light of the Soviet Union's deteriorating economic condition? Brezhnev's critics maintain that he was a captive of status quo forces. He led a corrupt and listless regime, drawn down by a growing bureaucracy that would have resisted meaningful reform. A more benevolent interpretation would be that economic reform is extremely difficult to impose on the Soviet bureaucracy. Significant reform cannot be carried through without an imposing mandate and without a general recognition that significant reform cannot be avoided. Brezhnev's choice was a "muddling through" approach—to hope that the prevailing system would generate sufficiently good performance to allow the Soviet Union to meet its highest-priority goals.

THE GORBACHEV YEARS

When Mikhail Gorbachev assumed power in March 1985, he was faced with a deteriorating economy and no ongoing reform to stem this decline. He quickly moved to consolidate his personal power and to devise a reform program that would halt the economy's precipitous slide. Gorbachev's economic reform program—called perestroika, or restructuring—will be discussed in detail in Chapter 14. For now, we can only deal with its basic outlines.

Features of Perestroika[33]

Many features of perestroika date to the reforms of the 1960s and are simply carryovers from earlier periods. Perestroika contains surprisingly few truly new ideas; many of perestroika's ideas have been recycled from the 1960s: greater emphasis on economic accounting, wholesale markets, profit incentives, and lesser intervention by planners. The recycled notions of the 1960s, the attention to sociological and political factors, and the seriousness of intent of the Soviet leadership, however, combine to make perestroika a truly interesting reform program. In presenting perestroika, Gorbachev has talked of the need for "radical" reform to distinguish perestroika from the now-defunct reforms and experiments of his predecessors.

The basic idea of perestroika is the same as that of the Kosygin Reform of 1965: more initiative should be exercised at the enterprise level. The amount of tutelage (*opeka*) exercised by state committees and ministries over enterprises is to be reduced. Ministries, instead of overseeing the routine operations of enterprises, are to concern themselves with long-term planning and with investment and technology policy. *Gosplan* is to concern itself more with long-term planning (the Five Year Plan is to be the dominant operational plan). The number of compulsory targets is to be reduced, leaving more leeway for enterprises to select their own output mixes. A system of state orders (*goszakazy*) is to replace compulsory output targets (although the distinction between state orders and compulsory targets is unclear), and enterprises are expected to produce goods and services above and beyond state orders. Higher-quality outputs are to be ensured by a system of state inspectors (*gospriemka*), who answer to higher authorities rather than to enterprise management. To encourage enterprises to take on ambitious targets, enterprises are to be judged on the basis of long-run plans and normatives. Instead of being given a whole series of compulsory input targets, enterprises will have to remain within norms set by the planning apparatus. The freedom of enterprises to engage in deal making is to be increased. Enterprises can trade goods among themselves, although the use of middlemen is discouraged. Interenterprise contracts will come to play a more important role. Goods that are exchanged on a negotiated contractual basis will be exchanged at prices agreed to by the exchanging parties. Enterprises will conclude output and delivery contracts, and the enterprise delivery plan (*plan postavok*) will become one of the enterprise's prime success criteria. Enterprise efficiency is to be improved by allowing enterprises to retain profits for managerial and worker rewards and for capital accumulation. Both enterprises and ministries will be placed on full economic accounting (*pol'ny khozrashchet*), which means that enterprises must cover their costs to remain in business. The old system of automatic subsidies for enterprises making losses is to be replaced. In recognition of the long-standing role of unplanned material exchanges among enterprises, such exchanges are to be made legal, and more private economic activities are to be legalized, although strict restrictions on the use of hired labor remain in effect.

To gain public support for perestroika, Soviet society is to become more open (glasnost). Workers are to be given more rights within their enterprises, even playing a role in determining the enterprise director. Widespread political reforms are to be implemented to render the party more of a policy-making body than an operational body in economic affairs.

Workers will be allowed to form cooperatives, which operate largely outside the planning system. Work in cooperatives is to be in addition to work at one's primary job in the public sector, but retirement-age people can work full time in the cooperative.

In agriculture, families will be allowed to lease land from the state for long periods of time (perhaps as long as 50 years). Although agricultural land remains state property, long-term leases should vest farm families with a sense of property rights.

Implementation of Perestroika

Soviet reformers caution that the transformation of the Soviet economic system will not take place overnight. The reform will be introduced in stages, and the restructuring process may not be complete until the first decade of the twenty-first century. The preparation stage was scheduled to be the period 1985–1987; the transition stage, the period 1988–1990; and the benefits from perestroika will be felt only after 1991. The most important perestroika decree to date, the Law of State Enterprise, was announced in February, 1987.[34] The Law of State Enterprise sets out the rights and obligations of state enterprises under the new system. A new ministry law remains to be drafted. Until then, it is presumed that ministries will continue to act according to established ministry laws.

Not all enterprises will be converted immediately to the new system. Gorbachev's reformers have called for extensive price reforms to ensure that enterprises will make their own decisions on the basis of "rational" prices. Despite its key importance to the success of perestroika, significant price reform is not expected until the early 1990s.

Opposition to Perestroika

Deciphering high-level maneuvering within the Politburo has always been difficult for Western observers. The late 1980s have seen a series of political maneuvers on the part of Gorbachev, which have been interpreted as moves to ensure political support for perestroika. High party officials who appear to be resistant to perestroika (or at least in favor of slowing down its pace) have been shuffled to less sensitive positions. Campaigns against Stalinism, ridicule of the stagnationist and corrupt Brezhnev regime, and rehabilitation of figures such as

Bukharin appear to be orchestrated attempts to solidify support for perestroika.

The most serious threat to perestroika may be the opposition of the entrenched bureaucracy. Perestroika calls for radical reductions in the size of the bureaucracy and for a lessening of bureaucratic authority. Yet it is the bureaucracy that must carry through perestroika, and previous reform efforts had shown that foot-dragging by the bureaucracy can negate economic reform.

The bureaucracy is not the only threat to perestroika. If the new enterprise law is strictly observed, subsidies will largely disappear from the scene. Failing enterprises will go under and workers will be unemployed. Soviet jobs will, for the first time, be insecure. Moreover, the disappearance of subsidies would mean substantial increases in consumer prices, especially of food. In the past, increases in basic consumer goods have met with resistance from the Soviet population.

The Soviet regime must also demonstrate that it can live with glasnost (openness). Various groups have used the increased openness of Soviet society to call for political actions (independence for non-Russian republics, opposition political parties, etc.) that clearly are not acceptable to the Soviet leadership. One possible reaction of the leadership would be to conclude that the reform has gone too far and to do away with both glasnost and perestroika in one action.

THE FUTURE

Gorbachev's perestroika program, if successful, has the potential of changing the face of the twenty-first century. There are enormous uncertainties associated with its implementation. There are no blueprints. The political risks are high. The proper staging of perestroika is complex. Perestroika will be closely watched, and, unlike many other phenomena of interest to academics, the course of perestroika will be played out in the world's press. In following perestroika, caution must be exercised. There has always been a gap between reform intent and reality. What is announced, even by the highest officials of the land, will not necessarily be implemented. The Western world desires real change of Soviet society and is often too optimistic in its assessment of change.

REFERENCES

1. For a discussion of the impact of the war in rural areas, see A. Nove, "Soviet Peasantry in World War II," in S.J. Linz, ed., *The Impact of World War II on the Soviet Union* (Totowa, N.J.: Rowman & Allanheld, 1985), pp. 79–92.
2. F. A. Durgin, Jr., "The Relationship of the Death of Stalin to the Economic Changes of the Post-Stalin Era," in R. C. Stuart, ed., *The Soviet Rural Economy* (Totowa, N.J.: Rowman & Allanheld, 1984), pp. 119–123.
3. R. Moorsteen and R. P. Powell, *The Soviet Capital Stock, 1928–1962* (Homewood, Ill.: Irwin, 1966), p. 615.

4. It is important to note two major issues relating to plan fulfillment in this era. First, the plans were changed so frequently that assessment of fulfillment is a difficult task, not to mention the problem of unrealistic plans developed to serve as an incentive for greater achievement. Second, Soviet official series on plan fulfillment and economic achievement during this period are based on 1926 prices. For a host of reasons, these prices are suspect as conveyors of relative scarcities of the 1940s. It is not surprising, therefore, that Western estimates of achievement during this period are lower, in some cases significantly lower, than official Soviet series. For a detailed discussion of these issues and citation of the various estimates, see E. Zaleski, *Stalinist Planning for Economic Growth, 1933–1952* (Chapel Hill: University of North Carolina Press, 1980), pp. 396–402.

5. For a detailed discussion of policy-making in the immediate postwar era, see T. Dunmore, *The Stalinist Command Economy* (London and Basingstoke: Macmillan, 1980).

6. For a useful survey of this period, see H. Schwartz, *The Soviet Economy Since Stalin* (Philadelphia: Lippincott, 1965).

7. There is a considerable amount of literature pertaining to Khrushchev and Soviet agriculture. For Khrushchev's own views, see N. S. Khrushchev, *Stroitel'stvo kommunizma v SSSR i razvitie sel'skogo khoziaistva* [The construction of communism in the USSR and the development of agriculture] (Moscow: Gospolitizdat, 1962), 8 vols. For a useful survey of this period, see J. F. Karcz, "Khrushchev's Agricultural Policies," in M. Bornstein and D. Fusfeld, eds., *The Soviet Economy: A Book of Readings*, 3rd ed. (Homewood, Ill.: Irwin, 1970), pp. 223–259. For a discussion of agricultural policy-making, see S. I. Ploss, *Conflict and Decision-Making in Soviet Russia: A Case Study of Agricultural Policy, 1953–1963* (Princeton, N.J.: Princeton University Press, 1965); and W. G. Hahn, *The Politics of Soviet Agriculture, 1960–1970* (Baltimore: Johns Hopkins Press, 1973). For a survey of agricultural campaigns, see J. W. Willett, "The Recent Record in Agricultural Production," in U.S. Congress, Joint Economic Committee, *Dimensions of Soviet Economic Power* (Washington, D.C.: U.S. Government Printing Office, 1962), pp. 91–113. For a discussion of organizational changes, see R. C. Stuart, *The Collective Farm in Soviet Agriculture* (Lexington, Mass.: Heath, 1972). For a discussion of monetary incentives, see F. A. Durgin, Jr., "Monetization and Policy in Soviet Agriculture Since 1952," *Soviet Studies*, vol. 15, no. 4 (April 1964), 381–407; and D. W. Bronson and C. B. Krueger, "The Revolution in Soviet Farm Household Income, 1952–1967," in J. R. Millar, ed., *The Soviet Rural Community* (Urbana: University of Illinois Press, 1971), pp. 214–258. The virgin lands campaign is discussed in detail in M. McCauley, *Khrushchev and the Development of Soviet Agriculture* (New York: Holmes & Meier, 1976).

8. McCauley, *Khrushchev and the Development of Soviet Agriculture*.

9. Ibid., pp. 79–83.

10. Ibid., Tables 4.5 and 4.6.

11. For a discussion of this strategy, see McCauley, *Khrushchev and the Development of Soviet Agriculture*.

12. J. Anderson, "A Historical-Geographical Perspective on Khrushchev's Corn Program," in J. F. Karcz, ed., *Soviet and East European Agriculture* (Berkeley and Los Angeles: University of California Press, 1967), Table 2. The data include corn for all uses.

13. For a discussion of organizational changes, see Stuart, *The Collective Farm*: and R.

D. Laird, "Khrushchev's Administrative Reforms in Agriculture: An Appraisal," in J. F. Karcz, ed., *Soviet and East European Agriculture*, pp. 29–56.

14. *Strana Sovetov za 50 let* [Country of the Soviets during 50 years] (Moscow: Statistika, 1967), p. 121; *Narodnoe Khoziaistvo SSSR v 1969 g* [The national economy of the USSR in 1969] (Moscow: Statistika, 1970), pp. 404 and 405.

15. For a detailed discussion of the evolution of the machine tractor stations, see R. F. Miller, *One Hundred Thousand Tractors* (Cambridge, Mass.: Harvard University Press, 1970).

16. For a discussion of rural/urban income differences during this period, see Bronson and Krueger, "The Revolution in Soviet Farm Household Income, 1952–1967."

17. U.S. Congress, Joint Economic Committee, *USSR: Measures of Economic Growth and Development, 1950–80* (Washington, D.C.: U.S. Government Printing Office, 1982), p. 193.

18. S. Butler, "The Soviet Capital Investment Program," in U.S. Congress, Joint Economic Committee, *Economic Performance and the Military Burden in the Soviet Union* (Washington, D.C.: U.S. Government Printing Office, 1970), p. 53.

19. For a discussion of the Sovnarkhoz Reform, see O. Hoeffding, "The Soviet Industrial Reorganization of 1957," *American Economic Review: Papers and Proceedings*, vol. 49, no. 2 (May 1959), 65–77.

20. Evsei Liberman's reform proposals had been made in the journal *Voprosy ekonomiki* [Problems of economics] as early as 1955. The original Liberman paper and the debate it generated are given in M. E. Sharpe, ed., *Planning, Profit and Incentives in the USSR*, vols. 1 and 2 (White Plains, N.Y.: International Arts and Sciences Press, 1966). For succinct statements of the Liberman proposal and its relation to a cost-profit calculus, see A. Zauberman, "Liberman's Rules of the Game for Soviet Industry," *Slavic Review*, vol. 22, no. 4 (December 1963), 734–744; G. R. Feiwel, *The Soviet Quest for Economic Efficiency* (New York: Praeger, 1972), chap. 5; Sharpe, *Planning, Profit and Incentives*, vols. 1–2.

21. U.S. Congress, Joint Economic Committee, *USSR: Measures of Economic Growth and Development, 1950–80*, pp. 193, 326.

22. This educational reform was complex, but generally the basic ten-year school was to be replaced by a basic eight-year school. After the completion of eight years of schooling, the student might take an additional three years of schooling as prerequisite to higher education or, as an alternative, might go directly to work or additional training of a technical nature. For a discussion of the reform and a comparison to prevailing U.S. patterns, see N. DeWitt, "Education and the Development of Human Resources: Soviet and American Effort," in U.S. Congress, Joint Economic Committee, *Dimensions of Soviet Economic Power* (Washington, D.C.: U.S. Government Printing Office, 1962), pp. 235–268.

23. U.S. Congress, Joint Economic Committee, *USSR: Measures of Economic Growth and Development, 1950–80*, p. 56.

24. For a general discussion, see F. D. Holzman, *International Trade Under Communism* (New York: Basic Books, 1976).

25. For a discussion of trade in the 1950s, see P. H. Thunberg, "The Soviet Union in the World Economy, " in U.S. Congress, Joint Economic Committee, *Dimensions of Soviet Economic Power*, pp. 409–438.

26. For a survey of the economic aspects of Khrushchev's downfall, see H. Schwartz, *The Soviet Economy*.

27. McCauley, *Khrushchev and the Development of Soviet Agriculture*, Table 4–9.

28. The original paper by Evsei Liberman can be found in M. E. Sharpe, ed., *Planning,*

Profit and Incentives in the USSR, vols. 1 and 2 (White Plains, N.Y.: International Arts and Sciences Press, 1966).

29. H. Schwartz, *The Soviet Economy Since Stalin* (Philadelphia: J. B. Lippincott; 1965).

30. Our discussion of the 1965 reform and its implementation is based on the following sources: F. I. Kushnirsky, *Soviet Economic Planning 1965–1980* (Boulder, Colo.: Westview Press, 1982); M. Kaser, "Kosygin, Liberman, and the Pace of Soviet Industrial Reform," in G. R. Feiwel, ed., *New Currents in Soviet-Type Economies: A Reader* (Scranton, Pa.: International Textbook, 1968); A. Kosygin, "On Improving Management of Industry, Perfecting Planning, and Enhancing Economic Incentives in Industrial Production," in Bornstein and Fusfeld, eds., *The Soviet Economy: A Book of Readings*, pp. 387–396; National Foreign Assessment Center, *Organization and Management in the Soviet Economy: The Ceaseless Search for Panaceas*, ER77-10769, Washington, D.C., December 1977; G. E. Schroeder, "Recent Developments in Soviet Planning and Managerial Incentives," in U.S. Congress, Joint Economic Committee, *Soviet Economic Prospects for the Seventies* (Washington, D.C.: U.S. Government Printing Office, 1973); G. E. Schroeder, "Post-Khrushchev Reforms and Public Financial Goals," in Z. M. Fallenbuchl, ed., *Economic Development in the Soviet Union and Eastern Europe* (New York: Praeger, 1976), pp. 348–367; National Foreign Assessment Center, *Organization and Management in the Soviet Economy*, pp. 1–22; A. C. Gorlin, "Industrial Reorganization: The Associations," in U.S. Congress, Joint Economic Committee, *Soviet Economy in a New Perspective* (Washington, D.C.: U.S. Government Printing Office, 1976); G. E. Schroeder, "The Soviet Economy on a Treadmill of 'Reforms,'" in U.S. Congress, Joint Economic Committee, *Soviet Economy in a Time of Change* (Washington, D.C.: U.S. Government Printing Office, 1979), vol. 1, pp. 312–340; E. Zaleski, *Planning Reforms in the Soviet Union, 1962–1966* (Chapel Hill: University of North Carolina Press, 1967); and M. E. Sharpe, ed., *Planning, Profit and Incentives in the USSR*, vols. 1 and 2 (White Plains, N.Y.: International Arts and Sciences Press, 1966).

31. This discussion is based on M. Bornstein, "Improving the Soviet Economic Mechanism," *Soviet Studies*, vol. 37, no. 1 (January 1985), 1–30; P. Hanson, "Success Indicators Revisited: The July 1979 Soviet Decree on Planning and Management," *Soviet Studies*, vol. 35, no. 1 (January 1983), 1–13; and N. Nimitz, "Reform and Technological Innovation in the 11th Five Year Plan," in S. Bialer and T. Gustafson, eds., *Russia at the Crossroads* (London: Allen & Unwin, 1982), chap. 7.

32. G. E. Schroeder, "Soviet Economic 'Reform' Decrees: More Steps on the Treadmill," in U.S. Congress, Joint Economic Committee, *Soviet Economy in the 1980s: Problems and Prospects*, part 1 (Washington, D.C.: U.S. Government Printing Office, 1982), p. 82.

33. This section is based on the following sources: D. Dyker, ed., *The Soviet Union Under Gorbachev* (London: Croom Helm, 1987); *USSR in a Time of Change* (Moscow: Progress Publishers, 1987); J. Berliner, "Organizational Restructuring of the Soviet Economy," Joint Economic Committee, *Gorbachev's Economic Plans*, vol. 1 (Washington, D.C.: U.S. Government Printing Office, 1987), pp. 70–83; J. P. Hardt and R. Kaufman, "Gorbachev's Economic Plans: Prospects and Risks," in *Gorbachev's Economic Plans*, vol. 1, pp. vii–xix; J. L. Felker, "Gorbachev's Economic Reform: A Soviet Economy Roundtable," *Soviet Economy*, vol. 3, no. 1 (January–March 1987), 40–53; Gertrude E. Schroeder, "Anatomy of Gorbachev's

Economic Reform," *Soviet Economy*, vol. 3, no. 3 (July–September 1987), 219–241; with comment by H. Levine, pp. 242–245; Timothy J. Colton, "Approaches to the Politics of Systemic Economic Reform in the Soviet Union," *Soviet Economy*, vol. 3, no. 2 (April–June 1987); Blair Ruble, "The Social Dimension of Perestroyka," same volume, pp. 171–183; E. A. Hewett, "Gorbachev at Two Years: Perspectives on Economic Reforms," *Soviet Economy*, vol. 2, no. 4 (October–December 1986), 283–288.

34. "Zakon o gosudarstvennom predpriiatii (obedinenii)" [Law of the state enterprises (trust)], *Pravda*, February 8, 1987.

SELECTED BIBLIOGRAPHY

A. Balinky et al., *Planning and the Market in the USSR: The 1960s* (New Brunswick, N.J.: Rutgers University Press, 1967).

J. S. Berliner, *The Innovation Decision in Soviet Industry* (Cambridge, Mass.: MIT Press, 1976).

———, "Planning and Management" in A. Bergson and H. S. Levin, eds., *The Soviet Economy: Towards the Year 2000* (London: Allen & Unwin, 1983), pp. 350–359.

———, "Organizational Restructuring of the Soviet Economy," Joint Economic Committee, *Gorbachev's Economic Plans*, vol. 1 (Washington, D.C.: U.S. Government Printing Office, 1987), pp. 70–83.

M. Bornstein, "Improving the Soviet Economic Mechanism," *Soviet Studies*, vol. 37, no. 1 (January 1985), 1–30.

K. Bush, "The Implementation of the Soviet Economic Reform," *Osteuropa Wirtschaft*, nos. 2 and 3 (1970).

S. F. Cohen, "The Friends and Foes of Change: Reformism and Conservatism in the Soviet Union," *Slavic Review*, vol. 38, no. 2 (June 1979), 187–202.

T. J. Colton, "Approaches to the Politics of Systemic Economic Reform in the Soviet Union," *Soviet Economy*, vol. 3, no. 2 (April–June 1987).

D. Dyker, ed., *The Soviet Union under Gorbachev* (London: Croom Helm, 1987).

N. Fedoryenko et al., *Soviet Economic Reform: Progress and Problems*, translated from the Russian (Moscow: Progress Publishers, 1972).

G. R. Feiwel, *The Soviet Quest for Economic Efficiency* (New York: Praeger, 1972).

J. L. Felker, *Soviet Economic Controversies* (Cambridge, Mass.: MIT Press, 1966).

"Gorbachev's Economic Reform: A Soviet Economy Roundtable," *Soviet Economy*, vol. 3, no. 1 (January–March 1987), 40–53.

A. C. Gorlin, "Industrial Reorganization: The Associations," in Joint Economic Committee, *Soviet Economy in a New Perspective* (Washington, D.C.: U.S. Government Printing Office, 1976), pp. 162–188.

P. Hanson, "Success Indicators Revisited: The July 1979 Decree on Planning and Management," *Soviet Studies*, vol. 35, no. 1 (January 1983).

J. P. Hardt and R. Kaufman, "Gorbachev's Economic Plans: Prospects and Risks," in *Gorbachev's Economic Plans*, vol. 1, pp. vii–xix.

A. Hewett, "Gorbachev at Two Years: Perspectives on Economic Reforms," *Soviet Economy*, vol. 2, no. 4 (October–December 1986), 283–288.

A. Katsenelinboigen, *Studies in Soviet Economic Planning* (White Plains, N.Y.: M. E. Sharpe, 1978).

W. Keizer, *The Soviet Quest for Economic Rationality* (Rotterdam: Rotterdam University Press, 1971).

A. Kosygin, "On Improving Management of Industry, Perfecting Planning, and Enhancing Economic Incentives in Industrial Production," in M. Bornstein and D. Fusfeld, eds., *The Soviet Economy*, 3rd ed. (Homewood, Ill.: Irwin, 1970), pp. 387–396.

E. G. Liberman, *Economic Methods and the Effectiveness of Production* (White Plains, N.Y.: International Arts and Sciences Press, 1971).

S. J. Linz and W. Moskoff, eds., *Reorganization and Reform in the Soviet Economy* (Armonk, N.Y.: M. E. Sharpe, 1988).

National Foreign Assessment Center, *Organization and Management in the Soviet Economy: The Ceaseless Search for Panaceas*, ER77–10769, Washington, D.C., December 1977.

A. Nove, *The Soviet Economic System* (London: Allen & Unwin, 1977), chap. 11.

P. Rutland, "The Shchekino Method and the Struggle to Raise Labor's Productivity in Soviet Industry," *Soviet Studies*, vol. 36, no. 3 (July 1984), 345–365.

K. W. Ryavec, "Soviet Industrial Management: Challenge and Response, 1965–1970," *Canadian Slavic Studies*, vol. 2 (Summer 1972), 151–177.

G. E. Schroeder, "Anatomy of Gorbachev's Economic Reform," *Soviet Economy*, vol. 3 no. 3 (July–September 1987), 219–241.

———, "The 1966–67 Soviet Industrial Price Reform: A Study in Complications," *Soviet Studies*, vol. 20, no. 4 (April 1969), 452–477.

———, "Recent Developments in Soviet Planning and Managerial Incentives," in U.S. Congress, Joint Economic Committee, *Soviet Economic Prospects for the Seventies* (Washington, D.C.: U.S. Government Printing Office, 1973), pp. 11–38.

———, "Soviet Economic 'Reform' Decrees: More Steps on the Treadmill," in U.S. Congress, Joint Economic Committee, *Soviet Economy in the 1980s: Problems and Prospects*, part 1 (Washington, D.C.: U.S. Government Printing Office, 1982), pp. 65–88.

———, "The 'Reform' of the Supply System in Soviet Industry," *Soviet Studies*, vol. 24, no. 1 (July 1972), 97–119.

M. Yanowitch, ed., *A Voice of Reform: Essays by Tatiana I. Zaslavskaia* (Armonk, N.Y.: M. E. Sharpe, 1988).

"Zakon o gosudarstvennom predpriatii (obedinenii)" [Law of the state enterprises (trust)], *Pravda*, February 8, 1987.

PART TWO

How The Soviet Economy Operates

Chapter 7

Planning, Finances, and Money

*I*n this chapter, we turn from the history of the Soviet planned economy to its operation. Although arrangements for allocating resources in the Soviet Union have changed over time, we shall concentrate on how the Soviet economy operated in the 1980s. The various Soviet economic reforms (discussed in Part Four) have at best brought about relatively minor changes in basic Soviet working arrangements. The Soviet economic system of the 1980s was not fundamentally different from the system put in place in the 1930s. The description of resource allocation arrangements that follows, therefore, does not depend heavily on the exact time period chosen.

INTRODUCTION TO SOVIET RESOURCE ALLOCATION

Our foremost concern in Chapters 8 and 9 is to elaborate how resources are allocated in the Soviet Union, in particular by what arrangements goods and services are produced and distributed and how the major factors of production (labor and capital) are allocated. Particular attention will be given to both the formal and informal means through which resource allocation is achieved. To analyze the matter of goods production, we consider in this chapter the planning apparatus, the relationship between the planners and enterprises, and the process of price formation. Chapter 8 examines the Soviet manager and the allocation of scarce capital among competing uses. In Chapter 9, we consider how the Soviet household functions in the planned economy, in its labor force and saving activities. This chapter also considers the unplanned second economy of the Soviet Union.

First, we outline the institutional framework in which the Soviet economy operates, since these institutions—the state economic hierarchy and the Communist Party—provide direction and control to the Soviet economy.

THE SOVIET ECONOMIC BUREAUCRACY[1]

The political system of the Soviet Union was described briefly in the introductory chapter. This chapter focuses on the Soviet economic bureaucracy, defined to include the economic activities of the ruling Communist Party, the state bureaucracy including the state planning apparatus, the industrial ministries, the trusts intermediate between the industrial ministries and the enterprises, and the enterprises at the lowest level.

The Party and State Economic Apparatus

The Communist Party of the Soviet Union (CPSU) is the dominant ruling force in the Soviet Union. The CPSU deals with a multitude of matters—propaganda, media control, foreign policy—in addition to economics. Its economic functions range from devising overall economic policy, to controlling key appointments in the economy, to monitoring economic activity at the highest to the lowest level. The CPSU plays a vital and ongoing role in the area of economics. At the highest level, the Department of Planning and Finance Organs (*Otdel planovykh i finansovykh organov*) of the Central Committee of the CPSU is responsible for issuing instructions to the highest state planning organs and for coordinating overall plan activity. This party department is staffed by professional party bureaucrats and plays a crucial role in staffing key positions in the state planning apparatus and in determining appointments and promotions in the upper echelons of the state economic bureaucracy. The

Central Committee also has industrial departments that supervise and monitor specific branches of the economy. For example, the Central Committee currently has separate departments of heavy industry, machine building, defense industries, chemicals, light industry and food, construction, transportation and services, and trade. These party industrial departments parallel the industrial departments of state planning organs and the industrial ministries themselves.

The CPSU exercises control over the economy not only from its apex in Moscow. Regional and local party organs—the *oblast'* party committees (obkoms), the city party committees (*gorkoms*), and the regional party committees (*raikoms*) are also involved in economic affairs. The first party secretary of a particular *obkom* oversees the economic affairs of his or her *oblast'* and is typically held responsible for the aggregate economic successes or failures of the *oblast'* economy. The first party secretary of a particular city (say, Moscow) tends to be judged according to the combined economic performance of enterprises in Moscow. This pattern is thought by political observers of the Soviet scene to lead to different goals pursued at the national and regional and local levels of the party organization. Whereas the Central Committee tends to be concerned with overall economic performance, regional and local party authorities tend to be concerned about the economic performance in the area of their jurisdiction. They are, therefore, prepared to intervene on behalf of local enterprises.

The primary party organizations (PPOs) of the enterprises represent party authority at the microeconomic level of the economy. Each enterprise has a PPO. In large enterprises, the PPO is headed by a full-time professional who is freed from other work responsibilities. In small enterprises, the PPO is more often headed by a party member who carries this responsibility on a part-time basis. Most political scientist agree that the power of the PPO is limited and does not strongly influence the operation of Soviet enterprises.

Whereas the CPSU involves itself in the making of economic policy, controlling key appointments, and in general monitoring and assistance, the state economic bureaucracy is charged with the formal implementation of party economic policy. Although there is an elected government, the Supreme Soviet, whose affairs are carried out by its presidium, the Council of Minister (*Soviet ministrov*) conducts the routine business of government in the Soviet Union. The Council of Ministers is the government bureaucracy of the Soviet Union. Each of the 15 union republics has its own state apparatus, the organization of which parallels the USSR state apparatus. The USSR Council of Ministers is staffed by the industrial ministers, the chairmen of various state committees, and the chairmen of other agencies with ministerial status. The chairman of the Council of Ministers occupies the most powerful position in the state apparatus.

Of the more than 20 state committees, the most important to planning and managing the national economy are *Gosplan* (the State Planning Commission), *Gosbank* (the State Bank), *Gossnab* (the State Committee for Material

Technical Supply), *Gosstroi* (the State Committee for Construction), *Gotsen* (the State Committee for Prices), *Minfin* (the Ministry of Finance), and the Central Statistical Administration. Although nominally responsible to the USSR Council of Ministers, *Gosplan* is by far the most important agency of the state economic bureaucracy. It maintains close ties with the Central Committee and is viewed by members of the Soviet economic bureaucracy as representing the will of the Central Committee. *Gosplan* itself is organized along functional lines in branch departments that parallel the various branches of the economy. For example, *Gosplan* has branch departments of coal, ferrous metals, machine building, and the like. In addition to branch departments, *Gosplan* has various summary departments (such as the departments of finance and costs, the department for the annual national economic plan, and the department of capital investment) which deal with issues that cross functional boundaries, such as the development of an integrated national plan. *Gosplan* is headed by a chairman, and its most important operational affairs are handled by *Gosplan's* collegium (staffed by the various department heads, the chairman, and the deputy chairmen). *Gosplan* USSR has branches in the 15 republics.

Gosplan, the State Planning Commission, was established in 1921 and engaged primarily in nonoperational long-term planning during the 1920s. During the 1920s, the role of *Gosplan* as the central coordinator of national planning was challenged by the People's Commissariat of Finance (*Narkomfin*), by VSNKh, and the ministerial planning bodies, but by the late 1920s, *Gosplan* was recognized as the principal planning body in the Soviet Union.[2] After its reorganization in 1928, it came to play an important coordinating function, especially after the ministerial system was introduced in 1932. Although the ministries themselves performed most of the current planning within the ministry, *Gosplan* was given the task of coordinating these ministerial plans by drawing up *material balances*, the basic planning system to be discussed shortly. The structure and functions of *Gosplan* have changed over the years, though to relate these changes in detail would be confusing and would not add significantly understanding Soviet planning.* In spite of continuing changes in the organizational structure of planning agencies, *Gosplan* has played a central coordinating

---

*In 1948–1949, *Gosplan* was weakened by the establishment of what had formerly been its material allocation department, technical department, and Central Statistical Agency as separate agencies. After Stalin's death, these departments (with the exception of the Central Statistical Agency) were returned to *Gosplan*. In 1955, *Gosplan* was split into two agencies: *Gosplan*, which was to concentrate on long-term planning, and the State Economic Commission, which was to be concerned with short-term plans. As a result of the regionalization reforms (the *Sovnarkhozy*) of 1957, *Gosplan* took on new possibilities. It absorbed the planning functions of the defunct ministries and was the crucial coordinating agency at the all-union level. In 1960, *Gosplan* was again split into the State Economic-Science Council, in charge of long-range planning, and *Gosplan*, in charge of current planning.

role throughout the plan period, especially with the application of material balance planning. *Gosplan's* main charge is devising national economic plans. Currently, *Gosplan* draws up both long-term plans (five years and longer) and annual economic plans. The annual economic plans are the plans according to which the economic bureaucracy operates, and *Gosplan's* planning work guides the activities of the other state committees that manage the nation's economy.

Gossnab, the State Committee for Material Technical Supply, is charged with managing the distribution of material inputs required to fulfill the national economic plan. *Gosbank* monitors fulfillment of financial plans and manages the credit and cash accounts of enterprises. *Gosstroi*, the State Committee for Construction, coordinates construction activity carried out throughout the national economy. The Ministry of Finance prepares the national budget, collect profit taxes and other levies, and monitors staffing. The Central Statistical Administration monitors plan fulfillment and gathers statistics for use by the state economic bureaucracy.

Ministries, Industrial Associations, and Enterprises

The ministries fulfill several functions. They supervise the productive enterprises that fall within their functional domain. The Ministry of Ferrous Metals, for example, supervises the enterprises in the economy that produce ferrous metals. The ministries break down the aggregated plan activities handed down by *Gosplan* into detailed targets for individual enterprises. The ministries are charged with carrying out the allocation of various supplies and materials among their enterprises. In the Soviet planning jargon, ministries are "fund holders" (*fondoderzhateli*). They, in effect, carry the responsibility for the orderly allocation of scarce inputs to their enterprises. Operational plans are a joint effort between *Gosplan* and the ministries. Soviet planning law clearly recognizes that planning is a joint effort between ministries and *Gosplan*.

The ministries are headed by a minister who has various deputy ministers. Each ministry is divided into chief administrations (or *glavks*) that are responsible for the different activities of the ministry. The ministry of construction materials, for example, is broken down into chief administrations that handle the different types of construction materials (cement, asphalt, brick, etc.) produced by the ministry's enterprises. The routine business of the ministry is handled by its collegium, which is staffed by the minister, the deputy ministers, the heads of the chief administrations, and the directors of major enterprises. The collegium deals with supply and output problems, makes personnel changes, and advises the minister. The minister is held responsible for the "final results" of the ministry's enterprises. The Collegium can only advise; the minister makes the final decisions.

Ministries are of three types. The all-union ministries manage directly from Moscow all the enterprises in that branch. Branches that are organized as all-union ministries tend to be key industrial branches (such as machine building, electronics, defense, and communication equipment) that maintain enterprises throughout the Soviet Union. The second type of ministry is the union-republican ministry, whose enterprises are subject to the dual subordination of the Moscow ministry and the republican ministry. Branches that tend to be organized on the union-republican basis are those in which production is concentrated in one or several republics (such as coal production and agriculture) or where activities are carried out broadly among the republics but on a more decentralized basis (such as construction). The third type of ministry is the republican ministry, which is charged primarily with managing enterprises producing for the local economy. Republican ministries also deal with construction projects of more local significance. In this latter activity, they share responsibility with the republican council of ministers.

The Soviet economic bureaucracy encompasses a large number of semi-independent consulting institutes, called scientific research institutes, project-making institutes, or scientific-technical institutes. These institutes can be subordinated to ministries, to *Gosplan*, to the Academy of Sciences, to republican organs, or to large enterprises. They contract with the various planning organs and ministries to perform detailed planning studies, feasibility studies for major construction projects, scientific input norm calculations, and the like. Much of the detailed planning work in the Soviet economy is actually carried out by these institutes.

Since 1973, increased emphasis has been placed on developing an intermediate management level between the ministries and the enterprises, called industrial associations. The industrial associations (*obedineniia*) are generally organized corresponding to the chief administrations, the *glavks*, of the ministry. In construction materials, for example, the industrial associations would be organized according to the main product lines handled by the main administrations. The industrial associations are, relatively speaking, a new phenomenon in the Soviet economic bureaucracy, and a number of operating rules remain to be firmly established. How much autonomy do individual enterprises that are members of the industrial association have? What supervisory and management tasks are left to the ministry? What tasks are carried out by the management of the industrial association? Apparently, the two motivating forces behind the ideas of the industrial association were the desire to involve technical ministerial experts in the direct administration of enterprises and to simplify the planning and management process by allowing planners to deal with combinations of industrial enterprises rather than individual enterprises.

The productive enterprises (*predpriiatiia*) form the microeconomic core of the Soviet economy. Much more will be said about them in Chapter 8. For now, we can say that Soviet enterprises are headed by a professional manager (director), who is aided by a management staff of accountants, engineers, designers, technologists, and economists. The enterprise runs on an independent accounting system, which means that it is supposed to cover its costs with its revenues and it is hoped to earn a profit. The enterprise operates according to detailed instructions from the ministry main administration and from the industrial association but retains considerable independent decision-making authority.

The Principal/Agent Problem and the Economic Bureaucracy

The Soviet economic bureaucracy is a complex, multilayered organization. It is organized according to hierarchical principles, with organization A being superior to organization B which is itself superior to organization C. The superiority of A over B and of B over C is evidenced by the fact that A can issue binding orders to B, and B can issue binding orders to C. In the Soviet case, these orders are instructions on what to produce and permission to use certain resources. In the language of modern economics, organization A is the *principal* and organization B is the *agent* of A. Organization B is the principal of C, or, stated otherwise, C is the agent of B. Organizations in the Soviet economic bureaucracy are tied together in *principal/agent relationships.*

When two organizations are involved in a principal/agent relationship, the agent is charged with carrying out the instructions of the principal according to an agreed-upon contractual arrangement. In market economies, principal/agent relationships of all kinds exist: a professional management team (the agent) represents the interest of the stockholders of a corporation (the principal). A home builder (the agent) carries out the orders of a family contracting to build a home (the principal). A professional baseball player is the agent of the team's owner. An *agency problem* arises when the agent fails to pursue the interests of the principal without formally violating the contractual agreement between the principal and agent. For example, the stockholders of a corporation wish to maximize the long-run market price of their shares, while the professional management team wishes to maximize job security. Accordingly, the management team resists corporate takeovers that benefit the stockholders. The contract between the stockholders and the management team does not prevent the agents from behaving contrary to the interests of the principal. The home builder may build a home that is of lower quality than the buyer perceives as contracted for, but the contract has been written in such a way that the agent has formally met his or her contractual obligations to the principal. When the interests of the principal and agent diverge, the principal must either devote resources to *monitoring* the contractual performance of the agent or attempt to devise an *incentive scheme* that causes the agent to pursue automatically the interests of the principal. Whether the principal chooses monitoring or automatic incentive schemes depends on the cost and feasibility of monitoring. If monitoring is costless, the agent simply watches every move of the agent to prevent the agent from acting contrary to the interests of the principal. When monitoring costs are present, perfect monitoring is typically not rational. The principal, therefore, must find incentive schemes that will encourage agents, who cannot be perfectly monitored, to pursue the principal's interest as closely as possible. In the real world, where monitoring costs are present, principals select a combination of monitoring and incentive mechanisms, the combination depending upon the costs of monitoring.

Agency problems are present in the Soviet context. Within the Soviet economic bureaucracy, principals issue orders and instructions to their agents, monitor the performance of agents, and reward or punish agents on the basis of established performance criteria. The Soviet economic bureaucracy is a complex organization. It is difficult to monitor the detailed activities of agent organizations, and information reported by agents tends to be distorted; so, principals in the Soviet system must combine performance monitoring with incentive mechanisms to encourage agents to act in the principals' interests. It is the task of the principal to find an incentive system that encourages agents to follow the spirit of the principal's instructions as closely as possible. The importance of the incentive system depend on the principal's ability to monitor the performance of the agent. The better the principal's monitoring, the less important the incentive mechanism.

Figure 7.1 gives an impressionistic picture of the various principal/agent relationships in the Soviet economic bureaucracy. In this discussion, we focus on the agency relationship between the Central Committee and *Gosplan* and the ministries and between the ministries and the enterprises. As the figure shows, there are a multitude of agency relationships that we cannot touch on in this discussion. The chief principals in the Soviet economy are the Central Committee and *Gosplan* (we know too little of their relationship to determine if an agency problem exists here). As the principal to the various industrial ministries, *Gosplan* issues directives to its agent ministries, telling them how much to produce (and in what assortments) and the resources (both real and financial) that will be made available to them. The principal would like the agent to meet these output targets with a minimal expenditure of society's resources (or to produce a maximum output with the allotted quantity of resources). Besides setting up monitoring procedures, it seeks to devise incentive schemes to encourage the agent ministries to pursue the interests of the principal. Within the general constraint of performance monitoring by the principal, the agent ministries wish to achieve maximal rewards from the established incentive scheme (either in the form of income, adulation, promotion, or job security). If the incentive scheme is imperfectly devised (and monitoring is imperfect), the agent ministries will engage in *opportunistic behavior* (such as achieving output targets at the sacrifice of quality or the wastage of resources) that is contrary to the interests of the principal as long as this perverse behavior is neither detected nor punished by the established incentive scheme.

The ministries, on the other hand, are the principals to the industrial associations and industrial enterprises that serve as their agents. They issue instructions to their agent enterprises concerning what they are to produce (and in what qualities and assortments) and concerning the real and financial resources at their disposal. The ministries cannot monitor their agents perfectly, and therefore, to supplement direct monitoring, they must devise incentive systems that encourage their agents to carry out instructions in the spirit of the principal. It is too costly to the principal to monitor all the activities of its many agents. The ministry would like its agents to produce the outputs ordered in the appropriate assortments and qualities with minimal expenditure of the ministry's scarce resources. Unless the incentive scheme is

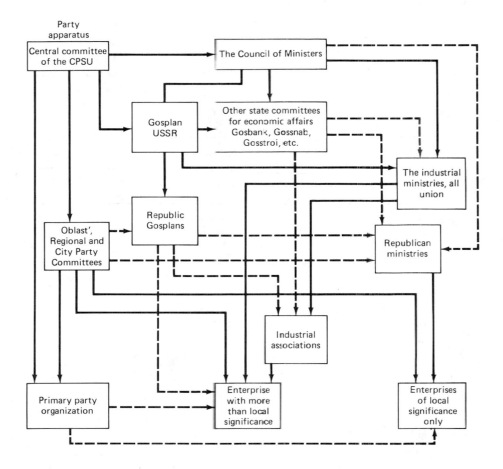

Figure 7.1 Relationships within the Soviet bureaucracy.

perfect, the agent enterprises will be tempted to earn the rewards offered by their principals (in the form of bonuses, promotion, etc.) by engaging in perverse behavior. If the principal's incentive system rewards output without rewarding quality or cost savings, the agent is tempted to sacrifice quality or cost savings in meeting its output directives.

The basic theme of this chapter and the next is how the Soviet economic system deals with the principal/agent problem. The agency problem provides a convenient framework for studying Soviet resource allocation practices. We first identify the major principal/agent problems in the Soviet economy. Second, we treat the various monitoring techniques used by principals. Third, we consider why the Soviet system tends to generate false information that raises monitoring costs. Finally, we discuss the different incentive systems that have been designed to treat the agency problem and show why it is difficult in the Soviet context to find incentive systems that eliminate agency problems. The chapters on economic reform (Chapters 13 and 14) describe the Soviet search for better incentive systems to ameliorate principal/agent problems.

SOVIET PLANNING: THE BASIC BALANCES

The official guide for Soviet economic planners emphasizes that planning in the Soviet Union proceeds from a a series of basic balances.[4] This chapter devotes most attention to two of these balances—the material balance and the income balance—but it is useful to begin with an overview of the basic balances of the Soviet planned economy.[5] In market economies, market forces achieve a number of balances: the supplies and demands for particular goods, services, and resources are equalized by the price system. The supply and demand for loanable funds are equalized through market interest rates. The aggregate supply and demand for goods and services are balanced by income adjustments and price level changes, and so on.

The Soviet planned economy must likewise achieve balances. There are negative consequences to underutilizing goods and resources. Resources are wasted if trained labor is standing idle due to lack of demand. If capital goods, produced at high opportunity cost, are not used, society has wasted its resources. Excess demands for goods, resources, and capital have similarly negative consequences. If the quantity of a good or resource demanded exceeds the quantity supplied, some means must be found to ration out the available supply in a reasonable manner to prevent chaos. This chapter and the next discuss in some detail how the Soviet planned economies achieve balances, largely without the aid of automatic market forces.

The Consumer Goods Balance

In the consumer goods market, planners aim to achieve a balance between the supplies and demands for individual goods and services at the micro level and between the aggregate supply and the aggregate demand for consumer goods at the macro level. There are reasons why Soviet planners would want a balance between the aggregate demand and aggregate supply of consumer goods. If there were excess demand that is not compensated by inflation, disappointed consumers might lose their interest in the monetary rewards offered by the economic system. For this reason, excess demand might have to be countered by inflation, which might unleash a political backlash against the system's leaders. If a macro imbalance is allowed to persist, consumers might respond by working less or accumulating forced saving. Soviet planners, therefore, seek a balance between the desired money outlays for goods and services of the population and the money value of goods and services offered to consumer markets. If planners wish to have stable prices and a general clearing of markets, then the two major means of bringing about this equality are to control the flow of income to the population or to control the output of consumer goods and services.

In notational form, a macrobalance is achieved in the consumer goods market (at established prices) when

$$\underset{\text{supply}}{PQ} \underset{=}{=} \underset{\text{Demand}}{wL + O - T - R}$$

where P = the prevailing price level
  Q = the real output of consumer goods
  w = the average annual wage rate
  L = average annual employment
  O = earnings other than wage earnings
  T = tax payment
  R = personal savings

the $wL + O - T$ term equals personal disposable income. When personal savings are subtracted from this term, we get the demand for consumer goods.

A macrobalance does not mean that each consumer market is in equilibrium. It simply means that, on average, the aggregate supply of consumer goods equals the aggregate demand at prevailing price levels.

The Labor Balance

In labor markets, planners desire to have microbalances between the supplies of the different labor services offered by the able-bodied population and the demands for these different labor services. Chapter 9 discusses how the Soviet labor market seeks to achieve microbalances. At the macro level, Soviet planners wish to have an aggregate labor force balance, whereby the aggregate demand for labor services equals the aggregate supply of labor services. In market economies, both the micro and macro labor balances are brought about by relative wage adjustments (especially in the long run). In the Soviet Union, both micro- and macrobalances are brought about by labor force planning (planning the supply of and the demand for professional and manual labor force) which uses relative wages as an instrument of labor force policy. Obviously, both micro- and macrobalances are desired because underutilized labor resources mean that the economy is producing below potential.

At the macro level, Soviet planners concentrate on balancing the demand for new positions in the economy with the flows of people into and out of the labor force. In notational form, a macrobalance is achieved when

$$\Delta D^L = E - R$$

where ΔD^L = new jobs projected by planning authorities
  E = new entrants into the labor market (primarily from the educational establishment)
  R = departures from the labor force (largely due to retirements)

The Credit Balance

Soviet planners must also aim for a balance of the demand for credit by Soviet enterprises and organizations and the supply of credit. In capitalist economies, this balancing is achieved primarily through interest rates, while in the Soviet Union, planners determine the credit needs of the economy and the State Bank supplies credit in accordance with credit requirements planned by the Ministry of Finance. The credit balance, like most other Soviet macrobalances, is achieved administratively, largely without adjustments in the opportunity costs of credit to the participants. One set of planners determines the credit needs of the microeconomic units, while another set of planners (theoretically working in tandem with the first group) supplies their credit needs.

In notational form, macrobalance is achieved in credit markets when:

$$D^c = S^c$$

where D^c = the aggregate demand for credit
S^c = the aggregate supply of credit

The Capital Goods Balance

Soviet planners are also charged with ensuring a micro- and a macrobalance of the demand for and supply of capital goods. The supply of capital goods is determined by the output of various capital goods (machinery, structures, and housing), while the demand for capital goods is determined by investment planners through investment plans for the various enterprises and organizations throughout the economy. In capitalist economies, the demand and supply of capital goods are balanced by adjustments in real interest rates. In the Soviet planned economy, the balance is brought about by administrative decree by those who plan the output and distribution of capital goods. As Chapter 8 will show, the microunit has surprisingly little to say about the process.

Although capital goods tend to be treated separately by Soviet planners, the investment goods balance is part of the material balance process. Soviet planners must ensure that the economy produces sufficient supplies of individual materials and capital goods to enable the enterprises to meet their production targets and to meet the demand for exports and for final consumption. The next section concentrates on material balance planning.

Material Balances[6]

Soviet planning authorities must balance the supplies and demands for the basic raw materials and commodities that either are used in the production process or flow to final consumers such as households or foreign exports. In any economy, there are literally millions of such goods (thousands of types of steel products, hundreds of different building materials, thousands of chemical products, a few grades of coal, and so on). In market economies, the supplies and demands for such goods are brought into balance by relative prices. If the quantity of coal demanded exceeds the quantity of coal supplied at prevailing prices, the relative price of coal will rise until the quantity demanded equals the quantity supplied. Under normal circumstances, users of materials in market economies do not have to stand in line to obtain materials; the price system allows buyers who are prepared to pay the going market price to buy the product.

In the Soviet planned economy, the supply and demand for materials are brought into balance by administrative procedures. One of the principal tasks of the Soviet planning apparatus is the achievement of balances of materials. *Gosplan* plays a key role in this activity—called material balance planning—and is assisted by the ministries and by *Gossnab* (the state supply committee). We shall begin with the idealized version of material balance planning reported by official Soviet texts on the subject.[7] We then turn to a discussion of how material balance planning is conducted in Soviet practice.

Our discussion begins with the construction of the annual plan.[8] The key to Soviet success in dealing with the enormous complexities of administrative planning is that only a limited number of commodities are centrally planned and distributed by *Gosplan SSSR*. Even then, industrial supply and distribution plans compiled by *Gosplan* have been known to total 70 volumes of almost 12,000 pages and to deal with well over 30,000 commodities.

The most important industrial products—such as steel, cement, machinery, and building materials—are called *funded commodities*. *Gosplan SSSR* is in charge of drawing up output and distribution plans for these funded commodities, which are specifically approved by the USSR Council of Ministers. Between 1928 and the present, *Gosplan* has developed annual balances for between 277 and 2390 separately funded product groups. In the mid-1980s, *Gosplan* prepared some 2000 balances. Output and distribution plans are also drawn up for two other categories of industrial products. *Planned commodities* are those industrial products jointly planned and distributed by *Gosplan*, *Gossnab* (State Committee for Material-Technical Supply), and the All-Union Main Supply and Sales Administrations, under the approval of the heads of these organizations. In recent years, 25,000 or more commodities have been planned according to this system. Finally, decentrally planned commodities are planned and distributed by the territorial administrations of *Gossnab* and by the ministries without the explicit approval of higher organs. In recent years, over 50,000 industrial products have been planned according to this system.

In addition to these three categories, the ministries plan and allocate "non-planned" industrial commodities, largely for internal use. In the 1970s, for example, the ministries allocated 26,000 products in this category.

An idealized version of *Gosplan's* planning of funded commodities through the industrial supply and output planning system is as follows (the breakdown into distinct steps is somewhat arbitrary, for there is considerable overlapping):

1. The first step in the planning process is for the party (the Politburo or the Central Committee) to establish its priorities for the forthcoming planning period. This is usually done in the spring preceding the planning period. The party expresses its priorities by setting output targets (generally in the form of desired

rates of growth) for a number of crucial funded commodities.

2. The second step is the control figure phase. Output targets are sent down through the state apparatus to *Gosplan*, which has been active gathering data on past plan fulfillment and bottlenecks. *Gosplan* then formulates a preliminary set of *control figures* (tentative output targets) for 200 to 300 product groups that fulfills the priorities set by the party. *Gosplan* also tentatively estimates, on the basis of past performance, the inputs required to achieve the control figures. The ministries are informed of their projected material "limits." At this stage, the planning departments of the ministries aid *Gosplan* in the formulation of the full set of control figures and project input requirements, a process that involves considerable negotiation and friction as the ministries bargain for reasonable targets and sufficient resources.

The objective of the next three phases is the preparation of a draft plan. Ministries react to their control figures and resource limits and bargain with *Gosplan*. Enterprises bargain with their ministries over their own control figures and proposed material limits.

3. The ministries send down control figures through the planning hierarchy via the ministerial organizations until they reach the individual enterprises. As the control figures progress through the planning hierarchy, they are disaggregated into specific tasks. For example, the all-union ministry will receive its control targets, which are then disaggregated by branches within the ministry, until each ministry enterprise receives its own control figures. At this stage, the planning office of the ministry will prepare a list of tentative input requirements, based on the ministry's control figures, for internal use by each enterprise.

4. Information now begins to flow up the planning hierarchy from the enterprise to *Gosplan*. The enterprise will relate its input requirements to its immediate superior, which in turn will aggregate the requirements of all enterprises under its control. These will be related to its superior, and so on, up to the ministry and then to *Gosplan*. At each stage in this process, the requested inputs are compared with estimated input needs, and the *correction principle* is used to adjust for differences between the two (after considerable bargaining among the various levels). If ministries propose higher material limits than those calculated by *Gosplan*, the ministers must "defend" their requests before *Gosplan*. Similarly, enterprises must "defend" requests for deviations from output and input targets before their ministries. An authoritative observer of this process reports a "siege" of *Gosplan* during the draft plan process as ministerial officials flood into *Gosplan* with their arguments and requests.[9]

5. After this phase of bargaining has been completed, *Gosplan* must check the consistency of the control figures, that is, determine whether an equilibrium exists. An equilibrium is achieved when the planned supplies of each commodity equal its targeted material input requirements and final uses. Assuming a total of 2000 funded commodities to be balanced, a material balance is achieved when

Exhibit 7.1

$$S_1 = D_1$$
$$S_2 = D_2$$

$$\vdots$$

$$S_{2000} = D_{2000}$$

where S = the planned supplies
             D = the estimated demands for the (2000) materials

The planned supply of the first commodity (S_1), for example, is the sum of its planned output (the control figure), denoted as X_1; available stocks (V_1); and planned imports (M_1). The total demand for the first commodity (D_1) is the sum of its intermediate (interindustry) demands $(X_{11}, X_{12}, X_{13}, \ldots X_{1,2000})^*$ and its final demand (investment, household demand, and exports), which is denoted as Y_1. From Exhibit 1, it is noted that a consistent set of control figures requires that

Exhibit 7.2

Sources   Distribution

$$X_1 + V_1 + M_1 = X_{11} + X_{12} + \ldots + X_{1,2000} + Y_1$$

$$X_2 + V_2 + M_2 = X_{21} + X_{22} + \ldots + X_{2,2000} + Y_2$$

$$\vdots$$

$$X_{2000} + V_{2000} + M_{2000} = X_{2000,1} + X_{2000,2} + \ldots + X_{2000,2000} + Y_{2000}$$

In most cases, planned production (the X_1) is the most important supply source, accounting for as much as 95 percent of the total supply of funded materials. On the other hand, imports are usually an insignificant source of supply. It is *Gosplan's* task to ensure that a material balance exists.

A simplified hypothetical material balance consisting of four product categories—coal, steel, machinery, and consumer goods—is provided in Table 7.1 to illustrate the concepts of intermediate demand, final demand, balance and so on.

---

*The X_{ij} refers to interindustry demands. For example, X_{13} would refer to the quantity of commodity 1 required to produce the planned output of commodity 3. In more general terms, X_{ij} would refer to the quantity of commodity i required to produce the planned output of commodity j. Such input requirements are also called *intermediate* inputs.

Table 7.1   A SAMPLE BALANCE OF MATERIALS

| | Sources | | | Intermediate inputs required by: | | | | Final use | |
	Output	Stocks	Imports	Coal Industry	Steel Industry	Machinery Industry	Consumer goods Industry	Exports	Domestic uses
Coal (tons)	1000	10	0	100	500	50	50	100	210
Steel (tons)	2000	0	20	200	400	1000	300	100	20
Machinery (units)	100	5	5	20	40	10	20	10	10
Consumer goods (units)	400	10	20	0	0	0	100	100	230

Note: Demonstration that a balance exists: Sources of coal: 1010 tons = uses of coal: 1010 tons. Sources of steel: 2020 tons = uses of steel: 2020 tons. Sources of machinery: 110 units = uses of machinery: 110 units. Sources of consumer goods: 430 units = uses of consumer goods: 430 units.

Usually, when *Gosplan* first compares supplies and demands, it finds that demands exceed supplies because of large interindustry requirements and taut planning in general. In those cases where excess demand prevails, the commodities are called "deficit" (*defitsitny*) commodities. *Gosplan* must then equate supplies and demands for deficit commodities by adjusting their different components (Exhibit 7.2). To illustrate this process in the simplest possible manner, assume that an overall balance has been achieved with the exception of the first commodity, which is, say, steel—that is, the supplies of all other commodities equal their demands, but the demand for steel exceeds its supply. This material imbalance can be corrected in five different ways:

1. *Gosplan could order an increase in the planned output of the deficit commodity (raise X_1).* This approach, however, could throw the remaining sectors out of balance because additional coal, electricity, and other inputs used to make steel would be required, and their targets would have to be increased accordingly, which would in turn require increased outputs of commodities used in producing them, and so on. If an output target is changed to achieve a balance, a chain of *secondary effects* is set off that affects balances in other sectors. For this reason, Soviet planners have generally been reluctant to use this approach to achieve a balance, finding it difficult to adjust for the secondary impacts of such changes. When Soviet planners have used this approach, they have tended to adjust only for secondary effects in obvious cases.[10] A more common approach has been to call for increased production without raising planned inputs , thus pressuring enterprises to economize on inputs and increasing the tautness of planning.

2. *Gosplan could increase imports (M_1) of the deficit commodity.* The major drawback of this approach is that it would make the consistency of the overall balance dependent on foreign suppliers and would require use of essential foreign exchange reserves (if imported from the

West). Even utilizing trade connections within the Communist bloc would be an uncertain alternative because of the risk that delivery deadlines will not be met. This second approach has generally been of limited importance in Soviet material balance planning, although during the first Five Year Plan (1928–1932), it was used to make up deficits of certain types of machinery; during the postwar period, it has been used to import grain and, in recent years, advanced technology products from the West.

3. *Gosplan could reduce interindustry demands for the deficit commodity* (X_{ij}). This could be done by directing enterprises to use substitutes not in short supply or by reducing their overall inputs. The danger inherent in this approach is that by reducing planned intermediate inputs or by forcing enterprises to use inferior substitutes, the affected enterprises may not be able to meet their own output targets, thus creating further bottlenecks.

4. *Gosplan could reduce final demands for the deficit commodity* (Y_1). This could be done by reducing either exports, household demand or investment demand. The positive feature of this approach is that household demand (such as coal for home heating) in particular can be treated as a residual in the planning process, with little impact on interindustry balances. Its negative feature is that such final demands are required to meet the material needs of the populace and could tend to be too readily sacrificed simply to achieve a balance of interindustry demands.

5. *Gosplan could draw upon stocks of the deficit commodity* (V_1). This approach is generally impractical because of either the lack of adequate stockpiles or the unwillingness of planners to draw down strategic supplies, and it has been used only rarely.

Gosplan has historically favored the third and fourth balancing techniques and has generally applied them within the context of a priority system, which has limited the flow of inputs to low-priority industrial branches (generally consumer goods) and has restricted the availability of final consumer goods. In the former case, planners have assumed that the neglect of low-priority consumer goods branches will not jeopardize plan fulfillment in the high-priority heavy-industry branches, which tend to be fairly independent of the consumer goods branches. For example, if a garment-producing enterprise were to fall short of its output goal owing to inadequate materials, this failure would not jeopardize plan fulfillment in the steel industry. In the latter case, if coal were in deficit, a simple balancing method would be to reduce coal available for household heating, which would have little immediate impact on the crucial interindustry balance. Over time (especially during the 1930s), the consumer sector has tended to be neglected for the sake of achieving balances, so much so that it has at times been called the "buffer" sector of the Soviet economy.

This neglect can be seen from Table 7.2. Soviet estimates for plan achievement in producer and consumer goods for the period 1928–1980 show that the

Table 7.2   FULFILLMENT OF PRINCIPAL GOALS OF SOVIET FIVE YEAR PLANS (5YPs): 1928–1980
Percent Fulfillment

	1st 5YP (1928–1932)	2nd 5YP (1933–1937)	4th 5YP (1946–1950)	5th 5YP (1950–1955)	7th 5YP (1959–1965)	8th 5YP (1966–1970)	9th 5YP (1971–1975)	10th 5YP (1976–1980)
National income								
Official estimate	92	96	119		98	101	95	95
Western estimate	70	67	84–90	94				
Industrial output								
Official estimate	101	103	117		102	101	97	93
Western estimate	60–70	76–93	84–95	97				
Producer goods								
Official estimate	128	121	128		106	100	100	
Western estimate	72	97	97	94				
Consumer goods								
Official estimate	81	85	96		99			
Western estimate	46	68	81	103		103	92	
Agricultural production								
Official estimate	58	63–77	90		77	97	92	98
Western estimate	50–52	66–78	76–79	80				
Labor productivity								
Official estimate	65		101					
Western estimate	36–42	86	81	85			96	
Retail trade								
Official estimate			86	109		106	96	91
Western estimates	39	54						

Sources: N. Jasny, *Essays on The Soviet Economy* (New York: Praeger, 1962), p. 266; E. Zaleski, *Stalinist Planning for Economic Growth: 1933–1952* (Chapel Hill: University of North Carolina Press, 1980), p. 503; A. Nove, *An Economic History of the USSR* (London: Penguin, 1969), p. 353; Department of Commerce, *State Five Year Plan for the Development of the USSR National Economy for the Period 1971–1975*, JPRS 56970-1, Washington, D.C., September 1972, part 1, p. 65, part 2, pp. 356–358; D. Green et al., "An Evaluation of the 10th Five-Year Plan Using the SRI-WEFA Econometric Model of the Soviet Union," in Joint Economic Committee, *Soviet Economy in a New Perspective* (Washington, D.C.: U.S. Government Printing Office, 1976), p. 305; *Narodnoe khoziaistvo SSSR v 1979 g* [The national economy of the USSR in 1979], (Moscow: Statistika, 1980).

achievement in producer goods has been substantially greater than that in consumer goods. Although in recent years there has been continuing emphasis on the need to improve both the quantity and the quality of consumer goods, plan adjustments and shortfalls still seem to predominate in the consumer goods sector.

After *Gosplan* achieves (or approximates) the balances, the final version of the plan is submitted to the Council of Ministers for approval (and sometimes modification), after which the finalized targets are sent down the hierarchy to the individual firm. In its final form, the enterprise plan is called the *techpromfinplan* (the technical-industrial-financial plan) and establishes enterprise output targets as well as input allocations, supply plans, delivery plans, financial flows, wage bills, and many other targets.

The final stage of material balance planning occurs during the actual operation of the finalized plan. During this stage, *Gosplan* checks plan fulfillment at the various levels and gathers information upon which next year's plan will be based. An important element of the plan fulfillment stage is the response of *Gosplan* and the ministries to bottlenecks, that is, their manipulation of available resources to ensure fulfillment of priority targets.

It would be a mistake to think that the process of resource allocation is completed with the approval of the final version of the plan. Rather, important shifts of resources occur during the course of plan fulfillment as the planning agencies respond pragmatically to crises and bottlenecks. The national economic plan is only the first stage of Soviet resource allocation. The real process of resource allocation commences with plan fulfillment. As bottlenecks develop, it becomes evident that certain targets must be sacrificed, and it is at this stage that centralized management supersedes centralized planning. As Table 7.2 indicates, plan fulfillment can vary dramatically by sector, even when one deals with broad aggregates. Those who control the flow of resources during plan implementation, therefore, play a crucial role in determining economic outcomes. The numerous adjustments that take place during the course of plan fulfillment have caused some experts to question whether Soviet economy is indeed a "planned" economy. This issue is discussed later in this chapter.

THE PLANNING PROBLEM: AN INPUT-OUTPUT FRAMEWORK

We have presented a sanitized version of Soviet material balance planning. Our description neglects what goes on behind the scenes as all the interested parties (*Gosplan*, the ministries, regional and local authorities, the enterprises, and party officials) struggle, bargain, and cajole for resources. As this process remains behind the scenes and out of Soviet textbooks, the Western observer can only imagine its intensity.

Soviet material balancing is carried out largely independently of the theoretically powerful input-output approach to planning, which could provide an alternative for Soviet plan formulation. Input-output planning facilitates understanding of present Soviet planning practices and points the way to future improvements in Soviet planning procedures.[11]

Conceptually, the basic problem of plan formulation is quite simple. In the Soviet case, the planner (*Gosplan*) receives plan directives from the Communist Party. At this level, plan objectives must be highly aggregated and require that the planner disaggregate them to an operational level. The planner might begin the task of plan formulation from a list of final demands for various products to be produced in various sectors of the economy. The planner must then prepare a plan relating inputs to outputs, bearing in mind two important considerations.

First, the plan must be *feasible*; that is, it must be capable of being achieved, given existing resource availabilities and the state of technology.

Second, it would be desirable that the plan be *optimal*. Among all plan variants that are feasible, the *best* should be chosen. A plan that is optimal would be one that achieves the maximum level of output for a given input—or what amounts to the same thing, a minimum input for a given level of output. The maximum level of output is that which yields the greatest level of "satisfaction" to the political authorities of the USSR. The implication here is that a number of variants of the plan should be prepared and the best variant (as defined above) be chosen. Given the fact that the preparation of a plan for an economy the size of the USSR is a massive task, the application of mathematical computerized techniques has obvious appeal. Indeed, the basic planning problem as we have outlined it is the classic case of maximization under constraints, for which a number of theoretical techniques are available.

A basic input-output (I-O) table such as Exhibit 7.3 is in essence a graphic presentation of the national accounts of an economic system, showing the interrelationships among the producing and the using sectors. The rows consist of producing sectors (in our simple example, industry, agriculture, and other sectors are shown) while the columns are consuming sectors. Each producing sector will generate output, some of which will be used as an *intermediate input* for the production of output by that sector and by the other sectors. The remaining output will be used to satisfy the various components of final demand, such as consumption, exports, and government. Exhibit 7.3 is divided into four quadrants. The interindustry transactions quadrant (upper left), for example, shows the amount of industrial output that is needed to produce agricultural output (X_{12}), a relationship that can be expressed as a technical coefficient (a_{ij}).

The technical coefficients are computed as follows:

$$a_{ij} = \frac{X_{ij}}{X_j}$$

where a_{ij} = the amount of commodity i required to produce one unit of commodity j

X_{ij} = the amount of good i actually used by industry j

X_j = the gross output of industry j

Such a coefficient can be computed for each cell of this quadrant and indicates the amount of item i that is needed to produce on unit of j. This technical relationship is crucial in the development of a plan, a point to which we return shortly.

The final-use quadrant (upper right of Exhibit 7.3) shows the distribution of production to final use, while the value-added quadrant (lower left) shows the contribution of the primary inputs (land, labor, and capital) to output. Finally, the direct factor purchase quadrant (lower right) shows the distribution of primary inputs to final users.

The matrix of technical coefficients is derived from the interindustry transactions quadrant and provides the planner with crucial information, namely, how much intermediate input is necessary to produce a unit of a particular

Exhibit 7.3

Hypothetical input-output table

Outputs: Producing sectors \\ Inputs: Consuming sectors	Industry	Agriculture	Other sectors	Total intermediate production	Consumption (C)	Exports (E)	Government and defense (G)	Total final demand (D)	Total gross output (GO)
Columns:	1	2	3	4	5	6	7	8	9
Industry	X_{11}	X_{12}	X_{13}	$\Sigma \chi_{1j}$	C_1	E_1	G_1	D_1	$D_1 + \Sigma \chi_{1j}$
Agriculture	X_{21}	X_{22}	X_{23}	$\Sigma \chi_{2j}$	C_2	E_2	G_2	D_2	$D_2 + \Sigma \chi_{2j}$
Other sectors	X_{31}	X_{32}	X_{33}	$\Sigma \chi_{3j}$	C_3	E_3	G_3	D_3	$D_3 + \Sigma \chi_{3j}$
Total intermediate use	$\Sigma \chi_{1i}$	$\Sigma \chi_{2i}$	$\Sigma \chi_{3i}$	$\Sigma \Sigma \chi_{1i}$	ΣC	ΣE	ΣG	$D_1 + D_2 + D_3$	
Labor	L_1	L_2	L_3	ΣL_i	L_C	L_E	L_G	ΣL	
Capital	K_1	K_2	K_3	ΣK_i	K_C	K_E	K_U	ΣK	
Land	LA_1	LA_2	LA_3	ΣLA_i	LA_C	LA_E	LA_G	ΣLA	
Total inputs	I_1	I_2	I_3	ΣI_i	I'_C	I'_E	I'_G	$\Sigma I'$	
Columns:	1	2	3	4	5	6	7	8	

Notes: $D_i = C_i + E_i + G_i$; $I_j + L_j + K_j + LA_j$; $I'_C - L_C + K_C + LA_C$ etc.

output. The use of the input-output model is limited (unless the I-0 table is re-computed regularly) insofar as it assumes constancy of these coefficients. Thus, it is assumed that the production functions underlying the relationship exhibit constant returns to scale and are without factor substitution. Although such assumptions may seem unduly restrictive, there has been considerable support for the use of this method of planning, at least in the short run. Let us return to the Soviet case, illustrating how a feasible plan could be formulated using the input-output approach.

Assuming that Soviet planners have a matrix of technical coefficients (*A*) derived from past performance, the plan process would begin with the specification by the planner of the final demands (*Y*) to be produced in the forthcoming plan year. The next step, matrix inversion, provides the planner with a list of gross outputs of each sector (*X*) that will, if produced, satisfy the planner's demand for final output.* The power of this model lies in the fact that, within reason, even for an economy disaggregated into a considerable number of producing and using sectors, the computation of sectorial outputs can be computerized. Furthermore, the matrix inversion process takes into account both initial *and* second-round effects (something material balancing cannot do), a feature crucial to the development of a balanced plan.

If the planner decides to increase the output of steel, obviously it will be necessary to increase the output of electricity, since electricity is used in the production of steel. However, when the output of electricity is increased, more inputs used in the generation of electricity will be needed, and so on. The process of matrix inversion is powerful in the sense that it can take into account all these second-round effects and, with the aid of a computer, permit the rapid calculation of a number of feasible plan variants. It is in this capability that the real power of the input-output method lies. The process of adjustment to changing outputs can be captured and the feasibility of numerous variants checked. If adjustments are necessary, the alternatives can be calculated quickly. The process of plan formulation is iterative or sequential. The input-

---

*If the matrix of technical coefficients is known, and the input-output table is entirely in physical units, then the consistency of a set of control figures can be checked almost immediately by using the formula $(I - A)X = Y$, where X is the proposed vector of control figures (in gross output terms), A is the familiar Leontief matrix of technical coefficients, I is the identity matrix, and Y is the vector of final outputs. An inconsistency in the proposed control figures would be indicated by a negative Y element, or by a Y element that is unacceptably small in light of planned investment, consumption, and exports. Thus, the internal consistency of alternative vectors of control figures could be readily determined simply by matrix multiplication.

If, on the other hand, Soviet planners desired to compute the vector of gross outputs (*X*) required to produce a proposed vector of final output targets (*Y*), then the following formula can be used: $(I - A)^{-1}Y = X$, where $(I - A)^{-1}$ is the inverse of $(I - A)$ and X is the set of required gross outputs. The feasibility of producing Y would be determined by considering the primary factor requirements (labor, capital, etc.) of the various programs relative to their availabilities.

output approach facilitates the rapid execution of a complicated iterative process.

If the input-output approach were the theoretical basis of material balance planning, it would provide a powerful basis for plan formulation. There are a number of basic problems with the input-output approach, all of which have tended to limit its practical application in the Soviet case.[12]

First, there has been an element of ideological bias against such methods, a bias that was particularly strong during the Stalin era but that has slackened in recent years. In the early years, when economic laws and the notion of balance and equilibrium were rejected, one can understand official distrust of input-output procedures.*

Second, the Soviet system of data gathering does not adapt itself well to input-output technology. Data are gathered on an administrative basis rather than on the product basis required to compute input-output tables. Material balances are prepared on an industrial-branch basis and result in concrete plans for the various industrial ministries. Yet these ministries tend to produce internally a broad range of products (steel, machinery, and consumer goods in one ministry, for example) that should show up in different commodity categories in an input-output table. A far more serious data problem is the generally poor and unreliable data base underlying both the construction of input-output balances and industrial planning. This tends to result in what one Soviet economist has termed "natural calamities"[13] when the technological coefficients are actually estimated.

---

*If the matrix B represents a matrix of primary resource coefficients, where b_{kj} represents the amount of the kth primary factor (land, labor, capital, etc.) required to produce one unit of output of commodity j, then

$$B(I - A)^{-1} = T$$

is the matrix of full primary resource coefficients. Each element of T (t_{kj}) indicates the amount of primary factor k required both directly and indirectly to produce one unit of commodity j. The price of j would, therefore, be computed by multiplying the p_k by the t_{kj}, where p_k is the price of the kth primary factor; and summing over the k's (assuming n primary factors) yields

$$p_i = \sum_{k=1}^{n} p_k \, t_{kj}$$

The "optimality" problem could be solved by determining all the Y vectors that meet the following condition:

$$TY = Z$$

where Z is the vector of primary resource availabilities. These Y vectors would represent a production possibilities schedule from which the optimal vector could be chosen as defined by the planners' objective function.

Third, it has proved difficult to compute complete input-output tables in physical terms. Most products are heterogeneous and must be aggregated in value terms. It is difficult to convert from the value figures (for example, rubles of steel) to the physical figures (for example, tons of steel...) needed by supply planners.

Fourth, material balance planners have traditionally derived balances for between 300 and 2000 materials. At the distribution stage, they have planned about 10 times the higher figure. Yet the Central Statistical Agency's 1959 national input-output table was a 73 by 73 matrix, and the 1966 and 1972 tables were 110 by 110.[14] Work has been done on a 600-branch national table by the Academy of Sciences (Siberian branch).[15] Input-output tables of much larger dimensions would have to be developed to preserve the current level of disaggregation of the material balance system. Given the current data-gathering capacity and computational sophistication of the Soviet Union, this has proved to be too complicated a task. Thus, the input-output tables used for planning will have to be at a higher level of aggregation than the material balance and industrial supply system. Soviet planners, who harbor no ideological dislike of input-output planning, must be concerned about its real-world applicability.

AN EVALUATION OF MATERIAL BALANCE PLANNING

The input-output approach is a powerful theoretical base for material balance planning. However, for a number of reasons that we have discussed, planning practice is really material balance planning. What are the strengths and weaknesses of the material balance approach?

On the positive side, by placing pressure on enterprises in the form of taut targets designed to strain enterprise capacity, Soviet planning brought about rapid growth of industrial output in selected priority sectors and presided over the vast and rapid transformation of the Soviet economy in the 1930s. The major strength of Soviet planning is its ability to direct resources into priority areas with more speed and force than can a market-directed economy. Taut planning does not mean chaos. Although taut output targets often exceed enterprise capacities and create supply shortages, ultimately planners can equate supplies and demands by directing available resources into higher-priority enterprises. The Soviets themselves stress that their planning system replaces the "anarchy of the market" by rational direction of resources.[16] Soviet planners recognized from the very outset of the industrialization drive that taut planning would result in severe strains and pressures on the economy, but they considered the risks well worth taking. Taut (*naprazhennye*) plans continue to be demanded by the Soviet leadership and remain a basic fact of industrial planning up to the present. For example, *Gosplan* was directed by the Central Committee of the CPSU to undertake three separate revisions of the ninth Five Year Plan (1971–1975) so as to uncover further "hidden reserves" of the economy—a euphemism for increasing the tautness of the plan. As growth continued to decline in the 1980s, *Gosplan* continued to be pressured into finding further "hidden reserves."

Taut planning is seen as enforcing plan discipline. The greater the degree of slack in the economy, the greater the flexibility exercised by managers at the local level and the greater the likelihood that production may stray from strict adherence to the priority system. In other words, taut planning is required to enable central authorities to maintain strict control over the economy.[17]

Second, arguments can be made for Soviet-style taut industrial planning on other grounds, using the theories of Western development economics. By setting taut (often unattainable) targets rather than setting moderate targets that avoid bottlenecks, enterprises will be forced to expand to the limits of their production possibilities and the economy will be pulled up to higher production levels in the process. This pressure, combined with an appropriate degree of administrative flexibility, could lead to more rapid economic growth than would have occurred under more "rational" balanced planning. In the language of Soviet planning, the plan should serve not to balance resources but to "mobilize" the economy.[18]

On the negative side, it is recognized that excesses result from the Soviet material balance system.[19] First, the pressured Soviet system forces Soviet managers to engage in dysfunctional behavior. Faced with overambitious targets and lacking supplies, managers engage in excessive stockpiling. They strive to build up emergency stocks as "safety factors," which they can use for future plan fulfillment or for trading, by overstating input requirements to their superiors. The economy loses from excessive stockpiling on two counts: scarce materials tend to stand idle (resources are wasted) and planners receive inaccurate information. On another score, the taut planning system has created a definite sellers' market, which has meant that managers can generally unload their output irrespective of its quality and design. This feature has been an important source of the quality problems so widely noted in the Soviet press.

Second, material balance planning is cumbersome and slow. Enterprises get their finalized targets well into the operating year (often as late as March) and must work without knowing what their targets actually are. When targets are received late, enterprises desperately attempt to meet production targets at the end of each period by *Shturmovshchina*—"storming"—a fairly inefficient method of scheduling production. Informal methods have been developed to get around the problem of late plans. One, the "correction principle," involves the use of advance estimates at each stage of the planning process prior to receipt of the information on the current production targets. Another is the "advance fund allotment," which gives enterprises a percentage of the previous period's input allotments to tide them over until the final plan is received. Ministries "reserve" a portion of material allotments to aid in combatting bottlenecks.[20] With planning delays and informal supply methods, Soviet administrators have found that planning is less of a problem when targets change only marginally from year to year. There is a built-in tendency in the Soviet planning system to avoid dramatic change. Soviet planning, as Igor Birman has emphasized, is "from the achieved level."[21] Because of planning complexity, *Gosplan* begins its projections with the output levels achieved in the past. It then adds on a growth factor (often arbitrarily) to determine current planned output levels. There is no opportunity to consider whether the "achieved level" from which planning begins is appropriate. At the enterprise level, the manager is reluctant to introduce new technologies that require a restructuring of established supply channels. In general, the introduction of new technology and of new ways of doing things is retarded by the material balance system.[22]

Third, the Soviet planning system, with its stress on output goals, generates dysfunctional behavior at various planning levels. The enterprise will pursue output targets even if they lead to clearly irrational results.[23] The ministry tends to be primarily concerned with the success of enterprises under its own control and places the input needs of its own enterprises over those of enterprises outside its control. The planning system does not foster concern for the environment, because enterprise managers are judged on the basis of output target fulfillment, not on the basis of environmental protection or conservation of natural resources. Also, the uncertainties of the material supply system have caused enterprises to adopt peculiar production patterns. Soviet enterprises integrate as many operations as possible to provide their own material inputs; it is not rare in the Soviet Union for machinery-producing enterprises to fabricate their own steel.[24] Thus, vital specialization of production is limited by the planning system.

A fourth criticism is that material balance planning requires a large bureaucracy. The theme of a rapidly growing cadre of administrative personnel is a subject of continuing complaint in the Soviet press.[25] At the same time, Soviet official statistics do not support the view that the administrative apparatus is especially large. A study by Gur Ofer came to the conclusion that the size of the administrative apparatus is smaller than one would expect, based on the evidence of development patterns in other countries.[26] Ofer's results have been challenged, but they suggest at a minimum that fears of a cancerous growth of the Soviet bureaucracy are overstated.

A final criticism is that material balance planning aims for *consistency*, not *optimality*. A consistent plan is one in which supplies and demands of funded commodities are equal. Consistency is a clear objective of the material balance system. If the plan were inconsistent, plan fulfillment would become a competitive struggle for deficit inputs that the planner would have difficulty controlling, even with the priority system. Instead, connections, prestige, and ability to maneuver (already important factors in plan fulfillment) would primarily determine who would be able to fulfill the target—a definitely undesirable situation in a controlled economy.

On the other hand, *optimality* should also be a desirable goal. To illustrate the concept of optimality, consider a situation where five different sets of control figures are consistent. From the point of view of the state, it would be desirable to be able to choose the "best," or optimal, figures; to do otherwise would be to misallocate scarce resources.* The Soviet material balance system works so slowly that planners are fortunate if they approximate just one consistent plan variant in the allotted planning period. Current Soviet balancing techniques, time, and manpower are inadequate to find several consistent plan variants from which to choose the optimal one, and the Soviets' disregard of the importance of optimality is a major weakness of material balance planning.[27]

IS THE SOVIET ECONOMY A "PLANNED" ECONOMY?

One long-time observer of the Soviet economy, Eugene Zaleski, argues that the Soviet economy is better described as a centrally *managed* rather than a centrally planned economy.[28] By this, Zaleski means that the construction of the plan is only the first step in the resource allocation process. The decisions made during the implementation stage are just as important. Moreover, much economic activity remains out of the purview of planners and is controlled by local officials, enterprises, and even private markets. The extent of economic activity not controlled by planners has caused observers to question whether the Soviet economy is "planned" after all.[29]

The discussion about whether the Soviet economy is "planned" has led to the search for fixed reference points in Soviet planning. If enterprises are able to bargain easily for adjustments in plan targets or manipulate their own plans, and if long-run plans are continuously violated by annual operational plans, are there indeed operational plans in the Soviet economy that are binding on their recipients? Moreover, if enterprises are punished for good plan performance by being given even more difficult plan targets in the next period, will not enterprises react counterproductively by holding plan fulfillment below potential? A *ratchet effect* exists when planners make current plan targets dependent on last year's plan overfulfillment (and thus discourage plan overfulfillment). The evidence (to be discussed in Chapter 8) is overwhelming that enterprise plans are not firm and that Soviet enterprises are subject to a ratchet effect.

David Granick maintains that ministerial output plans are firm binding plans even if enterprise plans are not. In this sense, Granick argues, the Soviet economy does operate ultimately on the basis of economic plans.[30] Moreover, Granick maintains that Soviet planners do not subject the ministries to the ratchet effect because of its known counterproductive long-run effects on economic performance. Granick notes that if plans are not firm, in the sense that plans depend on the actual performance of the planned agent, agents will manipulate their performance to change the plan to better suit the agent's inter-

---

*The optimal set of control figures could be defined in technical terms as the one that yields the maximum value of all consistent sets when entered into the planners' objective function; that is, the consistent set of control figures that the planners regard as the "best" in terms of their preferences and biases.

ests. With changing plans that depend on ongoing performance, the agent will engage in a gaming exercise to elicit more favorable plans from the principal. This gaming can take place with reference to the current period, and it can also take place with reference to future periods if next period's plan is dependent on this year's performance (the ratchet effect).

As Granick notes, it is an empirical issue whether Soviet planners assign firm plans to ministries. This issue is not easy to clarify because of the difficulty of relating actual plan fulfillment by the appropriate economic organizations to their original plan targets. Soviet economic data do not make this an easy comparison. Granick's own empirical analysis covering Soviet data for 1966–1977 suggests that Soviet ministries do tend to fulfill the plans assigned to them by superior planning organizations and that the next period's plan is not affected by ministry plan fulfillment in the current period. Granick's conclusion is supported by the empirical research for the same time period of Alice Gorlin and David Doane, who find that Soviet ministerial plans are firm and that the ministries do indeed succeed in fulfilling these firm plans.[31] Moreover, differences among ministries in plan fulfillment appear to be random and not systematically related to any explanatory factors. As in the case of many empirical issues, contrary evidence has been brought forth. Michael Keren maintains, using alternate econometric methods, that ministerial plan targets are indeed affected by ministerial plan fulfillment during the previous plan period. Keren also presents theoretical arguments as to why Soviet planners might be willing to base current plan targets on previous plan fulfillment, especially if they have a short time horizon.[32] Presumably, further study of this issue will eventually resolve the controversy over the firmness of ministry plans, but it does appear that, relatively speaking, ministry plans are firmer than enterprise plans.

MONEY AS A SOFT BUDGET CONSTRAINT

In some ways, money in the Soviet economy plays a role similar to that in other systems, namely, as a store of value, a medium of exchange, and a unit of account. There is, however, a very basic difference between money in the Soviet economy and in market economic systems. Money influences real economic activity in market systems; monetary policy influences real economic variables through interest rates, unanticipated inflation, and changes in relative prices. In the Soviet economy, there is little or no connection between monetary and real phenomena; money is *neutral* in terms of economic activity.

Janos Kornai has argued that in the Soviet Union, as in other planned socialist economies, money acts as a *soft budget constraint*.[33] Financial outcomes, such as profits or credits, do not affect real economic variables, such as output or employment. If an enterprise, for example, fails to cover its costs, automatic subsidies prop it up. The absence of profits does not alter enterprise output or employment. The availability of credit does not ensure that an enterprise will obtain real capital equipment because the decision on who will get the real capital is made by administrative decree, not according to the availability of credits.

RUBLE CONTROL

The enterprise *techpromfinplan* (technical-industrial-financial plan) includes a pervasive financial plan as well as physical input and output indicators. This financial plan parallels the physical section of the industrial supply and output plans and acts as a check on enterprise performance. The financial plan consists of a wage bill, planned cost reductions, and credit plans for purchasing inputs, along with many other targets. The amount of detail contained in the financial plan has varied over the years, but financial targets continue to serve as the monetary counterparts of enterprise output and input targets.

Soviet managers have tended to regard the fulfillment of financial plans (cost reduction targets, wage bills, credit plans, etc.) as less important than output plans. Despite this, financial targets enhance the planners' control over enterprise operations. In the Soviet terminology, this is called *ruble control (kontrol' rublem):* Because the financial plan is the monetary counterpart of a firm's input and output plans, deviations from the financial plan signal deviations from the physical plan. If a firm's labor input plan calls for the employment of 500 workers, the enterprise can draw only enough cash from its bank account to pay that number. If the input plan calls for 10 tons of steel, the enterprise can draw upon its funded input account only enough for that particular transaction, nothing in excess. If the firm is in need of working capital, short-term credit will be granted only if the transaction is called for in the plan. Reinforcing the system of ruble control is the fact that all (legal) interfirm transactions are handled by *Gosbank* (the State Bank), which supervises all such transactions and is the sole center for the settling of accounts.[34]

The Soviet manager, in response to this system of financial supervision, has developed informal sources of supply that do not require bank clearing operations and other informal devices to circumvent many financial controls.[35] Also, successful firms are often not strictly held to their financial plans. Financial controls are used primarily to detect significant deviations from planned activities, and desired corrections are normally made administratively. However, in recent years, state control over funds for wages has become very strict. The wage fund is, in many instances, a binding constraint. Despite the flexibility and circumventions of financial controls, ruble control remains an important monitoring device in the Soviet planning system.

PUBLIC FINANCE AND THE STATE BUDGET

The major allocation decisions in the Soviet Union are reflected in the annual budget of the USSR, which determines the allocation of total output by end use among private consumption, investment, public consumption, defense, and administration. The annual budget of the USSR is a consolidated budget, which encompasses the all-union budget, the state budgets of the republics, and the local budgets of provinces, regions, and districts.[36] It is a much more comprehensive system of accounts than the budget of the United States, which encompasses only federal receipts and expenditures.

As one might expect, a much larger portion of the Soviet GNP flows through its state budget than is the case with the American GNP. Between 1929 and the present, 10 to 30 percent of American GNP has been channeled through government budgets (including state and local government). In the Soviet Union, the cumulative average for the postwar period has been about 45 percent. The relatively greater importance of the state budget in the Soviet economy derives from the financing of most investment directly from the state budget and because communal consumption (public health, education, and welfare) represents a larger share of total consumption in the Soviet Union. Thus, the scope of public goods is broader in the USSR than in the United States. In a sense, one could argue that all products produced by the Soviet economy are public because they are produced by state or collective enterprises. However, in dealing with the Soviet economy, the convention is that if the enterprise operates on its own accounting system, independently of the state budget, it is not considered a public enterprise.

The budget of the USSR directs resources into consumption, investment, defense, and administration in the following manner: The state collects revenues from sales taxes (the so-called turnover tax), deductions from enterprise profits, direct taxes on the population, and social insurance contributions (see Table 7.3). The first two alone have consistently accounted for over 60 percent of total revenues throughout most of the plan period. These revenues are then directed through the national budget, the republican budgets, and provincial and local budgets to various uses: to finance investment in the form of grants, which at various times has accounted for between 33 and 64 percent of total expenditures (the "national economy" category); to finance communal consumption ("social and cultural undertakings"), which has accounted for from 14 to 36 percent of the total; and to finance defense and administration.

Although Soviet officials have claimed that the State budget has been balanced over the years, independent estimates show that the budget deficit has been between 2 and 8 percent of the Soviet GNP in the 1980s.[37] Large deficits were acknowledged by the Ministry of Finance in 1988. The budget deficits of the 1980s have been due both to falling revenues and rising expenditures. Declining growth has meant less revenue from profit taxes, falling oil prices have meant less revenue from foreign trade, and good subsidies have cut into turnover tax collections. In 1988, the budget deficit of 68 billion rubles was about 8 percent of GNP. More than half of this deficit was financed by monetary creation, the long-run effects of which could be inflationary. The inflationary effects of budget deficits are discussed below.

PLANNING FOR INFLATION

Once the overall allocation of budget resources into nonprivate consumption uses (investment, communal consumption, defense, and administration) is made and the physical outputs of consumer goods are specified by *Gosplan*, fi-

Table 7.3 THE BUDGET OF THE USSR, 1931–1988

	1931	1934	1937	1940	1950	1960	1970	1978	1984	1988
					Receipts (percent of total)					
Turnover tax	46	64	69	59	56	41	32	32	30	24
Deductions from profits	8	5	9	12	10	24	35	30	30	37
Social insurance	9	10	6	5	5	5	5	5	7	8
Taxes on population	4	7	4	5	9	7	8	8	8	9
Other revenue	33	14	12	19	20	23	20	25	25	22
					Expenditures (percent of total)					
National economy	64	56	41	33	38	47	48	54	56	—
Social and cultural undertakings	14	15	24	24	28	34	36	34	33	—
Defense	5	9	17	33	20	13	12	7	5	—
Adminstration and justice	4	4	4	4	3	2	1	1	1	—
Other expenditures	13	16	14	6	11	4	3	4	5	—

Sources: Narodnoe khoziaistvo SSSR v 1970 g [The national economy of the USSR in 1970], (Moscow: Statistika, 1971), p. 731; *The Soviet Financial System* (Columbus: Bureau of Business Research of Ohio State University, 1951), pp. 84–87; *Narodnoe khoziaistvo SSSR v 1978 g* [The national economy of the USSR in 1978] (Moscow: Statistika, 1979), p. 534; *SSSR v tsifrakh v 1984 godu* [USSR in figures in 1984] (Moscow Finansyi Statistika, 1985), pp. 50–51; Directorate of Intelligence, *USSR: Sharply Higher Budget Deficits Threaten Perestroyka*, Washington, D.C., SOV 88-10043U, September 1988, p. 18. As will be explained in a later chapter, the defense share is grossly understated by Soviet budget figures.

nancial authorities (the State Bank and the Ministry of Finance) must ensure that a macroequilibrium of supply and demand exists.

The objective of Soviet financial planning at the macro level is to balance the aggregate money demand for consumer goods with the aggregate supply at established prices. This is done centrally, because planning authorities must ensure the compatibility of the output of consumer goods at established prices with employment levels and wage rates. The smaller the planned output of consumer goods and the larger the number employed and the higher the wages, the more likely that aggregate money demand will exceed available supply at established prices.

An algebraic example illustrates this relationship. This example is the same as the consumer goods balance given above, but it is now broken down into consumer and producer goods. Assume that the output plan calls for enterprises to produce Q_1 "units" of consumer goods and Q_2 "units" of producer goods. The planners determine, through the use of labor input coefficients, that L_1 worker-years of labor are required to produce Q_1 and that L_2 worker-years are required to produce Q_2, and these employment levels are accordingly targeted by *Gosplan*. The workers are paid the prevailing wage rates in the consumer and producer goods sectors, respectively, and average annual wages are denoted in the two sectors as W_1 and W_2, respectively. In this manner, an annual wage income of $W_1L_1 + W_2L_2$ from public-sector employment is created.

The total demand for consumer goods, therefore, is that portion of total income that is not taxed away or saved. If personal taxes are denoted by T and personal savings by R, the total money demand (D) for consumer goods is

$$D = W_1L_1 + W_2L_2 + O - T - R$$

where O denotes other earnings (from interest or private-economy earnings). The total supply of consumer goods at established prices (S) is the total value of all consumer goods (denoted as P_1Q_1):

$$S = P_1Q_1$$

where P_1 denotes the existing consumer price level.

The task of the financial authorities is to strike an appropriate balance between consumer demand and supply at prevailing prices, that is, between $W_1L_1 + W_2L_2 + O - T - R$ and P_1Q_1.

The success of Soviet financial authorities in striking such a balance has varied over the years. In the 1930s, enterprises, faced with taut planning targets, bid among themselves for labor, driving up wages by over 500 percent between 1928 and 1937. At the same time, the shift of labor from agriculture to industry raised the full-time labor force. The shift in priorities to heavy industry caused the output of real consumer goods to stagnate or even decline. The net result was a substantial inflation (consumer goods prices rose over 700 percent between 1928 and 1937). Yet with the reduction of consumer goods output, inflation was not high enough to eliminate the gap between aggregate demand and supply. The 1930s were characterized by substantial *repressed* inflation. Soviet authorities simply allowed some of the excess consumer demand to persist. Despite rapidly rising retail prices, consumer demand still exceeded supply. Soviet authorities were therefore called upon to ration consumer goods either formally or indirectly during most of the 1930s. Such rationing proved necessary because Soviet financial authorities found it difficult to keep prices high enough to eliminate inflationary pressures in the face of the numerous unplanned wage increases and shortfalls in plan fulfillment in the consumer sector.

Rationing of essential consumer goods was introduced in the winter of 1928–1929, first on foodstuffs and then on manufactured consumer goods. To maintain labor incentives, to preserve the effectiveness of wage differentials, and to reward special groups, Soviet pricing authorities sanctioned a complex system of multiple prices during the early 1930s with higher prices paid in uncontrolled markets.[38]

While prices in state and cooperative stores doubled between 1928 and 1932, collective farm market prices, the only legal free-market prices, rose 30 times, a clear indication of the extent of repressed inflation. After 1932, this differential was reduced and nearly closed in 1937, but it was opened again by the outbreak of World War II. Because of the complex multiple price system, it is difficult to gauge trends in the general price level during the 1930s. What is known for sure, however, is that retail prices rose substantially, but not by enough to eliminate the excess consumer demand entirely—as is witnessed by the long queues and the multiple prices of the 1930s.

The substantial inflationary pressures of the industrialization drive of the 1930s and the war years subsided in the postwar era. The Soviet history of inflation is a chronological reverse of that of the capitalist West. In the 1930s, prices were generally falling in the West at a time when inflation was high in the Soviet Union. In the West, the postwar era saw accelerating inflation from the mid-1960s to the early 1980s at the time when inflationary pressures were easing in the Soviet Union. From the official price statistics published by Soviet statistical authorities, it appears that overt inflation has been virtually eliminated in the postwar era. According to official indices, Soviet retail prices declined substantially in the immediate postwar years. From 1965 to 1982 (the period of greatest price acceleration in the West), the official Soviet price index rose by only 8 percent. Soviet pricing and monetary authorities reduced (or even eliminated) inflationary pressures using a variety of measures.

Wholesale price increases were limited (such as in industry) or did not result in increases in retail prices (such as in agriculture). Over the 1965–1982 period, industrial wholesale prices rose only 15 percent, according to official statistics. In the case of agricultural products, where wholesale purchase prices were raised to make farm production profitable, retail prices of these products were raised, the difference being absorbed by the state as a subsidy. In other instances, the turnover tax rate was reduced, to allow wholesale prices to increase without commensurate increases at the retail level.

The consumer goods balance equation shows that inflationary pressures are determined by the relationship between money income and the output of consumer goods. Although the average monthly money wage grew steadily since the 1950s, so, too, did the output of consumer goods and services. Average annual wages increased by 90 percent between 1965 and 1982, while the real output of consumer goods increased by about 83 percent. In the postwar years, planners controlled inflationary forces better than in the 1930s and 1940s. No longer could enterprises draw excess funds for wage payments from their *Gosbank* accounts, and state control over wage payments increased. The upshot of these changes was that average annual wage increases were held to modest rates (by Western standards) throughout the mid-1980s. Wage inflation, a major source of inflationary pressure in the 1930s, has been kept under better control in the postwar years.

The 1980s have seen an acceleration of inflation. State retail prices rose at more than 2 percent per annum in the 1980s according to Western recalculations. More ominously, prices in collective farm markets were rising near double-digit rates in 1987 and 1988. The official plan fulfillment report for 1987 related that potatoes, fruits, vegetables, meat, and butter were selling at levels 2.5 to 4 times higher than in state retail outlets.[39]

Although Soviet inflation rates appear low by Western standards, the higher inflation rates of the 1980s are viewed with alarm by Soviet financial authorities. The inflation has been caused by a number of factors: plan shortfalls in consumer goods production, rising budget deficits, average wages rising faster than productivity. Rising inflation may also be a sign that the Soviet leadership has determined that overt inflation is better than repressed inflation with its accompanying rationing and queues. Even with higher inflation, rationing is still present. In September 1988, *Pravda* noted that rationing had been introduced in eight republics.[40]

It is difficult to determine what the actual rate of inflation in the Soviet Union has been over time. The official price indexes are for official prices in state retail outlets, and these prices have been held artificially low. Insofar as official prices generally have not cleared markets, consumer spending has spilled over into collective farm markets (in which prices are set by supply and demand) and into the "second economy"—the Soviet Union's underground economy. Soviet pricing authorities do publish periodic data on collective farm market prices, and one good indicator of repressed inflation is the differential between food price increases in official outlets and in collective farm markets. There are no official data on second-economy prices, so one can only guess as to the rate of inflation in the second economy.

Western experts have devoted considerable research to recalculating Soviet inflation rates.[41] Although these studies agree that official claims of extreme price stability are exaggerated, they nevertheless fail to uncover inflation rates that would be regarded as high by Western standards. The late 1980s may prove an exception in light of the exceptionally high inflation rates in collective farm markets during this period.

Soviet pricing officials face a dilemma in the 1990s. Over the years, they have been able to "buy" official price stability by allowing consumer purchases to spill over into collective farm markets and into the underground economy. This practice has created excess demand in official markets and a complex multiple price system where different prices are charged for the same good depending on the type of market in which the consumer buys. If Soviet authorities desire to eliminate such practices, they must bring prices in state stores in line with prices charged in free markets, and this would require a substantial increase in official prices, especially of food prices. The Soviet public, on the other hand, has resisted official price increases, perhaps because people have learned to live in this complex world of multiple prices. Substantial increases in official prices could lead to political backlashes, especially in a Soviet society that permits greater freedom of expression.

We would draw the following conclusion. The growth of disposable income has been kept more in line with the growth of the real output of consumer goods in the Soviet Union over that past quarter century. Thus, severe inflationary pressures in the sense of balance between aggregate demand and aggregate supply have been avoided. Official Soviet price indexes (and their recalculated versions) bear witness to this point. Such a macrobalance is not inconsistent with testimony on goods shortages. A macrobalance does not rule out severe microimbalances in which excess inventories of one type of good build up while there are long lines for other goods. Even with a macrobalance, Soviet consumers could form negative impressions about living standards when confronted with severe microimbalances in the consumer sector. We shall return to this point in our discussion of Soviet prices in Chapter 8.

BANKING AND MONETARY CREATION

The Soviet banking system plays an integral role in planning. Soviet banking is quite unlike its Western counterpart, for it is dominated by a single bank, *Gosbank*, which is a monopoly bank in its purest form. As a monopoly bank, *Gosbank* combines the functions of central and commercial banking, but owing to the absence of money and capital markets, some traditional banking functions (open-market operations, commercial-paper transactions, etc.) are not performed by *Gosbank*.

The tremendous scope of *Gosbank's* organization is difficult to conceptualize: it has more than 150,000 employees and more than 300 main offices, about 3500 local branches, and 2000 collection offices. *Gosbank's* customers include approximately 250,000 enterprises, 40,000 collective farm accounts, and nearly one-half million government organizations. Since 1954, *Gosbank* has been independent of the Ministry of Finance, and its director has ministerial status in the government. Since 1963, the savings bank system (with over 70,000 branches) has been incorporated into *Gosbank's* operations. The only other banks in the Soviet Union are the specialized banks: the Investment Bank (*Stroibank*) and the Foreign Trade Bank (*Vneshtorgbank*). The former is concerned with the disbursing of funds budgeted for capital investment, and the latter handles international transactions; neither competes with *Gosbank*.[42]

Throughout its history, *Gosbank* has had three functions: first, to make short-term loans for the working capital needs of enterprises; second, to oversee enterprise plan fulfillment and to monitor payments to the population by acting as the center of all accounts; third, to create money.

Each Soviet enterprise deals directly with a local *Gosbank* branch. It is dependent on *Gosbank* for short-term credit to finance inventories and working capital. Its receipts are automatically deposited at *Gosbank*, and it draws cash for wage payments at the discretion of the branch bank. In addition, the portion of its own profits that the enterprise is allowed to retain remains on deposit at, and under the supervision of, *Gosbank*. *Gosbank* is the sole legal grantor of short-term credit. Interfirm credit is forbidden, and a strict discipline on payments is enforced in interfirm transactions to prevent spontaneous interfirm lending. In addition, all interfirm transactions (except small payments) involving funds in enterprise accounts are handled by, and are subject to the supervision of, *Gosbank*.

As far as the control function of *Gosbank* is concerned, its supervision of enterprise accounts and its short-term lending operations are important. As the single clearing agent for the economy and the sole source of short-term credit, *Gosbank* is in a unique position to monitor the activities of enterprises. In drawing up short-term credit plans and in controlling enterprise accounts,

Gosbank plays a largely passive role by providing the monetary resources required to implement the physical plan. In making short-term loans for working capital, *Gosbank* has tended to grant production credit for specific purposes: if a particular transaction is called for in the input plan, the firm is automatically granted credit for this specific purpose. Not only is credit granted for specific purposes, but all interfirm transactions are cleared by *Gosbank,* and *Gosbank* must receive evidence of the transaction, such as a lading bill, before the clearing operation is completed. In this way, as the enterprise financial plan is the monetary counterpart of the physical plan, deviations from the physical plan will reveal themselves as deviations from the financial plan. This is a further extension of *ruble control.* Even if an enterprise builds up excess balances at *Gosbank,* this liquidity still does not represent a command over producer goods unless they are specifically called for in the plan.[43]

As the social accounting center monitoring cash payments to the population, *Gosbank* plays a role in the macroeconomic planning described previously. It provides financial authorities with data on disposable income for macroplanning. In case of a projected imbalance, *Gosbank* will try to limit the flow of wage payments to the population as much as possible, within the limits of the plan. This is accomplished primarily by restricting the convertibility of enterprise accounts into cash for wage payments and by permitting wage payments in excess of the planned wage bill only if the output target is overfulfilled.

The monopoly powers of *Gosbank* are seldom used to influence the flow of production. Instead, *Gosbank 's* audit operations serve primarily to reveal to planning authorities deviations from planned tasks, which are then corrected by the planners. Throughout its history, *Gosbank* has tended to automatically meet the credit needs of the economy (as specified in the plan) instead of regulating the flow of money and credit on a discretionary basis in order to direct the level of economic activity.

Gosbank, in conjunction with the Ministry of Finance, controls the supply of money in the Soviet Union.[44] How central banks control the money supply in the West is well known. How *Gosbank* determines the Soviet money supply is less well understood. The basic Soviet money supply consists of cash and currency outside the Soviet banking system. *Gosbank* primarily creates new money by authorizing enterprises to pay additional wage funds. Republican *Gosbank* branches have sufficient cash funds to meet wage payments of republican enterprises if cash inflows into the bank (as a result of consumer goods purchases, insurance payments, etc.) equal the outflow of cash funds required to meet enterprise wage bills. If cash inflows fall short of current wage bills for the economy as a whole, *Gosbank* must release fresh cash into the economy. Shortfalls in consumer goods sales can result in an increase in the money supply as money must be issued to meet wage bills.

Budget deficits can also result in monetary expansion. If government expenditures exceed government revenues (and the deficit is not offset by increases in household savings), *Gosbank* must release fresh cash into the economy, in effect, to pay the wages of those working on state budget accounts. In Western economies, budget deficits result in monetary expansion when the central bank monetizes the debt. Soviet state budgets lead as well to monetary expansion when *Gosbank* monetizes the debt by releasing additional cash funds.

Gregory Grossman and Igor Birman investigated the growth of the USSR money supply (data on currency in circulation are not published) and showed that monetary growth has been much more rapid than the growth of real output of consumer goods. Savings account data are published by the Soviets, and they do show substantial rises in household savings. From their investigation, Grossman and Birman believe that Soviet macroinflationary pressures have been greater than the average wage data cited above would cause us to expect.[45] Recent public release of data on state budget deficits (noted above) tend to confirm their study.

AN ASSESSMENT OF SOVIET PLANNING

This chapter has described only two parts of the Soviet planning system: output planning and financial planning. How prices are set, how capital is allocated, how the labor supply is allocated among competing ends, and how Soviet managers fulfill their plan targets will be covered in Chapters 8 and 9.

Weaknesses of the output and supply planning described in this chapter have prompted reform advocates to search for improvements and changes. The most prominent weakness probably is the slow-moving, cumbersome, and imprecise nature of material balance planning. Material balance planning must utilize and process an immense amount of information; it deals in terms of broad aggregates; and it is not able to handle qualitative differences. The official supply system that is an outgrowth of material balance planning has proven to be an unreliable source of supply, and enterprises have sought out ways to circumvent the official system. Financial planning has been viewed as being subservient to physical planning. Financial planning is designed more to provide information to physical planners than to independently influence real economic activity.

The challenge that reformers face is how to preserve the fundamental nature of a planned economy while allowing enterprises more freedom of action. What is the proper scope of planning? What decisions can be left to others, and what decisions must be made by the planners at the center?

REFERENCES

1. This section is based on the following sources: F. Kushnirsky, *Soviet Economic Planning, 1965–1980* (Boulder, Colo: Westview Press, 1982); A. Nove, *The Soviet Economic System* (London: Allen & Unwin, 1977), chaps. 1–4; W. J. Conyngham, *Industrial Management in the Soviet Union* (Stanford: Hoover Institution Press,

1973); W. J. Conyngham, *The Modernization of Soviet Industrial Management* (Cambridge: Cambridge University Press, 1982); A. C. Gorlin, "The Soviet Economic Associations," *Soviet Studies*, vol. 26, no. 1 (January 1974), 3–27; G. Grossman, "The Party as Manager and Entrepreneur," in G. Guroff and F. Carstensen, eds., *Entrepreneurship in Russia and the Soviet Union* (Princeton, N. J.: Princeton University Press, 1983), pp. 284–305; and P. R. Gregory, *The Soviet Economic Bureaucracy* (Cambridge: Cambridge University Press, 1989).

2.   E. H. Carr and R. W. Davies, *Foundations of a Planned Economy, 1926–1929*, vol. 1, part 2 (London: Macmillan, 1969), pp. 802–836.

3.   The principal/agent literature has been applied to the Soviet context by D. Granick, "Institutional Innovation and Economic Management: The Soviet Incentive System, 1921 to the Present," in G. Guroff and F. Carstensen, eds., *Entrepreneurship in Imperial Russia and the Soviet Union* (Princeton, N.J.: Princeton University Press), 1983, pp. 223–257; and by J. B. Miller, "The Big Nail and Other Stories: Product Quality in the Soviet Union," *ACES Bulletin*, vol. 26, no. 1 (Spring 1984), 43–58.

4.   Gosplan SSSR, *Metodicheskie ukazaniia razrabotke gosudarstvennykh planov i sotsial'nogo razvitiia SSSR* [Methodological directives to working out state plans and the social development of the USSR] (Moscow: Ekonomika, 1980). The authors are grateful to G. Schroeder for bringing this book to our attention.

5.   The notion of various macrobalances of the Soviet economy has been investigated by J. Millar, *The ABCs of Soviet Socialism* (Urbana: University of Illinois Press, 1981) and by J. Millar and J. Pickersgill, "Aggregate Economic Problems in Soviet-Type Economies," *ACES Bulletin*, vol. 19, no. 1 (Spring 1977), 5–20.

6.   The material presented here is largely based on the following sources: A. Bergson, *The Economics of Soviet Planning* (New Haven, Conn.: Yale University Press, 1964), chap. 7; Nove, *The Soviet Economic System*, pp. 87–96; R. W. Davies, "Soviet Planning for Rapid Industrialization, *Economics of Planning*, vol 6, no. 1 (1966); R. W. Davis, "Planning a Mature Economy in the USSR," *Economics of Planning*, vol. 6, no. 2 (1966); and M. Ellman, "The Consistency of Soviet Plans," *Scottish Journal of Political Economy*, vol. 16, no. 1 (February 1969). The last three are reprinted in M. Bornstein and D. Fusfeld, eds., *The Soviet Economy: A Book of Readings*, 3rd ed. (Homewood, Ill.: Irwin, 1970). See also H. Levine, "The Centralized Planning of Supply in Soviet Industry," in Joint Economic Committee,*Comparisons of the United States and Soviet Economies* (Washington, D.C.: U.S. Government Printing Office, 1959), pp. 151–176, reprinted in M. Bornstein and D. Fusfeld, eds., *The Soviet Economy: A Book of Readings*, rev. ed. (Homewood, Ill.: Irwin, 1965), pp. 49–65; M. Ellman, *Soviet Planning Today: Proposals for an Optimally Functioning Economic System* (Cambridge: Cambridge University Press, 1971); G. E. Schroeder, "The 'Reform' of the Supply System in Soviet Industry," *Soviet Studies*, vol. 24, no. 1 (July 1972), 97–119; G. E. Schroeder, "Recent Developments in Soviet Planning and Managerial Incentives," in Joint Economic Committee, *Soviet Economic Prospects for the Seventies* (Washington D.C.: U.S. Government Printing Office, 1973), pp. 11–38; M. Ellman, *Socialist Planning*, (Cambridge: Cambridge University Press, 1979), Nove, *The Soviet Economic System*; G. E. Schroeder, "The Soviet Economy on a Treadmill of 'Reforms,' " in Joint Economic Committee, *Soviet Economy in a Time of Change* (Washington, D.C.: U.S. Government Printing Office, 1979), vol. 1, pp. 312–340; E. Zaleski, *Stalinist Planning for Economic Growth, 1933–1952* (Chapel Hill:

University of North Carolina Press, 1980); and Kushnirsky, *Soviet Economic Planning, 1965–1980.*

7. As examples, see A. N. Efimov et al., *Ekonomicheskoe planirovanie v SSSR* [Economic planning in the USSR] (Moscow: 1967); and A. N. Efimov et al., *Metodicheskie ukazaniia.*

8. This chapter deals only with annual plans, which are the operational plans in the Soviet economy, and omits long-term "perspective planning," since historically there seems to have been little relationship between the perspective and annual plans. See N. Jasny, *Essays on the Soviet Economy* (New York: Praeger, 1962), essay 6. In theory at least, annual plans should be compiled on the basis of the five- or seven-year perspective plans, in such a manner that at the end of five (or seven) annual plans, the perspective plan targets are met. This was not generally the case for the first eight Five [Seven] Year Plans. The ninth and tenth Five Year Plans (1971–1980) apparently sought to remedy this situation by upgrading the role of the long-range plan by requiring more conformity between it and the annual operational plans. Although there was pressure during the 1970s to improve long-term planning, it is not clear that substantial gains were made. For evidence on this, see Schroeder, "Recent Developments in Soviet Planning," pp. 13–15, and Schroeder, "The Soviet Economy on a Treadmill of 'Reforms' " pp. 318–319.

9. Kushnirsky, *Soviet Economic Planning, 1965–1980,* p. 66.

10. In practice, Soviet planners have generally adjusted only for *first-order relationships* when output targets are changed because of the tremendous amount of time required to make the necessary computations. By first-order changes, we mean the additional coal, electricity, ore, and other commodities required to product the additional steel in our example. No account is taken of the additional resources required to produce the extra coal, electricity, and ore. For a detailed discussion of this point, see Levine, "The Centralized Planning of Supply," in Bornstein and Fusfeld, pp. 55–57.

11. For an introductory discussion on planning, see P. R. Gregory and R. C. Stuart, *Comparative Economic System,* 3rd ed. (Boston: Houghton Mifflin, 1989). For a discussion of the basic input-output model and its application to Soviet planning, see M. P. Todaro, *Development Planning* (Nairobi: Oxford University Press, 1971).

12. To what extent is input-output analysis actually used in the USSR? For a recent discussion and analysis of this point, see A. Tretyakova and I. Birman, "Input-Output Analysis in the USSR," *Soviet Studies,* vol 28, no. 2 (April 1976), 157–186; and V. G. Treml, "A Comment on Birman-Tretyakova," *Soviet Studies,* vol. 28, no. 2 (April 1976), 187–188. For more background material, see V. G. Treml, "Input-Output Analysis and Soviet Planning," in J. P. Hardt et al., *Mathematics and Computers in Soviet Planning* (New Haven, Conn.: Yale University Press, 1967), pp. 68–120; H. Levine, "Input-Output Analysis and Soviet Planning," *American Economic Review,* vol. 52, no. 2 (Many 1962); J. M. Montias, "On the Consistency and Efficiency of Central Planning," *Review of Economic Studies,* vol. 29, no. 81 (October 1962); B. N. Ward, *The Socialist Economy* (New York: Random House, 1967), chap. 3; V. G. Treml et al., "Interindustry Structure of the Soviet Economy, in Joint Economic Committee, *Soviet Economic Prospects for the Seventies* (Washington, D.C.: U.S. Government Printing Office, 1973), pp. 246–269; V. G. Treml et al., "The Soviet 1966 and 1972 Input-Output Table," in Joint Economic Committee, *Soviet Economy in a New Perspective* (Washington, D.C.: U.S. Government Printing Office, 1976), pp. 332–376; and D. M. Gallik et al., "The 1972 Input-Output Table and the Changing Structure of the Soviet Economy," in Joint

Economic Committee, *Soviet Economy in a Time of Change* (Washington, D.C.: U.S. Government Printing Office, 1979), vol. 1, p. 423–471.

13. Statement of S. Shatalin quoted in Treml et al., "Interindustry Structure of the Soviet Economy," p. 249.

14. *Narodnoe khoziaistvo SSSR v 1969 g.* [The national economy of the USSR in 1969] (Moscow: Statistika, 1970), pp. 50–75; Treml et al., "The Soviet 1966 and 1972 Input-Output Tables."

15. F. Baturin and P. Shemetiv, "Activities of Siberian Economists," *Problems of Economics: A Journal of Translations*, vol. 7, no. 7 (November 1969), 69. Translated from *Voprosy ekonomiki* [Problems of economics], no. 5 (1969).

16. M. Bor, *Aims and Methods of Soviet Planning* (New York: International Publishers, 1967), chap. 6.

17. R. D. Portes, "The Enterprise Under Central Planning," *Review of Economic Studies*, vol. 36, no. 106 (April 1969), 197–212. Also see M. Keren, "On the Tautness of Plans," *Review of Economic Studies*, vol. 39, no. 4 (October 1972), 469–486.

18. H. Hunter, "Optimum Tautness in Developmental Planning," *Economic Development and Cultural Change*, vol. 9, no. 4, part 1 (July 1961), 561–572. A similar argument has been made by A. Hirschman, *The Strategy of Economic Development* (New Haven, Conn.: Yale University Press, 1958), pp. 29–33. Hunter is careful to recognize that there is a level of "optimal tautness" and that Soviet planning may have exceeded this optimal limit. Western experts concluded that the ninth Five Year Plan, for example, went well beyond this optimal limit and that serious shortfalls in metals, timber, and electricity hindered its implementation. On this, see J. Noren and F. Whitehouse, "Soviet Industry in the 1971-75 Plan," in Joint Economic Committee, *Soviet Economic Prospects for the Seventies* (Washington, D.C.: U.S. Government Printing Office, 1973), pp. 207, 239–242. For a discussion of the pressure on planners to "mobilize" resources rather than formulate balanced plans, see Kushnirsky, *Soviet Economic Planning, 1965–1980.*

19. Hunter, "Optimum Tautness," pp. 567–571; and H. Levine, "Pressure and Planning in the Soviet Economy," in H. Rosovsky, ed., *Industrialization in Two Systems: Essays in Honor of Alexander Gerschenkron* (New York: Wiley, 1966), pp. 266–285. Reprinted in M. Bornstein and D. Fusfeld, eds., *The Soviet Economy: A Book of Readings* (Homewood, Ill.: Irwin, 1970), pp. 64–82.

20. Levine, "Pressure and Planning in the Soviet Economy," in Bornstein and Fusfeld, p. 73.

21. I. Birman, "From the Achieved Level," *Soviet Studies*, vol. 31, no. 2 (April 1978), 153–172.

22. J. Berliner has extensively investigated the problems of introducing new technology in the context of the Soviet planned economy; see J. Berliner, *The Innovation Decision in Soviet Industry* (Cambridge, Mass.: MIT Press, 1983).

23. In the oil industry, drilling enterprises are given targets in thousands of meters to be drilled. Theoretically, a dry hole is treated the same as a gusher. Enterprises therefore refuse to move their drilling equipment and continue to drill in the established fields. On this, see "Soviet Oil Expert Warns of Reliance on Old Fields," *New York Times*, February 13, 1980.

24. D. Granick, *Soviet Metal Fabricating and Economic Development* (Madison: University of Wisconsin Press, 1967), pp. 159–160; Schroeder, "The Soviet Economy on a Treadmill of 'Reforms,' " p. 336.

25. L. Smolinski, "What Next in Soviet Planning?" *Foreign Affairs*, vol. 42, no. 4 (July 1964), 604.

26. This evidence can be found in G. Ofer, *The Service Sector in Soviet Economic Growth* (Cambridge, Mass.: Harvard University Press, 1973). For more recent evidence, see F. L. Pryor, "Some Costs and Benefits of Markets: An Empirical Study," *Quarterly Journal of Economics*, vol. 91 (February 1977), 81–102. For additional discussion of this theme, see F. A. Durgin, "What Is Left for the Market Economy?" *ACES Bulletin*, vol. 16, no. 3 (Winter 1974), 41–51; G. E. Schroeder, "A Critique of Official Statistics on Public Administration in the USSR," *ACES Bulletin*, vol. 18, no. 1 (Spring 1976), 23–44; F. A. Durgin, "A Commentary on Gertrude Schroeder's 'Critique of Official Statistics on Public Administration in the USSR,' " *ACES Bulletin*, vol. 19, no. 1 (Spring 1977), 109–116; and G. E. Schroeder, "Reply," *ACES Bulletin*, vol. 19, no. 1 (Spring 1977), 117–118.

27. Schroeder, "The Soviet Economy on a Treadmill of 'Reforms,' " pp. 319–322, discusses the computerization of Soviet planning. About one-half of the calculations involved in the 1978 plan were aided by computers.

28. Zaleski, *Stalinist Planning*.

29. J. Wilhelm, "Does the Soviet Union Have a Planned Economy?" *Soviet Studies*, vol. 31, no. 2 (April 1979), 268–274; J. Wilhelm, "The Soviet Union Has an Administered, Not a Planned Economy, *Soviet Studies* vol. 37, no. 1 (January 1985), 118–130.

30. D. Granick, "The Ministry as the Maximizing Unit in Soviet Industry," *Journal of Comparative Economics*, vol. 4, no. 3 (September 1980), 255–273.

31. A. C. Gorlin and D. P. Doane, "Plan Fulfillment and Growth in Soviet Ministries," *Journal of Comparative Economics*, vol. 7, no. 4 (December 1983), 415–431.

32. M. Keren, "The Ministry, Plan Changes, and the Ratchet Effect in Planning," *Journal of Comparative Economics*, vol. 6, no. 4 (December 1982), 327–342.

33. J. Kornai, *Economics of Shortage* (New York: North Holland, 1980).

34. Our discussion of the role of money in the Soviet economy is based on G. Garvy, *Money, Financial Flows, and Credit in the Soviet Union* (Cambridge, Mass.: Ballinger, 1977); and A. Zwass, *Money, Banking, and Credit in the Soviet Union and Eastern Europe* (White Plains, N.Y.: M.E. Sharpe, 1979). For a history of money in the Soviet Union, see, for example, Z. V. Atlas, *Sotsialisticheskaia denezhnaia sistema* [Socialist monetary system] (Moscow: Finansy, 1969).

35. For an analysis of informal sources of supply, see A. Katsenelinboigen, "Coloured Markets in the Soviet Union," *Soviet Studies*, vol. 29, no. 2 (January 1977), 62–85.

36. M. V. Condoide, *The Soviet Financial System* (Columbus: Bureau of Business Research of Ohio State University, 1951), pp. 78–79; Nove, *The Soviet Economic System*, chap. 9. For a Soviet textbook on the subject, see M. K. Shermenov, ed., *Finansy SSSR* [Finances of the USSR] (Moscow: Finansy, 1977); R. Hutchings, *The Soviet Budget* (Albany: State University of New York Press, 1983); and I. Birman, *Secret Incomes of the Soviet State Budget* [Boston: Martinus Nighoff, 1981).

37. Directorate of Intelligence, *USSR: Sharply Higher Budget Deficits Threaten Perestroyka*, Washington, D.C., SOV 88-10043U, September 1988.

38. For discussions of financial planning in the 1930s, see F. D. Holzman, "Soviet Inflationary Pressures, 1928–1957: Causes and Cures," *Quarterly Journal of Economics*, vol. 74, no. 2 (May 1960), 176–180; Holzman, "Financing Soviet Economic Development," in M. Abramovitz, ed., *Capital Formation and Economic Growth* (Princeton, N.J.: Princeton University Press, 1955), pp. 229–287; A. Nove, *An Economic History of the USSR* (London: Penguin, 1969); V. A. Vinogradov et al., eds., *Istoriia sotsialisticheskoi ekonomiki SSSR* [History of the Socialist economy of the USSR] (Moscow: Nauka, 1978), vol. 4, chap. 13; and A. L.

Vainshtein, *Tseny i tsenoobrazovanie v SSSR v vostanovitel'ny period* [Prices and price formation in the USSR in the transition period] (Moscow: Nauka, 1972).

39. Directorate of Intelligence, *USSR: Sharply Higher Budget Deficits*, p. 5.

40. Ibid., p. 9.

41. For a discussion of Soviet price indices, see M. Bornstein, "Soviet Price Statistics," in V. G. Treml and J. P. Hardt, eds., *Soviet Economic Statistics* (Durham, N.C.: Duke University Press, 1972), pp. 355–396. The argument has been made that, over time, there has been a systematic and continuing disappearance of the lower price variants of a particular product, thus effectively raising the average retail price. See also G. E. Schroeder and B. S. Severin, "Soviet Consumption and Income Policies in Perspective," in Joint Economic Committee, *Soviet Economy in a New Perspective* (Washington, D.C.: U.S. Government Printing Office, 1976), pp. 620–660. Also see *USSR: Measures of Economic Growth and Development, 1950–1980* (Washington, D.C.: U.S. Government Printing Office, 1982), p. 334. For a discussion of this and other evidence on inflation, see J. Pickersgill, "Soviet Inflation: Causes and Consequences," *Soviet Union*, vol. 4, part 2 (1977), 297–313; see also J. Pickersgill, "Soviet Household Saving Behavior," *The Review of Economics and Statistics*, vol. 58, no. 2 (May 1976), 139–147. More generally, see M. Yves Laulan, ed., *Banking, Money and Credit in the USSR and Eastern Europe* (Brussels: NATO Directorate of Economic Affairs, 1973); and M. Yves Laulan, ed., *Economic Aspects of Life in the USSR* (Brussels: NATO Directorate of Economic Affairs, 1975). For evidence on recalculations of industrial price indexes, see J. E. Steiner, "Disguised Inflation in Soviet Industry," *Journal of Comparative Economics*, vol. 6, no. 3 (September 1982), 278–287; P. Wiles, "Soviet Consumption and Investment Prices and the Meaningfulness of Real Investment," *Soviet Studies* (April 1982), 289–295; and Directorate of Intelligence, *Revisiting Soviet Economic Performance Under Glasnost*, Washington, D.C., *SOV* 88-10068, September 1988.

42. G. Garvy, *Money, Banking and Credit in Eastern Europe* (New York: Federal Reserve Bank of New York, 1966); P. Gekker, "The Banking System of the USSR," *Journal of the Institute of Bankers*, vol. 84, part 3 (June 1963), 189–197; Garvy, *Money, Financial Flows, and Credit*; Zwass, *Money, Banking, and Credit*.

43. P. Hanson, *The Consumer Sector in the Soviet Economy* (Evanston, Ill.: Northwestern University Press, 1968), pp. 175–176.

44. P. Gregory, *The Soviet Economic Bureaucracy*, chap. 4.

45. I. Birman, *Secret Incomes of the Soviet State Budget* (Hague: Nijhoff, 1981); G. Grossman, "A Note on Soviet Inflation," Joint Economic Committee, *Soviet Economy in the 1980s*, part I (Washington, D.C.: U.S. Government Printing Office, 1982), pp. 267–286.

SELECTED BIBLIOGRAPHY

Political Institutions and Control of the Economy

W. Conyngham, *The Modernization of Soviet Industrial Management* (Cambridge: Cambridge University Press, 1982).

P. R. Gregory, *The Soviet Economic Bureaucracy* (Cambridge: Cambridge University Press, 1989).

J. F. Hough and M. Fainsod, *How the Soviet Union Is Governed* (Cambridge, Mass.: Harvard University Press, 1979).

A. Nove, *The Soviet Economic System* (London: Allen & Unwin, 1977).

L. Shapiro, *The Government and Politics of the Soviet Union* (Essex: Hutchison Publishing Group, 1978).

Supply and Output Planning

A. Bergson, *The Economics of Soviet Planning* (New Haven, Conn.: Yale University Press, 1964), chap. 7.

P. Bernard, *Planning in the Soviet Union* (Oxford: Pergamon Press, 1966).

M. Bor, *Aims and Methods of Soviet Planning* (New York: International Publishers, 1967).

R. W. Davies, "Planning a Mature Economy," *Economics of Planning,* vol. 6, no. 2 (1966), 138–153.

———, "Soviet Planning for Rapid Industrialization," *Economics of Planning,* vol. 6, no. 1 (1966), 53–67.

D. Dyker, *The Future of the Soviet Economic Planning System* (Beckenham-Kent: Croom Helm, 1984).

M. Ellman, "The Consistency of Soviet Plans," *Scottish Journal of Political Economy,* vol. 16, no. 1 (February 1969), 50–74.

———, *Socialist Planning* (Cambridge: Cambridge University Press, 1979).

F. Kushnirsky, *Soviet Economic Planning, 1965–1980* (Boulder, Colo.: Westview Press, 1982).

H. Levine, "The Centralized Planning of Supply in Soviet Industry," *Comparisons of the United States and Soviet Economies* (Washington, D.C.: U.S. Government Printing Office, 1959).

M. Manove, "A Model of Soviet-Type Economic Planning," *American Economic Review,* vol. 61, no. 3, part 1 (June 1971), 390–406.

J. Marczewski, *Crisis in Socialist Planning, Eastern Europe and the USSR* (New York: Praeger, 1974).

J. M. Montias, "Planning with Material Balances in Soviet-Type Economies," *American Economic Review,* vol. 49, no. 5 (December 1959), 963–985.

P. Rutland, *The Myth of the Plan* (LaSalle, Ill.: Open Court, 1985).

G. E. Schroeder, "Recent Developments in Soviet Planning and Managerial Incentives," in U.S. Congress, Joint Economic Committee, *Soviet Economic Prospects for the Seventies* (Washington, D.C.: U.S. Government Printing Office, 1973), pp. 11–38.

———, "The 'Reform' of the Supply System in Soviet Industry," *Soviet Studies,* vol. 24, no. 1 (July 1972), 97–119.

———, "Soviet Economic 'Reform' Decrees: More Steps on the Treadmill" in U.S. Congress, Joint Economic Committee, *Soviet Economy in the 1980s* (Washington, D.C.: U.S. Government Printing Office, 1982), vol. 1, pp. 312–340.

J. Wilhelm, "The Soviet Union Has an Administered, not a Planned Economy," *Soviet Studies,* vol. 37, no. 1 (January 1985), 118–130.

E. Zaleski, *Stalinist Planning for Economic Growth* (Chapel Hill: University of North Carolina Press, 1980).

Public Finance and Financial Planning in the Soviet Union

V. P. Diachenko, *Istoriia finansov SSSR* [History of USSR finance] (Moscow: Nauka, 1978).

Directorate of Intelligence, *USSR: Sharply Higher Deficits Threaten Perestroyka*, Washington, D.C., *SOV* 88-10043V, September 1988.

G. Garvy, *Money, Financial Flows, and Credit in the Soviet Union* (Cambridge, Mass.: Ballinger, 1977).

G. Grossman, "A Note on Soviet Inflation," in U.S. Congress, Joint Economic Committee, *Soviet Economy in the 1980s* (Washington, D.C.: U.S. Government Printing Office, 1982), pp. 267–286.

F. D. Holzman, "Financing Soviet Economic Development," in M. Abramovitz, ed., *Capital Formation and Economic Growth* (Princeton, N.J.: Princeton University Press, 1955), pp. 229–287.

———, "Soviet Inflationary Pressures, 1928–1957: Causes and Cures," *Quarterly Journal of Economics*, vol. 74, no. 2 (May 1960), 167–188.

———, *Soviet Taxation: The Fiscal and Monetary Problems of a Planned Economy* (Cambridge, Mass.: Harvard University Press, 1955).

R. Hutchings, *The Soviet Budget* (Albany: State University of New York Press, 1983).

M. Yves Laulan, ed., *Banking, Money and Credit in the Soviet Union and Eastern Europe* (Brussels: NATO Directorate of Economic Affairs, 1975).

F. L. Pryor, *Public Expenditures in Communist and Capitalist Nations* (Homewood, Ill.: Irwin, 1968).

A. Zwass, *Money, Banking, and Credit in the Soviet Union and Eastern Europe* (White Plains, N.Y.: M. E. Sharpe, 1979).

Management, Pricing, and Investment

*T*he enterprise manager plays a key role in the process of resource allocation in the Soviet Union. This role is especially important in a system in which managers are expected to execute plan instructions and achieve national objectives.

It should not surprise the reader that the Soviet system of enterprise management is different in important respects from that typically found in enterprises of Western industrialized market economies. In this chapter, we begin with a discussion of the Soviet enterprise, the framework in which managers work, after which we examine the managers themselves and the manner in which they respond to plan objectives under prevailing incentives and constraints.

ENTERPRISE MANAGEMENT IN THE SOVIET UNION

In the West, we are accustomed to analyzing the operation of the enterprise in a market setting, where the predominant task of management is guiding the enterprise as it responds to market forces. In the Soviet setting, managers are expected to respond to plan targets, although they are increasingly guided by economic rules derived from prices, profits, and so on. Accordingly, we will examine the nature and function of the Soviet price system and the potential impact of Gorbachev's reform program on prices and their role in the Soviet system.

Finally, we will examine the process of capital allocation in the Soviet economy and the role of the enterprise in this process.

The Soviet Firm

The enterprise is the basic unit of production in the Soviet economy. The enterprise is headed by a director (manager), who has a professional management staff. The management staff consists of a deputy director and a chief engineer, chief accountant, chief economist, and chief technologist. Structurally, the Soviet enterprise is specialized in the sense that the subunits, or shops *(tsekh)*, are organized to perform specific production tasks. The staff of the enterprise is broken down into white-collar and blue-collar components, and foremen are responsible for the routine activities of blue-collar workers at the shop level. The organizational structure above the enterprise is hierarchical. Managers receive directives from the planning apparatus. Directives come from the responsible chief administration *(glavk)* of the ministry, from the production association, and from *Gosplan*. It is the responsibility of the manager, within both formal and informal constraints, to achieve plan directives. Rewards, both monetary and nonmonetary, are designed to induce the appropriate managerial response to plan directives. Planning authorities recognize that managerial staff, like the staff of workers, require incentives to encourage work effort.

An authority on Soviet management, William G. Conyngham, notes that "Historically, Soviet management has been characterized by centralism, verticalism, and one-man management."[1] In effect, these are the basic principles underlying the Soviet managerial system.

Centralism refers to the concept of democratic centralism, long a basic feature of the Soviet political system. Under this concept, discussion is encouraged on any particular issue until a decision is formalized. At this point, centralism prevails, and the decision is binding on subordinates. Thus, enterprise managers can contribute to plan formulation through discussion of control figures and supply targets; once formulated, however, the plan is law. The Soviet system is a vertically organized hierarchy. Although Soviet enterprises can be subordinated to more than one external organization, for example, both to a ministry and to a local political (or state) unit, directives come from above, and the task of the manager is to achieve the wishes of those in power.

Although emphasis on the collective prevails in Soviet society, the principle of one-person management *(edinonachalie)* means that the enterprise manager is, in fact, responsible for the operations of the enterprise. "Edinonachalie" means that the manager has the authority to direct the labor and capital resources of the enterprise (within the constraints imposed by the plan). The manager's staff is obliged to obey the manager's directives, according to Soviet law. The principle of one-man management has been a key feature of the Soviet management system since the early 1930s. It clearly establishes the responsibility and authority of the Soviet manager over the collective of workers.[2]

This managerial structure is familiar to students of the Western corporation. It is a structure in which there is managerial input but where rules imposed from above are important. The manager is held responsible for the success or failure of enterprise operations and derives considerable personal benefit from successful operation. Success is not automatic. There are a number of risks and obstacles that make the managerial outcome uncertain. In this sense, Soviet managers, like their Western counterparts, operate under considerable pressure.

Enterprise Planning and the Soviet Manager

The operation of the Soviet industrial enterprise is governed in most respects by the *techpromfinplan* (technical-industrial-financial plan). This plan is the annual (semiannual, quarterly, monthly) subplan of long-term (five- to seven-year) "perspective" plans (although we have noted that the link between the two is often difficult to find) and is itself composed of subplans, each comprising a number of appropriate indicators or targets pertaining to the operation of the enterprise. In its broadest sense, the *techpromfinplan* sets forth the social goals—in the Soviet case, planners' preferences—that the enterprise is to implement. In a narrow sense, the *techpromfinplan* specifies output levels (in quantity and value terms), output assortment, labor and other inputs, productivity indexes, profit norms, and so on, which the enterprise is expected to observe.

The most important component of the *techpromfinplan* has been the production plan. Based on the capacity of the enterprise (normally defined as past performance plus some increment to incorporate planned capacity expansion), expected resource utilization, and estimated productivity increases, the production plan has typically specified the ruble value of output *(valovaia produktsia)*, the commodity assortment, and the delivery schedule of this output.*

---

*Enterprises producing homogeneous products often have their output targets stated in physical units rather than value terms—such as tons of cement, square meters of textiles, or tons of plastic—with a specified assortment. Later in this chapter, we will examine the impact of reform on management rules.

In addition to the production plan, the *techpromfinplan* includes a number of other component plans, the most important of which are the financial plan (the monetary expression of the physical plan), the plan of material and technical supply, the delivery plan, the plan of plant and equipment utilization, the plan of labor and wages, quality-improvement plans and, finally, indices of labor productivity.

One might conclude from this formal version of Soviet planning that the Soviet managers' freedom to make decisions is severely restricted. The *techpromfinplan* governs their choice of enterprise inputs and outputs, and they are morally and legally obligated to implement the plan, with bonuses geared to motivate them in this direction. Looking beneath the surface, however, one unearths a significant area of managerial flexibility. Due in large part to the inability of central organs to specify and control all details of local enterprise operation, Soviet managers do have a sphere of decision-making freedom.

Plan Execution by the Soviet Manager

Both formally and informally, one of the most important functions of the factory manager is the translation of state goals into daily tasks. If one considers the enterprise plan, it is readily apparent that the Soviet manager is confronted with both multiple targets (outputs, cost reduction, innovation, deliveries, etc.) and multiple constraints. Yet the enterprise plan fails to specify formally either the nature of the maximand (enterprise goal) or, for that matter, the nature of the trade-offs among possibly competing goals. The plan does not tell the manager which goals are more important than others, except informally—through party campaigns, bonuses, word of mouth, and other means. The manager is thus faced with a dilemma. If all plan indicators cannot be simultaneously and harmoniously achieved,* which ones should be met and which sacrificed, and to

---

*A common conflict under conditions of ambitious output targets occurs between profit maximization and output target fulfillment. The graph below illustrates how this conflict may arise. The enterprise's output target is Q', which it produces at an average cost above the price that it receives (and thus makes losses denoted by the area of the loss rectangle). To maximize enterprise profits, the enterprise would restrict its output to Q (and fail to fulfill its output target) but would maximize profits denoted by the profit rectangle.

what degree in each case?[3] This question is resolved in the capitalist enterprise by the use of profit as an enterprise goal and a set of scarcity prices such that the trade-offs among various objectives are readily apparent.

While profits have always formally been a part of the economic calculus of the Soviet enterprise, their maximization has generally not been an important enterprise goal either in theory or in practice. In fact, quite apart from the meaning of profit in the light of Soviet prices, profits have tended to be of minimal importance in the operation of an enterprise. What, then, replaces profits in the Soviet managerial calculus? In essence, the plan, the formal and informal constraints, and the managerial incentive structure have made *gross output*—and more recently, refinements such as "realized" gross output (sales) or net output—the most important indicator of enterprise performance. In short, managers have been rewarded primarily for the achievement of output targets, and accordingly, those targets not directly related to output have tended to be of secondary importance.

A frequent misconception should be cleared up at this point. Soviet enterprises do operate on an independent "economic accounting" (*khozraschet*) system, which is often taken to mean that Soviet enterprises operate to maximize profits. The *khozraschet*, or official managerial accounting system of the Soviet industrial enterprise, cannot, however, be understood to imply that profit and other monetary variables are of prime importance. Enterprise profits are calculated, but the *khozraschet* system simply guarantees that enterprises have financial relations with external organs such as *Gosbank* and, further, that their operations are elaborated and evaluated in terms of value indicators using official prices. The minimal practical significance of *khozraschet* to the Soviet economy must be understood, for in the first instance, the structure of Soviet prices makes such calculations suspect, and in the second, the results of such value calculations have had little impact on the present and future direction of enterprise activities. Future production targets are generally not a function of current profits. The traditional Soviet system has allowed enterprises to remain in operation even with persistent losses. In this sense, profits and losses have not served the disciplinary roles that they play in the West. One of Gorbachev's major reform themes (discussed in Chapter 15) has been to place Soviet enterprises in a "full" economic accounting system, whereby firms showing persistent losses must go out of business.

The Success Indicator Problem

The choice of gross output instead of profits as the crucial "success indicator" of managerial performance has generated a series of problems. In most cases, maximands relating to output (whether in value or quantity terms) cannot be defined in perfect detail by central authorities, and in the Soviet case in particular, gross production "success indicators" have led to considerable managerial freedom and often distortion. Where the weight of the output has been the success indicator in the production of castings, for example, castings tend to be made heavier than necessary, thus wasting scarce inputs. Where size has been the indicator, in the production of cloth, for example, managers favor large sizes and largely ignore assortment goals. These distortions, however, are only a part of what has been described as the problem of success indicators in Soviet industry.[4]

Planners estimate plant capacity—a crucial aspect of plan formulation—as a direct function of past performance plus allowances for productivity improvements. At the enterprise level, however, managers face a dilemma: if they significantly overfulfill output targets in the current year, they may receive a sizable bonus, but in subsequent years, targets will be substantially increased (the "ratchet effect"), thereby diminishing the likelihood of bonus earnings in the immediate future. As a result, managers tend to be cautious about overfulfilling plan targets even if overfulfillment is well within their grasp. Another problem arises from the stress on the expansion of output in combination with a bonus system that reinforces this narrow production-oriented conception of performance. A rapid expansion of physical output in a particular year is unambiguously "good" according to the success indicator, irrespective of poor performance in other areas. Thus, technological change, cost reduction, quality improvements, and on-time deliveries, all very important indicators for the Soviet economy as a whole, tend to be secondary considerations as far as the manager is concerned.

The uncertain supply system imposes risk and uncertainty on Soviet managers, who face continual pressure from above in the form of taut production targets. Therefore, management must rely heavily on the efficient functioning of the material and technical supply system, a system over which management has little formal control. Yet enterprise output depends to a great extent on the availability of appropriate inputs in the proper quantity and quality and at the appropriate time. In the absence of a genuine wholesale market, the enterprise must rely on all other supplier enterprises to meet its plan obligations, and a failure by a single enterprise can cause continuing reverberations throughout the system.[5] The supply system is crucial to enterprise plan fulfillment; yet its manifold weaknesses outlined above continue to impede enterprise target fulfillment.[6]

Informal Behavior Patterns

The emphasis on taut production targets has led to certain informal behavior patterns by enterprise management. First, managers must make decisions based on their perception of what is important to their superiors in the hierarchy. The astute manager uses plan directives, the bonus system, informal and formal communications from the party, and simple intuition as indicators of the prevailing priority structure.

Historically, the priority system has consistently signaled the priority of output performance over other plan targets. Thus, the priority system directs managers to emphasize output performance over other plan targets, with the resulting neglect of costs, innovations, quality, and so on. Second, the priority system signals to managers the relative importance of the various enterprises with whom they conduct business. If managers find themselves unable to meet delivery obligations to both enterprises X and Y, they must rely on their priority awareness to make their choice.

The major reason for the important role of priorities in the world of the Soviet manager is the existence of supply uncertainty, which itself is due to the tautness of planning and to planning errors. The priority system does have its positive aspect, because, in an imperfect system, it ensures that planners get their high-priority targets, irrespective of planning errors and supply deficiencies; yet it does force managers to seek informal sources of supply and to engage in dysfunctional practices.

A second informal behavior pattern is the safety factor phenomenon. The combination of ambitious targets, uncertain supply, and substantial rewards for fulfillment of priority targets causes the manager to search for organizational slack, or a safety factor, as it is called in the Soviet parlance. This search leads the manager into patterns of dysfunctional behavior, for example, the hoarding of material supplies (especially those most likely to be in short supply), thus immobilizing scarce resources.[7] This stockpiling is not totally dysfunctional, for the Soviet manager will use his *tolkach* (expediter) to barter and exchange stockpiled materials with other enterprises. Nevertheless, this informal supply system operated by the *tolkach* (and tolerated by planning and legal authorities) results in a weakening of centralized control over material allocation—a definitely undesirable feature from the planning authorities' point of view. Yet the toleration of the informal supply system indicates that the authorities have reluctantly accepted it as a necessary evil, required by the frequent breakdowns in the official supply system.

Third, under the existing priority system, there is a tendency for managers to avoid change, for the manager is not suitably rewarded for process and product innovation. Such innovations are considered risky because they might endanger plan fulfillment during the current period, and they carry little potential reward because output targets will simply be ratcheted upward if the innovations are successful. At the same time, quality, which is typically very difficult to incorporate effectively into quantitative indicators, has tended to be of secondary importance to the manager, who tends to be judged on the basis of *production*, not quality of product. Also, in a sellers' market, those searching for supplies will be less likely to complain about inferior quality. In this case, the economic facts of life dictate against the use of legal and other channels to seek redress of supply grievances pertaining to quality or quantity.

Fourth, the bonus structure has tended to penalize 99 percent fulfillment, but offers substantial rewards for 101 percent fulfillment. This discontinuous aspect of the bonus system, plus the other characteristics outlined earlier (especially supply inadequacy), lead to *storming*, or the production of a substantial portion of the monthly output in the final few days of the month. The result of *storming* is a reinforcement of other dysfunctional features—irregular delivery on supply contracts, improper utilization of capacity, poor quality, and so forth.[8]

Soviet Management and Incentives[9]

The basic problems of management are not peculiar to the Soviet industrial enterprise; their counterparts can be found for the most part in capitalist industrial enterprises. Given a set of goals (whether from a board of directors or a central planner), and given that appropriate information for both plan formulation and execution is held largely at local levels (in the branch plant of a capitalist enterprise, for example), how is a managerial environment and incentive structure to be constructed such that (1) managers know precisely what is expected from them, and (2) they are motivated to carry out the directives of their superiors in the true spirit of the directive?

The relationship between Soviet managers and their planning superiors is a classic principal/agent problem (see Chapter 7). The planning authorities (in this case, typically the ministry) want the manager (the agent) to implement a number of goals imposed by the principal. These goals, explicitly stated in the enterprise's *techpromfinplan*, translate into concrete targets given to the agent in proper assortment and qualities, with a minimal expenditure of the resources allocated by the principal. If the principal had perfect information about the operations of the enterprise and could perfectly monitor the actions of the agent, there would be no principal/agent problem. In fact, under these circumstances, there would be no need for a manager because the principal could directly manage the enterprise from above. Because the principal's information is not perfect and because the principal cannot perfectly monitor the agent, the agent must be given the flexibility to make certain key decisions concerning the output and inputs of the enterprise. With the agent able to exercise decision-making authority, the principal must devise a monitoring and incentive scheme to cause the agent to act in the best interests of the principal.

If the principal and agent have identical goals, there is no principal/agent problem because the agent will automatically act in the interests of the principal. However, if the agent has different goals from the principal, then it is up to the principal's monitoring and incentive schemes to ensure that the agent does not act contrary to the interests of the principal. If the main goal of managers is to achieve a quiet, secure life, the manager may wish to bargain for easy output targets and liberal input allocations, and may supply misleading information to the principal to convince the principal that the manager's requests are legitimate. The principal, however, wants the agent to produce the maximum output with minimum expenditure of resources. When the fundamental goals of principal and agent conflict, the principal must devise an incentive and a monitoring system to encourage the agent to pursue the goals of the principal, not the agent's own goals.

The Soviet answer to the principal/agent problem is a managerial framework that combines a relatively high degree of centralization of decision making within a rather formal bureaucratic structure with a significant degree of managerial freedom through informal decentralization. Thus, the hierarchical centralized planning structure implies that managers respond to "rules" while, at the same time, the *khozraschet* enterprise system implies that managers have a degree of local freedom and initiative in the operation of the enterprise.

It must be recognized that in almost any organization, there will exist both a formal and an informal sphere of managerial decision authority. In a sense, the latter oils the operation of the former. In the Soviet case, to the degree that the latter does not smooth the operation of the former, there exists a myriad of internal and external enterprise controls to reorient enterprise behavior along desirable paths. These controls will be examined as we consider the Soviet managerial reward structure.

Managerial Personnel and Rewards

Before considering the Soviet managerial reward system, let us consider the profile of Soviet industrial management. From the evidence gathered by Western authorities on Soviet management,[10] we know that the typical Soviet manager is probably well educated (usually at the college level)—most likely in the field of engineering, with minimal emphasis of finance and what we would describe as "business" courses. This is an interesting deviation from the American pattern where, for example, the manager has to be primarily conversant with financial and sales matters. Instead, the Soviet managers' engineering training prepares them more for technological production problems. While Soviet managers are typically not from a working-class background, they will, during the course of their educational experience and also throughout the period of managerial advancement, receive more practical training than their American counterparts.

The rewards for successful managerial performance can be significant. Although data in this area are limited, it is probably safe to generalize that the typical Soviet manager earns a base pay substantially higher than the average Soviet worker and, further, that monetary bonuses are a significant portion of total earnings. Bonus payments have varied substantially both over time and by region. In 1934, the share of bonus earnings in managerial incomes averaged 4 percent, rising to 11 percent by 1940. It was allowed to rise to 33 percent under wartime pressures but declined after the war to 12 to 15 percent in the mid-1950s. In 1961, the share dropped to 8 percent. The renewed emphasis on material incentives after 1961 caused the relative importance of managerial bonuses to rise again, to 16 percent in 1965 and to 35 percent in 1970.[11] Thus, bonus earnings are important for the Soviet factory manager, although, as a portion of aggregate managerial earnings, they were of no greater importance in the Soviet Union than in the United States in the 1960s.[12] It should be noted, however, that while participation in bonus schemes is generally universal for Soviet managerial personnel, such is not the case in the United States.

The bonus system has changed since 1965 in one important dimension. While gross output (or some variant thereof) remains an important determinant of bonuses, they are now awarded for the achievement of a variety of plan indicators, specified in advance of the operational period. The managerial bonus formula has changed over the years. During periods when labor productivity is of great concern, labor productivity performance is an important determinant of bonuses. During periods when concern about supply is high, fulfillment of the supply plan becomes more important. When planners are concerned with raising product quality, quality indicators become an important ingredient in managerial bonuses. In this sense, managers are aware of the importance placed by the planners on the achievement of various plan indicators. The inclusion of a number of indicators in the managerial bonus formula means that planning authorities wish managers to turn in a good performance for each indicator. It also means that managers can trade off one performance indicator for another. The weights attached to each indicator help determine the nature of this trade-off. David Granick, an expert on Soviet management practices, views the change in bonus-setting arrangements as being an important departure from past practices.[13]

Executive bonuses in the United States tend to be paid for achievement of both short-run and long-run objectives. For example, the American manager is expected to strike a proper balance between short-run and long-run profitability. Insofar as stock prices tend to reflect investor perceptions of long-run profitability, American corporate managers must pay attention to the effect of current actions on long-run profitability. In addition, bonus arrangements in the United States are more likely to be based on subjective evaluations of performance.[14] In the Soviet Union, however, bonus payments tend to be for short-run rather clearly defined tasks, such as the quantitative fulfillment of a specific output target or specific cost reductions. The short-run nature of Soviet bonuses tends to create an environment of pressure, and this in itself becomes a mechanism through which short-run priorities can readily be identified by managers. It is in this sense that some longer-run targets, such as quality, innovation, and new technology may well be set aside in favor of more rewarding short-run achievements.

In the Soviet case, the monetary bonus awards are normally awarded on a short-run basis (i.e., monthly), while the nonmonetary rewards are in greater measure long-run rewards, although they, too, can be thought of as defining priority goals and delineating the sphere of informal managerial behavior. Enterprises may, for example, provide the manager with living quarters and an automobile, the latter most likely with a driver. Both are significant amenities in present-day Soviet society when one considers the shortage of housing space (and the lack of a formal market for the purchase of same) and the prestige and convenience of an automobile. Finally, the enterprise manager can anticipate participation in local, state, and party organs, adulation in the press for particularly good performance, and also upward mobility to positions of greater prestige and reward.

While the Soviet manager's position is one of potentially significant monetary rewards, it is also one of significant risk. First, in an environment of uncertainty where the manager lacks decisive control over all inputs (for example, the delivery of material supplies to the enterprise on time), the manager is clearly in danger of not being able to meet priority targets. There are two possible consequences of such failure: loss of bonus, which represents a substantial portion of total income, or loss of job. A third consequence, execution or imprisonment, was widespread during the 1930s, when failures to fulfill targets were seen to be the work of saboteurs. Fortunately, Soviet managers no longer work under this threat. Executive turnover was very high in the 1930s, although it is clear that this pattern has changed significantly in recent years. Thus, for the postwar years, turnover of Soviet managerial personnel at both the middle and upper levels has been substantially less than that of comparable managerial personnel in American corporations. This represents significantly increased job security for Soviet managers of the 1960s, 1970s, and 1980s as opposed to the 1930s.[15] At the same time, it may suggest a degree of stagnation in the management system and the aging of managers, deemed an important factor in recent years.[16]

EXTERNAL CONSTRAINTS ON SOVIET MANAGERS

Numerous internal and external constraints on managerial flexibility make the job of the Soviet manager even more difficult. The planning and administrative bodies external to the firm also have to meet targets, which depend on the performance of subordinate enterprises. Regional and ministerial authorities are therefore interested in forcing enterprises under their control to exert themselves to the maximum. This relationship is significant, whether industry is arranged on a territorial or ministerial basis, for higher bodies will pressure the subordinate enterprises to ensure fulfillment of their own targets. The ministry practice of holding back enterprise supply allotments ("reserving") and of planning enterprise targets to exceed the aggregate ministry target are part of this pressure. In this manner, managers are subjected to increased pressure from their immediate supervisors. In addition, while the *khozraschet* system of management implies a degree of autonomy for the enterprise, it also suggests the establishment of financial rewards and connections with the State Bank—a further form of external control. The system of "ruble control" implies that the funds of the enterprise must be deposited in the bank and that the bank will exercise control over enterprise funds.

The role played by external forces is not necessarily negative. The regional or local party or state organization tends to be judged on the basis of the success or failure of enterprises under its jurisdiction. Thus, the local party organization is often prepared to represent the interests of local enterprise managers in disputes over input allocations or the lowering of plan targets. There is evidence that enterprises that experience plan fulfillment difficulties are able to get plan reductions *(korrektirovki)* and that the influence of the party can be helpful in this regard. The role of the supervising ministry remains unclear. The ministry is ultimately judged by the success or failure of the enterprises it supervises, so it would want to avoid the appearance of wide-scale failure. Thus, there are reasons to suspect that ministries would want to help out struggling enterprises. On the other hand, the ministry itself has targets that it must meet (such as producing a certain number of tons of steel, or trucks, or cement). If it is too easy on its own enterprises, then the ministry target will be jeopardized. An important research task of Western researchers is to determine the working relationships between the ministry and its enterprises. Recent research shows that Soviet enterprises can "fool" their superiors only at the margin.[17] Ministry staff personnel have had considerable production experience and are able to detect gross misreporting on the part of their enterprises.

INTERNAL CONSTRAINTS: THE TRADE UNION

Assessing the role of labor unions in Soviet society is a difficult task. In Western economics, labor unions are perceived as performing extra-market allocation functions. Since Soviet ideology views the objectives of the individual worker and the state as identical, one might question the role of an organization generally thought to defend the rights of the worker vis-à-vis the employer. Moreover, since Soviet trade unions do not have a formal role in wage setting and are not permitted legally to organize strikes, important functions of Western trade unions seem to be absent. What, then, are the nature and role of trade unions in the Soviet economic system?

As Blair A. Ruble, a Western authority of Soviet labor, notes, socialist unions in general and Soviet unions in particular ". . . have two divergent functions: On the one hand, they exhort workers to produce more; on the other, they defend the rights and interests of union members as those interests are defined by law."[18] The balance between those functions and the methods used for their achievement have varied over time. The postwar period has witnessed varying degrees of emphasis on incentives versus controls as a way to achieve desired objectives. Although recent changes in labor regulations seem to imply a growing support for controls over incentives, it is not this clear within the trade union movement, where the general issue of working conditions is paramount for the union.

Soviet trade unions are organized on the production principle, meaning that workers in a given sector of the economy will belong to a particular union. There are approximately 31 such unions, with a membership of roughly 130 million workers.[19] The structure of Soviet trade union is exceedingly complex, but it begins with general meetings of union members at the enterprise level culminating in the Congress of Soviet Trade Union—the All Union Central Council of Trade Union (AUCCTU) as the highest governing body.

Within the enterprise, a union chairperson is elected. This election is subject to a number of important constraints such as the *nomenklatura* procedure described in Chapter 1. Nevertheless, it is the fucntion of this union representative, now responsible to higher levels of union authority, to work within the additional confines of party and managerial authority. In the enterprise, then, the key relationship is among the enterprise director, the head of the party, and the union representative.

In a Soviet enterprise, the union and the manager negotiate a collective agreement operating under the general principle of democratic centralism, a concept discussed earlier. This agreement governs the conditions of labor in the enterprise. There is a formal and complex grievance procedure for those arguing that provisions of the agreement are not being implemented.

Understanding the formal structure of Soviet trade unions is a complicated task. Assessing their practical operation and impact is considerably more difficult, for a variety of reasons. There is little or no uniformity in collective agreements, so it is not surprising that reported outcomes of the union process differ significantly from one case to another. The nature of the union function is much more complicated than is implied by the traditional Western interpretation. On the one hand, it is true that with regard to important issues such as wages, Soviet trade union power is limited. It is also true that much of Soviet trade union activity at all levels is devoted to broad cultural issues, recreation facilities, and the like.[20] But in terms of the take-home pay of the Soviet worker, the trade union can have an impact not only at upper levels as pay scales are established, but also at local levels in terms of interpreting those pay scales and the many supplements (for example, bonus arrangements) that can and do vary locally.[21] Finally, the area of enforcement is also a matter of complexity. For example, safety is of major concern to Soviet trade unions. However, recent evidence seems to support the view that in spite of sometimes very successful trade union action in support of improved safety rules and conditions, Soviet safety standards and enforcement should be a matter of major concern.[22]

Soviet trade unions are complex organizations functioning in a peculiar environment. In recent years, there have been reports of labor unrest, although frequently these seem to be related to unenforced rights rather than efforts to make fundamental changes.[23] However, as the Soviet economy enters the 1990s, the Soviet trade union movement bears watching as it attempts to come to grips with increased worker unrest in countries such as Poland while at the same time motivating Soviet workers to work harder and be more efficient. Moreover, the Gorbachev reforms call for increased worker democracy in the workplace. Workers are to be given a role in selecting their managers. How the trade union will fit into this new scheme remains to be seen.

THE SOVIET PRICE SYSTEM

Thus far, our discussion of the Soviet planning system and the management structure has said little about prices, a major source of information for any manager in a Western setting. This treatment of prices in the traditional Soviet setting is not an oversight. As we have emphasized, the meaning of prices in the Soviet system, especially for the industrial enterprise, is changing. Extending beyond the effort of the immediate pre-Gorbachev era to tie managerial rewards more closely to enterprise performance, Gorbachev has strongly supported a substantially new regime for the enterprise. In this new regime, prices will play a much more important role than that of the past. Although the final substance of price reform in the Gorbachev era is far from known, it is nevertheless critical that we understand the nature of the Soviet price system—its past, present, and potential future posture.

We begin with a discussion of the traditional nature of Soviet prices, after which we consider recent trends.

Price Setting in the Soviet Union[24]

Most prices in the Soviet Union are fixed by central authorities rather than by the interaction of supply and demand. Price-setting responsibilities have at various times been shared by the Price Bureau of *Gosplan*, Ministry of Trade, the Ministry of Finance, the State Committee on Prices, the Union-Republican Councils of Ministers, and various republican and *oblast* authorities. The most important prices established by the forces of supply and demand have been the collective farm market prices. It is useful to discuss price setting in the Soviet Union in terms of four different types of prices, for the principles observed in each case are quite different: (1) industrial wholesale prices, (2) retail prices, (3) agricultural procurement prices, and (4) collective farm market prices.

Industrial wholesale prices Industrial wholesale prices perform less of an allocative function than other Soviet prices. Contrary to retail price setting, where an attempt is generally made to set market-clearing prices, industrial wholesale prices tend to serve primarily as accounting prices, used to add together heterogeneous inputs and outputs. That industrial wholesale prices play no real allocative role should come as no surprise, in view of our earlier discussion of industrial supply planning.

At the wholesale level, there are two important types of prices. First, the *factory wholesale price* is the price at which the industrial enterprise sells its product to the wholesale trade network. Second, the *industry wholesale price* is the price at which goods are sold to buyers outside the industry. In the latter case, a turnover tax will likely be included (on the average, about 8 percent of the industry wholesale price in heavy industry).[25] In the former case, there is seldom a turnover tax. Although the rules of price setting have changed somewhat over time, generally speaking, this function has tended to remain centralized. Thus, agencies in the planning hierarchy establish wholesale prices on the basis of *average branch cost* of production plus a small profit markup (generally 5 to 10 percent). Included in enterprise costs are wage payments, costs of intermediate materials, depreciation, insurance, and payments to overhead. Interest and rental charges are not normally included in costs, and depreciation charges do not include charges for obsolescence. While market prices in a competitive market system tend toward marginal costs, they are, in the Soviet case, average cost prices. Using average branch costs means that many enterprises will, in fact, take losses at the established prices because the cost figures are averages of low- and high-cost producers, and historically such has been the case. The consequences of such losses in the Soviet system have generally been small.

During the early years of planning, the prices of important industrial inputs were purposely kept low, and many industrial enterprises were operated under state subsidies. Since enterprise survival is not based on the profits or losses, as in a market system, such losses are of little particular importance, since subsidies are granted almost automatically to enterprises to cover operating losses. In these cases, minimization of losses (which might be a short-run objective for a capitalist firm) becomes a long-run criterion of operation and price setting in the Soviet Union.

Profit calculations have always existed in the Soviet schema; they simply have not been a dominant criterion of enterprise performance, and the presence or absence of profits has therefore not been the basis for action by Soviet planning authorities. A fundamental reason for this is the inability of pricing authorities to establish "fair" prices, under which the level of profits serves as a true indication of enterprise performance.

In some cases, especially the extractive industries, in which marked cost variations among producers occur, so-called accounting prices have been used. Producers, in effect, receive different prices (depending on cost differences) while all buyers pay the same price, with the state providing the intermediate cushion. Thus, the low-cost producers are, in effect, paying a differential rent to the state.

In rare cases, attempts have been made by pricing authorities to adjust the prices of close substitutes for differences in "use values," the most notable cases being the pricing of fuel oil and coal, and nonferrous and ferrous metals. In both instances, it was determined that the "use value" of fuel oil and nonferrous metals were higher than those of coal and ferrous metals, respectively; therefore, prices in excess of average branch costs were set for fuel oil and nonferrous metals (the difference between average branch costs and the wholesale prices being the turnover tax). Nevertheless, such instances are rare because generally it is difficult to distinguish among industrial commodities according to their "use values."

Further problems are created by the treatment of "new" products and of products bought and sold in Western markets.[26] If the labor theory of value is to be observed, "new" products produced by a new technology that results in labor savings should be priced relatively low. Enterprise directors who therefore take the risk of introducing new labor-saving technology face the prospect of having what would have been increased profits passed on to the users of their products in the form of price reductions. The reader can understand that such a pricing formula would not be conducive to technological innovation, and Soviet pricing authorities have (without great success) sought ways to exempt such "new" products from the labor theory of value formula. Cases of large differentials between domestic wholesale prices and world market prices have also been troublesome to pricing authorities. In the case of imports, planners may have to pass on to the Soviet enterprise at a low domestic price equipment that has been purchased at a high price in the world market. In the case of exports (oil, for example), the products may sell for a much higher price in the world market than the producing enterprise receives at home. Because of these discrepancies, there has been an increased tendency in recent years to adjust Soviet domestic prices on the basis of movements in world prices.

A major problem of industrial price setting is that, owing to the administrative complexities of price reform, industrial prices have seldom conformed to average branch costs. It has proved too difficult to change prices regularly along with costs. Instead, industrial prices have tended to remain rigid over long periods. As a result, general subsidies have often been required as the wholesale prices of many commodities have fallen gradually below rising costs. Industrial wholesale prices remained roughly constant between 1929 and 1936, despite rapidly rising wage costs, and by 1936, subsidies were the rule rather than the exception. A price reform in spring of 1936, sharply increased prices to cover costs, while in 1949, another large general price increase was required to eliminate subsidies. Despite the general rule that prices should cover costs, industrial prices remained virtually unchanged from the 1955 price reform to the 1966–1967 price reform despite changing wage costs and changing technology.[27] After the reform of 1966–1967, the next major price reform took place in 1982.[28]

Official Soviet industrial wholesale-price indices indicate a very modest degree of inflation throughout the postwar era, but there is reason to suspect that the official indices suffer from the same deficiencies as the retail-price indices. Yet Western recalculations also fail to reveal significant inflation in the industrial wholesale-price sphere.[29]

Retail prices   At the retail level, most prices are also formed by state planning authorities. They are basically designed to *clear the market* (to equate supply and demand), although this standard is often not met. This basic policy is in line with the Soviet policy of market distribution of consumer goods to preserve the incentive to work: For wage differentials to be meaningful, it is essential that they represent a differential command over consumer goods. In reality, retail prices have often tended to be somewhat below market-clearing levels, and thus queues have often served, in part, as a rationing device.

The retail price is simply the industry wholesale price, plus the retail margin (and costs, where additions to the product are generated at the retail level), plus the turnover tax. Unlike Western sales taxes, where consumers are generally aware of the tax rate they are paying, the Soviet turnover tax is included in the retail price without the purchaser knowing how large it is. The level of the tax is a function of supply-and-demand conditions in the given market and of the prevailing industry wholesale price. Where the price without turnover tax is below the market-clearing level, a tax sufficient to raise the retail price to the clearing level is added. In Figure 8.1, if the industry wholesale price is OP and the resulting equilibrium prices is OP, the turnover tax will be PP (or slightly

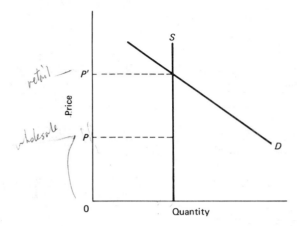

retail

wholesale

Figure 8.1   The Soviet turnover tax.

below if the price is set below clearing levels).* Thus, the level of taxation is price-determined rather than price-determining.

What happens if the industry wholesale price greater than *OP*? Obviously, in such a case there will be no turnover tax, and unless there is a subsidy that permits the setting of the retail price *below* the industry wholesale price, surplus unsold stocks will result. Two comments are in order. First, throughout much of the plan period, a sellers' market has prevailed—obviating the subsidy problem at the retail level. Second, the matter of unsold stocks is more fundamental than simply a question of price setting. In particular, as economic development proceeds and greater attention is given to consumer goods in the Soviet Union, one would expect the sellers' market to subside. Such indeed has been the case—for example, in the clothing industry and more recently in the consumer durables area.[30] In these cases, there have been unsold stocks in recent years, unlike the old sellers' market where producers could be unresponsive to consumers without losing sales. Thus, the current problem is a combination of matching output to consumer tastes and setting appropriate prices. In recent years, the simultaneous existence of surpluses of some commodities and shortages of others have demonstrated the magnitude of this structural problem. There are also financial implications involved: If stocks are unsold, the state is not able to collect the turnover tax—an important source of revenue. A

---

*The supply schedule in Figure 8.1 is drawn to be perfectly inelastic, under the assumption that the quantity of output is determined by the state plan, irrespective of price. This would apply largely to enterprises producing a single homogeneous product. For a multiproduct firm attempting to fulfill a gross output target, the supply schedule would likely be less than perfectly inelastic, that is, would have a positive slope.

fundamental problem of economic reform revolves around this question: When the sellers' market subsides, how can producers be made responsive to the consumer if the price system fails to provide effective information concerning consumer demand? What was not so much a problem in the past may well be an increasing problem in the future.

If retail prices are to serve as mechanisms to transmit consumer preferences to producers, fundamental changes will be necessary. In this regard, the two-tiered price system shown in Figure 8.1 is an obstacle. Because retail prices are essentially demand-determined and factory wholesale prices are cost-determined, it may happen that *relative* retail prices diverge significantly from *relative* factory wholesale prices. Yet producers will be more responsive to the relative wholesale prices that they receive rather than to the retail prices paid by consumers, which reflect consumer preferences. Thus, the signal sent by the consumer in the form of a market-clearing retail price is not received by the producer, who is paid a different factory wholesale price. For some products, the two-tiered system is being gradually and automatically eliminated, namely, in food processing and in clothing and textiles. Their retail prices have been held roughly constant in recent years, whereas their factory wholesale prices have risen along with rising wage and material costs, thus squeezing out the turnover tax.

Although there has been a continuing effort to vary prices on a zonal basis and to change them over time, this sort of variability has been highly restricted, given the magnitude of the administrative task involved. One can expect this problem to become more difficult in the future, as the economy grows more complex and the product range widens. Finally, it might be noted that the level of turnover tax (as one would expect) has varied widely among products and is as high as 80 percent of the price on some products. The average light-industry turnover tax in 1983 was 23 percent of the wholesale price, while it was 7 percent in heavy industry.[31] As we have seen, the revenue for this tax accounts for a substantial portion of state budgetary revenues and therefore remains an important consideration in both financial planning and price setting.

Agricultural procurement prices   Turning to agricultural pricing, we note that until 1958 (and again for grain after 1965), there existed a two-level pricing system for state purchases of agricultural products from collective farms. For compulsory deliveries, a low fixed price was paid, while for sales to the state above the compulsory level, a higher fixed price was established. Unlike pricing in the industrial sector, these prices, until recently, bore little relation to the production costs of the collective farm. There was no cost accounting whatsoever on collective farms until mid-1950s, at which time initial cost studies revealed that for most collective farms, production costs were substantially above even the above-quota prices. In this manner, state pricing policy was placing the collective farms in a most difficult financial position by purchasing output at less than cost. At the same time, the state farms, operating essentially as industrial enterprises, were receiving subsidies from the state to compensate them for the low procurement prices and were not financing their own capital investment, as were the collective farms.

The two-level system was abandoned in 1958 and, although revived in 1965 for grain and then some other products, the differential between the below- and above-quota grain prices has been small relative to earlier differentials. Most notably, however, throughout the 1950s and 1960s, purchase prices were raised substantially, so that average purchase prices would cover production costs. This pricing policy is in line with the agricultural policy that collective farm production should be "profitable" in the general sense of revenues covering costs. This policy remains in a state of active debate, since the problem of agricultural land rental charges remains unresolved. Finally, there has been a preliminary effort to revise agricultural purchase prices not only in terms of their levels but also in terms of their flexibility over time and in regions.

Collective farm market prices   The most significant example of a true market price in the Soviet economy is the collective farm market price. In these markets, the collective farmers sell their produce (from private plots and after meeting state targets) at prices determined by demand and supply. While these prices fluctuate, they have generally been substantially above the level of state food prices, a phenomenon explained in part by quality differentials and by the maintenance of state prices at artificially low (below equilibrium) levels. For example, collective farm market prices were on the average more than double state retail prices in 1940. After considerable variation throughout the postwar period, collective farm market prices were 63 percent greater than state retail prices in 1972.[32] The collective farm markets have been especially important in large cities, where standard sources of supply have been inadequate. How important are these markets? Although measurement is rather complex, collective-farm markets accounted for 13.9 percent of aggregate food sales in 1960 and for 8.8 percent in 1978. However, for certain products, these markets are of much greater significance. In 1957, for example, when the aggregate collective farm market share of food sales was 18.2 percent, they accounted for 63 percent of potato sales, 48 percent of egg sales, and 35 percent of meat sales. In 1970, they accounted for 67, 54, and 35 percent, respectively, of sales of these products.[33] In terms of production, in 1987, the private sector accounted for 26 percent of meat, 27 percent of milk, 29 percent of vegetables, and 58 percent of potatoes.[34]

Specialized Prices

The above classification of Soviet prices is traditional and useful for an understanding of the roles prices play in the Soviet economy. At the same time, there are a variety of what we might call specialized prices that do not fit neatly into the above framework. For example, foreign trade prices are established with only minimal connection to domestic prices. Wages, as we will see in Chapter 9, are set by the state under specific rules. Finally, in some sectors of the economy (for example, in the production of minerals and raw materials), the rules of price formation are more complicated, with differentials established to result in profitability for producing firms in spite of significant cost differences. These prices, a variant of wholesale prices, are termed settlement prices.

The Functions of Soviet Prices

Our discussion of the Soviet price system suggests that Soviet prices are formed quite differently from their market economy counterparts. However, to evaluate Soviet prices, we must consider them in the context of the various roles that prices are supposed to play in the Soviet command economy. To judge the Soviet price system exclusively as an instrument for allocating resources (as is sometimes done) would be a mistake, for Soviet authorities have generally not intended it to be used as such. Instead, industrial supply and output planning are supposed to allocate resources, with prices playing other roles. Soviet prices can be considered in terms of four possible functions: (1) allocation, (2) control, (3) measurement, and (4) income distribution. A biased picture of Soviet prices would inevitably be drawn if one were to concentrate only on the first function.

Allocation   In any economic system, prices can reflect relative scarcities on the basis of which economic decisions are made. As any standard economics textbook will explain, the profit-maximizing producer will employ inputs so as to equate marginal factor outlays and marginal revenue products. The utility-maximizing consumer will purchase goods and services so as to equate marginal utilities per dollar, and so on. In this manner, supply-and-demand schedules arise, and prices that reflect *relative scarcities* are determined. Under ideal conditions, such an arrangement will result in a maximum output produced at a minimum cost irrespective of the economic system and is, in this sense, optimal. It is only necessary for the consumer and producer to be aware of relative prices to respond correctly in such a system; no planner is required to tell either one how to behave.

Such perfect price allocation is scarcely to be found in either planned or market economies in the real world, since imperfect competition, price controls, public goods, government regulations, and so on, prevail almost everywhere.

What we have in the real world is a mixture of price allocation and administrative allocation. In the United States, for example, resource allocation is accomplished primarily through the price mechanism, though not necessarily in the optimal manner described above. In the Soviet Union, administrative planning bears the primary responsibility for allocation, although prices do play a limited role. Thus, while both systems have scarce resources to be marshaled toward the achievement of given (although different) goals—for which the price system might be utilized—the fundamental differences are, first, the extent to which prices are utilized for these purposes and, second the manner in which price formation is executed.

Soviet industrial wholesale prices, being centrally determined and based on the ideological definition of average branch costs, do not represent relative scarcities—as Soviet planners are well aware. This is one of the reasons why the administrative planning structure remains so much in charge of resource allocation and why there is so little price allocation in the Soviet Union. Like any generalization, there are exceptions. In the labor sector differential wages are used largely to allocate labor. Also, retail prices are used largely to distribute *available* consumer goods among the population, although such prices generally play an unimportant role in the decision to produce such goods. The most striking feature of the Soviet economic system remains the minor role that prices play in the allocative process. As we shall see in Chapter 15, this picture may well change, since Gorbachev seems to favor an economic system where prices, after major reform, might play a much more important role in the allocation process.

That Soviet prices generally fail to reflect relative scarcities is important despite their lack of use as allocative instruments, since Soviet prices do play other roles. This may sound rather abstract, but it is important. The Soviets have chosen administrative allocation over price allocation. Yet it is difficult to administratively allocate resources on a day-to-day basis without knowing relative scarcities, and it is even more difficult to relegate decision making to lower echelons without scarcity prices. How to introduce a degree of price allocation into such a system and how to make the prices themselves more "rational" are recurrent themes in the reform discussions in the Soviet Union and Eastern Europe.

Control The control function of prices is perhaps the most significant in the Soviet context. Even in a centralized economy, some delegation of authority and responsibility is required, ranging from the central planning agencies to the enterprises. This necessitates a mechanism for control of subordinates. In market economies, the profit mechanism and variants thereof can act as a control device as well as an allocative device. In the Soviet case, however, profits have played a very limited allocative role in the industrial enterprise. Nevertheless, many of the directives of higher planning authorities must be stated and verified in value terms—for example, rubles of steel output rather than tons. Thus, the extensive use of value categories—the most famous being *valovaia produktsia*, or *val* (gross production)—in Soviet planning means that prices have been used in a control function to evaluate and assess performance at all levels.

More recently (since 1979), *normative net output* has been adopted as a measure of enterprise output and thus enterprise performance. This performance indicator is an important control device because it departs from the past practice of relying so heavily on gross output or sales. Enterprise output, calculated in this new fashion, amounts to the physical quantity of output multiplied by a *net output normative*, a type of net price. In a recent study of these new rules, Morris Bornstein has noted that the net output normative per unit "... is essentially equal to planned branch average wage and social insurance cost plus profit."[35]

Measurement   The measurement role of Soviet prices is also important and is similar to the control function in various aspects. Prices are required to measure the results of economic activity, especially if one's scope extends beyond individual products: The measurement of economic activity requires the aggregation of dissimilar products, and aggregation requires valuation. Without prices, one cannot determine at what rate the economy is growing, whether the capital/output ratio is rising or falling, and so on, and these are important variables in the planning process. For example, the total output of the economy ("gross material product," as the Soviets call it) must be valued to be measured, and in an important sense, the results of this measurement will depend on the nature of the prices used. For example, the Soviets used 1926–1927 "constant" prices until the 1950s to measure Soviet total output. Over such a long period of time, these prices came to reflect prevailing prices and costs less and less, and eventually, because of their questionable economic significance, they were abandoned for a more up-to-date price base.

This illustration points out an important potential conflict among the various roles that a price system can play in the Soviet command economy, and this applies to both the control and the measurement functions. Control and measurement are more easily carried out when prices are not changed frequently. However, if prices remain unchanged, after awhile they will not reflect current cost relationships and therefore will be even less useful as a guide to allocation. Soviet authorities have been reluctant to change prices for two basic reasons. First, it is administratively difficult to gather the mass of wage and cost data required for a reform of prices. Second, it has proved a complex task to plan and evaluate when prices are in the process of change. In such a case, value targets must be stated in two variants—one for the old, the other for the new prices—and general confusion tends to reign until the new prices are firmly established.

Income distribution   Finally, Soviet prices play an important role in the distribution of income. In addition to the centrally determined wage scales that, of course, affect the distribution of income, pricing authorities can influence the distribution of real income through retail prices. In fact, some Soviet pricing policies can be partially explained in terms of their impact on income distribution. For example, low housing rents have been charged (despite a severe housing shortage) throughout the plan period, the below-equilibrium prices have generally been charged in state and cooperative shops for basic food products.[36] In line with these price-setting policies has been the practice of charging nothing or only nominal prices for health care and education.[37]

One can view the Soviet policy of setting low prices for necessities such as basic food products and health and education as an attempt to improve the distribution of real income. It is noteworthy that the most direct method of equalizing the distribution of income—the leveling of wage income—has not been used on the grounds that this would weaken the incentive system.

An Evaluation of Soviet Prices

Thus far, we have described the operation and functions of the Soviet price system. We now turn to a partial evaluation of Soviet pricing. Is the Soviet price system really unsatisfactory and "irrational," as many Western observers claim?[38] It is, of course, difficult to answer this question because the response depends to a great extent upon the criteria used to judge Soviet prices. If one accepts the criterion that "good" prices should smoothly allocate scarce resources among competing goals by equating supply and demand, then the Soviet price system will show up poorly. If, on the other hand, one judges the price system on the basis of how well it leads to the accomplishment of goals desired by leaders (say, Soviet planners), then the judgment may be quite different. While we cannot hope to provide conclusive answers to the relative "goodness" of Soviet prices, some plausible generalizations are in order.

We must recognize that when one judges the Soviet price system in absolute terms, it has become apparent to both Soviet and Western observers that the Soviet price system does not perform its postulated functions especially well. This dissatisfaction among observers on both sides is reflected in the long-standing criticisms of the lack of scarcity pricing and price inflexibility, and in the Soviet's own criticisms along these same lines. In particular, the conflict between the price flexibility required for scarcity pricing and smooth distribution of goods and the price inflexibility required for effective control and measurement has led to numerous problems. The absence of an interest charge on capital (prior to 1965) caused managers to treat capital as a free good, with ensuing capital wastage. For many years, natural gas was allowed to disappear into the air as a by-product of oil production. There are many more examples. Perhaps most disturbing have been the strict limitations imposed by the inflexible Soviet price system on the devolution of decision making through decentralization.

To evaluate Soviet prices on their own terms, one must determine to what extent the Soviet price system has promoted or retarded the attainment of the long-run economic, military, and political goals of the Soviet leadership. For example, has the Soviet price system furthered the Soviet economic goals of rapid economic growth, world military power, and the preservation of internal stability? From the leadership's point of view, flexible equilibrium prices may be generated only by allowing more decisions to be made at the micro level. The cost of Western-style prices may be the loss of decision-making authority. Are key decisions to be made administratively or by marketlike forces? There is a clear trade-off. The Soviets must recognize that dissatisfaction with goods scarcities is one of the most common concerns of the ordinary person. The inability to price consumer goods properly drives consumers into the second economy both as consumers and producers.

The major problem of the Soviet price system appears to be its inability to communicate relative scarcities to participants in the economy. Enterprise managers and ministry officials, for example, are not informed by Soviet prices of the true opportunity costs of their various inputs and outputs. Without such information, resources cannot be combined in an efficient manner. There is general agreement that Soviet prices do not provide accurate information on opportunity costs, but is there some substitute mechanism? Raymond Powell has argued that economic planners (in ministries, *Gosplan, Gossnab,* and the party industrial departments) may be in a position to gather and analyze information on relative scarcities.[39] Planners will be confronted with various kinds of information concerning relative scarcities: Enterprises will clamor more for one resource than another; long-time associates will informally tell their planning superiors that a particular goods shortage is more acute than others. Through a variety of signals, an experienced economic planner will learn how to detect true signals of high opportunity costs from false signals. Planners can, therefore, to a degree, substitute their own information for the opportunity cost information not provided by the price system. Accordingly, planners will be able, albeit imperfectly, to correct for gross misallocations of resources. It is Powell's claim that this ability to detect relative scarcities has prevented the Soviet economy from performing as poorly as might be expected in an economy in which relative scarcities are not known.

In the past, prices have simply not been important devices for influencing resource allocation in the Soviet Union. Will this posture change under Gorbachev? Although we leave an in-depth discussion of contemporary reform for Chapters 14 and 15, it is important to note that we may well see a changing role for prices in the Soviet economy and, in some respects, therefore, fundamental changes in the procedures for resource allocation. For example, recent reforms have emphasized a reduced role for plan directives, an increased role for the enterprise, and the need for financial self-sufficiency of the latter. In addition, there is a new emphasis on contracting, for example, between a user enterprise and a supplier enterprise at contracted prices to be established between the contracting parties under state rules.[40] These sorts of changes, if implemented, would imply major price reform and a greater allocative role for prices in the Soviet system.

THE ALLOCATION OF CAPITAL IN THE SOVIET ECONOMY: THE INVESTMENT DECISION

Investment Planning

By designating the physical outputs of the economy in the process of material balance planning, authorities must plan at the same time the expansion of enterprise capacity, that is, capital investment in plant and equipment.[41] To meet the expansion of output called for by either current or prospective plan, the capacity of the enterprise must be expanded accordingly to ensure the consistency of the output plan. Earlier, it was noted that enterprise output plans are based on past performance plus projected increases from additional plant and equipment. Although there has, at times, been an imperfect meshing of output and investment plans, the latter have been primarily determined by the former.

Most of the research and development (R&D) work in the Soviet Union is conducted outside of the enterprise, although large enterprises do have R&D facilities. They are more centralized than in capitalist economies. There are three types of R&D organizations. First, there is the research and development institute, which conducts applied research in a specialized technological area; there were 1700 such institutes in 1969. The second type of R&D establishment is the engineering design organization, which specializes in the design of new products and of production processes. It is called a project-making organization; in 1964, there were approximately 1000 engineering design organizations. The third type of R&D establishment is the construction engineering organization. It determines matters such as the location of the plant, the kind of equipment, and the scale of production; in 1970, there were 1400 such organizations.

Most of these R&D organizations are attached to ministries, and they are charged with the design and implementation of innovation and the expansion of existing facilities. Unlike capitalist enterprises, in which routine investment decisions and technological innovation are taken within the enterprise, in their Soviet counterparts such matters are handled by external R&D establishments, whose responsibility ends when the project design is completed. This explains, in part, the reluctance of Soviet managers to risk introducing new technology.

The task of the project-making organization is first to elaborate and then to choose among alternative projects that yield the expansion of enterprise capacity specified by higher planning authorities. In this section, we deal with how project-making organizations choose among alternative projects. In a broad sense, they actually have little to do with the basic allocation of capital among competing ends, for they are concerned primarily with allocating fixed amounts of investment in accordance with centralized directives within their own administrative unit. The allocation of capital *among* administrative units, which, after all, is the decision most basic to the allocation of capital, remains in the hands of higher planning authorities.

In the Soviet Union, an annual investment plan for the entire economy that has been formulated by *Gosplan*, the ministries, and various state committees is submitted to the Council of Ministers. Once approved, the various R&D organizations, *Gosplan*, and the ministries supervise its implementation by the project-making organizations. Just as the material balance plan has its financial counterpart, so does the investment plan. The Ministry of Finance provides a portion of the funds required to finance the various projects directly from the state budget; the financial institution directly in charge of disbursing such investment funds is the Investment Bank *(Stroibank)*, with *Gosbank* providing the funds for general repairs.[42] In this manner, the financial counterpart of the investment plan is used to locate deviations from the investment plan in much the same manner as it is used to monitor other enterprise operations. An over-commitment of investment resources (a situation where the materials and equipment required for approved projects exceed available supplies) will usually result in financial authorities providing insufficient financial resources to complete the project as scheduled. This practice tends to bring investment supplies and demands into balance but builds costly delays into underfinanced investment projects. One important source of this tendency to overcommit investment resources has been the ministries' desire to get as many projects started as early as possible so as to establish a priority claim on future investment supplies. For example, in a recent Soviet source, it was noted that "...25 percent of the construction projects currently under way were begun 10–12 years ago."[43]

Soviet investment policies began to change in the late 1970s. These changes continued into the 1980s and have become a cornerstone of the Gorbachev era. After discussion of the problems of investment choice, we will summarize the state of contemporary investment policies.

Problems of Investment Choice in the Soviet Economy

The choice among alternative investment projects, all of which yield the same increase in capacity, is not easy to resolve in the Soviet context. How is the project-making enterprise to choose among them? Ideally, a choice should be made that would minimize the consumption of scarce resources while achieving the required capacity expansion. On the surface, this seems like a simple criterion; yet for Soviet investment planners, it can be very complex.

First, there is an ideological constraint. The Marxian labor theory of value attributes all value to the current and past labor that has gone into the production of a commodity. From this, Soviet ideologists concluded during the early plan period that capital does not create value; therefore, enterprises should not pay interest charges for its use—a view that prevailed until the 1965 economic reform. Thus, using interestlike calculations to rank investment alternatives seemed out of line with Marxian ideology. As Alfred Zauberman has expressed it, "Where yield on capital is rejected as the motive force of the economy, its maximization could not serve as a guide for investment decisions."[44] In line with this reasoning, fixed capital from 1930 through 1965 was allocated to enterprises as an interest-free grant. Enterprises therefore came to regard capital as a free factor of production, to be sought after as long as its marginal productivity remained positive. The only legitimate capital cost definitely allowable by Marxian value theory is depreciation, which supposedly compensates the state for the past labor being used up in production. There is no room in this strict Marxian framework, however, for technological obsolescence that does not represent a using up of past labor. As a result, the sole capital cost to enterprises, depreciation, has generally been small because of the omission of charges for obsolescence.[45]

The conflict between the strict interpretation of the labor theory of value and Soviet growth strategy is obvious. Whereas Marxian value theory dictates that capital does not create value, the basis of Soviet growth strategy has been to direct as much additional capital as possible into growth-producing sectors such as electricity, machinery, and metallurgy. Rapid industrial growth is the objective of the system; yet the instrument crucial to generating this growth was said to create no value of itself and carried a zero price. In practice, this conflict between ideology and growth strategy was resolved by having Soviet planners allocate capital administratively according to a strict set of priorities and without reference to relative rates of return.[46]

The Soviet industrial price system represents a second problem. If more than one project yields the planned capacity increase, the project-making organization must generally evaluate the costs and benefits of alternative projects in value terms. If one of two equally expensive investment projects economizes on coal inputs while the other saves natural gas, the final choice will depend to a great extent on the relative prices of coal and gas. If these prices fail to reflect relative scarcities, then the "wrong" choice can be made. Because of the inconsistencies of the Soviet price system, one can understand the reluctance of planners to rely exclusively on value criteria in making investment decisions. Instead, most official guidelines suggest that value criteria be combined with physical indicators such as labor productivity and savings of specific material inputs, rather than relying exclusively on single value indicators.[47]

A third problem, closely related to the first, has been the lack of recognition of the importance of the time factor in capital investment decisions—a consequence of the absence of a recognized *time discount factor,* or interest rate. In market economies, investment projects that promise to yield large returns in the distant future will be ranked against projects yielding smaller but quicker returns by computing the present discounted value of each project using the interest rate as a common discount factor. A high interest rate (that supposedly reflects both society's time preferences and the scarcity of capital) will discourage long-term projects with delayed returns.

In the Soviet Union, there has historically been little recognition (at least until recently) of the time factor in choosing among alternative investment projects, and the perceived opportunity cost—either to the Soviet enterprise or to the ministry—of tying scarce resources down in long-term projects has been small. The lack of a time discount factor explains to a great extent the undue delays in the completion of investment projects (a problem frequently referred to in the Soviet press) and the tendency to select projects with long gestation periods (the gigantomania of the early thirties) despite the considerable scarcity of capital resources. Such behavior can be attributed, in part, to the expansion of planners' time horizons beyond sight during the "heroic phase of growth" during the 1930s.[48]

The Development of Investment Choice Criteria

Beginning in 1930, interest was outlawed as a capitalistic vestige no longer required when capital is the property of the state. In keeping with the general sentiment of the early 1930s, it was argued that the economic laws of capitalism were no longer operative and that capital should be allocated administratively, without resort to the economic criteria of the old capitalist order. Thus, Stalin argued that the allocation of investment according to rates of return or other profitability measures would be contrary to the interests of the state, for resources would then be directed away from heavy industry into light industry, where profit rates would be higher. In addition, it was argued in some quarters that the liberation from economic rules would permit planners to choose more advanced technology than would be justified if standard economic rules were strictly observed, and thus the rapid industrial transformation of the Soviet Union would be promoted.[49]

The intersectorial allocation of investment became an administrative decision of higher planning authorities after 1930, and open discussion of investment choice criteria at the economywide level disappeared. The practical problem of allocating investment funds within specific sectors led, however, even during the barren Stalin years, to the development of informal investment allocation rules that were eventually officially formalized between 1958 and 1960. During this early period, ministerial project-making organizations were forced to develop more specific rules for making decisions rather than simply choosing the investment variant yielding the lowest operating costs (the only rule officially sanctioned), since the ministry had a limited capital allotment that had to be stretched as far as possible. This problem was especially troublesome in the railroad and electrical power industries, where continuous substitutions between ever-increasing capital outlays and ever-lower operating costs were possible. Thus, project-making engineers and industry officials began to develop investment rules, for internal use that implicitly introduced rates of return and other capital profitability criteria into the investment decision. Disguised under such acceptable terminology as "effectiveness of investment" and "periods of recoupment," these investment criteria came into fairly wide use within selected ministries by the late 1930s.[50]

The use of such interestlike calculations was officially sanctioned in 1958 by an all-union conference on capital effectiveness, after roughly three decades of pioneering work by engineers and economists.[51] The appearance of the USSR Academy of Science publication *Typical Method of Determining the Economic Effectiveness of Capital Investment and New Technology* in 1960 further substantiated the official acceptance of interestlike criteria for allocating investment within administrative units. Let us turn to the rules suggested by this 1960 publication.

Investment Decision Rules, 1960–1969

The most important decision rule suggested by *Typical Method* was the *coefficient of relative effectiveness (CRE)*, which was designed to evaluate the trade-offs between capital outlays and operating expenses. Such a measure was easily rationalized in terms of Marxian value theory, since operating expenses ultimately reflect labor costs, and capital should be evaluated according to how well it economizes the use of labor. To illustrate how the CRE measure operates, we assume that a project-making organization must choose between two alternative projects, both yielding the planned capacity increase. The two differ in terms of initial capital outlays *(K)* and resulting annual operating expenses *(C)*, which, let us say, do not vary over time. Under normal circumstances, the higher the capital outlay, the lower the operating costs, and the CRE must evaluate this trade-off. It should be noted that a capital charge is *not* included in operating expenses—only a depreciation charge—an omission that may bias the CRE measure in favor of capital-intensive projects. In our example, the CRE is given by the following formula, where the *a* and *b* subscripts refer to two projects, *a* and *b*:

$$\text{CRE} = \frac{C_b - C_a}{K_a - K_b}$$

Thus, if project *b* costs 1 million rubles and project *a* costs 2 million rubles of capital outlay, [52] and the operating expenses of project *b* are 0.2 million and those of project *a* are 0.1 million, then the CRE of project *a* (relative, of course, to project *b*) would be 10 percent. This should be interpreted to mean that for every additional ruble of capital outlay on project *a*, 0.1 ruble of operating costs would be saved over project *b*.[53]

Typical Method further suggested the establishment of a norm—the standard coefficient of efficiency—for *each* branch. If a project's CRE fell below the norm, it should be rejected unless there were special reasons for not doing so. In this manner, a minimum profitability, or capital effectiveness, rate would be established for each branch. Because these norms varied by branch (with the higher the priority, the lower the profitability norm for a given branch), capital profitability rates would not equalize among branches, as had been advocated by several prominent Soviet economists and many Western economists.[54] This result, however, was to be expected, in view of the state's desire to promote priority industrial and military sectors independently of restrictive economic criteria. Although there is no definite evidence, the CRE norms actually established were most likely not high enough to equate the supply and demand for capital, and administrative capital rationing remained the primary mechanism for investment allocation, despite the CRE.[55]

Although the CRE was just one of many rules suggested between 1960 and 1969, it became the most important and most widely used. It is important to note how crude a measure it actually was, for it failed to come to grips with varying patterns of capital expenditures, different service lives of projects, risk differences, and different time spacing of operating cost economies, as well as a host of other problems.

An important question raised by the CRE criterion was whether a single, uniform standard coefficient should be established for the entire economy, promoting eventual equalization of marginal rates of returns on investment projects in all branches.[56] *Typical Method* was clearly in favor of differentiated standard branch norms. For the state to surrender its control over investment allocation and to replace it by a uniform mechanical rule was judged as contrary to the long-range vision of the Soviet leadership. The 1958 all-union conference on capital effectiveness leading up to the publication of *Typical Method* was quite clear on this point: "Some projects with smaller effectiveness may be approved . . . because they accelerate the solution of the basic economic problem, and are necessary for defense, political and other reasons . . ." and further, "capital investments are made on the basis of the economic laws of socialism which require the preferential development by the means of production. . . ."[57] An important point often overlooked in these discussions of the CRE is that the suggested rules generally pertain to the internal allocation of fixed sums of investment within a branch, and that only those investment alternatives yielding the planned increases in capacity would be evaluated. Also, the norms were generally not set to equate supply and demand, thus requiring a continuation of administrative rationing independently of the suggested rules. Thus, the leadership's acceptance of interestlike calculations in 1960 really represented no significant deviation from the centrally planned nature of the Soviet economy. Instead, the objective throughout was to make the allotted investment more effective and efficient within the context of planned choice.

Another common current running through official pronouncements during this period was the reluctance of planning authorities to rely too heavily upon a single criterion. For example, the 1958 conference report made it quite clear that while the conference favored the CRE measure, it was to be used in combination with a number of other indicators when the situation required. If industrial prices failed to reflect relative scarcities, physical indicators were to be used along with the CRE criterion. The possibilities of substantial delays in project completion were also to be considered, as well as the interrelation of the project with other branches. Social factors such as the workers' safety were to enter into the calculation as well. [58]

Revised Investment Rules, 1969

In September 1969, a new methodology for evaluating the relative effectiveness of investment projects was approved. The new *Standard Methodology for Determining the Economic Effectiveness of Capital Investments*[59] (referred to here as *Standard Methodology*) is identical to the CRE method, except for the acceptance of a *uniform* standard norm to apply to all branches of the economy. The measurement suggested for comparing alternative investment projects is the *comparative economic effectiveness of capital investments*, referred to here as the CEE. The CEE measure requires that investment projects be selected so that

$$C_i + E_n K_i = \text{minimum}$$

where C_i = the current expenditures of the ith investment variant
K_i = the cost of the investment project
E_n = the uniform *normative coefficient of effectiveness* of capital investments, which is the same for all branches

Standard Methodology suggests that this normative coefficient be set at 12 percent. Thus, *Standard Methodology* (like *Typical Method*) calls for evaluating investment projects on the basis of their *full* costs (operating costs plus imputed capital costs), with imputed capital costs calculated using a uniform coefficient for all branches.

An example of how the CEE method works would perhaps be helpful at this point. Assume three alternative investment projects (Table 8.1). As one might expect, there is a trade-off between operating costs and investment outlays in our example (the higher the K, the lower the C).

In our example, the projects should refer to investment projects within a branch or in different branches. Because the normative coefficient is uniform for the entire economy, this should make no difference in the evaluation process. The CEE investment criterion calls for the selection of the project having the lowest costs, that is, the lowest *full* cost (the sum of operating expenses plus a capital charge). In the table, the project with the lowest full cost, project 2, should be selected, for it yields the optimal trade-off between greater investment outlays and lower operating costs.*

Table 8.1 COMPUTATION OF THE "COMPARATIVE ECONOMIC EFFECTIVENESS" (CEE) OF THREE INVESTMENT PROJECTS

Project	Operating costs (C)	Investment outlay (K)	Uniform normative coefficient	Full costs (1 + 3 x 2)
1	300	510	12%	361.2
2	290	525	12%	353.0
3	285	590	12%	355.8

---

*The importance of differential normative coefficients in preserving the branch priority system can be illustrated using Table 8.1. Suppose that project 2 is in light industry, whereas projects 1 and 3 are in heavy industry. Instead of using 12 percent as a norm for light industry, a higher 30 percent rate is set. The CEE of project 2 now becomes 447.5, which eliminates it from selection.

In addition to establishing the CEE concept, *Standard Methodology* provides detailed discounting procedures for evaluating in present-value terms projects whose operating expenditures and capital outlays change over time. *Standard Methodology* suggests using a discount rate of 8 percent, which it claims is in line with current depreciation procedures.

On the surface, the use of a uniform normative coefficient for the entire economy would seem to violate the branch priority principle and call for the allocation of investment strictly on the basis of rates of return. This conclusion seems to be further supported by the fact that *Standard Methodology* calls upon the investment plan to allocate investment among branches according to a uniform coefficient of effectiveness. In fact, this may not prove to be so. First, the suggested normative coefficient (12 percent) will probably not be high enough to equate the supply and demand for capital—a point already noted by Soviet critics.[60] As long as this remains true, much capital allocation will be handled by administrative procedures. Second, *Standard Methodology* states that deviations from the normative coefficient may be approved by *Gosplan* in order to stimulate technological progress, to allow for differences in wage and price levels, and to promote regional development. For example, a lower (8 percent) normative coefficient was established for the Far North, and there is talk of establishing an 8 percent norm for electrical power generation. The generally liberal allowance for exceptions to the uniform coefficient rule quickly became a matter of concern to reform-minded Soviet economists, one of whom wrote that they "open the door to the broadest degree of arbitrariness" in investment decisions.[61] Third, *Standard Methodology* suggests that the CEE index be supplemented by further indexes—productivity of labor, capital/output ratios, capital investment per unit of output, and selected physical indexes—to "take account of the influences of the most important factors on the economic effectiveness of capital investments and to take account of the interaction of this effectiveness with other divisions of the plan."[62] Fourth, *Standard Methodology* states that the investment plan should follow the output plan of the national economy; for example, the allocation of investment among branches is still to be predetermined by the industrial supply and output plan. This statement seems to contradict one of the key provisions of the new investment rules, namely, that capital should be allocated among branches according to a uniform normative coefficient of effectiveness.[63]

Thus, the *Standard Methodology* was a step in the direction of investment allocation on the basis of rates of return irrespective of branch of production, but it clearly did not call for a clear break with investment allocation according to the priority principle. We emphasize that efficiency indices are brought into play only *after* the basic investment allocation decisions are made in the investment plan. Investment funds are allocated in the investment plan. The efficiency indices play a relatively minor role: They assist in selecting that investment project that yields the capacity expansion called for in the investment plan.

Investment Rules: Recent Changes

Decrees of 1974 reinforced the 1969 rule that capital projects should be selected to minimize the sum of operating costs and imputed annual capital costs ($C_i + E_n K_i = $ minimum). It was emphasized that this approach would be used to compare *project variants,* and it was not intended to change centrally determined investment priorities. However, discussion in the Soviet press has indicated that, in some instances, this criterion was interpreted more generally as a measure of overall effectiveness of investment.[64]

Throughout the 1970s, there was considerable discussion concerning the normative coefficients *(E_i)* to be used in project evaluation. A key question in these discussions was whether the normative coefficient would be the same for all branches. In 1981, a new *Methodology* (with no reference to being standard or typical) was published.[65] The 1981 *Methodology* elaborates the same basic method for evaluating project variants and suggests that for the period 1981–1985, normative coefficients should be set at 0.12. This apparently is the average rate, which will be allowed to vary from a minimum of 0.08 to a maximum of 0.25.[66]

David Dyker, in his analysis of Soviet investment rules, points out a difference in the 1981 *Methodology*: "The 1981 *Methodology* has laid down norms for levels of absolute effectiveness which are to operate as 'gateways' through which blocks of investment projects should have to pass."[67] In other words, investment projects should yield certain minimum rates of return to qualify for funding. Rate-of-return norms are not to fall below the actual average rate for the preceding five-year period. Dyker notes that the actual average rate for the period 1976–1980 was 0.14.[68] As the continuing flow of investment allocation rules indicates, Soviet authorities remain interested in injecting more rate-of-return decision making into the Soviet capital investment process. Yet the same authorities recognize that capital allocation determines the basic future direction of the economy. They remain reluctant, therefore, to turn such decisions over to "rules." Whether the 1981 rule of meeting minimum rate-of-return requirements will actually be implemented remains to be seen.

Investment Policies: Contemporary Perspectives

The issues surrounding capital investment policies remain at the center of reform discussion in the Soviet Union. In fact, beginning in the 1970s, important changes were made in investment policies.

First, the average annual rate of growth of investment has decreased markedly and rather steadily since the 1960s. For example, the average annual rate of growth of capital investment was 7.5 percent during the period 1961–1965, falling to 5.0 percent for the period 1971–1975 and finally 3.2 percent during 1981–1985. However, the rate increased to 3.9 percent on an average annual basis for 1986–1987 and is scheduled to increase to roughly 5 percent for the twelfth five-year plan, that is 1986–1990. Thus, while a policy of decreasing the rate of growth of capital investment was implemented through the end of the 1970s, this policy was debated and reversed in the 1980s, especially under the Gorbachev leadership.

Second, in the late 1970s, a renewed emphasis was placed upon the concept of self-financing. For example, in the Program to Improve Economic Management (PIEM) decree of 1979, emphasis was placed on using profits (at the ministry and lower levels) as a source of investment financing. Norms were to be used to designate what portion of profit would be used for investment purposes. However, in an analysis of this program, Morris Bornstein has noted that self-financing is difficult to apply insofar as planned profit might be insufficient, unstable, and in many instances unachieved.

Third, in the Gorbachev era, there have been changes both in the direction in which investment is to be placed and the manner in which it will be utilized. For example, investment devoted to new construction is to be curtailed, while modernization of existing facilities is to be emphasized. Machine building is to be a cornerstone of this investment policy, with the emphasis on modernization, specifically the replacement of old and obsolete equipment through faster retirement rates and the replacement of this outdated equipment with the latest equipment. According to a recent study of Soviet capital investment policies by Robert E. Leggett, the Soviets ". . . intend to enter the decade of the 1990s having replaced about one-third of the economy's stock of machinery and equipment and no less than 35 percent of the total industrial capital stock." This represents a major effort to improve capital productivity in the Soviet economy.

Finally, Gorbachev has announced a variety of other changes designed to intensify the use of the capital stock. For example, organizations have been instructed to monitor quality. The State Acceptance Organization will monitor quality in industry, while the State Construction Committee will oversee the work of the controversial construction sector. Moreover, new emphasis is being placed upon the need for the scientific establishment to do more applied work. The machine-building and metalworking sector has been a major target for this type of change.

Although Western authors have noted many of the shortcomings of the Soviet investment system addressed in recent policy changes, quick improvement will not be easy. Notably, the Soviet Union must either improve the quality of domestic machinery production and/or obtain the latest equipment from abroad. Obviously, there are difficulties to both approaches, though both can be utilized to a degree. In addition, long-standing problems of the Soviet economic system will inhibit change. Soviet managers have always been reluctant to interrupt production for the introduction of new equipment. The incentive structure will be a major problem.

RESOURCE ALLOCATION IN THE SOVIET ECONOMY

In the last three chapters, we have elaborated and analyzed the process of resource allocation in the Soviet Union. Has the process changed significantly in contemporary times? Although the simple answer to this question would probably be no, it is useful to summarize our discussion by contrasting the past with the present.

With several significant exceptions, we have observed that resources have been allocated largely by administrative means through the plan. Relative prices have not been important in the process of planning by balances. Moreover, financial forces have been largely passive, used like the Communist Party apparatus, as a mechanism to monitor plan fulfillment. Although managers do exercise some discretion in the operation of their individual enterprises, we have seen that their freedom is constrained by the plan, the ministries, the Communist Party, and other similar types of constraints. The managerial reward system has been geared toward output, not efficiency.

A major force for change in any economy, namely, capital investment, is influenced by forces largely external to the firm, whether it be the financing of investment or the allocation of given investment funds. Again, the decision is historically an engineering rather than an economic decision.

Although many of the systemic characteristics outlined above remain substantially intact through the 1980s, we will see later in our discussion of economic reform that important changes have been discussed and in some cases implemented.

For example, contemporary reforms would, if implemented, reduce the authority of the planning system and increase the authority of the individual enterprise over important decisions on outputs, inputs, and expansion. Moreover, the enterprise would operate in a setting guided more by what in Eastern Europe would be described as economic levers, specifically prices, costs, profits, and so on. Such changes, if the value categories come to have significant meaning, could shift the Soviet economy away from its primary reliance upon administrative mechanisms of resource allocation on both the input and the output side. We will pursue these issues in depth as we discuss the nature of economic reform in the contemporary Soviet economy.

REFERENCES

1. W. J. Conyngham, *The Modernization of Soviet Industrial Management* (New York: Cambridge University Press, 1982), p. 2.
2. H. Kuromiya, "Edinonachalie and the Soviet Industrial Manager, 1928–1937," *Soviet Studies*, vol. 36, no. 2 (April 1984), 185–204.
3. The phrase *success indicators* is a traditional reference to a wide array of problems pertaining to the assessment of Soviet managerial performance. For an early view, see A. Nove, "The Problem of Success Indicators in Soviet Industry," in *Economic Rationality and Soviet Politics* (New York: Praeger, 1964), pp. 83–98; for a recent view, see P. Hanson, "Success Indicators Revisited: The July 1979 Soviet Decree on Planning and Management," *Soviet Studies*, vol. 25, no. 1 (January 1983), 1–13; and

M. Bornstein, "Improving the Soviet Economic Mechanism," *Soviet Studies*, vol. 37, no. 1 (January 1985), 1–30.

4. Nove, "The Problem of Success Indicators," p. 88. A striking example of the possible distortion as pictured by the Soviet humor magazine *Krokodil* and cited by Nove is the nail factory whose gross output target is specified in *weight*. The month's output is one gigantic nail being hauled away with a crane. See A. Nove, *The Soviet Economy*, rev. ed. (New York: Praeger, 1969), p. 174.

5. Enterprise failures to meet delivery targets are generally not severely punished. Fines tend to be nominal and difficult to collect, and generally enterprises do not bother to pursue those who break contracts. Because of the lack of coordination of supply plans between the State Committee for Material-Technical Supply *(Gossnab)*, *Gosplan*, and the ministries, no particular agency has been willing to take the responsibility for contract violations. For Soviet discussions of these problems, see *Planovoe khoziaistvo* [The planned economy], no. 6, 1978, pp. 101–109, and *Pravda*, February 18, 1978.

6. For a discussion of the problems imposed by the supply system, see G. E. Schroeder, "The 'Reform' of the Supply System in Soviet Industry," *Soviet Studies*, vol. 24, no. 1 (July 1972), 105–107; G. E. Schroeder, "The Soviet Economy on a Treadmill of 'Reforms,' " in U.S. Congress, Joint Economic Committee, *Soviet Economy in a Time of Change* (Washington, D.C.: U.S. Government Printing Office, 1979), vol. 1, pp. 323–324; G. E. Schroeder, "Soviet Economic 'Reform' Decrees: More Steps on the Treadmill," in U.S. Congress, Joint Economic Committee, *Soviet Economy in the 1980's: Problems and Prospects*, part 1 (Washington, D.C.: U.S. Government Printing Office, 1982), pp. 65–88.

7. For a mathematical demonstration that supply uncertainty leads to overdemanding of inputs, see S. Linz and R. Martin, "Soviet Enterprise Behavior Under Uncertainty," *Journal of Comparative Economics*, vol. 6, no. 1 (March 1982), 24–36.

8. R. Hutchings, *Seasonal Influences in Soviet Industry* (London: Oxford University Press, 1971), pp. 187–195.

9. The discussion of Soviet management is based primarily on the following works: J. S. Berliner, *Factory and Manager in the USSR* (Cambridge, Mass.: Harvard University Press, 1957)—a study of the early years of Soviet management experience based primarily upon emigré interviews; D. Granick, *Management of the Industrial Firm in the USSR* (New York: Columbia University Press, 1954)—an in-depth study of industrial management of the 1930s, based primarily on a detailed reading of the Soviet local and specialized press; B. M. Richman, *Soviet Industrial Management* (Englewood Cliffs, N.J.: Prentice-Hall, 1965)—a general survey of material similar to that discussed by Berliner and Granick. More recent material on the Soviet as compared with other industrial managers can be found in D. Granick, *Managerial Comparisons of Four Developed Countries: France, Britain, United States, and Russia* (Cambridge, Mass.: MIT Press, 1972). For treatment of the Soviet managerial system in the language of organization theory, see D. Granick, *Soviet Metal Fabricating and Economic Development* (Madison: University of Wisconsin Press, 1967), chap. 7. The Soviet manager and innovation are treated in J. S. Berliner, *The Innovation Decision in Soviet Industry* (Cambridge, Mass.: MIT Press, 1976), part 3; G. Guroff and F. V. Carstensen, eds., *Entrepreneurship in Imperial Russia and the Soviet Union* (Princeton, N.J.: Princeton University Press, 1983); W. J. Conyngham, *The Modernization of Soviet Industrial Management* (New York: Cambridge University Press, 1982); J. C. Thompson and R. F. Vidmer, *Administrative Science*

and Politics in the USSR and the United States (New York: Praeger, 1983); H. Bhérer, *Management Soviétique* (Paris: Presses de la Fondation Nationale des Sciences Politiques, 1982); S. J. Linz, "Management's Response to Tautness in Soviet Planning: Evidence from the Soviet Interview Project," *Comparative Economic Studies*, vol. 30, no. 1 (Spring 1988), 65–103; and A. Freris, *The Soviet Industrial Enterprise* (New York: St. Martins Press, 1984).

10. Notably, Berliner, *Factory and Manager;* Granick, *Management of the Industrial Firm;* Granick, *Managerial Comparisons of Four Developed Countries;* and Richman, *Soviet Industrial Management.*

11. Richman, *Soviet Industrial Management*, pp. 134–135; Berliner, *The Innovation Decision*, pp. 478–484.

12. Granick, *Managerial Comparisons of Four Developed Countries*, chap. 9.

13. D. Granick, "Institutional Innovation and Economic Management: The Soviet Incentive System, 1921 to the Present," in G. Guroff and F. V. Carstensen, eds., *Entrepreneurship in Imperial Russia and the Soviet Union.* pp. 245ff.

14. Granick, *Managerial Comparisons of Four Developed Countries*, chap. 9.

15. Granick, *Managerial Comparisons of Four Developed Countries*, chap. 8.

16. For a discussion, see Conyngham, *The Modernization of Soviet Industrial Management*, p. 13.

17. S. J. Linz, "Managerial Autonomy in Soviet Firms, " *Soviet Studies*, vol. 40, no. 2 (April 1988).

18. B. A. Ruble, "Soviet Trade Unions and Labor Relations After 'Solidarity' " in U. S. Congress, Joint Economic Committee, *Soviet Economy in the 1980s: Problems and Prospects*, part 2, pp. 349–366. There is a large body of literature pertaining to Soviet labor unions. See, for example, B. A. Ruble, *Soviet Trade Unions* (New York: Cambridge University Press, 1981); A. Broadersen, *The Soviet Worker* (New York: Random House, 1966); E. Clark Brown, *Soviet Trade Unions and Labor Relations* (Cambridge, Mass.: Harvard University Press, 1966); D.C. Heldman, *Trade Unions and Labor Relations in the USSR* (Washington, D.C.: Council on American Affairs, 1977); P. Barton, "Trade Unions in the USSR," *AFL-CIO Free Trade Union News* 26 (September 1979), pp. 1–16; A. Kahan and B. R. Ruble, eds., *Industrial Labor in the USSR.*

19. Ruble, "Soviet Trade Unions and Labor Relations After 'Solidarity'," p. 355.

20. The major source of trade union income is membership dues. In 1981, just under 65 percent of union expenditure was for "mass cultural" and sports activities. See Ruble, "Soviet Trade Unions and Labor Relations After 'Solidarity', " p. 356.

21. The legal rights of Soviet workers are elaborated in Ruble, *Soviet Trade Unions*, chap. 4.

22. Ruble, *Soviet Trade Unions*, chap. 6.

23. For a recent discussion on worker influence over enterprise decisions, see D. Slider, "Reforming the Workplace. The 1983 Soviet Law on Labour Collectives," *Soviet Studies*, vol. 37, no. 2 (April 1985), 173–183; and E. Teague, "The USSR Law on Work Collectives: Workers' Control or Workers Controlled?" in D. Lane, ed., *Labour and Employment in the USSR* (New York: New York University Press, 1986), pp. 239–255.

24. For general treatments of Soviet pricing policies, the reader is referred to the following sources: M. Bornstein, "Soviet Price Theory and Policy," in M. Bornstein and D. Fusfeld, eds., *The Soviet Economy: A Book of Readings*, 3rd ed. (Homewood, Ill.: Irwin, 1970), pp. 106–137; P. Hanson, *The Consumer Sector in the Soviet Economy* (Evanston, Ill.: Northwestern University Press, 1968), chap. 8; M. Bornstein, "The Soviet Price Reform Discussion, " *Quarterly Journal of Economics*, vol. 78, no. 1 (February 1964), 15–48;

A. Bergson, *The Economics of Soviet Planning* (New Haven, Conn.: Yale University Press, 1964), chap. 8; M. Bornstein, "The Soviet Debate on Agricultural Prices and Procurement Reforms," *Soviet Studies*, vol. 21, no. 1 (July 1969), 1–20; M. Bornstein, "The Administration of the Soviet Price System," *Soviet Studies*, vol. 30, no. 4 (October 1978), 466–490; M. Bornstein, "Soviet Price Policy in the 1970s," in U.S. Congress, Joint Economic Committee, *Soviet Economy in a New Perspective* (Washington, D.C.: U.S. Government Printing Office, 1976), pp. 17–66; M. Bornstein, "The Soviet Industrial Price Revision," in G. Fink, ed., *Socialist Economy and Economic Policy: Essays in Honour of Friedrich Levcik* (New York: Springer-Verlag, 1985), M. Bornstein, "Soviet Price Policies," *Soviet Economy*, vol. 3, no. 2 (1987), 96–134.

25. Bornstein, "Soviet Price Theory and Policy, " p. 110; and *Narodnoe khoziastvo SSSR v 1978 g.* [The national economy of the USSR in 1978] (Moscow: Statiska, 1979), p. 141.

26. The problems of pricing "new" products and the impact of world prices on Soviet prices are discussed in J. S. Berliner, *The Innovation Decision in Soviet Industry* (Cambridge, Mass.: MIT Press, 1976), part 2; M. Bornstein, "The Administration of the Soviet Price System"; and V. G. Treml, "Foreign Trade and the Soviet Economy: Changing Parameters and Interrelationships," in E. Neuberger and L. Tyson, eds., *Transmission and Response: The Impact of International Disturbances on the Soviet Union and Eastern Europe* (New York: Pergamon Press, 1980).

27. A. Bergson and L. Turgeon, "Basic Industrial Prices in the USSR, 1928–1950," The Rand Corporation, Research Memorandum RM–1522, August 1, 1955; *Narodnoe khoziastvo SSSR v 1969 g.* [The national economy of the USSR in 1969] (Moscow: Statistika, 1970), p. 190.

28. For a discussion of the 1982 reform, see Bornstein, "The Soviet Industrial Price Revision."

29. For Western recalculations of industrial prices, see A. Becker, "The Price Level of Soviet Machinery in the 1960s," *Soviet Studies*, vol. 26, no. 3 (July 1974), 363–380; and J. E. Steiner, *Inflation in Soviet Industry and Machine Building and Metalworking*, SRM78–10142, Office of Strategic Research, Washington, D.C., 1978.

30. For example, sales of clothing and leather footwear grew at an annual rate of around 8 percent between 1968 and 1971. During the same period, clothing and footwear stocks grew at an annual rate of around 19 percent, largely because the types of goods produced failed to correspond to the wishes of the consumer. See *Planovoe khoziaistvo* [The planned economy], no. 10 (1972), pp. 5–7. This growing selectivity also applies to consumer durables. For example, the "Baku" refrigerator proved to be of such low quality that Azerbaijan SSR consumers refused to buy it. The quick-witted manager in charge of its production then changed the name and appearance and released it as a new model. For an account of this see *Sotsialisticheskaia industria* [Socialist industry], no. 14 (1969), p. 2.

31. *Vestnik Statistiki* [Journal of Statistics], no. 9 (1984), p. 80.

32. D. W. Bronson and B. S. Severin, "Consumer Welfare," in U.S. Congress, Joint Economic Committee, *Economic Performance and the Military Burden in the Soviet Union* (Washington, D.C.: U.S. Government Printing Office, 1970), p. 381.

33. Data from *Narodnoe khoziaistvo SSSR v 1978 g.* [The national economy of the USSR in 1978], p. 433; and J. F. Karcz, "Quantitative Analysis of the Collective Farm Market," *American Economic Review*, vol. 54, no. 4, part 1 (June 1964), 315–333; see especially the discussion on page 315.

34. E. C. Cook, "Household Plot Production and Contract Sales," in U.S. Department of Agriculture, *CDE Agriculture Report*, vol. 1, no. 6 (November/December 1988), 6–7.

35. Bornstein, "Improving the Soviet Economic Mechanism," pp. 9–11.

36. Political factors have also been important in maintaining low prices on basic foods such as meat and dairy products. In the post-Stalin era, the Soviet leadership risked popular discontent and sometimes civil unrest when such prices were raised. An example of this was the 30 percent increase in meat and butter prices in 1962. On this, see Hanson, *The Consumer Sector*, pp. 171–177. This issue has assumed increased importance in the Gorbachev era as price reform looms in the horizon, a reform that could attack the problem of growing subsidies and lack of enterprise interest in efficiency.

37. While charges for such services are generally very low, they do appear more substantial when considered as a portion of family income. Also, it is possible to contract some services—for example, those of a doctor—privately. In such cases, charges will be higher. For a discussion of this point, see R. J. Osborn, *Soviet Social Policies: Welfare, Equality, and Community* (Homewood, Ill.: Dorsey Press, 1970), pp. 89-94. The issue of private markets is discussed in Chapter 9.

38. For this view, see Bergson, *The Economics of Soviet Planning*, pp. 166–170.

39. R. P. Powell, "Plan Execution and the Workability of Soviet Planning," *Journal of Comparative Economics*, vol. 1, no. 1 (March 1977), 69–73.

40. For a discussion of the implications of contracting in the Soviet setting, see H. Kroll, "The Role of Contracts in The Soviet Economy," *Soviet Studies*, vol. 40, no. 3 (July 1988), 349–366

41. Investment choice in the Soviet Union has been discussed in a number of articles and books: Bergson, *The Economics of Soviet Planning*, chap. 11; G. Grossman, "Scarce Capital and Soviet Doctrine," *Quarterly Journal of Economics*, vol. 67, no. 3 (August 1953); A. Zauberman, *Aspects of Planometrics* (New Haven, Conn.: Yale University Press, 1967), chaps. 13 and 14; A. Abouchar, "The New Soviet Standard Methodology for Investment Allocation," *Soviet Studies*, vol. 24, no. 3 (January 1973), 402–410; Berliner, *The Innovation Decision*, chap. 21; S. H. Cohn, "Deficiencies in Soviet Investment Policies and the Technological Imperative," in U.S. Congress, Joint Economic Committee, *Soviet Economy in a New Perspective*, pp. 447–459; S. H. Cohn, "Soviet Replacement Investment: A Rising Policy Imperative," in U.S. Congress, Joint Economic Committee, *Soviet Economy in a Time of Change)*, pp. 230–245; M. Ellman, *Socialist Planning* (Cambridge, Mass.: Cambridge University Press, 1979), chap. 5; D. A. Dyker, *The Process of Investment in the Soviet Union* (New York: Cambridge University Press, 1981); J. Giffen, "The Allocation of Investment in the Soviet Union: Criteria for the Efficiency of Investment," *Soviet Studies*, vol. 32, no. 4 (October 1981), 593–609; R. E. Leggett, "Soviet Investment Policy in the 11th Five-Year Plan," in U.S. Congress, Joint Economic Committee, *Soviet Economy in the 1980s: Problems and Prospects*, part 1, pp. 129–152; S. H. Cohn, "Sources of Low Productivity in Soviet Capital Investment," in *Soviet Economy in the 1980's*, pp. 1969–1994; R. E. Leggett, "Soviet Investment Policy: The Key to Gorbachev's Program for Revitalizing the Soviet Economy," in U.S. Congress, Joint Economic Committee, *Gorbachev's Economic Plans*, vol. 1 (Washington, D.C.: U.S. Government Printing Office, 1987), pp. 236–256; D. Dyker, *The Future of the Soviet Economic Planning System* (London: Croom Helm, 1985), chap. 5; P. Goldberg, "Consistency in Soviet Investment Rules," *Journal of Comparative Economics*, vol. 12, no. 2 (June 1988), 244–247; A. Abouchar, "Western Project-Investment Theory and Soviet Investment Rules," *Journal of Comparative Economics*, vol. 9, no. 4 (December 1985), 345–62; A. Abouchar, "The Time Factor and

Soviet Investment Methodology, " *Soviet Studies,* vol. 37, no. 3 (July 1985), 417–427; R. C. Harmstone, "Background to Gorbachev's Investment Strategy," *Comparative Economic Studies,* vol. 30, no. 4 (Winter 1988), 58–91; B. Rumer, *Investment and Reindustrialization of the Soviet Economy* (Boulder, Colo.: Westview Press, 1984).

42. After the Kosygin reform of 1965, the importance of decentralized investment increased. However, in the 1970s, even where decentralized funds (for example, from enterprises) were financing investment, the distinction between centralized and decentralized investment lost its former significance, with central control being maintained over all investment. For a discussion, see Dyker, *The Process of Investment in the Soviet Union,* p. 31. This issue has remained important throughout the 1980s with a renewed push for self-financing at the enterprise level.

43. Cited in Leggett, "Soviet Investment Policy: The Key to Gorbachev's Program for Revitalizing the Soviet Economy," p. 247.

44. Zauberman, *Aspects of Planometrics,* p. 139.

45. The rapid retirement of obsolete equipment is an important thrust of the Gorbachev reform program. See R. E. Leggett, "Soviet Investment Policy: The Key to Gorbachev's Program for Revitalizing the Soviet Economy," pp. 245–246, R. C. Harmstone, "Background to Gorbachev's Investment Strategy," *Comparative Economic Studies,* vol. 30, no. 4 (Winter 1988), 58–91, M. J. Kohn and R. E. Leggett, "A Look at Soviet Capital Retirement Statistics: Unraveling Some Mysteries," *Comparative Economic Studies,* vol. 2 (1986), 29–31; R. C. Harmstone, "A Note on Soviet Fixed Asset Replacement in the 1970s and 1980s," *Soviet Studies,* vol. 3 (1986); and B. Rumer, "Some Investment Patterns Engendered by the Renovation of Soviet Industry," *Soviet Studies,* vol. 36, no. 2 (April 1984), 257-266.

46. For a detailed discussion of these points, see Grossman, "Scarce Capital," pp. 311–314, reprinted in F. D. Holzman, *Readings on the Soviet Economy* (Skokie, Ill.: Rand McNally, 1962).

47. "Recommendations of the All-Union Scientific-Technical Conference on Problems of Determining the Economic Effectiveness of Capital Investment and New Techniques in the USSR National Economy," *Problems of Economics: A Journal of Translations,* vol. 1, no. 9 (January 1959), 86–90, reprinted in Holzman, *Readings on the Soviet Economy,* pp. 383–392. Also see "Standard Methodology for Determining the Economic Effectiveness of Capital Investments," *Ekonomicheskaia gazeta* [The economic gazette], no. 39 (1969), pp. 11–12, translated in *ASTE Bulletin,* vol. 13, no. 3 (Fall 1971), 25–36.

48. Zauberman, *Aspects of Planometrics,* p. 139.

49. Nove, *The Soviet Economy,* p. 233.

50. For a discussion of the various techniques used during this period, see Grossman, "Scarce Capital," pp. 315–343.

51. "Recommendations of the All-Union Scientific-Technical Conference," pp. 86–90.

52. Capital outlay includes the cost of buildings, equipment, and installation but excludes the cost of the site: Zauberman, *Aspects of Planometrics,* p. 142.

53. An equivalent test would be: Let E be the "standard coefficient of efficiency." Then, the projects should be compared by comparing their full costs—including an imputed interest cost: $C_i + EK_i$ = minimum. The project with the lowest *full* cost would be chosen. See Bergson, *The Economics of Soviet Planning,* p. 254.

54. Bergson, *The Economics of Soviet Planning,* pp. 225–265; J. Thornton, "Differential Capital Charges and Resource Allocation in Soviet Industry," *Journal of Political Economy,* vol. 79, no. 3 (May–June 1971), 545–561.

55. Bergson, *The Economics of Soviet Planning,* pp. 262–263.

56. See Bergson, *The Economics of Soviet Planning*, p. 253, for a demonstration that a uniform norm will result in the equalization of the marginal productivities.
57. "Recommendations of the All-Union Scientific-Technical Conference, " p. 88.
58. Ibid., pp. 88–89.
59. "Standard Methodology for Determining the Economic Effectiveness of Capital Investments," translated in *ASTE Bulletin*, vol. 13, no. 3 Fall 1971), 25–36. It originally appeared in *Ekonomicheskaia gazeta* [The economic gazette], no. 39 (1969), pp. 11–12.
60. V. Cherniavski, "The Measure of Effectiveness," *Problems of Economics: A Journal of Translations*, vol. 15, no. 8 (December 1972); and L. V Kantorovich, *Essays in Optimal Planning* (White Plains, N.Y.: International Arts and Sciences Press, 1976), essays 8–10.
61. Quoted in V. Vainshtein, "On Methods of Determining the Economic Effectiveness of Capital Investment," *Problems of Economics: A Journal of Translations*, vol. 15, no. 3 (July 1972], 12.
62. "Standard Methodology," p. 31.
63. Abouchar, "The New Soviet Standard Methodology," p. 407.
64. This discussion is based on Giffen, "The Allocation of Investment in the Soviet Union: Criteria for the Efficiency of Investment," pp. 600–601.
65. "Methodika opredeleniia ekonomicheskoi effektivnosti kapital'nyich vlozhenii" [The method of determining the economic effectiveness of capital investment], *Ekonomicheskaia gazeta* [The economic gazette] (1981], pp. 2–3.
66. Dyker, *The Process of Investment in the Soviet Union*, p. 107.
67. Ibid., p. 108.
68. Ibid.

SELECTED BIBLIOGRAPHY

Soviet Enterprise Management

J.S. Berliner, *Factory and Manager in the USSR* (Cambridge, Mass.: Harvard University Press, 1957).

———, *The Innovation Decision in Soviet Industry* (Cambridge, Mass.: MIT Press, 1976).

———, "Managerial Incentives and Decision-making: A Comparison of the United States and the Soviet Union," in M. Bornstein and D. Fusfeld, eds., *The Soviet Economy*, 3rd ed. (Homewood, Ill.: Irwin, 1970), pp. 165–195.

M. Bornstein, "Improving the Soviet Economic Mechanism," *Soviet Studies*, vol. 37, no. 1 (January 1985), 1–30.

W. J. Conyngham, *The Modernization of Soviet Industrial Management* (New York: Cambridge University Press, 1982).

A. Freris, *The Soviet Industrial Enterprise* (New York: St. Martin's Press, 1984).

D. Granick, *Management of the Industrial Firm in the USSR* (New York: Columbia University Press, 1954).

———, *Managerial Comparisons of Four Developed Countries: France, Britain, United States, and Russia* (Cambridge, Mass.: MIT Press, 1972).

————, *The Red Executive* (Garden City, N.Y.: Doubleday, 1960).

————, *Soviet Metal Fabricating and Economic Development* (Madison: University of Wisconsin Press, 1967), chap. 7.

G. Guroff and F. V. Carstensen, eds., *Entrepreneurship in Imperial Russia and the Soviet Union* (Princeton, N.J.: Princeton University Press, 1983).

P. Hanson, "Success Indicators Revisited: The July 1979 Soviet Decree on Planning and Management," *Soviet Studies*, vol. 25, no. 1 (January 1983), 1–13.

H. Kroll, "The Role of Contracts in the Soviet Economy," *Soviet Studies*, vol. 40, no. 3 (July 1988), 349–66.

S. J. Linz, "Management's Response to Tautness in Soviet Planning: Evidence from the Soviet Interview Project," *Comparative Economic Studies*, vol. 30, no. 1 (Spring 1988), 65–103.

A. Nove, *Economic Rationality and Soviet Politics* (New York: Praeger, 1964), chap. 5.

B. M. Richman, *Management Development and Education in the Soviet Union* (East Lansing: Michigan State University Press, 1967).

————, *Soviet Industrial Management* (Englewood Cliffs, N.J.: Prentice-Hall, 1965).

The Soviet Price System

A. Abouchar, ed., *The Socialist Price Mechanism* (Durham, N.C.: Duke University Press, 1977).

A. Becker, "The Price Level of Soviet Machinery in the 1960s," *Soviet Studies*, vol. 26, no. 3 (July 1974), 363–380.

A. Bergson, *The Economics of Soviet Planning* (New Haven, Conn.: Yale University Press, 1964), chap. 8.

M. Bornstein, "The Administration of the Soviet Price System," *Soviet Studies*, vol. 30, no. 4 (October 1978), 466–490.

————, "The 1963 Soviet Industrial Price Revision," *Soviet Studies*, vol. 15, no. 1 (July 1963), 43–52.

————, "The Soviet Debate on Agricultural Prices and Procurement Reforms," *Soviet Studies*, vol. 21, no. 1 (July 1969), 1–20.

————, "Soviet Price Policy in the 1970s," in U.S. Congress, Joint Economic Committee, *Soviet Economy in a New Perspective* (Washington, D.C.: U.S. Government Printing Office, 1976), pp. 17–66.

————, "The Soviet Price Reform Discussion," *Quarterly Journal of Economics*, vol. 78, no. 1 (February 1964), 15–48.

————, "Soviet Price Theory and Policy," in M. Bornstein and D. Fusfeld, eds., *The Soviet Economy: A Book of Readings*, 3rd ed. (Homewood, Ill.: Irwin, 1970), pp. 106–137.

————, "The Soviet Industrial Price Revision," in G. Fink, ed., *Socialist Economy and Economic Policy: Essays in Honour of Friedrich Levcik* (New York: Springer-Verlag, 1985).

————, "Soviet Price Policies," *Soviet Economy*, vol. 3, no. 2 (1987), 96–134.

R. W. Campbell, "Marx, Kantrovich and Novozhilov: Stoimost' Versus Reality, " *Slavic Review*, vol. 20, no. 3 (October 1961), 402–418.

P. Hanson, *The Consumer Sector in the Soviet Economy* (Evanston, Ill.: Northwestern University Press, 1968), chaps. 7 and 8.

D. H. Howard, "The Disequilibrium Model in a Controlled Economy: An Empirical Test of the Barro-Grossman Model," *American Economic Review*, vol. 66, no. 5 (December 1966), 871–879.

R. Hutchings, "The Origins of the Soviet Industrial Price System," *Soviet Studies*, vol. 13, no.1 (July 1961), 1–22.

A. Nove, *The Soviet Economic System* (London: Allen & Unwin, 1977), chaps. 2 and 3.

J. Pickersgill, "Soviet Household Savings Behavior," *Review of Economics and Statistics*, vol. 58, no. 2 (May 1976), 139–147.

R. P. Powell, "Plan Execution and the Workability of Soviet Planning," *Journal of Comparative Economics*, vol. 1, no. 1 (March 1977), 69–73.

G. E. Schroeder, "The 1966–67 Soviet Industrial Price Reform: A Study in Complications," *Soviet Studies*, vol. 20, no. 4 (April 1969), 462–477.

J. E. Steiner, "Disguised Inflation in Soviet Industry, " *Journal of Comparative Economics*, vol. 6, no. 3 (September 1982), 278–287.

The Investment Decision

A. Abouchar, "The New Soviet Standard Methodology for Investment Allocation," *Soviet Studies*, vol. 24, no. 3 (January 1973).

———, "The Time Factor and Soviet Investment Methodology," *Soviet Studies*, vol. 37, no. 3 (July 1985), 417–427.

———, "Western Project-Investment Theory and Soviet Investment Rules," *Journal of Comparative Economics*, vol. 9, no. 4 (December 1985), 345–362.

A. Bergson, *The Economics of Soviet Planning* (New Haven, Conn.: Yale University Press, 1964), chap. 11.

F. A. Durgin, "The Soviet 1969 Standard Methodology for Investment Allocation Versus 'Universally Correct' Methods," *ACES Bulletin*, vol. 19, no. 2 (Summer 1977), 29–54.

D. A. Dyker, *The Process of Investment in the Soviet Union* (New York: Cambridge University Press, 1981).

———, *The Future of the Soviet Economic Planning System* (London: Croom Helm, 1985), chap. 5.

J. Giffen, "The Allocation of Investment in the Soviet Union: Criteria for the Efficiency of Investment," *Soviet Studies*, vol. 32, no. 4 (October 1981), 593–609.

P. Goldberg, "Consistency in Soviet Investment Rules," *Journal of Comparative Economics*, vol. 12, no. 2 (June 1988), 244–247.

P. Gregory, B. Fielitz, and T. Curtis, "The New Soviet Investment Rules: A Guide to Rational Investment Planning?" *Southern Economic Journal*, vol. 41, no. 3 (January 1974).

G. Grossman, "Scarce Capital and Soviet Doctrine," *Quarterly Journal of Economics,* vol. 67, no. 3 (August 1953).

R. C. Harmstone, "A Note on Soviet Fixed Asset Replacement in the 1970s and 1980s," *Soviet Studies,* vol. 3 (1986).

———, "Background to Gorbachev's Investment Strategy," *Comparative Economic Studies,* vol. 30, no. 4 (Winter 1988), 58–91.

M. J. Kohn and R. E. Leggett, "A Look at Soviet Capital Retirement Statistics: Unraveling Some Mysteries," *Comparative Economic Studies,* vol. 2 (1986), 29–31.

———, "Soviet Investment Policy: The Key to Gorbachev's Program for Revitalizing the Soviet Economy," in U.S. Congress, Joint Economic Committee, *Gorbachev's Economic Plans,* vol. 1 (Washington, D.C.: U.S. Government Printing Office, 1987), 236–256.

G. Leptin, *Methode und Efficienz der Investitionsfinanzerung durch Abschreibungen in der Sowjetwirtschaft* [Methods and efficiency of investment financing through depreciation in the Soviet economy] (Berlin: Osteuropa-Institut, 1961).

B. Rumer, *Investment and Reindustrialization of the Soviet Economy* (Boulder, Colo.: Westview Press, 1984).

———, "Some Investment Patterns Engendered by the Renovation of Soviet Industry," *Soviet Studies,* vol. 36, no. 2 (April 1984), 257–266.

A. Zauberman, *Aspects of Planometrics* (New Haven, Conn.: Yale University Press, 1967), chaps. 13 and 14.

———, *Mathematical Theory in Soviet Planning* (New York: Oxford University Press, 1976), chap. 4.

Chapter
9

The Soviet Household: Private and Public Work

*I*n this chapter we turn our attention to the household in the Soviet economy. Although the household is, in a sense, beyond the immediate grasp of the planner, it nevertheless remains of central importance both as a supplier of labor and as a consumer of goods and services.

We begin our discussion of the household as a supplier of labor, after which we turn to issues of saving and consumption. Our discussion follows a familiar pattern. We begin with an examination of the household as it fits into the formal economy, after which we turn our attention to the household in the informal or second economy.

LABOR ALLOCATION IN THE SOVIET UNION

The allocation of labor in the Soviet economy is accomplished through a combination of administrative controls and market forces. The latter, in the form of voluntary responses to wage differentials, primarily affect the supply of labor in various occupations and regions, whereas administrative controls have been used to affect both the supply and demand sides of the Soviet labor market, with the mix of market forces and administrative controls changing over time. Given the important role played by the market in labor allocation, we shall consider both the demand and supply of labor in the Soviet economy. Let us consider first the determination of enterprise demand for labor through the planning system.

Labor Planning in the Soviet Union

In the Soviet Union, the amount of labor required by an industrial enterprise is decided largely outside of the firm by superior authorities. In fact, the determination of enterprise labor staffing is an integral part of the general planning process. The enterprise *techpromfinplan* contains not only enterprise output and material input targets but also instructions on labor inputs. The amount of detail on labor staffing has varied over the years. However, throughout much of the plan era, *techpromfinplan* labor staffing instructions tended to be quite detailed, specifying the enterprise wage bills, the distribution of enterprise labor force by wage classes, average wages, planned increases in labor productivity, and so on. The Soviet manager has tended to exercise some discretion in the area of labor staffing within the constraints of the *techpromfinplan*; nevertheless, enterprise labor staffing is basically a decision made by planning authorities in accordance with the production plans that they also determine.

Gosplan determines a balance for the Soviet labor force just as it derives balances for material inputs. The most important part of such Soviet labor balancing is the estimation of available human resources, which is carried out by *Gosplan* with the help of regional and local governments and planning authorities. This is not an easy task, for the reserve labor force in agriculture must be estimated along with the potential reserves among the female population, in addition to existing urban labor resources. Also, demographic factors such as birth and death rates and migration rates between regions and between the countryside and towns must be considered.

Once the available supply (both actual and potential) of labor resources has been estimated, *Gosplan* must estimate the demands for labor resources. The labor requirements of the various economic branches are determined in much the same manner as material input requirements. The planning authorities estimate in detail (after considerable bargaining and consultation with lower echelons)—on the basis of coefficients (norms) relating labor inputs to outputs—the labor staffing required to produce the given output targets. As in the case of material inputs, enterprises and lower planning echelons have commonly exaggerated their labor staffing needs for the purpose of adding to their safety factor, and planning authorities have had to allocate labor resources below enterprise requests to balance supplies and demands. Another complication is the fact that labor productivity tends to increase over time, adding another variable to the problem of estimating required labor inputs.[1]

Once the planning authorities draw up the balance of labor resources, a second problem arises: How are they to bring the appropriate amount of labor into the various enterprises, or, to use the Soviet terminology, how are they to "guarantee the labor requirements of the national economy"?[2]

Population Growth: Long-Run Supply

The supply of labor to the Soviet economy depends on the population base decisions of households to participate in the labor force.[3] The Soviets inherited from the tsars a population that had been growing rapidly since the 1860s due to high fertility and declining mortality. Despite enormous losses during World Wars I and II, high rates of natural increase and territorial annexations caused the population of the USSR to grow at an annual rate of slightly under 1.5 percent between 1926 and 1985. During the early postwar period, Soviet population growth was especially rapid (1.7 percent per annum between 1951 and 1966). Since the early 1960s, there has been a sharp and continuing decline in the rate of growth of the Soviet population due to declining Soviet fertility. Although fertility levels reached their lowest point and began to increase significantly in the early 1980s, nevertheless the slowing of the population growth rate, the aging of the population, and the importance of regional differences are all factors influencing the availability of labor. With an average annual growth rate of the population at roughly 1.2 percent in the past two decades, the rate of expansion of the labor force has shrunk significantly. As the evidence in Table 9.1 suggests, the increments to employment, while positive, have decreased sharply in recent years. Moreover, the already very high participation rates preclude greater participation as a possible source of increased labor. Although those beyond the formal retirement age have been brought back into employment, this age group is also a source with limitations.

Beyond these overall demographic patterns, there are other factors that affect labor supply. In the Soviet case, regional redistribution has been important, most notably the outmigration from rural to urban areas. While the rural sector served as a major source of industrial labor in the past, its importance as a supplier of labor to urban areas has declined due to the aging of the rural population, the need to maintain the growth of agricultural output, and the difficulty of accommodating rural migrants in already crowded Soviet cities.[4] Although there are significant regional differences in the level of urbanization and hence the potential importance of rural migration as a source of labor, there are major problems with this source. Sixty-six percent of the Soviet population lived in urban areas in 1987, but by republic the level of urbanization varied significantly from a high of over 71 percent in Estonia to a low of just over 33 percent

Table 9.1   SOVIET POPULATION AND LABOR SUPPLY

Year	Total population (in thousands)	Able-bodied population[a] (in thousands)	Average annual employment: all sectors (in thousands)	Employment increment (in thousands)
1960	214,865	119,459	95,398	
1970	242,774	132,774	118,565	23,167
1980	266,410	154,472	136,350	17,785
1990	290,939	160,251	145,584**	9,234**
2000	311,637	172,616		

[a]Defined as females 16–54 years and males 16–59.
** Estimates by the authors.

Source: Population data from W. Ward Kingkade, "Demographic Trends in the Soviet Union," in U.S. Congress, Joint Economic Committee, *Gorbachev's Economic Plans,* vol. I (Washington, D.C.: U.S. Government Printing Office, 1987), pp. 166–186. Employment data from S. Rapawy, "Labor Force and Employment in the U.S.S.R.," in *Gorbachev's Economic Plans,* vol. 4, pp. 202–203.

in Tadzhikistan.[5] Unfortunately, the demand for industrial labor is not in the Central Asian republics such as Tadzhikistan. Moreover, although regional migration can be used to alleviate regional labor shortages, Soviet past experience suggests limited potential. In the case of Siberia, for example, higher wages have attracted new workers, but high turnover rates inhibit the development of a stable productive labor force. In Central Asia, the one region of the Soviet Union where the rate of growth of population remains high (and well above that prevailing in European Russia), migration to other republics of the able-bodied population has not been significant.

Soviet policies have been modified to encourage the greater participation of younger and older people in the labor force. For example, students are used to offset seasonal imbalances and for short-term needs in agriculture. Rules have been modified to enable older persons (specifically pensioners) to return to work yet still retain pension benefits.

All of these measures can make a contribution to increasing the Soviet labor supply and improving the regional distribution of labor. However, at the present level of labor productivity, the Soviet economy is perceived to have a significant labor shortage. According to existing demographic projections shown in Table 9.1, this problem will persist through the 1990s.

Differential Wages in the Soviet Union

There are a number of alternative means by which eligible participants could be induced to contribute effectively to the labor effort. First, administrative means could be used. In an extreme form, the state could conscript (or incarcerate) labor and assign it to particular regions and particular jobs. A second alternative would be the use of material and moral rewards, differentiated to attract labor to those regions and jobs where it is needed most. A third possibility, in part a variant of adjustment to the reward system, could be alteration of basic policy objectives, especially the full employment or job right concept. Finally, as a long-term variant, the supply of labor could be influenced through human resources training, education, and organized recruitment.

In the Soviet case, all of these mechanisms have been used. In times other than collectivization or war, market-type mechanisms—wages, education, and training—have been used to influence household decision making. Although the importance of controls has varied over the years, relative wages have been the most important factor influencing Soviet labor force allocation. At the same time, market forces have been constrained in a number of ways—such as closed cities, the passport system, and labor mobilization.[6]

Soviet wage-setting authorities have long recognized the allocative function of differential wages, and the principle has been accepted that wage determination should be governed by the needs of labor allocation rather than by considerations of equality.[7] Problems of poverty and income inequality should therefore be corrected by the social security system, not through differentials. Wage authorities point out that the "wrong" set of wage differentials adversely affects labor productivity and promotes excessive labor turnover. Ideologically, wage differentials are justified by the socialist distribution principle of "equal pay for equal work" and by Lenin's admonition against "equality mongering." Differentials are justified by Marx's labor theory of value, which recognizes that different types of labor must be converted into a common denominator. The Soviets call this the "principle of the reduction of labor." Insofar as labor consists of six dimensions—the length of time worked, the skill required, the region, the industry, the enterprise in which the work is performed, and working conditions—a socialist wage scale must differentiate among workers according to these dimensions.

Industrial wages are set by central authorities in the Soviet Union. Various agencies have over time participated in wage scale determination—the ministries, the Council of Ministers, the Central Council of Trade Unions, the State Committee on Labor and Wages, and many others—but the trend since 1956 has been toward increasing centralization and standardization. A nationwide reform of industrial wages ongoing from 1956 to 1965, but largely completed between 1958 and 1960, established a more simplified uniform system of industrial wages.[8] A later round of reforms between 1972 and 1976 extended the earlier reforms to other economic branches and continued the process of standardization of wage scales.

Industrial wage rates are set in the following manner: In each industrial branch, base rates (stavka) specifying the absolute wage of the lowest paid occupation are established. Then for each branch, a schedule (tarifnaia setka) is designated, which gives the wages of higher-grade occupations as percentages of the lowest-grade rate.[9] By altering the base rate, labor authorities can direct labor into and out of branches according to the plan. In this manner, high average wages in priority sectors such as machinery, metallurgy, electricity, and coal were used to effect the dramatic shifts of labor out of agriculture and light industry into heavy industry during the early plan era. During NEP, average wages in the consumer goods sector exceeded those in heavy industry. Beginning with the first Five Year Plan, average wages in heavy industry grew more rapidly than in light industry.[10] In the postwar period, a positive correlation existed between average branch wages and the national importance of the branch,[11] although wage authorities have attempted to reduce differentials between light and heavy industries.[12]

By manipulating the *tarifnaia setka,* the state can encourage workers to acquire the skills that it requires. Thus, Stalin established schedules in 1931 that heavily favored skilled workers, to encourage the then-untrained labor force to acquire industrial skills. As a result, large differentials were created between the earnings of skilled and nonskilled industrial workers. In fact, Soviet industrial wage differentials during the 1930s were larger than in the United States.[13] With the growing level of education of the labor force, the extreme differentials of the 1930s were gradually reduced after World War II, especially after 1956; and by the late 1970s, new ratios set the rates of the most-skilled categories at a maximum of 2.1 times those of unskilled categories—as opposed to the 4:1 to 8:1 ratios of the 1930s and 1950s. Two other factors have contributed to the leveling of industrial wages in the postwar period: Minimum wage rates have increased dramatically, and the numbers (and percentage) of workers making low wages have declined markedly. In 1982, industrial workers were divided into six *tarifnaia setkas,* with over 50 percent in the third and fourth categories. Some workers in ferrous metallurgy, iron ores, and machine building worked according to eight *tarifnaia setkas,* with 75 percent in the third through fifth categories.[14]

Industrial wages are also differentiated by region to encourage labor mobility into such rapidly growing areas as Siberia, Kazakhstan, Central Asia, and the Far North, which have harsh climates and lack the cultural amenities of European Russia. Such regional differentials are computed by means of a uniform system of coefficients, which are multiplied by the standard wage rates to yield regionally differentiated wages. For example, the coefficients used to compute wages in the Far North range from 1.5 to 1.7[15]; that is, wages between 50 and 70 percent higher than the standard rates are paid to workers in the Far North for performing the same basic tasks as workers in European Russia. Supplements are also used, which bring the basic wage rate in the Far North to as high as 2.8 times that in European Russia.[16] By 1970 there were 10 regional coefficients used to establish regional wage differentials—a much simplified system from the 90 regional coefficients that existed in the 1950s.[17] In addition to regional differentiation, some higher rates are provided in cases of dangerous work and work performed under arduous conditions. For example, underground mining occupations receive basic monthly wages 14 to 33 percent higher than those for above-ground occupations. In the chemicals industry, work performed under especially hot, heavy, and unhealthy conditions receives payment 33 percent above that for work performed under normal conditions.[18]

The *total* wage of Soviet industrial workers is actually the sum of two components. On the one hand, the worker receives the basic wage computed according to the *setka* and *stavka* system described above. This component does not vary relative to the performance of the individual or the enterprise, and is guaranteed by the state. In addition, the worker receives a variety of supplementary bonus and incentive payments that vary with performance. These supplementary payments are in the form of bonuses for overfulfillment of plan norms, of premiums paid from the wage fund or material incentive fund of the enterprise, and of supplements for special working conditions. In the 1970s, the basic wage accounted for 59 percent; bonuses, for 20 percent; premiums for norm overfulfillment, for 11 percent; and regional and special working conditions differentials, for 10 percent of average monthly earnings in industry.[19]

Prior to the general reform of wages that began in 1956, bonuses and incentive payments made up a larger share of industrial wages owing to the greater importance of piece rates and incentive schemes. During the early 1950s, such payments accounted for slightly more than 40 percent of average industrial incomes. By the 1970s, bonuses and supplements accounted for around 30 percent of industrial wage income. This decrease was a consequence of the substantial decline in the percentage of workers paid according to piece rates, which dropped from two-thirds to one-third of all industrial workers between 1957 and 1961. According to more recent statistics, the proportion of industrial workers working according to some form of piece rates was slightly above 50 percent in both 1972 and the early 1980s. Apparently, there has been a resurgence in piece-rate work since the early 1960s. In construction, the percentage of workers on piece rates was a much higher 80 percent in the early 1980s.[20]

The common current in Soviet wage policy dictates that wage rates should be set to equate supply and demand for labor. If the state wants an increase of employment in metallurgy, for example, wage rates should be raised to attract additional labor into metallurgy. If the state wants to develop the Far North, it must take labor supply factors into account and set a highly differentiated wage to overcome the worker's aversion to the region. As Leonard Kirsch has pointed out, in actual practice, the equation of supply and demand has been accomplished by combining centralized wage setting with enterprise flexibility in the area of incentive payments.[21] Thus, if the basic wage rates established by central authorities create labor shortages or surpluses at the enterprise level, managers have made needed adjustments at the local level by raising or lowering incentive payments.

In reality, Soviet managers operate with considerable flexibility. They can reclassify workers to higher occupation ratings. They can build up special bonus funds by placing bogus workers on their payrolls. Also, they can give workers fringe benefits such as housing or goods. Under Gorbachev, steps have been taken to increase wage differentials, especially by relating pay more closely to output, and granting enterprises the power to pay wage increases out of enterprise funds. These changes, in combination with a renewed emphasis on work discipline and the increasing use of the brigade system of labor organization, are all part of the "human factor" policies to be described in Chapter 15.

EXTRAMARKET CONTROLS OVER LABOR ALLOCATION

Although wage differentials have been used as the main instrument to allocate labor, extra market controls have been important as well. We turn now to an examination of the mechanisms used to control labor allocation, namely, education, organized recruitment, direct controls over labor mobility, the *nomenklatura* system, discipline campaigns, and Soviet labor unions.

The Education System

In the Soviet Union, the educational system provides an important centralized mechanism for control over the labor force.[22] Like other aspects of Soviet economic life, the educational training of qualified labor is planned by central authorities. The key actors are *Gosplan*, the ministries (most of which maintain the educational establishment), and the Ministry of Education. Education policy emanates from the highest levels of the CPSU. The main features of Soviet education policy are described below.

First, the completion of secondary education (through eighth grade since 1973) in general education schools is compulsory.[23] Beyond and in addition to this basic preparation, the Soviet Union has developed a large and complex net of specialized educational institutions under differing jurisdictions devoted to technical training, training in specialized subjects such as foreign languages, graduate training, and the like. At the highest level, universities and research institutes train higher-degree candidates. The rapid expansion of the Soviet educational establishment is an indicator of its priority (Table 9.2).

Second, Soviet education reflects the official view that the educational system must serve both the economy and Soviet society within a Marxist–Leninist framework.[24] Accordingly, there is no equivalent of what in the West would be described as a "liberal arts" education. Soviet education has been devoted to the development of the new Soviet person, Communist morality, and, above all, skills useful to the economy. Soviet education has emphasized science, engineering, and technical specialities and has restricted entry into the study of arts and humanities. Although career paths through the various types of schools create familiar problems of choice for Soviet students, service to Soviet society is a theme that remains strong to the present. In keeping with the emphasis on scientific and technical training, the Soviet educational establishment relies heavily on specialized secondary schools that provide professional vocational training to medical assistants, draftsmen, and skilled mechanics at a level between university and high school training.

Table 9.2   THE SOVIET EDUCATIONAL ESTABLISHMENT

	1960/61	1970/71	1983/84	1986/87
General education schools	224,000	190,000	141,000	138,000
Enrollment	36,187,000	49,193,000	44,479,000	43,900,000
Graduates (full completion: day and evening students)	1,055,000	2,581,000	3,628,000	3,039,000
Specialized secondary schools	3,328	4,223	4,438	4,506
Enrollment	2,060,000	4,388,000	4,503,000	4,485,000
Graduates	483,500	1,033,300	1,265,600	1,261,700
Vocational-technical schools	3,684	5,351	7,624	8,020
Enrollment	1,064,000	2,380,000	3,770,000	4,176,000
Graduates	741,000	1,638,000	2,518,000	2,583,000
Higher educational institutions	739	805	890	896
Enrollment	2,396,000	4,581,000	5,301,000	5,088,000
Graduates	343,300	630,800	849,500	839,500

Note: The data in this table are to be viewed as approximate. In most cases, the numbers are rounded. Some refer to the academic year (for example, 1970/71), while others refer to a calendar year (for example, graduates in 1970).

Source: TsSU, *Narodnoe khoziaistvo SSSR v 1983 g.* [The national economy of the USSR in 1983] (Moscow: Finansy i Statistika, 1984), 402, 484–504; Goskomstat, *Narodnoe khoziaistvo SSSR za 70 let* [The national economy of the USSR over 70 years] (Moscow: Finansy i statistika, 1987), pp. 422, 523–555.

Third, service to the economy is reinforced in other ways. For example, attempts are made at all levels of the hierarchy from *Gosplan* down through the local districts to plan in advance for labor requirements and, on this basis, to provide the educational capacity necessary to meet these planned needs. This feature is seen in the fact that the different education ministries take their orders from *Gosplan*. Moreover, there is a strong emphasis on vocational work experience in the Soviet school setting. Practical work experience was emphasized in the Khruschev years and resurfaced in later educational reforms such as efforts to expand "production training combines," whereby local enterprises build special workshops staffed by local students for the purpose of improving their technical skills and general work experience.[25]

Finally, Soviet authorities use a variety of control mechanisms to allocate labor, especially highly trained human resources. The most important of these is the work placement of graduates of higher and secondary specialized educational institutions. Decrees of the late 1970s and early 1980s have strengthened the role of the state in this regard. For example, graduates of vocational technical schools (since 1980) are required to complete two years of work assignment at a specified location.[26] Similar types of required assignments have been used for more highly skilled graduates and have been employed to offset labor shortages in areas such as Siberia.

In theory, state control of the educational system should be a powerful mechanism of guaranteeing the labor needs of the Soviet economy. The task of actually meeting these needs is, however, exceedingly difficult. For this and a host of related reasons, the system does not always work smoothly. The Soviet press contains accounts of university graduates whose specialities are no longer required by the ministry that ordered those specialities four years earlier. It also contains accounts of trained specialists who are working in areas outside their speciality. There are also reports of too many trained engineers.

Organized Recruitment

A second important mechanism for the administrative allocation of labor in the Soviet Union is organized recruitment.[27] Since 1976, the All-Union Resettlement Committee and the Administration for Organized Recruitment *(Orgnabor)* have gained substantial strength, having been placed under the State Committee for Labor and Social Problems *(Goskomtrud)*. During the 1930s, *Orgnabor* played a key role in transferring labor from countryside to the cities by recruiting labor for industrial enterprises from collective and private farms. Some 3 million peasants were transferred from the village to the city through *Orgnabor* contracts. After World War II, *Orgnabor* became more involved in the transfer of workers among industrial enterprises rather than from agriculture to industry; and by the late 1950s, *Orgnabor's* role in supplying industrial labor had become a limited one. Its major role, instead, became the recruiting of labor for vast construction projects and new industries located in the east and the north. By the late 1970s, only about 3 percent of job placements were handled by this agency.[28]

In the general task of worker placement, especially in the less desirable areas of the Soviet Union, the use of these formal mechanisms has always been supplemented by general appeals of the Communist Party and the Komsomol, the latter designed to attract youth to fulfill special tasks.

Labor Mobility: Legal Controls

The competitive bidding for industrial workers plus the vast influx into the cities of untrained peasants from the countryside created excessive job turnover during the 1930s. The average worker in the food industry changed jobs three times a year in 1930 and 1931; and for the economy as a whole, the average industrial worker changed jobs more than once per year.[29] Excessive turnover forced the state to adopt additional extramarket controls over labor mobility.

During the 1930s, a series of measures was adopted to reduce the excessive turnover. Absenteeism was deterred by severe penalties (eviction from factory housing and loss of social insurance benefits), "closed shops" were used to reward select groups of reliable workers, and enterprise control over limited housing was used as leverage to promote labor stability. After 1938, controls became even more severe. Labor books (in which a person's work record would be recorded) were issued to all employed persons, an internal passport system was used to monitor the movements of the population, and permission was required to change jobs (failure to comply being a criminal offense). Administrative controls over labor increased during the war with the mobilization of specialists, the lengthening of the workday, the making of absenteeism a criminal offense, and the establishment of labor reserve schools. Most of the laws pertaining to labor control during the war were passed in 1940. They were quite severe and resulted in numerous instances of criminal prosecution and imprisonment.[30] They remained on the books until their repeal in 1956, although they had actually fallen into disuse during the early 1950s. In 1956, the workday was shortened, criminal liability for leaving work without permission and for absenteeism was abandoned, and social benefits were raised. As an immediate response to this liberalization, turnover in industry rose to 38 percent in 1956, after which it declined to a fairly steady 20 to 22 percent, which was below comparable turnover rates in manufacturing in the United States.[31] The turnover rate of approximately one-fifth of the labor force annually seems to hold for the 1980s. However, it has been pointed out that in some sectors and regions, the turnover rate is much higher. For example, turnover rates have always been higher in Siberia. The loss of technically trained labor from rural areas has been a persistent problem for the agricultural sector.

The problem of "rolling stones" (workers who change jobs too frequently) remains a source of official concern, especially in the outlying republics where labor is quite scarce. This concern has been sufficiently serious for the state to introduce a series of measures—special bonuses for uninterrupted employment (1965), a labor code of 1971 giving reliable workers special privileges and priority in job advancement, and experimental programs in various urban areas to reduce job turnover—designed to combat what the state perceives as excessive job turnover. This theme, emphasized in the 1970s, has remained a point of focus in the 1980s under both Andropov and Gorbachev. Beyond the repetition of the general theme on the need to tighten labor discipline, specific steps have been taken to lessen turnover. In addition to the development of positive incentives (for example, expanded pension benefits for continuous service), negative sanctions have been increased. In the early 1980s, the notice period for voluntary separations was increased from two weeks to one month. Although Soviet labor authorities appear to believe that labor turnover has been excessive, David Granick finds that industrial labor turnover is not significantly different from that of industrial capitalist eonomies.[32]

Soviet authorities have taken further steps to lessen the impact of labor turnover. The role of labor placement bureaus, first introduced in the late 1960s, has expanded. Between 1977 and 1980, the number of such bureaus increased from 370 to 650, and in the 1980s they have been responsible for the placement of roughly 15 percent of the work force. Moreover, Soviet authorities have initiated scientific surveys of labor turnover in an effort to identify the sources of turnover. A study of the food-processing industry, for example, identified unattractive work conditions, overtime requirements, poor housing, inability to use specialization, and low wages as significant causes of turnover. The study found further that turnover was greatest among women, young people, persons on the job for less than one year, and manual workers.[33]

As we shall see in Chapter 12 when we examine Soviet economic performance, the rate of growth of labor productivity in the Soviet Union has declined significantly in recent years. While many factors can account for this outcome, there is no question that Soviet authorities place increasing emphasis on the need for better work discipline. Lack of work discipline is perceived to come from many sources, among them excess turnover, lack of adequate incentives, alcoholism, and the like. The evidence from recent years supports the view that in the face of a continuing slow growth of the labor force, considerable attention will be paid to various means for improving work discipline. Administrative means, especially controls of various sorts, may play an important role.

Penal Labor [34]

The most glaring deviation from the principle of a free labor market was the creation of a large penal labor force in the Soviet Union beginning in 1929. The number of prisoners in Soviet concentration camps (the *gulag* population) cannot be estimated with precision, but disparate sources—an occasional official reference, comparisons of official labor force figures with the able-bodied population, accounts of ex-prisoners, the materials published by Alexander Solzhenitsyn—all point to astonishing numbers of forced laborers. We shall never know the exact numbers, but there would be agreement on the following points: The *gulag* population received its first large influx with the collectivization drive, reaching 1 to 2 million in the early 1930s. The second large influx came with the Stalin purges of the mid- and late 1930s. Estimates for 1939 vary from 2 to 11 million. The camp population reached its peak size during World War II and its immediate aftermath. The figures for the 1945–1950 period range from 4 to 15 million. Ex-prisoners of war, resettled minorities, citizens of occupied territories, and many other groups were incarcerated during the war years. The official abolition of the *gulag* by Khrushchev in 1956 did not immediately spell the end of the large *gulag* population, the size of which was between 2 and 4 million in 1959. The proportion of the labor force in concentration camps was probably 5 percent in the mid-1930s and rose to over 10 percent during the war years.[35]

The legal foundation for mass political internments was provided by Article 58 of the 1926 Soviet criminal code, which declared actions directed toward weakening state power a crime against the state. Falling under this classification were a wide variety of offenses, including sabotage, propaganda, agitation, conscious failure to carry out one's duties, subversion of industry, and suspicion of espionage.

The internment of large percentages of the population in forced labor camps cannot be justified on moral and economic grounds. One may classify the *gulags* as the product of an irrational Stalin and his associates and not regard them as being consciously designed for economic purposes. The *gulag* population was put to work principally in mining and on construction projects in harsh climates to which free labor could not be attracted. Apparently, the state did seek to derive economic benefit from forced labor. However, the costs of this penal labor were immense. The high death rates in the concentration camps caused a substantial loss of population.

It is difficult to estimate the loss of life in the camps because of conceptual and data problems. One measure, however, is excess mortality between 1926 and 1939. "Excess mortality" measures the number of people alive in 1926 who died between 1926 and 1939 in excess of the number that would have died under normal circumstances. Excess mortality between 1926 and 1939 was likely in the range of 3 to 6 million.[36] Excess mortality is only one cost of the camps. The sense of alienation of former prisoners and their families (along with deteriorated health) would not render them enthusiastic "builders of socialism" after their release. Furthermore, it is likely that forced labor is less productive than free labor. The diversion of labor from the labor market into concentration camps more than likely caused a loss of output due to a general lowering of labor productivity. By the late 1980s, Gorbachev's *glasnost* policies even allowed Soviet publications to publish various estimates of the number of Stalin's victims.

Nomenklatura Controls

Another source of extramarket control over labor is the *nomenklatura* system described in Chapter 1. Under the *nomenklatura* procedure, the most important appointments in the economic system are filled from a party-nominated list of candidates. This list, maintained by the various cadres and departments of the Communist Party, allows the party to maintain direct control over most important administrative appointments. This control is important insofar as it can cover all aspects of the appointment process, whether it be technical skills required for the job or more general issues of party loyalty. The *nomenklatura* system requires that those individuals who desire high-level appointments demonstrate their acceptability to the party. This means following party directives, cultivating the favors of influential party officials, and avoiding behavior that would be frowned upon by the party.

AN EVALUATION OF SOVIET LABOR POLICY

One way to evaluate Soviet labor policy would be to consider its role in resource allocation. How well have Soviet authorities utilized available labor resources? Are there notable labor shortages or surpluses either by occupation or by region? Has aggregate unemployment been avoided? How well does the system correct structural unemployment? This is the criterion of *allocative efficiency*.[37] Although the allocative efficiency of the Soviet labor market is an important criterion, a broader criterion may also be in order. The effectiveness of Soviet labor policy may also be evaluated in light of its contribution to the economic and social goals of the state, which can be denoted as *goal achievement efficiency*.[38] Although these two efficiency measures are not necessarily incompatible, they may be in some cases. The restrictive labor policies of the late

1930s and World War II definitely reduced allocative efficiency in order to achieve the political, economic, and military objectives of the state.

In this section, we begin with a general evaluation of Soviet labor policy after which we summarize and assess contemporary trends.

Quantitative and Structural Changes

Despite the slower population growth after the revolution, the Soviets were able to expand their total labor force at an annual rate of 2.5 percent between 1928 and 1937,[39] a quite high rate by international standards.[40] Even more important than the overall rate of growth in employment was its sectorial distribution. In keeping with the state policy of rapid industrial transformation, the nonagricultural labor force expanded at an annual rate of nearly 9 percent, while the agricultural labor force contracted at an annual rate of –2.5 percent. Light industry suffered a decline in its labor force between 1928 and 1937 that was as dramatic as the shift of labor out of agriculture.

How did Soviet labor policy effect these shifts? The rapid growth of the total labor force can in part be explained by the large rise in the participation rate (the percentage of total population employed on a full-time basis).[41]

Various labor policies contributed to the high participation rate. First, low wages in agriculture, coupled with the organized recruitment of workers in agriculture by *Orgnabor*, resulted in the wholesale transfer of labor out of agriculture, where days worked per year were few relative to industry (owing to seasonal and other factors). Second, in the city, the authorities introduced moral and legal, as well as economic, inducements for all able-bodied individuals to work. "Parasitism" was subject to severe penalties. Such pressures increased throughout the 1930s and peaked in the late 1930s (during the Stalin purges), when cases are recorded of nonworking mothers with newborn infants being criminally prosecuted for "parasitism."[42] The low real wages of the 1930s made it necessary for both husband and wife to work to make ends meet.[43] By 1939, 71 percent of able-bodied women were members of the labor force.[44]

In 1926, 54 percent of the Soviet population over 60 years of age participated in the labor force; by 1939, this number had been reduced to 49 percent .[45]

Soviet wage policy was also used to effect the distribution of labor within industry. In particular, the setting of higher relative wages in heavy industry than in light industry, the use of "closed shop" privileges to reward workers in high-priority branches, and the setting of low piece rate norms to allow large supplemental earnings in heavy industry encouraged the rapid transfer of labor into priority branches. Of 17 industrial branches, average wages in coal and in iron and steel ranked tenth and thirteenth, respectively, in 1924. By 1940, they ranked first and second, respectively.[46] The rankings of the consumer goods branches declined generally. These dramatic shifts in relative wages go a long way toward explaining the radical shift of labor within industry.

The period 1928–1970 was characterized by rapid growth of industrial labor based on rising labor force participation, structural redistribution, and moderate population growth. The rapid growth of labor permitted the Soviet economy to grow extensively based on the expansion of inputs. This pattern ended abruptly after 1970.

The rate of growth of the Soviet population has declined significantly in recent years. For example, during the period 1950–1970, the average annual rate of growth of the Soviet population was 1.7 percent. The comparable figure for the period 1970–1985 was 1.00 percent with a projected decline to 0.78 percent for the period 1985–2000.[47]

This dramatic change in the growth rate of the Soviet population can be accounted for by changes in both birthrates and death rates. Soviet crude birthrates (number of births divided by population) have declined significantly, but they had a reversal in the mid-1980s. For example, in 1960 there were 25 births per 1000 population with a decline to 17 by 1970. By 1986, this number reached 20. Differences by region are important. The crude birthrate in 1986 varied from a low of 16 per 1000 in Estonia to a high of 37 per 1000 in Uzbekistan.[48]

The earlier decline in crude birthrates was in part a result of declining fertility and declining age-specific fertility. Put another way, there were fewer women of childbearing age, but in addition, women in this age group were choosing to have fewer children. However, after a long decline of fertility levels in the Soviet Union, they began to increase significantly in the early 1980s. The net result has been an increase in the natural rate of population growth from a low of 8.0 per 1000 in 1980 to 10.2 per 1000 in 1986.[49] There are significant regional differences in fertility levels, the highest being in Central Asia (although fertility levels there have declined recently), and the lowest in the Baltic republics.

On the other side of the coin, Soviet crude death rates, after a long decline through the 1970s, increased in the 1980s. Again, looking at Soviet official data, the crude death rate (deaths per 1000 population) increased from 7.1 in 1960 to 10.3 in 1980, declining slightly to 10.2 in 1986.[50] Recent increases have been studied by Murray Feshbach, who concludes that "the three major components underlying the increases are the aging of the population, infant mortality, and death rates for males aged 20–44."[51]

In part, then, increases in the Soviet crude death rate can be explained by an aging of the population. Also, it is important to note that this results in a growth in the size of the pension-aged population. While this increases the dependence ratio, it also provides a small but nevertheless additional source of labor.

More troubling, though, are the other factors accounting for the increase in the crude death rate. For example, between the late 1960s and the early 1980s, there were increases in age-specific death rates for most segments of the prime-aged population, and they are generally of greater magnitude for males than females.[52] Mortality differs significantly by region, and thus there are marked regional differences in life expectancies. The problem of increasing age-specific death rates has lessened in the 1980s, possibly due to social policies, for example, that against alcohol. But the concern for accident rates and various serious medical problems (especially coronary disease and cancer) remains.

Finally, the issue of infant mortality in the Soviet Union has received widespread attention.[53] This interest derives from the fact that infant mortality rates are frequently thought to be a commentary on the effectiveness of medical delivery systems. In the Soviet case, Western observers were surprised to see what at first appeared to be significant increases in the infant mortality rate in the 1970s and a cessation of publication of official statistics on the matter. Subsequent evidence seems to suggest that increases in the infant mortality rate in the early 1970s were probably in large part the result of better reporting from rural areas, where infant mortality rates are higher. By the mid-1970s, however, infant mortality rates again declined and by the mid-1980s had reached the levels that had prevailed in the late 1960s. Although the reported rates of infant mortality in the 1980s are probably more accurate than those of earlier years, they may still understate actual infant mortality rates.

From a quantitative standpoint, most of the growth of the Soviet labor force has and will continue to come from growth of the population in the age brackets 19–54 for women and 19–59 for men. In the 1970s, the aggregate Soviet labor force increased at an average annual rate of just over 2.2 million. This pace of growth declined to just over 1.0 million in the 1980s and is projected to increase to 1.4 million through the 1990s.[54] In addition to growth of the able-bodied population and selected increases in labor force participation rates, pensioners, a rapidly growing segment of the Soviet population, are estimated to be 12 percent of the Soviet labor force by the year 2000.[55]

The Regional Distribution of Labor

The regional distribution of labor in the Soviet Union has assumed much greater importance in recent years. This importance arises in several dimensions.

First, the rural-urban balance has always been a crucial aspect of labor allocation. The Soviet Union became a predominantly urban society in a relatively short period of time. The single most important source of this urban growth has been rural-to-urban migration.[56] Both administrative and market-type mechanisms were used to manipulate this process, and wage differentials were important in explaining the rural-to-urban shifts of the labor force.[57] In fact, rural-to-urban migration has been a crucial source of urban labor supply in the sense that it is rural youth who are most likely to migrate, motivated by the perception of better opportunities in the urban/industrial sector.

However, while the urban sector may have benefited, increasingly the rural sector has been facing a labor shortage, especially for peak season needs. Although there are important regional differences, the rural sector can no longer be viewed as a major source of incremental urban labor. In fact, policies have been implemented (for example, sharp improvements in rural levels of living) to make rural life more attractive and thus stem the migratory flows.

Second, a critical dimension of the contemporary Soviet labor force is its regional distribution. Whether we define a region in broad and general terms, related to specific economic characteristics, or simply in terms of political units such as the union republics, an examination of basic demographic patterns reveals major problems.

Fertility rates are sharply higher in the southern regions of the Soviet Union, broadly speaking, Central Asia and Kazakhstan (a territory of predominantly Muslim population), than in other areas of the Soviet Union.[58] The result is a significantly higher rate of growth of population, able-bodied population, and hence labor force in these regions. The implications of differential growth are important. For example, a Western study published in 1982 commenting on Central Asia and Kazakhstan concluded that "of the roughly 9.5 million workers who will be added to the labor force in the next decade, about ninety percent will come from these five republics."[59]

This picture presents both demand and supply problems. On the demand side, Soviet industrial capacity is not, of course, located in Central Asia, but rather primarily to the north.[60] This means that the demand for labor is not located where the labor supply is and will be available. Supply problems are also evident. Central Asia is a less developed region of the Soviet Union, with population and labor force characteristics reflecting this lower level of development. The labor force participation rate is generally lower than elsewhere, and there is a greater tendency to remain in rural activity. In addition, educational levels are lower, all of which suggests lesser market orientation, especially for women. Finally, the kinds of differences suggested here would lead one to doubt the possibility of significant migration, that is, of shifting the available labor supply from the south to the labor-short areas of the north.[61] Likewise, it is doubtful that Soviet planners will want to implement any major shift of industrial activity toward the south.

It is important to note that these regional imbalances result from basic underlying demographic and other relatively long-term factors. In this sense, the problem of regional labor imbalances is not likely to be solved in the near future.

Qualitative Changes

Soviet labor policy was successful in bringing about significant qualitative changes in the Soviet labor force. The Soviet labor force was poorly equipped to meet the needs of all-out industrialization. The 1897 census showed 78 percent of the over-15-year-old population as illiterate, with only 1.4 million having education beyond the seventh grade out of a population of 126 million and only 93,000 with completed higher education. The immediate preindustrialization figures of the 1926 census show considerable improvement preparatory to the industrialization drive: The illiteracy rate had dropped to 56 percent, 6 million had received education beyond the seventh grade, and roughly half a million had completed higher education.[62]

The major spurt in educational achievement occurred during the industrialization drive of the 1930s. By 1939, the illiteracy rate had dropped to 20 percent, 14 million had completed education beyond the seventh grade, and more than 1 million had completed higher education.[63] Thus, the Soviet educational system did a very significant job in meeting the labor needs of a modernizing economy.

Soviet labor policy contributed to this modernization of Soviet human resources in several ways. First, labor codes were put into effect forbidding the employment of younger people, a factor that enhanced the effectiveness of the universal education decrees. Large wage differentials were established between skilled and unskilled laborers, providing positive incentives for laborers to acquire highly rewarded skills. Stalin in 1931 cast aside "left equalitarianism" and introduced large incentives for skilled occupations. Wage differentials widened substantially between 1928 and 1934 and continued to increase throughout the 1930s.[64] The wage revision beginning in 1956 narrowed wage differentials, a policy made possible by the vast increases in skilled labor during the prewar period. For example, 4.5 percent of the Soviet labor force were specialists with a higher or secondary specialized education in 1928. By 1967, this ratio had risen to 14 percent. In 1983, 28 percent of the Soviet labor force were specialists with a higher or secondary specialized education.[65]

As we have already emphasized, education has been a major priority in the Soviet Union for many years. While this priority certainly remains, it is not clear that the qualitative labor force needs will be readily met in an era of changing rules of labor allocation. As we will see when we discuss issues of economic reform in greater detail in Chapters 14 and 15, educational reforms of the mid- and late 1980s have stressed the need for technical education.

Soviet Full-Employment Policies

Long-term aggregate unemployment should not be a serious problem in the Soviet planned economy. The output of goods and services is planned as a function of available capital and labor. Planners automatically plan to produce an aggregate level of output that provides employment for the able-bodied adult population. In fact, official Soviet concern is more about labor shortages (not having enough labor to meet the needs of the national economy). According to official statistics, unemployment was "liquidated" during the first Five Year Plan.* On the eve of the first Five Year Plan (1927–1928), unemployment averaged 8 percent of the Soviet labor force.[66]

Modern economic theory recognizes that frictional unemployment is required for a smoothly functioning dynamic economy. Of course, societies

*The Soviet figures on the liquidation of unemployment are as follows:

	Year	Unemployed (in thousands)
	1922	407
	1924	1344
	1929	1741
April	1930	1081
October	1930	240
December	1930	No unemployment

Source: L. M. Danilov and I. I. Matrozova, "Trudovye resursy ispolzovanie" [Labor resources and their utilization], in A. R. Volkova et al., eds., *Trud i zarabotnaia plata v SSSR* [Labor and wages in the USSR] (Moscow: 1968), pp. 245–248.

would like to keep the amount of frictional unemployment to a minimum, but the economy would be ill served if a zero percent unemployment rate were indeed achieved. In the course of economic growth, some branches rise while others decline. Some regions of the country grow, others lose population. A natural consequence of the ebb and flow of economic fortunes is that people change jobs; whenever there are job changes in a dynamic economy, frictional unemployment will result.

One cannot get an accurate picture of the extent of unemployment in the Soviet Union with the available data. A study by Peter Wiles, based on official turnover data from the late 1960s, suggests that Soviet short-term unemployment is in the neighborhood of 1 to 1.5 percent, a rate well below current short-term unemployment rates in the West but not far below rates achieved in the West in the 1960s. Other studies for the late 1970s find that the Soviet unemployment rate is between 1 and 2 percent of the Soviet labor force.[67] The Soviet long-term unemployment rate is well below recent Western experience but only slightly below the Western rates of the 1960s.

It should come as no surprise that there is unemployment in the Soviet Union. In any dynamic economy, there must be unemployment. The economy could not function without unemployment unless it was totally static.

A number of indications show that Soviet full-employment policies may have certain efficiency costs. First, the official Soviet concern with reducing labor turnover means that the Soviet leadership has set a goal of limiting the amount of frictional unemployment. Labor turnover has both its positive and negative sides. On the positive side, labor turnover allows the economy to adjust to differential growth patterns among employers. It allows workers to shift to employment where their productivity (and hence pay) will be higher. On the negative side, excessive turnover can raise training costs and employee search costs.

The major cost of a "job rights" economy (to use David Granick's term) is that guaranteed jobs result in efficiency losses. Outmoded factories cannot be closed, poor workers cannot be laid off, and so on.

Labor Policies: Contemporary Trends

Throughout much of the contemporary plan era, the Soviet economy has operated as if it had a labor shortage. We emphasize the presumed nature of the shortage because the evidence on this issue is difficult to interpret. On the one hand, there is evidence to suggest that in many sectors and regions of the economy, and sometimes on a seasonal basis, labor is in short supply. At the same time, the nature of Soviet enterprise rules and the insistence of full employment as a socialist policy combine to produce what in the West would be described as underemployment. Most phases of Soviet economic reform have addressed the issue of labor allocation in one way or another, and the Gorbachev era is no exception. However, changes in labor policies predate the Gorbachev era and deserve attention beyond our later focus on the Gorbachev reform process. We begin with the broadest approach to labor policy, move through changes in organizational arrangements, and finally examine policies within the individual enterprise.

As we will see when we examine the record of Soviet economic performance, a good share of the blame for the slackening of Soviet rates of economic growth has been placed on labor, specifically on the lack of discipline in the workplace.[68] In this context, Gorbachev has called for emphasis on the "human factor," in particular, changes designed to increase worker effort and, it is hoped, worker productivity.[69] Among these changes, a renewed emphasis on work discipline is a central focus. This emphasis includes general exhortations to Soviet workers, but it also includes more specific programs. In addition to changes in the payments system to be examined later, the organization of work has been changed to enhance work discipline and to tie effort more clearly to final result.

Beginning initially in the construction industry in the early 1970s, the brigade system for organizing labor has received widespread application.[70] Initially termed the Zlobin brigade, this form of organization has more recently been termed the *khozraschet*, or contract brigade system. The concept, with significant variation, involves the assignments of tasks to a relatively small group of workers with rewards tied to results. The group is intended to serve as a mechanism for discipline.

Although the brigade system was not without problems, it was expanded to industry in the mid-1970s. According to Soviet sources, by 1986, 77 percent of the workers in Soviet industry were organized by brigades.[71]

In addition to the introduction of the brigade system of organization, there has also been experimentation with the norms used to evaluate work. Although the reforming of the norm mechanism has not been widespread, success has been reported in developing norms that encourage rather than discourage achievement and overachievement.

A much broader attempt at reform of labor organization at the enterprise level, derived from the Shchekino experiment, a now well-known program to improve labor utilization, was begun at the Shchekino chemical factory in Tula in the late 1960s.[72] The basic idea behind this reform was simple: The wage fund would be fixed, enterprises would have the right to reduce the labor force by the removal of unneeded workers, and the remaining workers and the enterprise in general would benefit from the paring of unnecessary labor.

Understandably, there were difficulties with this concept. Soviet authors pointed out that the staffing freedom allowed by the Shchekino experiment could disrupt prevailing norms, break the normal relationship between productivity gains and wages, and create problems of regulating bonus funds. There probably was some lessening of interest in the Shchekino experiment in the 1970s, and thus the Western view of the program has generally been skeptical. This skepticism has been based on the apparent lack of widespread application of the program, a number of post-1967 regulations intended to alter the original concept, and, most important, the perception that such a program could not be implemented on a wide scale because it would introduce unemployment into the Soviet economy.

Recent evidence supports a more positive view of this program. In a major study of the original program, its changes, and its implementation, Peter Rutland finds surprising vitality. In the early 1980s, 3,300 enterprises were operating fully on the Shchekino method, with 21 million employed and 11,710 enterprises partially on the program.[73] He further reports that the Shchekino approach "saved" approximately one million jobs in the tenth Five Year Plan, not to mention a significant increase in labor productivity in those enterprises using this approach.

Rutland argues that Shchekino is now most appropriately considered an approach, or method, rather than a narrow experiment.[74] This importance stems not only from the number of specific applications noted above but notably from the fact that a number of elements of the method have, in fact, meshed with ongoing decision-making arrangements. Moreover, Rutland notes that while central rules under the general rubric of the Shchekino method are complex, in fact, there have been many local variations facilitating implementation.

To understand the changes of the 1970s, especially those that would be introduced in 1979 and thereafter, it is useful to note briefly the specific areas in which elements of the Shchekino approach have meshed with ongoing arrangements.

Soviet authorities have long been concerned with improvement in the organization and utilization of labor.[75] Much of this discussion, especially in the 1960s and thereafter, comes under the rubric of introducing *nauchnaia organizatsia truda* (NOT), or the scientific organization of labor. Two elements of this discussion are the issues of establishing labor norms and setting the wage fund. Moreover, there was great emphasis on the need to redefine labor norms, in effect, to move from the traditional coefficients to what is described as "normative" planning, or the setting of labor norms based on labor requirements per ruble of output. This issue would remain the subject of discussion throughout the 1970s and 1980s.

What, then, of the original Shchekino experiment? It would seem that the thinking of this approach has had an impact, indeed an impact that continues under constantly changing circumstances. Although the final chapter is yet to be written, Rutland argues that "there is no evidence that unemployment was a serious issue in the Shchekino method."[76]

In sum, the Shchekino experiment turned out to be much more than an experiment, and yet like other past reform efforts, it has not been wholly successful, in part due to the difficulties of adaptation in the Soviet setting. However, we could argue that a combination of changes begun in the 1970s and extended through the Gorbachev era may well alter the manner in which labor is organized and rewarded in the Soviet Union.

It is unclear where the line should be drawn between healthy and unhealthy turnover rates. Soviet policies may be aiming for too little turnover. The Soviet leadership has paid little attention to the legitimate role of employment exchanges; in a society that claims to have liquidated unemployment, state unemployment services are not necessary by definition. Local unemployment exchanges were abolished in the 1930s. Although local state and party organizations involve themselves in job placement (especially for graduates of local schools), there is little in the way of organized job information. In the postwar era, there have been efforts to reinstitute labor exchanges,[77] but most Soviet workers still find their jobs by informal means, such as inquiring at the factory gate, billboards, and information from friends.

Limited geographic mobility is another contributing factor to low turnover rates. About half the Soviet population reports never having moved since the date of birth. This very limited geographic mobility is likely tied to the difficulty of obtaining housing in faraway cities and to the internal passport system. Or it may be due to the limited financial incentives to move. In an economy that requires shifts in population to supply labor for new industries and to populate new regions, the limited geographic mobility of the Soviet population would be a problem; it also helps explain the low Soviet frictional unemployment rates. When people stick with prevailing housing and jobs, frictional unemployment is down.

The ultimate cost of Soviet full-employment policies is the widespread phenomenon of underemployment. Managers are reluctant to let workers go (although this is not a totally rare phenomenon).[78] Hoarding labor now often protects managers against overambitious plan targets in the future. Yet if workers know that it is unlikely they will be fired for mediocre performance, they will have little incentive to turn in their best performance. Guaranteed job tenure can definitely have negative effects on allocative efficiency.

Women in the Soviet Labor Force

An evaluation of Soviet labor and manpower policy would not be complete without reference to the role of women in the Soviet economy.[79] The traditional Western view prompted by Soviet writings has been that Soviet women have enjoyed relatively free access to the various occupations and professions, thus avoiding the allocative inefficiency that might derive from discrimination. This view has been supported by a rather general view of the role of women in the Soviet labor force—in particular, the high participation rates and child care and other support services to facilitate this role. In addition, it has been noted that women play an important role in key professions, for example, medicine.

In recent years, increasingly sophisticated analysis of Western labor markets and notably the role of women in these markets has led to a renewed interest in, and examination of, the role of women in the Soviet economy. Thus far, this reappraisal lends only partial support to the traditional scenario outlined above.

The overall participation rate of both men and women in the Soviet economy is very high, an aggregate rate of approximately 88 percent.[80] It is unlikely that the participation rate for women will increase. Although steps have been taken to increase female employment, increases are most likely to come from women in Central Asia, where female participation rates are lower than elsewhere in the Soviet Union.[81] At the same time, efforts are being made to stimulate larger families in non-Muslim areas, policies likely to reduce female participation rates, at least in the short run.

Although female labor force participation rates are very high in the Soviet Union, it has been pointed out that there tends to be an inverse relationship between the rate of pay and the proportion of women in a particular occupation or sector.[82] Women tend to predominate in sectors with relatively low pay. For example, in 1975, women accounted for only 21 percent of the labor force in construction and 21 percent in forestry, whereas they accounted for 76 percent in trade and services and 84 percent in health services.[83]

Furthermore, within these sectors, women occupy a lower proportion of the technical and higher-paying positions than would be true for the lesser-paying positions. Thus, the evidence suggests that women earn less than men due to their higher representation in lower-paying sectors and occupations.

A study of the Soviet urban sector (based on an emigré sample) provides strong, though rather preliminary, evidence to support the above view. This study, by Gur Ofer and Aaron Vinokur, concludes that the hourly pay for Soviet urban women is roughly 0.68 to 0.70 of that for men, a figure closely approximating the gap that is found for the United States.[84] Furthermore, these authors find that rather traditional factors such as the return to schooling and the role of experience are important in explaining these Soviet differences, just as they are in the United States.

A recent study of Soviet women conducted by Barbara Anderson and based on emigré data provides general support for the Ofer-Vinokur results but with some variations.[85] The Anderson study examines the earnings of Soviet women and compares them to the earnings of Soviet men, but does so using the "life course approach," that is, attempting to understand the impact of important events (sequence and timing) such as education, first entry into employment, and childbearing upon earnings. This study concludes that for those in the survey working full time and in the age bracket 25–54, women earn 70.1 percent of that earned by men. The comparable figure for American women in 1979 was 56.8 percent. Anderson concludes that while the factors associated with male-female differences (education, childbearing, and so on) are similar in the Soviet Union and in the United States, the differential in earnings between men and women in the Soviet case is less than in the American case.

Clearly, additional research will be necessary to elucidate the nature and causes of male-female earnings differentials in the Soviet Union and in other socialist countries.[86] However, the evidence presented above suggests that equality in the workplace may have to be a goal for the future. Econometric studies of Soviet earnings find a substantial residual of lower female earnings that is not explained by objective factors such as education or work experience.[87] In fact, the Soviet unexplained residual appears much like that found in studies on U.S. earnings differentials.

It will take considerable effort to unravel the forces underlying this pattern. Soviet women have enjoyed substantial achievement in terms of education and participation in the labor force. These achievements have, in part, been the result of changing values and policies, possibly also as a function of the industrialization experience. At the same time, the typical Soviet woman bears a rather high share of the household work burden. High participation rates may also be, in part, functions of a severe labor shortage and of the impact of World War II on the Soviet population. However, it remains true that Soviet women do not participate equally with Soviet men in the better-paying jobs and in jobs of administrative responsibility, such as enterprise director or farm head, where women are almost nonexistent.[88]

The role of women in the Soviet economy is rather different from traditional Western perceptions. It is true that women have participated actively in the economy through expansion of educational levels and participation in the labor force. At the same time, Soviet women seem to bear a double burden insofar as they are largely responsible for work in the home. Econometric evidence thus far seems to suggest that the overall role of women in the Soviet population, labor force, and home is not particularly unique, inasmuch as it exhibits patterns of behavior found elsewhere.[89] Moreover, as we have noted, it would appear that Soviet women tend to earn less than Soviet men, and for about the same reasons found to explain male-female earnings differences in the United States.

The Household and the Second Economy

Thus far we have examined the household as a source of labor supply, considering both the quantitative and qualitative aspects of population and labor supply. We turn now from the provision of labor to a different segment of the Soviet economy, specifically the second or peripheral economy. Although activities of the second economy are in fact intertwined with virtually every sector of the Soviet economy, much of this activity relates to the household and in this sense is appropriately considered in the context of household decision making.

The phenomenon of the second economy is common in planned socialist economic systems. Although extensive research has been done, it turns out that it is not easy to define the second economy with precision.[90] Gregory Grossman has suggested that second-economy activities must fulfill at least two of the following tests: (1) the activity is for private gain; (2) the activity knowingly contravenes existing law. In fact, these criteria turn out to be useful for understanding second-economy activity and the Soviet household.

Examples of second-economy activities are easily found in the Soviet press, court reports, and emigré interviews. A physician or dentist may treat private patients for higher fees. A salesperson may set aside high-quality merchandise for customers who offer large tips (bribes). A manager of a manufacturing firm sets aside the highest-quality production for sale to the black market. A collective farmer may divert collective farm land and supplies to his private plot ("theft of socialist property"). Black marketeers in port cities deal in contraband merchandise. Owners of private cars transport second-economy merchandise. In many cases, official and second-economy transactions are intertwined. A manager may divert some production into second-economy transactions to raise cash to purchase unofficially supplies needed to meet the plan. The official activities of an entire enterprise may serve as a front for a prospering second-economy undertaking. Workers may engage in private production on the job (repairing private automobiles in state garages). Private construction teams may build structures for private individuals. Information sellers (apartment brokers) may provide information on the availability of apartments or imported goods. The list could be expanded indefinitely. An important area of second-economy activity is bribery and corruption—influence buying, purchasing favors that only state and party officials can provide. Most second-economy activity involves money/commodity or money/service transactions.

According to available accounts, second-economy activities are concentrated in collective farms and in the transportation network. Apparently, the supervision of collective farms is more lax, and they therefore serve as better fronts for the second economy. Transportation enterprises are also critical to the second economy, for second-economy merchandise must be transported somehow. The increase in private ownership of automobiles has apparently enhanced the operation of the second economy and has led to a growing market in stolen gasoline.

We cannot establish how important the second economy is, say, as a percent of retail sales or GNP, but those who have studied the second economy argue that it is quite significant. Exact estimation of the importance of the second economy will never be possible, for measurement of an illegal activity is a virtually impossible task. To take one isolated example where estimates are available: In 1970, one-fourth of all alcohol consumed in the Soviet Union was produced and supplied through the second economy. In 1972, 500 million liters of stolen gasoline are estimated to have been sold by the second economy. Some 80 percent of the USSR fur market and 25 percent of fish sales are handled by the second economy. House repairs and decoration are dominated by the second economy. The most reliable information on the scope of the second economy comes from the emigré surveys conducted by Gur Ofer and Aaron Vinokur in Israel, which show that earnings derived from an activity other than that in the main place of employment account for some 10 percent of earnings.[91] The magnitude of the second economy would come as no surprise, for the official planning system has assigned low priority to "nonessential" services (beauty shops, appliance repairs, and so on), and expenditures on these items typically rise with rising income. Moreover, the official supply system has failed to offer the Soviet consumer sufficient supplies of quality merchandise, and the second economy would serve as a means of channeling available quality merchandise to the highest bidder. In addition, the Soviet taxation system imposes almost confiscatory marginal tax rates on professionals who are legally licensed to carry out private professional activity. As in many Western countries, the tax system of the Soviet Union drives professionals into the second economy. The immense power over resources placed in the hands of officials is another reason for the existence of the second economy. Officials rather than the market allocate many of the scarce commodities treasured by the Soviet consumer—automobiles and auto licenses, apartments, building permits, and so on. This situation opens up the possibility of bribery and corruption, much as it does in the West.

The second economy has its advantages and disadvantages as far as the planners are concerned. It helps to preserve incentives because higher wages and bonus payments can be spent in the second economy. Moreover, the second economy serves to reduce inflationary pressures in the official economy. On the negative side, the second economy diverts participants in the economy from planned tasks and loosens planners' control over the economy. The Soviets do not publish data on currency in circulation, and it is likely that second-economy transactions are conducted largely in cash. For this reason, studies of savings based on savings account deposits may be biased. The brisk market in jewelry and precious metals also provides the participants in the second economy with a means of storing value.

Much of the contemporary literature on the second economy is concerned with modeling the interaction between the second economy and the official, or first, economy. This is a subject of broader interest to which we now turn our attention.

Soviet consumer goods markets are usually studied in a demand-and-supply framework, assuming that there are pressures for markets to clear and for equilibrium to prevail. The assumption of equilibrium may be inappropriate in the Soviet setting where quantity rationing (quantity constraints) typically prevail. Accordingly, a large body of literature focusing on the explicit properties of consumer market disequilibrium setting has been used to analyze the socialist, especially the Soviet, case. The possibility of consumer market disequilibrium raises a series of questions: How does one determine whether a disequilibrium is present? What are the effects of disequilibrium on household labor supply and saving? In what ways does the second economy serve as a safety valve on consumer market disequilibrium?

The Household: A Disequilibrium Setting?

Thus far we have focused on the Soviet household as a largely unplanned supplier of labor. Although the Soviet economy is a controlled economy with significant nonmarket means for the distribution of goods and services, nevertheless households provide labor services in anticipation of income, this income to be used for consumption and savings. Although we will address the issue of Soviet consumption in our general assessment of Soviet economic performance, in this chapter we are concerned with the interaction between the supply of labor services, the generation of income, and its utilization for consumption and savings.

The importance of this topic lies in a popular conception about socialist systems in general and the Soviet system in particular: The Soviet economic system and economic policies have a bias against consumer goods. Moreover, even if more resources were poured into consumer goods, the Soviet economy would be incapable of producing an appropriate mix of goods. Finally, Soviet-type economies may have inherent disequilibria due to the nonprofit maximization nature of the economy.[92] Excess demand appears in the form of queues rather than price increases, the latter being common in market economic systems.

In addition to the immediate problem of a shortage, there are additional repercussions from excess demand in consumer markets. First, economic theory would suggest that under conditions of excess demand, consumption may be less than desired, and thus savings more than desired. Savings in this context is viewed as forced saving and an indication of repressed inflation rather than as a natural process of asset accumulation. High savings rates may indicate excess demand. Second, consumer market disequilibrium in official markets may be ameliorated by spillover effects in private markets. For example, if consumer demand cannot be satisfied in official markets, consumers may look to unofficial or second-economy markets to satisfy this demand. Third, if the Soviet income earner cannot use the income to satisfy demand, there may well be a tendency to withdraw labor services, at least at the margin. For example, worker attitudes towards overtime might change, or there might be reduced interest in having multiple wage earners in the family.

Consumer market shortages can lead to perverse and undesirable behavior, such as reduced labor supply or effort in a labor-short economy. Some experts have argued that this pattern has worsened considerably in recent years, especially since the late 1970s. What is the nature of the evidence on these issues?

In a recent and thorough survey of disequilibrium models, especially as they pertain to second-economy operations, Christopher Davis has suggested a threefold classification: (1) shortage economy models, (2) disequilibrium econometric models, and (3) other approaches to disequilibrium.[93] This classification aids in the understanding of differences of both approach and result in a literature that is large and growing.

Shortage models are unique in certain important respects. First, much of this modeling effort derives directly or indirectly from the work of Janos Kornai.[94] Second, Kornai did not approach the socialist economy with a view to modeling specific markets or cases, but rather began with an interest in modeling the socialist economy as a whole, differentiating it from the market capitalist system.[95] As such, Kornai's work focuses on a general model of the socialist economy from which numerous testable hypotheses have already been derived.

Disequilibrium econometric models are themselves broad in design and approach. One type of model is the "chronic (known) excess demand (or disequilibrium indicator) models," specifically the type applied to cases where chronic excess demand is known.[96] In this case, the models typically include a demand equation, a supply equation, and an equation specifying that the outcome is determined by the supply equation (supply less than demand).

A second type of disequilibrium econometric model, the "testable excess demand model," is similar to the indicator-type model.[97] A demand and a supply equation is specified, and a third equation specifies a minimum condition but with no assumption about whether there is or is not excess demand. These models derive from the familiar work of Barro and Grossman.

The third category includes those models that as Davis notes "...do not clearly fit into the shortage or disequilibrium modeling categories."[98] These models differ in their theoretical underpinnings, their specification, and the characteristics they attempt to capture. An important subset of these models consists of those concerned with the interaction between official and unofficial markets, especially the equilibrium characteristics of the latter under varying regimes.

With such a large and varying literature, it is difficult to characterize the results of the disequilibrium literature with either simplicity or certainty. There are, however, a number of contributions that have had a significant impact on our general perceptions of disequilibrium in the Soviet case.

An interesting and early variant of the testable excess demand model is represented by the work of D. H. Howard using the Barro-Grossman model.[99] The model, originally developed by Barro and Grossman, suggests that both labor supply responses and savings responses are influenced by the availability of consumer goods.[100] Thus, in a case of repressed inflation (excess demand), it is argued that an increase in the availability of consumer goods will lead to a decrease in savings and an increase in labor supplied. This model, with modifications, was applied to the Soviet case by Howard, who found that it explained the Soviet case quite well. Although this approach has been the subject of criticism, Howard found that with tightness of goods on the state or controlled market, there are indeed spillover effects. Moreover, he was able to rank the magnitude of these effects. Specifically, Howard argued that under shortage conditions in official markets, there would be a limited impact on labor supply (reduction), a moderate impact on the demand for products in the collective farm market and a strong impact on savings.[101]

Models of the chronic excess demand type, where known shortage cases are modeled, have generally produced confirmation of excess demand, although much of this modeling has been applied to Eastern Europe and not specifically to the Soviet Union. Although the modeling done by Richard Portes and others has not provided support for the repressed inflation hypothesis, this view is not widely held in the literature.[102]

Other investigations of the repressed inflation hypothesis, both formal and informal, have produced mixed results, although many would probably want to isolate the late 1970s and 1980s as a period when repressed inflation was more likely to have occurred. For example, the work by Joyce Pickersgill and the studies by Gur Ofer support the view that Soviet savings behavior can be explained by those forces found to be important for the explanation of savings behavior in any economic system.[103] Moreover, although these studies were done prior to the 1980s, they did not confirm the existence of an inordinately high level of savings by Soviet citizens. In fact, Pickersgill and Ofer find Soviet household saving behavior to be quite "normal" in terms of the experiences of other countries.

Igor Birman and Gregory Grossman have investigated the growth of the money supply in the USSR and suspect that it has been much more rapid than the growth of output of consumer goods.[104] Savings account data as published in official Soviet series do show significant growth, especially in the 1980s. From their investigations, Birman and Grossman believe that Soviet macroinflationary pressures are greater than the average wage data that we cite would cause us to expect. Recent emigré evidence supports this view, although from the viewpoint of citizen satisfaction, the main focus of complaint seems to be the lack of availability of consumer goods in stores, rather than other aspects of living standards such as housing.

Although the Soviet Union has probably been reasonably successful in creating macrobalance in the past, the evidence would suggest that this balance has been increasingly violated in recent years. Moreover, the existence of macrobalance does not rule out the possibility of severe microimbalances where in one case there are excess inventories while at the same time in other cases there are persistent shortages. In the Soviet case, there is no simply equilibrating mechanism.

REFERENCES

1. Detailed discussions of Gosplan's labor balances can be found in *Metodicheskie ukazaniia k razrabotke gosudarstuennykh planov ekonomichiskogo i sotsialnogo razvitiia SSSR* (Moscow: Ekonomika, 1980), chap. 19; A. N. Efimov et al., *Ekonomicheskoe planirovanie v. SSSR* [Economic planning in the USSR], (Moscow: 1967), chap. 6; and in Y. Dubrovsky, ed., *Planning of Manpower in the Soviet Union*, translated from the Russian (Moscow: Progress Publishers, 1975). For discussions of the construction of the labor balance for the 1971–1975 plan, see M. Feshbach and S. Rapawy, "Labor Constraints in the Five-Year Plan," in U.S. Congress, Joint Economic Committee, *Soviet Economic Prospects for the Seventies* (Washington, D.C.: U.S. Government Printing Office, 1973), pp. 485–507; and M. Feshback and S. Rapawy, "Soviet Population and Manpower Trends and Policies," in U.S. Congress, Joint Economic Committee, *Soviet Economy in a New Perspective* (Washington, D.C.: U.S. Government Printing Office, 1976), pp. 113–154; for an update, see S. Rapawy, "Labor Force and Employment in the U.S.S.R.," in U.S. Congress, Joint Economic Committee, *Gorbachev's Economic Plans*, vol. I (Washington, D.C.: U.S. Government Printing Office, 1987), pp. 187–212.
2. Efimov et al., *Ekonomicheskoe planirovanie*, p. 171.
3. For a discussion of population and labor force issues, see M. Feshbach, "Population and Labor Force," in A. Bergson and H. S. Levine, eds., *The Soviet Economy:*

Toward the Year 2000 (Boston: Allen & Unwin, 1983), chap. 3; A. Kahan and B. A. Ruble, eds., *Industrial Labor in the U.S.S.R.* (New York: Pergamon, 1979); J. Chinn, *Manipulating Soviet Population Resources* (New York: Holmes & Meier, 1977); A. Coale et al., *Human Fertility in Russia Since the Nineteenth Century* (Princeton, N.J.: Princeton University Press, 1979); S. Rapawy and G. Baldwin, "Demographic Trends in the Soviet Union: 1950–2000," in U.S. Congress, Joint Economic Committee, *Soviet Economy in the 1980s: Problems and Prospects*, part 2 (Washington, D.C.: U.S. Government Printing Office, 1982), pp. 265–296; and A. Goodman and G. Schleifer, "The Soviet Labor Market in the 1980s," in U.S. Congress, Joint Economic Committee, *Soviet Economy in the 1980s: Problems and Prospects*, part 2, pp. 323–348. The latest Soviet population census (1979) can be found in TsSU, *Chislennost' i sostav naseleniia SSSR* (Moscow: Finansy i Statistika, 1984). Recent population issues are discussed in W. W. Kingkade, "Demographic Trends in the Soviet Union," in U.S. Congress, Joint Economic Committee, *Gorbachev's Economic Plans*, vol. I (Washington, D.C.: U.S. Government Printing Office, 1987), pp. 166–186.

4. The urban labor force is discussed in W. Moskoff, "The Soviet Urban Labor Supply," in H. W. Morton and R. C. Stuart, *The Contemporary Soviet City* (Armonk, N.Y.: M. E. Sharpe, 1984), chap. 4. The specifics of rural to urban migration are developed in R. C. Stuart and P. R. Gregory, "A Model of Soviet Rural-Urban Migration," *Economic Development and Cultural Change*, vol. 26, no. 1 (October 1977), 81–92. General discussion of regional labor force problems can be found in S. Rapawy, "Regional Employment Trends in the U.S.S.R.: 1950 to 1975," in U.S. Congress, Joint Economic Committee, *Soviet Economy in a Time of Change*, vol. 1 (Washington, D.C.: U.S. Government Printing Office, 1979), pp. 600–617; regional issues are also discussed in A. Helgeson, "Geographical Mobility—Its Implications for Employment," in D. Lane, ed., *Labour and Employment in the USSR* (New York; New York University Press, 1986), pp. 145–175

5. Goskomstat, *Narodnoe khoziaistvo SSSR za 70 let* [The national economy over 70 years] (Moscow: Finansy i Statistika, 1987), pp. 373–375.

6. V. Zaslavsky and Y. Luryi, "The Passport System in the USSR and Changes in Soviet Society," *Soviet Union*, vol. 6, no. 2 (1979), 137–153.

7. This discussion is based on A. McCauley, *Economic Welfare in the Soviet Union* (Madison: University of Wisconsin Press, 1979), pp. 174–186.

8. L. J. Kirsch, *Soviet Wages: Changes in Structure and Administration Since 1956* (Cambridge, Mass.: MIT Press, 1972), pp. 1–8; J. G. Chapman, "Labor Mobility and Labor Allocation in the USSR," paper presented at the joint meeting of the Association for the Study of Soviet-Type Economics and the Association for Comparative Economics, Detroit, Mich., December 1970, p. 3; J. G. Chapman, "Soviet Wages Under Socialism," in A. Abouchar, ed., *The Socialist Price Mechanism* (Durham, N.C.: Duke University Press, 1977), pp. 246–281; and McCauley, *Economic Welfare in the Soviet Union*, chap. 8.

9. Prior to 1956, this system was extremely complex. In all, there existed around 1900 different *setka* schedules and about 1000 different *stavka* assignments. In the 1957–1961 system there were 10 *setka* schedules and 50 different *stavka* assignments. The 1972–1976 reforms reduced the number of *setka* to 3 and the number of *stavka* to 17. On this, see B. M. Sukharevsky, "Zarabotnaia plata i material'naia zainteresovannost" [The wage and material incentives], in A. P. Volkova et al., eds., *Trud i zarabotnaia plata v SSSR* [Labor and wages in the USSR] (Moscow: 1968),

p. 302; see also Kirsch, *Soviet Wages*, Table 4-2, p. 75; and McCauley, *Economic Welfare in the Soviet Union*, p. 202.

10. E. C. Brown, "The Soviet Labor Market," *Soviet Trade Unions and Labor Relations* (Cambridge, Mass.: Harvard University Press, 1966), pp. 11–37, reprinted in M. Bornstein and D. Fusfeld, eds., *The Soviet Economy: A Book of Readings*, 3rd ed. (Homewood, Ill.: Irwin, 1970), pp. 217–220.

11. A. Bergson, *The Economics of Soviet Planning* (New Haven, Conn.: Yale University Press, 1964), p. 115. Soviet labor experts have noted that this system tends to create excessive turnover problems in branches having low base rates. In the eastern regions during the 1960s, turnover was highest in the food industry, where wages were lowest, and lowest in ferrous metals, where wages were highest. Attempts were made to reduce the turnover problem in consumer branches by raising the minimum wage in 1968 and 1971. On this, see Chapman, "Labor Mobility," p. 13; and McCauley, *Economic Welfare in the Soviet Union*, pp. 200–207.

12. Sukharevsky, "Zarabotnaia plata," p. 292; and McCauley, *Economic Welfare in the Soviet Union*, pp. 206–207.

13. A. Bergson, *The Structure of Soviet Wages* (Cambridge, Mass.: Harvard University Press, 1944), chap. 8; and Sukharevsky, "Zarabotnaia plata," p. 291.

14. McCauley, *Economic Welfare in the Soviet Union*, p. 201; Kirsch, *Soviet Wages*, chap. 4; and M. Yanowitch, "The Soviet Income Revolution," *Slavic Review*, vol. 22, no. 4 (December 1963), reprinted in M. Bornstein and D. Fusfeld, *The Soviet Economy*, 2nd ed. (Homewood, Ill.: Irwin, 1966), pp. 228–241. See also Sukharevsky, "Zarabotnaia plata," p. 196; and *Vestnik Statistiki* [Herald of Statistics], no. 6 (1983), 61–62.

15. Brown, "The Soviet Labor Market," p. 219; and Sukharevsky, "Zarabotnaia plata," p. 302.

16. Chapman, "Labor Mobility," p. 23. Even these differentials have not proven sufficient to maintain an adequate labor force in the Far North and Siberia. Recent Soviet studies have suggested that the established regional differentials are not sufficient to compensate for cost-of-living differentials, not to mention the low level of services (child care, health, education) available in these regions. On this, see Chapman, "Labor Mobility," pp. 13–16.

17. Sukharevsky, "Zarabotnaia plata," p. 302; and McCauley, *Economic Welfare in the Soviet Union*, p. 202.

18. Sukharevsky, "Zarabotnaia plata," p. 292; and Kirsch, *Soviet Wages*, Table 6–1, p. 125.

19. McCauley, *Economic Welfare in the Soviet Union*, p. 248

20. Sukharevsky, "Zarabotnaia plata," pp. 297–302; Kirsch, *Soviet Wages*, chap. 2; and *Vestnik Statistiki* [Herald of Statistics], no. 6 (1983), 63–68.

21. Kirsch, *Soviet Wages*, chap. 8.

22. There is a large body of literature devoted to Soviet education. See, for example, M. Matthews, *Education in the Soviet Union: Policies and Institutions Since Stalin* (Boston: Allen & Unwin, 1982); R. B. Dobson, "Education and Opportunity," in J. Pankhurst and M. P. Sacks, eds., *Contemporary Soviet Society: Sociological Perspectives* (New York: Praeger, 1980); R. B. Dobson, "Soviet Education: Problems and Policies in the Urban Context," in H. W. Morton and R. C. Stuart, eds., *The Contemporary Soviet City* (Armonk, N.Y.: M. E. Sharpe, 1984), pp. 156–179; and National Foreign Assessment Center, *USSR: Trends and Prospects in Educational Attainment 1959–85* ER79–10344 (Washington, D.C.: June 1979).

23. Dobson, "Soviet Education," p. 156.

24. Ibid., pp. 172ff.

25. Ibid., p. 174. According to a recent Soviet source, 99 percent of day students in general education schools receive work-related experience as part of schooling. See TsSU, *Narodnoe khoziaistvo SSSR v 1983 g* [The national economy of the USSR in 1983] (Moscow: Finansy i Statistika, 1984), p. 490.

26. For a discussion of recent changes, see Goodman and Schleifer, "The Soviet Labor Market in the 1980s," pp. 336–339.

27. For a discussion of controls, see E. Nash, "Recent Changes in Labor Controls in the Soviet Union," in U.S. Congress, Joint Economic Committee, *New Directions in the Soviet Economy*, part 3 (Washington, D.C.: U.S. Government Printing Office, 1966), pp. 849–871; for recent evidence, see Goodman and Schleifer, "The Soviet Labor Market in the 1980s." For a discussion of controls from differing perspectives, see B. Arnot, *Controlling Soviet Labour* (London: Macmillan, 1988); and E. Teague, "The USSR Law on the Work Collectives: Workers' Control or Workers Controlled?" in D. Lane, ed., *Labour and Employment in the USSR* (New York: New York University Press, 1986), pp. 239–255.

28. Goodman and Schleifer, "The Soviet Labor Market in the 1980s," p. 338.

29. J. G. Chapman, "Labor Mobility and Labor Allocation in the USSR," paper presented at the ACES meeting, Detroit, Mich., December 1970, p. 8.

30. For a detailed discussion of labor controls from the mid-1930s to 1956, see A. Nove, *An Economic History of the USSR* (London: Penguin, 1969), pp. 195–198, 260–263.

31. Chapman, "Labor Mobility," pp. 7–8.

32. D. Granick, *Job Rights in the Soviet Union: Their Consequences* (New York: Cambridge University Press, 1987).

33. *Zaniatost' naseleniia: izuchenie i regulirovanie* [Employment of the population: study and regulation] (Moscow: Finansy i Statistika, 1983), pp. 49–65.

34. This discussion is based on the following references: S. Rosefielde, "How Reliable Are Available Estimates of Forced Concentration Camp Labor in the Soviet Union?" *Soviet Studies*, vol. 32, no. 4 (October 1981); D. Dallin and B. Nicolevsky, *Forced Labor in Soviet Russia* (New Haven, Conn.: Yale University Press, 1947); N. Jasny, "Labor and Output in Soviet Concentration Camps," *Journal of Political Economy*, vol. 59, no. 5 (October 1951), 405–419; A. Solzhenitsyn, *The Gulag Archipelago* (New York: Harper & Row, 1973 and 1974), vols. 1 and 2; S. Swianiewicz, *Forced Labor and Economic Development* (London: Oxford University Press, 1965); S. Rosefielde, "An Assessment of the Sources and Uses of Gulag Forced Labor," *Soviet Studies*, vol. 32, no. 1 (January 1981), 51–87; S. G. Wheatcroft, "On Assessing the Size of Forced Concentration Camp Labour in the Soviet Union, 1929–56," *Soviet Studies*, vol. 32, no. 2 (April 1981), 265–295; R. Conquest, "Forced Labour Statistics: Some Comments," *Soviet Studies*, vol. 34, no. 3 (July 1982), 434–439; S. G. Wheatcroft, "Towards a Thorough Analysis of Soviet Forced Labour Statistics," *Soviet Studies*, vol. 35 (April 1983), 223–237; and J. Barber, "The Development of Soviet Employment and Labour Policy, 1930–41," in D. Lane, ed., *Labour and Employment in the USSR*, pp. 50–65.

35. For a summary of estimates, see Rosefielde, "How Reliable Are Available Estimates?" Tables 1 and 4; and Wheatcroft, "On Assessing the Size of Forced Concentration Camp Labor," pp. 267–268.

36. S. Rosefielde, "Excess Mortality in the Soviet Union: A Reconsideration of the Consequences of Forced Industrialization 1929–1949," *Soviet Studies*, vol. 35, no. 3 (July 1983), 385–409; and B. Anderson and B. Silver, "Demographic Analysis and Population Catastrophes in the USSR," *Slavic Review*, vol. 44 (Fall 1985).

37. Our approach to allocative efficiency is quite intuitive and should not be confused with a formal development of Pareto optimality. The optimality of Soviet labor policy in terms of the Pareto conditions is discussed by Bergson, *The Economics of Soviet Planning*, pp. 118–126.

38. A similar standard is suggested by Kirsch, *Soviet Wages*, chap. 8.

39. R. Moorsteen and R. Powell, *The Soviet Capital Stock, 1928–1962* (Homewood, Ill.: Irwin, 1966), pp. 643, 648.

40. S. Kuznets, *Economic Growth of Nations* (Cambridge, Mass.: Harvard University Press, 1971), p. 74.

41. One finds varying estimates of trends in the Soviet labor participation rate. The reason is that prior to 1928, the major portion of the Soviet labor force was engaged in agriculture, and, by definition, just about all in agriculture are considered employed, even if they only work part time. Thus, the measure cited here is for full-time labor equivalents. See W. W. Eason, "Labor Force" in A. Bergson and S. Kuznets, eds., *Economic Trends in the Soviet Union* (Cambridge, Mass.: Harvard University Press, 1963), pp. 53–56; L. M. Danilov and I. I. Matrozova, "Trudcvye resursy i ikh ispol'zovanie" [Labor resources and their utilization], in A. R. Volkova et al., eds., *Trud i zarabotnaia plata v SSSR* [Labor and wages in the USSR] (Moscow: 1968), p. 247.

42. Nove, *An Economic History of the USSR*, p. 262.

43. Chapman, "Labor Mobility," p. 31.

44. Eason, "Labor Force," p. 57.

45. Ibid.

46. Bergson, *The Economics of Soviet Planning*, p. 115.

47. Computed from data in W. W. Kingkade, "Demographic Trends in the Soviet Union," in U.S. Congress, Joint Economic Committee, *Gorbachev's Economic Plans*, vol. I, pp. 166–186.

48. Goskomstat, *Narodnoe khoziaistvo SSSR za 70 let*, pp. 406–407.

49. Ibid.; TsSU, *Narodnoe khoziaistvo SSSR v 1982 g* [The national economy of the USSR in 1982] (Moscow: Finansy i Statistika, 1983), pp. 32–33.

50. Ibid.

51. Feshbach, "Population and Labor Force", p. 83.

52. Ibid.; Table 3.7. For a discussion of health issues, see M. Feshbach, "Issues in Soviet Health Problems," in U. S. Congress, Joint Economic Committee, *Soviet Economy in the 1980s: Problems and Prospects*, part 2, pp. 203–227; and C. Davis, "The Economics of the Soviet Health System," in *Soviet Economy in the 1980s: Problems and Prospects*, pp. 228–264.

53. For a discussion of infant mortality, see B. A. Anderson and B. D. Silver, "Infant Mortality in the Soviet Union: Regional Differences and Measurement Issues," *Population and Development Review*, vol. 12 (December 1986), pp. 705–738; E. Jones and F. W. Grupp, Infant Mortality Trends in the Soviet Union, *Population and Development Review*, vol. 9 (June 1983), pp. 213–246; C. Davis and M. Feshbach, *Rising Infant Mortality in the U.S.S.R. in the 1970s*, U.S. Bureau of the Census, series P-95, no. 74 (Washington, D.C.: U.S. Government Printing Office, 1980); M. Feshbach, "On Infant Mortality in the Soviet Union—A Comment," *Population*

and Development Review, vol. 10 (March 1984), pp. 87–90; and B. A. Anderson and B. D. Silver, "The Changing Shape of Soviet Mortality, 1958–1985: An Evaluation of Old and New Evidence," University of Michigan, Population Studies Center, no. 87–111 (June 1987).

54. Computed from S. Rapawy, "Labor Force and Employment in the U.S.S.R." in U.S. Congress, Joint Economic Committee, *Gorbachev's Economic Plans*, vol. I, pp. 187–212.

55. Ibid., pp. 188.

56. For a discussion, see R. C. Stuart, "The Sources of Soviet Urban Growth," in H. W. Morton and R. C. Stuart, *The Contemporary Soviet City* (Armonk, N.Y.: M. E. Sharpe, 1984), chap. 2.

57. For evidence, see Stuart and Gregory, "A Model of Soviet Rural-Urban Migration."

58. See M. Feshbach, "Trends in the Soviet Muslim Population—Demographic Aspects," in U.S. Congress, Joint Economic Committee, *Soviet Economy in the 1980s: Problems and Prospects*, part 2, pp. 297–322.

59. Goodman and Schleifer, "The Soviet Labor Market in the 1980s," p. 333.

60. The question of labor from Central Asia has received considerable attention. See, for example, Feshbach, "Trends in the Soviet Muslim Population—Demographic Aspects; M. Feshbach, "Prospects for Outmigration from Central Asia and Kazakhstan in the Next Decade," in U.S. Congress, Joint Economic Committee, *Soviet Economy in a Time of Change*, vol. 1, pp. 656–709; and S. E. Wimbush and D. Ponomarett, *Alternatives for Mobilizing Central Asian Labor: Outmigration and Regional Development* (Santa Monica, Calif.: The Rand Corporation, 1979).

61. The question of outmigration from Central Asia has been one of controversy. For an analysis, see Feshbach, "Prospects for Outmigration from Central Asia and Kazakhstan in the Next Decade."

62. N. DeWitt, "Education and the Development of Human Resources: Soviet and American Effort," in U.S. Congress, Joint Economic Committee, *Dimensions of Soviet Economic Power* (Washington, D.C.: U.S. Government Printing Office, 1962), p. 244.

63. Ibid.; p. 243.

64. Bergson, *The Structure of Soviet Wages*, chaps. 8 and 14; Sukharevsky, "Zarabotnaia plata," pp. 291–292; Kirsch, *Soviet Wages*, pp. 174–179.

65. Data are from *Narodnoe Khoziaistvo* 1983.

66. Bergson, *The Economics of Soviet Planning*, p. 105.

67. P. J. D. Wiles, "A Note on Soviet Unemployment in U.S. Definitions," *Soviet Studies*, vol. 23, no. 2 (April 1972), 619–628. The emigré unemployment rate data come from the Soviet Interview Project in a report by P. Gregory, "Unemployment and Job Security in the Soviet Union: Results from the Soviet Interview Project," SIP Working Paper, Summer 1985. For recent evidence, see P. R. Gregory and I. L. Collier, Jr., "Unemployment in the Soviet Union: Evidence from the Soviet Interview Project," *The American Economic Review*, vol. 78, no. 4 (September 1988), 613–632.

68. For a discussion of these issues, see P. R. Gregory, "Productivity, Slack, and Time Theft in the Soviet Economy," in J. R. Miller, ed., *Politics, Work, and Daily Life in the USSR* (New York: Cambridge University Press, 1987), pp. 241–278.

69. See E. Teague, "Gorbachev's 'Human Factor' Policies," in U.S. Congress, Joint Economic Committee, *Gorbachev's Economic Policies*, vol. 2 (Washington, D.C.:

U.S. Government Printing Office, 1987], pp. 224–239; and E. A. Hewett, *Reforming the Soviet Economy* (Washington, D.C.: The Brookings Institution, 1988), pp. 311–313.

70. Experimentation with the brigade system is discussed in B. Arnot, *Controlling Soviet Labour* (London: Macmillan Press, 1938), chap. 9; and M. M. Heinemeier, "The Brigade System of Labor Organization and Incentives in Soviet Industry and Construction," in U.S. Congress, Joint Economic Committee, *Gorbachev's Economic Plans*, vol. 2, pp. 272–281.

71. Goskomstat, *Narodnoe khoziaistvo SSSR za 70 let* [The national economy of the USSR over 70 years], p. 139.

72. For a discussion of Shchekino, see P. Rutland, "The Shchekino Method and the Struggle to Raise Labor Productivity in Soviet Industry," *Soviet Studies*, vol. 36, no. 3 (July 1984), 345–365; for a more critical view, see B. Arnot, *Controlling Soviet Labour*, chaps. 5–8; and B. Arnot, "Soviet Labour Productivity and the Failure of the Shchekino Experiment," *Critique*, vol. 15 (1981), pp. 31–56.

73. Rutland, "The Shchekino Method," p. 348.

74. Ibid., p. 345.

75. Ibid., pp. 353–357.

76. Ibid., p. 360.

77. A Soviet source from the early 1970s suggest that roughly one-half of industrial jobs are mediated by employment agencies in operation since the late 1960s. See F. D. Romma and K. P. Urzhinsky, *Pravovye voprosy podbora rasstanovki kadrov* [Legal questions concerning the selection and arrangement of cadres] (Moscow, 1971), chaps. 1 and 2; and Chapman, "Labor Mobility," chap. 4. Recent sources suggest that such agencies place about 15 percent of those employed in the *entire* national economy. See Goodman and Schleifer, "The Soviet Labor Market in the 1980s," p. 336 (footnote 14).

78. A 1978 study conducted by Soviet statistical authorities of the food-processing industry finds that 8.5 percent of the recorded separations were separations initiated by the enterprise administration for poor work. On this, see *Zaniatost' naselenie: izuchenie i regulirovanie* [Employment of the population: study and regulating] (Moscow: Finansy i Statistika, 1983), p. 57.

79. For the role of women in the Soviet economy, in addition to sources dealing with population and labor force, in general, the interested reader should consult N. T. Dodge, *Women in the Soviet Economy* (Baltimore: Johns Hopkins University Press, 1966); D. Atkinson et al., eds., *Women in Russia* (Stanford: Stanford University Press, 1977); M. P. Sacks, *Work and Equality in Soviet Society* (New York: Praeger, 1982); M. P. Sacks, *Women's Work in Soviet Russia: Continuity in the Midst of Change* (New York: Praeger, 1976); W. Moskoff, *Labor and Leisure in the Soviet Union* (New York: St. Martin's Press, 1984); G. W. Lapidus, *Women in Soviet Society* (Berkeley and Los Angeles: University of California Press, 1979); G. Ofer and A. Vinokur, "Earnings Differentials by Sex in the Soviet Union: A First Look," in S. Rosefielde, ed., *Economic Welfare and the Economics of Soviet Socialism* (New York: Cambridge University Press, 1981), pp. 127–162; P. R. Gregory, "Fertility and Labor Force Participation in the Soviet Union and Eastern Europe," *Review of Economics and Statistics*, vol. 64, no. 1 (February 1982), 18–131; B. A. Anderson, "The Life Course of Soviet Women Born 1905–1960," in Millar, ed., *Politics, Work, and Daily Life in the USSR*, pp. 203–240.

80. Feshbach, "Population and Labor Force," Table 3.9.
81. Goodman and Schleifer, "The Soviet Labor Market in the 1980s," pp. 329–330.
82. W. Moskoff, "An Estimate of the Soviet Male-Female Income Gap," *ACES Bulletin*, vol. 16, no. 2 (Fall 1974), 21–31.
83. *Vestnik Statistiki* [Herald of Statistics], no. 1 (1976), p. 85. Since 1976, the proportion of women in the labor force of various sectors is no longer published in *Vestnik Statistiki*, although the section in which the information appeared, *Zhenshchiny v SSSR* [Women in the USSR], appears annually in the January issue.
84. G. Ofer and A. Vinokur, "Earnings Differentials by Sex in the Soviet Union: A First Look," in S. Rosefielde, ed., *Economic Welfare and the Economics of Soviet Socialism* (New York: Cambridge University Press, 1981), pp. 127–162.
85. B. A. Anderson, "The Life Course of Soviet Women Born 1905-1960," pp. 203–240.
86. J. R. Moroney, "Do Women Earn Less Under Capitalism?" *Economic Journal*, vol. 89, no. 355 (September 1979), 601–613.
87. P. Gregory and J. Kohlhase, "The Earnings of Soviet Workers: Evidence from the Soviet Interview Project," *Review of Economics and Statistics*, vol. 70, no. 1 (February 1988), 23–35.
88. Discussions of the role of women in the Soviet rural economy are given in N. T. Dodge, "Recruitment and the Quality of the Soviet Agricultural Labor Force," in J. R. Millar, ed., *The Soviet Rural Community* (Urbana: University of Illinois Press, 1971), pp. 180–213; and R. C. Stuart, "Women in Soviet Rural Management," *Slavic Review*, vol. 38, no. 4 (December 1979). For an examination of the role of women in industrial management, see K. M. Bartol and R. A. Bartol, "Women in Managerial and Professional Positions: The United States and the Soviet Union," *Industrial and Labor Relations Review*, vol. 28, no. 4 (July 1975), 524–534.
89. P. R. Gregory, "Fertility and Labor Force Participation in the Soviet Union and Eastern Europe."
90. See A. Katsenelinboigen, "Coloured Markets in the Soviet Union," *Soviet Studies*, vol. 29, no. 1 (January 1977), pp. 62–85; D. K. Simes, "The Soviet Parallel Market," *Economic Aspects of Life in the USSR* (Brussels: NATO Directorate of Economic Affairs, 1975), pp. 91–100; G. Grossman, "The 'Second Economy' of the USSR," *Problems of Communism*, vol. 26 (September-October 1977), pp. 25–40; G. Grossman, "Notes on the Illegal Private Economy and Corruption," in Joint Economic Committee, *Soviet Economy in a Time of Change*, vol. 1, pp. 834–855; V. G. Treml, "Production and Consumption of Alcoholic Beverages in the USSR: A Statistical Study," *Journal of Studies on Alcohol*, vol. 36 (March 1975), pp. 285–320; G. E. Schroeder and R. Greenslade, "On the Measurement of the Second Economy in the USSR," *ACES Bulletin*, vol. 21, no. 1 (Spring 1979), 3–22; D. O'Hearn, "The Consumer Second Economy: Size and Effects," *Soviet Studies*, vol. 32, no. 2 (April 1980), 218–234; F. J. M. Feldbrugge, "Government and the Shadow Economy in the Soviet Union," *Soviet Studies*, vol. 36, no. 4 (October 1984), 528–543; B. Rumer, "The 'Second' Agriculture in the USSR," *Soviet Studies*, vol. 33, no. 4 (October 1981), 560–572; R. E. Erickson, "The 'Second Economy' and Resource Allocation Under Central Planning," *Journal of Comparative Economics*, vol. 8, no. 1 (March 1984), 1–24; and R. E. Erickson, "An Allocative Role of the Soviet Second Economy," in P. Desai, ed., *Marxism, Central Planning and the Soviet Economy* (Cambridge, Mass.: MIT Press, 1983).
91. G. Ofer and A. Vinokur, *Family Budget Survey of Soviet Immigrants in the Soviet Union* (Jerusalem: Soviet and East European Research Center, Hebrew University,

June 1977); and G. Ofer and A. Vinokur, *Private Sources of Income of the Soviet Urban Household* (Santa Monica, Calif.: Rand Corporation, R–2359–NA, August 1980).

92. J. Winiecki, *The Distorted World of Soviet-Type Economics* (London and New York: Routledge, 1988).

93. C. M. Davis, "The Second Economy in Disequilibrium and Shortage Models of Centrally Planned Economics," in *Berkeley–Duke Occasional Papers on the Second Economy of the USSR*, no.12 (July 1988).

94. See, for example, J. Kornai, *Growth, Shortage, and Efficiency: A Macrodynamic Model of the Socialist Economy* (Berkeley: University of California Press, 1983).

95. For a brief discussion, see P. R. Gregory and R. C. Stuart, *Comparative Economic Systems*, 3rd ed. (Boston: Houghton Mifflin, 1989), pp. 100–101.

96. Davis, "The Second Economy," pp. 70ff.

97. Ibid.

98. Ibid.

99. D. H. Howard, "The Disequilibrium Model in a Controlled Economy: An Empirical Test of the Barro-Grossman Model," *The American Economic Review*, vol. 66, no. 5 (December 1976), 871–879.

100. R. J. Barro and H. I. Grossman, "A General Disequilibrium Model of Income and Employment," *American Economic Review*, vol. 61, no. 1 (March 1971), 83–93.

101. Howard, "The Disequilibrium Model," pp. 876–877.

102. For a critical view, see, for example, L. Podkaminer, "Macroeconomic Disequilibria in Centrally Planned Economies: Identifiability of Econometric Models Based on the Theory of Household Behavior Under Quantity Constraints," *Journal of Comparative Economics*, vol. 13, no. 1 (March 1989), 47–60.

103. J. Pickersgill, "Soviet Inflation: Causes and Consequences," *Soviet Union*, vol. 4, no. 2 (1977), 297–313; J. Pickersgill, "Soviet Household Saving Behavior," *Review of Economics and Statistics*, vol. 58, no. 2 (May 1976), 139–147; G. Ofer and J. Pickersgill, "Soviet Household Saving: A Cross-section Study of Soviet Emigrant Families," *Quarterly Journal of Economics*, vol. 95 (August 1980), pp. 121–144.

104. I. Birman, *Secret Incomes of the Soviet State Budget* (Hague: Nijhoff, 1981); and G. Grossman, "A Note on Soviet Inflation," Joint Economic Committee, *Soviet Economy in the 1980s*, part I (Washington, D.C.: U.S. Government Printing Office, 1982), pp. 267–286.

SELECTED BIBLIOGRAPHY

Labor Allocation in the Soviet Union

J. Adam, *Employment Policies in the Soviet Union and Eastern Europe*, 2nd rev. ed. (London: Macmillan, 1987).

B. Arnot, *Controlling Soviet Labour* (London: Macmillan, 1988).

A. Bergson, *The Economics of Soviet Planning* (New Haven, Conn.: Yale University Press, 1964), chap. 6.

———, *The Structure of Soviet Wages* (Cambridge, Mass.: Harvard University Press, 1944).

E. C. Brown, *Soviet Trade Unions and Labor Relations* (Cambridge, Mass.: Harvard University Press, 1966).

J. G. Chapman, "Labor Mobility and Labor Allocation in the USSR," paper presented at the joint meeting of the Association for the Study of Soviet-Type Economics and the Association for Comparative Economics, Detroit, Mich., December 1970.

———, *Real Wages in Soviet Russia Since 1928* (Cambridge, Mass.: Harvard University Press, 1963).

———, "Soviet Wages Under Socialism," in A. Abouchar, ed., *The Socialist Price Mechanism* (Durham, N.C.: Duke University Press, 1977), pp. 246–281.

A. Coale et al., *Human Fertility in Russia Since the Nineteenth Century* (Princeton, N.J.: Princeton University Press, 1979).

W. W. Eason, "Labor Force," in A. Bergson and S. Kuznets, eds., *Economic Trends in the Soviet Union* (Cambridge, Mass.: Harvard University Press, 1963).

M. Feshbach, "Population and Labor Force," in A. Bergson and H. S. Levine eds., *The Soviet Economy Towards the Year 2000* (Boston: Allen & Unwin, 1983).

———, "Trends in the Soviet Muslim Population—Demographic Aspects," in U.S. Congress, Joint Economic Committee, *Soviet Economy in the 1980s: Problems and Prospects* (Washington, D.C.: U.S. Government Printing Office, 1982).

M. Feshbach and S. Rapawy, "Labor Constraints in the Five-Year Plan," in U.S. Congress, Joint Economic Committee, *Soviet Economic Prospects for the Seventies* (Washington, D.C.: U.S. Government Printing Office, 1973).

———, "Soviet Population and Manpower Trends and Policies," in U.S. Congress, Joint Economic Committee, *Soviet Economy in a New Perspective* (Washington, D.C.: U.S. Government Printing Office, 1976), pp. 113–154.

A. Goodman and G. Schleifer, "The Soviet Labor Market in the 1980s," in U.S. Congress, Joint Economic Committee, *Soviet Economy in the 1980s: Problems and Prospects*, part 2 (Washington, D.C.: U.S. Government Printing Office, 1982).

D. Granick, *Job Rights in the Soviet Union: Their Consequences* (New York: Cambridge University Press, 1987).

P. R. Gregory and I. L. Collier, Jr., "Unemployment in the Soviet Union: Evidence from the Soviet Interview Project," *The American Economic Review*, vol. 78, no. 4 (September 1988), 613–632.

M. M. Heinemeier, "The Brigade System of Labor Organization and Incentives in Soviet Industry and Construction," in U.S. Congress, Joint Economic Committee, *Gorbachev's Economic Plans*, vol. 2 (Washington, D.C.: U.S. Government Printing Office, 1987), pp. 272–281.

A. Kahan and B. A. Ruble, eds., *Industrial Labor in the U.S.S.R.* (New York: Pergamon, 1979).

L. J. Kirsch, *Soviet Wages: Changes in Structure and Administration Since 1956* (Cambridge, Mass.: MIT Press, 1972).

D. Lane, ed., *Labour and Employment in the USSR* (New York: New York University Press, 1986).

A. McCauley, *Economic Welfare in the Soviet Union* (Madison: University of Wisconsin Press, 1979).

M. McCauley, *Labor Disputes in Soviet Russia* 1957–1965 (Oxford: Oxford University Press, 1969).

S. Rapawy, "Labor Force and Employment in the U.S.S.R.," in U.S. Congress, Joint Economic Committee, *Gorbachev's Economic Plans* vol. I (Washington, D.C.: U.S. Government Printing Office, 1987), pp. 187–212.

————, "Regional Employment Trends in the U.S.S.R.: 1950 to 1975," in U.S. Congress, Joint Economic Committee, *Soviet Economy in a Time of Change*, vol. 1 (Washington, D.C.: U.S. Government Printing Office, 1979), vol. 1. pp. 600–617.

S. Rapawy and G. Baldwin, "Demographic Trends in the Soviet Union: 1950–2000," in U.S. Congress, Joint Economic Committee, *Soviet Economy in the 1980s: Problems and Prospects*, part 2 (Washington, D.C.: U.S. Government Printing Office, 1982).

B. A. Ruble, *Soviet Trade Unions* (New York: Cambridge University Press, 1981).

D. Slider, "Reforming the Workplace: The 1983 Soviet Law on Labour Collectives," *Soviet Studies* vol. 37, no. 2 (1985), 173–183.

M. Yanowitch, *Work in the Soviet Union* (New York: Sharpe 1985).

Women in the Soviet Union

B. A. Anderson, "The Life Course of Soviet Women Born 1905–1960," in J. R. Millar, ed., *Politics, Work, and Daily Life in the USSR* (New York: Cambridge University Press, 1987), pp. 203–240.

D. Atkinson et al., eds., *Women in Russia* (Stanford, Calif.: Stanford University Press, 1977).

K. M. Bartol and R. A. Bartol, "Women in Managerial and Professional Positions: The United States and the Soviet Union," *Industrial and Labor Relations Review*, vol. 28, no. 4 (July 1975), 524–534.

S. Bridger, *Women in the Soviet Countryside* (New York: Cambridge University Press, 1987).

G. K. Browning, *Women and Politics in the USSR: Consciousness Raising and Soviet Women's Groups* (New York: St. Martin's Press, 1987).

N. T. Dodge, *Women in the Soviet Economy* (Baltimore: Johns Hopkins Press, 1966).

G. W. Lapidus, *Women in Soviet Society* (Berkeley and Los Angeles: University of California Press, 1979).

J. R. Moroney, "Do Women Earn Less Under Capitalism?" *Economic Journal*, vol. 89, no. 355 (September 1979), 601–613.

W. Moskoff, "An Estimate of the Soviet Male-Female Income Gap," *ACES Bulletin*, vol. 16, no. 2 (Fall 1974), 21–31.

————, *Labor and Leisure in the Soviet Union* (New York: St. Martin's Press, 1984).

G. Ofer and A. Vinokur, "Earnings Differentials by Sex in the Soviet Union: A First Look," in S. Rosefielde, ed., *Economic Welfare and the Economics of Soviet Socialism* (New York: Cambridge University Press, 1981), pp. 127–162.

M. P. Sacks, *Women's Work in Soviet Russia: Continuity in the Midst of Change* (New York: Praeger, 1976).

————,*Work and Equality in Soviet Society* (New York: Praeger, 1982).

R. C. Stuart, "Women in Soviet Rural Management," *Slavic Review*, vol. 38, no. 4 (December 1979), 603–613.

The Second Economy in the Soviet Union

M. V. Alexeev, "The Underground Market for Gasoline in the USSR," *Comparative Economic Studies*, vol. 30, no. 2 (Summer 1988), 47–68.

F. J. M. Feldbrugge, "Government and the Shadow Economy in the Soviet Union," *Soviet Studies*, vol. 36, no. 4 (October 1984), 528–543.

G. Grossman, "Notes on the Illegal Private Economy and Corruption," in Joint Economic Committee, *Soviet Economy in a Time of Change* (Washington, D.C.: U.S. Government Printing Office, 1976), pp. 834–855.

————, "The 'Second Economy' of the USSR," *Problems of Communism*, vol. 26 (September-October 1977), 25–40.

————, *A Tonsorial View of the Soviet Second Economy* (Durham, N.C.: Berkeley-Duke Occasional Papers on the Second Economy in the USSR, December 1985).

A. Katsenelinboigen, "Coloured Markets in the Soviet Union," *Soviet Studies*, vol. 29, no. 1 (January 1977), 62–85.

G. Ofer and A. Vinokur, *Private Sources of Income of the Soviet Urban Household* (Santa Monica, Calif.: Rand Corporation, R–2359–NA, August 1980).

D. O'Hearn, "The Consumer Second Economy: Size and Effects," *Soviet Studies*, vol. 32, no. 2 (April 1980), 218–234.

Selected Topics on the Second Economy (Durham, N.C.: Berkeley-Duke Occasional Papers on the Second Economy in the USSR, April 1987).

D. K. Simes, "The Soviet Parallel Market," *Economic Aspects of Life in the USSR* (Brussels: NATO Directorate of Economic Affairs, 1975), pp. 91–100.

Studies on the Soviet Second Economy (Durham, N.C.: Berkeley-Duke Occasional Papers on the Second Economy in the USSR, December 1987).

V. G. Treml, *Alcohol in the Soviet Underground Economy* (Durham, N.C.: Berkeley-Duke Occasional Papers on the Second Economy in the USSR, December 1985).

————, *Purchase of Food from Private Sources in Soviet Urban Areas* (Durham, N.C.: Berkeley-Duke Occasional Papers on the Second Economy in the USSR, September 1985).

Soviet Population

B. A. Anderson and B. D. Silver, "The Changing Shape of Soviet Mortality, 1958–1985: An Evaluation of Old and New Evidence," University of Michigan, Population Studies Center, no. 87–111, June 1987.

————,"Infant Mortality in the Soviet Union: Regional Differences and Measurement Issues," *Population and Development Review*, vol. 12 (December 1986), pp. 705–738.

J. Chinn, *Manipulating Soviet Population Resources* (New York: Holmes & Meier, 1977).

A. Coale et al., *Human Fertility in Russia Since the Nineteenth Century* (Princeton, N.J.: Princeton University Press, 1979).

C. Davis and M. Feshbach, *Rising Infant Mortality in the U.S.S.R. in the 1970s*, U.S. Bureau of the Census, P–95, no. 74 (Washington, D.C : U.S. Government Printing Office, 1980).

H. Desfosses, ed., *Soviet Population Policy* (New York: Pergamon, 1981).

M. Feshbach, "Trends in the Soviet Muslim Population—Demographic Aspects," in U.S. Congress, Joint Economic Committee, *Soviet Economy in the 1980s: Problems and Prospects* (Washington, D.C.: U.S. Government Printing Office, 1982).

P. J. Grandstaff, *Interregional Migration in the U.S.S.R.* (Durham, N.C.: Duke University Press, 1980).

E. Jones and F. W. Grupp, "Infant Mortality Trends in the Soviet Union," *Population and Development Review*, vol. 9 (June 1983), pp. 213–246.

W. W. Kingkade, "Demographic Trends in the Soviet Union," in U.S. Congress, Joint Economic Committee, *Gorbachev's Economic Plans*, vol. I (Washington, D.C.: U.S. Government Printing Office, 1987), pp. 166–186.

S. Rapawy and G. Baldwin, "Demographic Trends in the Soviet Union: 1950–2000," in U.S. Congress, Joint Economic Committee, *Soviet Economy in the 1980s: Problems and Prospects*, part 2 (Washington, D.C.: U.S. Government Printing Office, 1982), pp. 265–296.

R. C. Stuart and P. R. Gregory, "A Model of Soviet Rural-Urban Migration," *Economic Development and Cultural Change*, vol. 26, no. 1 (October 1977), 81–92.

The Household

E. Jones and F. Grupp, *Modernization, Value Change and Fertility in the Soviet Union* (New York: Cambridge University Press, 1987).

M. Matthews, *Poverty in the Soviet Union: The Lifestyles of the Underprivileged in Recent Years* (New York: Cambridge University Press, 1986).

J. R. Millar, ed., *Politics, Work, and Daily Life in the USSR* (New York: Cambridge University Press, 1987).

W. Moskoff, *Labor and Leisure in the Soviet Union* (New York: St. Martin's Press, 1984).

The Disequilibrium Approach

W. Charemza and M. Gronicki, *Plans and Disequilibria in Centrally Planned Economies* (Amsterdam: North Holland, 1988).

C. M. Davis, *The Second Economy in Disequilibrium and Shortage Models of Centrally Planned Economies* (Durham, N.C.: Berkeley-Duke Occasional Papers on the second Economy of the USSR, no. 12, July 1988).

C. Davis and W. Charemza, eds., *Models of Disequilibrium and Shortage in Centrally Planned Economies* (London: Chapman and Hall, 1989).

D. H. Howard, "The Disequilibrium Model in a Controlled Economy: An Empirical Test of the Barro-Grossman Model," *American Economic Review*, vol. 66, no. 5 (December 1976), 871–879.

J. Kornai, *Economics of Shortage* (Amsterdam: North Holland, 1980).

———, *Growth, Shortage, and Efficiency: A Macrodynamic Model of the Socialist Economy* (Berkeley: University of California Press, 1983).

L. Podkaminer, "Macroeconomic Disequilibria in Centrally Planned Economies: Identifiability of Econometric Models Based on the Theory of Household Behavior Under Quantity Constraints," *Journal of Comparative Economics*, vol. 13, no. 1 (March 1989), 47–84.

R. E. Quandt, "Econometric Disequilibrium Models," *Econometric Review*, vol. 1 (1982), pp. 1–63.

———, "Tests of the Equilibrium vs. Disequilibrium Hypothesis," *International Economic Review*, vol. 19 (1978), pp. 435–452.

Chapter 10

Soviet Agriculture

The development of Soviet agriculture forms a very important part of the overall story of Soviet economic development. This importance stems, in part, from the role that agriculture has played in early Soviet development and the particular organizational arrangements utilized to fulfill this role. We have already considered this story.

Soviet agriculture is also of great importance to the contemporary Soviet economy for its ability to produce adequate food and fiber at reasonable costs in what is now primarily an industrial and urban society. In short, Soviet agricultural performance assumes major importance as Soviet leaders move toward the modernization of this traditionally controversial sector. Indeed, in most cases of economic reform in centrally planned socialist systems, changes in agriculture have generally played a prominent role. As we shall see, the Soviet attitude toward agricultural reform has been rather more conservative.

Westerners are accustomed to the notion that Soviet agriculture does not perform very well. This conception generally assumes sharp fluctuations in annual grain output, significant increases in the volume of Soviet grain imports, inadequate distribution of food products, periodic food shortages, rationing, and the like. How serious is the Soviet food problem and what contributes to it? If low productivity is a problem, why has the Soviet Union not reaped more benefits from all of the attention devoted to agriculture?

In this chapter, we consider four major themes. First, we examine the organizational arrangements of Soviet agriculture and the manner in which agriculture fits into the overall planning process. Second, we examine the performance of Soviet agriculture in terms of outputs, inputs, and associated factor productivity. Third, we consider more general performance considerations such as the contribution of agriculture to the Soviet diet and the role of agriculture in Soviet foreign trade. Finally, we examine contemporary developments in an attempt to chart possible dimensions and directions of future change in Soviet agriculture. Overall, our objective is an assessment of the performance of Soviet agriculture, the nature of its problems, and the prospects for its improvement.

SOVIET AGRICULTURE: ORGANIZATION AND PLANNING

As we have already noted, Soviet agricultural production takes place in a variety of institutions.[1] The most basic production units are the collective farm (*kolkhoz*) and the state farm (*sovkhoz*). In addition, agricultural production also takes place in the private or subsidiary sector that arises in both the state and cooperative sectors.

Beyond the *kolkhozy* and *sovkhozy*, in recent years there has been a tendency to integrate various facets of agricultural production, processing, and distribution in single administrative units broadly classified as agro-industrial enterprises. While difficult to measure in terms of simple numbers, integration, cooperation, and the development of more complex organizational arrangements have been a major and important theme in Soviet agriculture since the 1970s.

The importance of these various organizational arrangements can be measured in a number of ways. The basic indicators assembled in Table 10.1 prompt a number of observations.

First, as we noted in Chapter 5, in terms of simple numbers, state farms have been replacing collective farms since the 1940s. Both *kolkhozy* and *sovkhozy* are large by Western standards, though with some reversal of the shift to larger scale in the 1980s. Moreover, in terms of sown area, the growing importance of the *sovkhoz* and the minimal role of the private sector are both evident.

Table 10.1   THE ORGANIZATION OF SOVIET AGRICULTURE
            Selected Indicators

	1928	1932	1940	1953	1957	1960	1965	1970	1978	1983	1987
Number of collective farms (in thousands)	33.3	211.7	235.9	97.0	78.2	44.9	36.9	33.6	26.7	25.0	26.6
Sown area of collective farms as a portion of total sown area (%)	1.2	70.5[a]	78.3	83.9	68.4	60.6	50.2	47.9	44.2	43.75	43.83[b]
Size of collective farms (acres per farm)	237	2,218	3,530	10,374		13,302	15,067	15,067	16,549	16,055	15,947[b]
Number of state farms	1,407	4,337	4,159	4,857	5,905	7,375	11,681	14,994	20,500	22,313	23,300
Sown area of state farms as a portion of total sown area (%)	1.5c	n.a.	7.7	9.6	25.7	33.1	42.6	44.4	51.2	53.35	53.44[b]
Size of state farms (acres per farm)			30,134	32,357	60,021	64,714	60,762	51,376	43,472	41,002	39,293[b]
Number of interfarm enterprises and organizations							3,354	4,580	8,907	9.897	7,366[b]
Sown area of the private sector as a portion of total sown area (%)[d]	97.3	n.a.	13.0	4.4	3.8	3.3	3.2	3.2	3.0[e]	2.89	2.72[b]

[a]Based upon aggregate sown area for 1933.

[c]Includes state farms and other state agricultural enterprises.

[d]The private sector consists of three parts: (1) private plots of collective farm members; (2) private plots of workers in industry and other state organizations; (3) the private peasant economy. The last was of minimal importance after the 1930s.

[e]1975.

[b]1986.

Sources: Selected volumes of *Narodnoe khoziaistvo SSSR* [The national economy of the USSR]; *Sel'skoe khoziaistvo SSSR* [Agriculture of the USSR]; and *SSSR v tsifrakh* [The USSR in figures].

Second, the number of interfarm organizations and enterprises has grown significantly in recent years. Although these numbers are difficult to interpret, as we shall see shortly, they nevertheless represent an important contemporary trend. Indeed, according to official Soviet statistics, the capital funds of interfarm enterprises increased from just over 400 million rubles in 1970 to almost 9000 million rubles in 1986. For the same period, the average annual labor force of interfarm organizations and enterprises increased from just over 78,000 to 652,000 at a time when the overall agricultural labor force had been declining.[2]

If one considers the importance of various organizational arrangements in terms of their contribution to output, a different picture emerges (Table 10.2). In terms of the basic distribution of production activity, the roles of the *kolkhoz* and *sovkhoz* differ. For example, in the production of meat and vegetables, the roles of *kolkhozy* and *sovkhozy* are pretty similar, but with the private sector being a major though declining contributor. Finally, despite recent relaxation in attitudes toward the private sector (about which more later), the importance of the private sector has been great but has been slowly declining in recent years.[3] We now turn to a brief examination of each of the major organizational types.

The *Kolkhoz*

The *kolkhoz* is, in theory, a cooperative form of organization in which the peasants voluntarily join to till the soil, using the means of production contributed

Table 10.2   SOVIET AGRICULTURAL PRODUCTION BY TYPE OF PRODUCING UNIT
Percent of Total Production

Product	Year	Kolkhoz and inter-kolkhoz organizations	Sovkhoz and other state enterprises	Private sector
Meat	1965	30	30	40
	1975	33	35	31
	1985	30	42	27
Milk	1965	35	26	40
	1975	39	30	31
	1985	43	34	23
Eggs	1965	13	20	67
	1975	11	49	39
	1985	6	66	28

Note: Total production may not sum to 100 percent due to rounding. Data for 1985 may understate actual private-sector contributions due to the inclusion of contract sales in socialized-sector statistics.

Source: TsSU, Narodnoe khoziaistvo SSSR [The national economy of the USSR] (Moscow: Statistika), selected volumes.

by those who join but that now are owned jointly by all in the *kolkhoz*. Under the original *kolkhoz* charter developed in 1935 (a new charter was created in 1969), the means of production are said to be "*kolkhoz*-cooperative" property belonging to the *kolkhoz* in perpetuity. In addition to the socialized sector (land, equipment, buildings, etc.) belonging to the farm as a whole, the use of which is governed by a chairperson and a management board, each peasant household is entitled to cultivate a private plot.

In reality, much of the voluntary and cooperative nature of the *kolkhoz* has been lost. Those who depart from the *kolkhoz* to the city do not, in fact, receive their equity from the farm. Moreover, mobility has been limited because, until recently, members of collective farms did not possess internal Soviet passports.

Historically, the *kolkhoz* has been administered by a general meeting of its membership or, more recently, in large farms through a meeting of elected representatives. In theory, this general meeting elects the chairperson of the *kolkhoz*, although, in fact, the position of the chairperson is on the *nomenklatura* list and is therefore a local party appointee. In addition, the general meeting is supposed to select the operative management team and the management board, although here, again, the party-appointed chairperson and the party secretary are powerful.[4]

It is important to recall that prior to their abolition in 1958, the Machine Tractor Stations (MTS) played an important role in the day-to-day operations of the *kolkhoz*.[5] The MTS were responsible for the provision of machinery and equipment and agricultural specialists to the *kolkhozy*. Indeed, the fulfillment of *kolkhoz* tasks was the joint responsibility of the *kolkhoz* chairperson and the director of the MTS, a scenario described by Khrushchev as "two bosses" at the time of the abolition of these stations.

An important and distinguishing feature of any cooperative that is beyond its distinctive managerial system is its method of labor payment, normally a dividend, as opposed to payment of a wage. In this sense, the *kolkhoz* was distinctive until 1966, when a regular wage payment system was introduced.

Prior to 1966, all work tasks were rated in terms of a unit called the labor day, or *trudoden'*. The labor day was an artificial measure of labor input and bore little relation to the nature of the task. Thus, the labor days awarded for a particular task might differ from one farm to another and from one region to another, with little difference in effort required to complete the particular task. However, for each task assigned, the *kolkhoznik* would receive a specified number of labor days, the total to be recorded in an individual workbook. At the time of earning the labor day, its ultimate value in terms of money and product would be unknown. However, at the end of the year, when required state deliveries had been made, the value of each labor day would be determined simply by summing all of the earned labor days and dividing this sum into the available product remaining after fulfillment of state delivery obligations. After the value of the labor day had been determined, individual distributions in product and in money could take place. In light of the extreme uncertainty surrounding the eventual worth of a labor day at any time and place, it is not surprising that Khrushchev's moves to regularize payments were very popular. Moreover, distributions to labor were increasingly paid in money rather than in kind. In effect, the peasant was expected to expend effort now for an unknown future reward.

Western observers have tended to view the *kolkhoz* as an organization bearing little formal resemblance to a cooperative.[6] Moreover, the incentive system has been viewed as inadequate, with little immediate connection between effort expended and reward gained. However one views the *kolkhoz*, it is evident, as we have seen earlier, that it has been changed significantly such that the contemporary *kolkhoz* closely resembles a *sovkhoz* in many important dimensions.

The *Sovkhoz*

The second major form of production enterprise in Soviet agriculture is the state farm, or *sovkhoz*. The *sovkhoz* has always been structurally similar to a Soviet industrial enterprise. Specifically, this means that the *sovkhoz* is budget-financed (unlike the *kolkhoz*, which has been primarily self-financed), operates (or is intended to operate) under the *khozraschet* system of management, and pays a state-specified wage.[7] Ideologically, the *sovkhoz* with full state property is an organizational form favored over the *kolkhoz*. Moreover, the *sovkhoz*, directly under state control, has been favored where policy changes have necessitated implementing major changes in the countryside. Important examples are the virgin lands program discussed earlier and, more recently, the campaign to develop potato and vegetable specialization around large Soviet cities.[8] Finally, as we shall see, both forms of organization have played a role in agro-industrial integration, though the *sovkhoz* is the cornerstone of this program. It has been argued that, in the long run, the *kolkhoz* will eventually disappear to be replaced by the *sovkhoz* and other integrated forms of organization. Much of the available evidence supports this contention in the sense that changes within *kolkhozy* have made them increasingly similar to *sovkhozy*; many *kolkhozy* have been directly converted to *sovkhozy*; and, finally, many *kolkhozy* have lost their unique character in recently developed integration arrangements.

The Private Sector

As we have already noted, the private sector is important in terms of product contribution, but much less so in terms of the land area it occupies. By most indicators, the importance of the private sector has declined slowly over a relatively long period of time. This decline reflects, in part, a changing and generally hostile environment created by official attitudes and policies regarding the private sector. Recent modest changes in these policies may arrest past trends.

The private sector can be perceived in several different contexts. First, families on *kolkhozy* are entitled to the use of plots of land by virtue of their membership on the collective farm and their participation in the socialized sector of the farm. This allotment has varied over time and continues to vary on a regional basis. Its magnitude was reinforced in the 1969 charter as approximately 1.23 acres.[9] In addition, a small but generally limited number of animals may be held privately.

The products of the private sector may be consumed on the farm, they may be sold in farm markets, or they may be purchased by the state. State purchases of meat, milk, and eggs have generally represented a very small share of private output, although for some products—for example, wool—state purchases are important.

Second, workers and employees are also entitled to plots of land, although this entitlement varies depending on where they live and where they work. For example, after 1964, state farm workers are entitled to plots that ". . . should not normally exceed 0.30 hectare . . . ," or roughly three-quarters of an acre.[10] Workers and employees who live in rural areas but who do not work directly in agriculture have a small entitlement of roughly 0.37 acre.

Finally, workers and employees residing in urban areas are also entitled to garden plots varying from 0.15 to 0.30 acre, depending on whether the plot is located inside or outside city boundaries.

As we have noted, there has been considerable variability in these land allotments. However, in 1981, 13 million collective farm families held plots averaging just over three-quarters of an acre in size; 10 million state farm workers held plots averaging just over one-half acre; and finally, 10 million families of workers and employees held plots averaging 0.17 acre in size in urban areas and 0.42 acre in size in rural areas.[11]

In recent years, there has been a relaxation of official restrictions on private agricultural activity. Specifically, the limits on the numbers of livestock held in the private sector have been removed where such livestock is being raised on a contract basis for subsequent transfer to the socialized sector. Moreover, credits have been made available to finance this activity.

In spite of a more supportive attitude toward the private sector in the Brezhnev and post-Brezhnev years, it is not yet clear that the decline of private agricultural activity will, in fact, be reversed. Future trends will depend on the nature of future policies; the relative size of the constituent members of the private sector (the *kolkhoz*, from which much private activity derives, is gradually disappearing); and, finally, the nature and magnitude of the benefits that can actually be derived under recent changes to be discussed later.

Agro-Industrial Integration and Cooperation

Thus far, we have discussed the traditional organizational forms operative in Soviet agriculture—the *kolkhoz*, the *sovkhoz*, and private activity. However, various integration arrangements have been the essence of Soviet policy since the early 1970s.[12] Postponement of our discussion of these trends allows us to bring the story of organizational change up to date, to see what has happened to the traditional organizational units and what new arrangements have been introduced in recent years.

Soviet leaders have long tended to downplay basic differences between industrial and agricultural production, arguing that it is possible to "industrialize" agriculture. While there are varying perspectives on this theme, fundamentally it involves improving agricultural performance by industrial-type organizational and managerial arrangements. Moreover, as in industry, this argument represents an important theme in Soviet economic thought, namely, that benefits are to be derived from organizational change.

These ideas are not new in the Soviet Union. What is new is the intensity of application. For example, in the 1960s, there was continuing pressure to industrialize agriculture, but it found relatively limited application and only in a few regions, and only for selected types of activities. For example, construction was, and is, frequently organized on an interfarm basis. Selected types of production and/or processing activity, for example, wine making, might be organized on an industrial-type basis.

In the 1970s, however, there was a renewed emphasis on organizational change to reap the benefits of integration, both horizontal and vertical. These changes, of the 1970s and 1980s, have been developed and implemented with many important variations. There is no single, uniform mode of classification. Thus, we must be content with a broad picture to illustrate the major directions of change.

From a Western perspective, Soviet agro-industrial integration can best be understood by comparison with Western experience. For example, in American agriculture, integration would generally be termed the development of "agri-business." In this context, there may be vertical and/or horizontal integration in which a single administrative unit produces an agricultural product encompassing basic production, processing, and distribution. Horizontal integration may be achieved, for example, where a number of farms contribute a basic product to the integrated processing and distribution facility.

The process of "specialization and concentration of agricultural production on the basis of interfarm cooperation and agro-industrial integration" has become the operative phrase of Soviet agriculture in the 1970s and 1980s.[13]

Interfarm cooperation in the 1960s was largely associated with the development of inter-*kolkhoz* associations. These associations, initially in traditional areas such as construction, were expanded in the 1970s to include other activities and, in some cases, multiple activities. Although there were variations, the basic approach was the formation of an association with capital contributed by individual *kolkhoz* participants, with profit sharing based on a formula related to this capital contribution. Although affiliation with such an association was to be on a voluntary basis, important elements of managerial power from individual *kolkhozy* were shifted to the association level and vested in a representative assembly and a chairperson.

Integration, specifically vertical integration, received new impetus in the mid-1970s and involved the combination of industrial-type activity (for example, food processing) with constituent agricultural producing units. The latter were to be *kolkhozy, sovkhozy,* or a mixture of the two, although, in practice, *sovkhozy* tended to predominate. It is from this movement of the mid-1970s that the phrase agro-industrial integration and the notion of creating agro-industrial enterprises take on new importance.

Like the inter-*kolkhoz* associations, agro-industrial enterprises were formed with shareholder contributions managed by elected representatives, usually within the boundaries of a single *raion*.[14] *Sovkhozy* have predominated in this type of activity, in part because, in some regions, *sovkhoz* trusts had already been formed to bring *sovkhozy* together with other state enterprises and organizations into a single integrated unit. These units combined partially centralized management along with a degree of autonomy for participating individual *sovkhozy*.

In the late 1970s, statutes for agricultural production associations were formulated. These associations were to be broad-based, encompassing *kolkhozy, sovkhozy,* and other state agricultural and nonagricultural enterprises and organizations. Again, the association would operate as a legal entity with contributions to capital funds from constituents and mixed managerial powers at the association and the constituent levels.

Through the 1970s and into the 1980s, various forms of integration and cooperation continued to expand, though not without problems and reverses. Changes would be forthcoming.

Not infrequently, the distribution of decision-making authority, for example, in the areas of plan formulation and execution, remained unclear. Specialization, said to be important at the farm level, was not always promoted by upper-level associations. There were important regional variations.

The problems that arose in the 1970s were, in part, addressed by several major experiments conducted in various regions of the country. Ultimately, changes would be introduced as part of the Brezhnev "food program" of 1982.

While we leave for later discussion the economic aspects of the food program, in the administrative sphere, it called for the establishment of *raion* agro-industrial associations and a complete organizational hierarchy above the *raion* level. At the *raion* level, agro-industrial associations would incorporate *kolkhozy, sovkhozy,* state enterprises, and other state organizations. Management would be conducted by a *raion* agricultural council chaired by the first deputy chairperson of the *raion* Soviet executive committee. This council would serve as the management authority between the members of the association and upper-level administrative agencies. At the *oblast'* level (and in other similar regional units), a similar structure will be duplicated with an administrative council made up of members from the councils of constituent associations and agricultural officials from the *oblast'* level. In addition, in each republic, a commission was created to oversee the agri-industrial complexes subordinate to the presidium of the union republic council of ministers. Finally, a commission on agro-industrial complexes was created under the presidium of the USSR Council of Ministers.

Considerable power rests at the *oblast'* level, for example, in the areas of plan formulation and execution, redistribution of resources, suggestions for change, and the like.

Only time will tell to what extent these important changes, along with the Gorbachev reforms (to be discussed in Chapter 15), will fundamentally alter the Soviet agricultural system. They are aimed at basic problems such as the lack of specialization. While *raion, oblast',* and republic levels may better see the possibilities of specialization, the large and potentially unwieldy structure that has been created may make it difficult to oversee the best utilization of local resources. However, it is an attempt once again to handle the problems of territorial versus branch organization through integration and within a framework familiar to Soviet reform methods.

Organizational Arrangements: A New Era?

Until the late 1980s, it seemed that in many respects the reform movement had bypassed Soviet agriculture. For Western observers, possibly the most striking development was the emphasis by Gorbachev in mid-1988 and in a major address at the Party Plenum of March 1989 on considering the leasing of land for periods up to 50 years. This emphasis, however, reflected some basic changes made in the organizational arrangements of Soviet agriculture, albeit within the framework of the collective and state farms. Although the concept of leasing does not introduce private agriculture, it has important implications.

For many years, Soviet authorities have wrestled with what they believe to be a critical problem in agriculture: Tying reward to output. Along with a continuing series of changes in the reward system dating back to the 1950s and even before, recently there has been widespread application of the *podriad* system, essentially what Karl-Eugen Wädekin, a noted authority on Soviet agriculture, describes as a "contract production commitment." But, as Wädekin emphasizes, the *podriad* system is really a labor rather than a production contract. As such, it differs significantly by region, crop, and so on. Thus such a unit could be large, but it could also be small—for example, an individual family. It is in the latter context that the introduction of leasing could be important, especially if the *podriad* unit has reasonable freedom of input and output determination. While the *podriad* has been widely introduced in a formal sense, its impact remains to be understood.

SOVIET AGRICULTURAL PERFORMANCE

Earlier in this book, we considered the performance of Soviet agriculture by focusing on its sectorial contribution to economic development. Contemporary interest focuses on a different issue. To what extent does Soviet agriculture contribute adequate supplies of food and fiber to the Soviet population, with reasonable outlays of land, labor, and capital?

Our assessment of Soviet agriculture will be based on a variety of indicators. We begin with an examination of broad measures of output and input growth and thereafter turn to more sophisticated productivity measures.

In Table 10.3, we present evidence on basic output trends from the period 1960–1987. A number of observations seem relevant. First, a simple interpretation of these figures would suggest that there has been considerable output growth over these years. Although there are exceptions (for example, sunflower seeds and potatoes), the output of important agricultural products such as grain and meat has risen significantly.

Table 10.3　SOVIET AGRICULTURAL PRODUCTION, 1961-1987
Average Annual Basis[a]

Product	1961–1965	1966–1970	1971–1975	1976–1980	1981–1985	1986–1987
Grain (total)	130,335	167,562	181,554	205,028	180,301	210,700
Raw cotton	4,996	6,099	7,667	8,550	8,310	8,160
Sunflower seeds	5,068	6,389	5,975	5,309	4,969	5,700
Sugar beets	59,170	81,118	75,984	88,732	76,311	84,800
Potatoes	81,628	94,813	89,782	82,571	78,351	81,500
Vegetables	16,877	19,472	22,974	26,310	29,225	29,450
Meat	9,320	11,583	14,004	14,844	16,226	18,300
Milk	64,714	80,553	87,446	92,704	94,579	102,800
Eggs	28.7	35.8	51.4	63.1	74.4	81.4

[a] Unit of measure: One thousand metric tons except for eggs, which are in billions.

Sources: Compiled from U.S. Department of Agriculture, Economic Research Service, *USSR: Outlook and Situation Report* (Washington, D.C.: U.S. Department of Agriculture, various issues); Goskomstat, *SSSR v Tsitrakh v 1987 gody* [The USSR in figures in 1987], (Moscow: Finansy i Statistika, 1988).

Second, in spite of what seems to be, at first glance, a reasonable growth of output, closer examination of these figures indicates a slowdown in growth of output in the first half of the 1980s. For example, if we compare the average annual output for the period 1981–1985 against the same data for 1976–1980, we observe declines in five of the nine products considered in Table 10.3. In retrospect, one can appreciate the frequently expressed concerns about agriculture in the latter Brezhnev and early post-Brezhnev years. Fortunately, for important products, this downward trend was reversed in 1986-1987.

Third, year-to-year fluctuations, though not shown by our use of averages, are, nevertheless, important. For example, while the average annual output of grain for the period 1976–1980 was 205 million metric tons, annual output during this period varied from a low of 179 million metric tons in 1979 to a high of 237 million metric tons in 1978. This represents an output reduction of 24 percent, clearly a major change for a single production year. These sorts of fluctuations have continued. For example, in the period 1981–1985, average annual grain production was just over 180 million metric tons. However, annual output fluctuated from a low of 158 million metric tons (1981) to a high of 210 million metric tons (1986). In light of these fluctuations, it is important to develop an overall grain balance, including inventories and foreign trade, when assessing the grain question.[15]

Beyond an examination of aggregate output trends, it is also important to assess agricultural performance in terms of plan fulfillment. In Table 10.4, we have assembled plan targets and actual achievements for the 1980s. It is interesting to note that with some exceptions, targets are underfulfilled by significant amounts. However, while the early evidence of the late 1980s continues to show underfulfillment of all plan targets, the degree of underfulfillment (with the exception of meat and potatoes) has decreased.

Table 10.4   AGRICULTURAL PRODUCTION: PLAN AND PERFORMANCE
(Annual Average, 1981–1990)[a]

Product	Plan 1981–1985	Actual 1981–1985	Percentage fulfillment	Plan 1986–1990	Actual 1986–1987	Percentage fulfillment
Grain	238–243	180	75	250–255	210.7	83
Sugarbeets	100–103	76	75	102–103	84.8	83
Potatoes	82–89	78	91	90–92	81.5	90
Sunflower seeds	6.7	5.0	75	7.2–7.5	5.7	78
Meat	17.0–17.5	16.2	94	20.0–20.5	18.3	90
Milk	97–99	94.6	97	104–106	102.8	98

[a] Unit of measure: One thousand metric tons except for eggs, which are in billions.

Sources: U.S. Department of Agriculture, *USSR: Outlook and Situation Report* (Washington, D.C.: U.S. Department of Agriculture, various issues), Tables 1 and 5; *Current Digest of the Soviet Press.* "The Report on 1984 Plan Fulfillment," vol. 37, no. 4 (1985), 10–16; A. F. Malish, "The Soviet Food Program: A New Policy or More Rhetoric?" in U.S. Congress, Joint Economic Committee, *Soviet Economy in the 1980s: Problems and Prospects,* part 2 (Washington, D.C.: U.S. Government Printing Office, 1982), p 51; Goskomstat, *SSSR v tsitrakh v 1987 gody* [The USSR in figures in 1987] (Moscow: Finansy i Statistika, 1988).

Having examined output trends, we turn next to consider input patterns. Before we look at the Soviet case, it is important to bear in mind that during the process of economic development, we would expect factor substitution in agriculture. In particular, as urbanization proceeds, we would expect capital to substitute for labor along with a growing role for purchased inputs such as fertilizer. While the data assembled in Table 10.5 will help us to assess factor substitution, they do not provide us with a comparison of Soviet input levels with those found in other countries.

In recent years, there has been a significant growth of the volume of capital investment in Soviet agriculture while the land input has been roughly stable with a declining (though recently stable) labor force. In the early 1960s, capital investment in agriculture accounted for approximately 20 percent of total capital investment according to official Soviet sources, while according to Western estimates, roughly 34 percent of gross national product (at factor cost) originated from agriculture.[16] By the mid-1980s, however, the pattern was very different. Thus by the early 1980s, the share of total investment going to agriculture was roughly 27 percent, while agriculture accounted for roughly 20 percent of gross national product.

At the same time, there have been significant changes in the volume of purchased inputs. Although effectiveness of utilization remains an issue, there has nevertheless been significant continuing growth in the availability of fertilizers and the stock of equipment. The input patterns assembled in Table 10.5 can be interpreted in different ways.

Table 10.5   INPUTS TO SOVIET AGRICULTURE
Selected Indicators

Input	1966–1970	1971–1975	1981–1985	1986–1987
Mineral fertilizers delivered (thousands of metric tons nutrient weight basis)	8,452	13,802	22,156	26,957
Tractor inventory (thousands)	1,821	2,189	2,699	2,776[a]
Grain inventory (thousands)	578	661	792	827[a]
Truck inventory (thousands)	1,105	1,282	1,722	1,917[a]
Sown area (million acres; end year)	511	538	519	519[a]
Average annual labor force (millions; end year)	36.9	36.0	34.5	33.9[a]
Capital investment (billion rubles, end year in "comparable" prices)	19.8	31.6	42.6	46.0[a]
As a share of total investment (percent) end year	25	28	26	24.0[a]

[a] 1986.

Sources: U.S. Department of Agriculture, USSR: Situation and Outlook Report (Washington, D.C.: U.S. Department of Agriculture, various issues); Directorate of Intelligence, Handbook of Economic Statistics, 1988 (Washington, D.C.: Central Intelligence Agency, 1988); Goskomstat, Narodnoe khoziaistvo SSSR za 70 let [The national economy of the USSR over 70 years] (Moscow: Finansy i Statistika, 1987); U.S. Department of Agriculture, USSR: Agriculture and Trade Report: Situation and Outlook Series (Washington, D.C.: U.S. Department of Agriculture, 1988); Directorate of Intelligence; Handbook of Economic Statistics, 1988 (Washington, D.C.: Central Intelligence Agency, 1988).

For example, the growth of capital inputs along with purchased inputs might suggest increasing production costs given the limited changes in land and labor inputs in recent years. This is a theme of importance on which direct evidence will be presented later in this chapter.

In part, however, input substitution has been part of a continuing effort to raise agricultural productivity, about which more will be said later. Briefly, however, intensification has been an important component of agricultural policy, especially in recent years. A continuing effort has been made to improve input use, for example, better use of fertilizers, more attention to crop rotation, and timely use of pesticides.

Factor Productivity in Soviet Agriculture

To understand costs in Soviet agriculture, it is necessary to examine outputs, inputs, and associated changes in factor productivity. A study by Diamond, Bettis, and Ramsson examines these trends for the period 1951 through 1979.[17] The results are reported in Table 10.6. The figures in this table tell a familiar story. Output growth since the 1950s has been generally very good but has been declining markedly. The same can be said for the growth of inputs, though the slackening in the growth rate of inputs has been less than that for output. If we accept the traditional assumption that the growth of output results from the growth of inputs and the growth of factor productivity (better use of available inputs), it is apparent that the latter has accounted for a declining share of output growth. Indeed, according to the figures presented here, improvement of factor productivity accounted for approximately 44 percent of the increase in agricultural output during the period 1951–1960, while it accounted for approximately 11 percent during the period 1971–1979. The implication is that costs have increased. We turn to direct evidence.

Agricultural Costs and Prices

Since the 1950s when Khrushchev introduced cost accounting into Soviet collective farms, it has been widely recognized that cost/price ratios have been

Table 10.6   FACTOR PRODUCTIVITY IN SOVIET AGRICULTURE, 1951–1979

| | Average annual rate of growth | | | |
	1951–1960	1961–1970	1971–1979	1951–1979
Output	4.8	3.0	1.3	3.4
Inputs	2.7	2.1	1.3	2.1
Factor productivity	2.1	1.0	0.2	1.2

Source: D. B. Diamond, L. W. Bettis, and R. E. Ramsson, "Agricultural Production." in A. Bergson and H. S. Levine, eds., *The Soviet Economy: Toward the Year 2000* (London: Allen & Unwin, 1983), p. 146.

very unfavorable to agriculture. Specifically, for many products in many regions, state purchase prices simply did not cover basic production costs, leaving farms to make up the difference. Viewing the price/cost ratios as an important incentive for farm production and specialization, Soviet leaders have, over the years, increased prices with the objective of making agricultural production profitable. These increases have been designed to stimulate greater agricultural productivity.

For purposes of our appraisal, cost/price data are assembled in Table 10.7. Interpretation of Soviet agricultural cost and price data should proceed with caution, because the computation of both costs and prices is subject to complications.

Examination of cost price data reveals a number of important trends in Soviet agriculture. Obviously, production costs have risen, in some cases sharply. For example, the costs of meat, milk, and potatoes have roughly doubled. In addition, while the degree of profitability differs significantly from one product to another, generally speaking, crop production has been much more profitable than the production of meat-related products. Moreover, the general stability of food prices at the retail level has resulted in a large and growing agricultural subsidy.[18]

Soviet agricultural subsidies arise in several ways, though generally through efforts to hold down the price of purchased inputs and to raise procurement prices, making farms profitable. According to estimates compiled by Vladimir G. Treml, "since the system was introduced in 1965, subsidies have risen from

Table 10.7   COSTS, PRICES AND PROFITABILITY ON STATE AND COLLECTIVE FARMS

Commodity	1970			1980			1987		
	Cost[a]	Price[b]	Profitability[c]	Cost	Price	Profitability	Cost	Price	Profitability
Grain	51	103	102	80	110	38	101	173	71
Cotton	397	556	40	487	623	28	609	816	34
Sugarbeets	23	26	14	32	29	−10	35	50	42
Sunflower seed	58	181	212	93	173	86	107	413	286
Potatoes	67	70	4	129	130	0.5	154	163	6
Vegetables	88	105	19	112	124	11	138	164	19
Beef	1212	1539	27	2278	2050	−10	2740	2932	7
Pork	1161	1544	33	1909	1718	−10	2039	2182	7
Mutton	766	1011	32	1366	1216	−11	1824	2006	10
Milk	182	189	4	297	270	−9	340	428	26
Eggs	67	96	43	65	99	52	62	97	56

[a]*Sebestoimost'* (prime cost) in rubles per ton.

[b]Average producer price derived from Soviet cost/profitability data.

[c]Ratio of payments for sold output to prime cost.

Source: E. C. Cook, "Deriving Soviet Agricultural Producer Prices," U.S. Department of Agriculture, *CPE Agriculture Report,* vol. 1, no. 6 (November/December 1988), 8–12.

about 2 billion rubles to 37 billion rubles in 1980."[19] The latter figure, according to Treml, amounts to roughly 54 percent of the value of national income generated in agriculture.[20]

Recent evidence on procurement subsidies of the Soviet state budget indicates that such subsidies have more than doubled in the 1980s, amounting to over 60 billion rubles in 1986.[21] A major and growing component of subsidies relates to the agro-industrial complex.

The impact of the subsidy system on Soviet agriculture is a matter of substantial complexity. In general, however, it is clear that Soviet authorities have been unwilling to pass increases in the cost of production on to the retail level. At the same time, there has been continuing pressure to expand inputs to agriculture in the anticipation of output improvement. Clearly, the 1970s were years in which Soviet leaders paid a great deal of attention to agriculture. Agriculture seems to claim a growing share of the nation's resources; and yet, despite a reasonable long-term rate of growth of output, imports have risen significantly and the Soviet domestic agricultural product has become much more costly. Why have costs increased so rapidly in Soviet agriculture?

Recent studies of Soviet agriculture by a number of Western scholars shed light on this issue.[22] While cost increases can be traced to a number of factors, the bottom line is that Soviet agriculture does not use its inputs effectively, although the reasons for such a pattern are not always clear. Moreover, to the extent that Soviet agriculture has not been able to increase its efficiency, increases in output have been obtained with inordinate input increases, the prices of which have risen sharply. On both counts, the result has been an increasingly costly agricultural product. In light of these problems of input usage, it is not surprising that Gorbachev has placed so much emphasis on intensification.

Western studies have generally concluded that the effectiveness of resource utilization in Soviet agriculture is highly variable and not generally good. Although direct comparisons between the Soviet Union and other countries such as the United States involve a number of measurement difficulties, they are nevertheless instructive. In the postwar era, the capital stock of Soviet agriculture has increased much more rapidly than that of American agriculture. But, for the 1970s, the capital/output ratio of Soviet agriculture was three times that of American agriculture.[23] Labor productivity in Soviet agriculture is roughly 6 percent of labor productivity in American agriculture.[24]

Comparison of yields not only sheds light on the effectiveness of land utilization but also on the question of climatic impact both in the long term and on a year-to-year basis. It has been widely argued that Soviet climatic peculiarities (inadequate amounts and distribution of warmth and moisture) account for Soviet crop production difficulties, especially year-to-year variability.[25]

The evidence on this question is mixed. Analysts have studied crop yields using climatic analogs, that is, comparing Soviet yields with yields in other countries having similar climatic conditions. For example, when Soviet grain yields are compared with those in North America, Soviet yields are lower but generally quite good.[26] On the other hand, Soviet hay yields are at best one-half those obtained in climatically similar areas elsewhere.[27] Finally, if one examines technical crops, especially those of high priority such as cotton, yields are generally good.

What, then, of the role of climate? In his recent study of Soviet agriculture, D. Gale Johnson concludes that "there can be no doubt that climatic factors affect both the level of agricultural output and its variability in the USSR. But I believe that it has been shown that policy choices have influenced a significant proportion of these two effects."[28]

Recent evidence tends to confirm the view that while climate is an important element helping to explain output growth and variability, variations of input availability and usage must be considered to derive a full explanation. In this sense, the Gorbachev program of intensification will be critical for agricultural success into the 1990s.

Although it is difficult to clearly demarcate systemic and policy factors that may have influenced Soviet agricultural performance, plainly both are important. The organizational arrangements in Soviet agriculture have clearly been a factor that influences outcomes. Decision making has been historically relatively centralized, while agricultural activity must be guided in large part by the use of local information. This centralization stems, in part, from lack of effective decision-making procedures at the local level. From a technical perspective, Soviet agriculture at the local level has been poorly served by agricultural specialists in spite of efforts to make it otherwise. Historically, most specialists have found it both possible and attractive to work outside the rural economy. Moreover, from an economic perspective, local (and indeed upper-level) decision making must have been impaired by inadequate information. The development of useful cost information is a recent phenomenon, not to mention the perennial problem of pricing.[29] Thus, the concept of profitability has had little meaning; some activities have been highly profitable, while others have been persistently unprofitable, with neither having any relation to the achievement of desired objectives. While the capital stock of Soviet agriculture has been increased at a very rapid pace in recent years, we have seen that capital productivity is very low when compared to agriculture elsewhere. To take a case in point, the level of utilization of machinery and equipment is very low for a variety of reasons, not the least important of which is inadequate support facilities to keep equipment functional.

While it is difficult to offer firm figures, most observers of Soviet agriculture would argue that the agriculture infrastructure is a major problem. Whether one considers nonagriculture serving agriculture or the reverse, there are major problems. For example, Soviet economists have long argued that losses between the field and the table are great. Historically, processing and storage have been inadequate, and the transportation system (especially roads) is ill suited for the tasks at hand. On the input side, similar considerations prevail. To take another example, the production of chemical fertilizer has increased dramatically, and yet significant portions of this increase never find their way to the fields due to transportation and storage losses and the like.

These problems, in spite of reform efforts, tend to persist to one degree or another. They must have had a negative impact on the cost and the availability of the Soviet agricultural product.

Our earlier discussion of Soviet agricultural yields concluded with the argument that policy factors may have an important influence on Soviet agricultural performance. For example, it is argued that Soviet use of fallow land is inappropriate, namely, too low. D. Gale Johnson notes that "despite evidence from both foreign and Soviet sources of the merits of clean fallow for many agriculture areas, Soviet fallow area remains very low." [30]

Another example of policy failure is the evidence that Soviet seeding rates are inordinately high, especially for certain crops such as grain. As Johnson notes in his analysis of this issue, high seeding rates are inefficient, whether they result from ignorance or improper seeding procedures, or both.[31]

Finally, it is instructive to note that similar problems exist in the livestock sector production activity, where climatic and other unfavorable natural conditions should be of lesser importance than in crop production. As we have already noted, performance of the Soviet livestock sector, specifically, meat production, has been a matter of continuing concern. Efforts to expand meat production at a faster pace have resulted in sharp cost increases. Once again, problems in this sector can be found throughout the production process. Soviet hay yields are poor. More generally, animal fodder is deficient in protein content which, in combination with inappropriate feeding procedures and lack of specialization in the Soviet cattle sector, results in poor output per unit of input. This outcome is partly a result of Soviet organizational and other systemic arrangements, but it also results from questionable policies such as the lack of specialization.[32] It remains to be seen to what extend organizational and policy changes of the Gorbachev era can be effective in eliminating these problems.

ASSESSING THE RESULT: FURTHER EVIDENCE

We have now assembled sufficient information to return briefly to the theme developed at the beginning of this chapter. Has Soviet agriculture been able to supply adequate food and fiber for its population at reasonable cost?[33] But what are adequate amounts, and what is a reasonable cost?

One useful way to assess supply is to consider the ability of the system to meet self-imposed dietary norms. Evidence of dietary achievement is assembled in Table 10.8. The evidence in this table suggests that there has been a steady improvement in the Soviet diet, based on the extent to which official Soviet dietary norms have been achieved. Clearly, the achievement is variable, but it nevertheless reflects traditional trends away from starchy foods toward proteins.

From the point of view of caloric intake, the Soviet food situation looks pretty good.[34] Why, then, is there a steady flow of complaints about food, an

Table 10.8   SOVIET PER CAPITA FOOD CONSUMPTION AND NORMS
Selected Years, 1966–1990

	Meat and fat	Fish	Milk	Eggs	Potatoes	Grain	Veg.	Fruits
Norm	82	18.2	405	292	110	115	130	91
Actual 1966–1970	47	14.3	287	144	132	150	78	n.a.
Actual 1976–1980	57	17.3	318	227	116	139	92	39
Actual 1985	61	17.7	323	260	104	133	102	46
Plan 1990	70	19.0	330–266	260–266	110	135	126–135	66–70

Source: U.S. Department of Agriculture, *USSR: Outlook and Situation Report* (Washington, D.C.: U.S. Department of Agriculture, various issues).

issue that has become a centerpiece of reform success or failure? The answer lies in several dimensions.

First, the expectations of Soviet consumers have generally outstripped the realities of the food market. As domestic luxuries such as caviar become less available, a by-product of glasnost is greater consumer awareness of food consumption patterns elsewhere. It is not surprising that Soviet consumers have growing expectations in a setting where for many years they have been told on a daily basis of the great economic achievements of Soviet socialism.

Second, Soviet incomes have been growing at a pace that would allow expectations to be met if there were not losses, shortages, and imbalances in the supply system. Food supplies are simply not available on a regular and systematic basis. According to Western estimates, the growth of per capita food consumption has fallen steadily from 4.2 percent (1966–70) to 1.1 percent (1976-80) to 4.0 percent (1985-87).[35]

Third, aggregate data do not always reveal the full story from the perspective of the consumer. For example, in addition to distribution problems noted above, quality remains a problem. Moreover, the typical Soviet consumer would probably obtain protein from meat rather than bread.

According to official Soviet sources, the share of a worker's income devoted to food fell from 35 percent in 1970 to 28 percent in 1986.[36] There are, however, significant regional variations. Moreover, these sorts of data are difficult to interpret to the extent that retail food markets are characterized by disequilibrium, specifically excess demand.

The reader may well be puzzled at this point. We have observed that during the period 1950–1980, Soviet agricultural output grew at an average annual rate of roughly 3 percent, while Soviet population grew at an average annual rate of roughly 1.6 percent. Thus, on an average annual basis, there has been an increase of 1.4 percent in per capita food production. But how can the rate of improvement be maintained if the rate of growth of output has been declining in recent years? The answer lies in the increasing utilization of foreign trade.[37]

In Table 10.9, we present some basic numbers on Soviet agricultural trade. Western attention is frequently captured by the grain question. Obviously, grain is a crucial product of agriculture used for consumption, for industrial processing, and as animal food. During the 1960s, the Soviet Union was a net grain exporter, that is, it generally sold more than it purchased. In the 1970s, however, this position was reversed. Throughout the 1970s and 1980s, Soviet grain requirements exceeded domestic grain production; the difference was made up by a growing volume of imports. However, the data through 1985 may present an overly pessimistic view, at least for grain. Based upon preliminary estimates for recent years, it is likely that Soviet grain production for the years 1986 through 1988 will exceed 200 million metric tons. A major result of this improvement has been a reduction of Soviet grain imports from the 44 million metric ton range in 1984–1985 to roughly 26–28 million metric tons in the 1986-1988 period.[38]

Beyond grain, Soviet requirements have also exceeded Soviet domestic production in other critical areas, as the evidence in Table 10.9 indicates. At the same time, there have been products, such as cotton, where the Soviets have continued to be major net exporters. How should we interpret this trade posture?

Soviet agricultural trade in the 1970s and 1980s has been the focus of much attention, largely because of its impact on a number of different interest groups.[39] For the farmers of the major grain-exporting countries, for example, Canada, the United States, and Australia, sales to the Soviet Union provide a large if sometimes unpredictable market. Moreover, in this context, grain becomes a major issue in the more general framework of East–West relations.[40] United States grain sales to the Soviet Union have fluctuated considerably in

Table 10.9 TRENDS IN SOVIET AGRICULTURAL TRADE
(Net Balance in Thousands of Metric Tons)

Product	1975	1978	1980	1982	1983	1985	1986
Grain	−12,117	−21,014	−28,794	−37,429	−31,557	−41,789	−24,987
Meat and meat products	−471	−145	−786	−907	−960	−830	−903
Vegetable oil (edible)	+355	−18	−233	−752	−598	−678	−389
Cotton (lint)	+633	+743	+794	+923	+597	+444	+625
Hides and skins				+1,519	+952	+23,460	
Vegetable oil (edible)				−750	−598	−678	

Sources: U.S. Department of Agriculture, *USSR: Situation and Outlook Report* (Washington D.C.: U.S. Department of Agriculture, various issues), and U.S. Department of Agriculture, *USSR: Agriculture and Trade Report: Situation and Outlook Series* (Washington D.C.: U.S. Department of Agriculture, 1988).

spite of a long-term (five-year) grain agreement. New discussions have taken place to implement a replacement for the agreement, which expired in the fall of 1988.

Agricultural trade, and especially the large volume of grain sales to the Soviet Union, is of interest to trade economists as a major component of overall Soviet foreign trade with important implications for Soviet decision-making arrangements, payments mechanisms, and the like.

What does this trade posture tell us with respect to Soviet domestic agricultural production capability? There is nothing wrong with trade. Indeed, economists have long argued that specialization and exchange are rational. Moreover, the trends we have observed may not persist into the early 1990s. But the growing importance of Soviet agricultural imports suggests that domestic production has, in recent times, been increasingly incapable of meeting Soviet needs in spite of a growing effort by Soviet leaders to solve the agricultural problem. In this sense, it worries Soviet leaders, and it necessarily limits their available options.

SOVIET AGRICULTURE: CONTEMPORARY TRENDS AND FUTURE PROSPECTS

As we have emphasized, Soviet agriculture, despite continuing progress, remains a sector of major concern to Soviet leaders. Indeed, we are constantly reminded of this issue. Thus the grain harvest for 1988 was respectable at approximately 200 million metric tons, but the worst harvest in three years and some 40 million metric tons below plan. Projections suggest a final 1989 harvest of just over 200 million metric tons, specifically 208 metric tons.

While criticism of agriculture by the Soviet leadership is persistent, reforms of the 1980s have been quite modest, especially when compared to systems adopting more radical change, for example, China. Although more reform will undoubtedly be forthcoming, thus far Gorbachev has proceeded in a rather straightforward manner, building on the changes introduced in the late Brezhnev and immediate post-Brezhnev era. Although the areas of reform discussed by Gorbachev have frequently evoked images of dramatic change to come, for example, in the area of labor organization, in fact both reform substance and implementation have been rather modest.

In the late 1970s, Brezhnev was particularly critical of agriculture, especially the inability of the Soviet agricultural system to generate adequate food supplies for the Soviet people. The most prominent outcome of this criticism was the food program, announced in 1982.[41] Under this program, production and other goals through the end of the decade were announced, and reforms designed to achieve these goals were also announced.

The food program was not a dramatic departure from existing policies. Much of the emphasis from improvement was placed on the agro-industrial complex, especially improving decision making at all levels. At the upper level, a special commission on the agro-industrial complex (under the presidium of the Council of Ministers) was established. At the local level, the *raion* agro-industrial associations (RAPOs) were established. The RAPOs were supposed to coordinate differing agricultural and related activities at the local level. Although the RAPOs have been the object of criticism, their powers have been increased to include some price-setting authority and the ability to shift sales and investment targets among farms under their supervision.

Under the food program and associated legislation, there has been a relaxation of rules pertaining to the private sector in an effort to achieve closer integration between the private and the state sectors in agriculture. For example, the limit on the private holding of animals was eliminated provided that animals were held under a contract arrangement, purchased from the state to be sold back at a later date (after fattening, for example). In addition, provision was made to give the private sector easier access to needed inputs.

The food program called for better incentives at the farm level, including a closer connection between reward for effort expended and final product achieved. This connection was to be achieved through the implementation of collective contract brigades. These brigades have been the subject of considerable controversy. Although they were to become the dominant form of labor organization by the late 1980s, it is not clear that this has in fact been achieved. Moreover, while the original concept was to relate member pay to output, apparently the result bears little relationship to an autonomous type of brigade unit.

Finally, price reform was to be a major part of the food program. In particular, purchase prices for farm products were to be increased.

Agricultural reform under Gorbachev has moved along lines already evident from the food program.[42] Generally, Gorbachev, especially at the Party Plenum of March 1989, has stressed "intensification" to include the greater use of economic levers, movement away from the administrative command system and shifts in the allocation of agricultural investment to develop a better infrastructure. While the development of the agro-industrial complex has continued to be emphasized, upper-level management in agriculture has undergone important change. In 1985, a new organ of agricultural management, *Gosagroprom*, was created by combining five ministries, including the ministry of agriculture. *Gosagroprom* also includes some functions previously handled by other ministries and organizations, for example, food processing, and land reclamation. Although this new structure was intended to streamline agricultural decision making, it is not clear to what extent benefits have been achieved.

In addition to organizational change, Gorbachev (beyond strengthening the role of the RAPOs) has emphasized the need for greater self-sufficiency at the farm level (tighter controls on bank credit have been introduced). Also, farms have been assured of having stable long-term plans, an issue that dates from the 1960s. Moreover, in addition to the replacement of output quotas with sales quotas, farms are to have greater freedom in the disposition of above-quota deliveries.

Finally, Gorbachev has emphasized the need to shift capital investment away from traditional applications. For example, there has been a new emphasis on improving housing, distribution facilities, machinery and equipment, purchased inputs for intensive technology, and the like. The effectiveness of these sorts of shifts remains uncertain.

Only time will allow us to assess the effectiveness of recent changes in Soviet agriculture. Moreover, in critical areas, for example, price reform, we must await serious change in an overall price reform to come in the early 1990s. It is difficult to understand how serious improvements in farm decision making based on economic levers can be achieved under existing pricing arrangements. New farm purchase prices are to be introduced in 1990. In other dimensions, the pattern of reform is difficult to interpret. For example, as in the past, there continues to be a great emphasis on organizational change. At the same time, emphasis on better availability of food-processing equipment and the intensive technology programs suggest a serious commitment to modern agricultural techniques.[43] Possibly most important will be the outcome of ongoing discussions regarding new organizational arrangements, especially the leasing of land.

REFERENCES

1. For historical development, see D. J. Male, *Russian Peasant Organization Before Collectivization* (Cambridge: Cambridge University Press, 1971); R. G. Wesson, *Soviet Communes* (New Brunswick, N.J.: Rutgers University Press, 1963); R. W. Davies, *The Industrialization of Soviet Russia*, vol. 2 (Cambridge, Mass.: Harvard University Press, 1980). For a discussion of contemporary arrangement, see R. C. Stuart, *The Collective Farm in Soviet Agriculture* (Lexington, Mass.: D. C. Heath, 1972); K.-E. Wädekin, *The Private Sector in Soviet Agriculture* (Berkeley: University of California Press, 1973); and V. Litvin, *The Soviet Agro-Industrial Complex* (Boulder: Westview Press, 1987).
2. Goskomstat, *Narodnoe khoziaistvo SSSR za 70 let* [The national economy of the USSR over 70 years] (Moscow: Finansy i Statistika, 1987), p. 297. Recently, the amount of both labor and capital devoted to interfarm enterprises has declined as capital has been shifted to food processing and other areas.
3. For recent evidence on the private sector, see A. Lane, "U.S.S.R.: Private Agriculture on Center Stage," in U.S. Congress, Joint Economic Committee, *Soviet Economy in the 1980s: Problems and Prospects*, part 2 (Washington, D.C.: U.S. Government Printing Office, 1982), pp. 23–40.
4. For details, see Stuart, *The Collective Farm in Soviet Agriculture.*
5. The MTS are discussed in depth in R. F. Miller, *One Hundred Thousand Tractors* (Cambridge, Mass.: Harvard University Press, 1970).
6. There is a considerable body of literature on this issue. See, for example, E. D. Domar, "The Soviet Collective Farm as a Producer Cooperative," *American Economic Review*, vol. 56, no. 4, part I (September 1966), 734–757; W. Y. Oi and E. M. Clayton, "A Peasant's View of a Soviet Collective Farm," *American*

Economic Review, vol. 58, no. 1 (March 1968), 37–59. For recent analysis, see M. L. Wyzan, "The Kolkhoz and the Sovkhoz: Relative Performance as Measured by Productive Technology," in R. C. Stuart, ed. *The Soviet Rural Economy* (Totowa, N.J.: Rowman & Allanheld, 1983), pp. 173–198; and Clark Chandler, "The Effects of the Private Sector on the Labor Behavior of Soviet Collective Farmers," in Stuart, ed., *The Soviet Rural Economy,* pp. 223–237.

7 For a discussion of financing , see J. R. Millar, "Financing the Modernization of Kolkhozy," in J. R. Millar, ed., *The Soviet Rural Community* (Urbana: University of Illinois Press, 1971), pp. 276–313.

8. The virgin lands program is discussed in M. McCauley, *Khrushchev and the Development of Soviet Agriculture* (New York: Holmes & Meier, 1976). Urban specialization is discussed in F. M. Leversedge and R. C. Stuart, "Soviet Agricultural Restructure and Urban Markets." *Canadian Geographer,* vol. 19, no. 1 (1975), 73–93.

9. For a detailed discussion of rules, see Wädekin, *The Private Sector in Soviet Agriculture,* chap. 3.

10. Ibid., p. 35.

11. A. Lane, "U.S.S.R.: Private Agriculture on Center Stage," 24 (note 2).

12. For a discussion of integration, see E. M. Jacobs, "Soviet Agricultural Planning and Management and the 1982 Administrative Reform," in Stuart, ed., *The Soviet Rural Economy,* pp. 273–295; V. Litvin, "Agro-Industrial Complexes: Recent Structural Reform in the Rural Economy of the USSR," in Stuart, ed., *The Soviet Rural Economy,* pp. 258–272; R. C. Stuart, "Aspects of Soviet Rural Development," *Agricultural Administration,* vol. 2 (1975), pp. 165–178; A. Kahan, "The Problems of the Agrarian-Industrial Complexes in the Soviet Union," in Z. Fallenbuchl, ed., *Economic Development in the Soviet Union and Eastern Europe* (New York: Praeger, 1976), pp. 205–222; and K.-E. Wädekin, *Agrarian Policies in Communist Europe: A Critical Introduction* (Totowa, N.J.: Rowman & Allanheld, 1982), chap. 12.

13. E. Jacobs, "Soviet Agricultural Planning and Management and the 1982 Administrative Reform," p. 274.

14. This discussion is based on Jacobs, "Soviet Agricultural Planning and Management and the 1982 Administrative Reform," pp. 273–295.

15. For a grain balance through 1988/89, see U.S. Department of Agriculture, *USSR: Agriculture and Trade Report: Situation and Outlook Series* (Washington, D.C.: U.S. Department of Agriculture, 1988), p. 21.

16. These estimates are from Directorate of Intelligence, *Handbook of Economic Statistics, 1988* (Washington, D.C.: Central Intelligence Agency, 1988), p. 61.

17. D. B. Diamond, L. W. Bettis, and R. E. Ramsson, "Agricultural Production," in A. Bergson and H. S. Levine, eds., *The Soviet Economy: Toward the Year 2000* (London: Allen & Unwin, 1983), chap. 3.

18. For a discussion of recent trends, see V. G. Treml, "Subsidies in Soviet Agriculture: Record and Prospects," in U.S. Congress, Joint Economic Committee, *Soviet Economy in the 1980s: Problems and Prospects* (Washington, D.C.: U.S. Government Printing Office, 1982), pp. 171–186, and Y. Markish, "New Semenov Data on State Subsidies," U.S. Department of Agriculture, *CPE Agriculture Report,* vol. 1, no. 6 (November/December 1988), 27–29.

19. Treml, "Subsidies in Soviet Agriculture," pp. 171-172.

20. Ibid., p. 172.

21. Markish, "New Semenov Data on Soviet Subsidies," p. 28.

22. For a general discussion of factors underlying cost increases, see D. G. Johnson and K. McC. Brooks, *Prospects for Soviet Agriculture in the 1980s* (Bloomington: Indiana University Press, 1983). For a discussion of the livestock sector, see K. R. Gray, "Soviet Livestock: Stymied Growth, Increased Cost and Search for Balance," in U.S. Congress, Joint Economic Committee, *Soviet Economy in the 1980s: Problems and Prospects,* pp. 86–108; and Diamond, Bettis, and Ramsson, "Agricultural Production."

23. Johnson and Brooks, *Prospects for Soviet Agriculture in the 1980s,* p. 56.

24. Ibid.

25. Ibid., chap. 6 and pp. 123–128. See also R. A. Ambroziak and D. W. Carey, "Climate and Grain Production in the Soviet Union," in U.S. Congress, Joint Economic Committee, *Soviet Economy in the 1980s: Problems and Prospects,* pp. 109–123. For an attempt to isolate the impact of weather on Soviet agriculture, see also Directorate of Intelligence, *Modelling Soviet Agriculture: Isolating the Effects of Weather* (Washington, D.C.: Central Intelligence Agency, 1988).

26. Johnson and Brooks, *Prospects for Soviet Agriculture in the 1980s,* pp. 73–79. See also R. C. Stuart, "Wheat Yields in Socialist and Capitalist Economic Systems: A Statistical Comparison," *ACES Bulletin,* vol. 26, no. 1 (Spring 1984), 77–85.

27. Johnson and Brooks, *Prospects for Soviet Agriculture in the 1980s,* pp. 80–82.

28. Ibid., p. 91.

29. For empirical evidence on the rationality of Soviet factor proportions, see M. L. Wyzan "Empirical Analysis of Soviet Agricultural Production and Policy," *American Journal of Agricultural Economics,* vol. 63, no. 3 (August 1981), 475–483; E. M. Clayton, "Productivity in Soviet Agriculture," *Slavic Review,* vol. 39 (1980), 446–458; and Johnson and Brooks, *Prospects for Soviet Agriculture,* chap. 9.

30. Johnson and Brooks, *Prospects for Soviet Agriculture,* p. 41.

31. Ibid., pp. 41–44.

32. See, for example, K. R. Gray, "Improved Agriculture Location: Econometric Evidence from the Ukraine," in Stuart, ed., *The Soviet Rural Economy,* chap. 10; and K. R. Gray, "Soviet Agricultural Specialization and Efficiency," *Soviet Studies,* vol. 31, no. 4 (October 1979), 542–558.

33. K. R. Gray, "Soviet Consumption of Food: Is the Bottle 'Half-Full,' 'Half-Empty,' 'Half-Water,' or 'Too Expensive'?" *ACES Bulletin,* vol. 23, no. 2 (Summer 1981), 31–50.

34. For recent evidence on this issue, see Ann M. Lane, R. M. Marston, and S. O. Welsh, "The Nutrient Content of the Soviet Food Supply and Comparisons with the U.S. Food Supply," in U.S. Congress, Joint Economic Committee, *Gorbachev's Economic Plans,* vol. 2 (Washington, D.C.: U.S. Government Printing Office, 1987), pp. 79–99.

35. Directorate of Intelligence, *Handbook of Economic Statistics, 1988,* p. 65.

36. Goskomstat, *Narodnoe khoziaistvo SSSR za 70 let* [The national economy of the USSR over 70 years] (Moscow: Finansy i Statistika, 1987), p. 444.

37. According to a recent study, net imports of farm products in the 1970s replaced acreage as the second most important source of increased supply, with increases being the most important source when the 1970s are compared with the 1960s. See Diamond, Bettis, and Ramsson, "Agricultural Production," p. 151.

38. Data are from U.S. Department of Agriculture, *USSR: Agriculture and Trade Report: Situation and Outlook Series*, vol. 18, 33–34.

39. See, for example, P. L. Kelley, "Implications for World Food System Strategies with Special Regard to the Role of the United States," in K.-E. Wädekin, ed., *Current Trends in the Soviet and East European Food Economy* (Berlin: Duncker & Humbolt, 1982), pp. 339–361; K.-E. Wädekin, "Soviet Agriculture's Dependence on the West," *Foreign Affairs*; A. O. Byrne, J. E. Cole, T. Bickerton, and A. F. Malish, "U.S.–U.S.S.R. Grain Trade," in U.S. Congress, Joint Economic Committee, *Soviet Economy in the 1980s: Problems and Prospects*, pp. 60–85; and James R. Jones (ed.), *East–West Agricultural Trade* (Boulder, Colo.: Westview Press, 1986).

40. See, for example, the discussion of the U.S. grain embargo of 1980–1981 in J. C. Roney, "Grain Embargo as Diplomatic Lever: A Case Study of the U.S.–Soviet Embargo of 1980–81," in U.S. Congress, Joint Economic Committee, *Soviet Economy in the 1980s: Problems and Prospects*, pp. 124–140.

41. For a discussion, see A. F. Malish, "The Food Program: A New Policy or More Rhetoric?" U.S. Congress, Joint Economic Committee, *Soviet Economy in the 1980s: Problems and Prospects*, pp. 41–59; and K. Severin, "An Assessment of the Soviet Food Program," in Philip Joseph, ed., *The Soviet Economy After Brezhnev* (Brussels: NATO, 1984), pp. 85–112.

42. For a discussion of reform in agriculture, see U.S. Congress, Joint Economic Committee, *Gorbachev's Economic Plans*, pp. 1-130; U.S. Department of Agriculture, *USSR: Agriculture and Trade Report: Situation and Outlook Series*, pp. 13-17.

43. Recently responsibility for food processing equipment has been placed under the Ministry of Defense. For a discussion, see K. Gray and Y. Markish, "USSR: Guns Versus Butterchurns," in U.S. Department of Agriculture, *CPE Agriculture Report*, vol. 1, no. 3 (May/June, 1988), 8–11; M. Gorbachev, *On the Agrarian Policy of the CPSU in the Present Conditions* (Moscow: Novosti, 1989).

SELECTED BIBLIOGRAPHY

Josef C. Brada and Karl-Eugen Wädekin eds., *Socialist Agriculture in Transition: Organizational Response to Failing Performance* (Boulder, Colo.: Westview Press, 1987).

Center for Business and Economic Research, School of Business, Economics and Management, University of Southern Maine, *Newsletter for Research on Soviet and East European Agriculture* (Portland, Maine: RSEEA).

D. B. Diamond, L. W. Bettis, and R. E. Ramsson, "Agricultural Production," in A. Bergson and H. S. Levine, eds., *The Soviet Economy: Toward the Year 2000* (London: Allen & Unwin, 1983, chap. 5.

F. A. Durgin, Jr., "Monetization and Policy in Soviet Agriculture Since 1952," *Soviet Studies*, vol. 15, no. 4 (April 1964).

K. R. Gray, ed., *Contemporary Soviet Agriculture in Comparative Perspective* (Ames: Iowa State University Press, 1989).

K. R. Gray, "Soviet Agricultural Specialization and Efficiency," *Soviet Studies*, vol. 31, no. 4 (October 1979), pp. 542–548.

S. Hedlund, *Crisis in Soviet Agriculture* (New York: St. Martin's Press, 1984).

W. A. D. Jackson, ed., *Agrarian Policies and Problems in Communist and Non-Communist Countries* (Seattle: University of Washington Press, 1971).

N. Jasny, *The Socialized Agriculture of the USSR* (Stanford, Calif.: Stanford University Press, 1949).

D. G. Johnson and K. McC. Brooks, *Prospects for Soviet Agriculture in the 1980s* (Bloomington: Indiana University Press, 1983).

J. F. Karcz, ed., *Soviet and East European Agriculture* (Berkeley and Los Angeles: University of California Press, 1967).

R. D. Laird, ed., *Soviet Agricultural and Peasant Affairs* (Lawrence: University of Kansas Press, 1963).

R. D. Laird and E. L. Crowley, eds., *Soviet Agriculture: The Permanent Crisis* (New York: Praeger, 1965).

R. D. Laird, J. Hajda, and B. A. Laird, eds., *The Future of Soviet Agriculture in the Soviet Union and Eastern Europe* (Boulder, Colo.: Westview Press, 1977).

Z. A. Medvedev, *Soviet Agriculture* (New York: Norton, 1987).

J. R. Millar, ed., *The Soviet Rural Community* (Urbana: University of Illinois Press, 1971).

R. F. Miller, *One Hundred Thousand Tractors* (Cambridge, Mass.: Harvard University Press, 1970).

K. Severin, "An Assessment of the Soviet Food Program," in Philip Joseph, ed., *The Soviet Economy After Brezhnev* (Brussels: NATO, 1984).

R. C. Stuart, *The Collective Farm in Soviet Agriculture* (Lexington, Mass.: Heath, 1972).

———, ed., *The Soviet Rural Economy* (Totowa, N.J.: Rowman & Allanheld, 1983).

U.S. Congress, Joint Economic Committee, *Gorbachev's Economic Plans*, vol. 2 (Washington, D.C.: U. S. Government Printing Office, 1987), pp. 1–130.

U.S. Congress, Joint Economic Committee, *Soviet Economy in the 1980s: Problems and Prospects*, part 2 (Washington, D.C.: U.S. Government Printing Office, 1983), section VI.

U.S. Congress, Joint Economic Committee, *Soviet Economy in a Time of Change* (Washington, D.C.: U.S. Government Printing Office, 1979), vol. 2, part 3.

U.S. Department of Agriculture, Centrally Planned Economies Branch, Agricultural Trade Analysis Division, Economic Research Service, *CPE Agriculture Report* (Washington, D.C.: bimonthly).

U.S. Department of Agriculture, Economic Research Service, *USSR: Situation and Outlook Report* (Washington, D.C.: U.S. Government Printing Office, through 1987).

———, *USSR: Agriculture and Trade Report: Situation and Outlook Series* (Washington, D.C.: U.S. Government Printing Office, 1989).

L. Volin, *A Century of Russian Agriculture* (Cambridge Mass.: Harvard University Press, 1970).

K.-E. Wädekin, *Agrarian Policies in Communist Europe: A Critical Introduction* (Totowa, N.J.: Rowman & Allanheld, 1982).

————, ed., *Agriculture in Inter-System Comparison: Communist and Non-Communist Cases* (Berlin: Duncker & Humbolt, 1982).

————, ed., *Current Trends in the Soviet and East European Food Economy* (Berlin: Duncker & Humbolt, 1982).

Chapter 11

Soviet Foreign Trade

*I*n this chapter, we examine the role of the foreign sector in the Soviet economy. We begin with a discussion of trade in the Soviet planned economy—in particular, the state trade monopoly and the trade planning instruments utilized throughout the plan era. In addition to developing an understanding of how trade is conducted, it is necessary to examine both the volume and the structure of Soviet trade, especially its distribution among various trading partners in the world—notably among capitalist countries (developed and underdeveloped) and socialist bloc member countries of the COMECON organization. The Council for Mutual Economic Assistance, called COMECON or, alternatively, CMEA, is the Soviet bloc's equivalent to the European Common Market and will be discussed in this chapter. The member countries, in addition to the

USSR, are Bulgaria, Hungary, East Germany, Cuba, Mongolia, Poland, Rumania, and Czechoslovakia. These trends can give us a picture of how Soviet trade policies have functioned in practice and what role foreign trade has played in the Soviet development experience.

As most readers of this book will know, there has been a great deal of discussion of foreign trade in the Gorbachev era. However, unlike some other sectors of the Soviet economy, there were few if any changes in foreign trade in the middle and later years of the Brezhnev leadership. Moreover, the important changes suggested by Gorbachev represent recent proposals, dating mainly from the post–1986/1987 period. In light of the relative stability of Soviet foreign trade organizational arrangements and policies, it seems useful to begin with a reasonably complete presentation of the pre-Gorbachev Soviet foreign trade system. Thereafter, we will examine the Gorbachev foreign trade program in some depth, comparing suggested recent changes to the existing structure.

TRADE IN THE SOVIET PLANNED ECONOMY

The Organization of Foreign Trade Through the Mid–1980s[1]

The organizational mechanisms used to conduct Soviet foreign trade are numerous, and over the years they have grown in number and complexity. Altogether, these organizations comprise the foreign trade monopoly of the Soviet Union. The basic organization responsible for foreign trade is the Ministry of Foreign Trade, which itself is subordinate to *Gosplan*, and the USSR Council of Ministers (see Figure 11.1). The operative trade units, that is, the organizations that actually do the buying and selling in foreign markets, are Foreign Trade Organizations (FTOs)—or the All-Union Import-Export Associations, as they are described in Soviet parlance. These foreign trade organizations are usually subordinate to the Ministry of Foreign Trade and are financially independent, operating on a *khozraschet* basis. Most of the FTOs are organized by product. Thus, the FTO *Avtoeksport* ("auto export") deals in automobiles, and *Mezhdunarodnaia kniga* ("international book") deals in books. These organizations may handle imports, exports, or both. Reforms of the late 1970s were directed toward combining both the import and the export tasks within a single FTO. Moreover, as we shall see later, reforms promulgated in 1987 reduced the role of the Ministry of Foreign Trade, making it possible for a variety of Soviet organizations to deal directly with foreign buyers and sellers. In addition to those FTOs dealing with specific products, others exist for the servicing of foreign trade and conducting trade on a regional basis. An example of the former would be *Vneshtorgreklama* ("foreign trade advertising"), which handles advertising in foreign trade. An example of the latter would be *Vostokintorg*, which is the Eastern Trade Association.

The FTOs have within them the means of conducting foreign trade, and they provide necessary technical and financial services. Their revenue is calculated as a percentage of their foreign trade turnover (exports plus imports). In

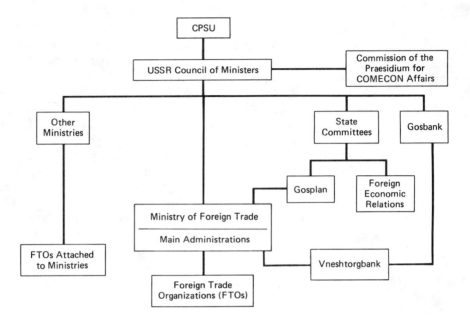

Figure 11.1 The organization of Soviet foreign trade. (*Source:* Compiled from V. P. Gruzinov, *The USSR's Management of Foreign Trade* [White Plains, N.Y.: M. E. Sharpe, 1979], pp. 26, 75, 79; E. A. Hewett, "Most-Favored Nation Treatment in Trade Under Central Planning," *Slavic Review,* vol. 37, no. 1 [March 1978], 28; Paul K. Cook, "The Political Setting," in Joint Economic Committee, *Soviet Economy in a Time of Change* [Washington, D.C.: U.S. Government Printing Office, 1979], vol. 1, no. 2, face p. 50.)

addition to the individual FTOs, the Ministry of Foreign Trade is divided into main administrations or branches that are concerned with a wide range of issues relating to foreign trade. These administrations provide technical and financial services, including research on foreign trade.

The financial arrangements for Soviet foreign trade are handled by a special bank, *Vneshtorgbank.*[2] Though traditionally under the jurisdiction of *Gosbank,* the *Vneshtorgbank* significantly expanded its powers and functions in the mid–1960s and early 1970s. It operates under policy guidance from *Gosbank,* but in close cooperation with the main foreign exchange administration of the Ministry of Foreign Trade. In addition to a large number of correspondent banks in foreign countries, *Vneshtorgbank* also operates through Soviet-owned banks abroad, for example, the Moscow Narodny Bank of London.

There are other more specialized organizations for the conduct of trade, the importance of which has grown over the years. A number of special FTOs do not fall under the jurisdiction of the Ministry of Foreign Trade. *Intourist,* the FTO responsible for Soviet tourism, falls within the jurisdiction of the administration for foreign tourism under the Council of Ministers. Another example was the Soviet Olympic Organizing Committee (SOOC), which operated independently of the Ministry of Foreign Trade and the FTOs but was fully empowered to sign agreements with foreign firms for the 1980 Olympic Games held in Moscow. The Soviet Union also has Joint Stock Companies, for example, Belarus Machinery Inc., which sells and services Belarus tractors in the United States. Finally, recent new legislation has been aimed at making joint ventures an important part of the Soviet foreign trade apparatus.

The Planning of Foreign Trade

Soviet foreign trade, like other sectors of the Soviet economy, has been managed as an integral part of the system of material balance planning.[3] Soviet foreign trade planners have tended to use imports and exports as balancing items in the national economic plan (imports where there were shortages and exports where there were surpluses). Planners have sought to avoid heavy reliance on trade to balance the plan for reasons discussed later in this chapter. In trade with COMECON countries, Soviet authorities planned for trade to play a more important role, namely, to promote the integration of these countries with the Soviet economy. Specifically, the Soviet Union was to serve as the basic source of raw materials for Eastern European development, with manufactured products supplied in return.

Although organizational reforms and enhanced interest in trade with the West have created an increasingly sophisticated foreign trade planning structure, the main features of foreign trade planning have remained basically intact since the 1930s.

Trade objectives are expressed in three plans: (1) an import-export plan, (2) a plan for support materials and services for Soviet projects outside the Soviet Union, and (3) a balance-of-payments plan. These plans are segregated according to region, and in the case of trade with COMECON, they are supposed to be coordinated with the general (and trade) plans of each member country. This coordination function is supported by long-range programs to promote joint planning among COMECON members—efforts to plan integration on a five-year time horizon in terms of industrial branches, projects, and joint ventures.

The foreign trade plans contain detailed plan targets. The import-export plan indicates the regional distribution of exports and imports, the tasks of each organization involved (the foreign trade and other ministries, the FTOs), and the schedule of deliveries. The balance-of-payments plan is developed by the Ministry of Foreign Trade in conjunction with the Ministry of Finance and shows both payments and receipts (on both a current and a credit basis) for various categories of goods and services distinguished by currency type—for example, by specific convertible currencies and transferable rubles. The transferable ruble (or *valuta* ruble) is used as an accounting tool and often has little relationship with internal ruble prices. In addition to the balance-of-payments plan, a capital plan is also prepared by the Ministry of Finance, *Gosplan*, and the *Vneshtorgbank*. It summarizes claims and credits on an annual basis.

The integration of the foreign trade plans and the national economic plan is incomplete in that there is no comprehensive plan that translates foreign trade flows into domestic prices. The trade plans are expressed in terms of foreign trade rubles, whose relationship to domestic prices is unclear. This separation of financial plans into those in *valuta* rubles and in domestic rubles has complicated Soviet economic planning.

Soviet foreign trade is conducted in a fundamentally different manner from a market economy. The most basic difference is that the foreign trade monopoly serves to isolate Soviet internal producers and consumers of export and import items, respectively, from direct contact with the outside world. From this basic difference stems a set of trading arrangements that are very different from those typically observed in the West. What has changed in the Gorbachev era is the extent of control exercised by the Ministry of Foreign Trade. As we shall see, this control has been relaxed.

The operative unit for carrying out the foreign trade plan is the FTO. The basic function of the FTO is to connect the internal producer or consumer with the external world. The FTO purchases authorized export items from the Soviet producer at internal ruble prices and sells them in foreign markets at agreed-upon (typically, world market) prices. Within COMECON, the sale will be transacted in transferable rubles. Likewise, an FTO will purchase authorized items in foreign markets at negotiated or world market prices, and the internal Soviet consuming firm will be charged the internal ruble price for the imported item. The financial side of these transactions is the responsibility of the various financial organs involved with foreign trade, along with the Ministry of Foreign Trade. If the imported item is sold internally at a higher price than that paid by the FTO, a surplus is created for the state budget. In the late 1970s, surplus earnings accounted for some 10 percent of state revenues.[4]

Soviet Foreign Trade Policy

Western observers have noted that the volume of Soviet foreign trade has been significantly less than one would find in market economies at similar levels of economic development.[5] This pattern is said to demonstrate a Soviet bias against trade or a "policy of trade aversion." Data on the volume of Soviet trade and trade proportions are given in Table 11.1. What factors explain Soviet bias against trade?

From the earliest days of the Soviet regime, the prevailing Marxist–Leninist ideology called for rejection of traditional Western arguments concerning the benefits to be gained from international trade—the thesis of *comparative advantage*—just as it has called for the rejection of other Western "economic laws." Western markets were viewed as subject to chaotic fluctuations that could jeopardize the planned nature of the Soviet economy. Moreover, it was argued that "socialism in one country" was possible due to the vast resources of the Soviet Union.

A second major factor explaining the Soviet policy of trade aversion was the early perception (and, in large part, reality) of a "hostile capitalist

Table 11.1 REAL VOLUME OF IMPORTS AND EXPORTS OF THE USSR (1913 = 100) AND TRADE RATIOS, 1913–1987

Year	Exports composite index	Imports composite index	Exports as percent of national income	Year	Exports composite index	Imports composite index	Exports as percent of national income
1913	100.0	100.0	10.4	1948	51.1	64.3	
1917	6.9	176.3		1949	58.2	72.4	
1918	0.5	7.7		1950	80.7	82.0	
1919	0.0	0.2		1951	94.6	101.4	
1920	0.1	2.1		1952	114.2	123.4	
1921	1.3	15.3		1953	120.0	133.1	
1922	5.4	19.6		1954	132.6	154.4	
1923	14.3	10.4		1955	142.3	149.2	3.0
1924	22.2	18.9		1956	150.7	173.8	3.0
1925	25.1	37.8		1957	179.2	186.7	3.6
1926	32.2	33.8		1958	184.2	223.8	3.1
1927	34.7	38.9		1959	242.9	264.7	3.9
1928	37.7	49.4		1960	242.6	290.1	3.7
1929	44.4	48.3	3.1	1961	265.7	299.4	3.9
1930	57.0	72.1	3.5	1962	311.8	334.6	4.3
1931	61.4	82.4	3.0	1963	321.7	364.3	4.4
1932	53.7	59.1	2.6	1964	333.9	378.9	4.4
1933	49.8	31.9	2.3	1965	371.5	401.5	4.5
1934	43.2	24.0	1.8	1966	422.9	396.3	4.6
1935	38.0	26.3	1.3	1967	453.0	423.0	5.0
1936	28.6	30.3	0.8	1968	503.4	479.5	5.9
1937	30.0	27.8	0.5	1969	558.8	514.1	6.0
1938	26.2	32.3		1970	590.8	552.9	6.3
1939	10.6	20.4		1971	608.5	586.1	6.4
1940	21.8	27.7		1972	626.3	685.6	5.7
1941	14.4	29.1		1973	714.9	785.1	6.0
1942	4.8	17.6		1974	809.3	812.8	6.5
1943	4.3	15.5		1975	833.0	962.1	6.3
1944	6.6	16.5		1976	898.0	1022.9	6.5
1945	15.5	20.0		1977	980.7	1039.5	
1946	27.2	49.4		1978	1028.0	1194.3	
1947	30.0	43.9		1980	1572.8	1528.3	
				1982	2004.6	1934.3	
				1987	2751.9	2087.6	

Sources: M. Kaser, "A Volume Index of Soviet Foreign Trade," *Soviet Studies,* vol. 20, no. 4 (April 1969), 523–526; *Vneshnaia torgovlia SSSR v 1978 g* [USSR foreign trade 1978] (Moscow: Statistika, 1979), p. 16; F. D. Holzman, "Foreign Trade," in A. Bergson and S. Kuznets, eds., *Economic Trends in the Soviet Union* (Cambridge, Mass.: Harvard University Press, 1963), p. 290; and V. G. Treml, "Foreign Trade and the Soviet Economy: Changing Parameters and Interrelationships," in E. Neuberger and L. Tyson, eds., *Transmission and Response: The Impact of International Disturbances on the Soviet Union and Eastern Europe* (New York: Pergamon Press, 1980). The indices are updated using official Soviet data on the real exports and real imports.

encirclement" which encouraged the Soviet regime to avoid reliance on foreign markets for its economic development. Events over the years have tended to bolster Soviet distrust of Western markets. In the immediate postwar era, the United States spearheaded a movement to restrict credits and the flow of "strategic" goods to the USSR. The United States has also cut off high-technology trade and, in 1980, of grain to punish the Soviets for political misdeeds.

Third, as a sector to be incorporated into an already complex planning system, foreign trade as a priority sector might significantly complicate the overall planning process—in particular, by introducing outside forces not directly controlled by Soviet planners and thus increasing the degree of plan uncertainty. One can find the tendency to avoid reliance on outsiders at all levels of the Soviet economy, and this reluctance is intensified when foreign suppliers (even ideologically compatible suppliers from COMECON) are involved. It is noteworthy that Soviet trade potential within COMECON remains "underutilized," although there have been no ideological objections to such trade.

Fourth, the Soviets stress that the capitalist countries have erected barriers against trade with the Soviet Union, beginning with the embargoes following the 1917 revolution to the present-day restrictions on lending, failure to grant tariff reductions, and controls on strategic commodities.

Fifth, it is important to note that in the early 1930s, the Great Depression was an important though uncontrollable factor influencing the terms of trade facing Soviet planners.[6] Specifically, the terms of trade turned against the Soviet Union as world market prices of Soviet exports fell more rapidly than world market prices of Soviet imports. This development must have had an impact on Soviet attitudes toward foreign trade.

Sixth, and possibly most important, the mechanisms for the conduct of Soviet foreign trade have themselves served to limit Soviet trade participation. As we will see later, it is in this area that Gorbachev has begun to implement important reforms. Before we discuss change, however, it is important to understand the nature of the system that has prevailed for so long. We turn next to a discussion of barriers to Soviet foreign trade.

Internal Barriers to Foreign Trade

We have already noted that the arrangements for conducting foreign trade and for pricing traded commodities have isolated Soviet enterprises from foreign market influences. If there is a difference between the internal ruble price and the foreign price of a particular product, this difference appears as a subsidy or as a revenue source in the state budget, with no immediate implications for the internal Soviet enterprise. This isolation of the Soviet enterprise both as a producer and as a consumer sets it apart from capitalist enterprises, which enter directly into foreign trade arrangements and can respond more readily to foreign markets. The isolation of Soviet producing enterprises makes it difficult for them to be competitive in world markets by not knowing what the changing world market requires. The Soviets' inability to compete in capitalist markets in the areas of manufactured goods and in the service fields is, in part, accounted for by this isolation.[7] The weak Western market for Soviet manufacturers has limited Soviet foreign exchange earnings over the years, which has, in turn, restricted Soviet imports from the West.[8] The Soviet Union has been unable (or unwilling) to expand its exports of petroleum products and other raw materials to offset its expanding import requirements from the West. Trade deficits vis-à-vis Western countries therefore have had to be financed with credits granted by capitalist countries.[9]

Existing trading arrangements inhibit trade in other ways. First, the Soviet ruble is an inconvertible currency, not listed on world currency markets and not accepted by (or available to) trading partners. Ruble inconvertibility, along with the Soviet system of centralized planning and price setting, means that the Soviet prices used in foreign transactions (*valuta* rubles) bear little relation either to relative scarcities in the domestic economy or to world market prices. There is, therefore, no common scale of value through which the potential advantages or disadvantages of trade can be measured. In the absence of an effective way to assess the costs and benefits of trade, bilateral agreements have to be negotiated between the Soviet Union and its trading partners, balanced usually in terms of some approximation of world market prices. The use of bilateral arrangements is almost inevitable, given Soviet internal controls over trade flows, the nature of Soviet prices, and the lack of meaning of the ruble (or any other socialist currency) in world markets.

Since the ruble is not a convertible currency, its real value in terms of other currencies (its exchange rate) is not known.[10] The exchange rate set administratively by the Soviet government tends to be arbitrary and not necessarily reflective of the relative purchasing power of the ruble. Thus, the exchange rate as a means to assess the benefits from trade is of little use in this case.

Unlike capitalist economies, where the gains from trade are obvious from comparisons of domestic and foreign prices, what goods should be traded and with what countries is not clear in the Soviet case. Internal Soviet prices themselves may not reflect domestic relative scarcities, and internal prices are difficult to compare with foreign prices due to the lack of appropriate rates of exchange. The absence of firm information on relative foreign and domestic costs and prices explains in part the depressed levels of Soviet trade. Even if there were substantial gains to specialization of production and exchange (say, trading Soviet machines for Bulgarian consumer goods) due to large differences in costs of production, this would likely not be evident to foreign trade planners. Thus, in the Soviet Union, an important pressure in favor of trade expansion is absent, namely, a clear appreciation of the fact that certain products can be obtained abroad with less sacrifice of resources than if produced domestically.

Soviet trade authorities (along with their COMECON counterparts) have sought to remedy this situation by developing criteria—Foreign Trade Efficiency Indices (FTEI)—for evaluating on a rational basis exports and imports.[11] The FTEI have been in use within COMECON since the mid-1960s and seek to provide rules for calculating the ratios of domestic to foreign costs of potential export and import items. Typically, FTEI are calculated separately for potential exports and imports. In simplified form, the *import index* is

$$X_{ie} = \frac{Z_i X_{i \cdot eq}}{V_i}$$

where

X_{ie} = the index of import effectiveness of the product
V_i = the foreign exchange cost of one unit of the product
Z_i = the domestic cost of producing one unit of the product
$X_{i \cdot eq}$ = the ratio of foreign exchange receipts from the country in question from exported goods to the domestic cost of producing these goods

The import effectiveness index is easy to understand except for $X_{i \cdot eq}$, which plays the role of a crude exchange rate. The Z values represent the internal ruble prices of imported items, and the V values represent foreign prices expressed in transfer (*valuta*) rubles. These transfer rubles are determined administratively and will vary for each of the USSR's trading partners. The problem is translating these foreign prices into domestic prices—a role played by exchange rates in capitalist countries. For this purpose, a form of opportunity cost measure is calculated for each trading partner. For this import index, this is the average domestic cost of producing goods domestically to earn the foreign exchange necessary to import the item from the particular country. It is calculated by taking the foreign exchange earnings from Soviet exports to that country and dividing by the domestic cost of producing these goods for export.

The general principle underlying FTEI formulas is that foreign trade prices should be translated into domestic prices by calculating the amount of domestic production required to earn the foreign exchange (*valuta* rubles) needed to purchase the foreign item (in the case of the FTEI, for imports). These formulas bear only a distant resemblance to the relative cost comparisons made by capitalist economies. To be an accurate index of the opportunity costs of domestic production versus foreign production, internal prices must reflect domestic relative scarcities, and the implicit exchange rates used in the indices must indicate the relative purchasing power of the foreign exchange accounting units. These conditions are not met. Moreover, the FTEI are used only as an aid for foreign trade planners. Most trading decisions are made administratively, without consulting foreign trade efficiency indices as a part of long-term agreements, and are often based on political decisions.

The second important consequence of Soviet trade arrangements is the difficulty of devising appropriate financial arrangements to handle the financing of trade imbalances. Specifically, since a nonconvertible currency cannot be used in payment for goods and services, Soviet trade with each partner must balance. If not, the Soviet Union must pay in gold or convertible Western currencies or arrange credit. In contrast, if the United States were to purchase more from

Canada than Canada buys from the United States, there would be no immediate problem, since Canada would be willing to accept U.S. dollars either for purchases in the United States or for use in other countries where dollars are readily acceptable at the established rate of exchange. Thus, the U.S. trade deficit with Canada is automatically financed, and a trade imbalance is possible. For example, if the Soviet Union were to have a trade deficit with Poland, the Soviet Union could not automatically finance the deficit by paying in rubles. Insofar as Poland cannot use rubles to freely purchase what it wants from the Soviet Union or another country, they are of no value to the Polish trade authorities. The tendency, therefore, is to balance transactions with all countries, even though a "rational" trading plan would call for surpluses or deficits vis-à-vis individual trading partners. In this manner, trade is restricted to the amount that one trading partner is willing to accept from the other in the form of barter transactions. Within COMECON, trade imbalances must be cleared by hard-currency payments, and in rare instances, credits are granted to finance deficits.

THE EXTERNAL ENVIRONMENT: THE SOCIALIST COUNTRIES

In terms of geographic distribution, the Soviet Union distinguishes between its trade with socialist countries (COMECON and others) and capitalist countries (developed and underdeveloped). The Council for Mutual Economic Assistance, COMECON, was established in 1949 on the initiative of the Soviet Union for the expressed purpose of integrating the socialist planned economies of Eastern Europe with the Soviet Union through the specialization of trade and production among member countries.[12] Trade with COMECON members has accounted for more than 50 percent of Soviet foreign trade throughout the postwar era (see Table 11.2), and the Soviet Union is in many respects the dominant partner in this organization. Although there have been some changes in the trading arrangements and cooperative agreements among COMECON

Table 11.2   SOVIET FOREIGN TRADE TURNOVER—GEOGRAPHIC DISTRIBUTION IN SELECTED POSTWAR YEARS
Percentages

	1946	1950	1953	1956	1959	1962	1965	1970	1975	1982	1987
1. Socialist countries[a]	54.5	81.1	83.2	75.7	75.3	70.2	68.8	65.2	56.3	54.3	66.9
COMECON member countries	40.6	57.4	59.3	49.6	52.0	57.5	58.0	55.6	51.7	49.1	61.7
2. Capitalist countries	45.5	18.9	16.8	24.3	24.7	29.8	31.2	34.7	43.6	45.7	33.0
Industrial	38.4	15.1	14.5	16.8	15.9	18.1	19.3	21.2	31.2	31.6	21.8
Less developed countries (LDCs)	7.1	3.8	2.3	7.5	8.8	11.7	11.9	13.5	12.4	14.1	11.2

[a] Includes China, Cuba, Vietnam, North Korea, and Yugoslavia.

Sources: Compiled from official Soviet foreign trade handbooks, in particular, from annual editions of Vneshnaia torgovlia SSSR [Foreign trade of the USSR] and Statisticheski ezhegodnik Stran-chlenov S.E.V. [Statistical yearbook of the member countries of S.E.V.]; Goskomstat, Narodnoe khoziaistvo SSSR v 1987 g [The national economy of the USSR in 1987] (Moscow: Finansy i Statistika, 1988), pp. 610-611.

countries since the 1960s, only a relatively limited degree of integration among these countries has been achieved, for a number of basic reasons.[13]

First, in spite of Soviet economic and political pressure for integration, the countries of Eastern Europe have focused on developing their own diversified industrial economies, including an adequate base of heavy industry.[14] During the postwar era, the COMECON countries have not been content to specialize in specific product lines as desired by the USSR, for they have viewed this as a loss of national economic independence. This stance is buttressed by the fact that COMECON possesses no supranational authority over its members. Each member has veto power, and various Soviet efforts to give COMECON supranational powers have been successfully opposed by other members.

Second, although some coordination has been developed, there has been less effective development of integrated planning arrangements, and only preliminary steps have been taken to develop common yardsticks (such as common costs and prices, and a convertible COMECON trading currency) to direct specialization and to achieve a more optimal pattern of bloc trade.[15] The most important efforts to date to promote COMECON integration are the Comprehensive Program of 1971, the Agreed Plan for Multilateral Integration Measures of 1975, and the Long-Term Special-Purpose Program for Cooperation signed in 1979. These cooperation programs are a series of bilateral agreements for bilateral economic and scientific cooperation and for joint economic planning among individual COMECON members. The agreement signed in 1979 called for cooperative programs to be implemented through 1990. The cooperative agreements of the 1970s and 1980s have focused on the development of Soviet energy and raw materials using Eastern European labor and capital.

Since the economic mechanisms and pricing arrangements are similar among the bloc countries (with the exception of Hungary, where major reforms have been undertaken), the USSR's COMECON trading partners conduct trade much like the Soviet Union does. Intrabloc trade is conducted largely on a bilateral basis, with five-year and one-year planning horizons. To facilitate multilateral clearing, the Bank for International Cooperation (IBEC) was created in 1964. However, most intra-COMECON trade is conducted in transferable rubles, a nonconvertible currency used basically in bilateral arrangements. Trade in hard currencies is small, and multilateral clearing is miniscule, perhaps 5 percent of the total.[16] Where there is a bilateral deficit, it is normally settled by adjusting future plan targets or by the shipment of "soft goods" (goods that are relatively unattractive because they are overpriced in COMECON relative to world market prices). Preference would be for "hard goods" that would have a market in the West, but hard goods are typically not offered to correct imbalances.

As with Soviet trade, the trade of bloc members is determined by their national planning agencies and with little or no cost-benefit frame of reference. The pricing of traded commodities in intrabloc trade has been complicated by the absence of a set of internal prices (say, USSR ruble prices) suitable for valuing transactions among member countries. As a general rule, the pricing principle for intrabloc trade has been to determine what the commodity would have cost in the world market. Such calculations are not easy to make in the case of machinery and equipment not sold in the West, since authorities can only guess at the price the commodity would command in world markets. This ambiguity has led to controversy between the Soviet Union and its COMECON partners over whether the terms of trade are "fair" and to claims that the USSR pays too little for manufactured imports from other COMECON countries. For example, Michael Marrese and Jan Vañous claimed that the USSR at times has deliberately subsidized Eastern Europe by selling Soviet raw materials at low prices to gain political leverage. On the other hand, Josef Brada finds that Soviet export pricing to Eastern Europe has been the natural result of relative resource endowments.[17] Most recently, Franklyn Holzman, a long-time analyst of Soviet foreign trade, has suggested that Soviet transfers to Eastern Europe may be explained by the fact that "...CMEA has many of the characteristics of a highly autarkic customs union."[18]

Prior to 1975, COMECON prices were fixed over the life of long-term national plans. According to the pricing formula agreed upon in Bucharest in 1958, the world market prices of 1957 were applied to intrabloc transactions until 1965. For the planning period 1966–1970, average 1961–1965 world market prices were used, and then average world prices of 1966–1970 were used for the period 1971–1975.[19] The explosion of energy and other raw material prices in the 1970s caused the USSR to change this pricing formula, as the Soviet Union remains the dominant supplier of energy to Eastern Europe. COMECON adopted in 1975 a new "sliding pricing formula," whereby average world market prices of the preceding five years are used. Thus, rising energy prices can be passed on to COMECON partners gradually over time. Also, provision was made to pay for Soviet energy deliveries above targeted levels in hard currencies at prevailing world market prices. These changes led to a substantial improvement in the USSR's terms of trade with Eastern Europe during the energy crisis of the 1970s.

In spite of attempts at reform of institutional arrangements, the basic problems of integrating the COMECON countries remain. It has proved especially difficult to integrate the industrialized members (the USSR, East Germany, and Czechoslovakia) with the less industrialized countries (Bulgaria and Rumania), due to the unwillingness of the latter to specialize in low-technology products and agriculture. Disputes among these countries have arisen, and with East European products finding a growing market in the West and with increasing hard-currency credits, imports of more advanced technology from the West (rather than from the Soviet Union) have become increasingly attractive. It is from this basic pattern that the problem of an expanding COMECON hard-currency debt has arisen, an issue we examine below.

As we have noted in Table 11.2, Soviet trade with socialist countries has grown significantly as a portion of total Soviet foreign trade. This trend in part derives from the inability of Eastern European countries to gain export markets in the West in the 1970s, a decade of difficult economic times for the Western capitalist systems. It derives from the dominance in Soviet–East European trade of certain commodities such as oil. Doubtless also it has been influenced by the continuing desire of the Soviet Union for closer integration of the Soviet and East European systems. This integration, however, has proven to be a difficult process under the Gorbachev regime. We will examine this theme in greater detail when we look at contemporary Soviet foreign trade policies.

SOVIET TRADE WITH CAPITALIST COUNTRIES

Soviet trade with capitalist countries has increased significantly during the years since World War II. If one excludes the atypical immediate postwar period, Soviet trade with capitalist countries as a share of total Soviet foreign trade has increased from roughly 19 percent in 1950 to 33 percent in 1988 (see Table 11.2). It is interesting to note that for several decades there was a tendency for the share of Soviet foreign trade with socialist countries to decline, and the share with capitalist countries to increase. This trend came to an end in the early 1980s. In fact, according to official Soviet sources, the share of Soviet trade with capitalist countries peaked in 1982 at 45 percent, declining thereafter to 33 percent in 1986.[20]

To examine Soviet trade with capitalist countries, it is useful to divide the latter into two broad groups, specifically the less-developed capitalist countries and the industrialized West (including North America, Western Europe, and Japan).

Soviet trade with LDCs has expanded from the very low levels of the 1950s, although in recent years there have not been significant changes, and has varied from 11 to 14 percent in recent years with a decline to around 11 percent in the 1980s. Asia is the dominant region, with India serving as the dominant partner in the region. Of secondary importance is Africa, with Latin America third. While Middle Eastern countries have been important (the Soviet Union imports oil from OPEC for reexport), Argentina has been an important Latin American trading partner primarily for the importation of agricultural products.

The commodity composition of Soviet trade with LDCs is of no great surprise. The Soviet Union exports primarily machinery and fuels, while primary products and food products are the important imports.

As we have already noted, Soviet trade with the industrialized capitalist countries grew relatively over a long number of years, after which, in the 1980s, it declined to a point some 10 percentage points below the peak of the early 1980s. This trend is in part explained by a slackening of world oil prices and thus a shrinking of Soviet hard-currency earnings. It is also explained by Soviet caution on hard-currency debt and a lack of willingness of the Soviet Union to become heavily dependent on Western capitalist countries for technology imports.

By the mid-1980s, the Soviet Union had a trade volume in hard currency (imports plus exports) of roughly $50 billion.[21] The bulk (three-quarters) of this hard-currency trade was with developed countries. The most important of these trading partners were West Germany, France, Italy, and Japan.

The commodity composition of Soviet trade with the industrialized capitalist countries presents no surprises. In the 1980s, Soviet hard-currency exports have been dominated by oil and oil-related products, natural gas, and military hardware (the last a major hard-currency export to OPEC nations). Of lesser magnitude have been machinery and equipment and chemicals. On the import side, agricultural products have accounted for roughly one-third of hard-currency imports, with machinery and equipment, chemicals, metals, and fuels accounting for the remainder. Soviet trade with Western industrialized countries has focused on growing Soviet demand for industrial technology and grain and a Soviet drive to expand exports to pay for these imports. It is in this context that the burden of Soviet hard-currency debt must be considered.

Soviet Foreign Debt

The growth of Soviet imports from the industrialized West has been concentrated in two broad areas—industrial goods and services designed to support the technological needs of the Soviet economy, and agricultural goods (largely grain and fertilizer) to offset serious harvest reverses and to stimulate agricultural productivity. Although Soviet hard-currency imports grew sharply in the 1970s, the dollar volume of these imports peaked in the early 1980s and declined through the mid-1980s. With a leveling and thereafter a shrinkage of hard-currency exports through the mid-1980s, the Soviet gross debt (that is, outstanding debt denominated in hard currency but not including Soviet hard-currency assets in Western banks) has grown significantly. Recent estimates suggest a gross debt of $11.5 billion in 1975, increasing to roughly $22 billion in the early 1980s and to $38 billion by the mid-1980s.[22] Should debt of this magnitude be an issue of concern?

The burden of Soviet hard-currency debt can be measured in different ways. A common measure of debt burden is to look at debt service ratio: the ratio of hard-currency debt payments (interest and principal payments) to total hard-currency earnings. Judged by this indicator, the Soviet hard-currency debt position is not of major concern. The pattern of the debt service ratio is of interest, however. From a low of just over 10 percent in the mid-1970s, the Soviet debt service ratio grew sharply through 1978, declining thereafter only to rise again in the 1980s. By the mid-1980s, the ratio stood at roughly 23 percent.

A second measure of debt burden is the ratio of gross hard-currency debt to hard-currency earnings. This ratio was 73 percent in 1980 and 115 percent in 1985.[23] The increase in Soviet hard-currency debt in the mid-1980s was the result of a slackening of hard-currency export earnings (in part the result of weak oil prices) and a resulting expansion of Soviet borrowing, largely through commercial debt.

In part, Soviet hard-currency debt has been kept within modest proportions (for example, when compared to hard-currency debt in Eastern Europe) through the sale of gold. However, in an era when further restriction of the growth of hard-currency imports may inhibit economic reforms, Soviet trade policy must aim for greater penetration of Western hard-currency markets. This effort has a number of dimensions.

First, even before Gorbachev's reform program, there was a long-standing effort to improve both the political and the economic bases of trade with Western countries such as the United States. The most significant breakthroughs came in commercial relations with Western Europe and Japan, in which the USSR gained tariff reductions and had relatively easy access to private and government credit. United States legislation on trade with the Soviet Union has remained restrictive, focusing especially on limiting sales of "strategic" goods, restricting governmental credits, and failing to grant general trade concessions. The 1960s and 1970s were a period of considerable discussion on trade matters between the Soviet Union and the United States, culminating in the negotiation of the U.S.-USSR Trade Agreement in 1972. This agreement, which was to grant most-favored nation (MFN) status, was annulled in 1975 by the Soviets when it was linked with the question of Jewish emigration. The question of granting MFN status remains up in the air, a matter of substantial emotional and political (though possibly dubious economic) importance to the Soviet side, especially when China was granted MFN in January 1980. The Soviets have argued that not being granted MFN has made their manufactured products less competitive in U.S. markets, but there is some controversy about the future effect of granting MFN on USSR exports to the United States.[24] In the mid-1980s, the U.S.-Soviet agreement on commercial relations was renewed and the volume of U.S.-Soviet trade increased. Although little progress has been made on the issue of granting MFN status, the Soviet Union has shown continuing interest in joining GATT—the multinational organization under which multilateral trade negotiations are conducted.

Second, the Soviet Union has been more aggressive in devising innovative arrangements for increasing imports from the West without an immediate increase in exports. For example, compensation agreements between the Soviet Union and Western firms that give foreign firms a share of output have increased in recent years. Compensation agreements were almost nonexistent in the 1960s but grew thereafter, involving Western Europe, Japan, and the United States.

Compensation agreements have been important insofar as Soviet law has not permitted private ownership, thus denying the Soviet Union the advantages of direct foreign investment. While the compensation agreement has been a substitute, we shall see that recent reforms, especially in the area of joint ventures, may lead to important changes with regard to direct foreign investment in the Soviet Union.

Another device for trade expansion has been direct investment by the Soviet Union in the West.[25] This phenomenon, which grew significantly in the 1970s, has been diversified geographically and by type of economic activity, varying from production (on a limited basis) through trade and service organizations to banking. However, with these organizations typically wholly owned, controlled, and managed by the Soviet Union, Western nations express the usual concern that one might connect with a multinational enterprise, adding the participation of a foreign and sometimes antagonistic government.

The future of Soviet trade with the Western industrialized nations and especially with the United States will hinge upon the fruitful development of these new strategies as well as the overall improvement of East-West relations. United States–Soviet trade has remained miniscule throughout the 1980s and remains a grossly underutilized commercial market. A new U.S.-Soviet trade agreement was under discussion in 1989.

Soviet Aid to LDCs

Assessing Soviet foreign aid is a difficult task for a number of reasons. First, beyond such categories as general development assistance, it is not always possible to define the content of aid with precision. For example, a considerable portion of Soviet aid to Cuba is in the form of subsidies on the purchase of sugar. Sugar subsidies are an indirect (and hidden) form of aid. Second, the valuation of Soviet aid in a common currency such as the U.S. dollar is difficult. Beyond the basic issue of valuing deliveries of, say, equipment, the issue of valuing subsidies remains complex. Third, aid agreements and actual aid disbursements can differ significantly over time. Finally and possibly most important in the present context, it is important to examine Soviet aid programs as they are concentrated on different recipient groups, specifically Communist and non-Communist countries. Motives, arrangements, and magnitudes differ significantly.

While assessing Soviet motives for economic interaction with socialist countries, it is useful to isolate the less developed from the more developed countries. In a recent study of Soviet aid to Communist countries, Fogarty and Tritle emphasize that "Moscow's economic program in the Communist developing countries (Cuba, Vietnam, Mongolia, North Korea, Laos, and Cambodia) differs dramatically in both content and implication from the penetration effort in non-Communist LDCs."[26] Specifically, the authors emphasize the need for the Soviet Union to reinforce political institutions and the fact that aid to Cuba, Mongolia, and Vietnam is arranged through full membership in COMECON, a status not shared by the other countries. Soviet aid to non-Communist LDCs has typically been quite concentrated, has often involved on-site implementation by Soviet personnel, and has focused on economic benefits sometimes through projects rejected by Western countries. To the extent that obvious political gains are not achieved by this type of aid (that is, the recipients are not in any sense socialist systems), the issue of economic gains has become increasingly important in the Gorbachev era as the focus on domestic growth becomes paramount.

The basic statistics on Soviet aid reinforce the above observations. According to recent estimates, Soviet economic aid to non-Communist LDCs between the years 1954 and 1987 amounted to just over $40 billion.[27] This compares to a figure of $157 billion for U.S. loans and credits to LDCs for a similar but slightly longer period (1946–1987). In the mid-1980s, U.S. aid averaged approximately $11 billion per annum, while Soviet aid to LDCs averaged approximately $3 billion per annum. The contrast between Soviet aid to LDCs and to Communist countries is striking.

For the period 1954–1987, Soviet aid to Communist countries amounted to just under $144 billion. On an annual basis, this aid package has fluctuated from a high (in the 1980s) of just over $20 billion in 1981 to a low of just over $8 billion in 1985.

The concentration of Soviet aid is striking. For example, of the $40 billion extended to LDCs over the period 1954–1987, fully 50 percent of the total can be accounted for by the five top recipients— India, Afghanistan, Turkey, Iraq, and Morocco — in order of amount of aid extended. The same pattern can be observed for aid to Communist countries. Of the roughly $144 billion in Soviet aid extended to Communist countries over the period 1954–1986, over 90 percent was extended to Eastern Europe and Cuba. In fact, one-third of Soviet aid to Communist countries has been aid to Cuba. Soviet aid to Cuba has averaged just over $5 billion annually in the 1980s, and has consisted of two major components: development aid and trade subsidies. Development aid accounts for roughly 26 percent of total Soviet aid to Cuba, while trade subsidies account for the remaining 74 percent of the total. Almost 80 percent of Soviet subsidies to Cuba can be accounted for by a single product— sugar.

Finally, military equipment is a major item to be considered in Soviet relations with LDCs. For the period 1980–1987, Soviet arms deliveries to LDCs (including Cuba) amounted to approximately $125 billion, or an average annual rate of $18 billion. United States military deliveries for the same period amounted to approximately $84 billion, or an annual rate of roughly $12 billion.

Soviet aid is striking in terms of its distribution and its magnitude. In assessing this aid, and especially when comparing it to U.S. aid, it is interesting to bear in mind that in the 1980s, the Soviet Union was supporting a very large aid system, heavily concentrated in Communist countries, from an economy whose per capita GNP was substantially lower than that of the United States.

Soviet Trade and Soviet Development

Trade can be a major contributor to economic growth and economic development. Indeed, in recent years, Gorbachev has begun major modifications of the Soviet foreign trade system designed to enhance trade's contribution to Soviet economic performance. We turn to an examination of trade in Soviet economic development, especially to the issue of what the Soviet Union has traded in the past and how it expects the commodity composition of trade to change in the future.

Western trade theory suggests that with varying resource availabilities in different countries, specialization of production and exchange with other countries can promote economic development. According to such theorizing, during the early stages of modernization, an LDC should export those goods and services in which it has a comparative advantage, and it should utilize export earnings to finance imports of goods needed for industrialization that would be produced at high relative cost domestically. As the economy grows more sophisticated over a long period of time, it will be able to substitute domestic production for imports and lessen its dependence on trade.

The role of trade in Soviet economic development was discussed seriously in the Industrialization Debate of the 1920s, with the right wing of the party emphasizing the comparative cost advantages of international trade. The trade strategy eventually adopted by Stalin during the 1930s rejected traditional comparative advantage principles and called for a policy of isolation from the outside world. It was argued that socialism could be "built in one country," without reliance on the capitalist world, and the Soviet Union's use of trade during the 1930s represents a case study of an industrialization with only minimal reliance on other economies.

A hallmark of Soviet economic development over the years has been the emphasis on self-sufficiency as a desirable economic goal. Self-sufficiency was most prominent during the 1930s, when trade proportions were negligible, but the policy of trade aversion continued into the postwar era. Soviet reasoning in support of self-sufficiency has already been described (capitalist encirclement, planning uncertainty, etc.), and the Soviet leadership's vision of capitalist world markets as chaotic underscored the theoretical legitimacy of trade aversion.

Possibly more important than such theoretical considerations was the Soviet development strategy of treating agriculture as a low-priority sector throughout the 1930s. Thus, the very nature of Soviet development strategy prohibited extensive reliance on foreign trade. As Bukharin has argued, a prosperous peasantry was the key to expanding trade; once the collectivization decision was made, the Soviet Union's role as a major supplier of grain and animal products to the world market was effectively terminated. Moreover, the Soviet economy of the 1930s had certain basic features that could support a minimal role for the foreign sector. With a favorable and varied resource base, a political mechanism to enforce high internal saving rates, and a reasonable scale for heavy industrial development, substantial reliance on foreign products and capital could be avoided. In particular, the existence of a state monopoly in foreign trade enabled the Soviet authorities to avoid noncritical imports (a pressing problem for many present-day LDCs) and to focus on those imports most crucial for economic growth—in particular, machinery and equipment and associated technology. Strict controls over exports and imports allowed the promotion of specific industrialization goals with relatively low foreign trade volumes.

Soviet trade patterns prior to 1917 were, as Franklyn Holzman has pointed out, "what one would have expected from such a nation." Exports were primarily agricultural products or semifabricates, while imports were mostly producer goods and raw materials. In 1913, for example, 60 percent of Russian exports were agricultural, 34 percent were raw materials and semifabricates, while 27 percent of imports were consumer goods, the remainder being raw materials and producer goods.[28]

Although trade was important in the period prior to 1900—for example, between 1886 and 1890, 46 percent of Russian wheat production was exported—this importance declined immediately prior to the revolution, due in large part to the onset of World War I. In addition, what had previously been a favorable balance-of-payments position—commodity exports typically exceeding commodity imports offset by capital inflows—was sharply reversed by 1917. The portion of grain output exported during World War I declined sharply, as did the foreign exchange earnings on this grain, largely due to growing competition in the world grain market.[29] In addition, while imports initially declined, by 1917 they were once again increasing, thus leading to an unfavorable Russian trade position and the expansion of Russian debts abroad.

From the relatively low levels of the immediate prerevolutionary period, the volume of Soviet foreign trade increased quite significantly between 1917 and 1928. However, the prerevolutionary trade level was not regained by 1928; trade volume that year was well below 50 percent of the 1913 level (Table 11.1). The instigation of the industrialization drive in that year significantly altered Soviet thinking on appropriate trade patterns and levels.

During the first three years of the first Five Year Plan (1928–1933), the volume of both Soviet exports and imports increased significantly. Thus, the volume of exports (1913 = 100) increased from 38 in 1928 to a high of 61 in 1931 while the volume of imports increased at a more rapid rate from 49 in 1928 to a high of 82 in 1931, declining thereafter (Table 11.1). The expansion of imports was directed almost exclusively to meeting the needs of heavy industry. In 1932, 66 percent of machine tools, 55 percent of metal cutting tools, and 77 percent of turbines and generators were imported.[30] Equipment was imported for two purposes: to generate electricity and to build other machines. In light of this significant expansion of foreign trade during the first Five Year Plan, it may well be that Soviet planners did not, in fact, initially plan to pursue a deliberate policy of autarky; rather, later economic events forced them into that course. The volume of Soviet foreign trade declined very sharply after the conclusion of the first Five Year Plan, but this trend was in some part the result of a collapse in world markets (especially grain prices) brought on by the world depression of the 1930s.[31]

After the onset of the depression, the prices of Soviet exports and imports declined significantly, though the rate of decline of the former greatly outstripped that of the latter. The index of the prices of Soviet exports fell from 100 in 1929 to 49 in 1931, while the prices of Soviet imports declined from 100 in 1929 to 68 in 1931. The result of these price changes was a substantial decline in the Soviet commodity terms of trade.[32]

Although the significant increase in the volume of trade during the first Five Year Plan must be considered important to the initial industrialization effort, the decline in the terms of trade must have been an important factor—in addition to ideological and strategy considerations—in leading the Soviet economy toward a different role for the foreign sector. After the first Five Year Plan, the volume of Soviet foreign trade declined sharply and steadily, increasing again only after World War II. For example, the share of exports in national income declined from 10.4 percent in 1913 to 0.5 percent in 1937.[33] Thus, at the peak of the forced industrialization drive of the late 1930s, the Soviets were operating a virtually autarkic economy. It was not until the early 1950s that the volume of trade turnover exceeded that of 1913, despite the fact that national income had been expanding at a rapid rate since 1928. Thus, the Soviet Union represents a case study of a country that was able to generate rapid growth of output and substantial shifts in the structure of output in the direction of heavy industry with only modest levels of industrial imports. Since the 1950s, there has been a significant growth in the importance of foreign trade in the Soviet economy. If autarky was an appropriate characterization for early Soviet attitudes toward trade, at most, trade aversion might describe trade policies of the Khrushchev-Brezhnev era. But, it is clear that in recent years the role of foreign trade in the Soviet economy has been reappraised by Soviet leaders. In part, as we shall see, this reappraisal has focused on changing the arrangement of foreign trade such that the trading posture of the Soviet Union more closely resembles that of a modern industrialized economy. Before looking at contemporary changes, we turn to an examination of the commodity composition of Soviet foreign trade.

THE COMMODITY COMPOSITION OF SOVIET FOREIGN TRADE

Over the years, the composition of Soviet trade has changed with the evolving requirements of the domestic economy. In 1913, imports were concentrated in three areas: raw materials (for the textiles industry), 22 percent; consumer goods, 21 percent; and machinery and equipment, 16 percent. On the export side, raw materials, grain, and animal products accounted for virtually all of Russian exports. In 1928, on the eve of the Five Year Plan era, the structure of exports and imports was much like that of the late tsarist era.[34]

The forced industrialization program of the 1930s brought about significant shifts in the structure of Soviet trade. On the import side, there was a distinct movement away from importing consumer goods and toward importing producer goods. Producer goods and consumption goods accounted respectively for 27 and 7 percent of aggregate Soviet imports in 1918; by 1931, the figures were 95 and 5 percent for production and consumption goods, respectively.[35] Also notable during the early years of Soviet industrialization was the increasing importance of imports of machinery and equipment. From a level of 16 percent of imports in 1913, machinery and equipment imports grew to account for 55 percent of imports in 1932.[36] This pattern changed significantly after the first Five Year Plan, basically through the development of domestic capacity in key industrial sectors. Nevertheless, if we look at the portion of Soviet utilization of key industrial commodities (those of crucial importance to the industrialization effort) accounted for by imports, the result is striking and suggests that foreign technology may have been a very important element in the industrial-ization process.[37] In 1930, for example, 89 percent of the aggregate Soviet con-sumption of turbines, boilers, and generators came from imports. In 1932, 66 percent of the machine tools used in the Soviet Union were imported.

Export patterns did not change radically during the early years of Soviet in-dustrialization. Fuels, raw materials, and consumer goods remained important as a portion of aggregate export volume. Exports of grain, which had virtually disappeared by 1928, increased significantly during the first Five Year Plan but fluctuated significantly thereafter, depending on the harvest. It is significant that grain exports were never again to regain the import role they played throughout the tsarist era.

Since the 1950s, there have been important shifts in Soviet commodity trade patterns on both the import and the export sides (Tables 11.3 and 11.4). These shifts have been a focus of concern by Soviet policymakers in the 1970s and 1980s and form one of the more important arguments in support of upgrad-ing the trade mechanism, a matter that we examined earlier in this chapter.

On the import side, there have been increases in the relative importance of machinery and equipment and of food-related items since the 1950s. In 1986, 41 percent of Soviet imports were for machinery. Since 1977, the Soviets have re-duced the detail of published trade data, so it is difficult to calculate the per-centage share of agricultural imports. We would guess that they represent nearly 20 percent of the total. Imported grains in the early 1980s accounted for about one-quarter of Soviet grain utilization.[38] On the export side, fuels have grown to a dominant position, along with the traditionally important exports of raw materials. In 1986, the two accounted for almost 60 percent of Soviet ex-ports. The aggregate data, however, hide the important underlying issue of geo-graphic distribution. In the hard-currency markets, fuels and raw materials are dominant, with machinery and equipment (exported mainly to Eastern Europe and the LDCs) playing only a very small role. Unless the Soviet Union can con-tinue to expand fuel and raw materials sales in hard-currency markets, trade di-versification in the direction of manufactures will be essential in the late 1980s and beyond.[39]

Finally, the development of Soviet foreign trade since World War II has been distinctive on several fronts, all of which deserve closer attention. The volume of trade has grown significantly—more rapidly than the economy. Thus, in 1950, exports and imports accounted for 2.1 and 2.9 percent, respectively, of GNP. By 1977, these shares had grown to 6.7 and 9.2 percent.[40] The rapid growth of trade volume has caused Vladmir Treml[41] to argue that the USSR has aban-doned at long last its policy of trade aversion. Does the Soviet Union still "un-derutilize" its trade potential, as it obviously did from the 1930s to the early 1970s? This question remains unresolved at this time because of the difficulty of translating foreign trade prices into domestic prices. What is clear is that the 1970s witnessed a dramatic increase in foreign trade volume, starting from ex-tremely depressed rates in the immediate postwar period. In 1960, for example, Soviet trade volume (imports plus exports valued in U.S. dollars at the official exchange rate) amounted to just over $11 billion.[42] By 1987, this volume

Table 11.3   THE COMMODITY COMPOSITION OF SOVIET EXPORTS
Percentages of Total Exports

	1950	1955	1960	1965	1970	1975	1977	1982	1986
Machinery	11.8	17.5	20.5	20.0	21.3	18.5	18.7	12.9	15.0
Fuels and energy	3.9	9.6	16.2	17.2	15.6	31.4	35.0	52.1	47.3
Metals, ores, minerals	12.3	18.6	21.6	23.2	21.5	17.0	13.1	5.5	8.4
Chemicals, fertilizer, rubber	4.0	2.7	2.9	2.8	3.5	3.5	2.8	2.5	3.5
Construction products	0.2	0.5	0.3	0.5	0.6	0.6	0.5	.1	—
Forest products, paper	3.0	5.0	5.5	7.2	6.5	5.7	5.0	2.4	3.4
Fibers	11.2	10.1	6.4	5.1	3.4	3.0	3.2	2.8	1.4
Agricultural raw materials	3.8	1.9	2.0	1.3	1.0	0.5	0.5	1.7	
Grain and oilseed	12.9	8.6	8.6	3.4	3.3	1.6	1.1		
Sugar	0.9	0.7	0.5	0.6	0.8	0.07	0.05		
Other foodstuffs	3.3	2.5	3.8	4.3	4.1	2.0	1.4		
Cloth, clothing, shoes	2.2	1.5	1.2	0.8	0.7	0.5	0.4	22.0	21.0
Small consumer durables	0.2	0.2	0.8	0.7	0.9	1.1	0.9		
Other consumer manufacturing	2.4	1.4	0.8	0.8	1.1	1.5	1.4		
Unclassified	27.7	19.0	8.8	11.8	15.5	12.9	15.7		

Sources: Computed from M. R. Dohan, "Export Specialization and Import Dependence in the Soviet Economy, 1970–77," in U.S. Congress, Joint Economic Committee, *Soviet Economy in a Time of Change* (Washington, D.C.: U.S. Government Printing Office, 1979), vol. 2, pp. 370–371; *Vneshnaia torgovlia SSSR v 1982 g* [Foreign trade of the USSR in 1982], p. 19; and Goskomstat, *Narodnoe khoziaistvc SSSR za 70 let* [The national economy of the USSR over 70 years] (Moscow: Finansy Statistika, 1987), p. 647.

Table 11.4   THE COMMODITY COMPOSITION OF SOVIET IMPORTS
Percentages of Total Imports

	1950	1955	1960	1965	1970	1975	1977	1982	1986
Machinery	21.5	30.2	29.7	33.4	35.1	33.2	37.5	34.4	40.7
Fuels and energy	11.5	8.1	4.2	2.5	2.0	3.9	3.6	4.6	4.6
Metals, ores, minerals	15.1	16.6	17.0	10.0	10.7	12.5	10.2	9.9	8.3
Chemicals, fertilizer, rubber	6.9	3.4	6.0	6.2	5.7	4.7	4.4	4.4	5.1
Construction products	1.4	0.6	0.8	0.7	0.4	0.3	0.4	n.a.	n.a.
Forest products, paper	3.9	3.0	1.8	1.9	2.2	2.1	1.8	1.5	1.3
Fibers	7.8	5.4	6.4	4.4	4.8	2.4	2.7	1.5	1.3
Agricultural raw materials	0.4	2.2	2.2	1.0	2.0	1.4	1.7	1.6	
Grain and oilseed	1.0	0.8	1.0	5.0	1.1	7.4	3.4		
Sugar	3.1	2.8	2.3	3.8	3.4	5.9	6.1		
Other foodstuffs	11.9	16.3	9.7	12.0	11.1	9.1	10.2		
Cloth, clothing, shoes	5.6	3.8	13.8	9.3	12.3	8.9	8.6	43.6	39.0
Small consumer durables	0.07	0.2	0.5	0.2	0.3	0.1	1.4		
Other consumer manufacturing	1.7	0.8	3.0	4.7	5.7	3.9	4.2		
Unclassified	6.5	5.5	1.5	5.0	3.0	4.0	5.0		

Sources: Computed from M. R. Dohan, "Export Specialization and Import Dependence in the Soviet Economy, 1970–77," in U.S. Congress, Joint Economic Committee, *Soviet Economy in a Time of Change* (Washington, D.C.: U.S. Government Printing Office, 1979), vol 2, pp. 370–371; *Vneshnaia torgovlia SSSR v 1982 g* [Foreign trade of the USSR in 1982], p. 18; and Goskomstat. *Narodnoe khoziaistvo SSSR za 70 let* [The national economy of the USSR over 70 years] (Moscow Finansy i Statistika, 1987), p. 647

reached just under $204 billion . For the United States, the comparable shift is from a trade volume of 37 billion in 1960 to just over 674 billion. However, in 1987, as measured above, Soviet foreign trade turnover represented approximately 8 percent of GNP, the comparable figure for the United States being approximately 15 percent.

SOVIET FOREIGN TRADE REFORM IN THE 1990s

Understanding the Soviet foreign trade mechanism and its impact on the Soviet economy is a difficult task. In addition to the serious problems of measurement, the workings of the Soviet foreign trade bureaucracy have not been open to the external observer. While the state has used the foreign trade monopoly to serve the immediate interests of economic development, the evidence suggests that in the aggregate, foreign trade has been underutilized. Moreover, this underutilization has been the result of observable factors, specifically the organizational arrangements of the Soviet foreign trade system, the policies pursued, and in some cases, forces external to the Soviet economy. The result in contemporary times is a foreign trade structure and outcome not well suited to the objectives of perestroika, let alone *uskorenie*, the acceleration of Soviet economic growth. In fact, Soviet trade patterns in some respects seem closer to those of a less-developed nation than those of an advanced industrial and military power. Although changing this system in significant ways will be a very difficult task, the 1980s have been an important decade in which significant beginnings have been introduced.

In the 1980s, new Soviet decrees were initiated to make major changes in two important areas. First, the power of the Ministry of Foreign Trade is being substantially reduced and dispersed among other organizations. Second, important new regulations have been introduced to govern joint ventures in the Soviet Union. Both issues deserve additional attention.

Although the restructuring of the Soviet foreign trade mechanism has been on the front burner since the mid-1980s, it is important to realize that earlier efforts, beginning in the 1970s, were made to increase the Soviet Union's competitiveness in export markets. For example, organizational changes were introduced to streamline the operation of FTOs, and Soviet authorities took steps to expand on-site Soviet operations in foreign markets.

The first important change of the mid-1980s was introduced in late 1986 to take effect in 1987.[43] Under a major decree, a significant number of ministries, state committees, and other organizations were granted the right to conduct foreign trade directly with foreign partners rather than through the Ministry of Foreign Trade. In fact, in a subsequent decree announced in late 1988, this right of direct entry into foreign trade was extended to all Soviet enterprises and organizations, to take effect in early 1989. Although the precise outcome of this relaxation is not clear, it does appear that there will still be close monitoring of foreign trade arrangements through a variety of channels and organizations, including the newly formed State Foreign Economic Commission. Moreover, the relationship between an organization engaging in foreign trade and, let us say, a domestic producer of an export product, is to be based on a contractual agreement with incentive arrangements designed to expand exports. In addition, heads of ministries who are operating in foreign markets will form the State Foreign Economic Commission, designed as a body to oversee foreign trade, along with the Ministry of Foreign Trade and other related organizations.

These changes are potentially significant in that they address aspects of the Soviet foreign trade system long criticized by Western observers. In addition to expanded incentives (for example, access to foreign currency by an exporting firm), the connection between a Soviet producing firm and a potential foreign user of the Soviet product may now be shorter and simpler than in the past.

A second major innovation has been decrees (effective in January 1987) to permit foreign firms to establish joint ventures in the Soviet Union. These decrees initially limited foreign ownership to 49 percent, but even this restriction was subsequently relaxed. Indeed, subsequent legislation has removed or relaxed a number of potential obstacles such as facilitating access by a joint venture to domestic supplies and labor. Western firms have been cautious, doubtless in part due to the difficulties experienced by Western firms attempting to penetrate Soviet markets in the 1970s. Clearly the Soviet joint venture legislation envisages specific and significant gains for the Soviet Union, not only in specified areas such as agricultural processing and distribution equipment, but also in the more general spheres of technology and managerial expertise.

Although Western firms have proven to be innovative in their dealings with the Soviet bureaucracy, the joint ventures do present special problems. For example, profit repatriation must come from exports, a potentially troublesome feature of the legislation. The new joint venture legislation is, however, a dramatic departure from Soviet practice in the immediate past. A number of Western firms in a variety of areas have either entered into agreements or have begun discussions on establishing joint ventures.

Beyond the specific initiatives noted above, the evidence of the 1980s would suggest that the Soviet Union envisages a new Soviet role in the world economy. Although the precise shape of this role remains to be seen, the Soviet Union has in the 1980s been increasingly aggressive in the world economy. As we have already noted, the Soviet Union has expressed interest in joining the General Agreement on Tariffs and Trade (GATT). Moreover, the Soviet Union has engaged in aggressive borrowing in Western credit markets in the 1980s, in part due to the desire to use foreign trade to stimulate the domestic economy at a time when export conditions, for example, oil prices, have been less than favorable to Soviet interests.

Do these changes signal dramatic departures for the Soviet posture in world markets? Do the Soviets envision a convertible ruble in the future? The Soviet Union has taken initial steps toward changing the historically artificial exchange rate between the ruble and Western currencies.[44] Recently, it was announced that effective in January 1990, the ruble will be devalued (specifically the dollar value of the ruble is to be doubled). Initially, the impact of this change will be reflected in Soviet accounting practices, although any connection to later potential Soviet price revisions remains unclear. Finally, this recent legislation also proposes new rules for enterprise access to and disbursement of foreign exchange, and the possibility of domestic foreign currency auctions.

There is little doubt that Soviet leaders have chosen a path of major change in the nature and operation of their foreign trade system. However, any observer of the East European effort in this area, albeit under different conditions, recognizes that the path to significant integration is long and difficult.

REFERENCES

1. For a general discussion of foreign trade in centrally planned economies, see F. D. Holzman, *International Trade Under Communism* (New York: Basic Books, 1976); and A. A. Brown, "Towards a Theory of Centrally Planned Foreign Trade," in A. A. Brown and E. Neuberger, eds., *International Trade and Central Planning* (Berkeley and Los Angeles: University of California Press, 1968), pp. 57–93. For a survey of the literature and basic issues, see F. D. Holzman, *Foreign Trade Under Central Planning* (Cambridge, Mass.: Harvard University Press, 1974), chap. 1. For details of organizational arrangements, see V. P. Gruzinov, *The USSR's Management of Foreign Trade* (White Plains, N.Y.: M. E. Sharpe, 1979). For details of recent organizational changes, see S. Bozek, "The U.S.S.R.: Intensifying the Development of Its Foreign Trade Structure," in U.S. Congress, Joint Economic Committee, *Soviet Economy in a Time of Change* (Washington, D.C.: U.S. Government Printing Office, 1979), vol. 2, pp. 506–525; and H. S. Gardner, *Soviet Foreign Trade: The Decision Process* (Boston: Kluwer-Nijhoff, 1983). An excellent discussion of recent developments can be found in U.S. Congress, Joint Economic Committee, *Gorbachev's Economic Plans*, vol. 2 (Washington, D.C.: U.S. Government Printing Office, 1987), pp. 429–556.
2. For more detail on financial arrangements, see G. Garvy, *Money, Financial Flows, and Credit in the Soviet Union* (Cambridge, Mass.: Ballinger, 1977), pp. 152–155.
3. This discussion is based on L. J. Brainard, "Soviet Foreign Trade Planning," in U.S. Congress, Joint Economic Committee, *Soviet Economy in a New Perspective* (Washington, D.C.: U.S. Government Printing Office, 1976), pp. 695–708; V. G. Treml, "Foreign Trade and the Soviet Economy: Changing Parameters and Interrelationships," in E. Neuberger and L. Tyson, eds., *Transmission and Response: The Impact of International Disturbances on the Soviet Union and Eastern Europe* (New York: Pergamon Press, 1980); H. Levine, "The Effects of Foreign Trade on Soviet Planning Practices," in A. A. Brown and E. Neuberger, eds. *International Trade and Central Planning* (Berkeley and Los Angeles: University of California Press, 1968), pp. 225–276; and *Metodicheskie ukazaniia k razrabotke gosudarstvennykh planov ekonomicheskogo i sotsial'nogo razvitia SSSR* [Methodological directives to working out the state plan of economic and social development of the USSR] (Moscow: Ekonomika, 1980), chap. 25.
4. Treml, "Foreign Trade." This surplus is the consequence of overvalued exchange rates used to translate *valuta* ruble prices into domestic prices and the rise in the world prices of Soviet raw material exports.

5. For empirical evidence on this point, see, for example, F. R. Gregory, *Socialist and Nonsocialist Industrialization Patterns* (New York: Praeger, 1970), pp. 119–120; and F. L. Pryor, *The Communist Foreign Trade System* (Cambridge, Mass.: MIT Press, 1963), chap. 1. According to Treml, "Foreign Trade," the Soviets in the 1970s abandoned their "policy of trade aversion" and now have a trade share of national income of 21 percent. The confusion lies in the manner of translating Soviet trade data in *valuta* rubles into domestic prices, and there is much controversy over this issue. On this controversy, consult Treml, ibid., footnote 1.

6. For a discussion, see M. R. Dohan, *Soviet Foreign Trade in the NEP Economy and Soviet Industrialization Strategy*, unpublished doctoral dissertation, Massachusetts Institute of Technology, 1969.

7. P. G. Ericson, "Soviet Efforts to Increase Exports of Manufactured Products to the West," in U.S. Congress, Joint Economic Committee, *Soviet Economy in a New Perspective*, pp. 709–727; and H. H. Kravailis et al., "Soviet Exports to the Industrialized West: Performance and Prospects," in U.S. Congress, Joint Economic Committee, *Soviet Economy in a Time of Change*, vol. 2, pp. 414–462.

8. F. D. Holzman, "Some Theories of the Hard Currency Shortages of Centrally Planned Economies," in U.S. Congress, Joint Economic Committee, *Soviet Economy in a Time of Change*, vol. 2, pp. 297–316.

9. P. G. Ericson and R. S. Miller, "Soviet Foreign Economic Behavior: A Balance of Payments Perspective," in U.S. Congress, Joint Economic Committee, *Soviet Economy in a Time of Change*, pp. 208–243.

10. For a discussion of the long-term impact of exchange rate prices, see F. D. Holzman, "The Ruble Exchange Rate and Soviet Foreign Trade Pricing Policies, 1929–1961," *American Economic Review*, vol. 57, no. 4 (September 1968), 807–812. For a discussion of how ruble-dollar exchange rates are determined, see Garvy, *Money, Financial Flows, and Credit*, chap. 7.

11. For discussions of FTEI, consult L. Brainard, "Soviet Foreign Trade Planning," pp. 701–707; C. H. McMillan, "Some Recent Developments in Soviet Foreign Trade Theory," *Canadian Slavonic Papers*, vol. 12, no. 3 (Fall 1970), 243–272; and A. Boltho, *Foreign Trade Criteria in Socialist Economies* (Cambridge: Cambridge University Press, 1971).

12. The members of COMECON are Bulgaria, Cuba (since 1972), Czechoslovakia, the German Democratic Republic, Hungary, Poland, Rumania, Mongolia, and the Soviet Union. For a more extensive discussion of bloc trade, see M. Kaser, *COMECON, Integration Problems of the Planned Economies*, 2nd ed. (London: Oxford University Press, 1967); F. L. Pryor, *The Communist Foreign Trade System* (Cambridge, Mass.: MIT Press, 1963); J. M. van Brabant, *East European Cooperation: The Role of Money and Finance* (New York: Praeger, 1977); and E. A. Hewett, *Foreign Trade Prices in the Council for Mutual Economic Assistance* (Cambridge: Cambridge University Press, 1974).

13. For discussions of the degree of integration of the COMECON countries, see J. Pelzman, "Trade Integration in the Council for Mutual Economic Assistance: Creation and Diversion, 1954–1970," *ACES Bulletin*, vol. 18, no. 2 (Fall 1976), 39–60; and J. van Brabant, "Trade Creation and Trade Diversion in Eastern Europe: A Comment," *ACES Bulletin*, vol. 19, no. 1 (Spring 1977), 79–98.

14. For a discussion of one particular but important case, see J. M. Montias, *Economic Development in Communist Rumania* (Cambridge, Mass.: MIT Press, 1967), chap. 4. Also see J. M. Montias, "Socialist Industrialization and Trade in Machinery

Products," in A. A. Brown and E. Neuberger, eds., *International Trade and Central Planning* (Berkeley and Los Angeles: University of California Press, 1968), pp. 130–158.

15. For a discussion of recent developments in the process of integration, see M. Bornstein, "East-West Economic Relations and Soviet-East European Economic Relations," in U.S. Congress, Joint Economic Committee, *Soviet Economy in a Time of Change*, vol. 1, pp. 291–311; A. Smith, "The Council for Mutual Economic Assistance in 1977: New Economic Power, New Political Perspectives, and Some Old and New Problems," in U.S. Congress, Joint Economic Committee, *East European Economies Post-Helsinki* (Washington, D.C.: U.S. Government Printing Office, 1977), pp. 152–173; and M. Lavigne, "The Soviet Union Inside Comecon," *Soviet Studies*, vol. 35, no. 2 (April 1983), 135–153.

16. For in-depth discussions, see van Brabant, *East European Cooperation*, chaps. 3 and 4; and M. Kohn and N. Lang, "The Intra-CMEA Foreign Trade System: Major Price Changes, Little Reform," in U.S. Congress, Joint Economic Committee, *East European Economies Post-Helsinki*, p. 137.

17. M. Marrese and J. Vaňous, *Soviet Subsidization of Trade with Eastern Europe: A Soviet Perspective* (Berkeley: University of California Institute of International Studies, 1983); and J. Brada, "Soviet Subsidization of Eastern Europe: The Primacy of Economics over Politics," *Journal of Comparative Economics*, vol. 9 no. 1 (March 1985), 80–85.

18. F. D. Holzman, "The Significance of Soviet Subsidies to Eastern Europe," *Comparative Economic Studies*, vol. 28, no.1 (Spring 1986), 54.

19. For a detailed discussion of these issues, see R. Dietz, "Price Changes in Soviet Trade with CMEA and the Rest of the World Since 1975," in U.S. Congress, Joint Economic Committee, *Soviet Economy in a Time of Change*, vol. 1, pp. 263–299; and Bornstein, "East-West Economic Relations," pp. 299–308.

20. TsSU, *Narodnoe khoziaistvo SSSR v 1982 g* [The national economy of the USSR in 1982] (Moscow: Finansy i Statistika, 1983), p. 534; and Goskomstat, *Narodnoe khoziaistvo SSSR za 70 let* [The national economy of the USSR over 70 years] (Moscow: Finansy i Statistika, 1987), p. 646.

21. For a discussion of recent developments, see J. F. McIntyre, "The USSR's Hard Currency Trade and Payments Position," in U.S. Congress, Joint Economic Committee, *Gorbachev's Economic Plans*, vol. 2 , pp. 474–488.

22. McIntyre, "The USSR's Hard Currency Trade and Payments Position," p.482.

23. Ibid., pp. 482–484.

24. For a discussion of this issue, see E. A. Hewett, "Most-Favored Nation Treatment in Trade Under Central Planning," *Slavic Review*, vol. 37, no. 1 (March 1978), 25–39; and H. Raffel, M. Rubin, and R. Teal, "The MFN Impact on U.S. Imports from Eastern Europe," in U.S. Congress, Joint Economic Committee, *East European Economies Post-Helsinki*, p. 1427.

25. This discussion is based on C. H. McMillan, "Soviet Investment in the Industrialized Western Economies and in the Developing Economies of the Third World," in U.S. Congress, Joint Economic Committee, *East European Economies Post-Helsinki*, pp. 625–647; and C. H. McMillan, "Growth of External Investments by the COMECON Countries," *World Economy*, vol. 2, no. 3 (September 1979), 363–386.

26. C. Fogarty and K. Tritle, "Moscow's Economic Aid Programs in Less-Developed Countries: A Perspective on the 1980's," in *Gorbachev's Economic Plans*, vol. 2, p. 538.

27. All the data on aid are from Directorate of Intelligence, *Handbook of Economic Statistics, 1988* (Washington, D.C.: Central Intelligence Agency, 1988), pp.143–189.
28. F. D. Holzman, "Foreign Trade," in A. Bergson and S. Kuznets, eds., *Economic Trends in the Soviet Union* (Cambridge, Mass.: Harvard University Press, 1963), p. 284.
29. Ibid., p. 286.
30. Ibid., p. 290.
31. For a discussion of the role of foreign trade in the preplan and early planning years, see M. R. Dohan, *Soviet Foreign Trade in the NEP Economy and Soviet Industrialization Strategy*, unpublished doctoral dissertation, Massachusetts Institute of Technology, 1969.
32. Holzman, "Foreign Trade," pp. 287–288.
33. Ibid., pp. 289–290.
34. Ibid., pp. 291–300.
35. Ibid., p. 297.
36. Ibid., p. 296.
37. It is important to recognize that the shift in trade patterns during the first Five Year Plan not only provided producer goods so necessary for the immediate expansion of output but also—and this may be the more crucial factor—provided prototypes of the best Western technology that could then be duplicated. For a discussion of the role of Western technology during the early years, see A. C. Sutton, *Western Technology and Soviet Economic Development 1930 to 1945* (Stanford, Calif.: The Hoover Institution, 1971).
38. A. Bryne, J. Cole, T. Brickerton, and A. Malish, "US-USSR Grain Trade," in U.S. Congress, Joint Economic Committee, *Soviet Economy in the 1980s*, part 2, p. 75.
39. For an elaboration, see Bozek, "The U.S.S.R.: Intensifying the Development of Its Foreign Trade Structure."
40. M. R. Dohan, "Export Specialization and Import Dependence in the Soviet Economy, 1970–77," in U.S. Congress, Joint Economic Committee, *Soviet Economy in a Time of Change*, vol. 2, p. 369. There is controversy over the share of imports of national income, with Treml, "Foreign Trade," Table 1, estimating the import share much above Dohan and other researchers. The share figures cited in Table 11.1 are those of Treml for the years 1955 to 1976.
41. Treml, ibid.
42. Data are from Directorate of Intelligence, *Handbook of Economic Statistics, 1988*. pp. 144–146, 164.
43. See J. F. McIntyre, "Soviet Efforts to Revamp the Foreign Trade Sector," in U.S. Congress, Joint Economic Committee, *Gorbachev's Economic Plans*, vol. 2, pp. 489–503.
44. See E. Stubbs, "Soviet Ruble Devaluation and Currency Convertibility (Providence, R.I.: Brown University Center for Foreign Policy Development, 1989), pp.1–7.

SELECTED BIBLIOGRAPHY

G. Adler-Karlsson, *Western Economic Warfare: 1947–1967* (New York: Humanities Press, 1968).

Q. V. S. Bach, *Soviet Economic Assistance to the Less Developed Countries: A Statistical Analysis* (New York: Oxford University Press, 1988).

A. Boltho, *Foreign Trade Criteria in Socialist Economies* (Cambridge: Cambridge University Press, 1971).

J. C. Brada, ed., *Quantitative and Analytical Studies in East-West Economic Relations* (Bloomington: Indiana University Press, 1976).

A. A. Brown and E. Neuberger, eds., *International Trade and Central Planning* (Berkeley and Los Angeles: University of California Press, 1968).

R. Campbell and P. Marer, eds., *East-West Trade and Technology Transfer* (Bloomington, Ind.: International Development Research Center, 1974).

C. C. Carvounis and B. Z. Carvounis, *U.S. Commercial Opportunities in the Soviet Union* (New York: Quorum Books, 1989).

M. R. Dohan, *Soviet Foreign Trade in the NEP Economy and Soviet Industrialization Strategy*, unpublished doctoral dissertation, Massachusetts Institute of Technology, 1969.

Z. Fallenbuchl and C. H. McMillan, eds., *Partners in East-West Economic Relations: The Determinants of Choice* (London: Pergamon Press, 1980).

C. Fogarty and K. Tritle, "Moscow's Economic Aid Programs in Less-Developed Countries: A Perspective on the 1980's," in U.S. Congress, Joint Economic Committee, *Gorbachev's Economic Plans*, vol. 2 (Washington, D.C.: U.S. Government Printing Office, 1987), pp. 532–541.

H. S. Gardner, *Soviet Foreign Trade: The Decision Process* (Boston: Kluwer-Nijhoff, 1983).

M. I. Goldman, *Soviet Foreign Aid* (New York: Praeger, 1967).

G. Grossman, "U.S.-Soviet Trade and Economic Relations: Problems and Prospects," *ACES Bulletin*, vol. 15, no. 1 (Spring 1973), pp. 3–22.

V. P. Gruzinov, *The USSR's Management of Foreign Trade* (White Plains, N.Y.: M.E. Sharpe, 1979).

P. Hanson, *Trade and Technology Transfer in Soviet-Western Relations* (New York: Columbia University Press, 1981).

H. W. Heiss, "U.S.-Soviet Trade Trends," in U.S. Congress, Joint Economic Committee, *Gorbachev's Economic Plans*, vol. 2 (Washington, D.C.: U.S. Government Printing Office, 1987), pp. 448–473.

E. A. Hewett, *Foreign Trade Prices in the Council for Mutual Economic Assistance* (Cambridge: Cambridge University Press, 1974).

———, "Most-Favored Nation Treatment in Trade Under Central Planning," *Slavic Review*, vol. 37, no. 1 (March 1978), 25–39.

F. D. Holzman, "East-West Trade and Investment Policy Issues," in *United States International Economic Policy in an Interdependent World* (Washington, D.C.: U.S. Government Printing Office, 1971), pp. 363–395.

———, "Foreign Trade," in A. Bergson and S. Kuznets, eds., *Economic Trends in the Soviet Union* (Cambridge, Mass.: Harvard University Press, 1963), pp. 283–332.

———, "Foreign Trade Behavior of Centrally Planned Economies," in H. Rosovsky, ed., *Industrialization in Two Systems: Essays in Honor of Alexander Gerschenkron* (New York: Wiley, 1966).

———, *Foreign Trade Under Central Planning* (Cambridge, Mass.: Harvard University Press, 1974).

———, *International Trade Under Communism* (New York: Basic Books, 1976).

———, "The Significance of Soviet Subsidies to Eastern Europe," *Comparative Economic Studies*, vol. 28, no. 1 (Spring 1986), 54–65.

M. Kaser, *COMECON: Integration Problems of the Planned Economies*, 2nd ed. (London: Oxford University Press, 1967).

M. Lavigne, "Soviet Trade with LDC's," in U.S. Congress, Joint Economic Committee, *Gorbachev's Economic Plans*, vol. 2 (Washington, D.C.: U.S. Government Printing Office, 1987), pp. 504–531.

J. F. McIntyre, "Soviet Efforts to Revamp the Foreign Trade Sector," in U.S. Congress, Joint Economic Committee, *Gorbachev's Economic Plans*, vol. 2 (Washington, D.C.: U.S. Government Printing Office, 1987), pp. 489–503.

———, "The USSR's Hard Currency Trade and Payments Position," in U.S. Congress, Joint Economic Committee, *Gorbachev's Economic Plans*, vol. 2 (Washington, D.C.: U.S. Government Printing Office, 1987), pp. 474–488.

C. H. McMillan, ed., *Changing Perceptives in East-West Commerce* (Lexington, Mass.: Heath, 1974).

———, *Multinationals from the Second World: Growth of Foreign Investments by Soviet and East European State Enterprises* (London: Macmillan, 1987).

A. Malish, Jr., *United States–East European Trade: Considerations Involved in Granting Most-Favored-Nation Treatment to the Countries of Eastern Europe* (Washington, D.C.: United States Tariff Commission, Staff Research Studies, no. 4, 1972).

P. Marer, *Soviet and East-European Trade (1946–1969): Statistical Compendium and Guide* (Bloomington: Indiana University Press, 1972).

M. Marrese and J. Vaňous, *Soviet Subsidization of Trade with Eastern Europe: A Soviet Perspective* (Berkeley: University of California Institute of International Studies, 1983).

J. M. Montias, *Economic Development in Communist Rumania* (Cambridge, Mass.: MIT Press, 1967), chap. 4.

B. Parrott, ed., *Trade, Technology and Soviet-American Relations* (Bloomington: Indiana University Press, 1985).

F. L. Pryor, *The Communist Foreign Trade System* (Cambridge, Mass.: MIT Press, 1963).

J. Quigley, *The Soviet Foreign Trade Monopoly: Institutions and Laws* (Columbus: Ohio State University Press, 1974).

G. A. Smith, *Soviet Foreign Trade: Organization, Operations, and Policy, 1918–1971* (New York: Praeger, 1973).

A. C. Sutton, *Western Technology and Soviet Economic Development 1917 to 1930* (Stanford, Calif.: The Hoover Institution, 1968).

———, *Western Technology and Soviet Economic Development 1930 to 1945* (Stanford, Calif.: The Hoover Institution, 1971).

———, *Western Technology and Soviet Economic Development 1945 to 1965* (Stanford, Calif.: The Hoover Institution, 1973).

V. G. Treml, "Foreign Trade and the Soviet Economy: Changing Parameters and Interrelationships," in E. Neuberger and L. Tyson, eds., *Transmission and*

Response: The Impact of International Disturbances on the Soviet Union and Eastern Europe (New York: Pergamon Press, 1980).

U.S. Congress, Joint Economic Committee, "Foreign Economic Activities," in *Soviet Economy in a New Perspective* (Washington, D.C.: U.S. Government Printing Office, 1976), part 3.

——, "Foreign Economic Activities," in *Soviet Economy in a Time of Change* (Washington, D.C.: U.S. Government Printing Office, 1979), vol. 2, part 4.

——, "Foreign Economic Relations," in *East European Economies Post-Helsinki* (Washington, D.C.: U.S. Government Printing Office, 1977), part 3.

——, "Foreign Economy," in *Soviet Economic Prospects for the Seventies* (Washington, D.C.: U.S. Government Printing Office, 1973), part 7.

——, *Soviet Economy in the 1980's: Problems and Prospects* (Washington, D.C.: U.S. Government Printing Office, 1982), papers by Goldman, Bryne et al., and part VIII.

J. M. van Brabant, *East European Cooperation: The Role of Money and Finance* (New York: Praeger, 1977).

J. Wilczynski, *The Economics and Politics of East-West Trade* (New York: Praeger, 1969).

P. J. D. Wiles, *Communist International Economics* (Oxford: Blackwell, 1968).

T. Wolf, *U.S. East-West Trade Policy* (Lexington, Mass.: Heath, 1973).

——, "Estimating 'Foregone Gains' in Soviet-East European Foreign Trade: A Methodological Note," *Comparative Economic Studies*, vol. 27, no. 3 (Fall 1985), 83–98.

PART THREE

Soviet Economic Growth and Performance

Chapter 12

Soviet Economic Growth and Productivity

*H*ow well the Soviet economy has performed relative to other economies is an important question. In fact, this is ultimately what the study of differing economic systems is all about: Which economic organization seems to function the "best"? Although we recognize that it is risky to generalize from the performance of one economy to the performance of the system,[1] that is, to treat Soviet economic performance as representative of the command socialist system as a whole, we compare the performance of the Soviet command economy with that of industrialized market economies in this chapter. Of special interest are the comparisons between the USSR and the United States, despite the different levels of development of the two countries. This is not to deny that other comparisons, such as the USSR with West Germany or Japan, are just as relevant.[2] The

United States and the Soviet Union are nonetheless the world's two largest economic powers, with fairly equal population sizes. Considerable research has already gone into Soviet-American comparisons, and the Soviets themselves tend to judge their economic performance relative to that of the United States. In this chapter, we emphasize long-run performance and concentrate on secular trends. The often considerable variation around the secular trend is not considered in detail.[3]

In addition to the traditional reasons for being interested in Soviet economic growth, the entire growth and performance issue has taken on new importance in the Gorbachev era. As we have emphasized in this book, much of the impetus for major economic reform derives from the fact that Soviet economic performance, measured by a variety of indicators, is unacceptable to Soviet leaders. If it were otherwise, the imperative of reform would be less important.

In comparing the economic performance of countries, there are two major problems. First, it is often difficult to measure the various economic performance criteria in an unambiguous manner. For example, measures of economic growth—frequently used performance criteria—are often dramatically affected by the choice of price weights—the index number problem. Thus, direct comparisons of growth rates tend to be difficult to interpret. It is difficult to evaluate the relative growth performance of countries, although one can narrowly define economic growth in rather specific terms. It is even more difficult to measure less easily quantifiable performance criteria, such as environmental quality or dynamic efficiency.

The second major problem is even more difficult to come to grips with. In view of the multitude of possible performance criteria—economic growth, environmental quality, efficiency of resource utilization, relative standards of living, equity of income distribution, military power, and so on—how can one rank the performance of one economy relative to another unless one economy outperforms the other in all categories? As an example, let us assume that the Soviet economy has outperformed the American economy in terms of growth and equity of income distribution, but that the United States economy has outperformed the USSR in all other categories. Which country deserves the higher overall rating? This depends, of course, on the relative importance of the various performance criteria, which is a matter of individual judgment, not of objective economics.[4]

In sum, there seems to be no unambiguous way to objectively evaluate the performance of one economy relative to another except in obvious (and rare) cases where one outperforms the other in all categories. Given, however, the wide-spread interest in performance evaluation, what can be done? Our answer is to examine the performance of the Soviet economy and market economies in terms of what we consider the most important performance criteria; the reader can then supply his or her own subjective weights to aggregate the individual performance indicators. In this chapter, we deal with the "conventional" economic success indicators commonly used to assess economic performance:

economic growth; static and dynamic efficiency; the equity of the distribution of income; consumer welfare, including both private and public goods; and economic stability (or security). Less conventional indicators of economic performance—military strength, environmental quality, and technological change—will be considered in Chapter 13. The stroke of our pen is quite broad: How well has the Soviet economy performed in each of these areas during the era of central planning (a time span encompassing 60 years) vis-à-vis the long-term performance of the industrialized capitalist countries? The time horizon of each comparison is dictated by the availability of data, and some series do not go back past World War II, but our objective is to assess the entire plan era with broad data aggregates. We also maintain special interest in contemporary performance issues insofar as these are, as we have noted, a driving force of perestroika. In this context, we will examine both long-term Soviet performance trends (comparing these with Western trends) and more recent trends influencing the reform scenario.

SOVIET ECONOMIC GROWTH

Although it is not widely recognized, measures of the long-term growth of real GNP are sensitive to the choice of constant price weights. If one measures the growth rate of an economy that has successfully transformed itself into an advanced industrial country, the computed real growth rate will often be much higher if constant preindustrialization prices are used as weights. This phenomenon is called *index number relativity,* or the "Gerschenkron effect," after Alexander Gerschenkron, who analyzed it in his study of Soviet industrial production.[5]

Although the explanation of index number relativity might seem a digression to the reader, we attempt to provide an explanation of this phenomenon because of its importance in evaluating USSR growth, especially during the 1930s. Moreover, index number effects play important roles in the assessment of Soviet military power (Chapter 13) and of the size of Soviet GNP relative to other countries.

An intuitive account of index number relativity would be as follows. In the course of industrialization, a negative correlation exists between the rates of growth of sector outputs and the rates of growth of sector prices. The fastest-growing sectors—machinery, electricity, transportation equipment—all tend to experience *relative* declines in prices (relative to the prices of the slowly growing sectors, such as food products and textiles) as advanced technology is introduced and economies of scale are achieved. Thus, if constant preindustrialization prices are used, the most rapidly expanding sectors will receive large relative weights, whereas the other sectors will receive small relative weights. Conversely, if post-industrialization prices are used, the rapidly expanding sectors will receive small relative price weights (which reflect the reductions in their relative prices), and the other sectors will receive large relative price weights. The same logic would apply to comparisons of the relative size of the total output of two countries, one "industrialized," the other "backward." The industrialized country produces larger relative volumes of "advanced" goods, whose relative prices are low, and produces relatively small volumes of "traditional" goods, whose relative prices are high. The backward country produces relatively large volumes of traditional goods at relatively low prices and relatively small volumes of advanced goods at relatively high prices. If the relative output of the two countries is calculated using the prices of the advanced country, the differential will be smaller than if the prices of the backward country were used. A hypothetical example is supplied in the accompanying note to assist the reader.[6]

This may seem quite academic to the reader, but Soviet 1987 GNP was 69 percent that of the United States in *dollar* prices but 41 percent that of the United States in *ruble* prices. Moreover, the annual growth rate of Soviet real GNP between 1928 and 1937, as calculated by Abram Bergson, was 11.9 percent using the preindustrialization prices of 1928 and 5.5 percent when calculated in postindustrialization prices of 1937.[7] The complexity of the question is increased when one realizes that comparable estimates of American growth in preindustrialization prices, say, of the 1800s, are not available.[8] What, then, is the "true" growth rate (or relative GNP) of the Soviet Union or of the United States? There is, in fact, no single "true" growth rate. Instead, there is a whole series of growth rates, one for each set of price weights, which yield a *range* of growth rates. Fortunately, for purposes of intercountry comparisons, truly significant differences arise only when comparing growth rates computed using pre- versus postindustrialization prices, owing to the large structural changes that occur during industrialization. Differences between growth rates in constant postindustrialization or constant preindustrialization prices tend to be smaller. Nevertheless, index number relativity continues to operate in industrialized countries, but only to a small degree.

With these reservations in mind, we shall contrast "comparable" Soviet and Western growth rates; in other words, we shall concentrate on growth rates that employ "late" year (postindustrialization) price weights. This method, however, does not eliminate all biases resulting from index number problems, but acts instead only as a crude adjustment. The cited Soviet growth rates have been estimated by American economists who have recalculated Soviet GNP using Western GNP definitions[9] to ensure the comparability of Soviet and American rates.[10] For reference purposes, we include the official estimates of growth rates of Soviet *net material product*, which differs from the standard Western concept by its exclusion of services not directly connected with physical production.

In Table 12.1, we supply annual growth rates of tsarist GNP (1885–1913), of Soviet real GNP during the plan era (1928–1983), and of the United States between 1834 and 1984. The Soviet figures to 1950 are based on the estimates by Abram Bergson, which are the most widely accepted Western estimates of Soviet growth. Bergson's figures are available through 1958. Estimates of the

Table 12.1   LONG-TERM GROWTH OF GNP IN THE USSR AND THE UNITED STATES
Annual Rates of Growth

USSR	American estimates	Official Soviet estimates (net material product)
1885–1913	3.3[c]	—
1928–1940	5.4[a]	14.6[d]
1950–1960	6.0[c]	10.1
1960–1970	5.1[c]	7.0
1970–1980	3.7[c]	5.3
1980–1984	2.0[c]	3.2
1928–1984	4.3[a]	8.8
1928–1984, effective years	4.8[b]	9.7
1950–1984	4.4[c]	7.6

United States	1860 prices	1929 prices	1958 and 1972 prices
1834–1843 to 1879–1888	4.4		—
1879–1888 to 1899–1908	3.7	3.8	—
1899–1908 to 1929	—	3.4	—
1929–1950	—	—	2.5
1950–1960	—	—	3.3
1960–1970	—	—	3.9
1970–1984	—	—	3.0
1929–1984	—	—	3.1
1950–1984	—	—	3.4

[a] 1950 prices.

[b] Combined index, 1950 prices 1928–1950, 1970 prices thereafter.

[c] 1970 weights.

[d] 1926–1927 prices.

[e] 1913 prices

Sources: A. Bergson, *The Real National Income of Soviet Russia Since 1928* (Cambridge, Mass.: Harvard University Press, 1961), p. 210; H. Block, "Soviet Economic Performance in a Global Context," in U.S. Congress, Joint Economic Committee, *Soviet Economy in a Time of Change* (Washington, D.C.: U.S. Government Printing Office, 1979), vol. 1, p. 135; P. Gregory, *Russian National Income, 1885–1913* (Cambridge: Cambridge University Press, 1982). Table 1; A. L. Vainshtein, *Narodny dokhod Rossii i SSSR* [The national income of Russia and the USSR] (Moscow: Statistika, 1969), p. 119; *Narodnoe khoziaistvo SSSR v 1978 g* [The national economy of the USSR in 1978] (Moscow: 1979), pp. 31–33; National Foreign Assessment Center, *Handbook of Economic Statistics 1984* ER79–10274, Washington, D.C., August 1984, p. 22; *The Economic Report of the President* (selected years); *Dostizheniia sovetskoi vlasti za 40 let v tsifrakh* [The accomplishments of the Soviet regime over 40 years in numbers] (Moscow: 1957), p. 327; R. Gallman, "Gross National Product in the United States, 1834–1909," *Output, Employment and Productivity in the United States After 1800* (New York and London: National Bureau of Economic Research, 1966), p. 26. The 1984 USSR figures are based on preliminary Soviet figures.

Central Intelligence Agency (CIA) are available for the entire postwar era and are used to extend the Bergson series.[1]

What conclusions can be drawn from Table 12.1 concerning Soviet growth performance relative to that of the United States? First, it is obvious that Soviet growth since 1928 has been more rapid than American growth during the same period. The average annual growth rate of the Soviet economy between 1928 and 1984 was 4.3 percent, whereas the rate for the United States between 1929 and 1984 was 3.1 percent. If one measures Soviet growth only during "effective years,"[12] that is, if one eliminates the war years, Soviet growth rises to 4.8 percent, 1.7 percentage points above the American annual growth rate.

Second, the Soviet growth rate during the postwar period (1950–1984) of 4.4 percent exceeded the comparable American rate of 3.4 percent (1950–1984)—a difference of 1.0 percentage point annually.

Third, Soviet growth in the postwar period has been declining, from a high of 6.0 percent between 1950 and 1960 to 3.7 percent between 1970 and 1980 and dropping further to a rate of 2 percent between 1980 and 1984. During this latter period, the worst growth years were 1963 (2.2 percent), 1969 (2.3 percent), 1972 (2.0 percent), and 1975 (1.7 percent).[13] As the table shows, growth was quite slow from 1980 to 1984. In each year, growth failed to exceed 2 percent. This declining growth rate has had a depressing effect upon the long-term Soviet growth rate, which is a combination of relatively rapid growth from 1928 to 1940 and from 1950 to 1960 and relatively slower growth after 1960. As the Soviet growth slowdown continues, the growth rate differential between the United States and the Soviet Union has declined.

Fourth, the official Soviet estimates of the growth of net material product in constant prices are much larger than the American estimates of Soviet growth using Western GNP concepts and different price weights. Such differences are greatest when comparing the 1928–1940 period, part of which is explained by the Soviets' use of preindustrialization 1926–1927 prices until 1950.[14] From the Soviet viewpoint, this is more than a matter of academic interest; it is difficult to determine how much Soviet growth has actually declined in recent years because the earlier rate (1928–1940) is difficult to interpret. Another cause of the differences between American and Soviet estimates is the Soviets' omission from net material product of selected service categories (such as passenger transportation, government employees, lawyers, housing), which have been among the slowest growing sectors in the Soviet Union.

Fifth, U.S. growth rates during early periods of industrial transformation are closer to the Soviet plan period rates than are the twentieth-century American rates. Thus, the American economy grew 4.4 percent annually between 1834–1843 and 1879–1888, which is 1 percentage point less than the Soviet rate during the 1928–1940 period and is roughly equal to the Soviet 1950–1984 rate.* In fact, the U.S. growth rate of 6.6 percent during the 1869–1878 to 1879–1888 period exceeded the Soviet 1928–1940 rate.

---

*In these comparisons, we use early-year price weights for the United States (1860 prices) and late-year price weights for the USSR—a seeming violation of the principle stated above. Index number relativity does not show up in these calculations for the United States, probably because of different calculation methods used by Gallman (the 1860 price estimates) and Kuznets (the 1929 price estimates). Note that for the same period (1879–1888 to 1899–1908), the 1929 price weights yield a higher growth rate (Table 12.1).

Sixth, whereas the Soviet growth rate of 6 0 percent between 1950 and 1960 was rapid by international standards, it was by no means unprecedented among the major industrial powers during this period. The annual West German growth rate between 1950 and 1960 was 7.8 percent, and the Japanese rate for the same period was almost 9 percent.[15] It may not be a coincidence that those major industrial powers that suffered the most extensive wartime destruction also experienced the most rapid growth rates in the immediate postwar period. More important, both Japan and West Germany (especially Japan) have been able to sustain high rates of growth after 1960 in contrast to the USSR's declining rate of growth. Since 1970, the USSR growth rate has been only slightly above that of Western Europe.

Seventh, Soviet growth rates during the plan era well exceeded the growth rate during the "industrialization era" of the tsarist period (1885–1913). In fact, the long-run Soviet growth rate during 1928–1984 was roughly 50 percent above the 1885–1913 rate. Thus, the Soviet period has seen an acceleration of economic growth. If the decline in the Soviet growth rate continues, however, the difference between the tsarist and Soviet growth rates could become negligible. In fact, the Soviet growth rate after 1970 (3.3 percent) is identical to growth during the late tsarist period.

Eighth, Soviet growth between 1928 and 1984 exceeded the long-term growth rates of the other industrialized economies, including the United States (Table 12.2). Only the long-term Japanese growth rate (4.5 percent) roughly equals the Soviet 1928–1984 rate. The above comparison does, however, assume that the 1928–1984 Soviet rate was indeed the long-term growth rate of the Soviet economy, although it is computed using a much shorter time period than the other rates. This assumption may eventually not prove to be the case,

Table 12.2   LONG-TERM GROWTH OF GNP OF SELECTED COUNTRIES
Average Annual Growth Rate

United Kingdom	1855–1864 to 1984	2.1
France	1831–1840 to 1984	2.4
Belgium	1900–1904 to 1984	2.2
Netherlands	1860–1870 to 1984	2.5
Germany (West Germany after 1945)	1850–1859 to 1984	2.8
Denmark	1865–1869 to 1984	3.0
Sweden	1861–1869 to 1984	3.0
Italy	1895–1899 to 1984	2.8
Japan	1874–1879 to 1984	4.5
United States	1834–1843 to 1984	3.4
Canada	1870–1874 to 1984	3.5
USSR	1928 to 1984	4.3–4.8

Source: S. Kuznets, *Economic Growth of Nations* (Cambridge, Mass.: Harvard University Press, 1971), pp. 11–14; and Table 12.1. The Kuznets figures are updated from *Handbook of Economic Statistics 1984,* p. 22, and *Economic Report of the President,* February 1985, p. 356.

in view of the declining Soviet growth pattern. For the other countries, however, there seems to be no consistent difference between early-period and late-
period rates,[16] so perhaps the shorter Soviet period does not distort our overall
conclusion that the long-term Soviet growth rate is the highest recorded (along
with Japan's). We emphasize that we are dealing with long-term rates, which
conceal the fact that growth rates as high or higher than the long-term Soviet
rate have been attained by many of these countries (Japan, the United States,
Germany, and others) during various subperiods in the past.

Thus, we conclude that Soviet economic growth during the plan era was
more rapid than American growth throughout the twentieth century and was
more rapid than the long-run growth of other industrialized countries—except
Japan. Soviet growth during the 1950s was rapid but was surpassed by the two
other major industrial powers—West Germany and Japan—which had also suffered extensive war damage. Only during its period of industrial transformation
did American growth approach the Soviet rate during the plan era. Soviet
growth was also above the growth rate of the tsarist economy after 1885. These
conclusions are probably sufficiently general not to be notably affected by the
index number problem and the other measurement problems mentioned above.

Let us now turn to a deeper question: To what extent was the rapid Soviet
growth a consequence of the Soviet economic system *per se* or of other special
factors unrelated to the system? This is a fundamental issue in appraising alternative systems, for we are interested in the merits of the system independent of
special circumstances.[17] In this regard, certain special factors probably affected
long-run Soviet growth performance. First, the Soviets industrialized late and
could, therefore, borrow more advanced technology from the West. Second, the
large Soviet population, concentrated as it was in agriculture at the beginning of
the plan era, provided, as we have seen, a plentiful supply of labor for industry.
Economies of scale could, therefore, be achieved in the course of Soviet industrialization without diminishing the marginal productivity of capital. On the
negative side, Soviet agricultural resources were limited relative to population,
with only a small proportion of land suitable for cultivation.[18] Although it is impossible to weigh the impact of each of these factors on Soviet growth, one can
speculate that the Soviets' borrowing of more advanced technology was an important factor in explaining rapid growth, especially during the 1930s and the
immediate postwar period.

Special factors aside, to what extent was the more rapid Soviet growth a
product of the Soviet system of central planning and political dictatorship? It
would seem that much of the superior Soviet growth performance can be explained by the substitution of growth-oriented planners' preferences for consumer sovereignty. In this manner, the state was able to opt for a pattern of development conducive to rapid economic growth by planning high investment
and labor participation rates and by expanding the education of the labor force.
In the case of educational levels, for example, in 1926 only 6 percent of the over-
15-year-old population (of 89 million) has received education beyond the seventh grade. By 1959, the percentage has risen to 39 percent (of 148 million).[19]

Moreover, educational levels have continued to increase. In 1959, the median years of schooling of the Soviet population over age 16 years was 5.9 years. This grew to a median of 9.9 years by 1985.[20] The high investment ratios (Chapter 4) and labor participation rates (Chapter 9) have already been discussed.

The growth bias of Soviet planning can be illustrated by comparing the pattern of Soviet growth (The growth of household consumption vis-à-vis gross investment) with that of the United States (Table 12.3). The major difference between the two is the much more rapid growth of investment than consump-

Table 12.3   DIFFERENTIAL GROWTH PATTERNS: GNP BY FINAL USE, USSR AND UNITED STATES
Annual Growth Rates

	Household consumption	Gross investment	GNP	(1 ÷ 2)
		USSR		
1928–1937[a]	0.7	14.5	5.5	0.05
1950–1955[a]	8.7	8.7	7.6	1.00
1958–1964[b]	4.8	7.4	5.9	0.65
1965–1969[f]	6.2	6.8	4.9	0.91
1970–1980[g]	3.1	4.8	3.2	0.64
1928–1955[a]	2.8	7.9	4.8	0.35
1983–1987[i]	2.4	4.2	2.0	0.57
		United States		
1834–1843 to 1879–1888[c]	4.0	6.5	4.4	0.62
1879–1888 to 1899–1908[d]	3.8	3.8	3.8	1.00
1899–1908 to 1914–1923[d]	3.1	3.0	3.1	1.03
1929–1950[e]	2.7	2.6	2.6	1.04
1950–1970[e]	3.6	2.0	3.6	1.80
1970–1984[h]	3.3	4.3	3.0	0.77
1929–1984[e]	3.2	2.9	3.1	1.10
1980–1986	3.5	5.6	3.1[j]	0.62

[a] 1937 ruble factor cost.
[b] 1958 adjusted factor cost.
[c] 1860 prices.
[d] 1929 prices.
[e] 1958 prices.
[f] 1955 prices.
[g] 1970 prices.
[h] 1972 prices.
[i] Factor cost: 1982 end-use weights.
[j] Gross domestic product.

Sources: Bergson, *The Real National Income of Soviet Russia*, p. 210; A. Becker, *Soviet National Income 1958–1964* (Berkeley: University of California Press, 1969), p. 256; *USSR: Measures of Economic Growth and Development, 1950–80*, pp. 66–67. S. Kuznets, *National Product Since 1869* (New York: National Bureau of Economic Research, 1946), Table 11–16; R. Gallman, "Gross National Product in the United States, *Output, Employment and Productivity in the United States After 1800*, (New York and London: National Bureau of Economic Research, 1966), pp. 26–34; *The Economic Report of the President* (Washington, D.C.: U.S. Government Printing Office, 1985); S. H. Cohn, "The Economic Burden of Defense Expenditures," in *Soviet Economic Prospects for the Seventies*, p. 151; Block "Soviet Economic Performance" p. 136; Directorate of Intelligence, *Handbook of Economic Statistics, 1988* (Washington, D.C.: Central Intelligence Agency, 1988), p. 61; The World Bank, *World Development Report 1988* (New York: Oxford University Press, 1988), Table 4.

tion in the USSR as opposed to the more rapid growth of consumption—with the exception of the very early 1834–1888 period and the period 1970–1984—in the United States. The most extreme case of this is the negligible growth of household consumption in the USSR between 1928 and 1937, a period when investment was expanding at over 14 percent annually. Although investment expanded more rapidly than consumption in the United States between 1834 and 1888 and between 1970 and 1984, the extreme differences noted in the Soviet case were avoided. This growth orientation is also reflected in the differential growth pattern of the various originating sectors of Soviet GNP (Table 12.4). The consumption-oriented sectors (trade, services, and agriculture) expanded more slowly than total output in the USSR, whereas in the United States they have expanded (during the period in question) at roughly the same rate as GNP, with the exception of agriculture.

DYNAMIC EFFICIENCY AND THE GROWTH OF PRODUCTIVITY

A second criterion for evaluating the performance of economies is *dynamic efficiency,* which "relates to the community's capacity to add to its technological knowledge and to exploit such knowledge with increasing effect."[21] We use this criterion in addition to economic growth because, as we just noted, the Soviet Union deliberately adopted a rapid growth strategy of high investment

Table 12.4   ANNUAL RATES OF GROWTH: MAJOR ECONOMIC SECTORS

	USSR, 1928–1982		United States, 1947–1984	
	Sector growth	Sector growth ÷ GNP growth	Sector growth	Sector growth ÷ GNP growth
Agriculture	1.5	0.32	1.2	0.36
Industry	6.8	1.45	3.2	0.97
Construction	6.5	1.38	1.9	0.58
Transportation and communications	7.9	1.68	3.5	1.06
Trade	4.1	0.87	3.5	1.06
Services	3.8	0.81	2.5	0.76
GNP	4.7		3.3	

Source: R. Moorsteen and R. Powell, *The Soviet Capital Stock, 1928–1962* (Homewood, Ill.: Irwin, 1966), pp. 622–624; S. H. Cohn, "General Growth Performance of the Soviet Economy," in U.S. Congress, Joint Economic Committee, *Economic Performance and the Military Burden in the Soviet Union* (Washington, D.C.: U.S. Government Printing Office, 1970), p. 17; *The Economic Report of the President, 1985* (Washington, D.C.: U.S. Government Printing Office, 1985), p. 245; Block, "Soviet Economic Performance," p. 135; *USSR: Measures of Economic Growth and Development, 1950–80*, p. 63; *Handbook of Economic Statistics 1983*, p. 63.

rates, high labor participation rates, borrowing of more advanced technology, and rapid expansion of education and training. Thus, one would be surprised if the Soviets has *not* attained relatively high rates of economic growth. This is not to detract from their growth achievement, but just to place it in its proper perspective.

Theory

In such a case, dynamic efficiency might prove a useful second performance criterion, for it measures the rate at which a country is able to increase the efficiency of resource utilization over time, that is, the rate of increase of the amount of output derived from a given amount of factor inputs. Dynamic efficiency can be measured only imperfectly and indirectly. Its most common measure is the rate of growth of output per unit of *combined* factor inputs.[22] A less general measure would be the rate of growth of output per unit of labor (or capital) input. One measures the rate of growth of output per unit of input by subtracting the growth rate of the input from the growth rate of output. For example, if GNP grows at 5 percent annually and combined factor inputs grow at 3 percent annually, the annual rate of growth of output per unit of combined factor input would be 2 percent.

From this decription of total factor productivity, one can see that it provides only an indirect link to dynamic efficiency because one can only imperfectly measure the rates of growth of factor input in both qualitative and quantitative terms. For example, it is extremely difficult to measure changes in the quality of Soviet capital and labor force relative to such changes in the United States or other countries. Further, how does one measure nonconventional inputs such as management? As a result, only conventional inputs such as land, labor, and capital can be measured and generally only in quantitative terms.[23] The danger, therefore, is that important changes in nonconventional inputs and qualitative changes of conventional inputs will be ignored, thus distorting the estimation of the growth of output per unit of input.

The Record: Long-Term Trends

In Table 12.5, we relate several measures of the rates of growth of factor productivity in the Soviet Union, United States, and selected other countries, both over the long run and for the postwar period. The table includes both the rates of growth of output per unit of combined (Capital and labor) input (column 5) and also the growth of output per unit of specific factor input, namely, labor productivity (column 6) and capital productivity (column 7).

Looking at the long-term trends in panel A, we see that the Soviet Union distinguishes itself from the United States and other countries by a more rapid growth of both labor and capital—2.2 percent and 7.4 percent, respectively, between 1928 and 1966. This reinforces our earlier point that one would expect more rapid Soviet output growth because of the more rapid growth of

Table 12.5 ANNUAL RATES OF GROWTH OF INPUTS AND PRODUCTIVITY: USSR, UNITED STATES, AND SELECTED COUNTRIES

Panel A: Long-term trends	(1) Output	(2) Labor, employment	(3) Fixed capital	(4) Combined inputs	(5) Output per unit of combined input (1–4)	(6) Labor productivity (1–2)	(7) Capital productivity (1–3)
USSR (GNP)							
1928–1966	5.5	2.2	7.4	3.5	2.0	3.3	-1.9
United States (GNP)							
1929–1969	3.3	0.8	2.0	1.1	2.2	2.5	1.3
United Kingdom (GDP)							
1925–1929 to 1963	1.9	0.8	1.8	1.1	0.8	1.1	0.1
France (GDP)							
1913–1966	2.3	-0.5	2.0	0.2	2.2	2.8	0.3
Canada (GNP)							
1926–1956	3.9	0.8	2.9	1.2	2.7	3.1	1.0
Norway (GDP)							
1899–1956	2.8	0.3	2.5	0.7	2.1	2.5	0.3

Panel B: Postwar trends	(1) Output	(2) Labor, employment	(3) Fixed capital	(4) Combined inputs	(5) Output per unit of combined input (1–4)	(6) Labor productivity (1–2)	(7) Capital productivity (1–3)
USSR							
1950–1960	5.8	1.2	9.4	4.1	1.7	4.6	1.7
1960–81	4.1	1.4	7.6	3.3	0.8	2.7	-3.5
1983–87	2.0	0.5	5.8	2.7	-0.7	1.5	-3.8
United States							
1948–1960	3.2	1.4	3.2	2.0	1.2	1.7	0.0
1960–1981	3.5	2.0	3.6	2.6	0.9	1.4	-0.1
Canada							
1960–1980	4.6	2.9	4.9	3.6	1.0	1.7	-0.3
Belgium							
1950–1962	3.2	0.6	2.3	1.2	2.0	2.6	0.9
Denmark							
1950–1962	3.5	0.9	5.1	2.4	1.1	2.6	-1.6

Table 12.5 *(Continued)*

Panel B: Postwar Trends	(1) Output	(2) Labor, employment	(3) Fixed capital	(4) Combined inputs	(5) Output per unit of combined input (1–4)	(6) Labor productivity (1–2)	(7) Capital productivity (1–3)
France							
1950–1962	4.9	.1	4.2	1.5	3.4	4.8	0.7
1960–1980	4.6	.8	5.0	2.3	2.3	3.6	-0.4
West Germany							
1950–1962	7.3	2.0	6.9	3.5	3.8	5.3	0.9
1960–1980	3.8	.0	4.8	1.7	2.1	3.8	-1.0
Italy							
1950–1962	6.0	.6	3.5	1.6	4.4	5.4	2.5
Netherlands							
1950–1962	4.7	1.1	4.7	3.1	1.6	3.6	0.0
Norway							
1950–1962	3.5	.2	4.2	1.6	1.9	3.3	-0.7
1960–1980	4.7	.5	4.1	1.7	3.1	4.2	0.6
United Kingdom							
1950–1962	2.3	.7	3.4	1.7	0.6	1.6	-1.1
1960–1980	2.3	.4	3.4	1.5	0.8	1.9	-1.1
Japan							
1953–1970	10.0	1.7	9.8	4.5	5.5	8.3	0.2
1970–1980	5.0	.9	8.4	3.5	1.5	4.1	-3.4
Greece							
1900–1000	6.1	.0	6.2	2.2	3.9	6.1	-0.1

Sources: Panel A: Moorsteen and Powell, *The Soviet Capital Stock*, pp. 38, 166, 315, 361–362, 365; A. Becker, R. Moorsteen, and R. Powell, *Soviet Capital Stock: Revisions and Extension, 1961–1967* (New Haven, Conn.: The Economic Growth Center, 1968), p. 11, 25, 26; Kuznets, *Economic Growth of Nations*, p. 74; E. Denison, *Accounting for United States Economic Growth, 1929–1969* (Washington, D.C.: The Brookings Institution, 1974), p. 54, p. 186; B. J. Wattenberg, ed., *The Statistical History of the United States from Colonial Times to the Present* (New York: Basic Books, 1976), pp. 257–258. Panel B: *Handbook of Economic Statistics* (various years), employment; U.S. Department of Labor, *Trends in Multifactor Productivity, 1948–81.* Bulletin 2178, September 1983, p. 22; *Growth Rates of Employment, Reproducible Capital, and Output:* E. Denison, *Why Growth Rates Differ* (Washington, D.C.: Brooking, 1967), pp. 42, 190, and chap. 21; E. Denison, *Accounting for United States Economic Growth, 1929–1969* (Washington, D.C.:Brooking Institution, 1974), pp. 32, 58; E. Denison and W. Chung, *How Japan's Economy Grew So Fast* (Washington, D.C.: Brooking Institution, 1976), pp. 19, 31; OECD, Department of Economics and Statistics, *Flows and Stocks of Fixed Capital, 1955–1980* (OECD: Paris, 1983), pp. 1–39; *Handbook of Economic Statistics 1980*, p. 47; *World Tables, 1980*, country tables and Table 5 (social indicators).

inputs—thus our hesitancy to use growth as our sole performance criterion. In the USSR, about 65 percent of long-term growth (column 1 ÷ column 4, panel A) is accounted for by growth of inputs, whereas in the United States and other countries (the United Kingdom is somewhat of an exception), a much smaller portion of growth can be attributed to the growth of inputs. The significance of this pattern is that Soviet growth has tended to be quite dependent upon an expanding labor force and capital stock, rather than upon expanding output per unit of input. Thus Soviet growth has tended to be *extensive* (based upon expanding inputs) rather than *intensive* (based upon better utilization of inputs)—a rather expensive growth pattern in terms of economic costs, for capital is expanded at the expense of current consumption and labor is expanded at the cost of leisure.

The postwar trends in panel B show that Soviet input growth was indeed rapid by international standards, but it was not unique. Canada (which experienced rapid labor force growth), West Germany (rapid growth of both labor and capital), and Japan (rapid growth of labor and capital) matched the Soviet postwar growth rate of combined inputs. It is notable that in the case of West Germany (1950–1962) and Japan (1953–1970), the payoff to rapid input growth was higher (in terms of growth) than in the Soviet Union.

Can one argue that rapid input growth forced the USSR into an extensive growth pattern? The example of Japan is instructive, for Japan was able to combine rapid input growth with a relatively intensive growth pattern. Some 60 percent of Japanese postwar growth is explained by increasing output per unit of input.

Turning to the rate of growth of output per unit of combined input (panel A, column 5), we see that the long-term Soviet rate (1928 to 1966) is perhaps somewhat below, or roughly equivalent to, the long-term productivity growth rates in the United States, France, Canada, and Norway. It is difficult to generalize on the basis of such narrow differences because the impact of wartime destruction on Soviet productivity is difficult to gauge; such estimates are quite sensitive to measurement errors. As far as the postwar period is concerned, while the annual rate of growth of output per unit of combined input in the Soviet Union 1950 to 1960—1.7 percent—exceeded the American rate of 1.2 percent, it was only average as far as Western Europe was concerned; it was well exceeded by France, West Germany, and Italy and dwarfed by the Japanese rate. After 1960, the Soviet factor productivity growth rate—0.8 percent—was below all the other factor productivity growth rates, just equaling the anemic English productivity rate. It was dwarfed by the Greek and Norwegian rates.

The long-term growth of Soviet labor productivity (3.3 percent annually) is slightly above the average rates in the other countries examined (but well above that of the United Kingdom). Soviet labor productivity growth in the early postwar period was extremely rapid (4.6 percent annually) and far exceeded the American rate. It was matched by the productivity growth in France, West Germany, and Italy but was dwarfed by the Japanese rate of 8.3 percent.

After 1960, Soviet labor productivity growth dropped to 60 percent of its earlier rate. At 2.7 percent per annum, it exceeded the American and English rates, but was well below France, West Germany, Japan, and Greece. Trends in Soviet capital productivity relative to the other countries (the rate of growth of output per unit of capital input) are interesting to note. The long-term growth rate of Soviet capital productivity is –1.9 percent annually, which indicates a rising capital/output ratio over the long run. Of the surveyed countries, none has a long-term negative rate of growth of capital productivity. In the early postwar era, the Soviet Union registered healthy growth of capital productivity at 1.7 percent per annum, exceeded only by the Italian rate. After 1960, Soviet capital productivity dropped at an annual rate of –3.5 percent. Most other countries also experienced slightly negative growth of capital productivity, but only Japan matched the Soviet Union's precipitous decline.

In sum, both the long-term and postwar comparisons show Soviet dynamic efficiency, as measured indirectly by the rate of growth of output per unit of combined input, to be neither exceptionally large nor small when compared to trends in the United States and other industrialized Western countries. Instead, Soviet productivity performance could be described as average. What these figures do indicate quite clearly is the extent to which the fast Soviet growth rate may be attributable to the policy of rapidly expanding inputs. The impersonal statistics of input and output growth rates veil a very significant point concerning long-term Soviet economic growth. The relatively low proportion of output growth explained by productivity growth means that Soviet growth was of the "high cost" variety. Rapid growth rates of labor and capital occasion significant sacrifice from the population in the form of lessened consumption, leisure, and "home production." If the USSR had been able to grow as "intensively" as the industrialized market economies (let us say, two-thirds of output growth accounted for by productivity growth), then the same long-term rate of economic growth could have been achieved with considerably less sacrifice demanded of the population. The USSR-Japanese postwar productivity comparison is notable, for it illustrates this point well. Both countries experienced roughly comparable input growth rates (equal sacrifice); yet the Japanese output growth rate for the 1953-to-1980 period was almost 2 percentage points above that of the Soviet Union. One cannot argue *a priori* that the Japanese experience is representative of capitalism under conditions of rapid input growth (just as one cannot argue that the USSR is representative of command socialism), but the Japanese counterexample must be recognized.

Soviet Economic Growth: The Contemporary Record

Comparison of Soviet and Western long–term growth trends is instructive for understanding the Soviet experience in a global perspective. However, of greater importance to our understanding of the contemporary Soviet economy is the recent growth record.

In Table 12.6 we have assembled evidence on Soviet economic growth in recent years. There are a number of important lessons to be derived from this evidence.

First, although there is considerable controversy about the various alternative measures of Soviet economic growth, this controversy does not say a great deal about recent trends. Accordingly, we leave this issue for the concluding section of this chapter.

Second, the measures presented in Table 12.6 demonstrate that there has been a significant and continuing downward trend in the rate of Soviet economic growth. As we have emphasized, this trend shows up in most estimates of Soviet economic growth, though obviously the exact magnitude of the trend will differ from one estimate to another.

Third, it is instructive to note that while the rate of growth of output has been declining, the rate of growth of inputs has also been declining. Notably, however, the former has been declining much more rapidly than the latter, hence a productivity problem to be addressed in the next section. It is this type of evidence, however, that underlies the discussion of Soviet difficulties in transforming their economy from an extensive pattern to an intensive pattern of economic growth.

This contemporary growth record worries Soviet leaders, and as we have emphasized, is a major force driving the reforms of the Gorbachev era. Although there is ample empirical evidence to suggest that rates of economic growth, as we define these concepts, tend to decline in economies at more advanced levels of economic development, the issue is nevertheless of great concern in the Soviet case.[24] The Soviet Union, however measured, is at a much lower level of economic development than most of the Western industrialized economies. Moreover, it is troubling to many that the system has been

Table 12.6   SOVIET ECONOMIC GROWTH: RECENT TRENDS
Average Annual Rates of Change

| Period | Output | | Inputs | | |
	Soviet officiala	CIAb	Labor in man-hours	Capital	Land
1961–65	6.5	4.8	1.5	8.8	0.2
1966–70	7.8	5.0	2.0	7.4	Negl.
1971–75	5.7	3.1	1.7	8.0	0.1
1976–80	4.3	2.2	1.2	6.9	−0.1
1981–85	3.6	1.8	0.7	6.2	−0.2
1986–87	3.2	2.2	0.4	5.3	−0.05

[a] National income produced.

[b] GNP adjusted for services— 1982 rubles sector of origin at factor cost.

Source: Directorate of Intelligence, *Handbook of Economic Statistics, 1988* (Washington, D.C.: Central Intelligence Agency, 1988), Table 37; Directorate of Intelligence, *Revising Soviet Economic Performance Under Glasnost: Implications for CIA Estimates* (Washington, D.C.: Central Intelligence Agency, 1988), Table 3.

incapable of greater efficiency at a stage well before basic consumer needs can be met. What are the common explanations for this growth record?

In a recent study of Soviet economic growth, Gur Ofer has provided an excellent summary of common explanations.[25] We outline these explanations dealing first with the more general ones, then with explanations for which empirical evidence may be available.

First, it has been argued that growth rates slow down because of the growing complexity of the economy. At earlier stages of economic development, there are fewer and more simply defined products being made by a smaller number of enterprises than at later stages of development. Thus, the problems of coordination, especially in a planned economy, may be simplified. This argument while interesting and intuitively appealing, is nevertheless difficult to quantify.

Second, although economists do not fully understand the relationship between incentives, effort, and performance, it is often argued that incentives in the Soviet Union are inadequate. Throughout the 1980s, this theme has assumed new importance as Gorbachev has stressed this aspect of the "social contract."[26] Later in this chapter, we will examine the Soviet record of consumption as part of our more general examination of performance criteria.

Third, Ofer has emphasized the issue of defense spending. Although there is a long and contentious literature pertaining to Soviet defense spending, much of this literature has focused on the magnitude of the Soviet defense establishment and the implications for U.S. and global security. Recently, the emphasis has shifted to some degree focusing on the issue of how the military and civilian economies interact in the Soviet case. While we defer to the next chapter on this general issue, Ofer notes that most Western estimates support the view that cuts in Soviet military spending will not make large contributions to the Soviet consumer sector.[27]

Fourth, a set of explanations relate to the specific characteristics of the Soviet system and the manner in which these characteristics may inhibit growth performance. For example, the Soviet economy has a sectorial structure requiring change. Possibly most important, both the structure of the economy (for example, capital intensity) and Soviet economic policies (for example, with regard to the implementation of technological change) seem to inhibit the growth of productivity. The productivity issue is indeed central to a more detailed examination of the growth slowdown and is obviously a fundamental basis of our more general examination of the performance characteristics of the Soviet economy.

Factors Behind The Productivity Decline

Table 12.7 provides a picture of combined factor productivity, labor productivity and capital productivity for the Soviet Union and selected other countries covering a fairly long span of time. This table provides greater detail and more recent productivity estimates for the Soviet Union both for the aggregate economy and for the industrial sector.

Table 12.7   SOVIET FACTOR PRODUCTIVITY, AGGREGATE ECONOMY, AND INDUSTRY
Average Annual Rates of Growth

	1961–1965	1966–1970	1971–1975	1976–1980	1981–1985	1986	1987
Factor productivity, aggregate economy	0.3	0.8	−1.2	−1.3	−1.1	1.4	−1.9
Labor productivity, aggregate economy	3.2	3.0	1.3	1.0	1.1	3.5	0.1
Capital productivity, aggregate economy	−3.7	−2.2	−4.6	−4.4	−4.1	−1.4	−4.6
Factor productivity, industry	−1.0	0.1	−0.1	−2.1	−2.3	−0.8	−1.4
Labor productivity, industry	3.5	3.1	3.9	1.3	1.2	2.3	1.7
Capital productivity, industry	−4.4	−2.3	−3.1	−4.7	−4.9	−3.1	−3.7

Source: Directorate of Intelligence, Handbook of Economic Statistics, 1988 (Washington, D.C.: Central Intelligence Agency, 1988), p. C3.

The importance of the productivity problem in the Soviet Union can be seen from the evidence in Table 12.7. The average annual rate of growth of factor productivity for the aggregate economy has been negative since the early 1970s (with the exception of the year 1986 in the periods for which we have provided evidence). Labor productivity has been positive, though with significant fluctuations from one period to another. Capital productivity has been negative since the early 1960s. While other countries have experienced problems with capital productivity, the Soviet experience must be especially troubling in light of the magnitude and persistence of the problem in a country whose level of economic development is generally below that of industrialized nations.

The productivity picture in Soviet industry has been broadly similar to that of the overall economy. The average annual growth of combined factor productivity for industry has been very modest or negative for much of the past 30 years. While the growth of labor productivity has been positive, the experience with capital productivity has been a major problem.

What has been the relative productivity performance of Soviet industry (the branch of highest official priority) relative to the industrialized capitalist economies? This appears to be the crucial test of the productivity of the Soviet planned economy. Abram Bergson has demonstrated that even if one uses a wide range of estimates of Soviet industrial technology (encompassing all positions in the debate), the annual growth rate of productivity has been roughly equal to the disappointing records of the United States and the United Kingdom (1955–1970) and well below the other industrialized countries.[28] As the growth rate of industrial output in the USSR was higher than that of the industrialized countries, this again points to an extensive pattern of industrial growth.

There has been a substantial debate in Western literature concerning the productivity performance of postwar Soviet industry, principally directed toward an explanation of its declining rate of growth. This discussion is highly technical and involves debates over the appropriate measurement of industrial output and the specification of Soviet industrial technology (via econometric and other methods). One explanation for the Soviet industrial productivity decline has been advanced by Martin Weitzman. Weitzman argues that the explanation lies in the difficulty of substituting capital for labor.[29] Throughout the postwar era, industrial capital has grown at a much more rapid rate than industrial labor (from 1960 to 1970, labor grew at 3 percent and capital at 10 percent per annum).[30] With such divergent rates of input growth, how successfully capital can be substituted for labor depends upon the technology ("production function") of Soviet industry. If capital can be easily substituted for labor, then these divergent rates should not impair the growth of output. If, however, it becomes increasingly difficult to substitute capital for labor (the technical measure is called the "elasticity of substitution"),* then one would expect a declining pattern of output growth. The measurement of the elasticity of substitution of Soviet industry is a complicated theoretical and econometric matter, as the debate over this issue suggests, and competing estimates have been offered, most of which suggest that Soviet industrial technology does not allow "easy" substitution of capital for labor. The whole point of this exercise is to demonstrate that the declining rate of growth of industrial output may (partially or fully) be the consequence of growing substitution difficulties rather than the result of declining productivity performance *per se*.

---

*A simple technical explanation of the substitution problem is as follows. The increase in output (dQ) can be decomposed (assuming a linear homogeneous production function and other "usual" assumptions concerning the shape of the production function) into that increase due to increase in labor (L) and capital (K) inputs and a residual due to technical progress (T). Thus,

$$dQ = \frac{\delta Q}{\delta L} \, dL + \frac{\delta Q}{\delta K} \, dK + dT$$

Dividing through by Q yields

$$\frac{dQ}{Q} = \eta_L \frac{dL}{L} + \eta_K \frac{dK}{K} + \frac{dT}{T}$$

where

$$\eta L = \frac{\delta D}{\delta L} \cdot \frac{L}{Q} \quad \text{and} \quad \eta K = \frac{\delta D}{\delta K} \cdot \frac{K}{Q}$$

are the partial elasticities of output with respect to each factor input. If the elasticity of substitution is less than unity, then it follows [Weitzman, "Soviet Postwar Growth," p. 679] that η_L will increase if K grows more rapidly than L (definitely true in the Soviet case). Thus, the weight of the slower-growing factor input (L) increases over time, while that of the faster-growing input (K) declines. The growth rate of combined factor inputs declines over time, therefore partially (or fully) offsetting the decline in the rate of growth of output.

Padma Desai offers a different interpretation of declining industrial factor productivity performance. Through a careful analysis of industry and the individual industrial branches, Desai concludes that the decline in factor productivity growth is not due to the difficulty of substituting capital for labor. In fact, Desai's estimated production functions indicate that capital can be readily substituted for labor in most industrial branches. The output decline is not due to substitution difficulties but rather to a declining growth rate of the unexplained productivity differential.[31]

If Desai's interpretation is correct, the decline in the growth of the productivity residual remains to be explained. Gertrude Schroeder has analyzed the industrial productivity slowdown between 1961 and 1982 at both an industry-wide and branch level and attempts to account for its precipitous decline, especially after 1975. Schroeder offers a number of explanations, not being able to single out any one as the dominant factor. First, she points to the decision of the central planners to reduce growth targets after 1976 in the hopes that reduced pressure would cause managers to use resources more efficiently. According to her analysis, this policy backfired in that output growth did indeed contract as planned but the efficiency of resource use did not improve. Second, the Soviet economy began to encounter severe shortfalls of key raw materials such as steel and coal after 1976 and was beset by transportation and energy bottlenecks as well. A third factor—the most difficult to quantify—may have been a decline in worker morale and discipline in the late years of the Brezhnev reign. Schroeder is able to rule out one factor—agricultural shortfalls—which she finds to be an insignificant factor behind the productivity slowdown.[32]

Growth and productivity slowdowns are difficult to understand in any setting. We imagine that Soviet and Western economists will never fully understand why Soviet output growth and productivity growth have declined so dramatically in recent years. The productivity slowdown is apparently so pronounced that it is readily recognized by emigrés from the Soviet Union who witnessed the productivity slowdown firsthand. They tend to blame a decline in material incentives for Soviet productivity problems.

SOVIET STATIC EFFICIENCY

Not only is the changing efficiency of an economy over time—*dynamic efficiency*—a valuable performance criterion, but one might also consider its efficiency at one point in time—*static efficiency*. The two concepts are interrelated in that an economy's dynamic efficiency in the long run will determine its static efficiency at a distant point in time, and static efficiency, in turn, may have an important impact on dynamic efficiency in the long run. In any case, the efficiency of the economy today is a matter of concern and interest. In this section, the focus is upon the static efficiency of the Soviet economy relative to that of the United States and selected other market economies.

Static efficiency is defined intuitively by Bergson as "the degree to which, *equity apart* [our italics], the community is, in fact, able to exploit the economic opportunities that are open."[33] The degree of static efficiency, therefore, will depend on the available stock of technological knowledge and on the effectiveness of its utilization, both of which serve to define the economic opportunities open to the community at a given point in time.[*]

How, then, is the relative static efficiency of the Soviet economy to be measured? Again, as in the case of dynamic efficiency, static efficiency can only be measured indirectly by comparing the magnitude of the output that is derived from a unit of "combined" factor inputs at one point in time. It is immediately obvious from our discussion of dynamic efficiency that such "factor productivity" comparisons measure static efficiency indirectly because inputs differ in quality, and some of them cannot be measured at all. In measuring output per unit of input at one point in time, differences in climate and soil fertility (an important factor in determining agricultural productivity), scale differences, cultural factors, and many other variables that may or may not affect productivity tend to be ignored, for they cannot readily be included.[34] In effect, by comparing factor productivities at points of time across countries and drawing static efficiency conclusions, we are assuming identical underlying production conditions. There is yet another problem: to compute the relative magnitudes—as opposed to rates of growth—of output per unit of combined factor inputs suitable for intercountry comparisons, both output and factor inputs must be measured in a common unit. Soviet output must either be valued in foreign prices (American prices, for example), or the output of the other country must be valued in ruble prices. The same is true of combined factor inputs (land, labor, and capital). As we have shown, index number relativity will affect such measurements because output mixes and relative prices vary among economies, and what one country produces in abundance at relatively low prices will likely be produced in smaller quantities at relatively higher prices by another country. In this manner, the relative GNP of one country valued in its own prices will be smaller than when valued in the prices of another country.[35]

---

[*]This static-efficiency concept can be illustrated in the figure below using the Production Possibilities Schedule (PPS). If the economy is operating on its PPS (point *A*), then it has attained maximum static efficiency. If it operates below the PPS (point *B*, for example), it has failed to attain maximum static efficiency. The available stock of technological knowledge, and the resource base of the economy will determine the location of the schedule, and an increase in this stock will move the schedule out. Thus, with an increase in the stock of technological knowledge, point *A* will now be below the new PPS, and if the economy is to remain statically efficient, it must advance to a higher point on the new PPS.

A further problem in the Soviet case is that combined factor inputs (capital, land, and labor), which are measured by the total cost of such inputs, cannot be measured directly because capital and land fail to generate rent and interest—under the labor theory of value—as they do under capitalism. Therefore, "synthetic" capital charges must be computed by applying an "arbitrary" rate of return to the value of net capital stock, and the choice of this rate of return can significantly affect the outcome of factor productivity comparisons.[36]

Despite all the shortcomings noted above, we relate Abram Bergson's estimates of national income per unit of combined factor (labor and reproducible capital) input in American prices to the Soviet Union, the United States, and several European countries in 1960 (Table 12.8). The United States price-weighted index was chosen because Soviet factor productivity makes its best showing using this variant.

The calculations of national income per unit of factor input show that the Soviet economy in 1960 derived slightly less than 50 percent as much output per unit of combined input as did the American economy, about 65 percent as much as France, West Germany, and the United Kingdom, and slightly below the output per unit of input in Italy. When the comparison is for industry alone, the Soviet productivity ratios improve (this is reflective of the relatively poor performance of agriculture and services). Soviet factor productivity in 1960 was roughly equal to that of Italy and the United Kingdom and was 80 percent that of France and West Germany. Although it is possible that a substantial portion of the computed productivity differentials could be accounted for by input quality differences[37] and by omitted factor inputs, such as land or entrepreneurship, this seems unlikely.[38]

Thus, one would have to conclude that the level of output power unit of combined capital and labor input in the Soviet Union was low relative to the other countries surveyed (except Italy) in 1960. These productivity rankings have changed significantly since 1960 (the West German ratio is likely equal to

Table 12.8   NATIONAL INCOME PER UNIT OF COMBINED FACTOR (LABOR AND REPRODUCIBLE CAPITAL) INPUTS, 1960 U.S. PRICE WEIGHTS
United States = 100

	National income	Industry
United States	100	100
France	63	71
West Germany	65	69
United Kingdom	64	61
Italy	47	60
USSR	41	58

Source: Bergson, *Productivity and the Social System: The USSR and the West* (Cambridge, Mass.: Harvard University Press, 1978), pp. 101, 111.

that of the United States in 1930), but the Soviet Union's ranking, as we have shown above, has not changed appreciably relative to the industrialized capitalist countries. The potential sources of low Soviet productivity have been described in Chapters 7, 8, and 9—the managerial bonus system, irrational prices, deficient investment allocation criteria, lack of incentives to innovate and to introduce new technology—and may be more severe than the sources of economic inefficiency in the industrialized West. It is interesting to note that Soviet estimates show Soviet industrial efficiency (output per production worker) to be slightly above one-half that of American industry.[39]

In a recent study, Abram Bergson has again examined the issue of productivity differentials between the socialist systems (the Soviet Union, Poland, Hungary, and Yugoslavia) and a sample of Western mixed economy countries focusing on the year 1975.[40] In this study, Bergson uses the basic Cobb-Douglas production function to relate output per worker, to capital per worker and land per worker all calculated relative to the United States. Dummy variable techniques are used to isolate the economic system effect, whether socialist or capitalist. In his conclusions, Bergson notes that output per worker in the socialist countries "… is found to fall systematically short of that in the Western mixed-economy (WME) countries. . ."[41] Specifically, the difference in output per worker between the socialist and WME samples varies from 25 to 34 percent, the socialist being lower than the WME countries, the amount depending on measurement assumptions—for example, the specific prices used.[42]

Just what does the low Soviet output per unit of input tell us about static efficiency in the Soviet Union? Can one attribute low productivity to weaknesses in the Soviet economic system or are factors independent of the economic system involved? On the one hand, it might be argued that low output per unit of input and low levels of economic development tend to go together, and the Soviet Union, like Italy, whose factor productivity is also low, is less developed (in terms of development indicators such as per capita income and percentage of rural population) than the other countries in Table 12.7. Thus, the Soviet productivity deficit should perhaps be regarded as a function of the low level of development of the Soviet Union and not as an indicator of its static inefficiency.* To

---

*The problem of comparing the productivity performance of two countries at different levels of development is illustrated in the figure below using the Production Possibilities Schedule (PPS). The country at a higher level of development would have a higher PPS (*aa*) than the country at a lower level of development (*bb*). If we define the PPS in terms of a combined unit of resources, then both countries may be operating at maximum static efficiency (at points *A* and *B*), yet the computed productivity at *A* will be greater than at *B*.

determine the extent to which low Soviet static efficiency is a product of the stage of economic development requires firm information on the relationship between efficiency levels and economic development. Moreover, if one attempts to make hypothetical adjustments for the level of development, the outcome in the Soviet case depends on which development indicator one employs. After examining this matter, Bergson concludes that "the low Soviet factor productivity does not seem fully explicable in such terms."[43] It is also not clear whether Soviet static efficiency should improve (in relative terms) as the stage of development advances, for the ability of the command economy to deal with the growing complexities of a modern economy remains to be demonstrated. The growth of Soviet factor productivity over time (Table 12.5) has been only average when compared with other industrialized countries; therefore, the Soviet Union does not seem to have reduced its productivity gap as it gradually closed its development gap—a result that one would expect if low productivity were solely the result of low economic development.

The low level of static efficiency in the Soviet Union has evoked considerable discussion among Western students of the Soviet economy. We summarize briefly two representative points of view. On the one side, Alec Nove and Peter Wiles,[44] both English economists, argue that the Soviets deliberately sacrificed static efficiency to achieve their long-run political objectives—the restructuring of the economy, the transformation of property relations, the expansion of military power, and rapid economic growth. Static efficiency, they argue, could have been achieved only at the expense of these goals, by adopting a more gradual marginalist approach and by eliminating political control over economic decisions. Thus, the static inefficiency of the Soviet economy today can be viewed as a deliberate policy decision, just as the rapid Soviet growth rate can be considered a deliberate policy choice of the Soviet leadership—with static inefficiency as the price that the Soviet leadership willingly paid for rapid economic development.

In opposition to this line of reasoning, Abram Bergson[45] argues that rapid economic development and static efficiency are not necessarily incompatible, as Nove and Wiles maintain, for an economy with greater static efficiency will produce a larger output and consequently a larger volume of savings (with the same savings rate), which will promote economic growth. Bergson does grant, however, that in a centrally planned economy, the state may opt to promote growth by autonomously increasing the savings rate through the introduction of forced savings, administrative economic controls, collectivization, and autarky—measures that may reduce static efficiency yet generate growth. If the state does so, however, it is at the expense of reduced living standards, which is in itself a significant cost to be considered in evaluating the performance of economies. According to Bergson, the basic question, therefore, should be: To what extent could similar rates of growth or slightly lower rates have been attained in the Soviet case through maximum utilization of resources (static efficiency) without sacrificing living standards?

One further aspect of the relative efficiency of the Soviet economy that fails to show up in output or input measures is that such figures often indicate output per unit of *employed* labor and capital inputs.[46] Although the Soviets do not publish aggregate unemployment figures, one can assume that aggregate unemployment in the Soviet Union is less than in the United States. Thus, unemployment is a major source of inefficient resource utilization in the United States that the Soviets have largely avoided, although the Soviets do suffer from "underemployment," an issue discussed earlier in Chapter 9 of this book. Moreover, with changing rules pertaining to labor allocation, the issue of unemployment will be important. For example, a recent study by Paul Gregory and Irwin Collier based on surveys of emigré responses for the 1970s places a lower bound on unemployment in the Soviet Union at 1.2 percent. This is an issue of major importance for the Soviet economy under Perestroika

A rather different issue is that of the Soviet management system and the extent to which the rules of this system facilitate waste and resulting inefficiency. It is difficult to predict the magnitude of the waste of capital resources in the Soviet Union that results from the stockpiling of fixed and working capital by the Soviet manager for the sake of building a safety factor and from poor choices of investment projects. In the American economy, such stockpiling adds to inventory costs and interest expenses, thereby reducing profits, and is therefore avoided as much as possible.

An even thornier issue in estimating factor productivity concerns the relative quality of output. Factor productivity measures relate the volume of output per unit of input, whereas the output measures (especially in the case of Soviet consumer goods) inadequately reflect the relative quality of output, which, according to numerous reports, is poor in the Soviet Union.[47] The production of a large quantity of defective goods using minimal inputs would show up well in factor productivity estimates, introducing a bias into such measures.

EQUITY OF INCOME DISTRIBUTION IN THE SOVIET UNION

A fourth performance criterion for evaluating economies is how "equitably" income is distributed among members of the population. Of all the suggested criteria, this is the most difficult to evaluate objectively because different individuals and different societies have different views on what constitutes an "equitable" or "inequitable" distribution of income. Some may argue that income is equitably distributed when divided equally; others may argue that equity requires large income differentials to reward risk, effort, and past frugality. Income derived from ownership of property is a very thorny question; in the United States, for example, large income differences among spending units result from differences in property income as opposed to wage and salary incomes. Whether it is equitable to allow such disparities in property income is a subjective judgment, yet it is crucial when contrasting equity in the Soviet Union and the United States. In view of these issues, we suggest that the definition of "good" or "poor" income distribution must remain subjective over a fairly wide range.

The Soviets have not published much data on the distribution of income among families. This is more likely the result of the relatively low priority attached to the gathering of such information than to any official policy of secrecy. The available data on income distribution have been analyzed extensively by Alastair McCauley, Peter Wiles, Stefan Markowski, Abram Bergson, Gur Ofer, Aron Vinokur, and Murray Yanowitch.[48] Although such data are far from complete and omit important income groups (the upper strata of the state and party bureaucracy, the state farmers), they do allow the researcher to draw certain conclusions. From the evidence that is available on industrial wage income, we note that Soviet wage differentials within industrial branches between high- and low-paid workers during the 1930s and early 1950s were probably greater than in the United States, but since the mid-1950s, Soviet differentials have been narrowed substantially until they are now probably smaller than American differentials. In general, the trend in recent years has been toward the concept of "equal pay for equal work," with wages to be determined by job content—working conditions, skill requirements, on-the-job incentives—rather than by some measure of productivity, which may be viewed as an attempt to introduce more equality into Soviet wage determination.[49] Such intercountry wage differential comparisons are quite crude and inexact, but the important point is that Soviet industrial wage differentials have at times been as large as in the United States. This result is in keeping with the Marxian theory of income distribution in the transitional stage of socialism, during which the workers' contribution to society should determine their share of society's output; inequality of income distribution would only be eliminated when society attained a higher stage of socialism—a stage of absolute abundance—when distribution would proceed according to need.[50]

Beginning in the early 1930s, the Soviet leadership waged a consistent battle against "equality mongering" (uravnilovka), a policy linked with utopian socialism and even Trotskyism. Indeed, during the 1930s, there was strong evidence of increasing inequality in the distribution of wage income, which persisted into the mid-1950s. Since the mid-1950s, there has been a remarkable decrease in such inequality. In 1956, the average wage earned by the top 10 percent of wage earners and salaried workers exceeded that of the bottom 10 percent by a factor of 4.4. By 1981, this ratio had been reduced to 3.0. For wage earners in industry, the ratio dropped from 3.36 in 1956 to 2.63 in 1972.[51] Although the move toward greater equality in the distribution of wage income has been justified ideologically by the "law of reimbursement,"[52] we suspect that economic considerations—namely, the greater supply of educated workers—served as the impetus for the leveling of wage incomes.

Comparisons of the *overall* distribution of income in the Soviet Union with that of other countries, both capitalist and socialist, is a risky business because of the omission of significant groups from the Soviet data and the questionable reliability of the data on included families.[53] With these reservations in mind, we cite some preliminary conclusions. The first is that the distribution of income probably became more equal between the late 1950s (1958) and the late 1960s (1967). This conclusion follows from evidence on state employees, a group accounting for 70 percent of all employment in 1967. It would be surprising if such a leveling had not occurred in light of the marked reduction in industrial wage differentials during this period. The second conclusion (derived from a measure of income distribution that does cover most, but not all, population groups) is that the overall distribution of money income after taxes (including income earned or retained by the farm population) in the USSR in 1967 was more unequal than in the other planned socialist economies of Eastern Europe.[54]

Third, the USSR distribution of income is not very different from the distributions of income in a number of industrialized capitalist countries, especially on an after-tax basis. The available evidence (gathered by Abram Bergson) is given in Table 12.9 for the USSR and for a number of industrialized capitalist countries. It should be noted that farm households are not included in the Soviet data, an omission that probably understates income inequality. Also, the incomes of the Soviet elite are not included, but their numbers are so small that this omission is likely not significant. As the income distributions show, the USSR 1972–1974 distribution looks very much like the Swedish, Norwegian, and U.K. after-tax distributions. The Soviet distribution is more equal than the U.S., Australian, French, and Canadian distributions. To quote Abram Bergson:

> Inequality in the USSR may not be much less than that in Norway and the United Kingdom, but is no doubt less than that in the United States and France. According to especially incomplete data, inequality in the USSR could sometimes fall short of that in countries at a comparable development stage, though that need not be markedly so in the case of Japan.[55]

Fourth, contrary to popular impression of the countryside, there is as much differentiation in the distribution of income among the farm population as among the city population.[56]

The final conclusion is a striking one: namely, the high incidence of "poverty" among the Soviet population, not only among the rural population and the pensioners but also among nonagricultural state employees. If one takes the Soviet's own "minimum material satisfaction budget" (the MMS budget), described as containing the "volume and structure of necessaries of life required for the reproduction of labor power among unskilled workers,"[57] then, McCauley estimates, in 1967, 42 million nonagricultural employees and their dependents, 5 to 10 million state farm families, and 32 million *kolkhoznik* families had incomes at or below the MMS level. These figures add up to an astonishing 79 million persons (or one-third of the Soviet population) living at or below the minimum material satisfaction budget. Given this large proportion, it is likely that the Soviet MMS budget is a liberal estimate of contemporary subsistence norms. However, if one adopts as the poverty norm one-half of the MMS budget, in 1967 approximately 25 million Soviet citizens (10 percent of the population) were living at or below the poverty level. From these figures,

Table 12.9   DISTRIBUTION OF INCOME, SOVIET UNION AND WESTERN COUNTRIES, HOUSE-
HOLDS BY PER CAPITA HOUSEHOLD INCOME

	Income share of			
	Lowest 10%	Lowest 20%	Highest 20%	Highest 10%
USSR, nonfarm households, before tax 1967 (McCauley)	4.4	10.4	33.8	19.9
USSR, urban households, after tax 1972–1974 (Ofer–Vinokur)	3.4	8.7	38.5	24.1
All households				
Australia, 1966–1967				
Before tax	3.5	8.3	41.0	25.6
After tax	3.5	8.3	40.9	25.5
Norway, 1970				
Before tax	3.5	8.2	39.0	23.5
After tax	4.7	10.5	35.6	22.4
United Kingdom, 1973				
Before tax	3.5	8.3	39.9	23.9
After tax	4.2	9.7	38.3	22.7
France, 1970				
Before tax	2.0	5.8	47.2	31.8
After tax	1.9	5.8	47.1	31.2
Canada, 1969				
Before tax	2.2	6.2	43.6	27.8
After tax	2.8	7.2	41.3	25.7
United States, 1972				
Before tax	1.8	5.5	44.4	28.6
After tax	2.3	6.5	42.5	26.8
Sweden, 1972				
After tax	3.5	9.3	35.2	20.5

Source: A. Bergson, "Income Inequality Under Soviet Socialism," Journal of Economic Literature, vol. 22, no. 3 (September 1984), pp. 1070, 1072. Bergson uses the work of McCauley, Ofer and Vinokur, and Aron Sawyer in his comparisons. Note: The posttax figures (except for Sweden) are calculated from the posttax/pretax ratios for total household income (Bergson, p. 1072).

McCauley concludes that "there are significant lacunae in the network of support provided by Soviet social welfare programs."[59] A recent account of poverty in the Soviet Union notes that the official Soviet poverty level (205 rubles per month for a family of four) is outdated.[60] But, according to this report, "Between four and five million Soviet families fall below the formal poverty level, according to Soviet officials, and a full 20 percent of the Soviet population lives on less than 75 rubles per month.[61]

The cited income distribution data are based upon money incomes and fail to incorporate social services provided free of charge and perquisites (the use of official cars, dachas, foreign vacations, and other fringe benefits). Moreover, they do not include the income of top government and party officials, but the number of Soviet elite is so small (maybe 0.15–0.3 percent of the population[62]) that their inclusion would be unlikely to change any of the above results. Moreover, most of their income comes to them in the form of payments in kind and perquisites (Katsenelinboigen's law[63] so that it would be difficult to incorporate them in the distribution. The distribution of noncash social consumption services (primarily education, child care, and medical services) received by Soviet workers cannot be specified with any degree of precision; such information must be culled from socioeconomic studies of workers at individual factories or municipalities. From this scattered information, it appears that noncash social services form a larger percentage of total family income among low-paid workers (as would be expected) but that higher-paid workers receive larger absolute benefits.

CONSUMER WELFARE IN THE SOVIET UNION

How well an economy meets the material wants and needs of its population with its *given productive capacity* is yet another way to evaluate economic performance. By "material wants and needs" we refer to those that can be satisfied through the consumption of material goods and services; items relating to mental and spiritual well-being are omitted, even though they are potentially important in determining overall welfare.

If one attempts to measure the level of consumer satisfaction in the Soviet Union relative to that of the United States or Western Europe, one encounters difficulties. First, the most frequently used measure of the relative level of consumer satisfaction is the per capita quantities of consumer goods and services made available to the consumer. According to this standard, either per capita quantities of selected consumer goods and services or aggregate per capita consumption may be compared. Both measures have their own deficiencies, aside from the almost impossible task of measuring quality differences. If one compares per capita consumption of selected commodities, one must realize that consumption patterns vary according to the level of development and cultural differences. For example, the per capita consumption of wheat products in the Soviet Union exceeds that of the United States, but the per capita consumption of most personal services and consumer durables in the United States exceeds that of the USSR. In this example, these differences are explained to a great extent by differences in per capita income, which means that single consumption indicators can provide misleading impressions of consumer welfare. The aggregative measure—total per capita consumption—must be computed in value terms; therefore, in comparisons between two countries, the prices of one country must be used to weigh the quantities of consumer goods and services available in both countries. Yet relative consumer prices vary among countries: commodities that are important consumption items in one country (where the price is relatively cheap) tend to be unimportant in another country (where the price is relatively expensive). Thus, the relative per capita consumption level of one country will be *higher* when valued in the prices of a second country and vice versa—another example of index number relativity.

A further problem in the measurement of consumer satisfaction is that *average* consumption figures veil the underlying distribution of goods and services among the population, and the nature of this distribution has a great deal to do with the level of consumer satisfaction. Prominent Western economists have argued that relative, not absolute, consumption levels are most important in determining consumer satisfaction, for individuals tend to judge their own economic well-being relative to the standard of living of their neighbors.[64] If income is distributed fairly evenly, the chances of feeling deprived relative to someone else are smaller than if income is unevenly distributed. For example, in 1957, the average personal income of the poorest fifth of American families was about the same as the *average* income in the Soviet Union.[65] Is, then, the conclusion proper that the American poor are as "well off" as the average Soviet citizen? In terms of how well both are provisioned with physical quantities of goods and services (index number problems aside), the answer may be yes. Yet in terms of perceived welfare levels, the answer is probably no, because the American poor feel relatively deprived because of the much higher living standards around them.

The point of this discussion is that, once a relatively comfortable standard of physical subsistence is reached, absolute measures of living standards may reflect the state of mental satisfaction less than relative measures do. In the foregoing section, we noted that a surprisingly large proportion of the Soviet population does not earn an income high enough to have a minimum material satisfaction budget. Does this mean that poverty is rampant in the Soviet Union? The answer is probably no, as perceived by the Soviet populace—a population that has experienced significant increases in its level of material well-being in recent years and that would be inclined to judge its contemporary well-being relative to its past experience. Insofar as the minimum material satisfaction budget has been recognized (tolerated?) by Soviet officialdom, this reflects the dissatisfaction of committees of specialists (health officials and sociologists) with existing consumption levels, which is itself a telling point.

Another problem in evaluating Soviet consumer welfare involves the relatively large share of communal consumption in the Soviet Union. Communal consumption—for example, communal services such as health care and education, provided free of charge—accounts for a substantial share of total consumption in the Soviet Union.[66] Such services are provided free of charge and are not subject to a market test as to the value of the satisfaction they provide. In fact, their value is determined by the costs of supplying them. Thus, it is difficult to compare the consumption levels of countries having different shares of communal consumption.

The foregoing discussion points to the loose relationship between the consumption of commodities and the level of satisfaction derived therefrom; yet it is perceived satisfaction that is of most interest. Thus, it is possible to argue (as the Soviets have done) that the underprovisioning of the Soviet consumer relative to American or Western European standards does not imply lower levels of satisfaction because of the new social consciousness of the Soviet people, who will accept this as a necessary cost of building socialism and whose recognition of their patriotism enhances their perceived level of welfare. The validity of such arguments is well outside the scope of this work.

With the above reservations in mind, we present estimates of total per capita consumption in the Soviet Union (including communal services) as a percent of total per capita consumption in the United States and several other countries (Table 12.10). All figures are calculated in United States prices to present the Soviet figures in the most favorable light (in view of index number relativity).

The striking feature of Soviet per capita consumption is that it is quite low relative to the United States, the United Kingdom, France, and West Germany, both in 1955 and in 1970. In 1955, it was roughly one-third of the American level and one-half of the British, French, and West German levels, and was more than three-quarters of the Italian level. Between 1955 and 1970, there was a catching up in relative terms. By 1970, Soviet per capita consumption was one-half that of the United States, 60–70 percent that of the United Kingdom,

Table 12.10   TOTAL PER CAPITA CONSUMPTION AND PER CAPITA GNP OF THE SOVIET UNION AS A PERCENT OF THE UNITED STATES AND OTHER COUNTRIES, 1955 AND 1970 Valued in U. S. Prices

USSR as a percent of:	1955		1970	
	Total per capita consumption	GNP per capita	Total per capita consumption	GNP per capita
United States	27	36	47	60
United Kingdom	41	53	67	88
France	47	59	61	73
West Germany	48	57	69	75
Italy	79	94	86	109
Japan	—	—	84	88

Sources: U.S. Congress, Joint Economic Committee, *Economic Performance and the Military Burden in the Soviet Union* (Washington, D.C.: U.S. Government Printing Office, 1970), pp. 14, 97; United Nations, *Yearbook of National Accounts Statistics* (1978); M. Gilbert and Associates, *Comparative National Products and Price levels* (Paris: Organization for European Economic Cooperation), p. 36; Irving Kravis et al., *A System of International Comparisons of Gross Product and Purchasing Power* (Baltimore and London: Johns Hopkins University Press, 1975), pp. 11, 189; and Imogene Edwards, Margaret Hughes, and James Noren, "U.S. and USSR: Comparisons of GNP," in U.S. Congress, Joint Economic Committee, *Soviet Economy in a Time of Change* (Washington, D.C.: U.S. Government Printing Office, 1979), vol. 1, pp. 378–379. The USSR-U.S. 1976 relatives are backcast to 1970, using GNP and consumption indices.

France, and West Germany, and 86 percent that of Italy. Data are available for Japan for 1970, with the Soviet level 84 percent of the Japanese level.

We suggested above that consumer welfare must be evaluated not in terms of absolute magnitudes but relative to productive capacity. Thus, one should ask to what extent the relatively low Soviet per capita consumption is a consequence of relatively low per capita GNP. Table 12.10 indicates that the major portion of the low Soviet per capita consumption can be accounted for by low per capita GNP, which shows that even if the Soviets had devoted the same proportion of their resources to consumption as the other countries shown, there would still be a substantial "gap" in Soviet per capita consumption.[67] In all cases, Soviet per capita consumption compares much less favorably than per capita GNP, which shows that the Soviets directed a relatively larger share of total resources to nonconsumption items such as investment and defense, and this was, of course, an administrative decision. In the Japanese case, the difference is small because of the similar allocation of resources in Japan and the USSR. As Table 12.11 indicates, the Soviets devote a much larger share of GNP to investment than the major Western countries. The sole exception is Japan, which devotes only a negligible proportion of its resources to defense.

The reader should now well understand the importance of using multiple criteria to evaluate economies. The Soviet economy grew at such a rapid pace largely because it was decided to devote labor and capital resources to this pursuit. Per capita consumption remained below levels attainable from Soviet productive capacity as a consequence of these policies—thus a trade-off between growth and consumption. In a long-run sense, the two are not incompatible, for economic growth will raise productive capacity, which can eventually be used to raise consumption levels.

Table 12.11   GROSS INVESTMENT EXPENDITURES AS A PERCENT OF GNP,
USSR AND SELECTED COUNTRIES,
Soviet Data in Factor Cost, Other Data in Market Prices

	1964	1978	1982	1986
USSR	35	31	33	33
United States	17	16	14	18
France	23	21	21	19
West Germany	28	22	23	19
United Kingdom	19	18	17	18
Italy	22	19	21	21
Japan	39	33	31	28

Sources: A. Becker, *Soviet National Income, 1958–1964* (Berkeley: University of California Press, 1969), pp. 220, 271; National Foreign Assessment Center, *Handbook of Economic Statistics, 1979,* p. 29; 1983, p. 62; World Bank, *World Tables,* 3rd ed. (Baltimore: Johns Hopkins, University Press, 1983). Directorate of Intelligence, *Handbook of Economic Statistics, 1988* (Washington, D.C.: Central Intelligence Agency, 1988), p. 62; and *World Bank, World Development Report 1988* (New York: Oxford University Press, 1988), Table 5.

The structure of Soviet consumption reflects both the relatively low per capita income of the Soviet Union and the efforts of the state to educate and keep the population healthy. Relative to the United States, Soviet per capita consumption compares more favorably in necessities such as basic food products and health care than than in nonnecessities such as durable goods. For example, in 1977, Soviet per capita consumption of food products was 54 percent that of the United States (up from 39 percent in 1955); education was 75 percent and health expenditures were 37 percent those of the United States (both down from 1955). On the other hand, expenditures for consumer durables were only 13 percent of the U.S. 1977 level.[68] A few individual comparisons bring this point home.

For example, in 1981, the daily caloric intake per person per day in the Soviet Union and the United States were similar at 3250 and 3410 calories respectively.[69] However, in the Soviet case, 47 percent of calories were provided by grain products and potatoes, while the comparable figure for the United States was 23 percent. At the same time, the caloric intake from meat, fish and poultry in the Soviet Union was less than 50 percent of the U.S. figure, ignoring possibly substantial quality differentials.[70]

The Soviet Union does not do well in the area of consumer durables. For example, in 1986 there were 570 automobile registrations per 1,000 persons in the United States; the equivalent number for the Soviet Union was 42. In 1976, the Soviet Union had 66 telephones per 1,000 persons; the equivalent number for the United States was 695.[71] However, the Soviet Union has more doctors and more hospital beds per 100,000 population than the United States.

In general, Western scholars have emphasized there is a significant service gap between the United States and the Soviet Union.[72]

Table 12.12   THE SERVICE SECTOR IN THE SOVIET ECONOMY: SELECTED INDICATORS

Average annual rate of growth, 1950–1980	USA	USSR	OECD
Per capita GNP	3.1	1.9	3.3
Household consumption	5.0	3.5	4.1
Employment share in services			
1950	22	–	34
1980	37	66	50
GNP–service share			
1950	38	58[a]	51
1980	40	64[b]	57

[a] 1960

[b] 1982

Source: G. Ofer, "Soviet Economic Growth: 1928–1985," Journal of Economic Literature, vol. 25, no. 4 (December 1987), Tables 2 4; The World Bank, World Development Report 1984 (New York: Oxford University Press, 1984), Table 3.

If there has been a "service gap" in the Soviet economy, it is worth investigating the extent to which the gap may have narrowed over time. The evidence in Table 12.12 is helpful in pursuing this issue.

It is interesting to note that while the average annual rate of growth of household consumption in the Soviet Union has been good, the share of services in gross national product has changed little and remains substantially below that of West European countries. Although employment shares in the Soviet service sector have increased significantly, this increase can be explained in large part by the decline in the agricultural labor force and population growth. There has been little change in the non-agricultural share of employment in services.[73] The share of total investment going to services of all types has changed relatively little since the 1950s and remains at just over 40 percent. Although problems of data and definition preclude accurate international comparisons, this investment share seems to be low compared to other countries. Although a new emphasis has been placed on the service sector in recent Soviet reform and plan documents, it remains doubtful that sufficient labor and capital will be made available to generate any significant and rapid narrowing of the service gap.

To sum up trends in Soviet per capita consumption, we note that per capita consumption in the Soviet Union is low compared to consumption levels in the United States and Western Europe. The major portion of the Soviet consumption gap can be accounted for by low per capita income, but some of it is attributable to the administrative decision to devote a relatively larger proportion of total resources to investment. The pattern of Soviet consumption also reflects the decision of Soviet authorities to deemphasize nonnecessities and to concentrate on essential goods and health and education, all of which are required to maintain and increase the productivity of the Soviet labor force. Looking at trends in Soviet consumption over time, one must conclude that the rate of growth of per capita consumption in the Soviet Union during the plan era has been quite respectable, exceeding comparable U.S. rates. Services have grown at roughly the same rate as gross national product, both declining. In recent years, the rate of growth of services has generally been faster in the United States than the Soviet Union suggesting that the "service gap" will not be narrowed significantly.

ECONOMIC STABILITY (SECURITY) IN THE SOVIET UNION

The ability of an economic system to provide economic stability to its population is yet another indicator of economic performance. Economic stability is an amorphous concept, but it conveys the notion of "reasonable" stability of employment and real incomes. The economic stability (or security) of a nation's citizens can be threatened by declines in real output (or a declining rate of growth of real output), resulting in significant losses of jobs, and by unanticipated inflation, which leads to substantial declines in the real incomes of population subgroups. The sources of economic instability can be either internal or external. In the latter category, one would have inflation transmitted into a country from abroad or by the interruption of petroleum deliveries. Economic stability, like consumer welfare, is a relative concept. In democratic countries, the electorate will determine "acceptable" and "unacceptable" levels of economic instability. In command systems, this function will be performed by political authorities, who may allow themselves to be influenced by public opinion. Different societies will have different attitudes, determined in part by past experience. American society is said to be more tolerant of inflation than German society because of Germany's experience with hyperinflation in the 1920s.

Three empirical measures are typically employed to quantify the degree of economic instability: the unemployment rate, the rate of inflation, and fluctuations in the growth of real output. These three measures are not independent, as the well-known short-run trade-off between employment and inflation attests.

We have already devoted considerable attention to issues of the labor force and need not repeat the discussion here. It is well known that Soviet authorities claim to have "liquidated" unemployment in the 1930s. However, no society can completely eliminate unemployment, at least not in terms of traditional meanings of the term unemployment. For example, frictional unemployment or the time spent changing jobs exists. However, it is generally argued that involuntary unemployment is much less than would be found in market capitalist systems. Recent empirical evidence suggests that such is probably the case, although longer term unemployment does exist in the Soviet Union.[74]

Labor allocation results in the Soviet Union are influenced both by Soviet economic policies and by the organizational arrangements of the Soviet economy. Soviet planners have deliberately pursued a policy of full employment planning. Enterprises' utilization of labor is planned, and regional authorities must ensure the full utilization of available labor resources. Historically, enterprises are not allowed to fail. Moreover, in a climate where enterprise cost reduction has not been a major success indicator and rules for dismissal have been very stringent, enterprise managers have had neither the means nor the motivation to reduce enterprise staffing.

Through the end of this century, however, the nature of labor allocation is likely to change in the Soviet Union. Gorbachev has been outspoken about the need to improve incentives and to improve the utilization of the labor force in a generally labor short economy. Since the 1960s, there have been numerous experiments implemented in varying degrees, all designed to emphasize market type forces in labor allocation. To the extent that resistance to such reform is overcome, changes in allocation procedures could face a major social obstacle—the belief in a full employment policy.[75]

The issue of inflation in the Soviet Union is one of great complexity. As we have already emphasized, Soviet official price indices reveal very little if any inflation in the recent past. For example, the Soviet official retail price index

(1940 = 100) increased to only 153 in 1986, an average annual increase of barely more than one percent.[76] Western analysts distrust these indices for a variety of reasons, the most important being the lack of inclusion of representative commodities and the problems of pricing new products. Moreover, there is considerable evidence to suggest that there is repressed inflation—lack of adequate consumer goods leading to long queues, the growth of savings deposits, and the like.

Unfortunately, in light of the form in which inflation seems to appear in the Soviet context, it is difficult to compare the Soviet experience with that of Western industrialized countries. Most would argue that inflation is a much more serious problem in the Soviet Union than official data would indicate. At the same time, it is doubtful that inflation in the Soviet Union has reached rates more generally found in the West, especially rates of the troubled 1970s.

One would not expect significant inflation in the Soviet case from wage inflation. Between 1960 and 1983, wages in the Soviet Union increased at an annual rate of 3.6 percent.[77] It only takes an annual growth rate of labor productivity of 2.1 percent to yield an annual rate of growth of unit labor costs of 1.5 percent, an inflation rate revealed by independent studies. Official Soviet policy has been to limit the increase in wages to increases in labor productivity. However, recent sharp declines in the rate of growth of labor productivity must have an impact on costs.

Recent evidence on overt inflation indicates significant acceleration in the recent past. For example, the official retail price index grew at a rate of 1.7 percent per year in 1986 and 1987, roughly twice the rate of the early 1980s.[78] Moreover, the Central Intelligence Agency has estimated that retail prices increased by 3.4 percent in 1986.[79] With savings increasing at record rates in recent years and sharp increases in collective farm market prices, monetary expansion to finance budget deficits may bear watching in the coming years. Particularly critical in this regard is the Gorbachev emphasis on the "human factor," involving a desire to stimulate motivation and effort in an economy still plagued by shortages of quality consumer goods.

Finally, what does the evidence tell us about fluctuations in the rate of growth of real output in the Soviet Union? Again, in spite of measurement complexities, there is general agreement that in the past, the Soviet Union has been able to avoid the more severe cyclical swings associated with the Western industrialized countries. However, the pace of economic growth in the Soviet Union has been subject to fluctuations and in recent years, a significant downward trend. Some have argued that in fact there was little real economic growth in the latter years of the Brezhnev era.

GLASNOST AND SOVIET ECONOMIC PERFORMANCE

Our discussion of Soviet economic performance has focused on traditional issues and measurement techniques. Throughout this book we have emphasized the general problems of assessing performance in a comparative setting and have also noted the specific problems associated with understanding and using Soviet statistics related to economic performance.

Controversies about the nature and interpretation of Soviet data are by no means new, nor are they likely to be brought to an end under glasnost. However, recent events in the Soviet Union have once again stimulated discussion of these issues.

First, a number of Soviet authors have published estimates of Soviet economic growth. For the most part, these estimates differ, in some cases significantly, from those available both from Soviet official and Western sources. Unfortunately, however, it is frequently difficult to assess the merits of these new estimates for reasons that are familiar, for example, lack of knowledge of underlying methodologies.

Second, although the Soviets have not generally revised past data series when methodological or other problems arise, there have been cases where revisions have been made. Probably the best known such case is the recent revision of the series for cotton production. In this case, a Soviet statistical handbook published in 1988 contained a new series on cotton production revising previous output data for the period 1976–1985 downward by almost 5 million tons.[80] Apparently, this was a case where production reports had been falsified.

In Table 12.13, we present a number of recent estimates of Soviet economic growth including the first Soviet estimates of gross national product using Western national income accounting. In the national income estimates, the downward trend in growth rates is evident. The estimates by Soviet authors (Selyunin-Khanin) and by Gorbachev's economic advisor (Abel Aganbegyan) are below both Soviet official and Western estimates but show the same sort of downward trend. Notably, these Soviet estimates are significantly below western estimates, although their reliability is uncertain. In Part, the differences result from differences in methodology, but they also result in frequently unknown differences in the prices used for aggregation. The latter issue remains critical in these sorts of estimates, especially given the likelihood that estimates of inflation have been understated.

Table 12.13   SOVIET ECONOMIC PERFORMANCE: RECENT ESTIMATES
(Average Annual Rates of Growth)

Period	National income			Gross national product		
	Soviet official	CIA	Selyunin-Khanin	Aganbegyan[a]	Soviet official	CIA
1961–1965	6.5	4.8	4.4	—	—	4.8
1966–1970	7.8	5.0	4.1	5.6	—	5.0
1971–1975	5.7	3.1	3.2	4.0	—	3.1
1976–1980	4.3	2.2	1.0	2.1	—	2.2
1981–1985	3.6	1.8	0.6	0.4	3.9	1.9

[a] Numbers are approximate. See *Revisiting Soviet Economic Performances,* fig. 2, p. 2.

Sources: Directorate of Intelligence, *Revisiting Soviet Economic Performance Under Glasnost: Implications for CIA Estimates.* (Washington, D.C.: Central Intelligence Agency, 1988).

SOVIET ECONOMIC PERFORMANCE: AN ASSESSMENT

It is quite evident from the data presented in this chapter that the Soviets have traded consumption (and leisure) for economic growth, the latter generally rapid by international standards. Had the Soviets adopted the input growth patterns of the West, their rate of economic growth would have been lower, ceteris paribus.

However, the evidence on productivity is clearly a major source of concern for Mikhail Gorbachev. Moreover, as our evidence on Soviet consumption patterns (especially the inadequate supplies and poor quality of Soviet consumer goods) improves, we learn about a cost of Soviet growth larger than previously anticipated. Clearly, Soviet economic growth has been "high-cost" growth. Roughly one-third of Soviet output growth has been accounted for by efficiency growth, while in the West, the share has generally been on the order of two-thirds. Possibly of greatest current import, the rate of growth of productivity has been declining significantly in recent years. It would seem that the Soviet economic system has thus far retained the characteristics of a system dominated by extensive rather than intensive economic growth. The transformation of the system from the former to the latter status is the major challenge facing Mikhail Gorbachev in the remainder of this century.

REFERENCES

1. P. Hanson, "East-West Comparisons and Comparative Economic Systems," *Soviet Studies*, vol. 22, no. 3 (January 1971), 327–343. We have shown that the performance of the USSR economy is in many respects different from that of other planned socialist economies. See P. R. Gregory and R. C. Stuart, *Comparative Economic Systems*, 3rd ed. (Boston: Houghton Mifflin, 1989), chap. 12.
2. A. Maddison, *Economic Growth in Japan and the USSR* (New York: Norton, 1969); A. Bergson, *Productivity and the Social System: The USSR and the West* (Cambridge, Mass.: Harvard University Press, 1978), chap. 11; A. Bergson, "Comparative Productivity," *American Economic Review*, vol. 77, no. 3 (June 1987), 342–357.
3. The reader interested in pursuing the question of cyclical instability in socialist economic systems should consult G. J. Staller, "Fluctuations in Planned and Free Market Economies,"*American Economic Review*, vol. 54, no. 4, part 1 (June 1964), 385–395; O. Kyn, W. Schrettel, and J. Slam, "Growth Cycles in Centrally Planned Economies: An Empirical Test," Osteuropa Institute, Munich, working paper no. 7, August 1975; J. Goldman, "Fluctuations and Trends in the Rate of Economic Growth in Some Socialist Countries, " *Economics of Planning*, vol. 4, no. 2 (1964), 89–98; C. W. Lawson, "An Empirical Analysis of the Structure and Stability of Communist Foreign Trade," *Soviet Studies*, vol. 26, no. 2 (April 1974), 224–238; and G. Roland, "Investment Growth Fluctuations in the Soviet Union: An Econometric Analysis," *Journal of Comparative Economics*, vol.11, no. 2 (June 1987), 192–206.
4. For a discussion of the success indicator issue, see A. Eckstein, ed., *Comparison of Economic Systems* (Berkeley and Los Angeles: University of California Press, 1971), parts 1 and 2; and J. M. Montias, *The Structure of Economic Systems* (New Haven,

Conn.: Yale University Press, 1976), chap. 4. For a contemporary analysis, see Gregory and Stuart, *Comparative Economic Systems*, Chap. 2.

5. A. Gerschenkron, "The Soviet Indices of Industrial Production," *Review of Economics and Statistics*, vol. 29, no. 4 (November 1947), 217–226.

6. For example, consider a hypothetical case in which the USSR in 1928 produced 100 "units" of textiles and 50 "units" of machinery, and that is all. The 1928 per unit prices of textiles and machinery were *1 R* and *2 R*, respectively. Assume further that in 1980, the USSR produced 200 "units" of textiles and 1000 "units" of machinery, and the prices of textiles and machinery had risen to *10 R* and *10 R*, respectively. If one values both 1928 and 1980 outputs in 1928 prices, 1980 output is *11 times* the 1928 output. If one values both 1928 and 1980 output, in 1980 prices, 1980 output is *8 times* the 1928 output. Formal analyses of the index number problem are found in R. Moorsteen, "On Measuring Productive Potential and Relative Efficiency," *Quarterly Journal of Economics*, vol. 75, no 3 (August 1961), 451–467; and G. W. Nutter, "On Economic Size and Growth," *Journal of Law and Economics*, vol. 9, no. 2 (October 1966), 163–188.

7. A. Bergson, *The Real National Income of Soviet Russia Since 1928* (Cambridge, Mass.: Harvard University Press, 1961), p. 261. The 1987 relative GNP figures are from Directorate of Intelligence, *Handbook of Economic Statistics, 1988* (Washington, D.C.: Central Intelligence Agency, 1988), p. 32.

8. Growth in the United States between 1834 and 1908 has been estimated in 1860 prices. See R. Gallman, "Gross National Product in the United States, 1834–1909," *Output, Employment and Productivity in the United States After 1800* (New York and London: National Bureau of Economic Research, 1966), pp. 3–75. These estimates are not comparable with the figures in 1929 prices cited in Table 12.1 because the two differ on current price estimates. Thus, these figures are not tests of the impact of index number relativity on the measurement of U.S. GNP.

9. Of course, there is the problem of valuation of Soviet GNP, because established prices often fail to reflect costs of production owing to substantial subsidies and indirect taxes. The figures cited employ the factor cost concept, which eliminates subsidies and indirect taxes. There is still a problem in that such factor costs fail to adequately reflect capital costs, but various adjustments show that overall growth rates are not substantially altered by the inclusion of capital costs. See Bergson, *Real National Income*, p. 219. For a discussion of conceptual differences in measures of aggregate output, see J. Pitzer, "Reconciliation of Gross National Product and Soviet National Income," *NATO Colloquium* (Brussels, July 1977). For a survey of estimates, see U.S. Congress, Joint Economic Committee, *USSR: Measures of Economic Growth and Development 1950–80* (Washington, D.C.: U.S. Government Printing Office, 1982).

10. For background on Soviet statistics, see V. G. Treml and J. P. Hardt, eds., *Soviet Economic Statistics* (Durham, N.C.: University of North Carolina Press, 1972). For a discussion of recent efforts to define the GNP of planned economies in dollar terms, see P. Marer, *Dollar GNPs of the Soviet Union and Eastern Europe* (Baltimore: Johns Hopkins University Press, 1985); for a discussion of Soviet statistics under glasnost, see Directorate of Intelligence, *The Impact of Gorbachev's Policies on Soviet Economic Statistics* (Washington, D.C.: Central Intelligence Agency, 1988).

11. The cited Bergson figures are in 1950 prices, and the CIA figures employ 1959 or 1970 weights; thus, this is a mixed index. Differences that arise as a result of the

mixed weighting scheme are most likely minimal. Differences between this index and one based on the Bergson 1937 price-weighted figures (to 1958) are negligible. Individuals associated with the Rand Corporation and various governmental agencies have made contributions to the estimation of Soviet GNP using Western accounting practices. See, for example, S. H. Cohn, "General Growth Performance of the Soviet Economy," in U.S. Congress, Joint Economic Committee, *Economic Performance and the Military Burden in the Soviet Union* (Washington, D.C.: U.S. Government Printing Office, 1970); A. Becker, *Soviet National Income, 1958–1964* (Berkeley: University of California Press, 1969). The most complete source is U.S. Congress, Joint Economic Committee, *USSR: Measures of Economic Growth and Development, 1950–80.*

12. The practice of computing Soviet growth for "effective years" was originated by Gregory Grossman, as a suggested measure of what long-term Soviet growth might have been in the absence of the war: G. Grossman, "Thirty Years of Soviet Industrialization," *Soviet Survey* (October 1958). One could perhaps argue that the Great Depression should be omitted from computing the long-term United States growth rate, except that it could be argued that the business cycle is inherent to the capitalist system and should be included.

13. Cohn, "General Growth Performance," p. 9; and H. Block, "Soviet Economic Performance in a Global Context," in U.S. Congress, Joint Economic Committee, *Soviet Economy in a Time of Change* (Washington, D.C.: U.S. Government Printing Office, 1979), vol. 1.

14. Bergson calculates Soviet growth between 1928 and 1937 as 11.9 percent annually in 1928 prices, compared with the official claim of 16.9 percent: Bergson, *The Real National Income of Soviet Russia*, p. 216. In recent Soviet publications, the official estimates of Soviet growth during the 1930s have been severely criticized as being unrealistic and inconsistent; on this, see Vainshtein, *Narodny dokhod Rossii i SSSR*, pp. 99–108. For a further discussion of the official Soviet figures, see A. Nove, "1926/7 and All That," *Soviet Studies*, vol. 9, no. 2 (October 1957), 117–130.

15. National Foreign Assessment Center, *Handbook of Economic Statistics 1979*, p. 22; and World Bank, *World Tables 1976* (Baltimore, Md.: Johns Hopkins University Press, 1976), pp. 262–263.

16. S. Kuznets, *Economic Growth of Nations* (Cambridge, Mass.: Harvard University Press, 1971), pp. 37–43.

17. On this point see A. Bergson, "Comparative Productivity and Efficiency in the USA and USSR," in Eckstein, ed., *Comparison of Economic Systems*, pp. 161–240.

18. Bergson, *The Real National Income of Soviet Russia*, p. 260.

19. N. DeWitt, "Education and Development of Human Resources: Soviet and American Effort," in U.S. Congress, Joint Economic Committee, *Dimensions of Soviet Economic Power* (Washington, D.C.: U.S. Government Printing Office, 1962), p. 244.

20. National Foreign Assessment Center, *USSR: Trends and Prospects in Educational Attainment 1959–85* (Washington, D.C.: Central Intelligence Agency, 1979).

21. A. Bergson, *Planning and Productivity Under Soviet Socialism* (New York: Columbia University Press, 1968), p. 52.

22. To determine the rate of growth of combined inputs—labor and capital—the individual growth rates of labor and capital, respectively, must be combined in some manner. In similar studies for Western countries, the two growth rates are generally combined by computing a weighted average, the weights being the labor and capital

shares of total income. In the Soviet case, capital does not generate income; therefore, there is no real "capital share" of total income. For this reason, "synthetic" factor shares have been used for the Soviet case, based largely on factor shares found in Western countries. For examples of the use of "synthetic" factor shares, see A. Bergson, *The Economics of Soviet Planning* (New Haven, Conn.: Yale University Press, 1964), pp. 341–343; and R. Moorsteen and R. Powell, *The Soviet Capital Stock, 1928–1962* (Homewood, Ill.: Irwin, 1966), pp. 264–266.

23. Attempts have been made to adjust for quality differences and to measure nonconventional inputs, but they rest very heavily upon rather tenuous assumptions made by the researchers themselves. See, for example, E. Denison, *Why Growth Rates Differ* (Washington, D.C.: The Brookings Institution, 1967); and E. Denison, *Accounting for United States Economic Growth 1929–1969* (Washington, D.C.: The Brookings Institution, 1974). For an attempt to adjust Soviet inputs for quality differences, see E. R. Brubaker, "The Age of Capital and Growth in the Soviet Nonagricultural Nonresidential Sector," *Soviet Studies*, vol. 21, no. 3 (January 1970), 350–359; and E. R. Brubaker, "Embodied Technology, the Asymptotic Behavior of Capital's Age, and Soviet Growth," *Review of Economics and Statistics*, vol. 50, no. 3 (August 1968), 304–311.

24. See, for example, A. Maddison, "Growth and Slowdown in Advanced Capitalist Economies," *Journal of Economic Literature*, vol. 25, no. 2 (June 1987), 649–698.

25. G. Ofer, "Soviet Economic Growth: 1928–1985," *Journal of Economic Literature*, vol. 25, no. 4 (December 1987), 1767–1833.

26. For a discussion of these issues, see E. Teague, "Gorbachev's 'Human Factor' Policies," in U.S. Congress, Joint Economic Committee, *Gorbachev's Economic Plans*, vol. 2 (Washington, D.C.: U.S. Government Printing Office, 1987), pp. 224–239.

27. See Ofer," Soviet Economic Growth: 1928–1985," p. 1815.

28. A. Bergson, "Notes on the Production Function in Soviet Postwar Industrial Growth," *Journal of Comparative Economics*, vol. 3, no. 2 (June 1979), 124. For example, Bergson finds the range of possible rates of growth of factor productivity in Soviet industry (1955–1970) to run from 1.6 to 2.3 percent per annum, depending on the elasticity of substitution and the method of calculating the rate of return to capital. Using the same procedures, Bergson calculates the following ranges for other countries (1955–1970): United States, 1.5 (no variation); France, 3.6–3.9; West Germany, 3.2–3.6; United Kingdom, 1.8–2.2; Italy, 4.2–4.7; Japan, 5.9–7.0.

29. This discussion was spurred by Martin Weitzman's seminal paper of 1970. See M. Weitzman, "Soviet Postwar Growth and Capital–Labor Substitution," *American Economic Review*, vol. 60, no. 4 (September 1970), pp. 676–692. Contributors to this debate are P. Desai, "The Production Function and Technical Change in Postwar Soviet Industry," *American Economic Review*, vol. 66, no.3 (June 1976), 372–381; S. Gomulka, "Soviet Postwar Industrial Growth, Capital-Labor Substitution, and Technical Changes: A Reexamination," in Z. M. Fallenbuchl, ed., *Economic Development in the Soviet Union and Eastern Europe* (New York: Praeger, 1976); S. Rosefielde and C. A. Lovell, "The Impact of Adjusted Factor Cost Valuation on the CES Interpretation of Postwar Soviet Economic Growth," *Economica*, vol. 44 (November 1977), 381–392; S. Rosefielde, "Index Numbers and the Computation of Factor Productivity: A Further Appraisal," *Review of Income and Wealth*, forthcoming; A. Bergson,

"Notes on the Production Function in Soviet Postwar Industrial Growth," *Journal of Comparative Economics*, vol. 3, no. 2 (June 1979), pp. 116–126.

30. National Foreign Assessment Center, *Handbook of Economic Statistics 1979*, p. 65; and F. D. Whitehouse and R. Converse, "Soviet Industry: Recent Performance and Future Prospects," in U.S. Congress, Joint Economic Committee, *Soviet Economy in a Time of Change*, vol. 1, pp. 402–422.

31. P. Desai, "Total Factor Productivity in Soviet Postwar Industry and Its Branches," *Journal of Comparative Economics*, vol. 9, no. 1 (March 1985), 1–23.

32. G. E. Schroeder, "The Slowdown in Soviet Industry, 1976–1982," *Soviet Economy*, vol. 1, no. 1 (January–March 1985), pp. 42–74.

33. Bergson, *Planning and Productivity*, p. 15. See also J. S. Berliner, "The Static Efficiency of the Soviet Economy," *American Economic Review*, vol. 54, no. 2 (May 1964), 480–490.

34. Hanson, "East-West Comparisons," pp. 332–343; Bergson, *Productivity and the Social System*, pp. 95–107.

35. An illustration and explanation of this phenomenon in American–Soviet GNP comparisons is found in R. Campbell, "Problems of United States–Soviet Economic Comparisons," in U.S. Congress, Joint Economic Committee, *Comparisons of the United States and Soviet Economies* (Washington, D.C.: U.S. Government Printing Office, 1959), part 1, pp. 13–30.

36. Hanson, "East-West Comparisons," p. 340, argues that perhaps Soviet labor was (for the period in question, the early 1960s) in "excess supply" because of labor hoarding in industry and seasonal unemployment in agriculture. A low weight should, therefore, be attached to labor and a high weight to capital. This would raise Soviet factor productivity considerably relative to the United States because the Soviet labor force is larger than the American labor force.

37. Bergson has made adjustments for quality differences in the Soviet and American labor forces, as indicated by the larger Soviet female labor force and lower educational levels of Soviet workers. These adjustments, which are admittedly very crude, raise Soviet factor productivity relative to the United States by about 10 percentage point but fail to alter the overall conclusion of the relatively low productivity of the Soviet economy. Bergson, *The Economics of Soviet Planning*, p. 342.

38. The major source of the low factor productivity of the Soviet economy seems to be the low productivity of the commerce and service sectors. On this, see E. R. Brubaker, "A Sectoral Analysis of Efficiency Under Market and Plan," *Soviet Studies*, vol. 23, no. 3 (January 1972), 443.

39. G. E. Schroeder, "The Economic Reform as a Spur to Technological Progress in the USSR," *Jahrbuch der Wirtschaft Osteuropas* [Yearbook of Eastern European Economics], vol. 2 (Munich: Günter Olzog Verlag, 1971), p. 346.

40. A. Bergson, "Comparative Productivity: The USSR, Eastern Europe, and the West," *American Economic Review*, vol. 77, no. 3 (June 1987), 342–357.

41. Ibid., p. 355.

42. Ibid.

43. Bergson, *Productivity and the Social System*, p. 104.

44. See A. Nove, "The Politics of Economic Rationality," in A. Nove, *Economic Rationality and Soviet Politics* (New York: Praeger, 1964), p. 53; and P. J. D. Wiles, *The Political Economy of Communism* (London: Blackwell, 1963), chap. 11.

45. See Bergson, *Planning and Productivity*, pp. 16–19, and *The Economics of Soviet Planning*, chap. 14.

46. Hanson, "East-West Comparisons," p. 338.

47. Bergson, *The Economics of Soviet Planning*, pp. 293–297, and P. Hanson, *The Consumer in the Soviet Economy* (Evanston Ill.: Northwestern University Press, 1968), p. 63.

48. P. J. D. Wiles and S. Markowski, "Income Distribution Under Communism and Capitalism: Some Facts About Poland, the U.K., the USA and the USSR," *Soviet Studies*, vol. 22, nos. 3 and 4 (January and April 1971), 344–369 and 487–511; P. J. D. Wiles, *Economic Institutions Compared* (New York: Halsted Press, 1977), p. 443; A. McCauley, *Economic Welfare in the Soviet Union* (Madison: University of Wisconsin Press, 1979); M. Yanowitch, *Social and Economic Inequality in the USSR* (White Plains, N.Y.: M.E. Sharpe, 1977); A. Bergson, "Income Inequality Under Soviet Socialism," *Journal of Economic Literature*, vol. 22, no. 3 (September 1984), 1052–1099.

49. L. J. Kirsch, *Soviet Wages: Changes in Structure and Administration Since 1956* (Cambridge, Mass.: MIT Press, 1972), chaps. 1 and 8; M. Yanowitch, "The Soviet Income Revolution," *Slavic Review*, vol. 22, no. 4 (December 1963), reprinted in M. Bornstein and D. Fusfeld, eds., *The Soviet Economy*, 2nd ed. (Homewood, Ill.: Irwin, 1966), pp. 228–241; Bergson, *The Economics of Soviet Planning*, pp. 106–120; Wiles and Markowski, "Income Distribution," pp. 501–507.

50. A. Bergson, "Principles of Socialist Wages," in *Essays in Normative Economics* (Cambridge, Mass.: Harvard University, Belknap Press, 1966).

51. Yanowitch, *Social and Economic Inequality* p. 25; Bergson, "Income Inequality Under Soviet Socialism."

52. The "law of reimbursement" means that workers should receive wages sufficient to cover the normal costs of production of labor power; for example, workers should receive sufficient income to cover their basic living requirements. Yanowitch, *Social and Economic Inequality*, pp. 27–28.

53. McCauley, *Economic Welfare*, gives surveys of available data on Soviet income distributions. The major omitted categories are the Soviet elite and state farm families.

54. This conclusion follows from McCauley, *Economic Welfare*, p. 66; and Wiles, *Economic Institutions Compared*, p. 443. Also see P. J. D. Wiles, *Distribution of Income: East and West* (Amsterdam: North-Holland, 1974), p. 48.

55. Bergson, "Income Inequality Under Soviet Socialism," p. 1092.

56. McCauley, *Economic Welfare*, pp. 59–61.

57. Ibid., p. 18.

58. Ibid., pp. 78–88.

59. Ibid., p. 74.

60. New York Times, January 29, 1989, p. 1.

61. Ibid.

62. M. Mathews, "Top Incomes in the USSR," in NATO Economics Directorate, *Economic Aspects of Life in the USSR* (Brussels: NATO, 1975), pp. 131–158.

63. A. Katsenelinboigen, *Studies in Soviet Economic Planning* (White Plains, N.Y.: M.E. Sharpe, 1978) p. 150. Katsenelinboigen contends that the proportion of total income received in the form of perquisites increases with the responsibility of the position. He believes this is a device used by the Soviet leadership to ensure the loyalty of high officials.

64. J. Duesenberry, *Income, Saving and the Theory of Consumer Behavior* (Cambridge, Mass.: Harvard University Press, 1949).

65. J G. Chapman, "Consumption," in A. Bergson and S. Kuznets, eds., *Economic Trends in the Soviet Union* (Cambridge, Mass.: Harvard University Press, 1963).

66. Between 1937 and 1964, communal consumption accounted for between 8 and 9 percent of Soviet GNP. In the United States, it accounts for about 3 percent (1956). See Bergson, *The Real National Income of Soviet Russia*, p. 237; Becker, *Soviet National Income*, p. 220; Chapman, "Consumption," p. 263.
67. For further evidence on the Soviet consumption "gap," see P. Gregory, *Socialist and Nonsocialist Industrialization Patterns* (New York: Praeger, 1971), p. 152.
68. J. Edwards, M. Hughes, and J. Noren, "U.S. and U.S.S.R.: Comparisons of GNP," in U.S. Congress, Joint Economic Committee, *Soviet Economics in a Time of Change* (Washington, D.C.: U.S. Government Printing Office), vol. I, p. 385.
69. A. M. Lane, R. M. Marston and S. O. Welsh, "The Nutrient Content of the Soviet Food Supply and Comparisons with the U.S. Food Supply," U.S. Congress, Joint Economic Committee, *Gorbachev's Economic Plans* vol. 2 (1987), pp. 81, 86.
70. Ibid., p. 92.
71. Directorate of Intelligence, *Handbook of Economic Statistics, 1988*.
72. Data are from Directorate of Intelligence, *Handbook in Economic Statistics, 1988*, Tables 2–3; data on telephones are from U.S. Congress, Joint Economic Committee, *Consumption in the USSR: An International Comparison* (Washington, D.C.: U.S. Government Printing Office, 1981), Table 10.
73. For a discussion of recent trends, see G. E. Schroeder, "U.S.S.R. Toward the Service Economy at a Snail's Pace," in U.S. Congress, Joint Economic Committee, *Gorbachev's Economic Plans*, vol. 2, pp. 240–71.
74. For recent evidence, see P. R. Gregory and I. L. Collier Jr., "Unemployment in the Soviet Union: Evidence from the Soviet Interview Project," *American Economic Review*, vol. 78, no. 4 (September 1988), 613–632.
75. See for, example, the discussion in B. Arnot, *Controlling Soviet Labour* (London: Macmillan, 1988).
76. Goskomstat, *Narodnoe khoziaistvo SSSR za 70 let* [The national economy of the USSR over 70 years] (Moscow: Finansy i Statistika, 1987), 480.
77. TsSU, *Narodnoe khoziaistvo SSSR v 1983g* [The national economy of the USSR in 1983] (Moscow: Finansy i Statistika, 1984), 393.
78. Directorate of Intelligence, *USSR: Sharply Higher Budget Deficits Threaten Perestroyka* (Washington, D.C.: Central Intelligence Agency, 1988), pp. 4–7
79. Ibid.
80. See U.S. Department of Agriculture, *USSR Agriculture and Trade Report: Situation and Outlook Series* (Washington, D.C.: U.S. Department of Agriculture, 1988), pp. 30–31.

SELECTED BIBLIOGRAPHY

Overall Evaluation Problems

A. Bergson "East-West Comparisons and Comparative Economic Systems: A Reply, " *Soviet Studies*, vol. 23, no. 2 (October 1971), 282–295.

———, *The Economics of Soviet Planning* (New Haven, Conn.: Yale University Press, 1964), chap. 14.

———, "National Income," in A. Bergson and S. Kuznets, eds., *Economic Trends in the Soviet Union* (Cambridge, Mass.: Harvard University Press, 1963), pp. 1–37.

R. Campbell et al., "Methodological Problems Comparing the US and USSR Economies," in U.S. Congress, Joint Economic Committee, *Soviet Economic Prospects for the Seventies* (Washington, D.C.: U.S. Government Printing Office, 1973), pp. 122–146.

A. Eckstein, ed., *Comparison of Economic Systems* (Berkeley and Los Angeles: University of California Press, 1971).

I. Edwards, M. Hughes, and J. Noren, "U.S. and USSR: Comparisons of GNP," in U.S. Congress, Joint Economic Committee, *Soviet Economy in a Time of Change* (Washington, D.C.: U.S. Government Printing Office, 1979), vol. 1, pp. 369–401.

P. Hanson, "East-West Comparisons and Comparative Economic Systems," *Soviet Studies*, vol. 22, no. 3 (January 1971).

L. Kurtzweg, "Trends in Soviet Gross National Product," in U.S. Congress, Joint Economic Committee, *Gorbachev's Economic Plans*, vol. 2 (Washington, D.C.: U.S. Government Printing Office 1987), pp. 126–165.

P. Marer, *Dollar GNPs of the Soviet Union and Eastern Europe* (Baltimore: Johns Hopkins University Press, 1985).

V. G. Treml and D. Gallik, *Soviet Studies on Ruble/Dollar Parity Ratios*, Foreign Economic Reports, no. 4, U.S. Department of Commerce, November 1973.

V. G. Treml and J. P. Hardt, eds., *Soviet Economic Statistics* (Durham, N.C.: University of North Carolina Press, 1972).

U.S. Congress, Joint Economic Committee, *USSR: Measures of Economic Growth and Development 1950–80* (Washington, D.C. U.S. Government Printing Office, 1982).

C.K. Wilber, "Economic Development, Central Planning, and Allocative Efficiency," *Yearbook of East European Economics* (Munich: Günter Olzog Verlag, 1971), pp. 221–246.

Soviet Economic Growth

A. Becker, *Soviet National Income, 1958–1964* (Berkeley: University of California Press, 1969).

A. Bergson, *Productivity and the Social System: The USSR and the West* (Cambridge, Mass.: Harvard University Press, 1978), part 3.

——, *The Real National Income of Soviet Russia Since 1928* (Cambridge, Mass.: Harvard University Press, 1961).

H. Block, "Soviet Economic Performance in a Global Context," in U.S. Congress, Joint Economic Committee, *Soviet Economy in a Time of Change* (Washington, D.C.: U.S. Government Printing Office, 1979), vol 1, pp. 110–140.

M. Bornstein, "A Comparison of Soviet and United States National Product," in M. Bornstein and D. Fusfeld, eds., *The Soviet Economy* (Homewood, Ill.: Irwin, 1962).

S. Cohn, *Economic Development in the Soviet Union* (Lexington, Mass.: Heath, 1969), chap. 7.

S. H. Cohn, "General Growth Performance of the Soviet Economy," in U.S. Congress, Joint Economic Committee, *Economic Performance and the Military Burden in the Soviet Union* (Washington, D.C.: U.S. Government Printing Office, 1970).

R. Greenslade, "The Real Gross National Product of the USSR, 1950–1975," in Joint Economic Committee, *Soviet Economy in a New Perspective* (Washington, D.C.: U.S. Government Printing Office, 1976), pp. 269–300.

Joint Economic Committee, *USSR: Measures of Economic Growth and Development, 1950–80* (Washington, D.C.: U.S. Government Printing Office, 1982).

G. Ofer, "Soviet Economic Growth: 1928–1985," *Journal of Economic Literature,* vol. 25, no. 4 (December 1987), 1767–1833.

G. E. Schroeder, "The Slowdown in Soviet Industry, 1976–1982, *Soviet Economy,* vol. 1, no. 1 (January–March 1985), 42–74.

Dynamic Efficiency and the Growth of Productivity

A. Bergson, "Comparative Productivity: The USSR, Eastern Europe, and the West," *American Economic Review,* vol. 77, no. 3 (June 1987), 342–357.

——, "Development Under Two Systems: Comparative Productivity Growth Since 1950," *World Politics,* vol. 23, no. 4 (July 1971), 579–617.

——, "Index Numbers and the Computation of Factor Productivity," *Review of Income and Wealth,* vol. 21 (September 1975), 259–278.

——, *Planning and Productivity Under Soviet Socialism* (New York: Columbia University Press, 1968).

——, *Productivity and the Social System: The USSR and the West* (Cambridge, Mass.: Harvard University Press, 1978), part 3.

E. Brubaker, "Embodied Technology, the Asymptotic Behavior of Capital's Age, and Soviet Growth," *Review of Economics and Statistics,* vol. 50, no. 3 (August 1968), 304–311.

R. Moorsteen and R. Powell, *The Soviet Capital Stock, 1928–1962* (Homewood, Ill.: Irwin, 1966).

F. D. Whitehouse and R. Converse, "Soviet Industry: Recent Performance and Future Prospects," in U.S. Congress, Joint Economic Committee, *Soviet Economy in a Time of Change* (Washington, D.C.: U.S. Government Printing Office, 1979), vol. 1, pp. 402–422.

Consumer Welfare in the Soviet Union

D. W. Bronson and B. S. Severin, "Consumer Welfare," in U.S. Congress, Joint Economic Committee, *Economic Performance and the Military burden in the Soviet Union* (Washington, D.C.: U.S. Government Printing Office, 1970), pp. 93–99.

——, "Soviet Consumer Welfare: The Brezhnev Era," in U.S. Congress, Joint Economic Committee, *Soviet Economic Prospects for the Seventies* (Washington, D.C.: U.S. Government Printing Office, 1973), pp. 376–403.

J. G. Chapman, "Consumption," in A. Bergson and S. Kuznets, eds., *Economic Trends in the Soviet Union* (Cambridge, Mass.: Harvard University Press, 1963), pp. 235–282.

——, *Real Wages in the Soviet Union* (Cambridge, Mass.: Harvard University Press, 1963).

"Consumption and Incentives," in U.S. Congress, Joint Economic Committee, *Gorbachev's Economic Plans*, vol. 2 (Washington, D.C.: U.S. Government Printing Office, 1987), pp. 219–352.

M. E. Denton, "Soviet Consumer Policy: Trends and Prospects," in U.S. Congress, Joint Economic Committee, *Soviet Economy in a Time of Change* (Washington, D.C.: U.S. Government Printing Office, 1979), vol. 1, pp. 759–798.

H. Herlemann, ed., *The Quality of Life in the Soviet Union* (Boulder, Colo.: Westview Press, 1987).

B. Q. Madison, "Social Services: Families and Children in the Soviet Union Since 1967," *Slavic Review*, vol. 31, no. 4 (December 1972), 831–852.

————, *Social Welfare in the Soviet Union* (Stanford, Calif.: Stanford University Press, 1968).

A. McCauley, *Economic Welfare in the Soviet Union* (Madison: University of Wisconsin Press, 1979).

R. J. Osborn, *Soviet Social Policies: Welfare, Equality, and Community* (Homewood, Ill.: Dorsey Press, 1970).

G. E. Schroeder, "Consumption," in A. Bergson and H. S. Levine, eds., *The Soviet Economy: Towards the Year 2000* (Boston: Allen & Unwin, 1983), pp. 311–349.

G. E. Schroeder and B. S. Severin, "Soviet Consumption and Income Policies in Perspective," in U.S. Congress, Joint Economic Committee, *Soviet Economy in a New Perspective* (Washington, D.C.: U.S. Government Printing Office, 1976), pp. 620–660.

U.S. Congress, Joint Economic Committee, *Consumption in the USSR: An International Comparison* (Washington, D.C.: U.S. Government Printing Office, 1981).

Economic Stability (Security) in the Soviet Union

M. Bornstein, "Unemployment in Capitalist Regulated Market Economies and Socialist Centrally Planned Economies," *American Economic Review, Papers and Proceedings*, vol. 68, no. 2 (May 1978), 38–43.

K. Bush, "Soviet Inflation," in M. Y. Laulan, ed., *Banking Money and Credit in Eastern Europe* (Brussels: NATO, 1973), pp. 97–105.

D. Granick, *Job Rights in the Soviet Union: Their Consequences* (New York: Cambridge University Press, 1987).

P. R. Gregory and I. L. Collier, Jr., "Unemployment in the Soviet Union: Evidence from the Soviet Interview Project," *American Economic Review*, vol. 78, no. 4 (September 1988), 613–632.

D. H. Howard, "The Disequilibrium Model: An Empirical Test of the Barro–Grossman Model," *American Economic Review*, vol. 66, no. 5 (December 1976), 871–879.

D. Lane, ed., *Labour and Employment in the USSR* (Brighton, England: Wheatsheaf Books, 1986).

J. Millar, ed., *Politics, Work, and Daily Life in the USSR* (New York: Cambridge University Press, 1987).

NATO Economics, Directorate, *Economic Aspects of Life in the USSR* (Brussels: NATO, 1976), contributions by G. E. Schroeder and A. Katsenelinboigen.

G. Ofer and J. Pickersgill, "Soviet Household Saving: A Cross Section Study of Soviet Emigrant Families," *Quarterly Journal of Economics*, vol. 45, no. 1 (August 1980), 121–144.

J. Pickersgill, "Recent Evidence of Soviet Household Saving Behavior," *Review of Economics and Statistics*, vol. 62, no. 4 (November 1980), 628–633.

———, "Soviet Household Saving Behavior," *Review of Economics and Statistics*, vol. 58, no. 2 (May 1976), 139–147.

R. Portes, "The Control of Inflation: Lessons from East European Experience," *Economica*, vol. 44 (May 1977), 109–130.

P. J. D. Wiles, "A Note on Soviet Unemployment in US Definitions," *Soviet Studies*, vol. 23, no. 2 (April 1972), 619–628.

Soviet Static Efficiency

A. Bergson, "Comparative Productivity and Efficiency in the USA and USSR," in A. Eckstein, ed., *Comparison of Economic Systems* (Berkeley and Los Angeles: University of California Press, 1971), pp. 161–218.

———, "Comparative Productivity: The USSR, Eastern Europe, and the West," *American Economic Review*, vol. 77, no. 3 (June 1987), 342–357.

———, *The Economics of Soviet Planning* (New Haven, Conn.: Yale University Press, 1964), chap. 14.

———, *Planning and Productivity Under Soviet Socialism* (New York: Columbia University Press, 1968).

J. S. Berliner, "The Static Efficiency of the Soviet Economy," *American Economic Review*, vol. 54, no. 2 (May 1964), 480–490.

E. Domar, "On the Measurement of Comparative Efficiency," in A. Eckstein, ed., *Comparison of Economic Systems* (Berkeley and Los Angeles: University of California Press, 1971), pp. 219–232.

Equity of Income Distribution in the Soviet Union

A. Bergson, *The Structure of Soviet Wages* (Cambridge, Mass.: Harvard University Press, 1944).

———, "Income Inequality Under Soviet Socialism," *Journal of Economic Literature*, vol. 22, no. 3 (September 1984), 1052–1099.

J. G. Chapman, "Earnings Distribution in the USSR, 1968–1976," *Soviet Studies*, vol. 25, no. 3 (July 1983), 410–413.

M. Ellman, "A Note on the Distribution of Earnings in the USSR Under Brezhnev," *Slavic Review*, vol. 39, no. 4 (December 1987) 669–671.

M. Matthews, *Privilege in the Soviet Union* (London: Allen & Unwin, 1978).

A. McCauley, "The Distribution of Earnings and Income in the Soviet Union," *Soviet Studies*, vol. 29, no. 2 (April 1977), 214–237.

————, *Economic Welfare in the Soviet Union* (Madison: University of Wisconsin Press, 1979).

A. Nove, "Income Distribution in the USSR: A Possible Explanation of Some Recent Data," *Soviet Studies*, vol. 34, no. 2 (April 1982), 286–288.

G. Ofer and A. Vinokur, "Earnings Differentials by Sex in the Soviet Union: A First Look," in S. Rosefielde, ed., *Economic Welfare and the Economics of Socialism: Essays in Honor of Abram Bergson* (Cambridge: Cambridge University Press, 1981), pp. 127–162.

P. J. D. Wiles, *Distribution of Income: East and West* (Amsterdam: North-Holland, 1974).

P. J. D. Wiles and S. Markowski, "Income Distribution Under Communism and Capitalism: Some Facts About Poland, the U.K., the USA and the USSR," *Soviet Studies*, vol. 22, nos. 3 and 4 (January and April 1971), 344–369 and 487–511.

M. Yanowitch, *Social and Economic Inequality in the USSR* (White Plains, N.Y.: M. E. Sharpe, 1977).

————, "The Soviet Income Revolution, " *Slavic Review*, vol. 22, no. 4 (December 1963).

Chapter 13

Soviet Performance: Military Power, Technology, and the Environment

*T*hus far we have assessed the performance of the Soviet economy in terms of conventional economic performance criteria: economic growth, efficiency, living standards, income distribution, and economic stability. This list is a restrictive one in the Soviet context because other goals, pursued consistently by the Soviet leadership, are not included. The first of these is the objective, first sought by an "encircled" Bolshevik regime in 1917, of achieving a degree of military power sufficient to protect the Soviet experiment from its capitalist foes and, later, to expand the Soviet sphere of influence. One can debate current Soviet military objectives—are they designed to achieve parity or dominance? But one thing is clear: There is a consistent priority assigned to military power. Soviet economic performance, especially in the postwar era, cannot be understood without an assessment of the resources devoted to the military and the military might these resources have produced, for these resources had to be diverted from consumption and investment. Trade-offs between military and civilian objectives would therefore be expected.

The second objective—the establishment of a high level of technology in the Soviet Union—is another that has been emphasized since the early days of the Soviet regime, when high-technology heavy industry was proclaimed the instrument through which socialism would be built. To what extent has this objective been achieved? Has the Soviet economy succeeded in creating and utilizing advanced technology to its maximum potential, given the resource constraints in which it has had to operate? To a limited extent, this issue has been addressed in Chapter 12, for efficiency gains will depend on the production and utilization of improved technology (including improved organizational arrangements). In this chapter, we examine this issue directly by considering the Soviet record in the technology area. Unlike other performance indicators, global measures of technological performance (other than measures of productivity) are not available; therefore we must make do with partial indicators of technological achievement. The manner in which new technologies are created and utilized by the Soviet economic system will be considered as well, for in the absence of accurate global measures of technological performance, analyses of Soviet "rules of the game" for technological innovation may provide insights overlooked by empirical measures. Moreover, in an era of economic reform, there is increased interest in the spillover of military technology and capabilities in the civilian economy.

The third performance criterion not encompassed in the conventional performance indicators is the degree to which the Soviet economy has been able to produce "environmental quality" or, expressed in the negative form, has been able to prevent "environmental disruption." Widespread concern and analysis of environmental disruption is a postwar phenomenon. Many LDCs still view environmental protection as a luxury that only affluent countries can afford; and as the Soviet Union was engaged in a program of rapid industrialization, and thereafter in a world war, one can understand that environmental concerns were of low priority during those early periods. Environmental disruption in the Soviet Union provides an interesting test case of the effect of the economic system on environmental quality, especially for those who have argued that environmental disruption is a product of capitalism.

SOVIET MILITARY POWER

We approach the topic of Soviet military power by posing two questions. The first is: How much military power have the Soviets been able to produce, given the limitations imposed by their economic base? This question is analogous to our earlier discussion of living standards, where we argued that per capita consumption levels must be judged relative to economic capacity. If one compares Soviet and American military power, it must be done with an appreciation of the different resource bases available to the two countries. To deal with this first question, we must above all have measures of military power, and as we shall point out, the measurement of military power raises severe conceptual and practical problems. The second question concerns the burden imposed on the Soviet domestic economy by the diversion of resources to military uses.

Problems of Measurement[1]

The military power of the Soviet Union can be quantified in two ways. The first is to list the physical quantities of the various inputs into the military power equation—armed service personnel, tanks, missiles, submarines, strategic supplies, and so on—and compare them with a similar list for the Soviet Union's major military competitors, the United States and its NATO allies and the People's Republic of China. In Table 13.1 such a compilation is supplied for the USSR and the United States.

Table 13.1   MILITARY STRENGTH: USSR AND USA, 1964

	1964	1978	1984	1988
USSR				
Intercontinental ballistic missiles (ICBMs)	200	1400	1398	1386
Submarine-launched ballistic missiles (SLBMs)	120	1015	981	944
Long-range bombers	190	135	143	175
Armed services personnel (millions)	3.4	4.2	4.3	4.3
USA				
Intercontinental ballistic missiles (ICBMs)	834	1054	1037	1000
Submarine-launched ballistic missiles (SLBMs)	416	656	592	640
Long-range bombers	630	432	297	337
Armed services personnel (millions)	2.7	2.1	2.1	2.3

Sources: These data are based on studies of the International Institute for Strategic Studies, London. They are cited in *The 1979 Hammond Almanac* (Maplewood, N.J.: Hammond Almanac, Inc., 1978), pp. 733–735; *The Official Associated Press Almanac 1973* (New York: Almanac Publishing Company, 1972), pp. 616–617; and *The World Almanac 1985*, p. 339. The Soviet armed services figures are from M. Feshbach and S. Rapawy, "Soviet Population and Manpower Trends and Policies," in U.S. Congress, Joint Economic Committee, *Soviet Economy in a New Perspective* (Washington, D.C.: U.S. Government Printing Office, 1976), p. 132; Hearings Before the Subcommittee on Priorities and Economy in Government, *Allocation of Resources in the Soviet Union and China—1978; Part 4: Soviet Union* (Washington, D.C., June 26 and July 24, 1978), p. 68. Recent data are from International Institute for Strategic Studies, *The Military Balance 1988–89* (Reading, England: Eastern Press, 1988), pp. 18, 33; *World Almanac and Book of Facts 1989* (New York: Photos Books, 1989), p. 758; Soviet military manpower (1988) from S. Rapawy, "Labor Force and Employment in the U.S.S.R.," in U.S. Congress, Joint Economic Committee, *Gorbachev's Economic Plans* (Washington, D.C.: U.S. Government Printing Office, 1987), p. 194.

Comparisons of physical quantities of military inputs are useful, and they confirm the general increase in Soviet military power vis-à-vis the United States. Yet such comparisons suffer from a series of deficiencies. Military hardware tends to be quite complex and heterogeneous; therefore, the simple counting of physical units will not reveal their contribution to military power. To make such a judgment, one must have detailed information on the (perhaps thousands of) characteristics of each type of military hardware. In the case of ICBMs, for example, one must know their payload, accuracy, speed of launch, degree of protection from nuclear attack, and so on. Even if this wealth of information were available, an *overall* measure of Soviet military power would still be lacking, for some means must be found of *aggregating* all the heterogeneous inputs (military personnel, tanks, bombs, ICBMs, strategic supplies, etc.).

The most straightforward means of converting physical indicators of military force into a common denominator is to multiply each by its price and then sum, that is, to compile a value aggregate of military power. Under ideal circumstances, relative prices will reflect both the opportunity cost of resources embodied in the commodity and the marginal rates at which defense planners are willing to substitute one item for another (holding the level of military power constant). In our earlier discussion of the Soviet price system, we noted that Soviet ruble prices rarely mirror the opportunity costs of production (or the marginal rates of substitution of users); and, in the case of pricing the defense commodities of the United States, it is difficult to know how rational such prices are (for example, until 1973, the wage rates of draftees were set well below opportunity costs). Thus, in making value comparisons of USSR and U.S. military power, one is unsure of the "rationality" of the prices used in aggregation.

In the case of compiling value aggregates of Soviet defense outlays, practical problems caused by data deficiencies are as serious as underlying theoretical issues. Official Soviet budgetary sources report defense spending as a single line item, and reported defense outlays are often manipulated to suit political needs. The announced state budget claims virtually no increase in defense spending (even prior to adjustment for inflation) between 1967 and 1978, a period when massive investments in military hardware systems were being made.[2] For these reasons, defense analysts in the United States have felt it necessary to make independent estimates of Soviet defense spending by employing U.S. defense budgetary practices. Two types of independent calculations have been made. The first, undertaken by the American intelligence community,[3] uses the "building block" approach, whereby the physical quantities of defense inputs (rockets, manpower, equipment, etc.) are multiplied by the presumed cost of producing the items in the United States (to obtain Soviet defense spending in U.S. prices for comparison with U.S. defense spending) and by Soviet ruble prices.[4] The advantages of the building block approach are that the estimates are independent of official Soviet budgetary data and that they are in a form suitable for comparison with U.S. defense spending. The disadvantages are that one cannot assess the reliability of intelligence data on Soviet military hardware and that it is difficult to determine accurately costs in the United States and the Soviet Union. The second approach calls for the estimation of Soviet outlays on military hardware by subtracting civilian uses of industrial production from the ruble value of industrial production; the resulting residual is presumed to equal defense outlays.[5] The accuracy of both types of estimates is subject to serious question (although they have tended to agree with each other in recent years),[6] and skepticism concerning their reliability was increased in 1976, when the Central Intelligence Agency raised its estimate of Soviet defense spending by 100 percent.[7]

Estimates of Defense Spending

Over the years, the CIA has derived estimates of the dollar cost of Soviet defense activities. According to estimates published in the late 1970s, the dollar cost of Soviet defense outlays as a percentage of U.S. defense outlays increased considerably from roughly 60 percent in the late 1960s to roughly 145 percent in the late 1970s.[8] According to these estimates, the dollar cost of Soviet defense spending came to equal the dollar cost of U.S. defense spending in the early 1970s. According to recent estimates calculated in constant 1985 dollars, the dollar cost of Soviet defense as a percentage of the dollar cost of U.S. defense has declined from roughly 125 percent in the early 1980s to roughly 108 percent in the mid-1980s.[9]

Expenditures on defense in any one year will not yield the total of military power, for military power is the product of cumulated past expenditures.[10] Therefore, a more accurate measure of Soviet military power vis-à-vis the United States would be the sum of military expenditures (in constant prices) over a substantial period of time. According to CIA calculations, cumulative Soviet defense outlays for the decade 1968–1978 exceeded American totals by 12 percent.[11] The implication of these findings is that the Soviet Union has overtaken the United States in its real defense spending, although the pattern of the 1980s has differed from that of the 1970s.

There is a range of considerable uncertainty surrounding these types of estimates, although the CIA believes its estimates are not more than 15 percent in error. For example, the CIA has made two substantial changes in its previous assessments of Soviet military spending. In 1976, the CIA increased its estimate of Soviet military spending in U.S. dollars as a consequence of raising its estimates of the dollar costs of Soviet procurement. In 1983, the CIA lowered its estimate of the growth of military spending after 1976 from 4 to 5 percent per annum to 2 percent per annum.[12] Given the problems of intelligence gathering and then of translating physical indicators into dollar or ruble values, one can understand why a substantial margin of error must be attached to these estimates. Second, the relationship between cumulated spending totals and military power is not clearly defined.[13] Military power depends not only upon sheer spending ability but also upon the wisdom of defense planners and the uses to which they put the expenditures. Third, there is the ambiguity introduced by the index number problem, which requires some comment.[14]

The dollar cost estimates of Soviet defense spending translate Soviet defense outlays into U.S. prices. Soviet ICBM systems are valued at U.S. prices, Soviet manpower is valued at U.S. military pay scales, fuels used by the military are computed in U.S. fuel prices. The United States is "rich" in advanced technology and "poor" in manpower relative to the Soviet Union; therefore, the prices of high-technology products will be low in the United States relative to Soviet ruble prices. The structure of Soviet defense outlays, however, is geared to domestic resource constraints, that is, Soviet defense planners will place relatively less emphasis on advanced technology (less use of advanced computer circuitry in ICBMs and greater use of large payloads) and more emphasis on labor-intensive military expenditures (larger armed forces). When Soviet defense outlays are translated into U.S. prices, products that play a relatively small role (advanced-technology computer products) are accorded a relatively low U.S. price, while those products that play a heavy role (manpower, rifles, etc.) are valued in relatively high U.S. prices. Thus, dollar cost estimates of defense spending will yield a higher relative value for the USSR than comparisons conducted in ruble prices. To this point, the most reliable estimates are those in dollar values, but the available estimates in ruble prices do confirm the expected relationship, namely, that if ruble prices are employed, the USSR spending advantage is reduced (to a 25 percent from a 45 percent advantage in 1978 according to the CIA). Franklyn Holzman has argued that the CIA grossly underestimates the effects of index number relativity.[15] He maintains that it is quite possible that the United States outspends the Soviets if ruble prices are correctly calculated. Holzman also emphasizes the fact that the higher quality of American manpower and military hardware is not captured by the CIA figures.

Despite these reservations, the conclusion to be drawn from figures on defense spending and physical indicators of military potential is that the Soviet Union has achieved an impressive degree of military might. Most analysts would agree that Soviet military might is at least equivalent to that of the United States, a nation that possesses considerably more economic power (as measured by the size of GNP). Soviet authorities have, therefore, achieved their objectives as far as the military power equation is concerned.

The Burden of Soviet Defense Expenditures

Obviously, these military power achievements have not taken place without sacrifice. The diversion of resources from the civilian economy has cost the Soviet economy production for consumption and investment. These costs can be illustrated in a number of ways: Soviet males reaching the age of 18 become subject to conscription; and in 1975, 87 percent of males turning 18 were drafted. It is projected that if current military manpower levels are to be maintained, over 100 percent of 18-year-olds must be conscripted in the 1980s, meaning that conscripts will have to be sought in other age groups.[16] Not only does Soviet defense require a drain of manpower from the civilian economy, it is also estimated that one-third of the product of the machine-building industry (the primary source of investment goods) is devoted annually to the defense sector.[17] In general, defense takes a large share of the highest-quality scientific, technical, and managerial talent, as well as having preferential access of scarce resources of all kinds.

The most frequently used measure of the total defense burden is the ratio of defense spending to GNP, as this denotes the share of total resources devoted to defense activities. Past estimates suggest that from 1967 to 1978, the Soviets devoted approximately one-eighth of their output to defense, versus 5 percent for the United States.[18] More recent estimates have not radically altered this picture. A recent recomputation of Soviet GNP by end use at factor cost places the defense share in 1986 at just over 15 percent.[19] The share of defense spending in U.S. GNP has been just over 6 percent in the early and mid-1980s.[20]

The exact cost of this military burden, as measured by the sacrifice of current consumption and the longer-run effects on growth of reduced investment, are not known, but econometric estimates suggest that they are substantial.[21] Projections into the future are necessarily uncertain, primarily because it is difficult to predict productivity gains, but the ultimate cost of Soviet defense spending may prove to be a growth rate unacceptably low to Soviet authorities. In fact, if the Soviets have indeed slowed down the rate of growth of defense spending in recent years, this may have been dictated by lagging economic growth. The defense burden had simply become too large.

THE MILITARY IN THE GORBACHEV ERA

We have emphasized that considerable controversy surrounds both the size of the Soviet military budget and changes in this budget over time. Most of this controversy stems from the fact that significant portions of Soviet military spending are not included in the Soviet defense budget. Moreover, although there have been hints that secrecy on this issue may be reduced under glasnost, only limited revelations about the size of the defense budget have been made thus far.

There is, however, considerable agreement on the notion that both the size of the military budget and its growth in earlier years (especially the 1970s) permitted slower growth (roughly 2 percent on an average annual basis) in the 1980s. Whether this slower growth in recent years was necessitated by poor overall economic performance or whether it in part represents policy changes is difficult to know.

Thus, from a significant base, the Soviet military has, in the 1980s, been able to sustain its claim on Soviet resources. However, during this past decade, and especially under the Gorbachev reform program, the issue of a trade-off between the military and the civilian economies has been an issue of growing importance.[22] There are a number of reasons for a renewed emphasis on the trade-off issue.

First, even within a wide range of error necessitated by measurement difficulties, there is little question that the military budget is a major burden to the Soviet economy and the Soviet population. Shifts of resources away from the military toward the civilian economy might well assist in the modernization of the Soviet economy, but the precise nature of this trade-off is unclear.

Second, Gorbachev has been outspoken in the area of potential defense cuts. If cuts were made in the Soviet defense commitment, and if a reduction of international tensions permitted the Soviet Union to pay less attention to the development of new weapons systems (for example, a response to SDI), both forces could have a major impact on the Soviet economy.

Third, and possibly most important in the short run, Gorbachev has clearly harnessed the military to his program of economic reform. The military is to have an important role in critical sectors such as machine building and food processing. In addition, the military is to be a major player in the overall strengthening of science and technology in the Soviet Union and, most important, the application of this new strength to modernizing the Soviet economy.

The precise direction of such changes remains to be understood fully. Whether military spending as such is or is not cut in some way, it is evident that Gorbachev is changing the role of the military in Soviet society.

SOVIET TECHNOLOGY[23]

The advancement of technology has received a great deal of attention in the Soviet Union in recent years. Although this attention was present in the Brezhnev era, it has received a new impetus under Gorbachev. In several dimensions, technological advancement is fundamental to Soviet economic reform policies.

First, when we turn to a detailed examination of perestroika, it will be evident that technological advancement is a key element of this reform program. While the concern for technology is broad, it also focuses heavily upon key sectors of the Soviet economy, for example, machine building, as a cornerstone of intensification.

Second, Gorbachev has chosen to enhance Soviet technological capabilities by borrowing, in part, from the military. This borrowing is represented by direct manufacturing assistance and also by replication of defense sector policies regarding technological change.

Third, while decentralized incentive-type mechanisms are being suggested for stimulating technological change, there is also a good deal of emphasis on more traditional organizational arrangements, especially planning, as used in the Soviet military.

In light of the growing emphasis on technology in the Soviet economy, and especially technology as a key element in Soviet economic reform, it is important that we understand the nature of technology and technological change in the Soviet setting.

Measurement of Soviet technological performance is, like the assessment of Soviet military power, a complicated problem. Direct measures of Soviet technological achievement relative to that of capitalist countries can be made only on an industry case study basis, and the researcher will not know whether such results are representative for the economy as a whole. Moreover, case studies require the evaluation of the operating characteristics of the technology (reliability, power/weight ratios, energy efficiency, etc.) and of the quality of the end products produced, and the number of such technical-engineering characteristics is so large that the evaluation may depend on the particular characteristics studied. Also, the characteristics of the technology will depend on the resource endowments of the country; so it may be optimal for one nation to adopt technology that is less "advanced" because factor proportions dictate such a choice.

Indirect measurement of technology represents the alternate to direct case studies. The relative factor productivity of the USSR vis-à-vis other countries can be calculated (Chapter 12), but the relationship between factor productivity and Soviet technological achievement is not clearly defined. It is not directly apparent whether low Soviet factor productivity is a consequence of lagging technological performance or of "omitted factors" (qualitative differences in inputs, economies of scale, and so on). A low technological level is only one of several explanations of low Soviet factor productivity, as the factor productivity calculation represents "a measure of our ignorance."[24] Further measures of the technology level (lead time to the utilization of a new technology, number of patents, volume of scientific papers, scientific awards, citations in scientific papers) supplement our understanding of Soviet technology, but all suffer from serious deficiencies.

Granted that no single measure of technological performance will be adequate, we can nevertheless cite some of the basic results of research on Soviet technology. First, we should refer the reader back to the factor productivity results (Chapter 12), which show Soviet factor productivity to be low relative to the advanced industrialized countries. This finding is consistent with the conclusion that Soviet technological performance is below that of the industrialized West, but such evidence is not conclusive by itself. Case studies of the technological level of Soviet industry (even when chosen so as to select priority branches) suggest as well a relatively low level of Soviet technology, although this conclusion applies less strongly to the defense and iron and steel industries. The most striking conclusion of case study research is that, in most sectors, "there is no evidence of a substantial diminution of the technological gap between the USSR and the West in the past 15 to 20 years, either at the prototype/commercial application stages or in the diffusion of advanced technology."[25] The conclusion is generally consistent with the factor productivity studies, which show the rate of growth of factor productivity in the USSR to be only average relative to the industrialized West.

The state of Soviet technological achievement is uneven. There are areas, for example, metallurgy and welding, where the Soviets are advanced. In other areas, lags are great. For example, in the critical area of computers, it has been estimated that the Soviet Union lags behind the United States by 9–15 years (main frames), 4–10 years (minicomputers), and 8–10 years (microcircuits).[26] In applied areas, for example, the development of automated management systems, progress has been uneven.

Another source of evidence concerning the relatively low technological level of the Soviet economy is its continued reliance on imports from the West to meet its advanced technology requirements. Case studies of computer and machine tool imports can be cited to confirm this continuing dependence.[27] Moreover, Marshal Goldman has noted that there may be pitfalls to reliance on imported technology.[28] Goldman argues that given the pace of technological change in advanced countries, and the growing complementarities among technologies, it may be increasingly difficult if not impossible to jump from behind simply by importing advanced technology. If such is the case, it will be increasingly important for the Soviet Union to emphasize domestic development of new technologies.

The technological level of a country will depend not only on the availability of new technology but also upon its diffusion throughout the economy. The limited evidence that is available suggests that the lead time between the granting of a patent for a new invention and its practical implementation are longer in the Soviet Union than in the United States and West Germany. In fact, the United States and West Germany tend to implement over one-half of their inventions in little more than a year, while the Soviets require three years to attain this ratio. The slowness of diffusion of new technology applies to imported technology as well as domestic inventions.[29]

What conclusions are to be drawn from this evidence? Our overall conclusion is that the information supplied by factor productivity studies, direct investigations of the technology of Soviet industry, reliance on high-technology imports, lead times, and diffusion point to a relatively low level of technological achievement in the Soviet economy (with the exception of the military). Moreover, data over time suggest that the Soviets' technology gap has not been narrowed over the past two decades. Put another way, Soviet technological achievement is generally inconsistent with Gorbachev's reform objectives. It is for this reason that new policies pertaining to industrial modernization in the Soviet Union bear close watching.

Microeconomic Causes of the Technology Gap

The probable causes of the Soviet technology gap have been identified by Joseph Berliner,[30] who argues that Soviet organizational structure, pricing system, and incentive rules discriminate against technological innovation. Although the Soviet economic system does have certain features favorable to innovation (patent restrictions do not limit the spread of an invention), other features inhibit technological innovation. The existing organizational structure gives maximal encouragement to decision makers to discriminate against innovations and to managers to shy away from doing new things. As noted in Chapter 8, Soviet managers have learned to minimize the risk of failure by developing secure channels of supply. Once a Soviet manager has established reliable supply relationships, the chance of failure is reduced. The installation of a new technology would change routine patterns and disrupt existing supply channels built up carefully over the years. New ways of doing things would also change established distribution arrangements and add another source of uncertainty to plan fulfillment. Moreover, most research and development work is done by research institutes and ministerial project-making organizations whose responsibility for a project ends when a new design is approved by the ministry. The need for enterprises to rely on an outside supply of R&D services compounds the risk of failure.

As Berliner points out, innovation does increase managerial risks; but if the rewards to managers for innovation were large enough, managers could more readily be induced to innovate. One way to reward managers would be to grant them high prices relative to costs of production (and thus larger profits) for new products and then to pay them bonuses, either directly for innovative activity or through an increased share in enterprise profits. The existing pricing and incentive structures do neither. The principle of pricing according to the labor theory of value discriminates against product innovation, for savings in labor costs are passed on to the user in the form of lower prices rather than to the producer as higher profits. Efforts to exempt new products from branch-average cost pricing have been largely unsuccessful, although some of the cruder disparities of earlier years have been eliminated.

The managerial bonus system also discourages innovation. Over the years, managers have been paid bonuses primarily for fulfillment of current year production targets. It was not until the mid-1950s that special bonuses for innovation were developed. But even after the introduction of a variety of rewards for innovation, it remains true that the managerial bonus still depends primarily on fulfilling basic enterprise plan targets. Moreover, the bonus system is geared to rewarding short-term results. Innovative activity, by disrupting existing channels of supply and distribution, typically causes a short-term reduction in enterprise output, which is compensated for by a long-term increase as an innovation comes on-stream. Yet during this period, the manager will lose bonus funds and will thus be discouraged from innovation.

Can Gorbachev change the posture of Soviet technology? Although it will take some years to form a definitive answer to this question, some patterns have begun to emerge. On the positive side, Gorbachev has clearly placed a new and important emphasis on technology. As we have stated, technology is a key element in the Gorbachev reform program. In addition, steps are being taken to improve inventive arrangements and to stress the need for quality as opposed to quantity. At the same time, Gorbachev has emphasized continuation of a number of past policies such as personnel changes, organizational changes, and the like. It remains to be seen whether there will be fundamental changes in the price system such that there will be a real incentive for technological change.

SCIENTIFIC LABOR FORCE IN THE SOVIET UNION

Berliner's work focuses on the microeconomic incentive problems of generating and implementing new technology in the Soviet economic system. This is one obvious cause of the Soviet technology gap. A second possible cause would be an inferior stock of trained science and technology (S&T) personnel, which would mean that the Soviet Union simply has not succeeded in creating the stock of S&T professionals required to bring about significant improvements in science and technology.

In the Soviet Union, the task of training S&T specialists is undertaken by the higher educational establishment, the so-called VUZ system. The VUZ system consists of traditional universities and a large number of scientific research institutes. The scientific research institutes may fall under the jurisdiction of the Soviet Academy of Sciences (and tend to concentrate on pure research), or they may fall under the jurisdiction of the various ministries (in which case they tend to concentrate on applied research). Both the universities and the scientific research institutes are charged with training advanced S&T professionals at the undergraduate and graduate levels. In fact, the specific positions opened to VUZ enrollees are determined through the interaction of *Gosplan*, the ministries, and the Ministry of Higher and Secondary Specialized Education. This interaction is to ensure that the VUZ system produce the S&T specialists required by the national economy.

The Soviet S&T training system can be judged according to its ability to select the most qualified candidates for advanced S&T training, by the quality of S&T training, by the rational placement of S&T personnel in the economy, and by the proper utilization of scientific and technical experts once they are at work in the nation's research network. As to the first point, it appears that admittance to advanced S&T training in the Soviet VUZ system is, with some exceptions, largely done on the basis of the scientific potential of the applicant. It is more difficult to judge the quality of Soviet S&T training at the VUZ level. Like in the United States, there is great variety among the best VUZs and the worst. The best higher educational establishments tend to be located in Moscow and Leningrad, and these institutions appear to offer advanced scientific training that is equal to the best training offered in the United States and Western Europe. On the other hand, the VUZs located in the provinces attract less-qualified candidates and function with less-qualified faculty; therefore, to draw an overall judgment is difficult. The Soviet S&T curricula tend to be highly standardized by central authorities, and examination of various S&T curricula suggests that they are on a par with S&T curricula in the West.

Long-run achievements of the Soviet S&T training establishment are impressive. High-level S&T personnel trends can be gleaned indirectly from the numbers of persons completing higher education because of the concentration of S&T in higher education training. In 1914–1915, 127,000 students were enrolled in higher educational establishments. By 1940–1941, this number had risen to 812,000; and by the 1980s, there were over 5 million students enrolled in higher education. In 1914, 136,000 people employed in the national economy had a higher education. In 1959, 3.8 million persons had a higher education. By 1987, this number had increased to 20.8 million. As for the over-10 population, the increase in the proportion of persons with higher education between 1959 and 1987 was from 2.3 percent to 9.0 percent.

The number of scientific workers with advanced degrees and titles tripled during the decade of the 1950s and tripled again during the decade of the 1960s. The 1970s saw a slowdown in the growth in the number of scientific workers with advanced degrees. The number increased from roughly 1 million to 1.5 million between 1970 and 1987.

The growth of Soviet higher educational establishments has been impressive. In 1914–1915, there were 105 higher education establishments in tsarist Russia of which 13 had the stature of university. By 1970, there were 805 higher education establishments (51 universities), and by 1987/88, there were 898 higher education establishments in the USSR. The number of teachers in higher education rose from 61,000 in 1940, to 263,000 in 1967, to approximately 510,000 in 1984. The last figure includes 19,000 doctors of science and 200,000 candidates of science.

Trends in enrollment in S&T higher education programs can be read from trends in overall enrollment in higher educational establishments. In 1976–1977, of the 4.95 million students in higher education, 1.6 million were enrolled in areas of study outside science and technology (teacher training, economics, law, arts, and humanities). Thus, about two-thirds of Soviet higher education enrollment tends to be in science and engineering (including medicine). Of the 768,000 graduates of higher educational establishments in 1987, roughly 50 percent were in science and technology.[31]

According to the best calculations available, the number of scientists and engineers employed in R&D in the United States around 1980 (some 600,000) was about three-quarters the number of R&D scientists and engineers employed in R&D in the USSR (about 830,000). The numerical superiority of the Soviet Union is a relatively new phenomenon dating to the late 1960s. In 1950, for example, the number of R&D scientists and engineers in the United States was around 50 percent higher than in the Soviet Union.

The number of R&D scientists with advanced degrees is more equal in the two countries, but the Soviet Union has clear numerical superiority. In the mid-1970s, the United States employed some 212,000 S&T specialists with advanced degrees, while the Soviet Union employed 271,000. The number of advanced-degree specialists in the physical and life sciences is about the same in the United States and the USSR, but the USSR has about twice the number of engineers as the United States.

Looking more generally at advanced-degree holders in both science and nonscience fields, we see that the United States devotes proportionally more resources to social sciences and humanities than the Soviet Union. A similar overall proportion of advanced degrees are in physical and life sciences. The major difference is that some 30 percent of Soviet advanced degrees are in engineering, while only 15 percent of American advanced degrees are in that field. The United States retains numerical superiority at the advanced-degree level only in the social sciences and humanities. The number of American advanced-degree specialists in the social sciences and humanities is about 60 percent greater than the corresponding Soviet number. The sole exception is economics, an area (due to the enormous task of managing a centrally planned economy) in which there are more Soviet advanced-degree specialists than in the United States. The relative figures on specialists with advanced degrees bring home the fact that, although both the United States and the Soviet Union train roughly similar numbers of advanced-degree specialists, the Soviets have chosen to concentrate their higher educational resources on training science and engineering specialists at the expense of social sciences and humanities.[32]

Most Western observers agree that the Soviet Union now has the world's largest science and training establishment. It is much more difficult to assess the quality of Soviet S&T education in similarly broad strokes. There is nevertheless some evidence that sheds light on this issue. Let us first consider the side of the ledger that points to quality achievements and then turn to evidence of quality deficiencies.

Studies of Soviet S&T training in different science and engineering specialties yield mixed results on the quality of Soviet graduates relative to American graduates. In the area of physics, for example, expert Western opinion suggests that Soviet university training in physics is comparable (or even perhaps superior) to that found in American universities. Other studies have produced mixed results on the quality of engineering training in Soviet and American engineering colleges, but there appears to be enough difference of opinion to suggest that differences in the quality of engineering training are not overwhelming. To quote from U.S. specialists on this matter:

> Comparisons of the level of training received in specific areas, however, indicate that the level of professional attainment of a science or engineering graduate of Soviet higher education establishments (in the full-time programs at least) is about the same as or occasionally higher than the level of attainment of a science or engineering graduate of a U.S. college or university.[33]

One caveat should be attached to the above conclusion: Just as in American science and technology education, there is variation in the quality of training among institutions. In the Soviet case, there is another source of quality variation—the quality difference between full-time training at higher education institutions and evening or correspondence training. There is universal agreement among Western and Soviet experts that the quality of evening and correspondence training is inferior. It will also be noted below that the majority of Soviet enrollment in higher educational establishments is in evening and correspondence programs, so this is a major adjustment that must be considered. On the matter of variation in quality among institutions, we have no way of knowing whether this variation is greater in the Soviet Union or in the

United States. Soviet S&T training is more strictly controlled and standardized by government authorities, so it may be that there is less variation in the Soviet Union, but this is only speculation. The conclusion that Soviet advanced-degree science training is roughly comparable to that of the United States is based on comparisons of the premier institutions in each country.

Other evidence on the quality of Soviet S&T training is fairly anecdotal, but may become a better established proposition as further studies of the third Soviet emigration are completed. There is some preliminary evidence that U.S. employers have found that the level of training of former Soviet citizens holding advanced degrees in science (based on full-time study programs) is roughly comparable to that of the U.S.-trained scientists with advanced degrees. Moreover, in-depth interviews with former Soviet scientists reveal that they personally rate the quality of their basic training as high.[34] This type of testimony is revealing because many Soviet emigré scientists have had an opportunity to compare themselves and their training with their American counterparts.

Additional evidence is derived from international scientific awards and citation indexes. In general, this evidence suggests that although Soviet scientists have received fewer prestigious science awards and are less widely cited by world scientists, they have achieved respectable world reputations in Soviet science priority areas. It must be emphasized that the relative numbers of international awards or citations are distorted measures of the qualitative achievements of Soviet science. There are obvious linguistic barriers; few world scientists read Russian. Soviet scientists tend to fall outside established scientific networks, and it is harder for Soviet scientists to obtain permission to travel to the West to establish contacts. Recognizing these problems, we note that in physics—a field in which Soviet scientists have historically excelled—Soviet scientists have captured seven Nobel prizes since 1950, as compared to the 31 captured by American-located physicists. In scientific fields not emphasized in Soviet resource allocation policies, Soviet scientists have performed less well.

Citation indexes reveal that Soviet scientists have established international reputations in mathematics, physics, and earth and space sciences. Despite language barriers, American mathematicians cite approximately as many Soviet mathematical articles as Soviet mathematicians cite American mathematical articles. The number of citations by U.S. scientists of Soviet publications in physics and earth and space sciences is also quite high, although the numbers of citations are far from parity.[35]

There is some evidence of weaknesses and flaws in the Soviet S&T training curriculum. In the standard Soviet University, 8 to 12 percent of classroom time is devoted to ideological training, and 4 to 6 hours per week are devoted to military training. Experts point out that Soviet scientists and engineers are trained in narrowly defined specialties (a comprehensive set of 499 numbered specialty fields) rather than receiving a broader scientific or technical background.[36] The extreme narrowness of Soviet S&T education may make it difficult for Soviet scientists to adapt to changes in scientific and technical fields. It may even lead to unemployed or underemployed S&T specialists when there are shifts in demand for the various specialties.

Another piece of evidence that points to systematic problems with Soviet S&T training is the bias in favor of passing students or graduating unqualified students. The Soviet press contains numerous complaints of grade inflation, lazy students, and the unwillingness of faculty to fail students. These complaints sound very much like those found in the American press, but the bias is possibly more systematic in the Soviet case. The reason is that Soviet educational establishments, like their factory counterparts, are judged on the basis of fulfillment of plans. The plans of higher educational establishments often consist of turning out target numbers of graduates in specific fields. If large numbers of students are failed, then the educational establishment fails to meet its plan. Moreover, activists in educational organizations (like activists in factory organizations) are judged on the basis of fulfillment of plan quotas. These pressures on the administration of higher educational establishments may lead to the release of poorly qualified S&T graduates on the R&D establishment.[37]

Although general conclusions of this sort are risky, we would conclude that the Soviet technology gap is not due to the low level of training and qualifications of Soviet S&T professionals. If anything, we would conclude that the Soviet economic system has done a relatively poor job utilizing the S&T personnel base with which it is working. It would thus appear that the microeconomic incentive problems emphasized by Berliner play the major role in explaining why the USSR, with its vast numbers of trained S&T experts, has not done a better job in closing the Soviet technology gap with the West.

SOVIET ENVIRONMENTAL QUALITY

Under capitalism, environmental disruption (ED) is thought to be caused by external effects. External effects arise whenever the private costs (or benefits) of a particular action diverge from its social costs (or benefits). If a profit-maximizing capitalist firm is able, for example, to pollute the air without being charged a price for this activity, the social cost of production will exceed the private cost and a greater than optimal level of environmental disruption will emerge. Only if private enterprises can be charged for the social costs (via a tax, for example) of their pollution or if such activities are internalized will the level of environmental disruption be optimal.* The optimality criterion is such that pollution should be allowed up to that level at which its marginal social cost equals the marginal cost of pollution abatement.[38] This is the standard adopted by most economists to the chagrin of many environmental groups, who deny the existence of "optimal" levels of pollution.

---

*Internalization occurs when costs that were previously external to the polluting enterprise become internal costs. For example, if all enterprises located along a river are merged, then the water pollution abatement costs of these enterprises become private costs.

Advocates of socialism have long argued on theoretical grounds that ED will not arise in a socialist society. Although specifics have varied, the essential thread is the *level* of decision making. Where decisions are centralized and the objective function—the outcome that planners are trying to achieve— includes environmental quality, there need never be externalities, since there is literally nothing external to the decision makers. A similar argument is made for local decision making if the planners develop an incentive structure that ensures the harmony of local decisions with central goals (assuming the necessary con- comitant of perfect information). It is necessary that appropriate resource valu- ations, which reflect central goals, be available to the central decision makers.[39]

Oskar Lange, a classic advocate of the socialist cause, argued in his famous article "On the Economic Theory of Socialism"[40] that under socialism, the price system will be more comprehensive and, in effect, a high value will be placed by the Central Planning Board upon a clean environment. Maurice Dobb makes a similar argument when he suggests that, although information availability and digestion may be a problem in the real world, socialist planners will tend to make decisions with maximum global vision and an eye to their environmental impact.[41] Jan Tinbergen, the noted Dutch economist, has also endorsed the no- tion that, in general, decisions made at the highest possible levels will mini- mize the problem of externalities.[42]

Quite apart from the theoretical arguments, most contemporary environ- mentalists would probably argue that ED is a growing and serious worldwide threat that has justifiably received increased attention in recent years.[43] Moreover, while the specifics of occurrence and reaction may differ from case to case, ED is largely a function of the drive for economic growth and economic development. As such, the problems arise in the East and West under widely differing circumstances, and comparison, analysis, and policy solutions are very difficult to generate. The comparison of ED across economic systems is difficult if not impossible.

Although it is difficult to make specific comparisons of ED between, say, the Soviet Union and the United States, there has been in recent years a grow- ing awareness in both the East and West of environmental problems in the Soviet Union. There are a variety of reasons for environmental problems in the Soviet Union.

First, as we have already emphasized, the primary and dominant focus of Soviet economic policy in contemporary times has been rapid economic growth. To the extent that the short-term costs of economic growth can be re- duced by in effect ignoring environmental costs, it can be attractive for a rela- tively poor country to achieve growth by postponing some of the real costs. Although policies for environmental preservation may exist, they mean little in a maximum growth environment.

Second, the ideological framework within which the Soviets work has prob- ably created an illusory optimism.[44] Marx said little about the environment, stressing the positive features of a new socialist order over the ills of the old capitalist order. Soviet thinking, expressed in a variety of ways over the years, has emphasized the ability of the Soviet system to master the environment, in effect to harness the environment with benefit rather than harm for the development of the economy and society. In this context, it is not surprising that the Soviet Union has pursued many grandiose and often controversial projects designed to harness nature. The Stalin plan for the transformation of nature and the contemporary river diversion projects are examples.

Third, although it is very difficult to isolate and examine the relationships between the economic system and environmental outcomes, undoubtedly Soviet organizational arrangements in combination with Soviet growth and related policies have had an impact on the environmental outcome in the Soviet Union. The potential for conflict between powerful ministries with differing objectives has been evident in the struggle for the preservation of Lake Baikal. Moreover, even where a degree of pluralism may exist at lower levels of the organizational hierarchy, it is not clear that local views will necessarily change central views and actions. The breakdown of the system may arise for a variety of reasons. Information channels may be inadequate, or as in the Soviet case, the absence of appropriate valuation of natural resources may put inappropriate or inadequate information into existing channels.

Finally, Soviet policies of secrecy have inhibited the development of an environmental lobby in the Soviet Union. Clearly, this aspect of Soviet policy has changed under Gorbachev, as the widespread discussion of the Chernobyl nuclear accident indicates.[45] It remains to be seen whether open discussion will fundamentally alter Soviet environmental policies. In spite of the serious nature of the Chernobyl accident, the development of Soviet nuclear power has continued as part of an overall plan for the fulfillment of Soviet energy needs.

Measurement of Environmental Disruption

To assess the Soviet record of environmental protection, one must begin with some notion of the stock of pollution in the USSR relative to the stock in the industrialized capitalist countries. Of all the performance criteria, we are on the most treacherous footing with regard to the measurement of pollution levels.[46] Although it may be possible to establish the physical quantities of harmful air pollutants, water pollutants, noise pollution, and radiation, there is no established system of weights that allows the researcher to aggregate environmental disruption into a single global measure. In place of a global measures, one must rely on various partial measures, the firmest of which are for air pollution. According to calculations by Victor Mote (for 1968–1969), the gross weights of air pollutants produced in the USSR were as follows: dust, 61 percent of U.S.; sulfur dioxide, 49 percent of U.S.; carbon monoxide, 19 percent of U.S.; and hydrocarbons, 22 percent of U.S.[47] Although these calculations relate to a period some 25 years ago, they are nevertheless suggestive of lower levels of Soviet air pollution relative to levels in the United States, a country with significantly higher levels of per capita income. Mote also emphasizes the fact that air pollution levels differ significantly by region in the Soviet Union. Industrial emissions are a problem, while automobile emissions are less serious. The reader should be aware that in 1987, the United States had 570 automobile registrations per thousand population, while the equivalent number for the Soviet Union was approximately 42.[48] Thus differences in the sources of pollution rather than differences in extent of effectiveness of solutions may largely explain differences in air pollution between the United States and the Soviet Union.

In a recent discussion of air pollution in the Soviet Union, Craig ZumBrunnen emphasizes the fact that while cars pollute the air in the United States, it is industrial smokestacks that pollute in the Soviet Union.[49] According to ZumBrunnen, as of 1983 air quality was monitored in nearly 500 Soviet cities. Newly constructed enterprises are supposed to have emission control equipment, although the available evidence suggests that the effectiveness of such measures is highly variable among the various Soviet industrial ministries and their enterprises. According to official Soviet statistics, the percentage of gaseous and particulate pollutants trapped by pollution equipment has increased from 75 in 1982 to 77 in 1987. Regional differentials are significant. For example, the effectiveness of pollution equipment as defined here ranges from a high of 93 percent in Estonia to a low of 33 percent in Turkmenistan.[50]

The management of water resources is a major environmental issue in the Soviet Union.[51] The importance of the water issue stems in part from the controversy over Lake Baikal, which first focused attention on Soviet environmental issues in a major way in the 1960s. More important, there is in the Soviet Union considerable regional imbalance between the demand for and supply of water, necessitating the development of major water diversion projects. Also, as in other countries, bodies of water such as the Black Sea are major dumping sites for untreated waste.

Of the total sums spent on environmental issues in the Soviet Union, those relating to water are by far the most important.[52] In recent years, there has been a tendency to question the grandiose water diversion projects, placing growing emphasis on, for example, the means for recycling water. Significant measures have been taken to purify industrial discharges, though with significant regional differentials.

In a study done in the mid-1970s, Craig ZumBrunnen found major water pollution problems in the drainage basins of the Black Sea and the Sea of Azov.[53] As the author notes, these drainage basins combine industrial development with high population density and low freshwater endowment. The experience here, it is noted, is similar to that found in any developing country context and seems to bear little relation to the particular organizational arrangements prevailing in the Soviet Union.

Finally, there has been, in recent years, growing Soviet interest in land preservation. In part, this interest stems from the need to reclaim land for agricultural purposes. It also includes a growing effort to set aside lands with a preservation status. Recently, a new category of preserved lands entitled State Nature Preserves has been created with significant results. The number of such parks has increased from 3 in 1976 to 19 in 1987. The land area occupied by such parks has increased from just under 200,000 hectares in 1976 to almost 2 million hectares in 1987. A similar growth has taken place in the number of nature preserves and hunting reserves. Their combined number has grown from 120 in 1975 to 161 in 1987, while the land area of these preserves has increased from just over 8 million hectares in 1975 to over 19 million hectares in 1987.[54]

Soviet Environmental Issues—Directions of Change

Western interest in Soviet environmental issues stems in part from general global concerns about environmental abuse. A major focus of interest, however, is the fact that Soviet organizational arrangements and economic policies differ from those with which we are familiar in the West. These factors, along with differences in the Soviet natural environment, present an environmental posture different from that found in many other countries.

Charles Ziegler, in a recent study of Soviet environmental policies, emphasizes the relatively recent nature of Soviet environmental concern.[55] This concern stems in large part from the discussions about the preservation of Lake Baikal, an issue that arose in the 1960s. Since that time, although there has been increased interest in environmental issues, the pace of growing interest has been slow and by the end of the 1970s, there was no superagency in the Soviet Union concerned with the environment. There is however, a significant body of Soviet legislation concerned with the environment. Moreover, in recent years the Soviet Union has started to publish data on expenditures related to the environment. As one might expect, expenditures have grown in recent years, although with significant variations by region and by use. The bulk of expenditures relate to water issues, with air conservation a secondary category.

Gorbachev has made it clear that the Soviet Union is to move from an extensive to an intensive pattern of economic growth. In doing so, conservation is to be a major force alleviating input shortages. In addition, cost-benefit analysis is to play a growing role in assessing the costs and benefits of environmental protection. This policy, however, necessarily must be based on price reform, an issue of continuing controversy in the Soviet Union.

Over the years, Soviet interest in environmental issues has grown, albeit unevenly. As the Gorbachev reforms unfold, it remains to be seen whether Chernobyl may turn out to be the catalyst of the 1980s as Baikal was the catalyst of the 1960s. Moreover, under glasnost, it will be increasingly difficult to ignore population involvement in environmental issues. These domestic forces, combined with the growing role of the Soviet Union in the international community, will most likely keep the Soviet Union moving forward in the environmental arena.

REFERENCES

1. This discussion is based on the following sources: A. Becker, "The Meaning and Measure of Soviet Military Expenditure," in U.S. Congress, Joint Economic Committee, *Soviet Economy in a Time of Change* (Washington, D.C.: U.S. Government Printing Office, 1979), vol. 1, pp. 352–368; H. W. Shaeffer, "Soviet Power and Intentions: Military-Economic Choices," in U.S. Congress, Joint Economic Committee, *Soviet Economy in a Time of Change*, vol. 1, pp. 341–351; W. T. Lee, *The Estimation of Soviet Defense Expenditures, 1955–1975* (New York: Praeger, 1977); National Foreign Assessment Center, *Estimated Soviet Defense Spending: Trends and Prospects*, SR78–10121 (Washington, D.C., June 1978); National Foreign Assessment Center, *A Dollar Cost Comparison of Soviet and U.S. Defense Activities, 1968–78*, SR79–10004 (Washington, D.C., January 1979); F. Holzman, "Are the Soviets Really Outspending the U.S. on Defense?" *International Security* (Spring 1980), 86–104; and U.S. Congress, Joint Economic Committee, *Gorbachev's Economic Plans*, vol. I, part IV (Washington, D.C.: U.S. Government Printing Office, 1987), pp. 367–485.
2. Hearings Before the Subcommittee on Priorities and Economy in Government, *Allocation of Resources in the Soviet Union and China—1978; Part 4: Soviet Union* (Washington, D.C., June 26 and July 24, 1978), pp. 11, 49.
3. National Foreign Assessment Center, *Estimated Soviet Defense Spending*; and National Foreign Assessment Center, *A Dollar Cost Comparison*.
4. There is no direct information on the ruble costs of military hardware, so analysts convert dollar values into ruble values using conversion rates for similar products (relative U.S.-USSR machinery costs, for example). For a critique of these conversions, see Holzman, "Are the Soviets Really Outspending the U.S. on Defense?"
5. This is the procedure used by Lee, *Estimation of Soviet Defense Expenditures*.
6. The various estimates for 1975, cited in Becker, "Soviet Military Expenditure," p. 362, are: official Soviet: 17.4 (billion rubles); CIA: 50–60; Lee: 72; French estimate: 42.3; Chinese estimate: 69.4.
7. P. Hanson, "Review of Estimating Soviet Defense Expenditures," *Soviet Studies*, vol. 30, no. 3 (July 1978), 403.
8. National Foreign Assessment Center, *A Dollar Cost Comparison of Soviet and U.S. Defense Activities*, 1968–78 (Washington, D.C.: 1979), p. 10.
9. U.S. Congress, Joint Economic Committee, *Allocation of Resources in the Soviet Union and China—1986* (Washington, D.C.: U.S. Government Printing Office, 1988), p. 127.
10. For a discussion of this point, see Becker, "Soviet Military Expenditure," pp. 352–366.
11. National Foreign Assessment Center, *A Dollar Cost Comparison*, p. 4.
12. *Allocation of Resources in the Soviet Union and China*, p. 37; and R. F. Kaufman, "Causes of the Slowdown in Soviet Defense," *Soviet Economy*, vol. 1, no. 1 (January–March 1985), 9–36.
13. See Becker, "Soviet Military Expenditure," pp. 352–358, for a discussion of the tenuous relationship between outlays and military power; also see Holzman, "Are the Soviets Really Outspending the U.S. on Defense?" pp. 86–104.

14. Holzman, "Are the Soviets Really Outspending the U.S. on Defense?" pp. 87–93.
15. See Holzman, "Are the Soviets Really Outspending the U.S. on Defense?" pp. 86–102, for a critique of estimates of defense expenditure shares.
16. M. Feshbach and S. Rapawy, "Soviet Population and Manpower Trends and Policies," in U.S. Congress, Joint Economic Committee, *Soviet Economy in a New Perspective* (Washington, D.C.: U.S. Government Printing Office, 1976), p. 150.
17. National Foreign Assessment Center, *Estimated Soviet Defense Spending*, p. i.
18. See Holzman, "Are the Soviets Really Outspending the U.S. on Defense?" pp. 86–102, for a critique of estimates of defense expenditure shares.
19. Directorate of Intelligence, *The Impact of Gorbachev's Policies on Soviet Economic Statistics* (Washington, D.C.: U.S. Government Printing Office, 1988), p. 79.
20. Directorate of Intelligence, *Handbook of Economic Statistics, 1988* (Washington, D.C.: U.S. Government Printing Office, 1988), p. 38.
21. For a simulation of the effects of defense spending during the 1960s, see D. Green and C. Higgins, *Sovmod I: A Macroeconometric Model of the Soviet Union* (New York: Academic Press, 1977), pp. 71–74. For a study of the 1970s and projections, see H. Bergendorff and P. Strangert, "Projections of Soviet Economic Growth and Defense Spending," in U.S. Congress, Joint Economic Committee, *Soviet Economy in a New Perspective*, pp. 394–430. Another important econometric study of the defense-consumption-GNP relationship is L. Calmfors and J. Rylander, "Economic Restrictions on Soviet Defense Expenditure," in U.S. Congress, Joint Economic Committee, *Soviet Economy in a New Perspective*, pp. 377–392; for a discussion of the potential impact of SDI, see G. G. Hildebrandt, *SDI and the Soviet Defense Burden* (Santa Monica, Calif.: Rand Corporation, 1988).
22. A. S. Becker, "Gorbachev's Defense—Economic Dilemma," in U.S. Congress, Joint Economic Committee, *Gorbachev's Economic Plans* (Washington, D.C.: U.S. Government Printing Office, 1987), pp. 372–387.
23. This discussion is based largely on the following sources: J. S. Berliner, *The Innovation Decision in Soviet Industry* (Cambridge, Mass.: MIT Press, 1976); J. Berliner, "Prospects for Technological Progress," in U.S. Congress, Joint Economic Committee, *Soviet Economy in a New Perspective*, pp. 431–446; R. Amman, J. Cooper, and R. W. Davies, *The Technological Level of Soviet Industry* (New Haven, Conn.: Yale University Press, 1977); J. R. Thomas and U. Kruse-Vaucienne, eds., *Soviet Science and Technology* (Washington, D.C.: George Washington University, 1977), parts 3 and 4; E. Zaleski et al., *Science Policy in the USSR* (Paris: OECD, 1969); J. Martens and J. P. Young, "Soviet Implementation of Domestic Inventions: First Results," in U.S. Congress, Joint Economic Committee, *Soviet Economy in a Time of Change*, vol. 1, pp. 472–509; J. Grant, "Soviet Machine Tools: Lagging Technology and Rising Imports," in U.S. Congress, Joint Economic Committee, *Soviet Economy in a Time of Change*, vol. 1, pp. 524–553; P. Hanson, "International Technology Transfer from the West to the USSR," in U.S. Congress, Joint Economic Committee, *Soviet Economy in a New Perspective*, pp. 786–812; R. Amann and J. Cooper, eds., *Industrial Innovation in the Soviet Union* (New Haven, Conn.: Yale University Press, 1982); B. Parrott, *Politics and Technology in the Soviet Union* (Cambridge, Mass.: MIT Press, 1983); and U.S. Congress, Joint Economic Committee, *Gorbachev's Economic Plans*, vol. 2, section VII, pp. 141–209.

24. A statement of R. Nelson cited by R. Amman, "Soviet Technological Performance," in J. R. Thomas and U. Kruse-Vaucienne, eds., *Soviet Science and Technology* (Washington, D.C.: George Washington University Press, 1977), p. 329.

25. This is the basic conclusion of the Amman, Cooper, and Davies study, conducted at the University of Birmingham, England. See Amman, Cooper, and Davies, *The Technological Level of Soviet Industry*.

26. For a general discussion of computing, see S. E. Goodman, "The Prospective Impacts of Computing: Selected Economic-Industrial-Strategic Issues," in U.S. Congress, Joint Economic Committee, *Gorbachev's Economic Plans*, vol. 2, pp. 176–184; for estimates of lags, see CIA/DIA, *The Soviet Economy in 1988: Gorbachev Changes Course* (Washington, D.C.: Joint Economic Committee, 1988), Figure 3.

27. Grant, "Soviet Machine Tools," pp. 524–553; K. Tasky, "Soviet Technology Gap and Dependence on the West: The Case of Computers," in U.S. Congress, Joint Economic Committee, *Soviet Economy in a Time of Change*, vol. 1, pp. 510–523; and S. E. Goodman, "The Prospective Impacts of Computing: Selected Economic-Industrial-Strategic Issues."

28. M. I. Goldman, *Gorbachev's Challenge* (New York: Norton, 1987), chap. 4–5.

29. P. Hanson, "The Diffusion of Imported Technology," in NATO Economics Directorate, *Economic Aspects of Life in the USSR* (Brussels: NATO, 1976).

30. This discussion is based on Berliner, *The Innovation Decision*, and Berliner, "Prospects of Technological Progress."

31. The above figures are from *Naselenie SSSR* [Population of the USSR] (Moscow, 1983), pp. 102–121; *Obrazovatel'naia i sotsial'no-professional'naia struktura naseleniia SSSR* [Educational and social professional structure of the USSR population] (Moscow, 1975), *Vestnik statistiki*, no. 11 (1984), 71; *Narodnoe khoziaistvo, SSSR za 60 let* [National economy of USSR for 60 years], p. 477; V. Yelyutin, *Higher Education in the USSR* (Moscow: Novosti, 1970), pp. 22, 79; *Narodnoe khoziaistvo SSSR v 1982 g*, p. 462; I. M. Makarov, "Povysit effektivnost nauchnykh issledovanii" [To raise the effectiveness of scientific research], *Vestnik vysshei shkoly*, no. 7 (1984) 4; *Vestnik statistiki*, no. 8 (1983), 63; and *Narodnoe khoziaistvo SSSR v 1987 g* [The national economy of the USSR in 1987] (Moscow: Finansy i Statistika, 1988).

32. These general conclusions are drawn from L. Nolting and M. Feshbach, "R&D Employment in the USSR," *Science*, vol. 207 (February 1980), 493–503; C. Ailes and F. Rushing, *A Summary Report on the Educational Systems of the United States and the Soviet Union*, SRI International, SSC-TN-7557-12, March 1980; S. Kassel and C. Campbell, *The Soviet Academy of Sciences and Technological Development*, Rand Corporation, R-2533-ARPA.

33. Ailes and Rushing, *A Summary Report*, p. 11.

34. M. Kuchment and H. Balzer, "An Interim Report on the Project: A Net Assessment of Soviet R&D Capabilities: Information and Insights from the 3rd Soviet Emigration," prepared for the National Council for Soviet and East European Studies, Washington, D.C., August 1981.

35. Based on data in the 1979 *Science Indicators*, published by the National Science Foundation and cited in U.M. Kruse-Vaucienne and J. Logsdon, *Science and Technology in the Soviet Union: A Profile* (National Science Foundation, George Washington University, Washington, D.C., 1979), p. 5.

36. M. Mathews, "Long Term Trends in Soviet Education," in J. J. Tomiak, ed., *Soviet Education in the 1980s* (New York: St. Martin's Press, 1983), pp. 1–24.

37. See, for example, *Current Digest of the Soviet Press*, July 4, 1984, for a typical series of complaints about Soviet university students.

38. R. McIntyre and J. Thornton, "On the Environmental Efficiency of Economic Systems," *Soviet Studies*, vol. 30, no. 2 (April 1978), 173–192.

39. A. Wright, "Environmental Disruption and Economic Systems: An Attempt at an Analytical Framework," *ASTE Bulletin*, vol. 13, no. 1 (Spring 1971), 11–12.

40. Lange's paper appears in B. E. Lippincott, ed., *On the Economic Theory of Socialism* (Minneapolis: University of Minnesota Press, 1938), pp. 103ff., reprinted by McGraw-Hill, 1964.

41. M. Dobb, *Welfare Economics and the Economics of Socialism* (Cambridge: Cambridge University Press, 1969), p. 133.

42. For a discussion of this point, see Dobb, *Welfare Economics*, pp. 133–134. For a survey of theorizing on environmental quality, see M. I. Goldman, *The Spoils of Progress: Environmental Pollution in the Soviet Union* (Cambridge, Mass.: MIT Press, 1972), pp. 12–22.

43. M. I. Goldman, "Externalities and the Race for Economic Growth in the Soviet Union: Will the Environment Ever Win?" *Journal of Political Economy*, vol. 80, no. 2 (March–April 1972); K. Bush, "Environmental Disruption: The Soviet Response," *L'Est*, no. 2 (June 1972); D. Kelley, K. Stunkel, and R. Wescott, *The Economic Superpowers and the Environment: The United States, the Soviet Union, and Japan* (San Francisco, Calif.: Freeman, 1976); W. A. Jackson, ed., *Soviet Resource Management and the Environment* (Columbus, Ohio: Anchor Press, 1978); V. Mote, "Environmental Protection and the Soviet Tenth Five Year Plan," *Geographical Survey*, vol. 7, no. 2 (April 1978); P. R. Pryde, *Conservation in the Soviet Union* (Cambridge, Mass.: Harvard University Press, 1972); F. Singleton, *Environmental Misuse in the USSR* (New York: Praeger, 1976); C. E. Ziegler, *Environmental Policy in the USSR* (Amherst: University of Massachusetts Press, 1987); and C. ZumBrunnen, "Gorbachev, Economics and the Environment," in U.S. Congress, Joint Economic Committee, *Gorbachev's Economic Plans*, vol. 2, pp. 397–424.

44. See C. E. Ziegler, *Environmental Policy in the USSR*, chaps. 1–3.

45. For a discussion, see T. Shabad, "Geographical Aspects of the Chernobyl Nuclear Accident," *Soviet Geography*, vol. 27, no. 7 (September 1986), 504–526.

46. For a discussion of measurement problems, see McIntyre and Thornton, "Environmental Efficiency," pp. 182–183.

47. Ibid., p. 181.

48. Directorate of Intelligence, *Handbook of Economic Statistics, 1988*, Tables 2–3.

49. See ZumBrunnen, "Gorbachev, Economics and the Environment."

50. *Narodnoe khoziaistvo SSSR v 1985 g.* [The national economy of the USSR in 1985] (Moscow: Finansy i Statistika, 1986), p. 386; and *Narodnoe khoziaistvo SSSR v 1987 g.*, p. 571.

51. ZumBrunnen, "Gorbachev, Economics and the Environment," pp. 399–407.

52. *Narodnoe khoziaistvo SSSR v 1987 g*, p. 577.

53. ZumBrunnen, "Gorbachev, Economics and the Environment," pp. 399–407.

54. Data are from *Narodnoe khoziaistvo SSSR v 1985 g*, p. 383; and *Narodnoe khoziaistvo SSSR v 1987 g*, p. 566.

55. Ziegler, *Environmental Policy in the USSR* chap. 3.

SELECTED BIBLIOGRAPHY

Soviet Military Power

A. Becker, "The Meaning and Measure of Soviet Military Expenditure," in U.S. Congress, Joint Economic Committee, *Soviet Economy in a Time of Change* (Washington, D.C.: U.S. Government Printing Office, 1979), vol. 1, pp. 352–368.

———, *Sitting on Bayonets: The Soviet Defense Burden and the Slowdown of Soviet Defense Spending* (Santa Monica: Rand Corporation, 1985).

H. Bergendorff and P. Strangert, "Projections of Soviet Economic Growth and Defense Spending," in U.S. Congress, Joint Economic Committee, *Soviet Economy in a New Perspective* (Washington, D.C.: U.S. Government Printing Office, 1976), pp. 394–430.

L. Calmfors and J. Rylander, "Economic Restrictions on Soviet Defense Expenditure," in U.S. Congress, Joint Economic Committee, *Soviet Economy in a New Perspective* (Washington, D.C.: U.S. Government Printing Office, 1976), pp. 377–392.

S. Cohn, "Economic Burden of Soviet Defense Expenditures: Constraints on Productivity," *Studies in Comparative Communism*, vol. 20, no. 2 (Summer 1987), 145–161.

J. M. Collins, *U.S. – Soviet Military Balance 1980–1985* (New York: Pergamon-Brasseys, 1985).

———, *US/Soviet Military Balance, Statistical Trends, 1970–1982* (Washington, D.C.: Congressional Research Service, 1983).

G. G. Hildebrandt, *SDI and the Soviet Defense Burden* (Santa Monica: Rand Corporation, 1988).

F. D. Holzman, *Financial Checks on Soviet Defense Expenditures* (Lexington, Mass.: Lexington Books, 1975).

M. Hopkins and M. Kennedy, *The Tradeoff Between Consumption and Military Expenditures for the Soviet Union During the 1980s* (Santa Monica: Rand Corporation, 1982).

International Institute for Strategic Studies, *The Military Balance 1988–89* (Reading, England: Eastern Press, 1988).

D. R. Jones, ed., *Soviet Armed Forces Review Annual* (Gulf Breeze, Fla.: Academic International Press, 1987).

R. E. Kaufman, "Causes of the Slowdown in Soviet Defense," *Soviet Economy*, vol. 1, no. 1 (January/March 1985), 9–31.

W. T. Lee, *The Estimation of Soviet Defense Expenditures, 1955–1975* (New York: Praeger, 1977).

National Foreign Assessment Center, *A Dollar Cost Comparison of Soviet and U.S. Defense Activities, 1968–78*, SR79–10004, Washington, D.C., January 1979.

———, *Estimated Soviet Defense Spending: Trends and Prospects*, SR78–10121, Washington, D.C., June 1978.

S. Rosefielde, *False Science: Underestimating the Soviet Arms Buildup: An Appraisal of the CIA's Direct Costing Effort* (New Brunswick, N.J.: Transaction Books, 1983).

H. W. Shaeffer, "Soviet Power and Intentions: Military-Economic Choices," in U.S. Congress, Joint Economic Committee, *Soviet Economy in a Time of Change* (Washington, D.C.: U.S. Government Printing Office, 1979), vol. 1, pp. 341–351.

U.S. Congress, Joint Economic Committee, *Gorbachev's Economic Plans*, vol. I, sect. IV (Washington, D.C.: U.S. Government Printing Office, 1987), pp. 367–485.

U.S. Congress, Joint Economic Committee, *Soviet Economy in the 1980's: Problems and Prospects*, part I, sect. III (Washington, D.C.: U.S. Government Printing Office, 1982), pp. 287–331.

J. Valenta and W. Potter, *Soviet Decisionmaking for National Security* (London: Allen & Unwin, 1984).

Soviet Technology

C. Ailes and F. Rushing, *A Summary Report on the Educational Systems of the United States and the Soviet Union*, SRI International, SSC-TN-7557-12, March 1980.

R. Amann and J. Cooper, *Industrial Innovation in the Soviet Union* (New Haven, Conn.: Yale University Press, 1982).

R. Amann and J. Cooper, eds., *Technical Progress and Soviet Economic Development* (New York: Basil Blackwell, 1986).

R. Amman, J. Cooper, and R. W. Davies, *The Technological Level of Soviet Industry* (New Haven, Conn.: Yale University Press, 1977).

A. Bergson, "Technological Progress," in Abram Bergson and Herbert S. Levine, eds., *The Soviet Economy: Toward the Year 2000* (London: Allen & Unwin, 1983), chap. 2.

J. S. Berliner, *The Innovation Decision in Soviet Industry* (Cambridge, Mass.: MIT Press, 1976).

J. Cooper, "Technology in the Soviet Union," *Current History*, vol. 85, no. 513 (October 1986), 317–320, 340–342.

M. I. Goldman, *Gorbachev's Challenge* (New York: Norton, 1987), chaps. 4, 5.

J. Grant, "Soviet Machine Tools: Lagging Technology and Rising Imports," in U.S. Congress, Joint Economic Committee, *Soviet Economy in a Time of Change* (Washington, D.C.: U.S. Government Printing Office, 1979), vol. 1, pp. 524–553.

P. Hanson, "The Diffusion of Imported Technology," in NATO Economics Directorate, *Economic Aspects of Life in the USSR* (Brussels: NATO 1975).

———, "International Technology Transfer from the West to the USSR," in U.S. Congress, Joint Economic Committee, *Soviet Economy in a New Perspective* (Washington, D.C.: U.S. Government Printing Office, 1976), pp. 786–812.

S. Kassel and C. Campbell, *The Soviet Academy of Science and Technological Development*, Rand Corporation R-2533-ARPA, p. 1.

J. Martens and J. P. Young, "Soviet Implementation of Domestic Inventions: First Results," in U.S. Congress, Joint Economic Committee, *Soviet Economy in a Time of Change* (Washington, D.C.: U.S. Government Printing Office, 1979), vol. 1, pp. 472–509.

M. Mathews, "Long Term Trends in Soviet Education," in J. J. Tomiak, ed., *Soviet Education in the 1980s* (New York: St. Martin's Press, 1983), pp. 1–24.

B. Parrott, *Politics and Technology in the Soviet Union* (Cambridge, Mass.: MIT Press, 1983).

A. C. Sutton, *Western Technology and Soviet Economic Development 1945 to 1965* (Stanford, Calif.: Hoover Institution, 1973).

————, ed., *Trade, Technology and Soviet American Relations* (Bloomington: Indiana University Press, 1985).

J. R. Thomas and U. Kruse-Vaucienne, eds., *Soviet Science and Technology* (Washington, D.C.: George Washington University Press, 1977), parts 3 and 4.

U.S. Congress, Joint Economic Committee, *Gorbachev's Economic Plans*, vol. 2, part VII (Washington, D.C.: U.S. Government Printing Office, 1987), pp. 141–209.

E. Zaleski et al., *Science Policy in the USSR* (Paris: OECD, 1969).

Environmental Quality

K. Bush, "Environmental Disruption: The Soviet Response," *L'Est*, no. 2 (June 1972).

M. I. Goldman, "Externalities and the Race for Economic Growth in the Soviet Union: Will the Environment Ever Win?" *Journal of Political Economy*, vol. 80, no. 2 (March/April 1972).

T. Gustafson, *Reform in Soviet Politics: Lessons of Recent Policies on Land and Water* (Cambridge: Cambridge University Press, 1981).

W. A. Jackson, ed., *Soviet Resource Management and the Environment* (Columbus, Ohio: Anchor Press, 1978).

B. Jancar, *Environmental Management in the Soviet Union and Yugoslavia* (Durham, N.C.: Duke University Press, 1987).

D. Kelley, K. Stunkel, and R. Wescott, *The Economic Superpowers and the Environment: The United States, the Soviet Union, and Japan* (San Francisco, Calif.: Freeman, 1976).

D. Marples, *Chernobyl and Nuclear Power in the USSR* (New York: St. Martin's Press, 1986).

————, *The Social Impact of the Chernobyl Disaster* (New York: St. Martin's Press, 1988).

R. McIntyre and J. Thornton, "On the Environmental Efficiency of Economic Systems," *Soviet Studies*, vol. 30, no. 2 (April 1978), 173–192.

V. Mote, "Environmental Protection and the Soviet Tenth Five Year Plan," *Geographical Survey*, vol. 7, no. 2 (April 1978), 25–34.

P. R. Pryde, *Conservation in the Soviet Union* (Cambridge, Mass.: Harvard University Press, 1972).

————, "The Decade of the Environment in the USSR," *Science*, vol. 220 (April 1983), 274–279.

B. A. Ruble, "*The Emergence of Soviet Environmental Studies*," *Review*, vol. 5, no. 1 (1980).

T. Shabad, "Geographical Aspects of the Chernobyl Nuclear Accident," *Soviet Geography*, vol. 27, no. 7 (September 1936), pp. 504–526.

F. Singleton, *Environmental Misuse in the USSR* (New York: Praeger, 1976).

J. Thornton, "Resources and Property Rights in the Soviet Union," in W. A. Jackson, ed., *Soviet Resource Management and the Environment* (Columbus, Ohio: Anchor Press, 1978), pp. 1–12.

C. E. Ziegler, *Environmental Policy in the USSR* (Amherst: University of Massachusetts Press, 1987).

C. ZumBrunnen, "Gorbachev, Economics and the Environment," in U.S. Congress, Joint Economic Committee, *Gorbachev's Economic Plans*, vol. 2 (Washington, D.C.: U.S. Government Printing Office, 1987), pp. 397–424.

Reform and Change: Prospects for the Future

Chapter 14

Soviet Economic Reform: The Early Years

We have focused attention on how the Soviet economy works and with what results. Our emphasis has been on what is actually done rather than on the theory of resource allocation in a centrally planned socialist economy. In part, this applied approach is dictated by the uncertain state of the literature on theoretical alternatives to the Soviet economic system. Alec Nove, a veteran observer of the Soviet economy has noted that the Soviets have had "virtually no theory to guide them; and no theory of planning emerged from their activities."[1]

In this chapter we turn our attention to the economic reform of the Soviet system. While many view economic reform as a phenomenon of the Gorbachev era, there have been many attempts to change the Soviet system, largely unsuccessful, before Gorbachev put his stamp of approval on change. To appreciate the dimensions of change in the present era, it is important to understand the events of the last 40 years. In effect, opportunities for economic reform began with the death of Stalin in 1953. The road leading to perestroika has been a winding one with many detours.

We begin with the theory of reform of a planned economy. Next, we consider the reform movement from the start of the post-World War II period to Gorbachev's ascension to power in 1985. In Chapter 15, we turn to Gorbachev's reform program.

THE CORE OF THE SOVIET SYSTEM AND ECONOMIC REFORM

It is useful to begin a discussion of economic reform with a simple question: Is there an irreducible "core" of the Soviet economic system that defines the limits of any economic reform? Are there basic features of the Soviet economic system that cannot be touched by economic reformers for political, economic, or ideological reasons?

Previous chapters elaborated the following core features of the Soviet economy:

1. The Soviet economy is a planned economy in which a national economic plan has replaced the market as the dominant mechanism for allocating resources. Although there is debate as to whether the plan itself or the subsequent resource management that occurs during plan fulfillment is the main resource allocation instrument, the fact remains that administrative orders rather than markets dominate. The Soviet literature has long emphasized that administrative allocation is superior to markets because of the "anarchy" of market allocation. Administrative allocation is especially important in the investment area because the allocation of investment determines the direction of development of the economy.

2. The Soviet economy is based on social ownership of the means of production as opposed to the predominantly private ownership of capitalism. The Soviet literature has emphasized the superiority of social ownership (either state or cooperative) over private ownership because it eliminates the exploitation of the worker by the owner of the means of production and because it reduces inequities in income distribution associated with the private ownership of wealth.

3. The Communist Party sets basic economic policy and priorities and monitors their fulfillment. The leading role of the party has been a key constant of the Soviet system throughout the years. The task of the state bureaucracy has been to implement the policies and priorities of the party.

A key question of Soviet economic reform is whether these core features of the Soviet economy define the limits of reform. Can economic reform indeed alter sacrosanct features of the Soviet system, such as public ownership, the predominance of administrative allocation, or the leading role of the party? Or must Soviet reformers work within these core features, taking them as givens while trying to make the system work better?

TAXONOMY OF ECONOMIC REFORM

There is no clear-cut theory of economic reform. *Economic reform* refers to a nontrivial change in the working arrangements of the economic system. Economic reform may change the organization of the economic system and/or its subunits, in which case we describe the reform as *organizational change*. A second type of economic reform aims at the *improvement of central planning*. If the economic system is changed in such a way as to shift the focus of decision making to lower units, a *decentralization reform* has taken place.

Organizational Reform

From a theoretical viewpoint, there is appeal to the idea that the system's organizational arrangements can be charged to best suit the needs of a particular economy at a particular stage of economic development. In a sense, one might think in terms of designing an optimal organizational structure, one that changes through time as economic conditions change.

In fact, in the real world, the drive for organizational change has been based on more pragmatic grounds. To take a case in point, associations were introduced in the Soviet Union largely because there was a feeling that the span of control for ministries was generally too great. Specifically, an organization was needed between the ministry and firms to supervise and to control more specific types of production activity, such as sheet steel and rolled steel rather than steel in general. Experiments with organizational change have been quite common in the course of Soviet reform. In part because the meaning of organizational change is difficult to assess, Western observers of the reform process have generally been skeptical of its potential effectiveness. They view organizational changes as a relatively meaningless reshuffling of offices and personnel rather than as a significant attempt to change the economic system.

Better Planning

The perfection of planning, though not a dominant reform type, represents a second type of socialist reform. Most planned socialist systems have relied heavily on national economic planning as the dominant mechanism for resource allocation. Moreover, planning is typically viewed as the mechanism that has, in the past, accounted for rapid economic growth. With such an ingrained faith in the planning mechanism, why would it be abandoned simply due to the need for improvement?

The case for improving the planning mechanism is based in large part on the perception that information flows can be improved and incentive mechanisms developed to harmonize local actions with central wishes. Faith in the potential for this type of improvement rests partially, though not exclusively, in the better utilization of computer technology. For example, to the extent that growing complexity is a problem, better computers would seem to present obvious benefits for providing decision makers with better information on a more systematic basis. This approach emphasizes the importance of planning as a means to allocate resources and looks to improvement in the planning mechanism to sustain its use even at advanced levels of economic development.

Decentralization Reform

There is no single concept of decentralization, the third theme of socialist reform. At the most obvious level, decentralization means the shifting of decision-making authority and responsibility down an established administrative hierarchy to lower levels in the hierarchy. Using this notion, decentralization occurs when a Soviet ministry makes decisions that were previously made by *Gosplan* or when an enterprise makes decisions that were previously made by the ministry. Because it covers such a broad range of activities, the hierarchical approach to understanding decentralization does not have much operational meaning.

Morris Bornstein draws a more useful distinction between *administrative decentralization* and *economic decentralization*[2]. Administrative decentralization occurs when local units (enterprises) are given increased authority to make decisions (previously made by higher administrative units) within a framework of rules and parameters set by higher administrative authorities. For example, the local unit may be given more authority to make its own input decisions based on the rule that managers should combine inputs in a least-cost fashion. To encourage the local unit to make "rational" input decisions, higher administrative authorities may reward the local unit on the basis of achieved percentage cost reductions. The key feature of administrative decentralization is that higher authorities control the parameters that the local unit uses to make its decentralized decisions. Higher authorities set input prices and the parameters of the local unit's reward structure. Administrative decentralization relieves the higher authority of much decision-making authority by permitting more decisions to be made by lower units. The higher authority, however, does continue to exercise authority and control over local units by keeping a firm hand on the parameters that motivate decentralized decisions.

Economic decentralization also allows the local unit to make more decentralized decisions but with the higher administrative authority setting fewer parameters. For example, higher authorities may allow input prices to be established by the forces of supply and demand in markets. They may allow the local unit to operate according to very general rules of the game, such as acting to maximize the economic well-being of the unit. Economic decentralization means that higher administrative authorities have given up more real authority to local units than under administrative decentralization.

The choice of administrative versus economic decentralization underscores the Soviet reform dilemma. As long as higher administrative authorities control the parameters that guide local decision making, they are in a better position to impose the state's will on microparticipants in the economy. In the 1930s, for example, administrative control and monitoring of local decision making may have been at their peak, and the Soviet economy was indeed transformed according to the preferences of the ruling elite. The micro units, who possessed local information as to how best to combine resources, were not allowed to exercise decentralized authority. Accordingly, numerous resource allocation mistakes were made that could have been avoided by enlightened micro–decision-making. In a setting in which the economy has already been transformed to conform to the preferences of the ruling elite, the elimination of resource allocation mistakes becomes more important. As efficiency becomes of paramount importance, local decisions must be better decisions; that is, they must achieve central wishes with a minimal expenditure of resources. If local decisions cannot be focused by centrally set rules, then local decision makers must be given a parametric framework in which their actions will be harmonized with central wishes.[3] It is here that a redefinition of managerial success indicators occurs.

Decentralization reforms aim to change the mechanisms by which decisions are made and judged. It is common in socialist economic reforms to characterize such changes as the introduction of new "economic levers" for the guidance of the economic system.

A common and controversial example of this type of reform is the increased reliance upon profit for the guidance of enterprise activity. While theoretically appealing, the meaning of profit guidance is often unclear in a system where prices bear little or no relation to relative scarcities. It is in this context, as an example, that the sequencing of reform components becomes a major issue. If profit is to be used as a guidance mechanism, how will the price system be reformed?

Optimal Mix and Sequencing

The theory of reform of the Soviet planned economy states that authorities should seek out an optimal mix of administrative and economic decentralization. Under the most ideal circumstances, a system would be put in place that encourages local units (utilizing the local information at their disposal) to combine resources in an efficient manner while, at the same time, encouraging local units to implement the stated plans of higher authorities. It remains to be seen, in both theory and practice whether these two objectives are compatible. Is the loss of centralized direction over local units the price that higher authorities must pay for better local decision making? Moreover, the adoption of the decentralized model may create macroeconomic side effects that the system's directors are unwilling to tolerate. For example, decentralized choice of inputs may cause enterprises to lay off redundant workers, thereby creating nationwide unemployment.[4]

Even if the theory of reform could specify the ideal economic system toward which the Soviet planned economy should strive, there remains the problem of moving from the prevailing system to that ideal system. No one will know for sure whether the proposed "ideal" system will work as the theory says it should; the system's managers know that they are taking risks when they move toward the new system. If the system's directors choose to move cautiously in a piecemeal fashion,[5] how will the system function during the transition?

It is difficult to understand how several firms will interact with each other when some are acting under the new set of rules while the remainder act under the old set of rules. If one firm is to be released from the plan when it comes to selling its products, then potential buyers must also be freed from the plan constraint of buying from a specified seller. The proper sequencing of economic reform is as difficult a theoretical issue as is the identification of the economic system the reform process is supposed to install.

These types of economic reform are clearly simplistic. However, we will see that they are useful as we trace the development of the reform process in the Soviet Union. We begin with a discussion of the major if largely unachieved reforms of the 1960s and thereafter.[6] In Chapter 15, we will turn to the reforms of the Gorbachev era.

BACKGROUND OF REFORM: 1920s TO 1960s

Although it is simplistic to classify reform in only two dimensions, it is useful to think of economic reform as either "centralizing" or "decentralizing." The centralizing approach is based on the notion that administrative planning can be perfected, that planners can improve information flows, and that subunits can be made to act "rationally" through better instructions and monitoring procedures.

The decentralizing school of reform argues that the effectiveness of planning is needlessly hampered by trying to make all decisions at the center. Important decisions can be made at the center; but to solve both information and incentive problems, more decisions must be made at local levels by individual producing units.[7]

This dichotomy between "decentralization" and "better centralization" can be traced all the way back to the discussions of the 1920s. The supporters of NEP were, in effect, advocates of the first approach: Let the routine day-to-day decisions be made by managers and "experts," with the state controlling the commanding heights. In the NEP environment, the bulk of economic decisions were made at micro levels, and the task of the planners was supposed to be limited to devising grand strategy. The mechanism that would make this all possible would be the market, which would coordinate the actions of producers and consumers. In the words of Stephen Cohen, the "first great reform in Soviet history was the introduction of . . . NEP in 1921."[8] The appeal of NEP as a model of reform persists, largely due to Lenin's writings in its support.

The coming demise of NEP forced Soviet planners and theorists to grapple with a different scenario, one in which the market was eliminated and resource allocation decisions were to be made administratively. The guiding mechanism of the market was absent, and new methods of rational resource allocation had to be sought.

The 1920s were a productive period of theorizing about the administrative planning option. During this period, rough outlines began to emerge that probably would have eventually led to full-fledged theories of socialist resource allocation through central planning. Talented economists and statisticians were busy estimating national balances, an example being the well-known 1923–1924 balance of the national economy prepared by the Central Statistics Board under the direction of P. I. Popov.[9] Such efforts, the intellectual predecessors of input-output techniques later sophisticated by Wassily Leontief in the United States, pointed the way toward the future development of mathematical planning techniques involving both balancing and optimization of resource allocation—an approach that was blocked by the harsh reaction against mathematical economics during the Stalin years. Nevertheless such efforts (premature, given the state of knowledge at the time were based on the premise that the socialist economy can be directed by mathematical planning models expressing input-output relationships among branches. It was not until the post-Stalin years that Soviet economists were allowed to return to their work and to develop the relatively sophisticated theories of mathematical planning in a centrally directed socialist economy.

With the establishment of the Stalinist dictatorship, discussion of the theory of Soviet planning ceased. The NEP system was anathematized, and the search for rational administrative planning procedures was halted by the brutal repression of economic science. Although the deficiencies of material balance planning and managerial behavior were likely known to the Soviet leadership, the Soviet economic system was declared infallibly directed by the planning principle. Criticism of the system became dangerous, and economic failures were attributed to individual mistakes and willful sabotage, not to the system itself. The "law of value"—supply and demand—was declared by Stalin not to operate in a socialist economy. Instead, a new economic regulator, the planning principle, had replaced the capitalist laws of supply and demand, and the tools developed by bourgeois economists to analyze capitalist economies were seen as unnecessary constraints no longer relevant to a socialist society. Such a socialist economy could be scientifically directed by technicians and engineers without observing "economic laws." This view came to be more firmly entrenched and is reflected in the growing disregard for market forces displayed by economic planners in the late 1920s.[10]

By the 1930s, it had become dangerous to argue for either the positive role of market forces or the existence of economic laws in a planned socialist economy.

Increasingly, planners shied away from concepts such as "equilibrium" and "balanced growth" as unnecessary constraints on their freedom of action, and most economic theorizing ground to a halt.[11]

Soviet economic science entered into a dark age during the Stalin dictatorship. The economic system that emerged under Stalin was an ad hoc response to practical problems and crises, and it evolved without the benefit of a calculated blueprint. But it was the product of the party (Stalin) and as such could not be criticized. It is no wonder that serious work on defining an optimal planning system or improving the existing system was discouraged, and theorists on economic reform and mathematical planning went underground, only to reemerge after Stalin's death. The two attempts by high officials to initiate reform (in 1933 and 1947) led to the execution of the ill-fated reformers.[12]

The death of Stalin in 1953 unleashed pent-up pressure to enact economic reform. To a great extent, Stalin's successor, Khrushchev was the embodiment of the reform ethos, and his overthrow in 1964 signaled the return to a more conservative approach to reform. The resurgence of interest in economic reform assumed several forms in the 1950s. First, there was a slight shift from blaming all economic problems on human shortcomings to a willingness to experiment with organizational reorganization changes. Although the inclination to deal with problems via organizational reorganization continues to the present day, it probably reached its peak in 1957 with Khrushchev's attempted shift from a ministerial to a regional system of economic management. Second, there was a resurgence of interest in mathematical planning techniques and theories of rational planning. Prominent Soviet pioneers in this area such as L. V. Kantorovich and V. V. Novozhilov suggested that resources could be utilized much more efficiently, without loss of central control, if optimal planning procedures were used.[13] In 1959, the book *The Use of Mathematics in Economics* was published under the editorship of V. S. Nemchinov. It contained the original papers on Kantorovich and Novozhilov, written during the repressive Stalin years. Since then, subsequent volumes in this series have been published, prestigious mathematical economics institutes of the Soviet Academy of Science have been established, and prominent Soviet mathematical economists were awarded the coveted Lenin Prize. Kantorovich even received the Noble Prize in economics.

A sign of the growing official toleration of reform discussion was the publication in obscure technical journals of papers suggesting various means to reform and improve the existing planning system by some decentralization (devolution) of decision-making authority.[14]

The official start of serious reform discussion in the Soviet Union can be dated to September 9, 1962, with the publication of the article "Plan, Profits and Bonuses" in *Pravda* by the then obscure economist Evsei Liberman.[15] The publication of Liberman's paper signaled official endorsement of open discussion of reform and initiated an important debate among orthodox planners, mathematical economists, and those advocating greater decision-making authority at the micro level. We shall return to this discussion and its outcome shortly, but first we must look at the reasons behind the party decision to allow open reform discussion.

THE INITIATION OF REFORM DISCUSSION IN THE 1960s

To understand the factors behind the first party endorsement of reform discussion, we must return to the scenario of the late 1950s and early 1960s. The 1950s was a period of heady growth of both agriculture and industry, and the Soviet leadership was emboldened to make rash claims about overtaking the United States and creating full communism. This optimism was nurtured by the perceived economic weakness of the United States, which had suffered mild recessions and slow growth throughout the 1950s. The pattern of declining growth of output and productivity that began to be perceived in the Soviet Union in the late 1950s and early 1960s provided the major impetus for discussions of economic reform.

Although Soviet economic performance in the early 1960s was quite good as measured by Soviet performance in the 1970s and 1980s, the faltering of growth of the early 1960s was interpreted as a sign of trouble on the horizon. We shall return to Soviet economic performance and its effect on economic reform in Chapter 15. For now, we can note that, although the 1950s and 1960s were decades of fairly good output and productivity growth, by the 1970s, it was apparent that output and productivity performance were steadily deteriorating. Both Western and Soviet estimates concur that there was a significant slowing down in the rate of growth of factor productivity since the late 1950s. Factor productivity growth slowed more dramatically than factor input growth, so declining factor productivity appeared to be the main culprit behind the growth slowdown.

The increasing recognition that the Soviet years of "easy" or extensive growth were over played a role in initiating reform discussion. In the past, much of the Soviet growth achievement had come from expanding labor and capital inputs. From the late 1920s to the 1970s, the capital stock grew at very rapid rates, the labor force participation rate increased to one of the highest in the world, and land inputs to agriculture expanded rapidly (especially in the 1950s) to act as a major source of increased production. Historical experience tells us that as a country becomes more mature, it must increasingly look to the better use of inputs—productivity growth—to generate overall economic growth. It cannot continue indefinitely to rely on rapid growth of labor, land, or capital inputs.

Rising consumer pressure for more and better goods and services became a more active concern to the Soviet leadership after Stalin. To the extent that monetary incentives are required to stimulate labor productivity, difficulties arise when there is persistent excess demand in some markets and unsold inventories in others. Since the 1950s, Soviet per capita consumption grew at a respectable average annual rate of 3 percent.[16] In the early 1970s, the growth rate of consumption dropped to 2.5 percent per annum, while for the late 1970s it declined to under 2 percent.[17] Declining economic growth has meant that the growth rate of consumption has had to decelerate. The growth rate of consumption, however, can provide a misleading picture of the growth of material living standards. If the economy fails to produce the goods and services desired by the population (and price them appropriately), the increased physical outputs of goods and services will not be transformed into higher levels of consumer satisfaction.

Interest in economic reform was also spurred by the growing complexity of the Soviet economy as evidenced by the growing number of interconnections among producers, consumers, and suppliers. In the early 1980s, there were 45,374 industrial enterprises in the Soviet Union.[18] If one adds wholesale and retail trade outlets and scientific and cultural organizations, the problem of coordinating Soviet economic activity is clearly awesome. As the Soviet economy grew, the number of sectors and the product range broadened. The priority principle became less and less useful. No longer could "steel blinders" be used.[19] Trucks, machines, missiles, and plants could now be built with steel, plastics, or other products. It was no longer clear which of these materials was "more important" to fulfill the economic goals of the Soviet leadership. Moreover, a more complex economy may be more vulnerable to mistakes in planning both in the sense that planning mistakes are more likely to be made and that, when made, they will be more serious as they reverberate throughout the system. With growing concerns over economic incentives, the use of consumer goods as a buffer sector became increasingly unattractive as a means to handle these problems.

Finally, the resurgence of economic theorizing in the Soviet Union in the post-Stalin era undoubtedly had an impact upon the party decision to initiate discussion in the 1960s and thereafter. Soviet economists in general and mathematical economists in particular claim that their preferred methods can improve the achievement of party objectives while leaving the determination of these objectives to the party. As Aron Katsenelinboigen writes: "When there is an urgent practical need for some method . . . Soviet leaders are in fact willing to sacrifice ideology."[20] In effect, the reform economists held up the prospect of substantial improvements in the Soviet economic system with relatively small ideological concessions.

The Liberman Proposals

The proposals of Evsei Liberman, a professor of engineering economics at Kharkov University, provide a starting point for the reform discussions of the 1960s. Although Liberman had been writing about enterprise performance and arguing for a reduction in the tutelage over managers since the 1920s, his ideas were brought to the level of public discussion in 1962 with the publication of his article, "The Plan, Profits and Bonuses" in *Pravda*.[21] Its publication in the party newspaper signaled an official sanctioning by the Soviet leadership of reform discussion.

Several facets of this early reform era deserve comment. First, Liberman gained prominence well out of proportion to the importance of his proposals.[22] In fact, Liberman served to some extent as the figurehead of the liberal "profit group," which included the eminent mathematical economist V. S. Nemchinov. Liberman's proposals remain unimplemented, and his renewed emphasis on profits—the aspect of his proposals that attracted most attention—was most limited. Liberman was quite clear in pointing out that the central planning of output would be maintained in full vigor and that profits would serve as a basis for managerial rewards only after the output targets for quantity and assortment had been met. If enterprises failed to meet their output targets, they would be "deprived of the right to bonuses."[23] Liberman did not propose that profits act as the fundamental guide for economic activity but rather that profits were to have a more important role along with success criteria and would be the source of bonus payments.

Liberman proposed that bonus payments (after fulfillment of the planned output target) should be an increasing function of the profit/capital ratio, thus encouraging the expansion of profits but the reduction of capital usage. Profitability norms established for each industry would serve as the basis for evaluating managerial performance. To encourage enterprise managers to set ambitious targets for themselves, rewards would be higher for successful fulfillment—or perhaps even underfulfillment—of an ambitious profitability plan than for the overfulfillment of an "easy" target.

The number of centrally planned enterprise directives would be limited to the quantity and assortment of output and its delivery. The enterprise itself would plan its own material, labor inputs, and new technology. This would prove possible under the new system, according to Liberman, because the new emphasis on profits would encourage managers to seek out cost economies and new reserves rather than build up excess stocks.

On the crucial issue of centralization versus decentralization of decision making, Liberman remained ambiguous. All the basic instruments of central planning—price setting, the state budget, ruble control, state control of large investments—would be maintained, along with the centralized planning of material supply.[24] How this system could be made compatible with enterprises planning their own inputs was not spelled out in detail by Liberman other than by his assertion ("with reasonable confidence") that the two would prove compatible.[25] Liberman's conservatism on the issue of supply was in marked contrast to "marketeers" such as Nemchinov and A. Birman, who advocated free trade in producer goods.[26] On the crucial issue of the price system, Liberman also equivocated,[27] although he did suggest that the current Soviet price system would act as a serious impediment to the actual implementation of his proposals by giving unfair profitability advantages to some producers while discriminating against others. Nevertheless, he believed that his system would force managers to press for more rational prices.[28]

The publication of the original Liberman proposals in 1962 sparked considerable controversy and a period of open discussion in the Soviet press and academic journals between 1962 and 1965.[29] During this period, the various factions—ranging from the conservative antireformers to the Liberman supporters and the more radical reformers, especially the mathematical school—were given the opportunity to state their positions. Delayed by a politically conservative leadership, considerable criticism over the issue of profit and its meaning in a socialist economy, and, in particular, a lack of willingness to let important decisions be made by the "anarchy" of the market, the official decision came at the party plenum in September 1965. Prior to the party decision, a series of experiments was undertaken to test various reform ideas on a partial basis.

Reform Experiments

Acting out of a sense of caution, the Soviet leadership authorized a series of experiments between 1962 and 1965 to test the ideas of the profit group and the advocates of more conservative economic reform.[30]

The conservative normative value of processing (NVP) experiment was initiated in the Tartar Republic in 1962 and then was broadened to selected consumer goods industries in other regions. The basic notion of the NVP experiment was to replace the much maligned gross output index by a new NVP index. The reader will recall that the use of gross output as the prime enterprise success criterion encouraged enterprise managers to meet their gross output targets by increasing their use of expensive materials. Stated in terms more familiar to Western economists, the NVP reform simply called for the substitution of enterprise value added (net output) for gross value of output.

The light-industry experiment was designed to provide a feedback mechanism between the consumer and producer. The lack of feedback was especially prominent in the clothing industry, where an accumulation of unsalable inventories had resulted. In a step to resolve this problem, an experimental program sanctioned by the Central Committee was begun in 1964.[31] The Bolshevichka factory in Moscow and the Maiak factory in Gorky were allowed to receive their production orders directly from a selected group of retail outlets rather than being assigned quantitative output targets. Unsold stocks or returned output would detract from plan fulfillment. In particular, attention was to be paid to consumer demand as a determinant of production, with bonuses (set between 40 and 50 percent of basic pay) dependent on fulfillment of delivery and profit plans, not output plans.

Although these experimental enterprises remained under centralized control of their material supplies, their performance was considered a success; and in subsequent years the program was expanded, even to heavy industry. By 1965, light-industry reform had been extended to 25 percent of the garment factories, 28 percent of the footwear factories, 18 percent of the textile mills, and 30 percent of the leather factories.[32]

The extent to which this reform, also dubbed the "direct links" reform was continued after 1965 is not known.[33] In fact, the light-industry experiments were subsumed by the official general (and more conservative) reform of September 1965, and thus this direction of change seems to have been blunted. Apparently, there remained a general lack of willingness to free these experimental enterprises from administrative controls, and hence many of the supply, incentive, and other problems of Soviet industry continued to plague these enterprises. When this experiment was applied more broadly, the inability of the trade network to anticipate consumer demand to coordinate orders with shifting consumer tastes became more apparent.

THE OFFICIAL REFORM OF 1965

The official economic reform was announced by Premier Alexei Kosygin in September 1965 as a general reform to be gradually implemented over the next five years. In light of the high expectations for significant change raised by the debates and experiments of the preceding years, the official response was disappointing to the proponents of decentralization of economic authority. However, the conservatism and caution of the party leadership should have been anticipated, given the power of status quo forces.

Enterprise Planning and Management

The basic thrust of the 1965 reform was a reduction in the number of enterprise targets to be set from above and, most important, replacement of gross output by "realized output" (sales) as the primary indicator of success for an enterprise. In addition, the number of indicators for labor planning—previously four—was to be reduced to a single wage fund indicator. Under the 1965 reform, an enterprise manager was to face the eight targets established within the central plan, compared to the earlier system of 20 to 30 targets:

1. Value of goods to be sold
2. Main assortment
3. The wage fund
4. Amount of profit and the level of profitability
5. Payments to and allocations from the state budget
6. The volume of investment and the exploitation of fixed assets
7. Main assignments for the introduction of new technology
8. Material and technical supplies

The 1965 reform decreed several changes in financial planning. An interest charge on fixed and working capital was implemented at a 6 percent rate.[34] In addition provisions were made for an enhanced role to be played by *Gosbank*. The importance of the state budget in financing of enterprise investment was reduced. *Gosbank* was given a new expanded role, especially in the provisions of investment funds at differentiated charges. Also, *Gosbank* was allowed to facilitate the clearance of debts among enterprises and their customers in the trade network.

The 1965 reform also placed increasing emphasis on enterprise self-financing. Ties to the budget as a source of investment finance and subsidies were reduced and a production development fund was to be established. This fund was to be fed from profits, amortization of equipment, and sales of unneeded equipment. Basically, enterprises that could not cover their costs were to be denied automatic subsidies.

Profits and Incentives

The changing role of profits called for in the September 1965 reform was relatively modest. Prices were to be reformed to allow enterprises to be profitable under normal conditions of operation in order to end one of the long-standing results of average branch cost pricing, namely, that a good many enterprises continually suffered losses. In addition, the role of profit was to change in two respects. First, profit was given a position of greater importance, along with the now more limited number (eight) of indicators of managerial success. Second, profits were to be an important source of funds for decentralized investment by enterprise managers (a 20 percent share for decentralized investment was projected) and were to be used as a source of funds for bonus payments.[35] Investment funds would be channeled through two funds—the production development fund and the fund for social welfare and housing (to build factory-owned apartments)—while the bonus funds would be channeled through a new material incentive fund. These three funds were to replace the old enterprise fund and were designed to enhance the importance of profits for enterprise activity in addition to giving enterprise managers greater freedom of decision making.

Prior to the 1965 reform, worker bonus schemes had been subjected to criticism not only because of the meager amounts involved but also because the funding was typically from the wages fund rather than from profits. The 1965 rules for the utilization of the new material incentive fund were complex.[36] Briefly, however, this fund was to be placed largely under the control of the enterprise itself and was to provide material incentive payments above and beyond those normally provided by the wages fund.

Two observations should be made concerning the role of profits in the 1965 reform. First, it was apparent that in terms of increasing the importance of profits as a success indicator for management, little change was envisioned. Output (now in the form of sales) remained the all-powerful indicator, and profits remained a secondary indicator of enterprise success, along with seven other targets. In addition, where managers might enjoy a measure of freedom in the utilization of profits, for example in the case of decentralized investment or worker bonuses, in many instances other constraints were erected, such as prohibiting management to contract for material supplies or tightening centralized regulations over bonuses.

Recentralization

The official 1965 reforms recentralized the Soviet economic bureaucracy. Power was returned to the ministries, and the regional economic councils (the *Sovnarkhozy*) put in place by Khrushchev in 1957 were abolished. Decision-making authority shifted from regional authorities to national authorities.

The 1965 reforms called for a variety of organizational changes in the economic management and planning system.[3] Key functions were centralized in three powerful new state committees: the State Committee for Material-Technical Supply (*Gossnab*), the State Committee for Prices (*Gostsen*), and the State Committee for Science and Technology (*Gostekhnika*). Industrial enterprises were to be combined into large associations, called "production associations," and research enterprises and institutes were to be grouped into "science-production associations." The rationale given for these associations was that they would yield economies of scale, reduce the bureaucracy, and assist in the planning process. *Gossnab* was given the primary responsibility for allocating producer goods, and the ministerial supply organizations that had dominated the rationing of funded goods were largely to disappear. *Gossnab* was to apply itself to the creation of a wholesale trade system based on direct contracting arrangements among suppliers and buyers.

Changes in the planning process were also proposed. There was to be an increased emphasis on long-term plans; the "scientific basis" of planning was to be upgraded through the use of computers, mathematical programming, and the like; and "complex planning" (the planning of regional complexes) was to be emphasized.

Enterprises were encouraged to propose "counterplans"—plans more difficult than those put forward by their ministries. Enterprises that took on difficult counterplans were to be rewarded by higher bonuses and were not to be penalized by even more difficult targets in subsequent years. Emphasis on long-term targets (that would not be ratcheted up) would encourage enterprises to engage in serious counterplanning.

REJECTION OF THE 1965 REFORM

The manner in which the 1965 reform was implemented provides a valuable case study of the barriers that stand in the way of Soviet economic reform. It reveals those areas of the system most resistant to change. Initially, two phases of reform implementation were anticipated. The first, or "extensive," phase was to be the phased conversion of nonagricultural enterprises to the new system. The second, or "intensive," phase, scheduled to begin in 1970, would be the one in which the true potential of the reform would be realized.[38] In terms of the original format, all industrial enterprises were to be converted to the new system by 1968 and the remainder of the economy by the end of 1970. The exception was agriculture, where the introduction of the reform was to take place at a slower pace.

The basic thrust of the 1965 reform was a reduction in the tutelage of the enterprise manager by the higher planning organs. The idea was to create a system that encouraged managers to respond spontaneously to various economic "levers"—profits, bonuses, increased authority over investment, and so on—to make the Soviet enterprise more efficient and release "hidden reserves." For these reasons, the number of plan targets was to be reduced, reliance was to be placed on more rational success indicators such as sales and profitability, and managers and workers were to become materially interested in the outcome of enterprise performance by tying bonus funds to enterprise activity.

Initially, the 1965 reform was viewed as a major attempt to decentralize decision making, that is, to shift decision-making authority and responsibility to the enterprise level. In retrospect, it may be more useful to interpret this reform not so much as decentralization but rather as an attempt to change the framework in which enterprise managers would make particular decisions.

Between 1965 and 1971, there was evidence of greater managerial spontaneity in response to these economic levers, especially as regards the disposition of bonus funds. As managers began to exercise their newfound authority, planners and bureaucrats began to react against "undesirable" spontaneous enterprise actions and to press for amendments to the 1965 rules. During the very period when the reform was scheduled to move into its "intensive" phase, amendments and modifications were introduced that significantly altered the content of the original reform. The particular shortcomings that these amendments sought to correct were the unduly large shares of bonus funds received by managerial personnel, the lack of attention to labor productivity and quality improvement, and the unwillingness of managers to request taut counterplans or to economize costs—many of the very shortcomings that the 1965 reform had sought to eliminate in the first place.

Starting in 1971, a number of changes were introduced that significantly modified the spirit of the original reform proposal. First, rigid regulations governing the size of enterprise incentive funds replaced the more flexible system called for in the reform. The ministry, based on limits determined by *Gosplan*, was allowed to determine the size of enterprise incentive funds by fixing planned incentive fund targets. The size of the various incentive funds came to depend on enterprise performance vis-à-vis planned indicators such as output, profitability, and labor productivity targets. Three additional targets—the plan for key products in physical units, the plan for consumer goods, and the plans for changes in product quality and new products—were introduced. Furthermore, the size of the incentive fund was tied to the tautness of the enterprise plan: The higher the output, profitability, and labor productivity targets, the larger the potential incentive funds. These restrictions on enterprise funds restored most authority to the ministries. The ministry again had the authority to determine the conditions under which incentive funds were to be accumulated and disbursed. Enterprises could be punished by fund reductions for failing to meet ministry targets.

Second, strict controls over enterprise incentive funds were introduced. In the new regulations, limits were placed on the rate of growth of managerial bonuses, average wages were not allowed to increase faster than labor productivity, and regulations were established to reduce bonus differentials among branches. Significantly, managerial bonuses were tied to fulfillment of sales and profitability plans *plus* the fulfillment of the physical assortment plan, and the ministries were allowed to add additional conditions if they so desired. The ministry could deny bonuses if delivery plans were not met.

Third, the manager's control over the production development fund (for investment) was circumscribed. Under the modified rules, the proportion of enterprise profits to be allocated to this fund was to be set by the ministry in accordance with bank credits planned for decentralized investments. The incentive effects of the enterprise investment fund were nullified. Under these decrees, the distinction between decentralized and centralized investment lost its meaning. On the one hand, managers were encouraged to invest on a decentralized basis, while, on the other hand, they were unable to purchase investment goods through the material supply network. These supply problems continued in spite of a system of fines for nondelivery and various attempts to develop the concept of "free sales."[39] The supply system remained largely centralized and out of reach of the typical enterprise manager.

Fourth, the envisioned expansion of the banking system as a supplier of credit did not materialize. Credits, though available, remained a minor source of finance. Bank financing of state centralized investment accounted for only 2.3 percent of all investment in 1973. Enterprises had surplus working capital resulting from the inability to spend production development and housing funds simply due to the absence of a mechanism for decentralized investment.

Fifth, the proposed changes in Soviet planning failed to materialize. The 1965 reform called for an enhanced role for long-term planning, seeking to establish the Five Year Plan as the basic operating plan of the national economy. Yet throughout the reform process, the annual economic plan remained the operative plan. Despite campaigns to promote counterplans, only 13,000 industrial enterprises engaged in counterplanning in 1977. As of 1981, only 6.6 percent of the industrial enterprises adopted counterplans. Moreover, managers proposed cosmetic counterplans that did not alter the substance of planned targets.[40] The lack of success of counterplanning perhaps reflects the continued fear of enterprise managers of the ratchet effect.

Sixth, many of the administrative changes proposed by the 1965 reform were not implemented.[41] During the early years of the reform, enterprises did not amalgamate into productive associations. It required a separate party government decree in April 1973 before the formation of production associations proceeded at a rapid pace. The purposes of the production association were to gain the advantages of economies of scale in management through the amalgamation of firms involved in similar lines of business and to economize on administrative personnel. In practice, the formation of industrial associations often meant little more than "changing the names on doors" in Moscow; supervisory power continued to remain in the hands of the main administrations of the ministries, and there was a 60 percent expansion in the bureaucracy between 1966 and 1977.[42] The ministries continued to be the centers of economic power, allocating materials and equipment, dictating the incentive systems of enterprises and industrial associations, and controlling investment. *Gossnab* was supposed to replace the ministerial supply organs, but *Gossnab* handled only one-half the value of rationed producer goods by the late 1970s. The market for producer goods failed to emerge, and the traditional system of material supplies and central balances continued to function.

Finally, and perhaps most important, the number of enterprise targets was expanded. New targets were reinstated in the 1970s: labor productivity, gross output, consumer goods assignments in heavy industry, quality targets, material and fuel economy targets, delivery obligations, new products, and the size of basic incentive funds. The tendency to introduce new targets goes against the intent of the 1965 reform, which was supposed to restrict the number of centralized targets. Apparently, new targets were introduced in response to the most pressing problem of the day. If low quality is perceived to be the most severe problem, planners reintroduce quality targets. Economist F. Kushnirsky refers to this practice as the planner's search for the perfect success criterion.[43]

Experts agree that by the mid–1970s, the 1965 reform was dead for all practical purposes. Nevertheless, Soviet authorities remained on a "treadmill" of reform. Scarcely a year passed without the announcement of a new reform or experiment heralded to solve long-standing problems. Experiments started in the late 1960s (such as the Shchekino labor experiment begun in 1967) continued.[44]

The thrust of the 1970s was toward the improvement of planning methods, for example, the greater emphasis on long-term plans, better norming, and increased use of automated methods and computerization. These changes shifted the focus of reform away from decentralization to the issue of "better planning." Soviet authorities ceased to be interested in decentralized levers; they were more interested in improvement of the planning mechanism. One Western student of the reform could write in 1973 that "after seven years of the reform, economic methods, or 'levers,' have been effectively converted into administrative 'levers' . . . as a consequence, centralized planning and administration are even more entrenched . . . ."[45]

THE JULY 1979 DECREE

In July 1979, a decree was issued entitled "On improving Planning and Strengthening the Economic Mechanism's Influence on Raising the Effectiveness of Production and the Quality of Work."[46] This decree, usually called PIEM, or Program to Improve the Economic Mechanism, was not a systematic program to change the economic system. Morris Bornstein, in a major study of PIEM, described the 1979 decree "as an attempt within the framework of a 'traditional' ('Soviet-type') socialist centrally planned economy to improve economic performance through changes in the arrangements for the choice of output, the allocation of resources to produce it, and the distribution of the associated personal income."[47] PIEM should not be viewed as a formal reform program but rather as an effort to change Soviet economic decision-making procedures. Rather, the aim of the PIEM program was ". . . to increase output; to reduce its cost, and particularly the use of materials and fuels; to improve quality, through the introduction of new products; to secure the timely delivery of output, according to the contracted product-mix; and to cut construction time and costs." These objectives were to be pursued through "a variety of measures affecting planning, performance indicators, incentives, and finance."[48]

Planning was to be improved in five general areas. First, enterprise capacity was to be better known through a "passport" system—a systematic effort to know more about production capability in each producing unit by requiring more information and on a regular basis. Second, the norming process was to be improved and was to replace "directive indicators" so that the planning process can be simplified and differing local conditions accounted for. Instead of an enterprise being specifically told how much labor could be used for a particular task, a predetermined norm would cover the particular application, and enterprise performance would be judged by the achievement of the norm. Third, enterprises were encouraged to operate under taut plans as measured by such indicators as the percentage use of capacity. Rewards would be provided for the enterprise adoption of "counterplans" that require more than the official plans.

Fourth, long-term planning was reemphasized, but with greater emphasis on plan coordination of one-year, five-year and regional plans. Overall, the emphasis was placed on the formulation of firm plan tasks that would not require constant correction.

Finally, the material supply system was to be improved largely through the expanded use of contracting. Enterprises were encouraged to establish supply contracts with user enterprises that fulfill the contract terms.

A crucial part of the 1979 decree related to performance indicators. Specifically, the decree addressed three traditional problem areas of Soviet enterprise performance: the overutilization of material inputs, the lack of enterprise interest in quality, and finally, neglect of product mix.

The emphasis on gross output as an enterprise success indicator has always led to the overutilization of material inputs. Under the new rules, labor productivity became a key indicator of enterprise performance, measured as net output per worker, as normed by planning authorities. The basic idea of "normed" net output was to calculate enterprise value added (net output) by subtracting planned costs from gross output. An enterprise that overused material inputs or substituted expensive inputs would be penalized because it could only use normed costs. Costs in excess of planned costs could not enter into the gross value of output.[49]

Quality was emphasized under the PIEM enterprise rules by making it an important indicator of enterprise performance, related to bonus payments. A commission was set up to categorize products according to quality, and enterprises were to be rewarded according to the share of better-quality products in their output. The assortment problem was attacked by better specification of output in the plan and by tying rewards to the completion of delivery contracts. Efforts were to be made to make the output specification more detailed so that deviations from plan could be spotted more readily.

PIEM decreed changes in bonus arrangements. Although enterprise profit remained as the main source of bonus funds, the rules for forming and disbursing bonus funds were changed and became more complex. The bonus system was to be more closely tied to labor productivity and quality indicators.

Finally, changes were decreed in the area of investment planning. The emphasis was placed on self-financing, especially at the ministerial level. Some ministries were placed on *khozraschet* and increasingly were to be accountable for their plan fulfillment. Ministries were to have profit plans; and after various payments to the state budget, retained ministry profits were to be used for investment.

From its inception, the 1979 PIEM decree aimed at improving the existing system. It proposed to improve planning procedures (focus on long-term plans and counterplans), manipulate levers (greater emphasis on productivity and quality indicators), and make the supply system more flexible by expanding the role of contracts. It sought to reduce waste by introducing net output normatives. These features can hardly be described as calling for significant changes in the Soviet economic system.

In her 1983 evaluation of the July 1979 decree and its implementation, Gertrude Schroeder concludes: "Planning is more centralized, rigid, and detailed than ever; the scope for initiative of the producing units is more circumscribed; producer goods are more tightly rationed; administratively set, inflexible, average cost-based prices are retained; and intricate incentive systems are tied to meeting plans for many potentially conflicting variables, with priority given to production plans expressed in physical units."[50]

It is interesting to note that these changes both reinforce and contradict earlier reform emphasis. For example, the emphasis on long-term planning, especially the stability of plans, was a theme of the 1965 reform. Counterplans were a part of the earlier reform, but they were implemented to only a modest degree. Yet a major emphasis of the 1965 reform, namely, reduction in the performance indicators, was reversed.

PRICE REFORM

An implicit factor in the Soviet reform discussion was the issue of industrial prices. As was pointed out in Chapter 8, industrial prices have been set to equal average branch cost of production (capital and rental charges often omitted) plus a planned profit margin without reference to demand. Such prices are not scarcity prices in the sense that they do not equate supply and demand, nor do they reflect marginal cost. In fact, more often than not, industrial prices have been allowed to diverge from costs owing to the administrative complexity of price reform, thus necessitating state subsidies for enterprises that sustain losses.

Against this background, one can understand the complexities of the decentralization issue, that is, the extent to which crucial economic decisions can be left up to enterprise managers without first having the primary information mechanism upon which such decisions are to be based—a "rational" price system. In this context, one can perhaps understand the relative willingness of Soviet authorities to give managers more discretion in the area of labor staffing, where prices tend to be based more on scarcity.

Such considerations culminated in a general reform of industrial prices during 1966–1967. Did this reform transform the Soviet price system into a more useful information mechanism for decentralization? The answer is quite simple: It did not.

The 1966–1967 price reform was conducted separately from the official reform of 1965, and, as we already noted, was not a major consideration in the earlier Liberman discussions. The goals of the 1966–1967 industrial price reform were quite modest. In view of the enhanced role of profits and monetary incentives envisioned in the 1965 reform, it was deemed essential to set industrial prices at average cost plus a profit margin sufficient to eliminate the pattern of subsidization of unprofitable enterprises. Thus, price revision was to become an important vehicle for implementation of the reform. No attempt was made to set prices to equate supply and demand—if this is possible at all in a planned economy. The more radical views—especially those of the mathematical school, advocating scarcity prices through linear programming models or through an auctioning process—were rejected. Prices were raised in 1966 and 1967, though still on the basis of average costs, and this reduced the number of planned loss enterprises and to some degree the profitability differentials among branches of industry.[51] In addition, a new centralized organ, the State Committee for Prices (*Gostsen*) was established, with rather broad powers, to administer the price system.

The reform of prices would be crucial to any attempt to enhance the role of profits (which, as we have seen, was not a major goal of the 1965 reform) and to resolve the problem of low-quality consumer goods (which was a major goal of the reform). The price reforms of 1966–1967 and a similar reform of 1982 failed to confront the basic issue with regard to profitability, namely, to set prices in such a manner that enterprise profitability would reflect managerial performance. If prices fail to include all legitimate factor payments (such as for superior equipment, locational advantages, favorable raw materials, etc.), then it is unclear whether high profits are the consequence of pricing foibles or of effective management. The 1966–1967 price reform did not come to grips with these issues and continued to use the traditional formulas for setting prices.

Ministries continued to redistribute profits from profitable to unprofitable enterprises. Some branches (food processing, for example) have prices that generally fail to cover average branch costs and require large subsidies. Thus, the failure to effect significant changes in the manner of price formation meant that profit-oriented reforms could not be put into practice even if the leadership were willing.

A whole series of measures was adopted after 1967 to encourage technological progress, the production of high-quality consumer and producer goods, and realistic regional price differentials. The procedures for setting "limit prices," "sliding prices," and quality differentials are complex and require lengthy explanations. It is sufficient to say that such measures have not brought about significant change in the Soviet price system.

As Gertrude Schroeder has noted, "The new prices, like those they replace, are calculated on the basis of average unit labor, material, and depreciation costs plus an average percentage profit markup over cost."[52] This adjustment was designed simply to bring prices into line with new evidence. Thus, while the changes were obviously important, the basic formula for price computation did not change, with the exception of some resource prices, where pricing at the margin is used.

ECONOMIC REFORM: THE EARLY YEARS

We have dated the beginning of contemporary economic reform in the Soviet Union to the Liberman discussions. We have traced the Soviet reform discussion through the end of the 1970s and into the 1980s, up to the beginnings of the Gorbachev era. A number of observations are relevant.

First, it is difficult to classify the Soviet experience as a pure form of economic reform. Clearly elements of all of our three reform categories were attempted in this period. The thrust of economic reform has been an attempt to improve the operation of the Soviet economic system through improvement of decision-making arrangements, rules, and organizational change. Clearly Soviet reform attempts have been mixed attempts.

Second, early Soviet reform was unquestionably very conservative. Indeed, if we think of reform as fundamentally changing the working arrangements of an economic system, then there was no reform at all, though obviously day-to-day operational procedures did change to some extent in the 1960s and the 1970s.

Third, to the extent that there were voices in the Soviet Union advocating the maintenance of central planning, these voices clearly won the day. Resource allocation in the Soviet economy of the 1980s was, as it had been earlier, primarily directed by the plan or administrative process.

Fourth, it was clearly evident from the early Soviet experience that whatever the reform blueprint, reform implementation would be quite another story. The reform blueprints were simply not implemented, though assessing the reasons for lack of implementation would turn out to be a difficult task. Were the blueprints inadequate, was the sequencing inappropriate, or was the resistance to change simply too strong?

There is the further question of whether economic reform can be introduced into the Soviet system within the context of existing objectives. Consider unemployment and inflation, well known in the West but officially banished from the Soviet system. If significant changes in Soviet working arrangements were made such as giving managers discretion over firing and hiring or allowing prices to be determined in markets, the consequences might be more inflation and unemployment than the authorities are prepared to tolerate. Most would probably agree that the Eastern European experience indicates that even limited introduction of market methods results in some sacrifice of these objectives. Unless a new and acceptable socialist term for "unemployment" can be invented, the unemployment outcome would be especially unacceptable to Soviet leaders.

Finally, Soviet bureaucrats are no different from bureaucrats elsewhere; they don't like change. Whether it be the ministries, the provincial party organizations, the local governments, or the enterprises, Soviet discussion of their reform programs reveals significant resistance to change at different levels where vested interests are threatened by reform.

How might we assess the state of economic reform in the Soviet economy? It is useful to quote the previous edition of this book:

> Does all of this mean that reform and change are dead issues? The answer is in the negative, though one might suggest a trend away from reform in the sense of major formal programs and toward change in the sense of continuous piecemeal adjustments. There are few signs of interest in changes in fundamental working arrangements. Instead, attention is focused on existing arrangements with an aim toward making them work better. Analysis of the evidence suggests such a commitment. In 1984, there was a reaffirmation of the need to continue pursuing the 1979 program. While in a formal sense much of the 1979 program has not been implemented, in an informal sense there has been considerable change with individual subunits in the system by adopting some parts of the intended change and modifying or ignoring other parts. The result is a substantial degree of diversification of prevailing decision-making arrangements. There is little evidence that such changes will be less popular in future years.

Few observers of early Soviet economic reform attempts would have predicted the onset of glasnost and/or perestroika. In Chapter 15, we assess the contemporary reformers.

REFERENCES

1. See, for example, L. Hurwicz, "Centralization and Decentralization in Economic Process," in A. Eckstein, ed., *Comparison of Economic Systems* (Berkeley and Los Angeles: University of California Press, 1971), pp. 79–102; L. Hurwicz, "Conditions for Economic Efficiency of Centralized and Decentralized Structures," in

G. Grossman, ed., *Value and Plan* (Berkeley and Los Angeles: University of California Press, 1960), pp. 162–183; L. Hurwicz, "On the Concept and Possibility of Informational Decentralization," *American Economic Review, Papers and Proceedings*, vol. 59, no. 2 (May 1969), 513–524; and T. Marschak, "The Comparison of Centralized and Decentralized Economies," *American Economic Review, Papers and Proceedings*, vol. 59, no. 2 (May 1969), 525–532. For a summary analysis of approaches to economic reforms, see P. Hare, "Economic Reform in Eastern Europe," *Journal of Economic Issues*, vol. 1, no. 1, 1987, 25–58.

2. M. Bornstein, "Economic Reform in Eastern Europe," in U.S. Congress, Joint Economic Committee, *East European Economies Post-Helsinki* (Washington, D.C.: U.S. Government Printing Office, 1977), pp. 102–134.

3. For example, a system that functions through imposed rules is the classic Weberian bureaucratic model. This model and its application to the Soviet case is discussed in D. Granick, *Management of the Industrial Firm in the USSR* (New York: Columbia University Press, 1954). The concept of a parametric framework implies rules, but not rules for each decision that has to be made. Rather, managers are given the authority and the responsibility to use locally available information to make decisions leading to some overall objective, for example, cost minimization. Such a framework generally implies the use of value parameters and hence gives great importance to the process of valuation.

4. This point is made by F. I. Kushnirsky, *Soviet Economic Planning 1965–1980* (Boulder, Colo.: Westview Press, 1982), pp. 41–42.

5. On this general issue, see Bornstein, "Economic Reform in Eastern Europe," p. 110.

6. Key references on reforms of this period are: A. Bergson, "Planning and the Market in the USSR: The Current Soviet Planning Reforms," in A. Balinky et al., *Planning and the Market in the USSR: The 1960s* (New Brunswick, N.J.: Rutgers University Press, 1967), pp. 43–64; G.E. Schroeder, "The 'Reform' of the Supply System in Soviet Industry," *Soviet Studies*, vol. 24, no. 1 (July 1972), 97–119; G. E. Schroeder, "The Soviet Economy on a Treadmill of 'Reforms,' " in U.S. Congress, Joint Economic Committee, *Soviet Economy in a Time of Change* (Washington, D.C.: U.S. Government Printing Office, 1979), vol. 1, pp. 312–340; G. E. Schroeder, "Soviet Economic 'Reform' Decrees: More Steps on the Treadmill," in U.S. Congress, Joint Economic Committee, *Soviet Economy in the 1980's: Problems and Prospects*, part 1 (Washington, D.C.: U.S. Government Printing Office, 1982), pp. 65–88; and A. Nove,*The Soviet Economic System* (London: Allen & Unwin, 1977), chap. 11.

7. For a discussion of alternative perceptions of decentralization, see Bornstein, "Economic Reform in Eastern Europe."

8. S. F. Cohen, "The Friends and Foes of Change: Reformism and Conservatism in the Soviet Union," *Slavic Review*, vol. 38, no. 2 (June 1979), 195.

9. On this, see V. S. Nemchinov's comments on the 1923–1924 balance in *The Use of Mathematics in Economics* (Cambridge, Mass.: MIT Press, 1964), pp. 2–10. Popov's original presentation of the 1923–1924 balance is translated in N. Spulber, ed., *Foundations of Soviet Strategy for Economic Growth* (Bloomington: Indiana University Press, 1964), pp. 5–19. For a discussion of the early Soviet mathematical economics school, see L. Smolinski, "The Origins of Soviet Mathematical Economics," in H. Raupach et al., eds., *Yearbook of East-European Economics*, vol. 2 (Munich: Günter Olzog Verlag, 1971), pp. 137–154.

10. E. H. Carr and R. W. Davies, *Foundations of a Planned Economy*, 1926–1929, vol. 1, part 2 (London: Macmillan, 1969), pp. 787–801.

11. Spulber, *Soviet Strategy for Economic Growth*, chap. 2; G. Grossman, "Scarce Capital and Soviet Doctrine," *Quarterly Journal of Economics*, vol. 67, no. 3 (August 1953), 311–315; R. Dunayevskaya, "A New Revision of Marxian Economics," *American Economic Review*, vol. 34, no. 3 (September 1944), 531–537; and Smolinski, "The Origins of Soviet Mathematical Economics," pp. 150–151.

12. Cohen, "The Friends and Foes of Change," p. 196.

13. For a review of Kantorovich's and Novozhilov's contribution, see R.W. Campbell, "Marx, Kantorovich and Novozhilov: Stoimost' Versus Reality," *Slavic Review*, vol. 20, no. 3 (October 1961), 402–418. For a general survey, see M. Ellman *Soviet Planning Today: Proposals for an Optimally Functioning Economic System* (Cambridge: Cambridge University Press, 1971); and A. Zauberman, *The Mathematical Revolution in Soviet Planning* (Oxford: Oxford University Press, 1975). For an insider's view, see Aron Katsenelinboigen, *Studies in Soviet Economic Planning* (White Plains, N.Y.: M. E. Sharpe, 1978), chap. 3. Also see L. Smolinski, ed., *L. V. Kantorovich: Essays in Optimal Planning* (White Plains, N.Y.: International Arts and Sciences Press, 1976).

14. Evsei Liberman's reform proposals had been made in the journal *Voprosy ekonomiki* [Problems of economics] as early as 1955.

15. The original Liberman paper and the debate it generated are given in M. E. Sharpe, ed., *Planning, Profit and Incentives in the USSR*, vols. 1 and 2 (White Plains, N.Y.: International Arts and Sciences Press, 1966).

16. U.S. Congress, Joint Economic Committee, *USSR: Measures of Economic Growth and Development, 1950–80* (Washington, D.C.: U.S. Government Printing Office, 1982), p. 22.

17. Ibid.

18. *Narodnoe khoziaistvo SSSR v 1983*, p. 118.

19. This was Khrushchev's often quoted criticism of planning during the Stalin years. See M. Goldman, "Economic Growth and Institutional Change in the Soviet Union," in P. Juliver and H. Morton, eds., *Soviet Policy-Making: Studies of Communism in Transition* (New York: Praeger, 1967), pp. 63–80, reprinted in M. Bornstein and D. Fusfeld, eds., *The Soviet Economy: A Book of Readings*, 3rd ed. (Homewood, Ill.: Irwin, 1970), p. 350.

20. A. Katsenelinboigen, *Studies in Soviet Economic Planning*, p. 79.

21. Translated in M. Bornstein and D. Fusfeld, eds., *The Soviet Economy: A Book of Readings*, 3rd ed. (Homewood, Ill.: Irwin, 1970), pp. 360–366. Translations and analysis of Liberman's other writings are in Sharpe, *Planning, Profit and Incentives*, vols. 1 and 2. For succinct statements of the Liberman proposal and its relation to a cost-profit calculus, see A. Zauberman, "Liberman's Rules of the Game for Soviet Industry," *Slavic Review*, vol. 22, no. 4 (December 1963), 734–744; Felker, *Soviet Economic Controversies*, pp. 58–62; G. R. Feiwel, *The Soviet Quest for Economic Efficiency* (New York: Praeger, 1972), chap. 5; and Sharpe, *Planning, Profit and Incentives*, vol. 1, introduction.

22. For a discussion of Liberman's career, see R. C. Stuart, "Evsei Grigorevich Liberman," in G. W. Simmons, ed., *Soviet Leaders* (New York: Crowell, 1967), pp. 193–200.

23. Liberman, in Bornstein and Fusfeld, *The Soviet Economy*, p. 361. Also see E. G. Liberman, *Economic Methods and Effectiveness of Production* (White Plains, N.Y.: International Arts and Sciences Press, 1971).

24. Liberman, in Bornstein and Fusfeld, *The Soviet Economy*, pp. 362–363.

25. Ibid., p. 363.

26. Nove, *The Soviet Economic System*, pp. 309–310.

27. According to Nove, *The Soviet Economic System*, p. 309, Liberman never developed a coherent pricing model. Prices, in Liberman's own words, were to be "fixed and flexible."

28. M. Kaser, "Kosygin, Liberman, and the Pace of Soviet Industrial Reform," in G. R. Feiwel, ed., *New Currents in Soviet-Type Economies: A Reader* (Scranton, Pa.: International Textbook, 1968), p. 334.

29. For further English translations of the major contributions to the debate, see M. E. Sharpe, ed., *The Liberman Discussion: A New Phase in Soviet Economic Thought* (White Plains, N.Y.: International Arts and Sciences Press, 1965). For chronological accounts of the 1962–1965 debate, see Kaser, "Kosygin, Liberman," pp. 330–343; and Felker, *Soviet Economic Controversies*, chaps. 3 and 4.

30. These experimental programs are discussed in Feiwel, *The Soviet Quest for Economic Efficiency*, chap. 5.

31. For a discussion of this experiment, see Goldman, "Economic Growth and Institutional Change," p. 322; Kaser, "Kosygin, Liberman," pp. 337–338; and E. Zaleski, *Planning Reforms in the Soviet Union, 1962–1966* (Chapel Hill: University of North Carolina Press, 1967), pp. 122–140.

32. Goldman, "Economic Growth and Institutional Change," p. 357; and Feiwel, *The Soviet Quest for Economic Efficiency*, pp. 242–250.

33. See A. Kosygin, "On Improving Management of Industry, Perfecting Planning, and Enhancing Economic Incentives in Industrial Production," in Bornstein and Fusfeld, eds., *The Soviet Economy: A Book of Readings*, pp. 387–396.

34. This rate could be lower for unprofitable enterprises. See Zaleski, *Planning Reforms*, p. 143.

35. K. Bush, "The Implementation of the Soviet Economic Reform," *Osteuropa Wirtschaft*, no. 2 (1970), 67–90; and no. 3 (1970), 190–198.

36. L. J. Kirsch, *Soviet Wages: Changes in Structure and Administration Since 1956* (Cambridge, Mass.: MIT Press, 1972), chap. 7.

37. For discussions of the organizational aspects of the 1965 reform, see Kushnirsky, *Soviet Economic Planning*; and National Foreign Assessment Center, *Organization and Management in the Soviet Economy: The Ceaseless Search for Panaceas*, ER77–10769, Washington, D.C., December 1977.

38. G. E. Schroeder, "Recent Developments in Soviet Planning and Managerial Incentives," in U.S. Congress, Joint Economic Committee, *Soviet Economic Prospects for the Seventies* (Washington, D.C.: U.S. Government Printing Office, 1973), p.12.

39. Goldman, "Economic Growth and Institutional Change," p. 323; and Schroeder, "Recent Developments in Soviet Planning," pp. 107–111. On the lack of material supplies as a brake on decentralized enterprise investment, see, for example, D. Allakhverdian, "O finansovykh problemakh khoziaistvennoi reformy" [About the financial problems of economic reform], *Voprosy ekonomiki* [Problems of economics], no. 11 (1970), 63–74.

40. S. J. Linz, "Managerial Autonomy in Soviet Firms," *Soviet Studies*, vol. 40, no. 2 (April 1988).

41. This discussion is based on M. Bornstein, "Improving the Soviet Economic Mechanism," *Soviet Studies*, vol. 37, no. 1 (January 1985), 1–30; Schroeder, "Soviet Economic 'Reform' Decrees"; Schroeder, "Recent Developments in Soviet Planning

and Incentives," pp. 11–38; Schroeder, "The Soviet Economy on a Treadmill of 'Reforms,' " pp. 312–340; Schroeder, "Post-Khrushchev Reforms and Public Financial Goals," in Z. M. Fallenbuchl, ed., *Economic Development in the Soviet Union and Eastern Europe* (New York: Praeger, 1976), pp. 348–367; National Foreign Assessment Center, *Organization and Management in the Soviet Economy*, pp. 1–22; A. C. Gorlin, "Industrial Reorganization: The Associations," in U. S. Congress, Joint Economic Committee, *Soviet Economy in a New Perspective* (Washington, D.C.: U.S. Government Printing Office 1976), pp. 162–188; and Kushnirsky, *Soviet Economic Planning.*

42. Schroeder, "The Soviet Economy on a Treadmill of 'Reforms,' " p. 314.
43. Kushnirsky, *Soviet Economic Planning*, chap. 1.
44. For a discussion of the Schlekino experiment, see P. Rutland, "The Shchekino Method and the Struggle to Raise Labour Productivity in Soviet Industry," *Soviet Studies*, vol. 36, no. 3 (July 1984), 345–365; B. Arnot, "Soviet Labour Productivity and the Failure of the Shchekino Experiment," *Critique*, vol. 1, no. 5 (1981), 32–56; and B. Arnot, *Controlling Soviet Labour* (London: Macmillan Press, 1988), Chaps. 5–8.
45. P. K. Cook, "The Political Setting," in U.S. Congress, Joint Economic Committee, *Soviet Economic Prospects for the Seventies.*
46. This section is based on Bornstein, "Improving the Soviet Economic Mechanism"; Schroeder, "Soviet Economic 'Reform' Decrees"; P. Hanson, "Success Indicators Revisited: The July 1979 Soviet Decree on Planning and Management," *Soviet Studies*, vol. 35, no. 1 (January 1983), 1–13; and N. Nimitz, "Reform and Technological Innovation in the 11th Five Year Plan," in S. Bialer and T. Gustafson, eds., *Russia at the Crossroads* (London: Allen & Unwin, 1982), chap.7
47. Bornstein, "Improving the Soviet Economic Mechanism,' p. 2.
48. Ibid. p. 23
49. For a detailed discussion, see Bornstein.
50. Schroeder, "Soviet Economic 'Reform' Decrees," p. 82.
51. G. E. Schroeder, "The 1966–67 Soviet Industrial Price Reform: A Study in Complications," *Soviet Studies*, vol. 20, no. 4 (April 1969), 464ff.; M. Bornstein, "Soviet Price Policy in the 1970s," in U..S. Congress, Joint Economic Committee, *Soviet Economy in a New Perspective*, pp. 17–67; and J. S. Berliner, "Flexible Pricing and New Products in the USSR," *Soviet Studies*, vol. 27, no. 4 (October 1975), 525–544.
52. Schroeder, "Soviet Economic 'Reform' Decrees,' p. 76

SELECTED BIBLIOGRAPHY

A. Balinky et al., *Planning and the Market in the USSR: The 1960s* (New Brunswick, N.J.: Rutgers University Press, 1967).

J. S. Berliner, *The Innovation Decision in Soviet Industry* (Cambridge, Mass.: MIT Press, 1976).

———, "Planning and Management," in A. Bergson and H. S Levine, eds., *The Soviet Economy: Towards the Year 2000* (London: Allen & Unwin, 1983), pp. 350–359.

M. Bornstein, "Improving the Soviet Economic Mechanism," *Soviet Studies*, vol. 37, no. 1 (January 1985), 1–30.

K. Bush, "The Implementation of the Soviet Economic Reform," *Osteuropa Wirtschaft*, nos. 2 and 3 (1970).

S. F. Cohen, "The Friends and Foes of Change: Reformism and Conservatism in the Soviet Union," *Slavic Review, vol. 38, no. 2 (June 1979), 187–202.*

N. Fedoryenko et al., *Soviet Economic Reform: Progress and Problems*, translated from the Russian (Moscow: Progress Publishers, 1972).

G. R. Feiwel, *The Soviet Quest for Economic Efficiency* (New York: Praeger, 1972).

J. L. Felker, *Soviet Economic Controversies* (Cambridge, Mass.: MIT Press, 1966).

A. C. Gorlin, "Industrial Reorganization: The Associations," in U.S. Congress, Joint Economic Committee, *Soviet Economy in a New Perspective* (Washington, D.C.: U.S. Government Printing Office, 1976), pp. 162–188.

P. Hanson, "Success Indicators Revisited: The July 1979 Decree on Planning and Management," *Soviet Studies*, vol. 35, no. 1 (January 1983).

A. Katsenelinboigen, *Studies in Soviet Economic Planning* (White Plains, N.Y.: M.E. Sharpe, 1978).

W. Keizer, *The Soviet Quest for Economic Rationality* (Rotterdam: Rotterdam University Press, 1971).

A. Kosygin, "On Improving Management of Industry, Perfecting Planning, and Enhancing Economic Incentives in Industrial Production," in M. Bornstein and D. Fusfeld, eds., *The Soviet Economy: A Book of Readings*, 3rd ed. (Homewood, Ill.: Irwin, 1970), pp. 387–396.

E. G. Liberman, *Economic Methods and the Effectivenes of Production* (White Plains, N.Y.: International Arts and Sciences Press, 1971).

S. J. Linz, "Managerial Autonomy in Soviet Firms," *Soviet Studies*, vol. 4, no. 2 (April 1988).

National Foreign Assessment Center, *Organization and Management in the Soviet Economy: The Ceaseless Search for Panaceas.* ER77–10769, Washington, D.C., December 1977.

A. Nove, *The Soviet Economic System* (London: Allen & Unwin, 1977), chap. 11.

P. Rutland, "The Shchekino Method and the Struggle to Raise Labour Productivity in Soviet Industry," *Soviet Studies*, vol. 36, no. 3 (July 1984), 345–365.

K. W. Ryavec, "Soviet Industrial Management: Challenge and Response, 1965–1970," *Canadian Slavic Studies*, vol. 2 (Summer 1972), 151–177.

———, "Soviet Industrial Managers, Their Superiors and the Economic Reform: A Study of an Attempt at Planned Behavioral Change," *Soviet Studies*, vol. 21, no. 2 (October 1969), 208–229.

G. E. Schroeder, "The 1966–67 Soviet Industrial Price Reform: A Study in Complications," *Soviet Studies*, vol. 20, no. 4 (April 1969), 462–477.

———, "Recent Developments in Soviet Planning and Managerial Incentives," in U.S. Congress, Joint Economic Committee, *Soviet Economic Prospects for the Seventies* (Washington, D.C.: U.S. Government Printing Office, 1973), pp. 11–38.

———, "The 'Reform' of the Supply System in Soviet Industry," *Soviet Studies*, vol. 24, no. 1 (July 1972), 97–119.

————, "Soviet Economic 'Reform' Decrees: More Steps on the Treadmill," in U.S. Congress, Joint Economic Committee, *Soviet Economy in the 1980's: Problems and Prospects*, part 1 (Washington, D.C.: U.S. Government Printing Office, 1982), pp. 65–88.

————, "The Soviet Economy on a Treadmill of 'Reforms,' " in U.S. Congress, Joint Economic Committee, *Soviet Economy in a Time of Change*, vol. 1 (Washington, D.C.: U.S. Government Printing Office, 1979), pp. 312–340.

M. E. Sharpe, ed., *Planning, Profit and Incentives in the USSR*, vols. 1 and 2 (White Plains, N.Y.: International Arts and Sciences Press, 1966).

L. Smolinski, ed., *L. V. Kantorovich: Essays in Optimal Planning* (White Plains, N.Y.: International Arts and Sciences Press, 1976).

E. Zaleski, *Planning Reforms in the Soviet Union, 1962–1966* (Chapel Hill: University of North Carolina Press, 1967).

A. Zauberman, "Liberman's Rules of the Game for Soviet Industry", *Slavic Review*, vol. 22, no. 4 (December 1963), 734–744.

————, *The Mathematical Revolution in Soviet Planning* (Oxford: Oxford University Press, 1975).

Chapter 15

Prospects for Perestroika

M ikhail Gorbachev inherited a wide range of pressing economic problems when he became general secretary of the Soviet Communist Party in March 1985. The Soviet Union's economic problems have been enumerated in earlier chapters: the alarming decline in the growth of output and factor productivity, growing dissatisfaction with consumer goods availability and quality, a disturbing technology gap with the West, a restive population that is scarcely reproducing itself in the European republics, rising mortality associated with a possible deterioration of Soviet health care and with alcoholism, and finally, a serious food problem. This collection of problems represents most recently the legacy of the Brezhnev regime, which began with the unseating of Nikita Khrushchev in 1964 and ended with the death of Konstantin Chernenko in

1985. In the Soviet terminology of the 1990s, the 1970s to the mid-1980s was a period of "stagnation" (*zastoi*) that was a consequence of the lack of innovation and the presence of corruption during the Brezhnev years. This stagnation also reflected the failure of the "administrative-command" model instituted by Stalin in the early 1930s and perpetuated by Brezhnev and his associates.

STAGNATION: BREZHNEV'S LEGACY

Although the Soviet Union's stagnation during the Brezhnev regime can be captured by a variety of statistical indicators, comparisons of U.S.-USSR economic performance over the last three decades brings the point home in eloquent fashion. In Table 15.1 we compare Soviet output, input, and factor productivity growth with that of the U.S. for the period 1961–1988. This evidence shows that from 1961 to 1970, Soviet output growth exceeded or equaled that of the United States, although for this decade, Soviet productivity growth was below that of the United States. The relatively high Soviet output growth of the 1960s was a product of its exceptional input growth (Soviet input growth was more than double that of the United States). Soviet output growth still exceeded U.S. growth in the early 1970s (the onset of the West's energy crisis), but from the mid-1970's on, Soviet output growth has fallen short of that of the United States. Soviet input growth remained slightly above that of the United States, but the margin of superiority has narrowed. Moreover, there is a suspicion that official statistics overstate Soviet economic growth during this period as noted below. Most alarmingly, Soviet factor productivity growth has

Table 15.1   OUTPUT, INPUT, AND PRODUCTIVITY GROWTH, USSR –U.S. 1961–1988

	USSR			United States		
Period	Growth of output	Growth of factor productivity	Growth of inputs	Growth of output	Growth of factor productivity	Growth of inputs
1961–1965	4.8	0.3	4.5	4.8	2.8	2.0
1966–1970	5.0	0.8	4.2	2.8	0.9	1.7
1971–1975	3.1	−1.2	4.3	2.3	0.6	1.7
1976–1980	2.2	−1.3	3.6	3.3	0.3	3.0
1981–1985	1.8	−1.1	3.0	3.0	0.9	2.1
1986–1988	2.0	−0.3	2.5	3.2	1.6	1.6

Sources: Directorate of Intelligence, *Handbook of Economic Statistics, 1988* (Washington, D.C.: CPAS 88–10001, September 1988), p. 63; "Reproducible Tangible Wealth in the United States," *Survey of Current Business,* vol. 68, no. 8 (August 1988), 36; and *Economic Report of the President* (Washington, D.C.: U.S. Government Printing Office January 1989), p. 360. Figures for 1988 are preliminary.

been negative since the early 1970s, while U.S. productivity growth rates have risen. These comparisons are particularly troublesome for the Soviet case when one considers that the Soviet Union is substantially less developed than the United States, suggesting that slower growth rates accompanying maturity must be unacceptable to the Soviet Union at this time. Moreover, as we know, the 1970s was a decade during which much domestic concern in the United States focused upon U.S. productivity problems.

The comparison of USSR–U.S. growth performance provides ample evidence of stagnation of the Soviet economy and explains why Gorbachev has been required to take the question of economic reform so seriously. Gorbachev assumed power in the midst of a substantial economic expansion of the Western economic powers, an expansion that began in the early 1980s. The burgeoning economic performance of the West obviously played a role in Gorbachev's negative assessment of Soviet economic performance of the recent past. The 1970s was a decade of energy shocks, stagflation, and uncertainty for the capitalist West. The Soviet leadership, confronted with its own economic problems in the 1970s, could at least take some comfort from the West's own economic problems. The West's uninterrupted business expansion of the 1980s, however, intensified the relative magnitude of the Soviet Union's economic problems. The superior economic performance of Western capitalism appeared to be forcing Gorbachev's hand.

GORBACHEV'S REFORM THEMES

With the ascendancy of a vigorous leader, young enough to be untainted by a Stalinist past, the Soviet Union was presented with a rare opportunity to break with the "administrative-command system" — to pursue meaningful economic reform that would force the economy out of its "stagnation" mode.[1]

The major themes of Gorbachev's reform policies were developed in the first four years of his regime (1985–1989).[2] At the Twenty-Seventh Party Conference in February 1986, he explicitly called for "radical reform" (*radikal'naia reforma*). Gorbachev's call served notice of his conviction that Soviet economic problems were not to be solved by the minor tinkering characteristic of earlier reform. However, it should be emphasized that prior to 1987, although there were a variety of reform decrees, there was no general reform package. Many in this early period would question whether Gorbachev had a grand vision that could be translated into legislation.

The year 1987 would prove important for the reform process. In February, the draft law on the state enterprise (assocation) was published in *Pravda*, spelling out many of the key features of Gorbachev's reform program. The critical watershed, however, was the June 1987 Plenum of the Central Committee of the Communist Party. This plenum approved the general decrees (Osnovnye Polozheniia) that outlined the general principles of Gorbachev's economic, political, and social programs. Although the publication of these decrees has generally been regarded as presenting a reasonably comprehensive reform program, it would be wrong to treat these decrees as complete.

As late as the summer of 1989, Gorbachev's reform proposals were far from complete, even as legislation. Draft laws on foreign trade zones were still to be drafted, and major decisions concerning property relations in agriculture remained to be resolved.[3] Little progress had been made on issues of price reform. Moreover, new laws defining the role of ministries remain to be written. Although the pace of developing economic reform proposals appears brisk by the standards of the past, it must be noted that Gorbachev has not moved at breakneck speed with either inception or implementation. He has allowed for a span of at least six years in order to get his reform proposals in place. In fact, there is serious concern that Gorbachev will not be able to meet his original deadline for reform implementation — January 1991.[4]

The spirit of Gorbachev's reform program is captured by three slogans that, remarkably, have entered the vocabulary of most languages: *perestroika*, *glasnost*, and *demokratizatsiia*.

Perestroika means a restructuring of the Soviet economic system to reverse declining output and productivity trends and to raise its technological level. Thus, under the concept of perestroika are subsumed the economic aspects of reform. *Glasnost*, on the other hand, is a broader concept and refers to the increased openness of Soviet society, for example, through the Soviet press, in literature, and in daily life. *Demokratizatsiia* refers to the increased democratization of Soviet society. For example, there have been fundamental and important changes in the Soviet political process, including an opening of the electoral process.

The Gorbachev reform leadership hopes that the combination of perestroika, glasnost, and demokratizatsiia will result in an acceleration (*uskorenie*) of economic performance that will reverse the long-term decline of growth/production and especially the period of stagnation.

Gorbachev's three reform slogans make it evident why he refers to his reform program as "radical" reform. Unlike earlier attempts at economic restructuring, current economic reform has been coupled with wide-ranging social and political reforms. In effect, Gorbachev has concluded that narrow economic reform will fail unless it is accompanied by fundamental changes in Soviet political and social institutions.

Although this chapter focuses primarily on Gorbachev's economic program, it is vital to understand why the new Soviet leadership has linked economic reform with political and social reforms. A number of explanations can be offered.

First, Gorbachev has concluded that "human factors" contributed significantly to the stagnation of the Brezhnev years. Any reform effort that fails to deal with human motivational factors, therefore, stands little chance of success.[5] If people are poorly motivated, if they are alienated by the social and political system they encounter daily, they are unlikely to contribute to the Soviet restructuring effort. If workers have an increasing say in enterprise affairs and even in local and national affairs, they are less likely to be alienated from the Soviet system.

Second, if ordinary Soviet citizens are to support perestroika policies, they must have a better understanding of the benefits and costs of economic reform. Economic restructuring will have both costs and benefits, and greater openness and candor will be required to build the necessary public support for reform policies. Increased candor about the deficiencies of the policies of the past can also serve to weaken political opponents — in the upper reaches of the party or in the entrenched bureaucracy. Open criticism of the failures of past leaders associated with the failed administrative-command system that Gorbachev is attempting to change — Stalin and Brezhnev, for example — strengthen Gorbachev's own position. Soviet critiques of the official growth statistics of the 1970s illustrate how glasnost can be used to strengthen Gorbachev relative to opponents associated with the earlier regime.[6] Glasnost- inspired critics have embarked on a broad-based reevaluation of Soviet economic performance, with some critics (Abel Aganbegian and Grigory Khanin and Vasily Seliunin) concluding that past Soviet growth was significantly lower than that claimed by official statistics.

Third, the democratization of Soviet life, by giving ordinary citizens a say, should make them more willing to bear the costs of restructuring. Democratization also offers the opportunity to give the public a chance to discredit politicians and bureaucrats associated with the politics of the past. Democratization at the workplace may help to overcome the morale problems associated with human factors. Soviet citizens have long been promised material betterment if they will work hard to build socialism. Although living standards have clearly improved, effort in the contemporary Soviet economy apparently carries insufficient reward to be considered seriously.

Fourth, democratization and openness will enhance Gorbachev's standing in the world community. Key features of perestroika, such as overcoming technological backwardness, require the active support and participation of the industrialized capitalist nations. Having the Soviet Union regarded as a regular member of the world community with social and political policies that more closely resemble those of a Western democracy would definitely contribute to perestroika's success.

Although many features of the perestroika program represent ideas that have been tried before (without great success), even the skeptics grant the seriousness of Gorbachev's intent. In fact, the seriousness of the Soviet Union's economic position confirms that the Soviet leadership has little choice but to be serious about this reform effort. The most striking indicator of the seriousness of intent is the fact that truly fundamental changes were made in the social and political sphere prior to the introduction of real economic reform. In effect, the political and social change that took place between 1985 and 1989 might be regarded as Gorbachev's declaration of intent with regard to economic reform.

Gorbachev may be interpreted as offering Soviet citizens a "New Deal" to replace the "Little Deal" they had under Brezhnev.[7] Gorbachev's New Deal offers Soviet citizens openness, democratization, and an improving standard of living in return for more responsibility and risk-taking on the part of ordinary citizens.

LESSONS FROM EARLIER REFORMS

Chapter 14 examined the reform experiments of the 1960s and 1970s. Reform discussion in the Soviet Union literally began with the Liberman discussions of the early 1960s; a series of experiments followed (the light-industry experiment, the Shchekino experiment); modest official reforms were put in place (in 1965 and 1979) and subsequently rejected. The earlier reform experience is important to understanding perestroika because many reform ideas from this earlier period have been revived by Gorbachev. Moreover, the system's rejection of earlier reforms reveals how the economic system has reacted to change in the past and the obstacles that the current reform is likely to encounter.

Recurring Themes from Earlier Reforms

We noted in Chapter 14 the recurring themes of earlier Soviet Reforms. An idea would find its way from the theoretical literature into practice, be abandoned, and then be resurrected in a subsequent reform. The fact that these themes appear to have a life of their own suggests that they may eventually be put into real practice. What are the recurring themes?

First, there is the idea that Soviet enterprises should have more autonomy. There should be less "petty tutelage" (opeka) on the part of ministries and state committees; enterprises should have increased freedom to make their own output and input decisions. Ministries and planning bodies should concern themselves more with broad policy matters (such as investment and technology) and less with the details of enterprise operations.

A second recurring theme is that enterprises should be held responsible for their final results. The enterprise that cannot make a profit should not count on an automatic bailout by higher authorities. Not only should enterprises cover their costs; they should also create reserves for investment finance and for incentive bonuses.

A third recurring theme — often termed "direct links" — is the notion that enterprises should be tied more closely to their customers. An enterprise that produces for the consumer should know what that customer wants. An enterprise that produces materials for other enterprises should deal directly with its customers to learn what they want and when they want it. Enterprises that produce shoddy, low-quality materials that are of little use to their customers should receive no credit for this production. Tying enterprises to their customers implies a reduction in tutelage from above. If decisions are made by voluntary contracts among the parties that are directly involved, the role of bureaucratic intermediaries must diminish.

The reader will quickly recognize that these areas of concern, along with pervasive problems of economic reform such as price setting, have been dominant in the Soviet version of socialism.

Obstacles to Past Reforms

The system's rejection of past reforms reveals the obstacles that a successful Gorbachev must surmount. The government reforms of 1965 and 1979 were rejected by the economic system in a number of ways, both direct and subtle. In each case, one encounters initial public enthusiasm for reform from virtually all official circles; yet it has proven difficult to convert this professed enthusiasm into action. The natural forces that appear to cause bureaucratic resistance are as follows.[8]

First, there are natural conflicts between enterprise decision makers and their ministerial superiors. When enterprise managers began exercising their new authority to disburse incentive funds, ministry superiors found it difficult not to second guess their actions. Ministry officials concluded that enterprise managers were rewarding managerial staff too well and were neglecting worker bonuses. Accordingly, new rules were introduced to limit managerial autonomy. In a bureaucratic economy that has grown accustomed to dictating enterprise actions, it has proven difficult for superior organs to abide by local decisions that the superiors feel are contrary to larger social interests.

Second, previous reforms have not been able to shift the focus of planning from the routine to larger policy matters such as investment and technology. Moreover, previous reforms have not succeeded in breaking the stranglehold of the ratchet effect. Enterprise managers have not been convinced that they can reveal their true capacity through the much-heralded counterplans without being handed even more difficult tasks in subsequent years. The system's inability to move away from planning detail and the presence of the ratchet are not simply symptoms of a bureaucratic hunger for power. As long as ministries must fulfill concrete production targets and are assigned material input limits, ministries themselves feel obligated to deal with routine matters. Moreover, Soviet planners have never been able to concoct an operational concept of long-term planning (which must somehow be coordinated with the annual state budget).[9] Enterprise distrust of avowals that good enterprise performance will not result in tauter future targets appears rational. In an information-poor economic system, it is difficult for planners not to incorporate such valuable information in their future plans.[10]

Third, the Soviet system has proven resistant to reductions in the number of planned indicators. In fact, there appears to be a game of musical chairs among planned indicators. One indicator will be eliminated to be replaced by another, only to reappear several years later. Fyodor Kushnirsky has provided a logical explanation as to why it is so difficult to limit centrally set targets.[11] In the course of previous Soviet reforms, the removal of one indicator allows enterprises to engage in opportunistic behavior. If, for example, labor productivity targets are eliminated, enterprises begin to make decisions that aid them in other areas of enterprise operations but lower labor productivity or, at best, pay little attention to productivity indicators. Hence, planners feel compelled to deal with the problem by reintroducing labor productivity targets. If quality targets are not handed down from above, enterprises will neglect quality for quantity, and their superiors deal with the problem by introducing quality control targets. The persistence of gross output targets (val) can be attributed in part to the fact that ministries have been judged on the basis of gross outputs; hence they continue to demand specific gross outputs from their enterprises. Soviet authorities introduce planned indicators as a form of crisis management: Each new crisis requires a new set of indicators to deal with the crisis.

Fourth is the question of the degree of enthusiasm for reform, even among those who appear to benefit from it. Enterprise managers must learn a new set of rules, establish new supply relationships, and incur new risks. Experience with previous reforms suggests that enterprise managers, even of profitable firms, have resisted reform.[12]

Fifth, the pattern of past Soviet reform has been one of phased or piecemeal reform. A reform typically begins with limited-scale experiments; if the experiment is successful, the reform is broadened to other enterprises and branches. Then a general reform is announced, calling for a phasing in of various sectors over time and for the implementation of the various measures over a period of time. The 1965 reform called for a series of reform measures to be followed by a general price reform. Typically, the phasing-in stage of reform has been chaotic, with some branches operating under the old system and others operating under the new system. The chaos has allowed reform opponents the chance to contravene the reform by introducing emergency measures. Unfortunately, such a pattern seems to be typical of socialist economic reform efforts.

Gorbachev's Lessons from the History of Reform

Gorbachev and his reform advisors must have learned from the earlier rejections of economic reforms both at home and in other centrally planned economies. The failure of past reforms would have taught him that bureaucratic opposition represents a serious obstacle to reform. Hence, it is vital to weaken the power of the entrenched bureaucracy (especially of the ministries), which can be accomplished by putting reliable reform-minded specialists in high bureaucratic positions and by mobilizing public opinion against bureaucratic opposition through glasnost and democratization. Second, past experience would cause Gorbachev to be wary of piecemeal reforms— Soviet economic problems are not to be solved by the discovery of a magic new success indicator. Third, grass-roots support of reform at the enterprise level may not be as strong as would be expected. Enterprise managers dislike certain features of the administrative-command system, but they have learned to live comfortably with its other aspects. Fourth, quite apart from political will and the issue of general support, Socialist economic reform raises critical and difficult economic issues, the resolution of which is exceedingly complex.

THE BLUEPRINT OF PERESTROIKA

Many of Gorbachev's perestroika policies will be familiar to the reader; they were proposed in earlier reforms, and they were largely rejected in the course of past reform efforts. The initial reaction, therefore, of many Western specialists to perestroika was one of skepticism. Much of what Gorbachev was proposing had been tried before. But the combined package of political, social, and economic reforms provides convincing evidence of the seriousness of intent of the reform leadership. Seriousness of intent does not, however, guarantee a successful economic reform. We turn to an examination of the main features of perestroika.

Reduction in Enterprise Tutelage

As in the 1965 reform, perestroika calls for a reduction in the amount of intervention by ministry and planning officials in the routine affairs of enterprises. Enterprises are to have increased freedom to choose their own outputs and inputs.[13] Ministry and planning officials are to concern themselves with longer-term policy matters such as investment and technology planning. Enterprises are to be given increased freedom to enter into supply and delivery contracts with other enterprises without requiring permission or approval from enterprise superiors. At least initially, enterprises will have to devote a portion of their capacity to producing obligatory state orders (*goszakazy*), for which they receive materials through the centralized supply network, but the share of state orders should decline over time.

The ministries and planning bodies are to influence enterprise actions not through directives (other than state orders) but through the indirect instruments of rules, norms, and laws. Directives are to be severely limited, and superior organs are to influence enterprise operations indirectly through the "rules of the game" they create. Moreover, local party organs (*obkom, gorkom*, etc.) are to cease their tutelage of enterprises operating in their region. They can no longer redistribute materials among local enterprises; they can no longer require enterprises to perform civic tasks as before.

Insofar as "direct links" among enterprises will replace much of the traditional administrative supply system, increased attention will be paid to contract enforcement. Central authorities will determine whether enterprises have indeed fulfilled their supply plan (*plan postavok*) as expressed by the terms of product assortment and timeliness of delivery. In fact, perestroika proposes to elevate the fulfillment of the supply plan to one of the most important indicators of enterprise performance. Legal sanctions for contract violations are to become more severe.

A new state committee, Gospriemka, will be given the authority to reject low-quality output, thereby forcing enterprises to concentrate on higher-quality production. Notably, Gospriemka will be independent of enterprises, both hierarchically and financially. Therefore Gospriemka workers can act as true independent auditors.

These sorts of changes, if implemented, will fundamentally alter the nature of Soviet resource allocation arrangements. At the same time, it will be difficult to follow implementation closely. There is, for example, a fine line between traditional plan targets and state orders. Will targets really disappear, or will they simply exist under a different name?

Enterprise Accountability

Perestroika makes enterprises responsible for final results. Each enterprise must be self-financing over the long run. It must meet its wage payments and other obligations from its revenues. The enterprise must meet its investment financing needs out of retained earnings or bank borrowing and must generate its own bonus funds out of profits.

In the words of perestroika, Soviet enterprises are to be placed on a system of full economic accounting (*pol'ny khozraschet*). Full economic accounting means, quite simply, that unprofitable enterprises must eventually go out of business either through a bankruptcy proceeding or by another enterprise taking over its assets. Perestroika proposes to put an end to the automatic subsidies arranged by the ministries by redistributing profits within the ministry. If implemented to the letter of the law, it would spell the end of guaranteed job rights in that unprofitable enterprises would no longer be able to guarantee the jobs of their employees. Bear in mind, however, that the rhetoric of enterprise accountability (*khozraschet*) has long existed in the Soviet system. Whether it will come to have significant meaning in the new reform package remains to be seen.

Whereas enterprise managers are to be freed from excessive intervention from above, perestroika puts in place a new level of managerial responsibility. Soviet enterprises are to operate on a self-management basis (*samoupravlenie*) in which enterprise management must be periodically reelected and management must work with a workers' council in determining enterprise policy.

The increase in enterprise responsibility is supposed to ensure that enterprises act in an economically rational manner. Enterprises that produce shoddy products for which there are no customers will not be able to cover their costs. Enterprises that overdemand materials or hoard labor will have excessive costs that will eventually drive them out of business. If enterprise management performs poorly, workers can elect new management. The emphasis on full economic accounting will replace at long last the "soft budget constraint" that Soviet enterprises have traditionally faced with a "hard budget constraint."

Relative prices will guide enterprise activities along with the indirect "rules of the game" devised by planners.

Enterprise Rewards

Enterprise managers and workers will bear new risks (bankruptcy, job loss), but they will benefit from good enterprise performance. Managers and workers will have strong financial incentives. Enterprises must surrender to the state a portion of their profits in the form of a uniform tax rate.[14] The after-tax portion of enterprise profits will be available for reinvestment or for worker or managerial bonuses. On the other hand, an enterprise that fails to earn a profit will lack funds for investment (and presumably have a limited borrowing potential) and no funds for worker or managerial bonuses.

Cooperatives, Private Activity, and Property Rights in Agriculture

Perestroika calls for an enhanced role for private and cooperative economic activity. The law on private economic activity, passed in November 1986 (which went into effect in May 1987) allows individuals to engage in a wide range of private economic activities that had previously been (at least officially) illegal.[15] Examples of newly legalized private activities are private taxicabs, dry cleaning, restaurants, and repair activities. The main restriction on private activity is that it must be carried out by able-bodied individuals on a part-time basis (in addition to a main job in the state sector) or by students, housewives, or pensioners who are permitted to work full time. Individuals who work in private activity must have a license from local government and must pay a license fee. Originally, the law on private economic activity called for a discriminatory income tax on private earnings, but apparently this proposal has been abandoned.

Regulations on cooperative economic activity, issued in the fall of 1986 and early 1987, authorized state employees in their spare time, housewives, students, and pensioners to form cooperatives for the production of consumer goods and services. Cooperatives, such as cooperative restaurants or auto repair services, are licensed by local authorities. Their net income goes first to payments for a state income tax, and the residual is available for distribution by cooperative members in the form of profit sharing.[16] Cooperatives are free to contract for services and materials and to set their own prices. The major restriction on cooperatives is that they cannot be a full-time activity of able-bodied adults.

In effect, Gorbachev's encouragement of private and cooperative activity represents a recognition that immediate consumer benefits can be obtained from the encouragement of private initiative. Moreover, it is a recognition that private economic activities emerge spontaneously in a setting of shortage and low-quality consumer goods. The legalization of private activity is simply a de facto recognition of the inevitability of such activities and that important consumer benefits can be obtained if their efforts are productively harnessed. However, it remains to be seen whether Soviet citizens will accept increases in income inequality that will inevitably result from successful and expanded private activity.

Property rights in agriculture remain one of the most sensitive issues in the reform process. Will property rights be expanded beyond the small-scale private plots in Soviet agriculture? Will collective agriculture be abandoned? Gorbachev's agricultural policy remains to be fully elaborated, but its preliminary outlines appear to be as follows: First, collective and state agriculture are to be retained. Although more radical reformers have called for a return to the private-property arrangements of NEP, party plenums in 1989 concluded that collective agriculture should be retained, largely for the purpose of guaranteeing state orders of major agricultural products. Second, a form of quasi private property is to be created through a system of long-term leases (perhaps as long as 50 years) of state land to family units. How this leasing arrangement will work remains to be elaborated, but it is likely that the amount of leased land will be strictly limited so as not to deprive collective lands of farm labor.

The Opening of the Soviet Economy

Perestroika calls for a significant opening of the Soviet economy to the outside world. Previous chapters taught that Soviet foreign trade has been handled by a foreign trade monopoly that intermediated between the domestic and foreign firm and handled the necessary financing arrangements. Perestroika proposes to relax the foreign trade monopoly by allowing ministries and enterprises to deal directly with foreign customers. Soviet enterprises are supposed to be free to negotiate deals directly with foreign firms and will be free to expend from their own supplies of hard currencies. Foreign Trade Organizations (FTOs) are to be attached to productive ministries, whose enterprises can strike deals directly with foreign firms. Although organizational roles are as yet unclear, the powers of the Ministry of Foreign Trade would seem to be significantly reduced under these new arrangements. Moreover, in mid-1986, the State Commission for Foreign Economic Relations was created. This body will presumably serve to coordinate foreign trade decisions under new, more decentralized arrangements.

In 1986, a decree was passed that permitted Soviet export firms to retain a significant portion of their hard-currency earnings for their own use—as an incentive fund to stimulate hard-currency exports. In 1987, 200 million rubles of soviet foreign trade turnover were accounted for by direct links between foreign and Soviet firms. Direct foreign links were strongest for Soviet firms located in the Baltic republics, Belorussia, and the Far North.[17]

Beyond changes in the organizational arrangements of the Soviet foreign trade apparatus, there have been significant developments with regard to joint ventures. Since 1987, foreign firms have been encouraged to establish joint ventures in the Soviet Union. The legislation permitting these new arrangements was initially quite restrictive with regard to important issues such as foreign equity, repatriation of profits, and so on. Recently, however, earlier restrictions have been relaxed, for example, permitting majority foreign ownership.

As we have noted earlier in our discussion of Soviet foreign trade, Soviet leaders seem to have specific objectives in mind, ranging from help with the development of agricultural processing and distribution equipment to more general areas such as the importation of technology and managerial expertise. It is important to realize that this new joint venture legislation represents a major change of Soviet foreign trade policy and practice. At the same time, there are a host of reasons, ranging from the difficulties of profit repatriation to problems of access to domestic resources, all of which make Westerners very skeptical about deriving significant benefits from joint ventures.

At the discussion stage are more radical changes in the conduct of foreign trade. Gorbachev's reform advisors have recommended that the USSR join the various international organizations that manage the rules of international trade and its financing (such as GATT, the World Bank, or the International Monetary Fund).[18] Gorbachev's advisors talk of the Soviet Union having a convertible ruble within the next ten years.[19] Moreover, legislation is purportedly being prepared to create free trade zones in the Soviet Union in which Western firms can operate with only limited restrictions. Indeed, there has been discussion of a devaluation of the ruble in 1990 in part to provide joint ventures more favorable access to domestic resources and materials. There has also been discussion of currency auctions, where presumably the State would auction hard currencies for rubles, permitting Soviet firms access to foreign currencies.

The changes in the Soviet foreign trade sector are important and potentially far-reaching. In many respects, they represent a rationality long advocated by observers of the socialist reform process. At the same time, whether it is doing business in the Soviet Union or simply attempting to expand the volume and change the direction of foreign trade, it is extremely difficult to open up an economy so long closed to the forces of world trade.

Technology Policy

Gorbachev's top industrial policy is industrial modernization—to raise the technological level of Soviet industry to that of the United States and Western Europe by the end of the 1990s.[20] Success in the technology area is clearly crucial to the overall success of the reform program. Modernization requires the extensive retooling of production facilities and marked improvement in specialized machine tool production. The managerial resistance to new technology (discussed in earlier chapters) must be overcome. The perennial problems of construction (low quality, interminable delays) must be solved. Enterprises must be encouraged to retire capital on a more rational basis. Systems must be created to reward product quality, and scientific and technical personnel must be rewarded in more innovative ways for successful R&D work. In a nutshell, the Gorbachev approach focuses on improving the quality (technological level) of the capital stock rather than further additions to capital.

Gorbachev's response to the technology gap has been twofold: First, Gorbachev has encouraged an opening of the Soviet economy to foreign technology through joint ventures and other efforts to attract Western capital and technology. Second, Gorbachev's technology policies have been directed toward improving the technological level of Soviet industry and making capital resources go further. Generally speaking, Gorbachev's technology policies have been conservative compared to other aspects of his reform program. Specifically, Gorbachev has chosen to adopt a Japan-like industrial policy in which specific sectors—plastics, robotics, and precision machine tools—are to be singled out for emphasis. In addition, perestroika manipulates the enterprise reward formula to encourage technological progress by placing greater emphasis on material economies, accelerated retirement of equipment, and the meeting of specific assortment targets. Gorbachev has also resorted to outmoded organizational solutions, such as the creation of superorganizations that centralize R&D work from basic research to its implementation. Gorbachev seeks to improve the utilization of scarce investment resources by emphasizing renovation over new plant construction and by making the authorization of new construction more difficult. In light of our earlier discussion of Soviet capital productivity, this aspect of the Soviet reform program must be viewed as fundamental to the long-term success of that program.

Price Reform

It is obvious to all observers that, if Soviet industrial enterprises and other local organizations are to make rational decisions on the basis of their newfound freedoms, a system of relative prices that reflect relative scarcities will be essential. As noted in Chapter 14, the price reforms of the past have been of an extremely conservative and routine nature. The goal of previous price reforms has been to set wholesale prices roughly equal to the average branch costs of production with relatively little attention paid to demand conditions. Unfortunately, a major price reform is critical, and yet it is precisely in the area of price reform that past reform efforts have failed. Moreover, even in those cases where reform would be considered moderately successful, for example, Hungary, price reform has proven to be a major difficulty in the overall reform process.

The perestroika program, like previous reforms, calls for a significant reform of wholesale and retail prices, but under a timetable that will stretch into the early 1990s. The intent is to create an industrial wholesale price system in which a relatively few nationally important commodities have centrally set prices. The bulk of wholesale prices will be formed by negotiated contracts between the buyer and seller according to price-setting rules and limits set by pricing authorities. A number of wholesale prices (presumably those with the lowest national importance) will be set freely according to contracts or market conditions independently of existing pricing rules.[21]

Retail prices will also be reformed. Because a large number of basic commodities are subsidized—for example, agricultural products (to cover the gap between the agricultural wholesale price based on farm cost and the low subsidized retail price)—a major goal of retail price reform will be the elimination of price subsidies.

It is noteworthy that the most substantial delays in the implementation of perestroika have occurred in the area of price reform. These delays have a number of explanations: First of all, it is recognized that price reform is a very complex matter. In an economy in which a number of key materials markets are dominated by one or two producers, what is to prevent monopoly prices from being charged? What type of price-setting rules should be established? Should the Soviet government introduce antitrust laws before allowing price-setting autonomy? All these matters require considerable thought and preparation. Second, it is unclear whether Soviet authorities are indeed prepared to turn price formation over to the impersonal forces of the market. Soviet reformers continue to talk of price reform in terms of cost-plus formulas instead of market clearing. Third, the political costs of retail price reform will be high. There are serious equity considerations. Soviet consumers, accustomed to a diet of heavy subsidies, will resist substantial increases in the prices of staples. It is unclear whether Gorbachev is prepared to risk a decline in his personal popularity in the early years of a difficult reform process.

In the early years of the Gorbachev era, many argued that there was no complete reform package. As we enter the 1990s, the reform plate is certainly full and carries with it the major changes encompassed by glasnost. But, while 1986 was a good year in terms of economic growth, performance was much more modest. Moreover, the Soviet consumer awaits a bigger share of the pie. Will perestroika fail? Where do we stand in the 1990s?

WILL PERESTROIKA FAIL?

Gorbachev has warned that the benefits of perestroika will not be felt until well into the 1990s. The full complement of reform programs is not scheduled to be in place until the early 1990s. The world press finds it difficult to distinguish concrete perestroika actions (such as the new enterprise law) from speculations on actions that may or may not be approved (such as ruble convertibility). Hence it is premature to judge perestroika's results. What is clear is that Soviet growth performance has not rebounded during the process of shifting to the new economic system. Factor productivity growth remains negative, and GNP growth remains a low 2 percent per annum. The gains offered by perestroika remain to be enjoyed in the future.

The road to a successful restructuring of the Soviet economy is steep with unknown detours and curves. Reforms have failed in the past, and the probabilities that perestroika itself will fail are not low. Although we do not have a simple barometer with which to judge the ongoing effectiveness of perestroika, it is useful to enumerate some of the most important factors (both positive and negative) associated with the implementation of perestroika.

Negative Factors

Pessimists can point to a whole range of reasons why perestroika will ultimately fail. As we have emphasized, the experience of the past shows that the Soviet planned system is very adept at rejecting reform. In fact, a number of familiar rejection signs can already be seen.

Prices   Soviet reformers appear unable and unwilling to deal decisively with the issue of retail and wholesale price reform — to take the giant step of turning price formation over to the impersonal forces of the market, indeed, a market that does not really exist. There are a number of economic and political reasons for delaying this step. The public outcry against retail price reform would be deafening. Allowing impersonal market price formation in a sellers' market (*diktat potavshchika*) could lead to monopoly prices that do not reflect relative scarcities. Yet without relative prices that provide a reasonable approximation of relative scarcities, it makes little sense to decentralize economic decision making. The pricing problem illustrates the circularity of reform: Scarcity prices are required to decentralize decision making, but scarcity prices cannot be known until the economy is decentralized. Must price reform and decentralization be implemented simultaneously?

Another serious question is the timing of retail price reform. As noted above, Soviet reform authorities have determined to avoid biting the bullet of retail price increases for several years. Thus, the creation of a "rational" retail price system has had to be postponed. In the meantime, the price gap between state and private (or cooperative) prices will grow, and there will be a public outcry against the high prices charged by the private sector.[22] One possible outcome is for the state to respond with a suppression of the private sector, either outright or in the form of price controls. A similar reaction occurred during NEP: When free-market prices diverged significantly from state prices, the stage was set for suppression of private markets.

Moreover, the mere anticipation of price reform can cause problems. Reports indicate that consumer goods shortages intensified in 1989 due to hoarding and panic buying. This suggests that Soviet citizens anticipate that retail prices will be raised in the near future and are therefore disposing of their hoard of savings. The increase in monetary velocity has therefore intensified consumer-market disequilibrium at the very time when it should be disappearing. Moreover, one might suggest that consumer expectations in the Soviet setting will be different from those found in a market economy.

Efficient rule making   Deciding the optimal level of bureaucratic intervention in the new economic system will prove very difficult. If bureaucrats are to set the "rules of the game" instead of issuing directives, how are they to distinguish efficient from inefficient rules? In effect, Soviet policymakers must devise an entirely new set of "rules of the game" to replace a significant portion of the administrative allocation system. Rule makers must devise a new tax system, antitrust policy, regulatory policy, and so on within five years' time. In market economies, the economic rules of the game (common law, antitrust legislation and court interpretations thereof, government policy toward natural monopolies) evolved over centuries. Many of these rules have withstood the test of time; nevertheless, inefficient rules continue to plague private decision making in the West. It remains to be seen how well Soviet rule makers can perform this difficult task.[23]

Bureaucratic resistance   Bureaucratic resistance served to scuttle past Soviet economic reforms. The attention Gorbachev has devoted to preventing perestroika from suffering the same fate demonstrates his deep fear of such resistance. Bureaucratic resistance is often described, in both the Western and Soviet literatures, as motivated solely by a fear of loss of authority and prestige. Obviously, such fears represent important motivating factors. Bureaucrats resist reform for a number of more rational reasons.[24] Ministerial personnel resist decentralization as long as they continue to be held responsible for enterprise results under the traditional rules of the game. Ministers, as long as they must meet physical output goals, will be reluctant to end their tutelage of enterprises whose combined results determine ministerial success. The ministry applies its levers—profit redistribution, reshuffling of supply limits—to ensure that it meets its own targets, not because it necessarily enjoys doing so.

The fact that the responsibilities of the ministry remain to be defined suggests that Soviet reformers are having a difficult time determining the appropriate role of the ministry. The same comments apply to local party officials. As long as they continue to be held responsible for the economic results of their region, they will be tempted to use the levers that they have traditionally applied to local enterprises.

Surviving the transition   The transition from the traditional command system to the mixed perestroika system will likely be a time of confusion and chaos. Planners and ministry officials have been taught to think in terms of administratively determined balances, not in terms of balances that emerge from negotiated exchanges at market-clearing prices. In an environment of relatively free exchange, enterprises may continue initially to overdemand resources out of habits formed during the soft-constraint period, and excess demand will likely characterize many producer goods markets. The temptation to intervene to make administrative corrections to such imbalances will be strong. It will also be difficult to differentiate between a necessary intervention to correct true chaos and a situation in which temporary imbalances correct themselves through market-clearing processes. Intervention may take a variety of forms, though all will most likely serve to limit the implementation of perestroika. Where new arrangements do not initially work well, it is tempting and familiar to revert to previous practices.

Prior to the creation of a rational price system, decentralization will lead to decisions that are obviously irrational. A well-managed enterprise may be forced to close simply because it has had bad luck in drawing irrationally high input prices and irrationally low selling prices. Lacking faith in the price system, planners are placed in a position of having to decide what decentralized decisions are so patently wrong that they should be overturned.

Meshing private and state markets   Perestroika calls for a delicate mix of private and planned decision making. State enterprises are to produce state orders using the traditional administrative supply system while simultaneously producing on a decentralized basis according to contracts. This requires a blending and coordination of two types of supply networks. Moreover, state and private or cooperative firms will find themselves in competition, both for resources and for customers. Cooperative firms will be free to charge higher prices and will be more flexible in providing higher quality products. The higher profits of private and cooperative enterprises will tend to lure resources, particularly labor resources, out of the state sector. Even though regulations—such as restrictions on full-time work in private or cooperative enterprises—are present to limit this flow, individuals will succeed in circumventing such restrictions.[25] Whether Soviet authorities will tolerate the loss of resources to private or cooperative ventures remains to be seen.

Basically, Gorbachev's intent appears to be close to Lenin's conception of a commanding heights economy—an economy in which the commanding heights of industry remain under strict state control and supervision, while the routine affairs of the economy (especially in light industry) are conducted on a decentralized basis. The system of state orders ensures that the economy will continue to produce the key industrial and agricultural materials demanded by the state. In effect, Gorbachev is aiming for a mixed system that bears some resemblance to the NEP economy of the 1920s. The inability of NEP to find the optimal coexistence of market and plan, therefore, should be recalled. Whether Soviet officialdom will be able to tolerate a rather free competition for resources between the state and private sectors represents a key question for the implementation of perestroika.

Positive Features

The most positive force in favor of the eventual success of perestroika is the seriousness of intent of the Soviet leadership. It has shown its resolve by embarking on an ambitious program of political, social, and economic reform. In fact, some experts would argue that this reform is irreversible—the Soviet Union no longer has the option of returning to the discredited administrative-command system. If this is the case, necessity will be the mother of invention. When one aspect of perestroika fails, the Soviets must find a new solution rather than reverting to the old system.

There is some evidence that perestroika is more than a routine economic reform. Industrial ministries have experienced significant staff cuts, some equivalent to one-half of the ministry's staffing.[26] Press reports contain accounts of enterprises that have declared their independence of ministries and that have demanded compensation for the ministry's failure to live up to the rules of the new enterprise law.

In addition to the seriousness of intent accompanying perestroika, this reform attacks many of the major economic problems facing the Soviet economy, and it does so with a degree of rationality. Few would argue against the desirability of changing the conduct of foreign trade or the rules of enterprise guidance. The problem is the design and implementation of reform, necessarily a process of long duration taking place against the pressure of unmet consumer demand.

Furthermore, it is not necessary that Gorbachev demonstrate major achievements in all facets of the reform process. Although the sequencing of reform implementation is itself a complex issue, Gorbachev could undoubtedly sustain domestic strength if he is able to demonstrate a sufficient degree of achievement in important areas, for example, in the production and distribution of consumer goods.

Finally, the domestic impact of the international dimensions of Soviet domestic reform is difficult to judge. One could argue that Gorbachev buys a measure of domestic support for his aggressive posture on the world stage. To what extent the average Soviet citizen is willing to substitute pride for meat is not clear, however.

Where is perestroika as we enter the 1990s? If we examine the trends of the mid- and late 1980s, some patterns emerge. The initial years of the Gorbachev reform process have resulted in a continuation of modest Soviet economic performance. Although the economy has been troubled by factors beyond the control of Soviet leaders, for example, the serious earthquake in Armenia, most of the performance difficulties relate to familiar causes, including fluctuations in the agricultural sector. The growth of gross national product, apart from a good year in 1986, has remained at between 1 and 2 percent annually.

Beyond the issue of economic performance *per se*, Gorbachev has found it difficult to implement many of his programs. There has been retrenchment on the alcohol campaign, and the modernization of the capital stock, while proceeding, does so at a very slow pace. The lack of consumer goods remains an issue of major importance. At the same time, budget deficits have increased significantly in the late 1980s as opposed to their level in the early 1980s, putting additional stress on the economy.

While reform implementation is proceeding, it is doing so at an uneven pace. There appears to be the emergence of a general view that the reform will unquestionably take considerably longer to implement then originally anticipated. Thus the uneven pace is evident. For example, a full discussion of the very complex issue of price reform has yet to take place, while in 1989 significant attention has been paid to reform in agriculture. Recognition of continuing problems in the provision of consumer goods led to the announcement in 1989 of increased consumer goods imports to alleviate shortages on a short-run basis.

Finally, it is worth noting that the role of military spending in the Soviet economy is a major uncertainty as we enter the 1990s. In several speeches, Gorbachev has proposed numerous changes in the Soviet military posture. Thus far, our best evidence suggests little change in the size of the Soviet military budget. Should this policy change, and if Soviet leaders are able to divert military spending to civilian uses, a new and significant element would be introduced into the reform discussion.

In the meantime, it would seem that Gorbachev will continue to press for reform implementation, hoping that various steps can be taken to convince restive consumers that they will see improvement in the immediate future.

Whether perestroika succeeds or fails is perhaps the most important issue of the second half of the twentieth century. If it succeeds, the Soviet Union will, in effect, join the community of Western nations as a normal trading partner and a responsible actor on the world scene. If perestroika fails, the Soviet Union could revert back to its traditional command-autarkic model. The stakes are high, indeed much higher than those for previous reform efforts. The need for better Soviet economic performance is pressing. Moreover, perestroika has been coupled with glasnost, an approach and commitment very different from that of previous Soviet reform efforts.

REFERENCES

1. For a discussion of the events immediately preceding the Gorbachev era, see E. A. Hewett, *Reforming the Soviet Economy* (Washington, D.C.: Brookings Institution, 1988), chap. 6. See also comments made by E. Domar in A. Bergson and H. Levine, eds., *The Soviet Economy Toward the Year 2000* (London: Allen & Unwin, 1983), pp. 445–446.

2. The discussion of Gorbachev's political-economic program is based upon E. A. Hewett, *Reforming the Soviet Economy*, chap. 7; P. Desai, *Perestroika in Perspective: Design and Dilemma of Soviet Economic Reform* (Princeton: Princeton University Press, 1989), chaps. 1–3; S. J. Linz, ed., "A Symposium on Reorganization and Reform in the Soviet Economy," *Comparative Economic Studies*, vol. 29, no. 4 (Winter 1987); D. Dyker, ed., *The Soviet Union Under Gorbachev: Prospects for Reform* (London: Croom Helm, 1987); "Soviets Planning Economic Zones to Draw More Foreign Investment," *Wall Street Journal*, May 2, 1989.

3. For a discussion of recent developments in agriculture see K. E. Wädekin, "Re-Emergence of the Kolkhoz Principle," *Soviet Studies*, vol. 41, no. 1 (January 1989), 20–38; and U.S. Department of Agriculture, *USSR Agriculture and Trade Report: Situation and Outlook Series* (Washington, D.C.: U.S. Dept. of Agriculture, May 1989).

4. Recent Soviet discussions of reform implementation seem to imply that the timetable for reform will be significantly longer than originally planned. See Hewett, *Reforming the Soviet Economy*, p. 332.

5. Some of Gorbachev's key reform advisors are sociologists by training, such as Tatiana Zaslavskaia. Advisors of a sociological bent have convinced Gorbachev of the importance of human factors. On this, see A. Aslund, "Gorbachev's Economic Advisors," *Soviet Economy*, vol. 3, no. 3 (July–September 1987), 246–269.

6. Directorate of Intelligence, *Revisiting Soviet Economic Performance Under Glasnost': Implications for CIA Estimates*, SOV 88–1988, September 1988 .

7. The "Little Deal" is an expression coined by Vera Dunham to refer to the accommodation the Brezhnev regime reached with the Soviet middle class. The regime implicitly agreed to the privilege, material incentives, and perquisites of the middle class (in place of sacrifice and revolutionary fervor). Gorbachev can be conceived of as offering a New Deal that consists of more openness and democratization in return for more responsibility and risk. On the issue of the "Little Deal", see V. S. Dunham, *In Stalin's Time: Middleclass Values in Soviet Fiction* (New York: Cambridge University Press, 1976); and J. Millar, "The Little Deal: Brezhnev's Contribution to Acquisitive Socialism," *Slavic Review*, vol. 44, no. 4 (Winter 1985) 694–706.

8. The following discussion is largely based on P. R. Gregory, "The Soviet Bureaucracy and Perestroika, "*Comparative Economic Studies*, vol. 31, no. 1 (Spring 1989), 1–13.

9. For a statement of the difficulty of compiling operational long-term plans, see "K voprosu o planirovanii" [To the question of planning], *Planovoe khoziaistvo* (September 1987), 95–100.

10. On this matter, see M. Keren, "Optimal Tautness," paper presented at conference in honor of Holland Hunter, Haverford College, March 1989.

11. F. Kushnirsky, *Soviet Economic Planning 1965–1980* (Boulder, Colo.: Westview Press, 1982), chaps. 1–2.

12. P. R. Gregory, *The Soviet Economic Bureaucracy* (Cambridge: Cambridge University Press, 1990), chap. 8.

13. The basic rights of enterprises are enumerated in Draft Law of the Union of Soviet Socialist Republics. On the state enterprise [association], published in *Pravda*, February 8, 1987.

14. According to one of Gorbachev's influential advisors, the enterprise profit tax should be "neutral" in the sense that priority enterprises will not be given lower tax rates than nonpriority branches. On this, see A. Aganbegyan, *The Economic Challenge of Perestroika* (Bloomington: Indiana University Press, 1988), pp. 117–118.

15. Hewett, *Reforming the Soviet Economy*, pp. 340–341.

16. Ibid., p. 341.

17. A. Aganbegyan, *Inside Perestroika* (New York: Harper & Row, 1990), chap. 3.

18. L. J. Brainard, "Soviet International Financial Policy: Traditional Formulas or New Innovations?" Joint Economic Committee, *Gorbachev's Economic Plans*, vol. I (Washington, D.C.: U.S. Government Printing Office, 1987), pp. 100–115.

19. For an insider's view of the possibilities of ruble convertibility, see Aganbegyan, *Inside Perestroika*, chap. 3.

20. This section is based on "Industrial Modernization" (papers by P. Gregory, R. Legett, F. Kushnirsky, C. Pedersen, B. Rumer and Y. Vatkin, C. Harris, M. Sagers, and T. Shabad, J. Braithwaite, and P. Hanson), *Gorbachev's Economic Plans*, part I, pp. 231–366.

21. Hewett, *Reforming the Soviet Economy*, pp. 330–331.
22. In the spring of 1989, a good portion of space in popular satirical magazines was devoted to the evils of the price-gouging cooperatives.
23. P. R. Gregory, "Soviet Bureaucratic Behavior: Khoziaistvenniks and Apparatchiks," *Soviet Studies*, forthcoming 1990.
24. P. R. Gregory, *The Soviet Economic Bureaucracy* (Cambridge: Cambridge University Press, 1990).
25. Interviews conducted by one of the authors in Moscow in the spring of 1989 conform this competition for resources. Ministerial officials in light-industry ministries complained about the loss of enterprises to cooperatives. Line officials, moreover, complained about restrictions that prevented them from forming cooperatives and expressed bitterness about not being able to earn the high profits of cooperatives.
26. Interviews conducted by one of the authors in Moscow in the spring of 1989 confirmed that ministries have indeed suffered enormous staff cuts, handled largely through natural retirements and nonreplacement of vacant positions. Moreover, ministry staff personnel express concern about their lack of responsibilities under the new regime.

SELECTED BIBLIOGRAPHY

A. Aganbegyan, *The Economic Challenge of Perestroika* (Bloomington: Indiana University Press, 1988).

———, *Inside Perestroika* (New York: Harper & Row, 1990.

A. Aslund, "Gorbachev's Economic Advisors," *Soviet Economy*, vol. 3, no. 3 (July–September 1987).

A. Bergson and H. Levine, eds., *The Soviet Economy Toward the Year 2000* (London: Allen & Unwin, 1983).

L. J. Brainard, "Soviet International Financial Policy: Traditional Formulas or New Innovations?" Joint Economic Committee, *Gorbachev's Economic Plans*, vol. I (Washington, D.C.: U.S. Government Printing Office, 1987).

P. Desai, *Perestroika in Perspective: Design and Dilemma of Soviet Economic Reform* (Princeton, N.J.: Princeton University Press, 1989).

Directorate of Intelligence, *Revisiting Soviet Economic Performance Under Glasnost': Implications for CIA Estimates, SOV 88–1988*, September 1988.

V. S. Dunham, *In Stalin's Time: Middleclass Values in Soviet Fiction* (New York: Cambridge University Press, 1976).

D. Dyker, ed., *The Soviet Union Under Gorbachev: Prospects for Reform* (London: Croom Helm, 1987).

B. Eklof, *Soviet Briefing: Gorbachev and the Reform Period* (Boulder, Colo.: Westview Press, 1989).

P. R. Gregory, "The Soviet Bureaucracy and Perestroika," *Comparative Economic Studies*, vol. 31, no. 1 (Spring 1989).

———, "Soviet Bureaucratic Behavior: Khoziaistvenniks and Apparatchiks," *Soviet Studies*, forthcoming, 1990.

————, *The Soviet Economic Bureaucracy* (Cambridge: Cambridge University Press, 1990).

M. I. Goldman, *Gorbachev's Challenge: Economic Reform in the Age of High Technology* (New York: Norton, 1987).

P. Hanson, "The Shape of Gorbachev's Economic Reform," *Soviet Economy*, vol. 2, no. 4 (December–January 1986), 313–326.

E. A. Hewett, *Reforming the Soviet Economy* (Washington, D.C.: The Brookings Institution, 1988).

"Industrial Modernization" (papers by P. Gregory, R. Legett, F. Kushnirsky, C. Pedersen, B. Rumer and Y. Vatkin, C. Harris, M. Sagers and T. Shabad, J. Braithwaite, and P. Hanson), U. S. Congress, Joint Economic Committee, *Gorbachev's Economic Plans*, part I (Washington, D.C.: U.S. Government Printing Office, 1987).

T. A. Jones, *Perestroika: Gorbachev's Social Revolution* (Boulder, Colo.: Westview Press, 1989).

P. Juviler and H. Kimura, eds., *Gorbachev's Reforms: U.S. and Japanese Assessments* (New York: Aldine de Gruyter, 1988).

"K voprosu o planirovanii" [To the question of planning], *Planovoe khoziaistvo*, September 1987.

M. Keren, "Optimal Tautness," paper presented at conference in honor of Holland Hunter, Haverford College, March 1989.

F. Kushnirsky, *Soviet Economic Planning 1965–1980* (Boulder, Colo.: Westview Press, 1982).

S. J. Linz, ed., "A Symposium on Reorganization and Reform in the Soviet Economy," *Comparative Economic Studies*, vol. 29, no. 4 (Winter 1987).

Z. A. Medvedev, *Gorbachev* (New York: Norton, 1986).

A. Melville and G. W. Lapidus, eds., *The Glasnost' Papers* (Boulder, Colo.: Westview Press, 1989).

J. Millar, "The Little Deal: Brezhnev's Contribution to Acquisitive Socialism," *Slavic Review*, vol. 44, no. 4 (Winter 1985).

"Soviets Planning Economic Zones to Draw More Foreign Investment," *Wall Street Journal*, May 2, 1989.

G. W. Weickhardt, "Gorbachev's Record on Economic Reform," *Soviet Union*, vol. 12, no. 3 (1985), 251–276.

M. Yanowitch, ed., *A Voice of Reform: Essays by Tatiana I. Zaslavskaia* (Armonk, N.Y.: M. E. Sharpe, 1989).

Conclusions and Prospects

More than half a century after the introduction of command planning, the Soviet economy presents a mixed picture of both substantial achievement and significant shortfall. Indeed, the challenge for present and future Soviet leaders is how to preserve the achievements while eliminating the shortfalls. Probably at no time in recent Soviet history has the pressure for change been so great and the potential costs of failure so high.

Throughout this book we have demonstrated how the Soviet economic system allocates resources, the extent and the ways in which this allocation differs from that commonly found in market capitalism, and finally, with what observable result.

At this juncture it is useful to isolate and identify what we feel are the main strengths and weaknesses of the contemporary Soviet economic system. Having made this assessment, we are then in a position to ponder the future of the Soviet economic system in light of the Gorbachev reforms.

ACHIEVEMENTS

International comparisons of economic achievement present formidable difficulties. However, if we compare the Soviet economy of the early plan era (1928) with the contemporary Soviet economy, we find impressive long-run achievements. In 1928, Soviet gross national product was roughly one-quarter that of the United States; by the late 1980s, this ratio has risen to roughly three-quarters. This improvement in relative position has been the result of a more rapid rate of economic growth than in the industrialized West, where only Japan has rivaled the long-term Soviet growth record. Soviet achievements in the area of military power have also been significant. The Soviet military system rivals that of the United States, a country with a substantially large GNP.

The introduction of central planning appears to have accelerated rates of economic growth. The historical rate of economic growth of the tsarist economy during its industrialization era (1885–1913) was slightly in excess of 3 percent per annum. From 1928 to 1980, Soviet gross national product grew at an average annual rate of 4.4 percent. We cannot rule out the possibility that capitalist Russia would also have experienced a rapid increase in its relative economic position after 1917, as did the United States in the nineteenth century and Japan in the twentieth century, but such cases are rare in world economic history.

What features of the Soviet economic system and Soviet economic policies were responsible for Soviet growth achievements? Simply stated, the plan mechanism was able to accelerate economic growth by allocating resources in such a manner as to maximize the growth of capital and labor inputs and to allocate these inputs to growth-generating sectors. If factor inputs had continued to grow at rates of the late tsarist era, it is unlikely that an acceleration of economic growth of this magnitude would have taken place. The mechanisms for maximizing the growth of factor inputs have been described in detail in earlier chapters. Administrative allocation allowed producer goods to be favored at the expense of consumer goods; both administrative and market-type mechanisms were used to maximize labor force participation and to encourage a rapid flow of labor out of low-priority into high-priority sectors; the use of the turnover tax and direct access by the state to sources of accumulation provided investment funds; the use of controls in agriculture provided the state with secure sources of grain on terms unlikely to prevail under market conditions.

The Soviet economic experience was unique in the sense that the state, through the planning mechanism and state ownership, took control of the resources and harnessed them to achieve state objectives. In important ways, these objectives differed from those of market capitalist systems, where policy objectives are developed in a more pluralistic manner. Most would agree that while economic growth and structural change were achieved, the short-term and the long-term costs were substantial. The long-term costs are especially relevant as we assess the likelihood for the current Soviet leadership's success in transforming the system of an earlier era.

THE COSTS OF SOVIET ECONOMIC GROWTH

Economic growth is not without costs, although some costs may be difficult to measure. What is important, however, is the magnitude of the costs relative to the benefits, the distribution of the burden among participants, and the distribution of costs over time.

The rapid expansion of Soviet economic and military power was certainly obtained at the expense of the growth of living standards. The Soviet consumer, both in the city and in the countryside, bore the burden of rapid industrialization. The growth of living standards was virtually halted if not reversed in the 1930s. Although the growth of consumption was substantially better in the post-Stalin era, it is not clear that the promises of the 1930s were kept. Current complaints about the inadequate supplies and assortments of food and other consumer goods suggest that the sacrifices of more than one generation have been required for the growth achievements, and in particular for the emphasis on heavy industry and the military.

Although the impact of a heavy-industry bias on consumption can be readily observed, there is a different long-term cost that is more difficult to assess. The contemporary Soviet Union, even after many years of attempted change, sustains a sectorial structure unlike that which we observe in market capitalist systems. Put another way, the patterns that we have described earlier (bias against consumption, bias in favor of heavy industry, etc.) remain to the present day. These ingrained biases may well be a major stumbling block to significant economic reform. The success of perestroika requires substantial increases in labor productivity, yet the enhancement of labor productivity requires better incentives in the form of more and better-quality consumer goods. The Soviet economic system has not been programmed to meet this task.

The relationship between productivity and the economic system remains poorly understood. However, it is possible to make some reasonable generalizations. Soviet economic growth has been, as we have noted, extensive in character. The expansion of inputs rather than the growth of factor productivity has been a primary source of output growth. While such a pattern is reasonable and indeed likely at early stages of economic development, presently advanced countries have been able to shift to an intensive mode where productivity achievement is the major source of output growth. Indeed, the need to improve productivity growth to ensure reasonable rates of growth of living standards is recognized by the industrialized capitalist countries.

The issue of technology remains critical to Soviet economic performance, both actual and potential. The Soviet Union began the era of central planning with a large technology gap relative to the countries of the industrialized West. However, since 1928, the rate of growth of factor productivity in the Soviet Union has not been higher than in these industrialized countries. There is no evidence to suggest that the Soviet Union has closed the technology gap it inherited from its tsarist predecessors in spite of substantial borrowing of technology from abroad and a domestic policy emphasis on technology, especially evident in recent years. One exception is military technology, where there has been a significant closing of the gap. It remains important to understand why one sector can close the technology gap, and what implications there may be for technology transfer into the lagging civilian economy. Expert studies cited in this book conclude that in the past three decades, there has not been a noticeable reduction in the technological backwardness of the Soviet Union. The Soviet Union's technological backwardness has important implications for reform in the Gorbachev and post-Gorbachev eras.

The major failing of the Soviet system has been its inability to create a major transformation to intensive growth, that is, growth based on increases in efficiency rather than increases in inputs. In the industrialized West, generally more than half of the growth of output can be accounted for by increases in factor productivity, while in the Soviet Union, productivity improvement accounts for roughly one-third of output growth. The impact of this fact is simply that Soviet economic growth has been high-cost growth, achieved at the expense of leisure and consumption. While the relationship between productivity and the availability of consumer goods is not fully understood, many would argue that years of deprivation of adequate consumer goods has created serious problems of morale among Soviet workers. It is no accident that Gorbachev has paid so much attention to the issues of consumption and morale.

While most countries grow extensively in the early stages of their industrialization, the transformation to intensive growth must take place if living standards are to continue growing. If one examines input use in the Soviet case, it becomes quickly apparent that further growth from input expansion is simply not possible. Investment ratios are already among the highest in the world. Investment cannot be further increased at the expense of lagging consumption. Moreover, the same can be said for labor force utilization. With labor force participation among the highest in the world, how can more labor be derived from greater participation? Possibly most important, however, even if more capital could be made available, recent experience has shown that it will be unproductive under existing utilization arrangements and factor proportions. In short, the Soviet Union, unless it is willing to accept long-term stagnation, really has no option but to raise factor productivity. Yet planners cannot simply decree increases in productivity like they can decree increases in outputs. How productivity grows—through enhancement of knowledge, economies of scale, better management, and the like—remains a "residual" in our knowledge of economic growth. The forces that influence productivity growth are still not well understood, even in a market setting.

A major cost of the Soviet economic system is its rigidity. While a planner can dictate where a steel mill is to be placed, the same planner cannot dictate technological change. Planners cannot legislate away technological backwardness because the system provides inadequate managerial rewards for innovative activity. The pervasive emphasis on short-term output goals does not create an environment in which economic efficiency is promoted.

THE SOVIET ECONOMY IN THE 1980s

The 1970s was a decade of turmoil for the world economy. Energy shocks, recessions, and stagflation appeared to threaten the stability of the world economic order. However, the 1980s was a decade of considerable economic achievement, even for the laggards such as Great Britain, accustomed to economic crises. While problems of debt and trade imbalance remain, for many industrialized systems, the 1980s was generally a good decade. The same cannot be said for the Soviet Union.

As we have already noted, by almost any measure, the growth rate of Soviet *GNP* declined steadily from the 1950s through the 1980s. Moreover, the growth of total factor productivity also declined steadily through the 1980s. In fact, the growth of total factor productivity became negative in the late 1970s and 1980s due to declining rates of capital productivity.

Although the growth of labor productivity was positive through the 1970s, it also declined. Moreover, capital productivity has been negative (with fluctuations from one period to another) since the late 1950s.

These declining rates of growth of output and factor productivity must be viewed by the Soviet leadership with great alarm. They are not simply cyclical responses to adverse conditions, but rather show a long-term downward trend that under existing arrangements can be reversed only by enormous additional burdens on the population. Moreover, it is by no means clear that placing additional pressure on the population would be sufficient to reverse the downward trend. Under these circumstances, one can fully understand the reform imperative of the Gorbachev era.

In the 1970s, the Soviet Union turned increasingly outward to meet its increasing need for grain and advanced technology. A country that once was a net exporter of grain became a net importer, on a significant scale and on a continuing basis. The proportion of imports to GNP increased significantly, with Western credits becoming an important source of finance. Soviet hard-currency indebtedness remained within manageable bounds, with Soviet exports of oil and raw materials being a major source of hard-currency earnings. Although the declining ability to rely on petroleum exports could be countered initially by tightening up on exports to COMECON countries, Soviet authorities began to realize that there was a significant constraint on imports from the West. Moreover, the Soviet failure to gain trade and credit concessions from the United States in the 1970s worsened the Soviets' prospects of competing effectively in Western manufacturing markets.

The 1970s also brought home the fact that economic reform, as implemented in the Brezhnev era, would simply not release the "hidden reserves" so often discussed in the Soviet media. Faced with the alternative of significant economic reform or maintenance of the status quo, the Brezhnev leadership chose the latter.

The adverse trends of the 1970s continued through the 1980s. The population dilemma persisted—slowing rates of growth and sharply decreased expansion of the labor force except in the Central Asian Republics, which lack a significant industrial base. Although continuing emphasis on education will increase the quality of the labor force, the process is slow and uncertain.

The 1980s has been a decade of mixed economic performance. With significant year-to-year fluctuations, GNP has grown at an average annual rate under 2 percent while consumption has grown at an average annual rate of approximately 2 percent, the lowest in years. Moreover, this rate of growth decreased in the late 1980s. The gap between plan targets and actual achievements has generally been wide.

While the share of investment in GNP remains high, the growth of capital investment has declined steadily over the years from roughly 13 percent per annum in the late 1950s to around 2 percent in the 1980s. Capital productivity problems remain, largely resulting from inappropriate policies and an economic system incapable of generating effective capital use.

Throughout the 1980s, defense has remained a large claimant of Soviet resources, although Gorbachev has indicated intentions to reduce the defense committee.

Finally, Soviet hard-currency debt, though very manageable, has grown steadily in the 1980s from roughly $10 billion in the early 1980s to $26 billion in the mid- and late 1980s.

In sum, it is evident that the Soviet economy has in a sense reached a plateau of economic achievement. To what extent are the reforms of the Gorbachev era likely to shift the Soviet economy off the plateau such that performance achievements of an earlier era can be restored?

THE SOVIET ECONOMY: LOOKING AHEAD

We have already discussed the Gorbachev reform program in some detail. No observer of the Soviet economy, no matter how well informed, can predict with any surety the outcome of the present reform process. Predicting the outcome is even more difficult because the Gorbachev reform is more than an economic reform; it is in the framework of glasnost, a remaking of Soviet society. If narrow economic reform programs are difficult to prejudge, then economic reforms combined with social change must be of a significantly higher order of difficulty.

In a recent study of the reform process, Ed Hewett suggests four possible outcomes, which he describes as "success," "high growth," "high quality," and "failure." Most would agree with some such characterization, though most interesting are the intermediate possibilities, since many would probably reject the extremes of full success and total failure. Interestingly enough, the two middle scenarios suggested by Hewett focus on growth and productivity improvement on the one hand, and improvement in the quality and availability of goods and services on the other hand. Thus in the high-growth scenario, the rate of growth of output and productivity are significantly improved, while there is only limited improvement in the quality and availability of goods and services. This, as Hewett notes, is in a sense an anti-reform scenario.

In the high-quality scenario, growth is modest and improvements in productivity are modest, but achievements in the quality and availability of consumer goods are significant.

While additional alternative scenarios could be sketched out, the four scenarios provide a convenient framework in which to go beyond specific outcomes to the forces that will mold these possible outcomes.

First, as we have already emphasized, the Soviet reform combines uncertain economic change with even more uncertain social change. The interactions between economic and social change are poorly understood. Whether social change will be compatible with economic change remains to be seen. Western economists have long argued that the social and political system affects the economic system. A degree of political freedom and pluralism is required in order for decentralized markets to function. Soviet reformers must therefore coordinate the pace of social, political, and economic reform.

Second, the intertwining of the consumer and the economic system in the reform process is no accident. Unless the reform can bring significant improvement (how significant is a matter of debate) for the Soviet consumer, the reform is likely to fail. While there exists a number of alternatives to achieve this end, most would agree that the participants in the Soviet system will become increasingly restless unless the long-promised benefits of socialism become reality.

Third, in the Soviet case as in other reform settings, the resistance to change can be expected to be significant. Quite apart from bureaucratic resistance from those who favor the old system, the difficulties of changing the Soviet system are major. For example, even the single task of price reform and the development of "market forces" must be very difficult in a system that has rejected markets and an allocative role for prices for 50 years. But even more important, price reform, as difficult as it will be, must be combined harmoniously with other facets of reform, such that the modus operandi of the system can change.

Fourth and possibly most important, significant economic reform may well necessitate a reassessment of Soviet economic objectives, a reassessment that could be fundamental and possibly intolerable for Soviet consumers, at least in the short run. In a sense, Soviet leaders would like the efficiency of the market capitalist system with the equity of the socialist economic system. To the extent that such a combination of systems and system goals is very difficult,

Soviet consumers may come to learn that formerly "inexpensive" housing is not inexpensive after all, and that "free" health care cannot be free if the price system and economic rationality are to be the mechanisms to deliver housing and health care. The Soviet worker may come to learn that "job rights" are incompatible with changing market forces and efficiency requirements.

Barring some unforeseen incident such as a change of leadership, it is likely that the Soviet reform process will continue. It is not likely to be successful in the sense that Hewett has defined success. On the other hand, as we have noted, complete failure is unlikely if rigidly interpreted. A more likely scenario is a reform that is sustained with a delicate balance between gradual and hard-won improvements in basic economic indicators and a gradual if uneven improvement in the position of the Soviet consumer. If the experience of other planned socialist systems is any indicator of outcomes, the process of improvement will be slow, difficult, and uneven.

Finally, should we care about the outcome of the reform process in the Soviet Union? It is important to realize that while the Soviet Union is very different from the smaller East European economies, obviously the progress of reform in the former will affect the process of reform in the latter. Possibly more important from a Western point of view, the Soviet Union as part of its reform strategy has already and will unquestionably make further changes that will be of vital importance to Western interests. The Soviet leadership has already recognized the link between the military and economic reform. Moreover, a major part of the reform process involves playing a new and larger role in world markets and in the organizational arrangements of world trade. It would be difficult and inappropriate for Western countries not to be participants in this process of change. In this sense, the success of Soviet economic reform can be closely tied to the nature and behavior of the Soviet political process. Both bear close watching as the substance of the Gorbachev reform process unfolds in the 1990s.

SELECTED BIBLIOGRAPHY

A. Bergson and H. S. Levine , eds., *The Soviet Economy: Towards the Year 2000* (London: Allen & Unwin, 1983).

P. Desai, *Perestroika in Perspective* (Princeton, N.J.: Princeton University Press, 1989).

E. A. Hewett, *Reforming the Soviet Economy* (Washington, D.C.: The Brookings Institution, 1988).

U.S. Congress, Joint Economic Committee, *Gorbachev's Economic Plans*, vols. I and II (Washington, D.C.: U.S. Government Printing Office, 1987).

Index